Sex and Power in History

By the same author:

THE AMERICAN EMPIRE
THE SOUL OF INDIA
THE SOUL OF CHINA
THE COMING CAESARS
ROOF OF THE WORLD

Sex and Power in History

AMAURY de RIENCOURT

David McKay Company, Inc.

NEW YORK

SEX AND POWER IN HISTORY

Copyright © 1974 by Amaury de Riencourt

LIBRARY OF CONGRESS CATALOG CARD NUMBER: 74-82989
ISBN 0-679-50490-7
MANUFACTURED IN THE UNITED STATES OF AMERICA

Contents

Introduction

Since the dawn of conscience, the existence of two different sexes cleaving their species into two distinct, cooperating, and conflicting halves has mystified human beings. What is male, what is female, how should they relate to one another? These are great basic questions, central to the quest for the meaning of life—and this is an attempt to answer them.

Essentially this work is an all-inclusive interpretation of history from end to end, as seen through the interplay of the primary biosocial forces that have shaped it—the *yin* and *yang*, the female and male principles that are the warp and woof of an intricate tapestry. This interplay underlies the natural evolution of practically all living organisms, including humankind. But the *yin-yang* dialectic also permeates the historical development of all cultures and civilizations, all mythologies, religions, philosophies, arts, political and social organizations, economic doctrines, and structures.

Only the sick feel their limbs and organs. The acute consciousness of a predicament in the relations between the sexes is probably the most significant element in the overall crisis of contemporary civilization, because it subsumes all the others. What follows is an endeavor to analyze this crisis by going back to its remote sources and giving a coherent account of the weaving of this planetary fabric: the human race.

For the first time, in the following pages a study of human evolution focuses primarily on the female of the species and presents a comprehensive view of the influence, social position, economic status, and cultural influence of women throughout the ages. The main articulations of this spectral analysis can be delineated as follows:

Using the fundamental dimorphism between the sexes generated by the hunting way of life, the prohibition of incest (connected with the birth of language) triggered, through the matrimonial exchange of women, communications between far-flung groups of human beings. Crossing a major mental threshold, Paleolithic males began to worship womanhood (Mother Earth), looking upon the opposite sex as the intermediary between man and nature's mysteries.

At some point, however, men gradually substituted a male god for the former Mother Goddess when they discovered the connection between sex and procreation, and their *biological* paternity. This *patriarchal revolution*, which swept the whole world some thirty-five hundred years ago, was preceded in the collective unconscious by the mythological metamorphosis known as *solarization*, the victory of the male sun god over the female moon goddess. In turn this implied the collapse of the female-oriented *cyclical* fertility cults and the rise to supremacy of the male concept of *linear* history consisting of unrepeatable events, messianism, and eschatology, with Zoroaster and the Hebrew prophets.

Alongside this metaphysical transformation, Greek rational thought broke away from magic thought processes, and symbolically transferred the center of creative power from the female womb to the male brain (symbolized by Athene's birth from the forehead of Zeus), creating the great Western cultural distortion that is still with us today, by giving greater value to culture than to nature, to the abstract *Idea* than to concrete *Life* itself. This entailed that, while the masculine Promethean drive was exalted, while Greek thinkers became the pioneers of philosophy and discursive thought, the *psychological* degradation of the female principle (*physiological* creation of new life) led to the debasement of woman's *social* position and status, which reached its nadir at the time of Pericles. This cultural distortion—unknown in Eastern civilizations where a somewhat harmonious balance between the two *sexual principles* was maintained—disrupted the Western human ecology by depicting females as inferior or *incomplete* males (biblical Eve, Greek Pandora, and Aristotle's philosophic rationalizations) instead of granting them their *different* specificity, as was done in China or India.

The first feminist revolt known to history was the consequence, starting in Greece with Euripides and culminating with women's liberation movements in Rome. In turn, this eventually destroyed Roman society's ethical framework and family structure, lowered the birthrate drastically, and wrecked Roman civilization from within *before* the barbarians destroyed it from outside—a historical phenomenon that had no parallel in India or China.

This cultural imbalance was temporarily overshadowed by the birth of Christianity's new set of values, the great *synthesis* of the first millennium A.D.—not only in terms of an amalgamation of Hebrew faith and

Greek philosophy, but also in terms of a synthesis between these two masculine trends (historically minded and rational) and the female-oriented cyclical fertility worship whose main themes were preserved and incorporated in the allegories of the *New* Testament. They permeate the sacrifice of Christ in its symbolic reenactment of the ritual death and rebirth of the Neolithic kings and male gods—while the Virgin Mary became the reincarnation of all the former goddesses.

A study of all the other creeds of mankind—Islam, Hinduism, Buddhism, Taoism—leads to a contrasted analysis of the two fundamental forms of religious expression—*female* mysticism and *male* prophetism.

The birth of romantic medieval love implied that man's *sublimated* love for woman symbolized the search for his own soul—as the Paleolithic fear of his remote ancestors of femalehood symbolized his fear of nature's mysterious forces.

A study of the leading types of womanhood—the medieval woman, the virago, the witch, the reformed woman and the cultured woman—underlines the great historical watershed of the sixteenth century. Christianity's male-female synthesis broke down with:

1. The Reformation. During this period the female component of Christianity (the Virgin) was expelled and it reverted to the unadulterated patriarchalism of the Old Testament.
2. The Renaissance. Breaking with medieval *symbolic* thought, this movement reverted to classical Greco-Roman thought and its emphasis on the supremacy of the rational, scientific attitude—that is, once again, the supremacy of the Mind over the Life which gives birth to it and is generated by woman's physiological processes.

The historical result of this cultural revolution was the explosive development of modern science and its offshoot, the industrial revolution, the unleashing of vast social changes, the breakdown of the extended family as a unit, as well as the increasing separation of the sexes and the generations resulting from urbanization and industrialization.

The feminist revolt started with this social metamorphosis, gathering momentum with the idling of large segments of middle-class women, now lowered to the rank of mere status symbols with all the frustration and loss of true identity this entailed.

The *cultural* devaluation of woman's life-creating function was thus compounded by a *social* deactivation of bourgeois women as economic producers, as if they were obsolete machinery. This gave further impetus to the feminist revolt which, if not understood and coped with at its *cultural root*, could destroy Western society as a similar movement destroyed Roman civilization.

The problem is now made more acute by the *biological revolution* which could, if pushed to its ultimate potential, alter the human race beyond recognition, or lead to its virtual destruction, while still giving the impression that scientific thought can fully comprehend and master that which generated it—Life.

The contemporary woman's liberation drive toward a *decrease* in sexual differentiation, to the extent that it is leading toward androgyny and unisexual values, implies a social and cultural death-wish and the end of the civilization that endorses it. The scientific and historical record shows that all the way from unicellular organisms to human beings, progress in evolution has been stimulated by the *increase in sexual differentiation.*

Social engineering and legislative tinkering will not solve the problem. The present dilemma can be overcome only if a profound *cultural* change takes place and an entirely new set of values replaces the traditional values that Western civilization inherited from both biblical and Greek patriarchal sources. These new values will be effective only to the extent that they are based on respect for the different specificities of the sexes and the same reverence for the creation of Life as for the creations of the Mind.

Part I

BEFORE HISTORY:
THE ETERNAL FEMININE

CHAPTER

I

Anthropoids and Humans

It all started a few million years ago, when our distant anthropoid cousins became hunters. Toward the end of the Pliocene epoch and the beginning of the Pleistocene, a gradual reduction in rainfall began to deforest parts of Africa south of what is now the Sahara Desert. Rain forests changed into grassland savannas. While the ancestors of present-day gorillas, baboons, gibbons, and chimpanzees retreated with the forest and clung to its arboreal shelter, other anthropoids were compelled to face boldly the challenge of the grasslands' open spaces with its dangers and terrors—presumably pushed out of the dwindling groves by the stronger forerunners of the great apes.

From food gatherers, ground anthropoids were constrained to become hunters under the spur of this ecological change; inevitably, their diet also changed. Around the Middle Pleistocene, manlike apes changed into apelike men by becoming omnivorous, which implied a remarkable increase in their capacity for survival in all environments. Herbivores gather food exclusively for themselves; most carnivores tend to *share* food. Carnivores also do not consume their game on the spot but bring it back to be apportioned among the other members of the group. And since hunting could not be carried out by all members, food procurement became a specialized task, left to the strongest and cleverest young males. Specialization automatically implied group cooperation and sharing the fruits of the hunt with females and infants: food sharing became the "outstanding functional criterion of man," the trademark, as it were, of the human condition among primates.[1]

One of the main by-products of this revolution was that the search for food—much more difficult under the new circumstances, but also much more rewarding energy-wise—became the primary preoccupation in this new way of life, relegating sex and the choice of mates to a secondary role. The sexual impulse had to be brought under control in order to serve a *socially* useful purpose: the protection and strengthening of the family and tribal group, achieved by a strictly prescribed code of behavior, or by a behavior pattern imposed by the new living circumstances.

But when the *Australopithecines,* the bipedal apelike men of Southeast Africa, extended hunting to medium- and larger-size animals (antelopes, wild pigs, hyenas, and buffalos) other evolutive changes took place: while a premium was still put on physical strength and agility, an even higher premium would be put on the development of *intelligence* and the ability to solve problems. Learning and intelligence began to take over from the vanishing animal instincts. This evolving male primate began to emerge and stand slightly apart from nature as a thoughtful, problem-solving, tool-making, immensely adaptive protohuman capable of abstract thinking. Big-game hunting became the decisive organizing activity that shaped all the morphological, physiological and intellectual traits that characterize our species to this day. It was not only a new food-procurement technique but a new way of life that generated a new species—and it should be kept in mind that man has been a hunter during 99 percent of mankind's lifespan.

More than anything else, hunting required not only the aggressiveness of a predator but also *cooperation* between the male hunters during the hunting season. The early weapon-wielding apelike men were pack hunters, very much like wolves. Unlike wolves, however, they were equipped with a powerful brain and were able to devise elaborate methods of cooperation and group communications. Moving toward bigger and more dangerous game and increasingly lengthy hunting expeditions, they gradually gave up their nomadic ways and began to build semipermanent home bases for females and offspring, along with storage facilities for the food brought back from the hunt.

The most important consequence of the new big-game-hunting way of life in the open savannas, however, was to trigger an asymmetric evolution in the activities and social standing of the sexes.[2] While herbivorous male primates need not provide food for females—food gathering (mostly fruit-picking) is easy for both, and all except small infants can provide for themselves—hunting anthropoids had to provide for females and offspring in their new way of life. Menstruation, pregnancy, and the care of children were not compatible with the hunt, which thus became an exclusively male occupation, leaving females in charge of food gathering whenever possible and convenient. As a result of this new division of labor between the sexes, the cooperative instinct of the hunting males developed rapidly, giving protohumans an inestimable advantage over other noncooperating animals. The new way of life had another consequence: the development of pair-bonding, a rare occurrence among primates. Indeed, the long expeditions required by the hunt made it imperative that sexual rivalry between males be reduced to the minimum—hence the allotment of one female for one male on a semipermanent basis. In turn, this pair-bonding allowed for a great increase in hunting cooperation, in what can be termed male-bonding. Obviously, the weaker males could no longer be frustrated by the stronger ones as among other primates; successful hunting required the cooperation of all males, all of whom had to be sexually satisfied.

Perhaps the most important result of pair-bonding was the birth of the nuclear monogamous family structure for the benefit of the young: one male provided for a specific female and her offspring. Pair-bonding was undoubtedly related to a radical change in sexual posture: unlike other primates, whose males approach the females from the rear and mount them from behind, the typical mating procedure of our species is face-to-face. Rear-end copulation without any frontal body contact depersonalizes sex, making the identity of the female mounted a matter of small concern to the male. The hominids, on the contrary, *personalized* sex by adopting face-to-face mating; in this posture, sexual signaling is closely connected with identification signaling—something that is of utmost importance in pair-bonding because it links the specific partners more intimately. In other words, the sexual act had to become far more attractive if it was to lead to a capacity for forming a strong emotional bond with one specific member of the opposite sex, and maintaining that bond during the long period of time required to raise a family.

This new way of life had other important consequences, notably a physiological alteration of the human female: the disappearance of the heat period during which she was sexually receptive in favor of a more permanent, year-round receptivity to the amorous inclinations of the male. With the fade-out of the estrous cycle, hormonal control was replaced by mental control. The greater permanency of the female's sexual attractiveness throughout the year must have made a stable union between one male and one female that much more stimulating and valuable. Man's own sexuality and other instinctual impulses were gradually brought under cortical control, putting an end to the promiscuousness inherited from his primate ancestors.

Increasing sexual dimorphism made the female more dependent upon the male than ever. Hunting inevitably enhanced the physical and mental development of the male by making greater demands on him, and he increased in body size, muscular strength, and speed, as well as in intelligence, imagination, and knowledge—in all of which the female hardly shared. To that extent, the world became increasingly a man's world; and this remained true until very late. Only some ten to twelve thousand years ago did a new, agricultural way of life appear on the planet.

It may be highly relevant to look now at some contemporary primates that traveled part of the evolutionary way for the same ecological reasons, before reaching a dead end. While male-female dimorphism is slight among forest-dwelling primates, it increases drastically among the baboons roaming the more dangerous savannas of southern Africa —not because they took up hunting as their protohuman cousins did so long ago, but because they must defend themselves and their brood. It comes as no surprise, therefore, to learn that selective evolution has operated among these baboons in favor of a great increase in the size and strength of the males, who are physically equipped to defend their females and offspring. What is striking, however, is that evolution has propelled them along a road of development that parallels that of primitive man; social links are established among the males, links that appear to be connected with some form of "political" domination, which in turn is connected with a certain sexual predominance—the exclusive possibility for the dominant males to have access to the females in heat.[3]

Quite clearly, a selective process is at work in favor of those males who are capable of establishing durable and complex links with other males. This in turn enables them to have privileged access to females in heat and to mate with them; these links, if solid and durable, appear to be the foundation of some form of social and political power structure.[4] What is still more striking is that, among such primates, the females appear incapable of forming such links with other females, unable to group themselves for any purpose whatsoever. Order, stability, and defense of the group depend entirely on the political power structure formed by the associated males. It becomes obvious that Darwinian selection requires the complex ability of the dominant males to establish *sexual* links with the chosen females and *social* links with the chosen males, the two being concomitant. Further observation has disclosed that this type of organization is highly conducive to good upbringing for the young males and contentment for the females.

A true system of parenthood apparently operates among apes, with some form of social stratification and definite class structure, completely divorced from any form of property or ownership. This suggests that the distant biological roots of our primitive human institutions can still be found, at the subhuman level, among certain groups of contemporary primates. Nevertheless, it took the hunting way of life to develop these traits to the full in the human species.

Hunting cooperation and specialization are essentially *human* innovations. Whereas among subhuman primates the distribution of work between the sexes is concerned only with defense and rudimentary politics, among the hominids it began to include economics. Thus started, at a later stage, a distribution of the work load between males and females that has often appeared arbitrary—certain groups allot to women a type of labor reserved for men in other groups—but has always aimed at separating the sexes during work. It would seem that mixing the sexes functionally introduces a disturbing element that reacts unfavorably on the quality of their economic activity. The most important consideration, however, is that for any work that is considered important or dangerous, males exclude females in order to associate themselves undisturbed and establish strong male-to-male links, unperturbed by female intrusion and sexual preoccupations. It appears quite probable that the Australopithecine transmitted a genetic code to his descendants, according to which males and females are bound to specialize in *different* tasks, whatever they may be; and that the male's "animal nature" at its deepest level is phylogenetically "programmed" so as to enable him to form associations with other males, to the exclusion of the females. At the very root of mankind's emergence from the animal kingdom as a new species lies a remarkable *increase* in sexual dimorphism.

Sexual dimorphism was also enhanced by another masculine characteristic that must have become phylogenetically programmed. The human male's typical aggressiveness must have been developed by the need to have two different motivational systems—one for the hunt itself, and the other for eating. Unlike the forest-dwelling primate for whom food collecting is almost simultaneous with eating, the hunting primate sees hunting and eating as two widely separate activities. The hunt itself has to provide its own pleasurable stimulation. Killing the prey must produce its own enjoyment, quite apart from its nutritive value. The male of the species became a killer who enjoyed killing for its own sake; he still does.[5]

The division of labor brought on by the new hunting way of life and the ensuing sexual dimorphism was decisive in accelerating human evolution in the sense that it allowed a far more prolonged development of the human child than was and is the case among other primates. This in turn increased the human infant's capacity for learning, while strengthening its affective bonds with parents and family. The lengthening of infancy enabled *neoteny* to take place and become a permanent feature of the human race's genetic programming: infantile characteristics are extended into adult life, thanks to the retention of embryonic tissues with great potential for change and development. This "fetalization" enabled the brain to grow steadily through an extended childhood, unlike that of other primates whose brains at birth have already reached two-thirds of their ultimate size, because the sutures of their skulls close too early. Because of this innovation, the interacting symbiotic relationship between mother and child became far more important and long-lasting in humans than in other animals. The precarious state of immaturity in which the human infant is born, and its very long period of dependency, inevitably entailed all the traits that characterize the human animal—the instinct for cooperation, and conjugal and parental devotion and affection.

To sum up, the human revolution consisted in the following concomitant subrevolutions: an amazingly rapid trebling of the brain capacity between 500,000 B.C. and 150,000 B.C., an increase that could not possibly take place in the womb but had to occur after birth; the lengthening of childhood in order to enable the enlarging brain capacity to substitute for the vanishing instincts and store information with which to cope with the problems of human adulthood; and, as a social framework, the establishment of family bonds that had to survive the mating season and become permanent in order to allow full emotional protection for the long development of the human child.

The rain forest had abandoned mankind's primate ancestors, but this was a blessing in disguise. The days of leisurely fruit picking were over; now it was cooperative prey killing all the way. Man was at last free from his cozy arboreal protective prison; from being an earthbound quadruped, he became erect and was able to scan the distant horizon of the primeval grasslands. Fleet on his feet, wielding weapons of his own invention, carnivorous, and fired with the extra energy that higher-calorie food provides, he was blessed with freedom of choice but cursed with the threat of constant danger and the imperative need to use his brain to the utmost. He became an innovative predator feeding on lower forms of animal life. All this, however, affected the male of the species rather than the female; she evolved physiologically with the end of the estrous cycle, but remained psychologically behind man in a solipsistic world. While the more cerebral male began to emerge from nature and look at it, to a certain extent, from outside, she remained largely within its confines—she was part of nature and nature was part of her.

CHAPTER

2

Incest and Communication

Man was now master of his fate—with a more-or-less permanent help-mate at his side; the monogamous pair-bond had come into existence. Pair-bonding, and its natural sequel, the monogamous marriage, is the first, original, and universal form of mating ever since humankind branched out in the animal kingdom. As Bronislaw Manilowsky states it, "Monogamy is, has been and will remain the only true type of marriage."[1] Polygamy is merely an extension of the monogamous pair-bond, a successive monogamy rather than joint domesticity.

The success of pair-bonding, however, depended on breaking the old atavistic habit of the stronger adult male eliminating younger and weaker rivals and mating with his female relatives. But on what basis, according to what rules or tradition, did males and females choose each other as life partners? The record shows that at least one rule was almost never violated anywhere in the world—the prohibition against incest, the strictest of all forms of sexual control. It appears probable that while this prohibition, compelling all families to exchange their female members, became the most respected social rule (with some limited exceptions among the ruling classes of Egypt, Peru, Hawaii, and Madagascar), its roots are sunk deep in some form of psychological compulsion, springing from the need to avoid a destructive sexual competition within the group or clan. Wherever or whenever the ruling classes discarded this taboo in connection with their own families, they made certain that it was sternly enforced by the rest of the population. In ancient Peru the prohibition was harsh:

> We, the Inca, order and decree that no one shall marry his sister or his mother, nor his first cousin, nor his aunt, nor his niece, nor his kinswoman, nor the godmother of his child, under penalty of being punished and of having his eyes pulled out . . . because only the Inca is allowed to be married to his carnal sister. . . .[2]

The avoidance of incest is definitely not a biologically rooted instinct, nor are the alleged eugenic drawbacks soundly based. Inbreeding can be beneficial; selective inbreeding is widely used in animal and plant husbandry to good effect. Even among humans, incest among the Egyptian Ptolemies was not always harmful.

As a general rule, the incest taboo implies the transition from the *natural* fact of consanguinity to the *cultural* and social fact of matrimonial alliance; below the human level, even among the higher primates, there appears to be no feeling for or against incest. But if nature left copulation to chance, culture was bound to introduce order and restriction in the midst of haphazard disorder. Culture's primary role was to preserve the continued existence of the group and substitute deliberate organization for chance; it is from the incest taboo that all the various forms of matrimonial arrangements known to anthropology and history have sprung.

By leading to strict rules of exogamy, this prohibition has had far-reaching *social* implications. In effect, by compelling marriage between outsiders, it has led to the social integration of diverse, and sometimes far-flung, groups within enlarged social organisms, requiring the active collaboration of groups hitherto foreign to one another, ensuring their cooperation in war and peace. This prohibition is not so much designed to prevent consanguineous marriages with mother, sister, or daughter as to compel their being given away to others; it is essentially a rule of *gift*, in return for a similar gift. This exchange triggers new friendships and alliances, widens the social circle, and, as a primordial integrating societal development, may well have originally started human social life on a grand scale.

This rule against incest still obtains among all primitive as well as civilized people. Margaret Mead, interviewing some Arapesh people, reached the root of the matter when she discovered that underneath the actual prohibition, they were mostly concerned with the positive effects—the actual acquisition of brothers-in-law brought about by marrying outside the family and giving one's sister away, brothers-in-law who become allies and friends, boon companions, fellow hunters.[3] In a sense, therefore, the incest taboo is a social device whereby the male cooperative instinct, first developed by the onset of big-game hunting, became institutionalized throughout the world.

Survival of the group or tribe depends primarily upon two things: food supply and the procreation of children. Hence, the close assimilation of woman to food and the fundamental function of the regulation of matrimonial alliances on the basis of an exchange of goods—grain, cattle, or land, as the case may be. Although this assimilation of woman to food and goods may seem derogatory to our contemporary way of thinking, nothing of the sort was implied from the standpoint of primitive mentality, for which there was, and still is, direct continuity between organic sensations of the human body and the sociosexual organization of the tribe. In primitive economies of scarcity, food appears as the source of the most intense feelings and emotions, the basis for abstract notions and, eventually, religious metaphors.[4] It is easy to wax indignant when one reads that in the matrimonial vocabulary of the early Slavs of Great Russia, the groom was known as the "merchant" and the bride as the "merchandise," but, again, nothing disparaging was implied.

Marriage, in primitive society, is more an economic problem than an erotic one; sexual problems that spring from a shortage of women or some form of polygamy can be, and are, solved with the help of homosexuality or the loan of women. The economic problem revolving around the economic cooperation between the sexes is of far greater importance and can be easily apprehended if one looks at the situation of the male bachelor in primitive society—a poor, ostracized wretch who lives on the fringes of society like a despised pariah and can hardly provide for himself. It is not only the Pygmies who despise bachelors and state that "the greater the number of women, the more food there is";[5] all over the world, contempt for bachelors prevails. South American Indians, the Kachins of Burma, the Papuans of New Guinea, all agree: "For a man without a woman, there is no heaven in the sky nor on earth. . . . If woman had not been created, there would be neither sun nor moon; there would be no agriculture and no fire."[6]

Marriage is, first and last, a *social* necessity to which the individual (male or female) and his family must subordinate their own private interests and inclinations. The prohibition of incest and the strict rules governing matrimonial alliances imply the supremacy of social over natural order, of the collective group interest over that of the individual, of deliberate organization over chance and hazard. Hence the complex regulations concerning exogamy and endogamy, setting strict limits as to what is permissible and definite compulsions to marry outside a clan but inside a tribe, as is the case today with the Australian aborigines.

In all primitive societies, marriage automatically implies an economic transaction, an exchange of goods. All matrimonial regulations were originally set up in order to establish a system of *exchanges*, in which food and women were initially the only available commodities; but it would be a great error to see in it a mere "commercial" transaction. It should be understood, as it is by the primitive mind, as an *exchange of gifts* rather than a trade, an exchange that is of far greater importance in these societies than in our "civilized" world because gifts always have vast *symbolic* significance. As anthropologist Marcel Mauss puts it, these exchanges represent "total social facts" whose significance is at once religious, magical, social, economic, ethical, juridical, and sentimental.[7] Sharing gifts is customary during all the great events of life; there is no real commercial intent attached to these exchanges for the simple reason that, for the primitive mentality, commodities represent far more than their mere economic usefulness; they are tools and conveyors of a much greater array of ideas and feelings —power, status, sympathy, emotion. These exchanges form an extremely complex system of communication, replete with maneuvers involving not only matrimony but also alliances, rivalry, war, and peace. This ceremonial exchange of gifts, like the *potlatch* ceremonial of some American Indians, has a definite supraeconomic character that springs from the primitive notion that it is the *distribution* rather than the possession and retention of goods that confers prestige and status —to the point of willful destruction of precious commodities on great ceremonial occasions. No one can really *possess* a symbolic object since the prime function of symbolism is not accumulation and retention, but *communication* by way of exchange.

In primitive society, the rule of exchange is primordial—whether it be of goods, words, or women. But whereas the symbolic role of the exchange of goods has considerably diminished in favor of more strictly commercial transactions, it has preserved its full importance in the case of women—partly because women are the supremely desirable commodity, but also because they are a natural stimulant, stimulating the one instinctual desire—sex—whose satisfaction can be *postponed.* The transformation from stimulant to sign and symbol that is carried out in the matrimonial exchange characterizes the transition from nature to culture, and constitutes the basis for the most enduring social institution of the human race.

Since sexual relations are only part of a total, comprehensive exchange that takes place at the time of marriage, it is clear that this exchange does not really concern the newlyweds as much as the two social groups standing back of them. And since social authority (unlike family authority) rests invariably in the hands of men, marriage is really a transaction between two groups of men, the woman being only one of the objects traded in the barter. Concerning her feelings in the matter, she may, of course, make it easy or impossible to conclude the deal; but she cannot change the *terms* of the deal, for the simple reason that the reciprocal link that establishes marriage is not set between men and women but between men *by way of* women. Women are merely means to an end—the strengthening of ties between men, who, as males, always remain in full control of all important social arrangements.[8]

Here again, the very rare instances of societies that are both matrilinear (filiation through the maternal line) and matrilocal (marital residence at the wife's house) merely demonstrate that the wretched husband (known among the Menangkebau of Sumatra as *orang samando* or "borrowed man") is replaced by males of the wife's family—uncle, brother, or older son.[9] Under no circumstances are women ever in control of social life or public authority in rudimentary political organisms. While there were, and are still, a substantial number of matrilinear societies, matrilocal ones are extremely rare, which confirms the fundamentally asymmetrical relationship between the sexes; most matrilinear societies are simultaneously patrilocal. One outstanding exception that survived into the twentieth century was that of the Nāyars of Travancore and Cochin (Kerala) where a man's sister's sons were his heirs, rather than his own sons; where the wife remained in her own *tarawād* (household), was visited from time to time by her husband, and raised their children in her house. But again, all authority rested in the hands of the eldest male *(karanavan)* of the clan, who conducted the entire management of the *tarawād*'s estate.[10]

As soon as societies grow larger and political power becomes important enough to take precedence over traditional forms of social organization, patrilinear filiation predominates. And as soon as patrilinear and patrilocal institutions are firmly established, with all that they imply for the future bride condemned to an exile in a foreign settlement, which is theoretically without appeal, a feminine compensation also becomes institutionalized (especially in southern Asia); the dominant personality at the time a matrimonial alliance is concluded is the bridegroom's father's sister—not the father, who is sometimes even excluded from the wedding procession.[11] Besides indicating a possible survival of ancient matrilinear customs, this fact points to a rudimentary female solidarity that counteracts, to a point, male dominance in primitive societies. It may represent an atavistic survival going all the way back to the days when man was not aware of his biological role as inseminator of new life, when biological filiation was believed to proceed exclusively through the mothers.

Many customs that are still prevalent—among the Kachins of Burma, for instance—not only point to a latent tension between female and male lines of descendants, but also to the far greater attachment of women for the family into which they were born than for that into which they marry. The whole Gilyak mythology, for instance, is female-oriented—its tales concern the human maternal ancestors contrasted with the animal paternal forefathers, uncles saving their sisters and nieces from the claws of the dreaded bear; all depicting the feminine outlook on primitive marriage, which includes as well the viewpoint of the brothers of the bride, who tend to overestimate the loss of their sister while downgrading their own gains of wives as a result of this "loss." In fact, it is the mythology of the linear system of filiation as opposed to the agnatic (filiation through the father) one—again, a survival of ancient times when filiation was exclusively through female lines.

As the patrilinear and patrilocal system came to prevail throughout most of the world, the most powerful feelings engendered in women by the rules of exogamy were the dread of expatriation, exile, loss of protection of their own families, and the difficulties encountered in settling down to married life in an alien environment in order to start a new family. Marriage implied leaving one's kin and friends, as well as constant struggle to establish a close understanding with the husband's family. Among the ancient Chinese of the Shang era, as well as among the "barbarians" dwelling beyond their borders, marriage became final only after three years of wedlock; it was often said that three years were required before the wife would smile at her husband for the first time. Attachment to the family out of which the girl marries is usually extremely strong—good understanding with the husband is often compared to "fraternal" understanding, with the jealous brothers always in the background. Perhaps the greatest symbol of this attitude is the custom, known as *chotunnur* among the Yakuts of Siberia, of brothers deflowering their sisters before their marriage.[12]

In institutionalizing the union of opposite sexes, human society sets itself above the natural order. And the following remark can apply to all human societies: "The most fundamental religious notion deals with the difference between the sexes. Each is perfectly normal in its way, but contact between them is pregnant with danger for both of them."[13] Marriage is a dramatic meeting between nature and culture, between kinship and alliance; and it is only through strict regulations, all of which spring from the primordial prohibition of incest, that human society came into being, through *social* control of its biological instincts. All the rules of kinship and matrimony aim at the same goal: the integration of the biological family into the social group. This in turn enables mankind to overcome its biological limitations in order to build increasingly complex social organizations.

In this sense, exogamy and language fulfill the same purpose: *communication* with others and integration of the social group. By compelling the exchange of women, the incest taboo, in effect, acts as a nonverbal discourse. As Claude Lévi-Strauss remarks, this taboo is as universal as language, and the link between the two is not as arbitrary as it sounds: words are just as much *gifts* as are brides and goods. In fact, their close connection in the primitive mind gives us the key to its ultimate understanding of woman's social role. The primitive mind groups linguistic and incest prohibitions under the same overall heading, language being understood, not merely as strings of meaningful words, but as verbal power and action, as symbolism—that is, etymologically, link, bond, intercourse. In New Caledonia, for instance, "bad word" means adultery. Primitive mentality has a great respect for word power and frowns on any kind of linguistic distortion: quantitative (immoderate laughter, loud play, excessive display of feelings) and qualitative (reacting to meaningless sounds that are not words, calling someone by a name that is not his, talking to something that only *appears* to be human). In all cases, the common feature is the concept of a misuse of something sacred: language. Prohibition of such misuse is grouped with the incest taboo and judged to be of equal importance. And this in turn can imply only one thing: women themselves are treated as symbols or signs used for social communication, and they are misused when they are not handled as symbols or signs are meant to be handled—that is, when they are not *communicated,* exchanged. Language and exogamy both represent equivalent solutions to the problem of communication between human societies, and a kinship system is, in effect, a matrimonial dialogue, its members being exchanged like words.[14]

But these two means of communication have evolved quite differently over the years. While language has reached a high degree of power of abstraction and quality of communication, words have largely lost, except in poetry, their quality as *value* in order to become merely signs. Along with the progress of scientific understanding and greater depth of abstraction, the development of language has definitely robbed words of most of their aesthetic, affective, and magical connotations.

But if we shift from speech to matrimonial alliance, the situation presents itself quite differently. While the emergence of symbolic thought required that women, like words, should be exchanged, it could never reduce women to mere signs. Under her two conflicting aspects as object of desire on the part of a male ego and simultaneously subject to the desire of others, woman was bound to become an instrument of communication and alliance with others. But, as producer of signs herself and as a bona fide human being, woman retained not only her quality as sign but also as *value*—dependent on her ability to play her part in all the intimate roles of matrimonial life. Thus it is that the relationship between the sexes has retained all the affective magic and the unfathomable mystery that has disappeared, except for poetry, from verbal communication.

It is largely to the taboo of incest that the human race owes its unity and universality, inasmuch as that prohibition gradually knitted together increasingly large but scattered populations and, through intermarriage and cross-fertilization, gave some social cohesion to ever-vaster aggregates of human beings. It could be said, metaphorically, that the unification of the human race was so structured that the males constitute the individual bricks and the females the mortar of this vast biological unit destined to spread eventually over the entire surface of the planet.

CHAPTER

3

The Rise and Fall
of the Great Mother

*In the beginning the Great Mother created the heaven and the earth. . . .
And the Great Mother said, let there be light: and there was light . . . and
the Great Mother divided the light from the darkness.*

Had the biblical Genesis been written some tens of thousands of years
ago, this would probably have been its rendering, since every evidence
points to the fact that the male stood in awe of the female, as he did
of all natural phenomena—storms, lightning, earthquakes, volcanic
eruptions. Weak, relatively defenseless, and more or less isolated in
small, scattered groups, yet increasingly capable of abstract thought,
primitive man was afraid of nature's mysterious displays of grandiose
power. In exactly the same way, he stood in awe of the mysteries of
gestation and childbirth because they were *natural* manifestations of
creative power. Social forces he understood, since he, as a hunting
male, was the originator of social organizations and customs, but all
natural phenomena were invested by him with magic significance—
they were mysteries. Men's rites were social customs, but all rights of
protective isolation applicable to women were men's *social* attempts to
cope with, and control, *natural* mysteries. The weird menstrual cycle,
the flow of blood, the magical birth of new life, made woman part of
those forces of nature that he did not understand and feared, and the
necessary *intermediary*, not only between man and man (via the incest
taboo) but also between man and nature.

Some idea of this dependence of man on woman as intermediary can
be gathered from certain traditions still maintained by primitive communities in this century. In an extraordinary account of the magic
ceremonies celebrated by African Pygmies in preparation for hunting
antelopes in the Kongour forest, Leo Frobenius described a scene that
must be as old as the men of the Stone Age:

At dawn, accompanied by a woman, the Pygmies climbed to the top of a hill, where they cleared and flattened a small patch of ground. When this had been done, one of the hunters drew with his finger on the ground the outline of an antelope, while his companions murmured incantations. Then came an expectant silence, and at the moment when the sun rose over the horizon one of the men, bending his bow, came up to the bare patch. A few minutes more and the sun's rays touched the drawing. At that very moment the following extremely rapid scene took place: the woman raised her hands as if to seize the sun, muttering words, while the bowman shot his arrow into the silhouette traced on the ground. Again the woman muttered, and then the hunters, with their weapons, bounded off into the undergrowth. The woman remained a few moments longer and then went back to the camp. . . . When evening came the Pygmies brought back an antelope, killed by an arrow through its jugular vein.[1]

Womanpower and magic control over nature were closely interconnected in the mind of early man, as is still the case with Frobenius's Pygmies. Is it any wonder, then, that the earliest objects of worship uncovered by archeological research were naked *female* forms, small figurines with great thighs, big breasts, and large bellies, representatives of the earliest ritual art? Whenever the male figure appears, it is usually clothed, ornamented, and masked. Man already felt cut off from nature, and woman was the obvious intercessor; was there not a close and observable correlation between her menstrual cycle and the phases of the moon or the movements of the tide?

This new awe and fear, unknown among other primates, must have been generated by an abrupt increase in knowledge and understanding, implying a decisive crossing of a threshold of self-consciousness, the rapid development of a new awareness and a new feeling of reverence for human life and its transmission—probably linked with the dawn of a tragic understanding of the inevitability of death. Magic worship and propitiation of the mysterious forces of nature began. Humankind took a giant leap forward when symbolic thought emerged, that is, when thoughts and experiences were crystallized, reproduced, and preserved in artifacts, the very beginning of artistic expression. Primitive man overcame the world of immediate appetites and sensations, began to remember the past and anticipate the future, extend his mental domain and fill it with widely accepted and comprehended symbols whose meanings and values were acknowledged by the whole group. Symbolism created a mental duplicate of the understandable universe and gave man some feeling of the orderliness that underlies the processes of nature—and, eventually, some degree of control over those cosmic processes that affected him directly.

Hence the little figurines that began to dot the primeval landscape, dramatic expression of man's awe at woman's physiological power to create new life, apparently unassisted by man. Many statuettes were found ensconced in shrines, which implies that they were the objects of a magic cult rather than samples of primitive erotica. In the very early Paleolithic epoch, Homo sapiens began to roam the vast Eurasian plains stretching from Spain to Lake Baikal. The great icefields of the fourth glaciation were just beginning to recede and he hunted the woolly mammoth in what was then arctic tundra. His main objects of worship were these female statuettes, such as are still carved by Siberian reindeer hunters. The Yakuts and Ostyaks worship these diminutive Venuses in the Siberian taiga and provide an instance of unbroken continuity all the way back to the remote Paleolithic past:

> . . . from the point of view of the history of thought, these Late Paleolithic Venus figurines come to us as the earliest detectable expression of that underlying ritual idea which sees in Woman the embodiment of the beginning and continuance of life, as well as the symbol of the immortality of that earthly matter which is in itself without form, yet clothes all forms.[2]

Early cosmologies must have closely resembled that of the Delaware Indians who believed that, originally, men lived as embryos or larvae in the body of the Mother, that is, deep in the bowels of the earth; adding to a similar belief, the Iroquois believed that, one fine day, man found an opening in the Earth's crust and crawled out onto the surface, and began to enjoy living in the open air. In Navajo language, the earth was named *Naëtsán,* the "recumbent Woman," and Navajo cosmology tallies closely with the previous one: a complete homology between the condition of the newborn baby with that of their remote, underground-dwelling ancestors.[3] The same myth prevailed in Peru as in Mexico that the first men came out of the earth—*Pachamama,* Peruvian Earth Mother, or the Mexican Mother of All, also known as *Centeotl,* goddess of the maize, nourisher of men, and bringer of children.[4]

The mammoth-hunting Paleolithic man's dwelling places during the Aurignacian period were widely scattered but comparatively stationary. Within these semipermanent dwellings, as in the warmer subtropical dwelling places farther south, woman's role and influence must have been considerable, inciting man's jealousy, resentment, and desire to gain control over this mysterious female power. To this day, a number of primitive populations, notably the Ona and Yahgans of Tierra del Fuego, entertain legends to the effect that, in ancient times, women ruled men by witchcraft, and that it was only relatively recently that men reasserted their authority.[5] This legend is widespread in primitive communities and points to some kind of tension between the sexes. Whatever the scant evidence of such tension in prehistoric times, however, some hostility may well have existed. Prehistoric man worshiped the little goddesses, but probably more in superstitious fear than in adoration.

In those Aurignacian days, the climate of the Eurasian plain was arctic; the icefields were retreating at a very slow pace (southern Norway was still under the icecap). Hunting rhinoceros, reindeer, and mammoth from his relatively stationary dwellings, Aurignacian man appears to have been, more or less willingly, completely under the spell of the naked goddesses, that is, of Mother Earth in her various guises. From the celebrated Venuses of Willendorf (Austria) and Lespugue (France) to the twenty-odd statuettes found at Mal'ta, near Lake Baikal, the great northern plains are strewn with Aurignacian remains indicating the prevalence of a female-oriented worship; such carved evidence has also been unearthed on Kostienki Island and at Yeliceevici, in Russia; at Mézin, in France; at Vistonice and Prědmost, in Czechoslovakia, and at Mainz, Germany. These rudimentary works of art always represent heavily breasted, stout women in advanced stages of pregnancy, presumably the work of Aurignacian and Gravettian sculptors illustrating fertility magic.[6]

But the shattered remains of female statuettes in the rock shrine at Laussel, almost certainly the victims of willful aggression, bear witness to a deep-seated male antagonism. Other such shattered remains were found in scattered Paleolithic encampments, pointing to a deliberate attempt to destroy the magic power of these female figurines, preparatory to the substitution of the male shaman for the female goddess as wielder of magic powers.[7]

Time passed, the icecap retreated farther, and the climate and ecology of the Eurasian plain changed. Humid tundra became dry steppe, and new hunting game (wild ass, antelope, wild horse, bison) required a more nomadic way of life, and a consequent decrease in the importance and influence of women. Pursuing the great herds required "more of the running-muscle than of the sitting-fat."[8] Magic worship began to shift, at the western end of the broad plain, from the vagina to the phallus, and from "an essentially plant-oriented to a purely animal-oriented mythology." This was the area of the great Paleolithic hunt, when the bison, and no longer the mammoth, was the main game. When wide-ranging nomadism replaced the relatively stationary mammoth-hunting encampments, animal-oriented magic cults took over, eliminating the female-oriented cults of former days.

To this monumental shift we owe the great mural paintings of the temple caves in Spain and southern France; while in Russia and Siberia the mammoth remained for thousands of years, along with the female figurines. Certain it is, however, that in Europe these figurines disappear completely at the close of the Aurignacian epoch. In the Magdalenian period that followed, they are replaced by the magnificent cave paintings in which we find a rich representation of animals and human males dressed as shamans—the extraordinary murals of the Trois Frères, the grotto at Tuc d'Audoubert, and the caves at Lascaux, with their dancing shamans, bulls, and bisons. It is worth noting, however, that these grottoes, caverns, and underground labyrinths were still viewed as the multiple vaginas and wombs of the Earth Mother, and that even this masculinization of the *Zeitgeist* could not do away completely with the Primordial Mother to whose entrails Magdalenian man entrusted his most precious pictorial creations. But, by and large, this was now a hunting world, in which the masculine psyche prevailed and remained predominant until the close of the Bronze Age. In the great hunting plains of Europe, the Earth Mother's magic power was broken and male shamanism took over.

What, basically, is a shaman? In real terms, a shaman is a medicine man who applies a psychoanalytic cure to organic or psychosomatic ailments. Primitive man fully accepts the reality of a world of good and evil spirits, magic animals, supernatural monsters, and malignant dwarfs, since he makes little distinction between objective reality and subjective feeling. But his acceptance is qualified to the extent that this, to us, crazy universe is, to him, a coherent system that he understands fully. What he refuses to accept are incoherent and arbitrary sufferings that have no place or explanation in his mental universe. The function of the shaman is to call in the myth, as valid explanation, and strip the suffering of its arbitrary meaninglessness and its incoherent aspect. For us, today, the valid explanation of an ailment relates a germ or virus to the disease, but it is an *external* relationship between cause and effect. The shaman, on the other hand, relates the disease to some mythological monster which is *internal* and lurks in the mind of the patient, establishing a relationship, not between cause and effect, but between symbol and thing symbolized, or signifying to signified; he provides the patient with a *language* in which the disease can be expressed, understood, and therefore controlled or even mastered. Unlike the psychoanalyst, however, the shaman does the talking and actually cures the patient by taking an active part in the battle between the beneficent spirits that he leads into the diseased organ and the malignant monsters who symbolize the disease.[9] In other words, the shaman incarnates a new, essentially masculine spirit that seeks to overcome forcibly the ills imposed by Mother Nature, instead of submitting to them with fatalistic resignation. He is the one who puts to flight the feminine spirit of Mother Earth and breaks the female figurines that symbolize it.

While the masculine ethos came to dominate completely in the northern plains stretching from Spain to central Russia, another type of primitive culture developed farther south, in the tropics and subtropical areas stretching from East Africa, Egypt, Syria, Mesopotamia,· all the way to India and Southeast Asia. Here, an entirely different type of social and religious structure prevailed, initiated by the transition from hunting and food collecting to cultivation. In horticultural economies, women are the main food producers, besides being the child bearers; all the magico-religious power is theirs. The lowered status of males in this type of organization, enhanced by their ignorance of their biological role as inseminator of the female, must have been strongly resented by the men: "Small wonder . . . if, in reaction, their revengeful imaginations ran amok and developed secret lodges and societies, the mysteries and terrors of which were directed primarily against the women!"[10] Such secret societies had nothing in common with those devoted to initiation in hunting tribes; they spread far beyond the local tribe, indulged in antifeminist propaganda, and their membership had nothing to do with kinship but was recruited through election. Even today, in West Africa and Melanesia, for instance, these primitive freemasonries recruit their members in widely scattered and different tribes. In such organizations, ritual cannibalism and homosexuality are prevalent, along with odd skull cults and an elaborate paraphernalia of drums and masks.

With all that, it often happened that the prevailing deities worshiped in these woman-hating societies were still female. The Supreme Being was pictured as the Great Mother—the prevailing female-oriented atmosphere being so powerful that even woman-hating males were compelled to bow to the ultimate female, the Earth Mother. It is probably from these gardening cultures in the tropical belt that the female-oriented outlook penetrated the Middle East when protohistory picks up the tale.

The Neolithic cultures came into being in the Fertile Crescent (Mesopotamia and Syria) at the junction of the hunting world of the great northern plains and the southern tropical belt of planting cultures. From about 10,000 to 5,000 B.C. human progress advanced rapidly, almost explosively, with the beginning of the domestication of animals and the new pastoral way of life it entailed in the northern plains, of agriculture in the southern subtropical areas. The conjunction of these dramatic advances in economic output led to a mixed barnyard economy in which grain agriculture (wheat and barley) and stock breeding (sheep, ox, pigs, and goats) complemented each other. Based on this extraordinary increase in affluence, human skills progressed at a swift pace: carpentry, house building, weaving, and pottery began to flourish. Farming altered from plot cultivation by women with hoes to agriculture by men with heavy plows pulled by harnessed oxen—a socioeconomic alteration that had already taken place before the oldest Egyptian and Sumerian documents could record the fact.

The foundations of the old matrilinear, "mother-right," kinship structure were shaken to the ground by the Neolithic revolution. A multiplicity of technical inventions contributed to this revolution: harnessing domesticated animals, the sail, the wheel, and the potter's wheel. The discovery of irrigation and the rising fertility of the land allowed the farmers to grow increasingly large surpluses of food which sustained increasingly elaborate and complex societies living in fast-growing urban centers.

The beginning of large-scale agriculture must have been psychologically traumatic, and more than one future agriculturist must have echoed the following words, uttered late in the nineteenth century by a North American Indian, Smohalla of the tribe of Umatilla:

> It is a sin to wound or cut, to tear or scratch our common mother by working at agriculture. You ask me to dig in the earth? Am I to take a knife and plunge it into the breast of my mother? But then, when I die, she will not gather me again into her bosom. You tell me to dig up and take away the stones. Must I mutilate her flesh so as to get at her bones? Then I can never again enter into her body and be born again. You ask me to cut the grass and the corn and sell them, to get rich like the white men. But how dare I crop the hair of my mother?[11]

Archeological evidence indicates that it is in the relatively high and well-protected valleys of southern Anatolia and Iran that human civilization first achieved its major breakthrough, a complete mutation in the human way of life which took place between the tenth and sixth millennia B.C., leading progressively to the first city-states of the Fertile Crescent during the High Neolithic (4500–3500 B.C.). During this entire period, the centerpiece of mythology and worship was the Great

Mother.[12] In southeastern Europe and the Mediterranean, in Iran, Egypt, and Syria, Neolithic societies molded female figurines in clay, or carved them in bone and stone—all symbolic representations of the Great Goddess of fertility, from whose bosom grain sprouts when she is propitiated correctly. Like all females (man thinks), she can be bribed by sacrifice and beseeched by prayer, although she can also be brought under some form of control by ritual magic and assorted incantations.[13]

Recent excavations in the higher valleys of southern Anatolia have thrown new light on the Great Mother Goddess's origins and on life during the Upper Paleolithic. Dating back to the seventh millennia B.C., large settlements amounting almost to small cities such as Çatal Hüyük display wall paintings and plaster reliefs of goddesses and animal heads, all having ritual rather than merely decorative significance. Bull heads appear between stylized female breasts protruding like knobs from the walls. A scene frequently depicted is that of the birth of the bull god from the body of the goddess; long before Sumer ever existed, the stalacmitic underground caverns of the Taurus were understood to be the dreaded haunts of the Great Goddess. The partly aniconic figures unearthed at Çatal Hüyük represent her in her awesome chthonic aspect as ruling the realm of the dead who are back in her womb. Sometimes she is pictured as "Mistress of Animals"—numerous clay figurines depicting the goddess, supported by two felines (usually leopards), giving birth to a bull deity or, sometimes, a ram.[14]

There are also numerous figures of the Twin Goddess—two heads, two pairs of breasts but a single pair of arms—representing the two aspects, mother and maiden, of the Great Goddess, "predecessors of the 'Two Ladies' of the Knossos texts, the famous ivory from Mycenae, and the Demeter and Kore of Classical Greece."[15] It is significant that at Çatal Hüyük, somewhere around the fifty-eighth century B.C., hunting ceased and agriculture took over, a process which started in Çatal Hüyük II and was completed later in Hacilar—and with it there came an almost complete disappearance of male statues in the cult, witness to the tight connection existing between the supremacy of the male psyche and a hunting culture.[16] Whenever the divine family was represented (sculptures in the round), its four members were always depicted in order of decreasing importance—mother, daughter, son, and father, which are in fact reducible to two: the Great Goddess herself and her son who is also her paramour.

Sex is nowhere depicted in the figurines, statuettes, wall paintings, or plaster reliefs of either Çatal Hüyük or Hacilar. The capital point is that in these settlements there were no phallic symbols, no representation of the vulva, in strange contrast to other Upper Paleolithic and Neolithic cultures in the Balkans and other parts of Anatolia where phalli of clay and stone had already begun to appear. The point is crucial in that an emphasis on sexual organs in artistic representation betrays the supremacy of the male impulse over that of the female. Here, on the contrary, the supremacy of the reproductive, motherly, but asexual female principle is clearly asserted: breast and pregnancy symbolize the female, horned animal heads the hunting male. Especially after hunting ceased, the female principle dominated completely with its repetitive theme of conservation and propagation of life, a purely vegetative, lunar-cyclical, and largely passive outlook—all the mysteries of life and death were hers, not his. All over the world, this metaphysical supremacy of the female principle has asserted itself whenever horticultural production and human reproduction were linked. The Orinoco Indians of South America always left horticultural work to the women, since "as women know how to conceive seed and bear children, so the seeds and roots planted by them bore fruit far more abundantly than if they had been planted by male hands." The South American Jibaros firmly believe that "women exercise a special, mysterious influence on the growth of cultivated plants." The Ewe of Africa entertain the same belief.[17]

In the Middle East, however, this outlook was eventually doomed. As the male was slowly overcoming his awe and fear of the complex female-nature, the masculine principle, inherently aggressive, was gradually emancipating itself in a Promethean drive to become master of what had awed him: nature and the Great Mother. The psychological struggle lasted several millennia; but in Çatal Hüyük and Hacilar we can see only the faint outline of the beginning of the process. The great merit of the existence of these ancient settlements is that they have provided us with the missing link between Upper Paleolithic art (as expression of hunting magic as well as female symbolism) and the forthcoming fertility cults of the Neolithic Middle East with their supremacy of the Great Goddess and her successive reincarnations, all the way to Cybele, Artemis, Diana, and Aphrodite. In Anatolia's high valleys, the hunting masculine spirit met for a while with the Great Mother; with the end of hunting, the Great Mother smothered that spirit for a while—that is, until the final, irrevocable patriarchal revolution set in, thousands of years later.

In *The Palace of Minos,* Arthur Evans, the discoverer of Cretan civilization, claimed that the innumerable images of goddesses discovered by him represented "the same Great Mother with her Child or Consort whose worship under various names and titles extended over a large part of Asia Minor and the Syrian regions beyond"[18]—a claim which was substantiated later by further excavations and deciphering of Cretan documents. In the same way, continuity between Cretan, Mycenaean, and classical Greek representations of the Great Goddess is also unquestionable.

In early Sumerian mythology, her supremacy is clearly established, at least as far as the mythological sequence is concerned. On a tablet listing the Sumerian deities, the goddess Nammu is given priority; she is written with the pictograph standing for the primeval "sea" and is depicted as "the mother, who gave birth to heaven and earth," eternal and uncreated.[19] In turn, heaven and earth were depicted as being originally united in the form of a mountain, Anki, of which heaven, An, was a male deity and earth, Ki, female; from their union was begotten the air god, Enlil, who in turn separated his parents from one another; and from his union with his mother sprang human beings, animals, and plants.

Mythologies are never static but always in a process of evolution, especially as regards nomenclature. The original Earth Goddess, Ki, became in time Nintu ("the Lady who gave birth"), Ninmah ("the Exhalted Lady"), and finally Ninhursag. In the early days of Sumerian culture she was supreme, although she lost rank later on; and in those early days, all Sumerian rulers described themselves as "nourished by the trustworthy milk of Ninhursag"—mother of life itself, unassisted procreator of man. Her shrine, uncovered at Obeid in southern Mesopotamia, had an oval shape undoubtedly designed to symbolize female genitalia.[20]

In the form of the Twin Goddess, she was first of all Inanna, Queen of Heaven (transmuted later in classical Greece into Aphrodite), who, as tutelary goddess of the city-state of Erech, successfully stole all the divine laws from Enki, tutelary god of the city of Eridu; her female-organ-shaped sanctuary was eventually uncovered at Khafajah. But she was also the dreaded Ereshkigal, Queen of the Underworld (later Persephone in classical Greece). The god Dumuzi-abu, lover of Inanna in life and of Ereshkigal in the underworld, was the forerunner and counterpart of the Greek Adonis. This triad became, in the forthcoming mysteries of Eleusis, Demeter (Mother Earth), Persephone (Queen of the Underworld), and Triptolemus, their foster child. The overall continuity is well established between Sumer and post-Homeric Greece, via Crete and Mycenae.

From all available documents, it is quite clear that in the Bronze Age Middle East, the prevailing view of life was essentially a nonheroic, fatalistic, rhythmic lunar-vegetal one. The Great Goddess, the "Original Mother without a Spouse," was in full control of all the mythologies. From Minoan Crete to the Indus Valley civilization of Mohenjodaro and Harappā and even the China of the Shang era, she held full sway. She was the Earth itself, and all that came from her womb was semantically assimilated to the female organs—the Babylonian *pû* meant both the source of a river and the vagina; the Egyptian expression *bī* stood for both a mine's underground gallery and, again, the vagina. In fact, the vagina was equated in most Middle Eastern languages with underground features or water; the Sumerian *buru,* for instance, implied both vagina and a river; and the ores extracted were probably assimilated to embryos—the Babylonian *an-kubu* translates either as "embryo" or "abortion"; metallurgy and obstetrics were closely correlated.[21] The Earth Mother was creative by parthogenesis and was in no need of fertilization or impregnation by a male entity —a view that lasted well into the classical Greek era when Hera was presumed to be able to conceive unassisted and give birth to Ares, Typhon, and Haephastos.[22] In this Bronze Age matriarchal symbolism, there was no room for original sin, divine wrath, and an all-powerful godhead; the male gods were merely sons, later promoted to consorts, of the Great Goddess.

It is perhaps in Minoan Crete rather than Sumer that the female-oriented life outlook was most in evidence—the enormous preponderance of goddesses and female cult officiants, the emotional nature of the religion, which is evident in the tree cult scenes that have been excavated; also, the complete absence of any phallic symbols or references to sexual activity:

> We see the women depicted as often as, if not more often than the men, whereas in Assyria they never appear at all. Probably in Minoan Crete women played a greater part than they did even in Egypt. . . . It is certain that they must have lived on a footing of greater equality with the men than in any other ancient civilization, and we see in the frescoes of Knossos conclusive indications of an open and easy association of men and women. . . .[23]

Following the Egyptian custom, women were painted white and men red; both sexes were elaborately dressed, with flying hair of the same length. Women were unveiled, usually in décolleté with arms and necks bare.

As in Mesopotamia, Minoan architectural symbolism emphasized the supremacy of femaleness—tombs shaped according to female anatomy (death being merely the blessed return to Mother Earth's womb), labyrinth and maze symbolizing the female's internal organs, illustrating the twin principles of (female) defensive exclusion and (male) penetration. The Cretan labyrinth symbolism, "somehow to be associated with maidenhood," was brought out in bold relief by the legend of Theseus' penetration of the maze and his extraction thanks to Ariadne's thread.[24] This outward projection into space of symbolized sexual organs is in a sense analogous to the outward projections of given societies' political institutions or mythological beliefs—the circular schema of Sioux villages, or the layout of roads and temples in the Inca Empire.

Minoan culture and mythology appear to have set fast at an earlier stage of Bronze Age civilization than those of Mesopotamia and Egypt —milder and more gentle, uninterested in great feats of arms and heroics, living life to the full in their cities without protective walls. But Minoan culture was by no means limited to the island of Crete; it spread to the entire Aegean world and continental Greece. Mycenae, to a large extent, was a crude replica of Knossos; ornaments and vessels found in Mycenaean graves were the work of Minoan craftsmen —signets, representations of the Cretan flounced skirt and masculine drawers; as in Crete, the Great Mother Goddess was depicted surrounded by her Minoan paraphernalia: the dove, the double axe, the horns of consecration, and the sacred pillar.[25] Yet there was at Mycenae the very beginning of a more masculine spirit—a greater martial atmosphere than in Crete, fortified citadels, and large numbers of weapons. Mycenaeans worshiped the Great Mother Goddess out of atavism; but the barbaric Mycenaean spirit definitely prefigures the forthcoming patriarchal revolution.

In Bronze Age matriarchal symbolism, placid and optimistic, the motherly stress was on unification and conservation; in the subsequent patriarchal era, the stern, fatherly stress would be on dissociation and change. The fundamental psychological reason is obvious: a girl gradually approaches her ultimate role of motherhood with rising sureness, thanks to identification with her mother. A "girl finds that the reinterpretation of impregnation and conception and birth fits easily into her early experience with the intake of food, while the boy with the same initial experience can at most use it to interpret the female role, but will find himself heavily confused if he attempts to use it to interpret his own."[26] For the boy, the process is reversed; he must realize himself as *different* from his mother, must "turn out of himself" and find expression through the bodies of others. As Margaret Mead states it, a girl's femininity is

> concealed deep within her, nothing that she can touch and see, depend upon or flaunt. . . . The small boy struts, sometimes with

emphasis on his penis, more often carrying hatchet, knife, stick, pole, in upward positions as he marches, parries, performs. His behavior, however symbolic, is to the extent that he is male a concentrated phallic exaggeration, while his sister's is more diffuse and involves the whole body. The little boy is sure about his specific maleness, but seems not to be so sure of his adequacy to operate it. He supplements with various symbolic objects.[27]

A further difference lies in the fact that a woman experiences sharp and dramatic cleavages in her life course, sharp transitions between defloration, pregnancy, childbirth, and menopause; man's life course knows no such abrupt thresholds, its various stages shading impercep- tibly into one another from childhood to old age. As a result, woman places greater emphasis on *being,* and man on *doing,* on proving that he is a man, that he is *different.*[28] The female-motherly outlook, cyclical and rhythmic, dissolves all duality, including life and death, in a warm, consoling embrace; nature and spirit are not divorced, immanence and mystical feeling prevail. Life and death are only two episodes in the essential being of Mother Earth—life merely implying a temporary detachment from the planet's womb, death a return home.

Keeping this view in mind makes it easier to understand what hap- pened when, at the end of the Bronze Age, a monumental psychologi- cal shift took place and the prevailing female-oriented outlook disinte- grated. In remote times, the mysterious menstrual cycle, pregnancy, and the birth of new life out of woman's body made a profound impres- sion on the masculine mind, greatly enhanced by the fact that preg- nancy and the sexual act were not understood to be connected. Appar- ently, *man had no part in the creation of new life.* It was female magic and the reincarnation of ancestral spirit that thrust new life into the woman's womb, not man's semen. Even in the advanced civilization of early Minoan Crete, where divinity was worshiped in the shape of sacred motherhood—the heavy-buttocked clay figurines prefiguring the forthcoming Great Goddess were usually in a state of advanced pregnancy—the biological role of the father does not seem to have been fully understood.[29]

Man was therefore father only in a legal and social sense. Men were related through mothers, not fathers: until very recently, for instance, among matrilineal Bantu tribes, kinship ties were based on the fact of being "born from the same womb," or "suckled at the same breast." All the father did was to *legitimize,* as it were, almost adopt his own children. And the fact that they thought that the fetus was merely a seed placed in woman's womb through contact between her and some animal or sacred object stripped man of all participation in the life- creating process. Since they believed that before birth their soul or

spirit dwelt in caves, trees, wells, or rock crevices before being ushered
into woman's womb by some magic or other, they were far more
closely related to, and yet fearful of, nature than they have been ever
since: "We might say in a sense that *man was not yet born,* that he did
not yet realize that he belonged wholly to the biological species he
represented. It might be better to consider that at this stage his life was
in a pre-natal phase: man still continued to share, directly, in a life that
was not his own, in a 'cosmico-maternal' life."[30]

This seems to have been a worldwide fact. In Athens, traditional lore
had it that, before Cecrops (the mythical founder of the city), children
were ignorant of their fathers. In early China, it was commonly believed that a woman could become pregnant from a dragon's saliva.[31]
Even in contemporary times, the Trobriand islanders' language had no
word for "father" because the very concept did not exist. It was the
missionaries who taught the incredulous islanders the facts of procreation, which they had believed, until then, to be attributable to the
entrance of a ghost, *baloma,* into the womb, usually when the woman
was bathing. New Zealand's Maoris claimed that "the moon is the real
husband of all women." Some Australian tribes restrict the role of the
husband to merely "opening the woman," while Hudson Bay's Es-
kimos believe that, although the child actually crawls into the womb,
man's semen is required to "feed the child."[32] Other Central Australian aborigines, the Arunta, Luritcha, and Ilpirra, understand the
connection but claim that the child is not the direct result of coitus;[33]
as far as they are concerned, sexual congress does not *cause* pregnancy
but is merely a required preparation for the introduction of the child's
spirit in the womb.[34]

It seems quite probable that, under those circumstances, the woman
did not suffer from any Freudian penis envy but that the men suffered
from "uterus envy," a female-protest within men who were awed by
the apparently exclusively female power of creation of new life.[35] This
is perhaps the origin of the widespread ritual known as *couvade,* which
was highly popular in many parts of the world, from France to China,
and was mentioned in Roman times by Diodorus and Strabo. The
ritual still survives among some South American Indian tribes: either
before or at the birth of a child, the father takes to his bed or hammock
for days or weeks and receives the kind of care usually reserved for
women in an advanced stage of pregnancy. This ancient tradition was
probably inspired by such uterus envy, as well as by a desire to affirm,
however artificially, the existence of a bond between father and child
which nature, alone, did not seem to establish. Those were times when
woman's main desire was not marital bliss but fertility and procreation.

One modern psychologist, Karen Horney, even asserts that this male envy of female procreativity has served, and still serves, "as one, if not as the essential, driving force in the setting up of cultural values." And she adds:

> Is not the tremendous strength in men of the impulse to creative work in every field precisely due to the feeling of playing a relatively small part in the creation of new living beings, which constantly impels them to an over-compensation in achievement?[36]

Undoubtedly. And even more so when, in ancient times, they believed that they played *no part* at all. And this in turn explains why cultural production and symbol making became an almost exclusively male function. In the remote days when the Great Mother ruled supreme, there was little cultural outlet for the humbled male. It is only when phallic symbolism appeared that it became evident that a profound psychological shift was taking place and that a culturally induced "penis envy" began to haunt female psychology.

In the early stages of Minoan art, divinity was thought of so exclusively in terms of motherhood that the typically divine couple was mother and son—Mother Earth giving birth without need of a male assistant. The slender, youthful boy-god depicted so often in earlier Minoan art represents the annual birth, growth, and decay of vegetation, the typically cyclical conception of a gardening culture. In the early stages, Cretan art portrays the boy-god seated on his mother's lap, then growing up toward puberty. And then, in the Late Minoan Age, the boy-god "seems to have lost prominence before the slow advance of procreative ideas"[37]—probably the very beginning of an understanding of the crucial role played by the sexual act in the procreating process. The boy-god is replaced by a full-fledged consort; the Great Mother acquires a spouse—first step on her way to ultimate dethronement. Some similar shift took place in Sumer; from being the supreme deity, ranking before Enki in the god-lists, the goddess Ninhursag slowly declined in prestige and influence before the air god, Enlil—originally her son.[38]

There appears, therefore, to be a close connection between the disintegration of the female-oriented outlook and increasing knowledge of man's biological role in the procreating process. In order to understand the psychological nature of this dawning awareness, it is essential to remember that early man did not think in logical terms as we do; causality was unknown to him. Even when some connection between sex and procreation was finally established, this connection was not, at first, a *causal* one. Prelogical thinking is not exclusively focused on practical aims; its main goal is to satisfy *intellectual* require-ments. Primitive man, then and now, can no more live in mental chaos than we can; an intellectual frame of reference is required at all times. The greatest curse, that which induces insanity and has destroyed many primitive cultures under the impact of an alien civilization, is *mental disorder*, the inability to classify things and ideas, and connect them, and thus introduce some order in man's mental picture of the universe. Any form of classification is preferable to chaos, even classi-fying at the level of mere appearances is a step in the direction of rational order.[39]

Therefore, the main objective is not, for instance, the knowledge that a specific herb cures a specific ailment, but what kind of congru-ence can be established between herb and ailment, how they can be made to "go together"; this congruence, when established, becomes the general mental framework within which the cure effected by the herb becomes only one of its practical applications.[40] Quite obviously, a phenomenon such as the interdependence between lovemaking and pregnancy is not grasped in terms of cause and effect but in terms of symbol and phenomenon symbolized or in terms of signifying and signified.[41] The sequence cause-and-effect implies an awareness of *temporal succession* that is not available to prelogical man, bathing as he does in an atmosphere of timeless cyclical myth.

Magical thought can establish congruences between the most dispa-rate and incongruous elements. Primitive minds can homologize by establishing strict correspondences between social and natural phenomena; for instance, the Australian Murngin tribe's world-picture is made up of two alternating halves, corresponding to the sexes and the seasons—male, pure, sacred, fertilizing (rain), superior, and the snake; female, impure, profane, fertilized (earth), inferior, and the incestuous Wawilak sisters. Life can exist only because of their collabo-ration with one another; and if it had not been for the mythical crime of incest committed by the sisters, there would be neither life nor death, and no seasonal rhythm.[42]

Linguistic evidence illuminates this metaphorical framework—for instance, the extremely widespread linguistic analogy established be-tween sex and nourishment, marrying and eating; even today, in Yoruba as in French (*consommer*), the word for both acts is the same. This, of course, is biologically sound, since it is well established that the sexual impulse is a development of the nutritive, and that nutri-tional libido and sexual libido are so closely connected that they proba-bly branch out of a common stem. In other instances, among the Australian Koko Yao of Cape York, the expression *kuta kuta* signifies both incest and cannibalism.[43] While as a rule the male is the eater and the female the eaten, on the mythological plane a strange inversion often occurs with the theme of the *vagina dentata*, betraying the unconscious fear of some males (in the Far East especially) that, through copulation, the female drains away into herself their vital strength.[44]

There is hardly any doubt that magic thought is rather the shadow preceding the body than a timid, inarticulate form of pseudoscience. It is not just a beginning or a modest attempt at scientific thought but a vast, well-articulated mental system, comparable in every respect with that of modern science, except for its inferiority in practical results. Myths and fables were not destined to push away reality but, quite the contrary, to preserve observations and thoughts adapted to the world as perceived by primitive man, to discoveries of a specific type—those prompted by the organization and exploitation of an intensely concrete world in concrete terms.

It seems clear, therefore, that the gradual awareness of man's biological role in determining pregnancy, understood in terms of rough *causality*, implies that sometime between the fifth and third or second millennia B.C. (depending on the culture and the geographic location), man crossed a *mental threshold* from magico-symbolic thought processes to rational thinking: the same fact (connection between coitus and pregnancy) that had been observed for some time was now understood quite differently in *causal*, and no longer magical, terms. It gradually dawned on Late Bronze Age man that this connection was not only essential but was also the only one that created new life. To give an instance of the conclusions reached by relatively primitive cultures when that mental threshold was reached, we have the widely prevalent view among the Lepchas of Sikkim (but also known to the Turks, Mongols, ancient Chinese, and Indians since the distant days of the Mahābhārata) that the bones and brain come from the father's semen and the flesh and blood from the mother's vaginal secretions—hence the necessity of the prohibition of incest, in the light of this new knowledge, failing which it is presumed that bones become brittle and the offspring sickly.[45]

Crossing this threshold must have also implied that man began to realize that he belonged to his own specific biological species. His relationship with the whole of nature was changing under the spur of the Neolithic revolution and its technical discoveries. Man left the "cosmico-maternal" life that had been his for hundreds of thousands of years. One of the most significant symbols of this metamorphosis in mental outlook was a complete change in burial customs, the beginning of cremation, of the swift and utter destruction of the physical body which appeared in Neolithic times among Aryan tribes.[46] This signified a typically male urge to escape from the timeless bondage to the earth, an attempt to get away from Mother Earth's eternal clutches so that the soul could soar toward the wide-open spaces of the firmament rather than descend into her bowels. Instant destruction of the body freed the imprisoned soul whereas customary burial left it attached to a slowly rotting body of flesh and bones, haunting the earth as an unhappy ghost, chained to a decomposing corpse being slowly reabsorbed into the muddy bosom of Mother Earth. Cremation was a male revolt, a decisive symbol of masculine emancipation from thralldom to the Great Mother—the opposite of the earthbound outlook of female-oriented cultures in which the corpses were carefully buried in fetal position as if returning to the womb.

When man became fully aware, in a rational sense, of his biological role in the process of creating new life, he must have completely reevaluated the importance of his part in conjugal life and come to the conclusion that, through this knowledge, he was, in fact, in full control of the fate of woman. By now, male agriculture had replaced female horticulture, enhancing the male's economic importance. Just as the farmer plowing the Earth Mother sows his seed purposefully, knowing that a plant will grow out of it, so does the male penetrate the female and discharge his semen (from the Latin "to sow") in the full knowledge that an offspring will grow out of it. The identification of the plow with the phallus and of semen with seed became widespread in all agricultural communities, that is, quasi-universal.[47] While the Indian *Videvdāt* compares fallow land to a barren woman, in many Eastern and Western tales the woman who cannot beget children cries that she is like a field on which nothing grows. The great Syrian god Ba'al was termed "the spouse of the fields" and the Qur'ān of Muhammad states that "your women are unto you as fields." The Indian Laws of Manu bluntly declared that "the woman is the field and the male is the bestower of the seed." By and large, woman was identified with a furrow and the phallus with spade and plow—which came into being as "anthropo-telluric" concepts only when the true nature of conception was understood. The Hindus compared the vulva (*yoni*) with the furrow, the spade or plow with the male organ (*lingam*), and the seed with the *semen virile*.[48] When the Hindu god Indra marries Urvara, her meaning is "fertile land"—symbol standing for the invasion and taking over of a foreign country, implying the marriage between the invading king and the plowed land.[49]

It is in the amazing metamorphosis of the old matriarchal mythologies that the depth and importance of this profound psychological revolution can be best understood. All the mythologies were taken over and stood on their head; all the female-oriented myths were reinterpreted patriarchally. What had been good became bad, former heroes became demons, and the remarkable coincidence was that this metamorphosis happened more or less simultaneously, over a period of time, in the Indo-European and Semitic worlds, in Greece as in India, and in China as well as in Palestine and Mesopotamia. It is to this exceptional conjunction of a changing male outlook in the ancient agricultural societies and an irresistible tidal wave of nomadic patriarchal invaders that history owes this global revolution.

Actually, it was a slow revolution by our contemporary standards, and we can trace its outline in the mythological metamorphosis that took place at the time—the victory of the sun god. The sun arose in the mythical consciousness of Paleolithic man as the great hunter par excellence, whose appearance at dawn chases away the stars and moon as the roaring lion (perennial symbol of the sun) scatters the weaker animals around him. The divinity of the sun, lord of time and space, was essentially masculine—the phallic sunbeams striking down on Mother Earth—a maleness whose rays impregnate the earth and cause the seed to germinate. From Spain to China, the prehistoric sun stood for maleness, individual self-consciousness, intellect, and the glaring light of knowledge, as against the moon, ruler of the tide, the womb, the waters of the ocean, darkness, and the dreamlike unconscious. Even today, thousands of years and many civilizations later, Carl Jung has found that the sun still symbolizes, in the dreams of the modern unconscious, the *individual* consciousness.[50]

So it was that, in a strange process of psychological mutation known as *solarization,* the entire symbolism of former times was reversed; the moon and the lunar bull, symbols of female supremacy, were overthrown by the sun and the lion, the male principle. In the mythological belief of the Semitic Babylonians, this translated itself in the decisive victory of the sun god Marduk over his female ancestor Ti'amat; a victory that appears to date back to the days of the great Hammurabi. The ascent of the male principle is clearly visible in this strange mythology with its shift from the earlier emphasis on a nondual state which precedes creation and identification with the forces of nature, to one that emphasizes greater self-awareness, individualism, the ascent of the intellect, a sharper understanding of the time process and of rudimentary causality, a greater focusing on combat and power, strife, and effort.

In Egypt, the same process took place. At the earlier stage, as depicted in the Narmer palette (circa 2850 B.C.), the horizon was bounded by the four legs of the cow goddess Hathor ("Hathor of the Horizon"); she was conceived as straddling the earth, her legs the pillars of the four quarters, her belly the sky. The sun god Horus entered her mouth every evening at dusk and came out again the following morning; upon entering, he was "the bull of his mother," symbolizing the insemination of the cow; and upon emerging the following morning symbolized his birth from his consort's loins. He was thus his own father, while Hathor was both his consort and his mother.[51] In the aspect of the bull-father, Horus was also Osiris, symbol of the Pharaoh's dead father; however, as plain Horus, the falcon-son, he was also the living Pharaoh himself.

A decisive shift took place a few hundred years later and, as evidenced by the famous step pyramid of Pharaoh Zoser (circa 2630 B.C.), a new mythological age dawned when the same process of solarization took place in Egypt as was taking place in Mesopotamia. The myth of the lunar bull was gradually superseded by the solar mythology of the lion. With the Fifth Dynasty, a new myth appeared to give mythopoeic expression to this solarization: the sun god Re, no longer the son as Horus but the father of Pharaoh, presides over this change of outlook. From now on, a strongly masculine spirit pervades Egyptian mythology and cosmology. The concept of Pharaoh as god-king disappears, to be replaced by an eternal, more elevated, and transcendental solar principle of radiant light, one which never dies and of which the living Pharaoh is only the obedient son: the sun is eternal and is always there, either in the world or in the netherworld. The old female-lunar dialectic of alternating light-and-darkness, life-death-rebirth, fades away; a male, transcendental god emerges. Yet Pharaoh still partakes of divinity, in a subordinate way, and divinity is still immanent in the glorious land of the Nile. A certain optimism still prevails in Egypt that has disappeared in the gloomy mythology of Babylonia—and it was from this somber atmosphere, rather than the more optimistic one of Egypt, that the Hebrews drew their own cosmogenesis.

Among the first items we read about in the biblical Genesis, the "evil" serpent who tempts Eve is in fact a reverse adaptation of the old snake god, a revered deity in many lands from Sumer to pre-Aryan India. Living in the bowels of the earth, able to cast off its skin and rejuvenate its body year in and year out, to bite and kill instantly, the snake became the prime symbol of cyclical fertility, and therefore, immortality. It also became a prime phallic symbol, especially when diving into water, the primordial symbol of femaleness. The water-female symbolism was fully retained in the biblical account—"The Spirit [wind] of God was moving over the face of the waters"—but the serpent lost its lordly position to become the repulsive incarnation of a newly conceived (Satan). In the biblical rendering, the snake now becomes "more subtle than any beast," is "cursed above all cattle, and above every beast of the field" by a wrathful Yahweh who condemns him to crawl, thereafter, on his belly and eat dust "all the days of thy life." So much for the former symbol of maleness whose major fault, presumably, was to live in the bowels of Mother Earth. His former position is now occupied by the wind—the wind becomes spirit, the dynamic masculine, seminal, and creative power, while the sluggish waters remain female: Moses floating in his basket on the Nile symbolizes the child in his mother's womb (basket) floating in the amniotic fluid (river). The baptismal rites still symbolize this "birth from water," the maternal waters.

The Garden of Eden was taken wholesale by the Hebrews from the Paradise depicted by the Sumerians in the mythological poem titled "Enki and Ninhursag": Dilmun, the Sumerian Eden, is a land that is "pure," "clean," and "bright," a "land of the living" where sickness and death are unknown, and in which the Great Goddess Ninhursag cultivates eight plants.[52] The villain is the water god Enki, who orders the two-faced god Isimud to pluck off the plants and bring them to him, whereupon he eats them. Enraged, Ninhursag pronounces upon him the curse of death. Enki falls desperately sick and none of the other male gods seems to be able to cope with the disease; suddenly, Ninhursag reappears, forgives him, and heals him—a striking contrast with the unforgiving harshness of the biblical account. Every item of the biblical description of the Garden of Eden appears to be borrowed from the Sumerian myth but reinterpreted in its own fashion—the existence of Eden itself, located by the Bible *eastward* as was Dilmun (probably southwest Iran); the watering of Dilmun inspired the biblical ". . . there went up a mist from the earth, and watered the whole face of the ground"; so was the painless birth of several goddesses turned upside down: "Unto the woman He said, I will greatly multiply thy sorrow and thy conception; in sorrow thou shalt bring forth children"; Enki's eating the plants and being cursed foreshadows the biblical episode of the Tree of Knowledge, the eating of the apple, and Yahweh's subsequent cursing of all concerned. But, this time, the woman is at the wrong end of the stick; instead of being the benevolent, all-powerful Ninhursag who forgives Enki and restores him to good health, wretched Eve is condemned to subservience to Adam: "And thy desire shall be to thy husband, and he shall rule over thee"—some slight consolation for the fact that Adam, too, was cursed and banished from the Garden of Eden.

Even the fashioning of Eve out of one of Adam's ribs, a symbol of man's priority, is an adaptation of a Sumerian play on words—the

Sumerian for rib, *ti*, also means "to make live."[53] In the Sumerian account, there is no sign of implacable divine anger, no knowledge or awareness of guilt, no forbidden fruit. Knowledge is there to be plucked and enjoyed by all those who attempt to secure it in the proper way. The concept of a "fall" is unknown, and so is the curse of Original Sin. A seemingly idyllic spirit of innocence prevails in Dilmun, a joyful acceptance of all the bounties of nature, a feeling of mystical union binding all living things—a hymn to Life itself, the typical mythology of a female-oriented culture; the old Sumerian seals depict a world-outlook of fundamental cosmico-maternal peace and accord.

It is easy to recapitulate the metamorphosis of the concept of cosmic creation—from the universe born of a goddess without a spouse, to that born of a Great Goddess in need of a male consort, and through the concept of the universe formed out of the earthy body of the slain goddess by a male deity (the Babylonian concept), to the ultimate downfall of the goddess in the biblical account. In conjunction with the gradual fade-out of the female principle and the rise of the male principle to mythological supremacy, another striking development takes place: the increasing strength of the male per se, in that the son becomes invariably more powerful than the father. The begotten one overcomes the begetter, implying the birth of the masculine notion of progress: Enlil, the air god, become stronger than his father, An, god of heaven; later, Marduk, the great god of the Semitic Babylonians, becomes mightier than his father, Enki.[54]

Finally, in the biblical account, the universe is created by the male godhead alone, unassisted by a female deity; even matter, the earth, was created by God since, as John tells us in his Gospel, "In the beginning was the Word." It is, perhaps, by studying the remote origins of the "Word" as creative power that one can see the gradual emergence of the supremacy of man's autonomous *mental* power over that of the female's physiological, material creativity. As far back as one can see, it appears to have started with the Sumerian expression for "word," *enem*, the voice of Enlil, "Lord of the Storm," among other things. However, the same pictogram is also used for *gu*, "voice" or "thunder." In later Canaanite mythology, this assimilation is amplified: the storm god, Ba'al or Haddu (Hadad), creates the thunder-bolt, *baraqu*, so that his subjects may hear his commands. The Semites translated the Sumerian *enem* by *awatu*, and it is at this juncture, it seems, that a decisive shift of concept took place. The vague notion of "Creative Word" acquired added precision when associated with thunder.[55] The "Sumerian *enem* is therefore the most likely root of the

Greek *lógos,* although the same concept began to appear more or less simultaneously in Egypt, as stated in the Memphite text: "Ptah the Great is the heart and tongue of the gods"—heart meaning "mind" and tongue the "spoken word."[56] The creator god Ptah "pronounced the names of all things" and thus created them *ex nihilo:* from now on, cosmic creativity belongs to the mind rather than the womb. Eventually, the Stoic philosophers of the Hellenistic Age went one step further and conceived "creative reason," *lógos spermatikós,* as the origin of the supreme divine element. From now on, the power of original creation was assigned to man's natural ability for *seminal thought.*

In Freudian terms, this revolutionary "transference upward," this sublimation, was to be symbolically represented in Greek mythology by the birth of Athene from the forehead of Zeus; and henceforth, sexuality and spirituality were to be sharply opposed as irreconcilable enemies.

What happened in the Semitic Middle East found its echo in Greece during the transition from Minoan-Mycenaean culture to post-Homeric times. In Minoan Crete, as in the entire Aegean world, the pre-Homeric outlook on life was essentially female-oriented, a peaceful acceptance of the entire cosmic process, an organic, unheroic view of human destiny that was in stark contrast with the dramatic Homeric vision to come. The iron-bearing Dorian invaders, patriarchal to the core, despised this world-outlook and consigned it to the netherworld. In classical Greece as in Hebrew Palestine, the reversal was total; in Greece as in Palestine, all the old elements were taken over and turned upside down. In the new patriarchal myths, all that was good belonged to the new heroic male gods, shifting the Great Mother Goddess's natural powers to the murky underworld of Tartarus—Mother Earth's now-despised bowels. Needless to add, even the social position of women began to suffer in this new mythological environment.

It is easy to follow, in the dreamlike sequence of the Homeric myths, the overthrow of the old order by the shining knights of the new patriarchal one: the victory of Zeus over Typhon, youngest son of Gaea (Mother Earth), and the crushing defeat of the Titans, her sons, defeat which secured sovereign rule for the new gods on Olympus while the defeated Typhon was hurled into Tartarus—from where he revenged himself and his mother by stirring up dreadful storms, volcanic eruptions, and earthquakes. And so it was, too, in Vedic India after the Aryan invasions when Indra, the Indian counterpart of Zeus, triumphed over the cosmic serpent, Vritra.[57]

From then on, in Greece as in Palestine as in India, in the throes of barbaric invaders who patriarchally upheld the warlike value of the male individual and the unique worth of the autonomous personality, the old female-oriented order disappeared or went underground; in the dark mystery cults of classical Greece, we can find all the distorted remains of the old outlook. But from now on, the prevailing outlook focused on the principles of free will and *moral* responsibility of the individual: the revolution was directed against the worship of the Earth and its natural fertility. Man's attention in Greece focused on himself (leaving woman to her closer affinity with nature), or on his relationship with the godhead in Palestine. But there was a difference: while the biblical outlook expelled all traces of feminine influence, and through its one-sided, uncompromising monotheism, all references to earlier worships, classical Greece proved more tolerant. In the mysteries of Demeter and the Orphics, the earlier, pre-Homeric deities survived and retained part of their former influence. Greek religion became a blend of the emotional, mystical temper of the pre-Hellenic population and the more sober, intellectual faiths of the Indo-European patriarchs who had invaded the land. Indeed, the Olympic gods married the female deities of the land, rather than annihilating them in biblical fashion—although even in Palestine, the Great Mother retained some of her hidden power for a long time, to the great displeasure of the prophets. And in the rest of the Middle East she survived quite successfully into the Christian era as Isis, Ishtar, Cybele, Diana, Venus-Aphrodite, and many other incarnations. But henceforth it is the patriarchal, transcendental God that rules supreme and makes history, relegating the immanent goddesses and female immanentism to the dark underground of the unconscious and the subterranean caves of the earth.

In the new patriarchal *Weltanschauung*, the female principle has been systematically degraded, as if in revenge for its former predominance.[58] Nothing illustrates this better than the mythology surrounding the epic Trojan War; in the Judgment of Paris, the feminine is debased in an atmosphere of beauty contest, cheating, and bribery which has left its stamp on the Western conception of true feminity—a concept to which Western women ever since have tried to live up, in spite of temporary revolts.

The downfall of the Great Mother some three to four thousand years ago was a psychological event of the first magnitude. It took place in the collective unconscious of these early cultures and shaped the relationship of the sexes of the species in such a way as to assure the complete predominance, not always or necessarily, of men, but of the masculine principle—in the West far more than in the East. Even more than the great invasions of the iron-wielding warrior tribes, it was the crossing of this mental threshold that set the stage for the beginning of history proper—some four thousand years of turbulent rise and fall of civilizations, of wars and revolutions, of strife and anguish and cataclysmic progress.

We shall now step aside from our historical account to take up woman's role and characteristics in three disiciplinary contexts—sociology, biology, and psychology—that have affected her behavior in the historical evolution of the Iron Age which follows.

CHAPTER

4

The Past That Survives

The exact position of woman in the Paleolithic and Neolithic social organizations is far more difficult to determine than the shifting position of the eternal feminine in the mythological framework of these societies. It would seem logical to conclude that, under the sway of the Great Mother, when the life-giving female principle was enthroned and worshiped as the supreme metaphysical entity, women as such enjoyed greater prestige and influence than they did after the patriarchal revolution—for the simple reason that their own *being* as females was identified by the fearful males with all the mysterious forces of nature. It must have seemed to thoughtful males that Mother Earth and Woman were one united, compact telluric force that had to be propitiated with magic rites and ceremonies. If any harm came to Woman, nature was sure to retaliate with storms, earthquakes, starvation, and the end of procreation.

The fog that enshrouds the distant past can be partly lifted and dispelled by anthropology and ethnology. The remote Paleolithic epoch is, to an extent, still alive, represented by countless primitive societies scattered throughout the world, mostly on the geographical periphery of "civilized" societies; as such, they undoubtedly form a link with that remote past and help us understand how our distant ancestors must have evolved. It seems clear, for instance, that today, and probably in the past as well, there never was a true matriarchate from a sociological viewpoint. Contemporary anthropologists are unanimous in this respect, and the ethnographic data are irrefutable: whatever their influence within the family, women never ruled the first tribes or rudimentary states, nor was their social position ever higher than that of the males, whether in matrilineal or patrilineal societies. The Australian aborigines have both types of social structure and the position of women is no different in either of them; the same is true in Melanesia. In matrilineal organizations authority is not wielded by the wife but by her uncles or brothers. Even in polyandric societies, such as those of the Marquesa Islands in Polynesia, where upper-class wives have several husbands, women have little power and authority, and always remain subservient to one of the husbands who acts as undisputed chief of the household.

The nonexistence of matriarchal rule is perfectly consonant with the fact that it was the hunting male who originally created social and political links, at the exclusion of the females; even his subsequent worship of the female creative principle as supreme cosmic entity did not entail his handing over to woman any part of his political prerogatives. No wonder that, as a noted ethnologist puts it, "a genuine matriarchate is nowhere to be found, though in a few places feminine prerogatives have evolved to a marked degree in certain directions."[1] Bachofen's primeval "telluric gynecocracy," in which the mother dominated the social order, is a myth as far as sociology is concerned. Matrilineal descent and matrilocal residence do not imply female superiority but only the superiority of the female's male kin. The females' status as women is not a bit affected, although they probably enjoy more dignity; they merely shift from the domination of one set of men to another. In all cases, men are ultimately in full social and political control of the women, who must rest content with whatever power and authority they may wield in the home.

But when all has been said, it still remains that in the matrilineal type of social structure traditionally known as "mother-right," which must have prevailed in prehistoric times throughout the nonhunting subtropical belt in gardening or hoe cultures, woman as such is raised to a certain dignity because the entire social organization revolves around her procreative function; the rights of all members of the society are determined by a relationship traced through the mother— the father being more or less inconsequential. At its utmost, this implies that descent, which regulates membership in the social group, is matrilineal; that the concept of kinship is traced solely through the mother; that children inherit nothing from the father's side—although, strangely enough, in this case women inherit nothing at all, are debarred from holding property altogether, although property is transmitted from man to man *through* them. In this sense, women are usually better off in a patriarchal system which often guarantees their rights as individuals. To all these attributes of the mother-right system must be added that succession, in terms of rank, dignity, or office transmitted, goes from the male incumbent to his sister's sons.[2] As for authority, with the exceptions mentioned earlier, it is usually vested in the oldest male in the household, sometimes in the mother's brother (avunculate). The last, and extremely important although rare, feature is the matrilocal rule, according to which the husband either lives with the wife's family or becomes only an occasional visitor at his wife's home—the "borrowed man" of Sumatra's Menangkebau.

All such features still exist, more or less mixed with patriarchal elements, in primitive communities scattered around the world. It is interesting to note that the most extreme forms of mother-right, in terms of descent, inheritance, and succession, existed among the North American Indians, and that among some tribes (Iroquois, Huron, Pueblo, Pawnee, Creek, Choctaw, and Seminole), woman's place in the social scheme almost deserved to be called a full-fledged matriarchate. This is the exception that confirms the general rule, according to which social and political power is, ultimately, always vested in men. Last but not least, the extreme forms of mother-right characterize the more backward people, in terms of cultural level, with very few exceptions; along with those who practice a horticultural economy (the maize country in North America and parts of West Africa). Typical of the hoe culture are the North American Hopi, organized along matrilocal as well as matrilinear lines, but here again, it is not the mother but the maternal uncle who is in control and disciplines the children; the chiefs are men, not women.[3]

It may be worth our while to take a closer look at one outstanding exception mentioned earlier, that of the Iroquois as the early colonists knew them in the seventeenth and eighteenth centuries. The striking aspect of the social structure of the Six Nations was that while the women were *sedentary,* the men were *nomadic;* while the women lived permanently in their "longhouses" and cultivated their cornfields in the neighborhood, the men roamed for months, and sometimes years on end, from the Hudson and Delaware to the Mississippi and from Hudson's Bay to the Carolinas, engaged in hunting, trading, or warring. In other words, traveling was the Iroquois male's full-time business. Inevitably, inheritance of lineage membership was matrilineal and residence matrilocal; although monogamy was firmly established, women could have a number of husbands in their lifetime, the obvious result of the precariousness of the husband-wife relationship caused by the husband's long absences. Often enough, she found herself another mate in the meantime; if, upon his return, her former spouse attempted to retrieve her, he could do so only with her explicit consent, and was usually strongly encouraged to find himself another wife among the unmarried girls—while his former wife kept the children.[4]

So far, so good; this was an extreme case of mother-right. What set it apart from other such structures and engaged it much deeper toward a mitigated form of matriarchate was that on three important occasions women wielded *direct political power:* the senior woman of the lineage he represented designated the successor of anyone of the League of Iroquois' forty-nine chiefs after his death; although they were not allowed to indulge in public speaking, women took part in town and tribal meetings on equal footing with the men and caucused behind the scenes; women were entitled to declare war formally by compelling the men to fight for revenge when next of kin were murdered. This quasi-matriarchate was both the cause and the consequence of the fact that the males lived on the periphery of their settlements, and that their long journeys deprived them of effective authority within the community. The disintegration of the Iroquois' marital relations was related to a number of accessory causes—easy promiscuity, drunkenness of the males and harshness of the women, frequent abortions of the wives with their mothers' connivance.

All this eventually came to an end after the American Revolution when the Iroquois were confined to reservations and prevented from roaming their great forests at will. Reservation life made matriarchy intolerable and most of its outstanding features disappeared. Handsome Lake, the remarkable Seneca prophet who reorganized Iroquois society, reestablished marital stability in the nuclear family, broke the tight bonds that traditionally linked mother and daughter (directed against son-in-law and husband), and restored men to their role as heads of family—although he left alone matrilineality and part of women's political prerogatives.

One aspect of the matrilineal-patrilineal dichotomy deserves special comment: it is one thing for woman to be under her husband's control, an important part of which is *sexual* control, and an entirely different one to be under her uncle's or brother's control which, because of the universal incest taboo, is completely asexual. In a sense, sex and power over woman are completely divorced in the mother-right type of structure; obviously, woman's sex life with a socially downgraded and powerless husband is a very different thing from lovemaking with an all-powerful, patriarchal one—possibly a more satisfying relationship for woman. In the former state, the complete divorce between sex and socioeconomic power deprives woman of her sexual leverage; in the latter, she can use sex as a means to socioeconomic power *through* man —and over the ages she has often used it with considerable skill. On the whole, it may be said, and this is proved by the evidence at our disposal, that in the former she had more *dignity,* and in the latter, she had far greater potential for actual *power,* however indirectly.

In the more general state of patriarchalism that has prevailed now for thousands of years, the actual status of woman depends on a great many variables. One thing is certain: while the social position of woman is one thing, it is not necessarily connected with her legal status nor with her economic position. In Central Asia, for instance, the connection between work and legal status is disproved by the examples of the Kirgiz and Altai Turks. The Muslim Kirgiz women, while apparently worse off than their Altai counterparts, are actually, and in spite of an unfavorable Islamic law code, better off. Altai women are at work all day long, in the house and outside, tending the cattle, milking cows, bringing in the fuel, manufacturing the tools, cultivating barley plots, etc., while the men work hardly at all. Kirgiz men, on the other hand, share the work equally with the women. As a result, Kirgiz women enjoy far more actual freedom than their overworked Altai sisters, even though their legal status is inferior.[5] The fact is clear that there is often a considerable gap between theory and practice, between woman's legal status and her de facto position and influence.

In areas such as South America and southern Africa where women plant and harvest and play an important part in the economic life of their societies, they remain, nevertheless, in a subordinate position; in some hunting tribes, however, such as the Andaman Islanders, women play a small economic role and yet have achieved near social equality with the males. It remains true, however, that woman's position in stock-breeding tribes and among pastoral people in general is completely subordinate—probably because the domestication of animals was a male achievement to start with, but also because cattle breeders tend to be more nomadic. And although among horticultural populations women's role and influence had been greater, they declined again when agriculture came in—since plow culture was also a masculine invention. It still holds true that the link between economic activity and status is tenuous, at best, and that a great deal of the apparatus of traditions and customs probably originated in a few geographical spots long ago, to spread from one tribe to another by a sort of cultural contagion.[6]

The problem of the extent of cultural diffusion is one that plagues modern anthropology and makes it difficult to establish a precise correlation between the economic and social factors. As the noted ethnologist Robert Lowie states it, "I myself believe that the forces of suggestibility and mental inertia are shown to be so powerful by anthropological evidence that the propagation and preservation of an accidental complex is entirely possible."[7] This probably explains why and through what kind of accidental diffusion it happens that sex equality is the rule among the pastoral Hottentots while the neighboring Bantu women who till the soil enjoy a lower social position.

The causal relationship between economic activity and woman's social position is almost impossible to determine. A tribe may well adopt only part of a diffused complex and be influenced by other considerations, including location, climate, and religious beliefs. In fact, woman's position is often determined by historical relations and cultural traditions rather than present-day economic considerations. The evidence is all around us; the Chukchi women of east Siberia, in spite of the introduction of the reindeer, enjoy a status far superior to that of the Ostyak women of western Siberia because the Chukchi woman's status is fixed in large part by her cultural tradition, which a change in economic circumstances can affect only in part. Oceania and Australia provide even clearer evidence that woman's social standing is strongly connected with the historical traditions of the people concerned; so do the Indian tribes of North America. In fact, and at least in the contemporary world, economic structures are only one among other codeterminants.

Nor is there any precise correspondence between the status of woman and the degree of civilization of the people concerned—or, if there were any, it would tend to indicate an increasingly lower status as the degree of civilization rises. If we travel with the mind's eye from simple hunting communities such as the Andaman Islanders and the Vedda, where sexual equality is the rule, through the more civilized Bantu tribes, where women are definitely subordinate, to the fully civilized Central Asians, where women are definitely viewed as inferior, we see clear *reverse* correlation between the two factors: "George Eliot and Mme. Recamier, in spite of their social influence, did not even remotely approach the legal position of the average Iroquois matron." In fact, the ethnographic evidence culled from surviving primitive societies clearly corroborates, in its own way, the momentous historical shift that took place at the end of the Bronze Age when the status of woman declined as the degree of civilization increased sharply.

The explanation for this state of affairs has already been hinted at. Unlike women, men go through life without experiencing the sharp cleavages caused by menarche, defloration, pregnancy, childbirth, and menopause which punctuate the female life-course. Since nature did not supply man with physiological landmarks, culture has to do so— his culture, which he created out of his own estrangement from nature, which he developed out of his original uterus envy when the Great Mother ruled supreme. There is no precise moment, defined physiologically by nature, when a boy can say that he is now a man, so his culture has to determine it. Hence the numerous initiation ceremonies which take place all over the world when adult males accept the adolescent into society as a full-grown man—a *social* affair, not a natural one, sanctified by incisions or scarification surrounded by a sacred ritual. The exclusive and highly emotional attachment of the son for the mother and compensating oedipal hostility to the father eventually has to be broken. For this reason, initiation ceremonies emphasize identification with the male community, rooted as they probably are in the atavistic male solidarity inherited from the early days of the great hunt. Initiation precludes any regression toward the early infantile dependence on the mother and emphasizes the development of a strong masculine identification. Nature makes the physiological *male*, but culture and the ritual of initiation makes the psychological *man*.

If there is one inescapable conclusion to which all ethnological study comes, it is that primitive woman is generally well treated and regarded, and that it is often among the most primitive tribes that she reaches practical equality with man. Cultural and technical progress usually works to her disadvantage and lowers her status and influence. What difference there was, and still is, was due to the impact of two sets of facts: First, historically, the growing intelligence of Homo sapiens and his increasing awareness of his biological role as inseminator of new life; second, the physiological realities as disclosed by the development of our scientific knowledge, which has given us an almost symbolic picture of sexual differentiation at the very root of organic life.

CHAPTER

5

The Biological Roots

The microcosmic root of sex lies very close to the root of life itself; elements such as viruses, which are themselves on the threshold of organic life, can actually mate when in a host cell.[1] Sex, as such, is not absolutely indispensable for the existence of organic life; single-celled organisms can also reproduce by fission without any recourse to sexual mating. But this elementary form of asexual reproduction leads to an evolutionary dead end; it is sexual reproduction in more complex monocellular organisms that allowed, in the past, for a rapid acceleration of evolutionary progress. The reason is obvious: increasing sexual differentiation leads to conjugation or *fusion*, the precise opposite of fission, in that two cells which normally multiply by fission are attracted to one another and join together, internally exchange elements of their anatomy, and merge into one single organism. From that point on, multiplication by fission is resumed anew by the invigorated organism:

> Biologists have long recognized that, after many generations of multiplication by fission, cells will often show decreasing vigor and increasing somnolence. In time, they may seem near death. If, at this point, conjugation can occur between two such cells, the resulting organism has great new vigor. . . . Why does conjugation invigorate? The answer is that through mating, an organism, weakened by the prolonged reinforcement of its own weakest "family" genes, now receives a therapeutic transfusion of strengthening new, dominant genes.[2]

In fact, the basic function of sexual reproduction is to endow the given species with far greater genetic variability and plasticity by combining mutants that would remain isolated from one another in asexual reproduction, imprisoned, as it were, in their various respective lines without the possibility of combining with each other.

49

The next step up the evolutionary ladder is an increase in complexity; cells find it advantageous to gather together and group themselves in colonies, the first stage on the road to the formation of multicellular organisms. But then arises the problem of how to impart the precious information concerning the advantages of colony grouping to their offspring if all member cells continue to multiply by solitary fission without any exchange of information-bearing material. The solution is to appoint a specialized cell, a preserver of the plan with the coded information of the colony structure inside itself, to reproduce sexually by fusion with another specialized cell, imparting the required information to the next generation. By ensuring the perpetuation of the colony through the device of giving birth to cells already genetically predisposed to colony life, they create the embryos of the complex multicellular organisms. Sexual differentiation, leading to complexification and increasing specialization, leads to reproduction of more highly integrated organisms.

To sum up: The purely functional distinction between male and female soon becomes a structural one, transmitted phylogenetically when the function splits into two distinct organisms, and eventually two individuals. Sexuality is thus one element, but the most important element, in evolutionary progress.

On the way up the ladder leading from the lower to the higher organisms, one meets with great varieties of sexual organizations. While sexual differentiation, in general, increases into sharp separation between male germ cells (pollen grain in plants, spermatozoa in animals) and female cells (ovules in plants and ova in animals), some weird combinations occur. For instance, the eggs of insects such as bees and wasps can develop by parthenogenesis, in which case they grow into males; on the other hand, if fertilized, they grow into females.[3] The interesting consequence in this case is "social": the female controls the fertilization, or lack of it, in the sense that she stores a considerable number of spermatozoa which she can release at will. This type of sex determination, which no longer results in a rough numerical equilibrium of the sexes, allows for a variety of proportions that can range from an all-female to a predominantly male brood—a great asset in a social structure where one queen bee reigns over hundreds of drones and thousands of workers; but where the workers rule in the sense that they determine, by the technical device of building cells of specific proportions, the sex ratio of the next generation —they guide the queen in her egg-laying activity. And although, like the queen, they develop from fertilized eggs and are genetically female, they remain sexually undeveloped, and therefore sterile, thanks to the low-protein diet on which they are raised. Now that mankind is rapidly approaching the time when it will be technically possible to predetermine the sex of its offspring, the relevance of the insect type of social organization stands out in bold relief.

Sex determination is not always a "genetic mechanism." Many plants are hermaphroditic in the sense of harboring both male and female sex organs; the same is true of some animals (earthworms and snails), which renders them capable of both self- and cross-fertilization. Cattle, too, display some peculiar features: when cows give birth to twins of different sexes, the female is often a sterile "freemartin" whose internal sex organs are halfway between the male and the female types—this occurs because male hormones produced in the twin embryo flow into the female through a connection between the embryonic blood vessels. Even environmental influences can sometimes become sex determinants: oysters are male at low temperatures and female at high ones.

It can be said by way of generalization that sexual behavior (union of egg and sperm) for reproductive purposes is universal, from unicellular organisms all the way up to the most complex multicellular ones, with the exception of three phyla (sponges, coelenterates, and echinoderms); this implies that the presence of male and female elements, at the most microscopic level of living stuff, is a fact, but also that the sexual division of any given species is not always sharp and clear-cut.[4] No individual organism is all male or all female, and some are hermaphrodites—the gynandromorph among the insects, for instance, whose head can be male while its body is female, or vice versa. The essential feature at the very level of bacteria, however, is that the male represents the active, eager, aggressive, variable principle, and the female, the passive, stable, receptive one[5]—all the way up to the plants where it is the mobile pollen of the stamen, male organ of flowering plants, that falls on the stationary female pistil. In animals, as a rule, and in humans, this distinction is even more clear-cut: the general evolutionary tendency in higher animals is toward increasing dimorphism between the sexes, the males becoming more active and aggressive, the females more passive and receptive. The phylogenetic basis lies in the fact that while the female organism, as carrier, maintainer, and protector of the future of the species is characterized by *anabolism*, or constructive use of energy, the male is essentially characterized by *catabolism*, or destructive use of the same energy.[6]

We now turn to sexual reproduction in the human race as disclosed by the data of embryology. The controlling, decisive element in the process of sexual selection is genetic inheritance, that is, the chromosomal apparatus. Sex is determined at the very moment of conception by the differentiating chromosome carried by the spermatozoon. The striking feature of this process is that, already in the womb, the male appears to be embryologically *more differentiated* than the female; indeed, the embryo can very well be female without ovaries, but a male absolutely requires testicles in order to be male. Far from being an incomplete form of maleness, according to a Western tradition stretching from the biblical Genesis through Aristotle to Thomas Aquinas, femaleness is the norm, the fundamental form of life.

From an embryological standpoint, therefore, the male appears to be *more evolved* than the female, in the sense of being farther removed from the initial, neutral type. This is why, referring to sex reversal among some lower forms of animal life as an adaptive reaction to an altering environment, a scientist could state that "the individual is a female when it may and a male when it must."[7] Indeed, the morphology of gametes displays, in almost symbolic form, this sexual differentiation at the time of fertilization—the enormous difference between the heavy female cell, ten thousand times larger than the male cell and relatively motionless, contrasted with the tiny, agile spermatozoon, competing against anywhere from 200 million to 500 million rival male cells flowing up the oviduct, any one of which has only one choice: to win the race and "rape" the passive female cell, or die.

If we now take up endocrinology, we find that our main topic of interest lies in the impact of sexual difference on the hypothalamus; the hypothalamic region contains some of the important centers controlling the autonomic nervous system, which are under the inhibitory influence of the cortex—sympathetic and parasympathetic centers. Clinical observations have shown that this region is closely connected with the control of fat and carbohydrate metabolism, sleep, heat regulation, and sex.[8] The important point is that the hypothalamic centers synthesize some neuro-hormones of great importance known as "releasing factors"; and while they release them *continuously* to the male, they do so cyclically to the female:[9] while the male's testes receive continually from the pituitary gland the "interstitial-cell-stimulating" hormone (ICSH) which induces them to secrete testosterone, the female ovaries receive cyclically, from the same source, a follicle-stimulating hormone (FSH) as well as a luteinizing hormone (LH), which prompts them to release female sex hormones, estrogen and progesterone.[10]

The functioning of the hypothalamus is regulated differently for males and females, and appears to be the area of the brain most directly affected by sexual differences. While this differentiation in regulation seems to be of genetic origin, the administration of testosterone to a newborn female can masculinize the hypothalamus by abolishing its feminine rhythmiclike regulation and alter the entire character of the female by stimulating in her deportment aggressiveness and imagination, since the entire cerebral chemistry is under the influence of sexual hormones.

Sexual difference in the brain goes further than that, however; it already shows at the microscopic level of the nerve cell. In a female, the nuclei of nerve cells contain a sex chromatin known as "Barr body" (also found in a variety of other tissues) which does not occur in cells taken from males: "In the female a body about one millimicron in diameter appears as a small satellite to a large nucleus in all types of nerve cells examined. In the male, a nucleolar satellite is seldom seen distinctly. There is evidence that male nerve cells contain a nucleolar satellite so small that it lies at the limits of resolution with standard optical equipment."[11] If one reflects that every one of the millions of neurons in the brain alone is, even slightly, different in males and females, one cannot wonder at the fact that mental functions differ according to sex.

Not only nerve cells but many other body cells as well differ according to whether they belong to a male or female body; it has now become possible to tell which sex any piece of skin or drop of blood comes from. For instance, biologists have discovered in some of the white blood cells (polymorphonuclear leucocytes) of females an element known as "drumsticks" which is absent in the blood cells of normal males.[12] All of which goes to show that basic sexual differences lie at the basal level of the billions of cells that make up the average human body. In fact, sexual differentiation permeates the entire somatic being of the individual, not only in terms of greater muscular development of the male, but also in terms of certain cerebral functions.

Of the actually known instances of such differentiation in mental functions, one of the most interesting is brought to light by studies of conjugate-lateral eye movement (CLEM). Staring with the observation that women are not as often either left-movers or right-movers (i.e., they are more likely than men to move their eyes in both directions), it has been observed that there are less differences in alpha-wave production between female right- and left-movers than between males of both types:

> I have found evidence at the neurological and physiological levels that there are sex differences—that there may be more hemispheric integration in women than in men . . . studies of cortical-

evoked potentials show evidence of sex differences in the asymmetrical organization of the brain. These differences in the lateral organization of the central nervous system may account for observed cognitive and affective differences between the sexes.[13]

The scientific verdict appears to be clear-cut: the structure and functioning of the brain in males and females are not identical; comparisons between the two disclose important differences, albeit qualitative ones rather than quantitative. This may explain the fact that in primitive societies, hunting man's greater muscular development gave him an edge over woman in the contest for public power and authority, while in more civilized societies, where the premium was increasingly put on creative intelligence, masculinity showed itself in quite a different way—in the fact that, while woman is creative on the physiological plane, man is creative on the *mental* plane. Masculine thinking appears to be both more analytical and more original; it seems to display greater ability to think in abstract terms and, simultaneously, far greater gifts for mental creativity and power of invention. Whatever the relative importance of the respective parts played by chromosomes, cellular structures, and hormones, they affect profoundly not merely some disconnected organic parts but the whole physiology of the body, and more especially the central nervous system and all mental functions.

If we go back to hormonal functions, we can see that male sex hormones influence the whole body through increased retention of phosphorus, sodium, potassium, and sulfur, all of which play a considerable role in tissue formation.[14] Testosterone stimulates muscular development; if large doses of such male hormones are injected into a female, it will artificially induce in her the aggressive behavior which comes naturally to the male, as well as greater sexual urges. This implies that testosterone has a decisive influence on libido in *both* sexes —that the sexual urge is fundamentally male in both sexes. Adrenalectomy, removing the adrenals where male hormones are manufactured, drastically lowers sexual desire in woman; but ovariectomy, which takes out the ovaries that secrete female hormones, hardly affects her sexual impulse.

While these differences are duly emphasized, it remains true that all human individuals are embryologically, genetically, and hormonally bisexual. In the higher organisms, including humans, sex determination within an individual is, to an extent, a statistical matter. In terms of genetics, sex is determined by a definite, but after all slight, preponderance of one combination—only one out of twenty-three pairs of chromosomes; but, again, it does so in *every* cell. The same is true of hormones, since males and females produce small amounts of the hormones of the opposite sex. And even the absolute opposition between male and female hormones is more apparent than real; recent research has disclosed many instances of strange inversions of hormonal effects, whereby antagonistic hormones display a functional synergy.[15] In other words, the purely *human* characteristics far outweigh the differences of sex differentiation. The fundamentally androgynous nature of all human beings can no more be denied than the fundamental differentiation between the two *sexual principles* that appear at the dawn of life itself—as two polar opposites, or rather two complementary principles forever attracted to one another. It is well known, for instance, that the masculine and feminine components of the individual vary according to age—that, physiologically as well as psychologically, older women develop masculine qualities whereas men tend to display feminine traits as they advance in age.[16] What we are dealing with, therefore, are two complementary principles that happen to be distributed in the human race in such a way that all individuals are, in a statistically greater or lesser proportion, predominantly representative of one or the other.

But the bisexual nature of each and every human being should not be overstressed, either. Woman has less emotional equilibrium than man—a lack of "homeostasis" that is intimately connected with the tidal-like ebb and flow of hormonal forces induced by menstrual functions. Hence the far greater variety of her emotions, her hypersensitivity reaching, on occasion, the level of outright hysteria. It is a well-attested fact that the workings of female hormones (estrogen) increase sensory perceptions and cause women to be far more sensitive to the conditioning of social pressures and traditional values than the coarser and more individualistic men, who are less affected by the opinions, moods, and feelings of others.[17] Woman's preoccupation with her intracorporeal sensations precisely derives from a far greater internal sensitivity which finds its external reflection in her greater sensitivity in social relations. Man, being less involved with his own physiological being, is also less sensitive to other human beings: his body and his mind are more independent of one another, and he therefore "senses" himself and others far less than she does.

On the whole, men usually display definite tendencies toward power, stamina, energy, aggressiveness, hunting instinct, conquest, and domination, whereas females are more oriented toward submissiveness, passivity, sensitivity, tenderness, intuition, receptivity. Undoubtedly these traits are partly induced by education and social pressure, but the biological basis cannot be denied. The Recent tests carried out in high schools and colleges bring to light a fundamental difference between male and female thought processes: male thought is more analytical, female thought more "global," in that it takes into account all the elements in the field. In fact, observations carried out in various cultures, all the way from Western Europe to Hong Kong, show conclusively that women are far more dependent on the general "field" than men are.[18] Other tests show that men have greater ability to "restructure" a situation in order to study it anew; women tend to "conserve" the preestablished structure. When asked to group elements together, women tend toward "functional grouping"—for instance, doctor, nurse, and wheelchair—while the more analytical men will make up groups on the basis of one detail common to all the pictures, "analytical grouping," or one might say, "concept grouping."[19]

Women tend more toward conformity than men—which is why they often excel in such disciplines as spelling and punctuation where there is only one correct answer, determined by social authority. Higher intellectual activities, however, require a mental independence and power of abstraction that they usually lack, not to mention a certain form of aggressive boldness of the imagination which can only exist in a sex that is basically aggressive for biological reasons.[20]

To sum up: The masculine proclivity in problem solving is analytical and categorical; the feminine, synthetic and contextual. Out of abstract thought, man creates norms, ethical systems, and codes of law that often appear to woman to be inpedimenta and obstacles to achieving immediate happiness and well-being—hence, the inherently anarchistic and emotionally volatile temper of woman when she revolts. But, in a reverse dialectical twist, man, the arch-individualist, is the first one to break the abstract framework he has created, whereas under normal circumstances, woman remains the arch-conservative who intuitively understands and adapts with great flexibility to overpowering external circumstances—which are usually social and cultural structures created by men. Deep down, man tends to focus on the object, on external results and achievements; woman focuses on subjective motives and feelings. If life can be compared to a play, man focuses on the theme and structure of the play, woman on the innermost feelings displayed by the actors.

We are now driven back from all these considerations to the fundamental question: To what extent is the apparent supremacy of the male of the species due to *cultural* traditions that discriminate socially and politically against the female from the cradle to the grave, and to what extent is it due to biological elements? In a sense, there is no argument at all. All social behavior is ultimately rooted in biology; all cultural traits derive from genetic and hormonal influences; all social and cultural behavior is imbedded in the biosocial and biocultural.[21] If we go back beyond the appearance of the first humans to the more evolved primates, we can already perceive among these animals certain physiological facts of great importance that seem to anticipate similar developments among primitive human communities—greater size and strength of the male; inclination of the males to get together to the exclusion of the females; link between this male instinct for cooperation, sexual domination, and procreative privileges; political dominance of the males; and social stratification. Added to this in the case of primitive man are all the developments resulting from the hunting way of life—reinforced sense of male cooperation, greater development of the male intellect triggered by the need to solve hunting problems, and development of an aggressive attitude far in excess of that found among most other species.

All this suggests that, deep down in human nature, both males and females are phylogenetically programmed according to what some anthropologists call a human "biogrammar" in such a way as to assure male predominance in certain fields of importance.[22] If men are basically "joiners" and tend to form associations that exclude women, it is essentially the result of their physiological predisposition. It would seem that women's own physiological endowments make it difficult for them to form equivalent all-female associations that could possibly compete with male organizations. The problem does not lie in the question of whether "sisterhood" is powerful or not; the real question is whether sisterhood exists at all. From the numerous all-male secret societies that are found in so many primitive and civilized communities, from Africa to India and China, to the contemporary societies, organizations, and clubs in Europe and America, we have to conclude that the natural instinct of the male is to associate, except for sexual functions, with his own sex. If any secret society begins to include women and becomes heterosexual, it tends to lose most of its inner cohesion and is likely to disintegrate. It seems clear that men's refusal to include women in their various associations is motivated by something profoundly rooted in biological reality, rather than mere prejudice and desire to discriminate against them. This ostracism springs from the unconscious; probably, through some immensely old biological programming, it goes all the way back to the prehuman primates in whose days, millions of years ago, this form of sociosexual exclusivism ensured the survival of the group.

The main reason for the persistence of this discrimination is undoubtedly the fact that man-woman relationships are of a different, and far more explosive, nature than those binding men—affectionate, passionate, emotional, and of such strength and intensity that they always threaten to disrupt the social order. In fact, they are downright antisocial. Male-female pair-bonding implies the exclusion of the rest of mankind from consideration in order to focus every ounce of devotion on one individual; it implies the desire to flout laws and regulations, if need be, in order to strengthen this pair-bond. This extremely disturbing element is not only of truly explosive strength; it can also be extremely transitory, adding the upsetting factor of its ephemerality to its perturbation of the social order. It is no wonder that most of the laws and traditions governing human society, from the most primitive to the most sophisticated, focus, first of all, on the controlling and disciplining of the male-female relationship—by integrating it into the social structure and assuring the permanence of the pair-bond, regardless of the transitoriness of the feelings of mutual attraction.

If men have a definite tendency to link up and form associations from which women are excluded, they also tend to use these associations to deal with sociopolitical macrostructures concerned with war, hunting, sports, politics—leaving women to deal with social microstructures. These microstructures linking women, to the exclusion of men, are smaller, less permanent, and less complex, but evidence going all the way back to the evolved primates indicates that they play an essential part in maintaining the *continuity* of the group from one generation to the next, and in many cases influence decisively the selective process whereby the male leaders are chosen.[23] It would seem that in the transition from primate to man, a certain harmonious balance between the sexes was lost, probably because most primates, regardless of sex, collect their own food individually, whereas, when man began to hunt and became the provider for the female and the young, he began to form exclusively male associations and apportion other tasks to the females, inaugurating an unequal distribution of social roles and work load between the sexes. From then on, the pendulum swung back and forth between higher or lower status, greater or lesser economic importance, depending on the nature of the culture and social structure, but it was always a cooperative undertaking in which the respective roles of the sexes were always different and sharply separated. As Margaret Mead points out:

> We know of no culture that has said, articulately, that there is no
> difference between men and women except in the way they con
> tribute to the creation of the next generation; that otherwise in

all respects they are simply human beings. . . . However differently the traits have been assigned, some to one sex, some to the other . . . although the division has been arbitrary, it has always been there in every society of which we have any knowledge.[24]

In sum, the weight of evidence suggests that social structures are not so much the cause as the effect of biological considerations—even though, by a certain feedback process, some social customs can influence physiology in a minor way. As Simone de Beauvoir puts it:

It has been well said that women "have infirmity of the abdomen"; and it is true that they have within them a hostile element —it is the species gnawing at their vitals. . . . From puberty to menopause woman is the theater of a play that unfolds within her and in which she is not personally concerned. . . . It is during her periods that she feels her body most painfully as an obscure, alien thing.[25]

In other words, it would probably be true to say that, physiologically, whereas man lives, woman *is lived* by the "species gnawing at her vitals."

6

Sex and Psyche

The androgynous nature of all human beings is a biological fact that finds its counterpart in the realm of psychology. The psyche is bisexual, a fact that even Freud accepted under the spur of his doctor friend, Wilhelm Fliess; the latter's medical research had convinced him that anatomically, embyrologically, and chemically, human beings were normally bisexual.[1] But having accepted this fact, Freud interpreted it as implying the introduction of a source of potential conflict within the psyche when the subject was called upon to assume its proper sexual and gender role.[2] According to his theory of repression and inhibition, the repressed material is invariably the "vanquished sex," the second and weaker component of the androgyn rejected by the stronger one. As far as women were concerned, Freud never deviated from the traditional view, his convictions bolstered by the twin cultural influences that weighed upon him—Victorian patriarchal puritanism and the male-oriented Jewish outlook of his forebears: the masculine element in woman, far from being a positive factor, is a negative one, to be rejected at all costs. And his disciple Sandor Ferenczi emphasized that "every female patient, if her neurosis is to be regarded as fully disposed of, must have got rid of her masculinity complex and must emotionally accept without a trace of resentment the implications of her female role."[3]

Freud had no hesitation in interpreting the young female's psychology from a strictly male point of view, that is as being dominated by penis envy, the frustration of being an incomplete human being, of wanting to be a male. Quite naturally, since most early psychoanalysts were men and most of their patients were women, the libidinal concepts were drawn from the male viewpoint and failed to account for the female outlook. Freud even went so far as to assert unequivocally:

> As we learn from our psychoanalytic work, all women feel that they have been injured in their infancy and that through no fault

of their own they have been slighted and robbed of a part of their body; and the bitterness of many a daughter towards her mother has as its ultimate cause the reproach that the mother has brought her into the world as a woman instead of a man.[4]

And searching for an explanation of the fact, already mentioned, that in some primitive societies it is a man other than the husband who performs the act of defloration of the bride, he pointed out again this female resentment at her femaleness; as his biographer Ernest Jones, spells it,

> Freud traced it to the transition the woman passes through in exchanging her original clitoritic (masculine) attitude for the vaginal (feminine) one of adult life. An ancient part of her mentality resents her being made into a woman and generates hostility towards the man who brings it about. It is from this hostility that the custom in question protects the future husband.[5]

This overvaluation of the masculine phallus blinded Freud and deprived him of the insights brought out by his erstwhile friend and collaborator Carl Jung. Even with Freud's later amendments such as *Beyond the Pleasure Principle,* his overemphasis on sexuality limits arbitrarily the meaning and scope of the libido. Ernest Jones points out:

> The accent falls, as throughout his writings, on the importance of the male impulse. He maintained that the female child's libido is more male than female, because her autoerotic activity concerns predominantly the clitoris. He even made the obscure suggestion that perhaps all libido, being like all impulses in its nature active, is essentially male.[6]

We have already pointed out that recent hormonal research has proved him correct on this point. Where he erred was in advocating the elimination of the masculine component which is present in all normal women.

The Jungian outlook is far more profound, free from overemphasis on sheer sexuality, and appears to come much closer to the complex psychic reality. To Jung, "the unconscious is the *mother* of consciousness. Where there is a mother there should also be a father, but he seems to be unknown. Consciousness, the frail youngster, may deny his father, but he cannot deny his mother."[7] From the start, therefore, it would appear that the unconscious, qua unconscious, is feminine, whereas the conscious mind would tend to display more masculine characteristics: and if, as Jung puts it, "the conscious mind is based upon, and results from, an unconscious psyche which is prior to consciousness and continues to function together with, or despite, consciousness,"[8] it is clear that the conscious mind emerges from the unconscious as the child from the mother's womb. But the unconscious cannot be merely a chaotic medley of instincts and images; it must have some kind of structure: "Its center cannot be the ego, since the ego was born in the conscious mind and turns its back on the unconscious, seeking to deny it as best it can."[9]

The unconscious has indeed a structure, a complex one resulting from the existence of two apparently contrary sexual components in the human person. Dubbing the psychic component of the second, complementary sex within each individual *animus* and *anima*, Jung looked upon them as "natural 'archetypes,' primordial figures of the unconscious which gave rise, thousands of years ago, to all the mythological gods and goddesses."[10] *Animus*, the "man in a woman," and *anima*, the "woman in a man," in Jung's own terms, are contrasted by him with the *persona* (mask worn by Roman actors) as the unconscious soul, the inner personality, is contrasted with the conscious, external personality. Inner and outer personalities within the human individual have a *complementary* relationship, comparable to the formal one that divides, and yet joins, males and females in human society. As Jung puts it, "whereas logic and objective reality commonly prevail in the outer attitude of man, or are at least regarded as an ideal, in the case of woman it is feeling. But in the soul the relations are reversed: inwardly, it is the man who feels, and the woman who reflects." Hence, the feeling of mental "pregnancy" in the creative man who is about to give birth to an original work of art or science.

Having stated that our psychic makeup is fundamentally androgynous, Jung adds that it is the inevitable consequence of a biological reality; furthermore, the weaker sexual component produces a corresponding portion of the personality that, because of its weakness, remains unconscious and repressed. What sets Jung sharply in opposition to Freud is that he advocates *integrating* the secondary sex *(animus* or *anima)* rather than eliminating it. The therapeutic method suggested by Jung consists in recognizing it by discriminatory separation from its opposite, and then consciously integrating it in what is bound to become an androgynous personality, with mere predominance of one side or the other. From what could be termed the "passive" catharsis of Freud, we reach an "active" catharsis that implies a conscious effort of free will; and this active catharsis is nothing less than a dialectical reconciliation of opposites. Jung has understood and stated that the psyche, like life itself, requires polarity; and that, whatever its problems, these cannot be "solved" but can be dialectically *overcome* by integration of supposedly incompatible elements, and then by *individuation*, "the process that makes a human being an 'individual' —a unique, indivisible unit. . . ."[11]

Jung also terms the general psychic energy flowing from one pole to the other *libido*, the meaning of which, in his interpretation, is not limited to sex but implies more generally longing, desire, urge. Libido flows between the polar opposites from one extreme to another; these polar opposites (consciousness and unconsciousness, extraversion and introversion, thinking and feeling) being subsumed under the heading of *animus* and *anima;* and he accepts the fundamental psychological law of *enantiodromia*, a running contrariwise, the regulative function of opposites, thanks to which, sooner or later, everything runs into its opposite. Thus, the libido moves forward and then backward, progresses in satisfying the demands of consciousness, then regresses in order to appease the unconscious.[12]

Individuation implies the integration of the opposites within the personality, when consciousness (which implies selection, discrimination, and exclusiveness) and the unconscious both accept each other's partnership and form a harmonious whole. Whenever the unconscious is frustrated, it rebels and destroys the ego-consciousness that attempts to repress it. The reason for this undoubted power of the unconscious is that it has immensely deep roots in the remote past, "in the phylogenetic substructures of the modern mind, the so-called *collective unconscious.*"[13] Thus, an entirely unknown and strange psychic life, supra-individual, supports our ephemeral ego-consciousness: "This psychic life is the mind of our ancient ancestors, the way in which they thought and felt, the way in which they conceived of life and the world, of gods and human beings." Hence Jung's extensive studies and psychological interpretations of all myths and legends, East and West. Quite rightly, he berates Freud for not recognizing that many of his "discoveries" consist merely in putting new labels on old bottles: "Freud's idea of the super-ego is a furtive attempt to smuggle in the time-honored image of Jehovah in the dress of psychological theory." And Jung adds: "When one does things like that it is better to say so openly: for my part, I prefer to call things by the names under which they have always been known."[14]

It is in the remote, partly inaccessible (to ego-consciousness) phylogenetic substructure of the unconscious that *anima* and *animus* live,

in a world where the pulse of time beats ever so slowly, where the birth and death of individuals count little, and where ten thousand years ago is yesterday. No wonder that their aspect is strange—so strange that their intrusion into consciousness often blasts into fragments the all-too-feeble brainpans of unfortunate mortals. Anima and animus contain the greater part of the material which appears in insanity, more especially in schizophrenia.[15]

Whenever a typically feminine disturbance, hysteria for instance, also occurs in a male, it is his female component, his *anima* acting up and breaking through a too-weak male predominance. In his work *Character Analysis*, Wilhelm Reich expounds on this topic:

> The hysterical character . . . represents the simplest type of character armoring. Its most outstanding characteristic is an *obvious sexual behavior*, in combination with a specific kind of *bodily agility* with a definite sexual nuance. This explains the fact that the connection between female hysteria and sexuality has been known for a very long time. In women, the hysterical character type is evidenced by disguised or undisguised coquetry in gait, gaze and speech. In men, there is, in addition, softness and over-politeness, feminine facial expression and feminine behavior.[16]

Jung's concept of *collective* unconscious goes much further than Freud's, for whom the unconscious was mostly individual, although he was quite aware of "its archaic and mythological thought-forms," without really being able to account for them.[17] Later, Freud even went part of the way toward the acceptance of Jung's position and stated that "the content of the unconscious is collective anyhow."[18] As far as Jung is concerned, while the *personal* unconscious is only the superficial layer, the deeper collective unconscious is filled with *archetypes* which, over thousands of years of prehistory and history, have been objectified in terms of communicable symbols, transferable myths, fables, and legends; a great deal of the symbolism of esoteric teachings is based on objectified archetypes: ". . . myths are first and foremost psychic manifestations that represent the nature of the psyche," and not some arbitrary constructions of the mind.[19] Therefore, it comes as no surprise that the

> anima is not always merely the feminine aspect of the individual man. It has an archetypal aspect—"the eternal feminine"— which embodies an experience of woman far older than that of the individual. This anima is reflected, of course, in mythology and legend. It can be siren or wood nymph, Grace or Erlking's daughter, lamia or succubus, who infatuate young men and suck the life out of them.[20]

> Unlike the *anima*, the *animus* tends to be represented by a *group* of men, like "an assembly of fathers or dignitaries of some kind who lay down incontestable 'rational' *ex cathedra* judgements."[21] Whenever aroused, the *animus* prompts woman to seek power and behave aggres-

sively, and even tyrannically; blind to reason, it prevents woman from thinking objectively and without prejudice.

It is a striking fact that Jung studies the *anima* in great detail, but deals far less with the *animus;* but then, as he points out, "traditional symbolism is chiefly a product of the masculine psyche and is, therefore, not a suitable object of imitation for woman."[22] The importance attributed to the *anima* springs from the fact that the male psyche has developed the *anima* archetype to a far greater extent and given it fundamental importance; it is not the dogmatic soul but a natural archetype that stands behind language, mythology, and religion, an a priori element in every spontaneous manifestation of psychic life from which consciousness arises. "With the archetype of the anima we enter the realm of the gods or of metaphysics, for everything in which the anima appears takes on the quality of the *numen—* that is becomes unconditional, dangerous, taboo, magical."[23] According to Jung, coming to terms with one's *anima* is a "masterpiece" of bravery, a great act of courage, "a test by fire of all a man's spiritual and moral forces."[24]

The important point is that the *anima*, when thoroughly understood, consists of several contradictory layers and that the deeper layers only reveal themselves to him who is willing to come to terms with it:

> If a man comes to terms with the anima, its chaos and caprice give him occasion to suspect a secret order, to sense a plan, meaning and purpose extending beyond its existence. . . . It is only when this hard task has been faced that he comes more and more to recognize that, behind all the anima's cruel sporting with human fate, there lies something like a secret intention which seems to spring from a superior knowledge of the laws of life. Just the most unexpected, just the alarmingly chaotic, in such psychic experience, reveals the deepest meaning. And the more this meaning is recognized the more does the anima lose its impetuous, impulsive, and compulsive character. Dams against the flood of chaos slowly arise, for the meaningful divides itself from the meaningless. . . . Thereby a new cosmos arises.[25]

But this is not the end of the story; something else is needed before a new cosmos arises out of chaos, a new archetype, here defined by Jung: "Only when all supports and crutches are broken . . . does it become possible to experience an archetype that up till then had lain concealed in the anima's significant senselessness. It is the *archetype of meaning*, as the anima is the archetype of life itself." This archetype, in Jungian terminology, is the *wise old man*, an essentially masculine principle which identifies itself psychically as king, hero, savior, messiah, or shaman who "penetrates the chaotic darkness of mere life with the light of meaning."[26]

In a psychoanalytical sense, the overthrow of the Great Mother Goddess's supremacy at the end of the Bronze Age represents the sinking back of man's *anima* into the depths of the collective unconscious and the rise to supremacy of the "wise old man" archetype— in other words, the rise to supremacy of man's autonomous thought, of the *lógos spermatikós*, seminal thought; in fact, the triumph of the blinding light of man's creative intellect at the terrible cost of downgrading the *anima,* that is, Life.

And so we are brought back, after this excursion in the realms of sociology, biology, and psychology, to the threshold of history, at the beginning of the Iron Age when the Wise Old Man takes over the leadership of mankind's development from the defeated Great Mother.

Part II

THE AXIAL PERIOD:
WOMAN AND RELIGION

❀

I

The Patriarchal Revolution

With unfailing regularity during their dazzling New Year's festival, Babylonians reenacted the famous cosmic victory won by the male over the female principle—the victory of the great god Marduk over the powers of darkness symbolized by the goddess Ti'amat. This was an age of transition. The still insecure male ethos was just beginning to assert its predominance, yet it recognized the formidable power of the female's cyclical principle which, after all, stood for birth, death, and rebirth—fundamental facts of the life cycle. Male preeminence could not assert itself fully until the mythopoeic view of the world was replaced by a rational and logical one. All through the metamorphosis of the early myths, one perceives the discursive power of the mind attempting to awaken and break through the primeval dreamlike forms of mythological understanding.

During the Bronze Age, the mind had not fully awakened. Man was not yet aware of any sharp separation between his species and that of other animals. As far as the Egyptians were concerned, foreigners were not "people" and the notion of mankind as a separate species was unknown. Foreigners could become human (i.e., Egyptian) only if they dressed and behaved like the Egyptians. The world of man and the world of nature were so intertwined as to be impossible to distinguish one from the other; natural phenomena were understood in terms of human experience, and human experiences were understood in terms of natural phenomena. Bronze Age men did not conceive of the external world around them as object, as an impersonnal "it," but as a "thou," as a world pregnant with life. The world of nature was never viewed as inanimate but as teeming with life and symbolic meaning, and every phenomenon was invested with willful individuality and personality—stones, lightning, thunderstorms, flowing rivers, earthquakes. There was no sharp separation between the subjective and the objective; the two were inextricably mixed.

The important point here is that the I-thou relationship, as distinguished from the object-subject opposition, implies an intuitive or instinctive "understanding" of external phenomena as we "understand" and share other people's feelings and emotions through empathy—fear, greed, anger. The relationship itself was the important feature of this thought process, absorbing the objective and subjective poles within itself. This was made easy because of the subject's own lack of inner unity, its consciousness's participation in external phenomena, and their own intrusion into the inner core of the personality. This intermingling is a fundamentally passive, *feminine* form of understanding, based on impressions received directly, a form of participatory knowledge that is essentially emotional and inarticulate. When determining the nature of an object, on the other hand, a person is essentially active, and yet detached. This intellectual form of understanding, which is essentially *masculine* and analytical, is based on emotionally indifferent but discursive knowledge.

The emancipation of human thought from the "feminine" mode of understanding was an exceedingly slow process. It required, at the outset, a true mental revolution within the context of the mythologies in which the traditional wisdom of the various cultures was expressed. In this mythopoeic view of the world, a gradual shift had to occur—and it did take place—which dethroned the female principle in favor of the male. After this, and then only, did it become possible for the masculine mode to come to the fore and begin the steady progression that was to lead to an entirely different *Weltanschauung*. The first step was the emergence of reflective thought, *reflection*, the ability of an individual consciousness to turn around and look upon itself as an *object*, no longer simply to know but to become conscious of the fact of knowing, to think that one is thinking; this involves detachment from external circumstances and emotional participation. This triumph of Greek speculative philosophy consisted in focusing on the *ob-jectum* as something alien projected against the thoughtful subject, that is, its opposite. What surrounds the subject becomes an objective environment, independent from it.

From an I-thou relationship based on the fact that "thou" is always unique, unclassifiable, and unpredictable, and has to be experienced intuitively in a reciprocal relationship, the human mind progressed slowly to a "subject-object" form of understanding based on the fact that, stripped of the "thou" personalism, the objectified "it" can be scientifically related to other objects, become part of a series, and be amenable to universal, impersonal *laws*—again, an essentially masculine approach. Man questions the external world, no longer in terms of "who" but of "what."

True myth, the expression of the collective dream world of a given culture, is not mere childish fantasy but is endowed with the compelling authority that always springs from the unconscious. In this outlook, or psychological disposition, the contrast between reality and appearance becomes meaningless; whatever moves feelings, will, mind, is automatically considered real and has to be dealt with as such —in which case, dreams are at least as real as impressions received in the waking state. From the spontaneous symbolism of the dream world springs the religious and artistic symbolism expressed in mythological thought. It is in mythology, first of all, that the momentous patriarchal revolution took place, long before it began to become visible in historical events—in the deep, dark unconscious of Bronze Age men: "Myth is a form of poetry which transcends poetry in that it proclaims a truth; a form of reasoning which transcends reasoning in that it wants to bring about the truth it proclaims; a form of action, of ritual behavior, which does not find its fulfilment in the act but must proclaim and elaborate a poetic form of truth."[1]

We are now in a position to understand what happened in the collective dream world of Babylonia when the cosmological outlook inherited from Sumer began to change into a more patriarchal one. Ti'amat, the Great Mother, is still at the origin of everything, having given spontaneous birth to innumerable beings, including all the gods and goddesses. As described in the famous Akkadian mythological work, *Enuma elish*, the birth of the gods from the womb of Ti'amat, which stands for the sea and chaos, introduced a new principle in the universe—masculine activity, dynamic movement, sharply contrasted with the forces of chaos symbolizing feminine passivity and inactivity out of which they emerged.[2] The male gods, attempting to organize a cosmos out of the primeval chaos of Ti'amat, challenge her and decide to come together in order to dance—symbol of activity:

> The divine companions thronged together
> and, restlessly surging back and forth, they
> . . . disturbed Ti'amat's belly,
> dancing within [her depth] where heaven is founded.
> Apsu could not subdue their clamour,
> and Ti'amat was silent . . .
> but their actions were abhorrent to her
> and their ways not good . . .

The challenge is flung and the struggle is on. Apsu, symbolizing the sweet waters flowing into the sea, begetter of the great gods, and now their antagonist, goes to see Ti'amat:

Apsu began to speak
saying to pure Ti'amat:
"Abhorrent have become their ways to me,
I am allowed no rest by day, by night no sleep.
I will abolish, yea, I will destroy their ways,
that peace may reign [again] and we may sleep."[3]

The gods are frightened and desperate until the wisest among them, Ea-Enki, manages to cast a spell on Apsu and kills him—the spell being an authoritative command, a word of power—first ghostly outline of what will eventually become the Logos. But the struggle is not over yet. Ti'amat's awful brood of monsters and dragons are set loose on the terrified gods—chaos threatening to overwhelm and destroy the youthful cosmic order. Ea and several other gods fail to rout Ti'amat and her brood and, in despair, eventually choose Marduk, Ea's son, to champion their cause. At the head of a formidable host, Marduk marches against the forces of chaos and scatters them; only Ti'amat stands firm, fearless:

Spreading his mighty net, Marduk envelops Ti'amat in its meshes. As she opens her jaws to swallow him, he sends in the winds to hold them open. The winds swell her body, and through her open mouth Marduk shoots an arrow which pierces her heart and kills her. . . . When complete victory has thus been achieved, Marduk returns to Ti'amat's body, crushes her skull with his mace, and cuts her arteries; and the winds carry her blood away. Then he proceeds to cut her body in two and to lift up half of it to form the sky.[4]

As noted earlier, the symbol of the wind is of prime importance— essentially it is the new masculine symbol of power, activity, relentless force in contrast with the water, the eternal, primordial female. As the biblical Genesis has it, "and the spirit of God moved upon the face of the waters." Already in Sumerian mythology, we recall, the goddess Nammu, the "mother who gave birth to heaven and earth," was depicted with the ideogram "sea"—the female primeval expanse of water.[5] As against the stagnant water, whether it be the Greek *pneuma* or Hebrew *ruach*, the new masculine principle expresses simultaneously the wind, breath, and spirit, remote ancestor of Christianity's Holy Spirit.[6] Again, Genesis states that God "breathed into his [man's] nostrils the breath of life," implying that *ruach* is just as well the spirit of life. The Old Testament states: "Thou takest away their *ruach* and they die, and return to their dust. Thou sendest forth Thy *ruach* and they are created."[7] God's *ruach* is almost synonymous with His Word, and is just as creative. In Psalm 33:6 we find that "by the word of the Lord were the heavens made: and all the hosts of them by the *ruach* of his mouth." If anything was required to testify as to the essentially masculine spirit of the mythological revolution taking place in Babylonia, this is it—the triumph of the male wind over the female water, slowly metamorphosed at a later stage into the spiritualization of the human breath and its equivalence with the creative Word.

Thus it is that the symbols of movement and activity, the male gods and the winds, overcame those of female inertia and watery stagnation. From now on, organization can proceed and civilization be established; human society comes into being along with the political state. With Ti'amat's defeat, the matriarchal outlook begins to dissolve like the morning fog—under Marduk's divine auspices, the great Babylonian King Hammurabi sets up his famous code of laws. Yet, the mythopoeic form of knowledge still rules supreme. The prevailing religious outlook is still largely female-oriented in that it focuses on the *immanent* nature of spirituality. Whereas the forthcoming Bible of the Hebrews was going to affirm the uncompromising *transcendentalism* of their faith when it states that "the heavens declare the glory of God; and the firmament sheweth his handiwork," the Egyptians still view the heavens as the "divine mother through whom man was reborn," and the Mesopotamians look upon the firmament as being the majestic god Anu himself.[8] The divine was still immanent in nature; human society and its cultures are still conceived as emanations of nature, and still embedded in it. Regardless of the victory of Marduk over Ti'amat, the female psyche still ruled; Mother Earth, the Great Mother of fertility, Nin-tu, the "Lady who gives birth," was still worshiped as the consort of Anu, god of Heaven.

While the male principle had risen high enough in mythopoeic thought to challenge the female supremacy, it had not yet succeeded in destroying it altogether; it had reached a rough equality with it. Mother Earth's warm, passive embrace had survived the death and destruction of Ti'amat's body and held Middle Eastern cultures tight to its bosom. But in the middle of the second millennium B.C., momentous events were to take place that would transform this steady retreat of the female principle into a rout: the great invasions.

In the meantime, social changes had been taking place in different areas of the Middle East that seemed to point in another direction. It is true that in Egypt, for instance, there remained firm traces of "mother-right" kinship and matrilinear organization, which had already completely disappeared in Babylonia—the Egyptian "Lady of the House" stood higher in her sphere than the husband, known merely as the "Male."[9] True also that Hittite women enjoyed a much higher social position than they did anywhere in the Middle East; their queen appears to have enjoyed special prerogatives that could not be taken away from her,[10] and the supreme tutelary deity that protected the Hittite state was the sun-goddess of Arinna, "Queen of the land of Hatti, Queen of Heaven and Earth, mistress of the kings and queens of the land of Hatti, directing the government of the King and Queen of Hatti."[11]

Portent of things to come, however, the deity of Arinna at some point changed its sex and became masculine, probably when the entire mythological outlook of the Middle East underwent the process of "solarization"; this was now a male god to whom King Muwatallis addressed his prayers.

What appeared to point in another direction, however, was that increasing social differentiation and inequality, caused by the vast numerical expansion of human societies, had one noteworthy consequence, unheard of in smaller tribal communities: the rise to social and political power of women from the higher social strata. If patriarchalism was making steady inroads at the end of the Bronze Age, the female sex could at least find partial compensation in the fact that some of its more socially prominent members were at times in the position of lording it over great numbers of men, especially as rulers of considerable kingdoms, and at times, of great empires. Social inequality cuts across sexual differences, pushing into the background the problem of the equitable distribution of gender roles, and often allowing individual women to rise far above average men in terms of public power. This explains why the rise of democratic egalitarianism brings out this problem, places it in the foreground, and sharpens the bitterness of an unequal distribution of political and social power between the sexes.

The early rise to power of some women is remarkably illustrated by the life history of the original female ruler, the ancestress of all queens and empresses, the great female Pharaoh Hatshepsut who snatched the throne from her husband, Thutmose III, in the sixteenth century B.C. and "thus became king, an enormity with which the state fiction of the Pharaoh's origin could not be harmonized," as James Breasted puts it.[12] Known as the "female Horus," she must have been a formidable character inasmuch as the husband she eclipsed during her lifetime became, after her death, the greatest pharaoh in history. She ruled with extreme competence a vast Egyptian empire stretching from the Nile's Third Cataract to the Euphrates, and like any good housewife, she developed the economic resources of the empire as few male rulers ever did. Being female, however, she contradicted all the sacred religious lore concerning the essentially divine maleness of all pharaohs, and this sacrilegious contradiction itself is a measure of her remarkable achievement.

In the temple she built at Der el-Bahri for her own glorification, she had herself depicted as specifically designated for the job by Amon's divine will—Amon being the reincarnation of the sun god Re, according to Theban theology, but "the artist who did the work followed the current tradition so closely that the new-born child appears as a *boy*, showing how the introduction of a woman in the situation was wrenching the inherited forms."[13] After her death, her embittered husband, Thutmose III, wreaked terrible vengeance against her memory. Ridiculed and confined to puerile functions in her lifetime, he proceeded to have her name erased and her figure hacked out from every monument, while her obelisks at Karnak were concealed by a masonry sheathing. Again, this pettiness has to be put alongside the fact that Thutmose became, upon Hatshepsut's death, the greatest of the empire-building Pharaohs:

> His reign marks an epoch not only in Egypt but in the whole east as we know it in his age. Never before in history had a single brain wielded the resources of so great a nation and wrought them into such centralized, permanent and at the same time mobile efficiency. . . . The genius which rose from an obscure priestly office to accomplish this for the first time in history reminds us of an Alexander or a Napoleon. He built the first real empire, and is thus the first character possessed of universal aspects, the first world-hero.[14]

It is against such an overpowering character, kept in leash for so long against his will by her will, that the forceful greatness of Hatshepsut has to be measured.

None of her female successors to rulership could hold a candle to her. The Middle East came to know a good many famous queens, from Cleopatra to the great Zenobia of Palmyra, who stood fast against the Roman imperium, fierce defender of the downtrodden Aramean-speaking world. Zenobia appeared in the third century A.D. as a dazzling comet who, for a short time, carved for herself an empire out of the eastern part of the Roman Empire in the name of her minor son, Wahab-Allāth—"gift of the goddess al-Lāt." Claiming blood relationship with Cleopatra, she was learned enough to write a history of the Orient and, female though she was, stands in history as a precursor of Islam in its role as destroyer of most of what was to become the Byzantine Empire and liberator of its Syrian and Egyptian dominions.

Cleopatra had a different claim to fame from Zenobia, being the progeny of a long line of incestuous ancestors. Incest had become traditional among Egypt's ruling Ptolemies, a device intended to perpetuate their dynasty and keep their enormous wealth within the clan. Ptolemy II, for instance, was practically compelled by his sister Arsinoē (known also as Philadelphos, "brother-loving") to repudiate his legal wife and marry her—which caused a tremor throughout the Hellenistic world but prompted Theocritus to compare a brother-sister marriage to similar arrangements among the Olympian deities: "He and that fine noble spouse, who maketh him a better wife than ever clasped bridegroom under any roof, seeing that she loveth with her whole heart brother and husband in one."[15]

On the threshold of history, woman achieved one noteworthy end in spite of the forthcoming patriarchal revolution: to reach, as a privileged individual, direct access to power and to rule millions of men and women whenever circumstances were favorable and her talent measured up to the job.

From the microscopic roots of organic structures to the highest forms of life, the male element has been essentially the active, mobile, dynamic, expansion-oriented element; it is basically a centrifugal element—in stark contrast with the more passive, wooed, selective, absorbing, retentive, and possessive female element with its fundamentally centripetal character. The vast Eurasian steppes and Arabian deserts favored the nomadic pastoral, stock-breeding way of life and the violent centrifugalism of a patriarchal outlook, whereas the agricultural, gardening types of culture spread out in the Middle East, and India favored, under the aegis of what was left of the Great Mother, a typically centripetal outlook. The physical collision between the two principles in the shape of the great invasions, the dynamic aggression of the centrifugal patriarchals tearing into the vitals of the peaceful centripetal cultures of the settled populations, was shattering and historically decisive: an irresistible masculine force subjugated, violently penetrated, and inseminated the female-oriented cultures strewn from one end of the Eurasian continent's periphery to the other, marrying the far greater evolutionary power of the masculine-mobile invaders to the more highly civilized and formative but passive sedentary populations.

The epoch that stretches from the seventeenth to the fourteenth century B.C. is probably the sharpest cleavage in history—an era of *Völkerwanderung* on a gigantic scale, involving countless populations stretching from North Africa to India and China. After twelve or thirteen centuries of continuous historical records in Egypt and Mesopotamia, there is a complete interruption. Egyptian inscriptions virtually disappear between 1730 B.C. and 1580 B.C. (the Hyksos period); after the fall of Babylon around 1530 B.C., inscriptions also disappear in Babylonia and are not resumed until 1400 B.C. Assyrian records vanish between 1720 B.C. and 1400 B.C. Hittite inscriptions suffer the same fate for more than a century.[16] In short, a catastrophic hiatus occurred throughout the Middle East, a sort of Dark Ages brought about by multiple invasions of iron-bearing, horse-drawn, chariot-riding barbarians of obviously terrifying mien and disposition.

The great invasions of patriarchal warriors all over the civilized world wrecked countless states, kingdoms, and even empires, and destroyed more than one rudimentary civilization. Knossos, capital of Minoan Crete, collapsed into ruins at the close of the fifteenth century; the Mycenaeans, for a while, replaced the Minoan Empire with their own Achaean seapower and policed the seas as King Minos used to. The final break in cultural continuity came in the twelfth century when the Dorian invasions took place—overwhelming Mycenae, destroying the Hittite Empire, sweeping away everything and everyone that stood in their path until they reached Egypt where, in 1188 B.C., they were stopped at the Battle of the Nile. This great invasion had been preceded in the fourteenth century by tidal waves of Semitic barbarians sweeping into Canaan and Syria from the North Arabian deserts; and in the thirteenth century by repeated invasions of the Nile Delta by warriors coming across the Western desert from Tunisia and Sicily.

These invasions changed the entire ethnic landscape by triggering massive migrations: Cosseans rushed down from their mountains into Mesopotamia, while Hurrians invaded Syria; non-Semitic invaders (refugees from Crete) flooded into Palestine to collide with the Semites; the intrusion of Phrygian-speaking people into Asia Minor pushed the Carians down the Maeander valley, whose inhabitants, in turn, shoved the Lycians all the way down to the toe of the Anatolian peninsula. On the other side, the Dorians overwhelmed the Greek mainland, pushing the Ionians onto the Aegean islands and Ionia on Anatolia's west coast. In Syria, the Semitic Amorites were drowned under waves of Hittite refugees who fled up the Orontes valley, compounded by another tidal wave of Aramean Semites springing from northern Arabia. Except for Phoenicia, the coast was taken over by Philistine refugees fleeing the Aegean, while inland, the Hebrews streamed into Canaan.

Almost simultaneously, farther afield, Iranian tribes of Indo-European stock swarmed across the Caucasus and Transoxiana and invaded the Persian highlands south of the Caspian Sea; the eastern branch coming in from Transoxiana could not get across the Hindu Kush and turned west across Bactria and up to the eastern Persian plateau. The reason for their failure to cross the Hindu Kush into India was that they had been preceded in the Punjab by another branch of Indo-European cousins who founded Vedic India; for centuries after, they fought the Vedic tribes in the east for possession of Arachosia and eventually Iranized it.

The most momentous invasion was that of India itself by the easternmost branch of the Aryans. There was little to destroy on the Iranian plateau where scattered populations had not reached a high level of culture. But in India the great civilization of Harappā and Mohenjodaro was still in full swing—a civilization that had been closely connected with Sumer, and whose religious outlook was essentially focused on the Great Mother. The numerous clay figurines of females found in the Punjab and Baluchistan testify to this worship. This great civilization collapsed about the middle of the second millennium B.C. under the onslaught of the patriarchal Aryan warrior tribes; urban life disappeared, cities crumbled into dust, and India entered a Dark Age at just about the time Homeric Greece did.

China was not spared in the great *Völkerwanderung* sweeping the civilized world. During the Shang era, stretching from the middle to the end of the second millennium B.C., the matriarchal outlook seems to have been as predominant as elsewhere; the earth was identified with the Great Mother, whose consort was Shang Ti, the sky god.[17] About the middle of this Shang era, irresistible invasions of patriachal Turko-Mongol horsemen equipped, like the Aryan invaders, with war chariots, plunged the Shang realm into a barbarian age during which they became the feudal lords of the decaying realm. The female-oriented culture disappeared, along with the matrilinear social structure and the cults of agrarian fertility.

From this massive shift of populations sweeping everything in its wake from Spain to China, destroying old matriarchal-oriented civilizations, tearing apart mighty empires as well as small kingdoms, and plunging most of the known world into an era of simultaneous Dark Ages, dates the patriarchal supremacy.

Iran and Israel: The Spiritual Breakthrough

The great patriarchal revolution at the dawn of the Iron Age set the stage for the rise of the higher cultures, and for what Karl Jaspers calls the "Axial Period." This was the era that started with Zoroaster and the Magians of Persia, a relatively short era during which the most momentous events that started history proper on its course were concentrated—the age of Confucius, Lao-tzu, and the great Chinese schools of philosophy; the age of the Upaniṣads and the Buddha in India; of Socrates, Plato, and Periclean Athens; of the great Hebrew prophets in Palestine, Elijah, Isaiah, and Jeremiah—all between 800 and 200 B.C., "the most deepcut dividing line in history."

In this new patriarchal age, mythology, the mythology that had prevailed in the old days of the Great Mother's preeminence, was put to flight by a new, masculine, unmythical thought process, relying increasingly on rationalism and logic: it was *lógos* against *mythos*, male abstract thought against female concrete feeling, conscious thinking instead of unconscious myth making. Religion became ethical; myths were reshaped into parables; and uncertainty, spiritual questing, took the place of the quiet, passive acceptance of nature and destiny. In Jasper's words, "the calm of polarities becomes the disquiet of opposites and antinomies."[1] It was the first age of *philosophy*, of speculative thought. The overthrow of the female-centered outlook allowed mankind as a whole to take a giant step forward: tension replaced repetitive rhythm. Everything was now in flux: the first "universal empires" and male-oriented cultures appeared, along with a new historical consciousness, and catastrophic and eschatological views of life and death, original sin, heaven and hell, final judgment. From now on, all was guilt, effort, struggle, danger, violence—but also thirst for individual freedom, quest for personal development, enlightenment, and spiritual salvation. Power of creation was mythically transferred from the womb (the lotus goddess, Padma, in India) to the navel (Viṣṇu's) or to the brain (Athene springing from Zeus's head). Hence the creative power of the "word," Lógos or its Indian equivalent, *manasa putra* ("mind-born child" according to the Purāṇas)[2]; the transfer was quite a natural one, the mouth being assimilated to the vagina and the "word" to the newborn child. In all patriarchal myths, whenever they survived the onslaught of discursive thought, the significance and function of the female were systematically downgraded in a cosmological and symbolic sense. But this revolution was also a major breakthrough, the birth of a new man endowed with a Promethean drive to master the forces of nature and dominate the earth.

Detached and psychologically free of the powers of nature in whose physiological clutches he left woman, man at last became conscious of consciousness, able to reflect on himself and, simultaneously, to ask radical questions concerning his destiny. Set loose from the mythical age with its calm and gentle stagnation, he set out on an anxiety-filled journey of exploration armed with the essential tools of masculinity: philosophic thought in Greece, cosmological thought in Iran, driving willpower among the Hebrews. Even in India and China, philosophers were basically unmythical in their creative intellectual power, although tolerant of surviving mythologies. Men began to rely on themselves in an individual sense, as free, autonomous personalities: "Man proved himself capable of contrasting himself inwardly with the entire universe."[3] The sharp opposition between *subject* and *object* finally dawned on him, along with a newborn mystical urge to overcome this sharp opposition which his increasingly acute mind had been able to perceive for the first time since mankind came into existence. In fact, as Jaspers points out, "this overall modification of humanity may be termed spiritualization."[4]

Inasmuch as Persian culture had a profound impact on Judaism after Cyrus freed the Jews from their captivity in Babylon, the Zoroastrian creed must be viewed as probably the first one to have achieved the decisive spiritual breakthrough—the overthrow of the cyclical fertility cults tied to the rhythm of seasonal change and female physiological laws. For the first time, a purely "masculine" concept of the unidirectional flow of time achieved a breakthrough by dramatically emancipating itself from the tight grip of the lunar-vegetal cycle and setting up the flow of time, *history*, as the great battlefield between good and evil. In Greece and China, historical happenings were still viewed as cyclical and without metaphysical meaning; in India, historical insight was altogether smothered in much vaster cosmological schemes, equally based on endless cyclical repetition of *yugas* and astronomical *mahā-yugas*—all of them unconscious metaphysical extensions of fertility concepts based on the rhythmic alternation of seasons and crops.

Now, for the first time, history is viewed as a *linear* progression with a beginning, a middle—the present—and an end, and therefore with profound metaphysical significance. The distinction between past, present, and future, hitherto blurred by endless cyclical repetitions, is now sharply perceived. Emancipated from nature's grip, from the primeval "once upon a time," man begins to see history as a linear development of unique and unrepeatable events, all endowed with moral significance. As Martin Buber states, "in Babylon the cult calendar might carry on its eternal cycle above and immune to the vicissitudes of history; in Israel history with its own hand transcribed the calendar into the stupendous signs of the unique."[5] The development of the consciousness of the personal ego leads to a sharpened awareness of its finiteness, of death looming at the end of the earthly pilgrimage; death becomes the main preoccupation of metaphysics.

It is to the Persians and the Hebrews that all subsequent monotheistic creeds owe this fundamental insight; Nietzsche was not far wrong when he more or less dedicated his *Also Sprach Zarathustra* to Persia, and as he pointed out, "I had to do a *Persian* the honor of identifying him with this creature of my fancy. Persians were the first to take a broad and comprehensive view of history."[6]

While the Indo-European tribesmen who invaded the bleak Persian highlands retained for a long time the same patriarchal gods that their Vedic cousins worshiped in the warm subtropical plains of India, the symbolism and personality of these deities underwent a profound metamorphosis. The Indo-Aryans slowly blended their masculine religion with the female-oriented creeds of the defeated civilization of Harappā. Their Persian cousins strengthened their own patriarchal outlook; their Magian religion's numerous deities began to fade into the background when Zoroaster preached his reformist creed. It is significant that Zoroastrianism, alone among the world's major religions, never developed any kind of mysticism—the essentially feminine component of all religious feeling. It was essentially an *ethical* creed, focusing on masculine morality, one whose ethical severity almost matched that of the Hebrews. But it was not a religion aiming at man's adaptation to the inscrutable Will of God, in Hebrew fashion; it was a cosmology seeking to give a rational, coherent, and comprehensive explanation of the nature of the universe. To this Magian component, Zoroaster added a prophetic and exhortative message that appealed to moral sentiment as well as the intellect. Its broad dualistic theology can be summed up succinctly in Zoroaster's words:

> The two primal spirits who revealed themselves in vision as twins are the Better and the Bad in thought, word and action. And between these two the wise knew to choose aright, the foolish not so.[7]

Moral choice comes into play as a result of the basic freedom granted to man, to choose between good and evil which between them cleave the universe into two halves.

God (Ahura Mazdā, later Ohrmazd), identified as the principle of goodness, is locked in deadly combat with Satan (Angra Mainyu, later Ahriman), the principle of evil. The battlefield is the world of creation, the material universe itself which Ohrmazd has created, as he created man, as a trap in which to imprison, and eventually destroy, Ahriman. Thus the divine Ohrmazd is not infinite, inasmuch as he is limited by his demonic rival *in space*. Nevertheless, along with space he has also created *time* and the historical process that gives it substance—and it is the flow of time that will, in due course, destroy Ahriman and close the historical process itself; in other words, Ahriman "was and is, yet shall not be."[8] In short, the divine Ohrmazd is eternal and identified with infinite *time*, not with infinite *space* which he has to share, a while longer, with satanic Ahriman—unbounded by time and yet bounded by space, whereas Ahriman is bounded by *both* time and space.

The crucial feature here is that when the two antagonistic spirits, Ohrmazd and Ahriman, agree to engage in a nine-thousand-year-long battle, the divine Ohrmazd actually *knows* that at the end of this period Ahriman will be completely annihilated[9]—because, by its very essence, evil has neither memory nor foresight whereas goodness remembers and foresees; because, caring neither for past nor future, evil lives only for the benefits of the present: evil has no consciousness of time, is fundamentally ahistoric.

The moral justification is plain. Originally, God was finite, limited by Satan, a dualistic situation that could have lasted eternally had it not been that Satan's inherently evil nature made him attack: he became the aggressor, and this fact alone, compelling God to counterattack in self-defense, makes it possible for God to become what he was not initially—infinite. Satan, being the principle of death, has no such possibility; thus, *history* and the flow of time that encompasses it is the tale of the perfecting of an originally imperfect God.

This is where man comes in—as the divine Ohrmazd's agent and ally in the forthcoming destruction of evil. Man's role is to lead a virtuous life and avoid temptation, to indulge only in good thoughts, good words, and good deeds. Quite naturally Zoroastrianism was adamantly opposed to the basic ingredients of all mystical experiences that are artificially contrived—asceticism and monasticism, and celibacy in general. It was man's imperative duty to take a wife and procreate in order to further the divine Ohrmazd's cause in his cosmic struggle with Ahriman; celibacy is unnatural and evil in itself. Evil is personified as the "Lie" *(drauga, druj)*, while righteousness is essentially "Truth" *(arta)*. Most of the metaphysical paraphernalia of this remarkable religion was eventually incorporated into Christianity—the immortality of the soul, the host of angels and demons surrounding the good and evil deities, the resurrection of the body at the end of time when evil is finally annihilated, and its incorporation in the "Final Body," the reestablished macrocosmos from which all evil will have been expelled— this being brought about by the *Saoshyant,* the Saviour, a title that Zoroaster appropriated for himself and which became Christ's dignity alongside that of Jewish Messiah.

Woman, the eternal female, comes into play primarily as an ally of the diabolic Ahriman, as the "Demon Whore" who boasts that she will take away the dignity of the Blessed Man, Gayōmart, the Persian version of primordial Adam. In a striking passage that echoes the thought of many contemporary Greeks deploring the impossibility of procreating without woman's assistance, the divine Ohrmazd is made to lament that "had I found another vessel from which to make man, never would I have created thee. . . . But I sought in the waters and in the earth, in plants and cattle, in the highest mountains and deep valleys, but I did not find a vessel from which blessed man might proceed except woman. . . ."[10] Time and again in the sacred texts of the *Bundahishn* it is made plain that the reproduction of males rather than females is essential for the defeat of Ahriman—woman, who, "though created by Ohrmazd, chose to play the harlot with Ahriman," has no sense of history or of ethics.

While it is clear that woman was looked down upon by the Zoroastrians, her reproductive function was nevertheless of such importance (from a theological standpoint) that she was blessed as mother and housewife. But the contrast between the Blessed First Man, Gayōmart, and the First Woman, the "Demon Whore," brings out vividly the uncompromising patriarchalism of the Zoroastrian creed. Again, as the *Bundahishn* states it, woman was originally created by the divine Ohrmazd but fled to Ahriman and became his consort. From this satanic embrace sprang menstruation, a condition deemed repulsive and impure by the Persians: "Thus man is defiled by woman and ever will be so till the final Resurrection when both sexes are called to share in the universal bliss."[11] Until then, however, she is polluted by her satanic association and forever subjected to man; and it is thanks to this subjection that the demonic Ahriman is to be finally destroyed at the end of time.

While this view may appear uncompromisingly hostile to woman, the feminine principle is somewhat redeemed by Spandarmat, daughter-wife of the divine Ohrmazd, "Queen of Heaven, Mother of Creation," in other words old Mother Earth—woman in her reproductive, motherly aspect which counterbalances beneficently the evil aspect of the Demon Whore. Try as it may, the patriarchal spirit cannot deny the eternal feminine in her motherly aspect, especially when the patriarchal spirit shuns asceticism and puts a premium on human procreation: it claims that evil is introduced into the world by the feminine element but is compelled to grant that it cannot be all evil. Distrust for the female, however, should be instilled in all men, as is usually the case in all creeds that are, like Zoroastrianism, primarily ethical. It was left to Ādhurbādh, who lived much later, in the fourth century A.D. under the reign of Shāpūr II, to urge his Zoroastrian followers: "Put not your trust in women lest you have cause to be ashamed and to repent. Do not tell your secrets to women lest [all] your toiling be fruitless."[12]

The social status of woman in Persia could not have been anything but a reflection of this metaphysical outlook. Before the arrival of the Aryans, the original inhabitants of Iran were organized along matrilinear lines. It seems that in some areas women were even in command of the armed forces—among the Guti of Kurdistan, for instance.[13] But all this changed when the invaders settled on the highlands: the status of woman declined as Persian civilization rose. By the seventh century B.C. no trace of matrilinear organization was left, as the strictly patriarchal organization of Persian society took shape: the principle unit was neither the restricted family (nmāna) nor the large tribe (zantu) but the medium-size, intermediate clan (vis). Under the Achaemenids, large harems were already in existence, harems that included not only wives and concubines but all the women of the household—mothers, sisters, aunts, nieces.[14]

Zoroastrianism fought with success against the atavistic nomadism of the Persians, but while they settled and became sedentary, they retained the typical nomadic and pastoral view of woman as beast of burden. Zoroastrianism itself, however, was largely diluted in Mazdaeism and had to compromise with an irrepressible polytheism in which the goddess Anāhitā, at once "Lady of Waters" and "Lady of Birth," ranked high—polytheism invariably implying a strong female component that pure monotheism never accepted.

The Zoroastrian religion remained dualistic to the end; the Magians simply could not conceive that a benevolent God Almighty could be responsible for evil and suffering. Much later, in Sassanian times (third century A.D.), fruitless attempts were made, under monotheistic pressure, to derive the two principles of good and evil from a common source, viz. Infinite Time (Zurvān Akarana). The sect was short-lived and disappeared when Islam swept over Iran.

It was left to a small Semitic people to conceive of an uncompromising monotheism, which entailed a most brutal emancipation from the clutches of the mythological outlook. But even the Hebrews could not dispense entirely with mythopoeic thought processes and expressions, most of which are in full evidence in the Book of Genesis—the last-born of a long series of Genesis accounts. The Ancient Testament's account follows, in the main, the pattern of previous mythological accounts in Sumer and Babylonia but turns them upside down. While all the ingredients (serpent, primeval woman, Garden of Eden, genesis of procreation, and death) are similar, the general outlook is quite different. The early female-oriented mythologies are placid and optimistic; they know nothing of Original Sin, the Fall, or Exile. The ritual murder of the earlier agricultural myth, according to which the Earth Mother gives the early Cain his strength, is reversed in the Bible and is now used to reemphasize the theme of the Fall. Cain is condemned to wander on the face of an implacably hostile earth; furthermore, Cain, the matriarchally oriented agriculturist, is condemned in favor of Abel, the patriarchally oriented shepherd—the Hebrews were pastoral nomads and the Canaanites agriculturists. This remarkable reversal of the symbolism becomes even more striking if one refers to a Sumerian cuneiform text (circa 2050 B.C.) that depicts the goddess Inanna as, quite naturally, biased in favor of the sedentary farmer.[15]

Another instance illustrating the impact of the masculine mental disposition to *dissociate* (the analytical disposition), as against the feminine to *unite* (the synthetic), is the radical dissociation between Almighty Yahweh and the world he created ex nihilo—symbolized in the Bible by the dissociation between the Tree of Life and the Tree of Knowledge (which becomes inaccessible to man); in earlier mythologies they are one and the same tree. There can be no confusion here: the absolute transcendence of God makes it impossible to entertain the slightest pantheistic or immanentist interpretation of the divinity; not quiet happiness and contentment but toil and sorrow are the lot of human beings on earth.

Most of the other borrowed myths are similarly made to fit into the new patriarchal mold—the Deluge, or the reversal of the function of the Mesopotamian *ziggurat* in the Tower of Babel. It is mostly the atmosphere conveyed that is completely opposed to the earlier placid, serene, comfortable one—the existence of an all-powerful, absolutely transcendental, wrathful God, the calamitous Fall, Original Sin, and Exile; but also the supremely satisfying, and extremely masculine, dissociating notion based on exclusivism of belonging to the Chosen People.

Originally, all Semites were organized in matrilinear clans; the mother's, and not the father's, bloodline determined kinship. Goddesses rather than gods were worshiped as prime deities. But at some point in history a massive transfer altered the sex of most deities from female to male; the rule of kinship also changed from matrilinear to patrilinear.

In the earlier days of female kinship and widespread polyandry, the Great Mother was supreme; under one guise or another, she survived for a long time in the patriarchal era. The Carthaginians worshiped a Great Mother identified with Tanith-Artemis—the "heavenly Virgin" which Augustine, much later, reidentified with the unmarried mother of the gods in his *De Civitate Dei*. The Arabian goddess al-Lāt was worshiped by the Nabateans at Petra, as described by Epiphanius:

> Divine motherhood, like the kinship of men and gods in general, was to the heathen Semites a physical fact, and the development of the corresponding cults and myths laid more stress on the physical than the ethical side of maternity, and gave a prominence to sexual ideas which was never edifying, and often repulsive.[16]

The change in kinship laws transferred authority from uncle to father, from brother to husband. Women fell under the authority of their new lord and master from another family; their children became members of his kinship group, not of theirs. And along with this social metamorphosis in sexual relations went the theological metamorphosis already alluded to; in Canaan and elsewhere, Ishtar reappeared as Astarte (Ashtoreth to the Hebrews), but now only as a subservient consort to the supreme, all powerful, masculine Ba'al. Whenever the identity of the goddess was too well established to be altogether discarded or associated with a new male deity, she changed her sex, as in southern Arabia where Ishtar was transmuted into the masculine 'Athtar. Whatever emotionalism there was in Semitic paganism always focused on the worship of goddesses, both in the sexual and the motherhood aspects. The male deity appealed rather to more austere and rigidly ethical feelings—and it was among the Hebrews, latter-day beneficiaries of this vast upheaval in the Semitic world, that this ethical aspect of religion received its most uncompromising formulation.

The struggle toward monotheism among the Hebrews implied far more than the mere elimination of polytheism; it suggested intense concentration on morality and, as a consequence, on a degradation of the feminine element that found its natural counterpart in woman's low status in ancient Israel. A wife called her husband *ba'al* (master) or *'adôn* (lord), addressing him as a slave adresses his master; the Decalogue ranks a wife among her husband's possession. While *he* could repudiate *her*, she could not ask for divorce and remained legally a minor through life. Wives and daughters did not inherit, except in the absence of male heirs.[17]

From all this, it should not be gathered that women were without protection or influence; again, as in Persia, they were well protected by law and tradition in their capacity as generators of new life. As is still the case under rabbinic law, children's Jewishness was determined by the mother's bloodline, not the father's. Women performed most of the hard work at home, but in times of national stress they often took part in public life—heroines such as Deborah and Jael, rulers like Athaliah in Judah, prophetesses after the pattern of Huldah who was consulted by the king's ministers, national saviors in the mold of Judith and Esther. The wife won increasing respect when she became a mother, especially of male children:

> The social and legal position of an Israelite wife was, however, inferior to the position a wife occupied in the great countries round about. In Egypt the wife was often the head of the family, with all the rights such a position entailed. In Babylon she could acquire property, take legal action, be a party to contracts, and she even had a certain share in her husband's estate.[18]

In fact, only among Jewish colonies in foreign lands, such as Elephantine in Egypt, was the social position of women improved.

Strangely enough, many women must have appreciated this subordination because far more women than men were converted to Judaism. It certainly could not be because of the high regard expressed for women in the Torah, which spells out quite clearly that "he who instructs his daughter in the law, instructs her in folly"; or by the Talmud which enjoined men not to speak to women in public; or by the traditional Jewish prayer in which the male beseeched, "O God, let not my offspring be a girl, for very wretched is the life of woman"[19] —and added daily, "Blessed be thou, O Lord our God, for not making me a woman."

One root of this discrimination appears traceable to Jewish traditional stress on the fact that woman's sexual drive was probably greater than man's, and that it was usually woman who led man into sexual misbehavior; this is a recurrent theme from the Old Testament to the Talmud. With all that, talmudic legislation always enjoined the husband to give adequate satisfaction to his wife's sexual requirements and specified that, in the case of polygyny, a husband could not possibly satisfy more than four wives—a prefiguration of Islam's legislation on the matter. Although Eve's daughters were legally bound and fettered in every conceivable way, the Hebrew-Jewish tradition held woman-as-mother in high, if subordinate, regard. Jewish faith and culture could never have displayed such remarkable power for survival through the ages if this had not been the case.

It is true that a widower might be the sole heir of his departed wife, although, conversely, a widow might not inherit from her deceased husband; that if there were sons, daughters inherited only what their brothers saw fit to leave them; that girls might not be sent to school; and that the authority of the father could be almost as absolute as that of the ōld republican Roman *paterfamilias*—yet, Jewish women still benefited from both the healthy puritanism of the Judaic life style and the extremely tight bonds uniting the family. Sexual lewdness, commonplace in the Middle East, and later in Greco-Roman civilization, and later again in Islamic civilization, was almost unknown among the Jews. Women were bound to benefit from the general excellence of parental relations, the reverence for the elders, and the stern but loving upbringing of the young. In the sanctity of family life, the Jewish mother probably found greater affective fulfillment than the forthcoming "emancipated" women of Greece and Rome. The vital part played by the mother-child relationship for the healthy development of the individual was always acknowledged, best symbolized by the profound talmudic statement according to which, since the Almighty could not be everywhere, He created mothers and, so to speak, delegated part of His creative power to them.[20]

There was a definite relationship between the early Hebrew temper and the geographical setting in which it developed most of its culture. The early Hebrews were essentially nomads who lived not in the great boundless desert but on the border of settled lands, between the desert and the sown. It is not by accident that the pastoral way of life is more highly valued in the Bible than the agricultural. While the settled farmer accepted and even revered a distant bureaucratic authority that regulated the flow of irrigation for the benefit of his crops, while inflicting all the constraints of living as a humble subject in a large kingdom or empire, the proud nomad sought to preserve his freedom to come and go as he pleased. The farmer's enslavement to the phenomena of nature's growth and decay and his worship of fertility were repellent to the free-moving nomad. The latter, rejecting the complexities and fetters of settled agricultural life, gained freedom but lost communion with the world of natural fertility, with the world of cyclical rhythm and form. Whereas the farmer, in his worship of fertility, saw the divine as *immanent* in the phenomenal world, the pastoral people quite naturally could see nothing in the vast stillness of the confines of the desert where nothing grows and nothing decays but *transcendence*—transcendence of God beyond all concrete phenomena. Furthermore, there was no need to bend and adapt to a complex human society, or to the agricultural rhythm and growth and decay, to become enmeshed in a complex set of religious-magic observances, rituals, and fertility celebrations. In the desert, sheer human *will* prevailed, free, unattached, and constantly strengthened by the need to overcome all the tribulations of a hard life—Yahweh's divine Will being the projection beyond space and time of that primitive human will. In such a setting, the male psyche prevails absolutely.

Quite naturally, Yahweh, although originally a Midianite volcano god of rather barbarous disposition, soon metamorphosed into a completely transcendent Almighty of righteousness, an exclusive and *universal* God completely distinct from His own creation in time and space; pure Being, unconditioned, ineffable. The distance between Yahweh and His creation is infinite, yet He is the ground of all existence; He is the height of abstraction, the first example in history of a complete emancipation from the mythopoeic thought process—but this applies only to the latter part of the Ancient Testament; the earlier part is still largely immersed in mythology. In fact, the biblical account itself, from end to end, is but one long historical process of *progressive emancipation* from the shackles of mythology.

Unlike the Greeks, however, the Hebrews did not get over the I-thou mental framework; but the new "thou" of the Hebrews—Yahweh—was no longer in nature but way beyond it, an unfathomable spiritual entity who led the Chosen People through the desert by virtue of a special compact between them. Thus, as fast as one mythology was destroyed, a far more abstract ideology expressed as parables took its place: the concept of the Chosen People fulfilling the Will of God. Nature faded into the background since Yahweh transcended it completely. History, the irreversible flow of time, became the new phenomenal dimension in which the Almighty's Will revealed itself, since the will always refers to the future—the tribulations of the wandering tribes searching for the Promised Land. Man was the servant, the interpreter of God's capricious Will—not His proud assistant and collaborator as in Zoroastrian Persia. In a more humble way, man was a modest helper of the Almighty, destined to strive to realize His divine Will on earth. The pathetic atmosphere in the biblical accounts of the stress and sufferings of inadequate, weak men trapped into making endless efforts is in stark contrast with the calm serenity of former mythologies dating back to the bygone days of the Great Mother. Man was far more free in the biblical account than in any previous one, but he was also crushed by the weight of his new individual responsibility, his loneliness, and his feeling of guilt. A spirit of intense drama pervades the account of Abraham facing the sacrifice of his son, Jacob; Moses leading his people out of Egypt; the appalling miseries of Job; the tragic fate of Saul.

In the old female-oriented atmosphere of ancient times, man was deeply enmeshed in the coils of nature, soothed by its cosmic rhythm, free from individual responsibility and moral qualms, carried along by his harmonious, magic relationship with the supreme cosmic entity, the Great Mother in whose consoling embrace he longed to seek refuge after death and return to Mother Earth's womb. There is nothing of all this in the dramatic biblical atmosphere where *disharmony* prevails absolutely—man alone facing his stern Maker. Nature is no longer of any account, only history-in-the-making, Hebrew man's history of his relationship with Yahweh dating back to the Exodus and the forty years in the wilderness where he tempered his willpower. With the end of the female principle's supremacy, individualism was born, but also its inevitable consequences—guilt feelings, anguish, endless striving, and constant strife.

From the start, the masculine spirit of the Hebrews expressed itself primarily as overdeveloped *will* looking toward the future, whereas the Greek male outlook emphasized timeless *reason*. One aspect of the contrast has been neatly pinpointed by Miguel de Unamuno in *The Tragic Sense of Life*:

> The will and the intelligence seek opposite ends: that we may absorb the world into ourselves, appropriate it to ourselves, is the aim of the will; that we may be absorbed into the world, that of intelligence . . . the intelligence is monist or pantheist, the will monotheist.[21]

The Hebrew-Jewish view was that man had to know and follow the Law which had come to be known through divine *revelation*, not through a rational mental process. Any transgression was condemned, not because it was irrational or illogical but because it was a *sin* against the Almighty. This connection between willing and sinning is no accident; Kant has clearly demonstrated that morality is a product of our willing (*Critique of Practical Reason*) just as truth is a product of our understanding (*Critique of Pure Reason*). Here, in Hebrew land, was no Cartesian *cogito ergo sum;* man's highest faculty was not his mental ability but his willpower—he *is* his will, his sinfulness is willful, and he shall be sternly judged as one who is endowed with complete freedom of choice between good and evil. In turn, this extraordinary development of the Hebrew will was the direct outcome of the tension generated by the striking contrast between the belief of belonging to the Chosen People and the patent, empirical inadequacy of the human individual who is almost nought compared to his all-powerful Maker.

According to Schopenhauer's pregnant distinction, while the plastic arts—painting, sculpture, architecture—are reflections of ideas, that is, epiphenomena of the will, music is pure reflection of the will itself. How right he was is proved by the fact that whereas the Greeks developed plastic arts to a pitch of perfection because their major organ of perception was the eye, the Hebrews' organ of perception was the ear: they did not *see* Yahweh but *heard* him, and therefore never reproduced his likeness in painting or sculpture. It is the "voice" of Yahweh that is perceived and only his effulgence is seen directly; in the cave of Horeb, the prophet Elijah heard God's "still small voice" without ever seeing him.[22] While the Greeks never developed the solitary song, the Hebrews' major art form was the psalm and nothing could be further from Greek marble than the lyrical expression of Hebrew singing—the direct artistic expression of the will, with its attendant striving, tension, and sense of the unidirectional flow of time. In turn, the will applied itself to the conquering of this tension, almost unbearable at times. Unlike the Greeks, "the Jews found conciliation not in the contemplation of knowledge but in the exertion of the will"[23]—its greatest expression being the relation of Hebrew man to the Almighty as a contest of antagonistic willpowers—divine Will against human obstinacy in sin.

Compare the willful arbitrariness of Yahweh with the virtual impotence of Greece's Olympian deities who, time and again, even Zeus, must yield to implacable fate. Greeks were primarily thinkers who looked for, and found, in nature general rules of impersonal law which limit freedom of both gods and men. Yahweh, on the other hand, is the quintessence of arbitrariness, and his rule has nothing to do with impersonal law; standing above everything, including nature, creator of the universe ex nihilo, he embodies absolute, pure Will—which entails man's own freedom to will as he chooses. This *liberum arbitrium* compels man to submit to a freely chosen, or God-imposed (which amounts to the same thing in this context) code of ethics; morality has no meaning without freedom of choice. The divine legislation, the Ten Commandments, are not laws derived by human reason and logic from an observation of nature's own impersonal laws but commands dictated by the Almighty Creator, and his echo, man's inner conscience. Masculine will, expressed by the Hebrew prophet, thus sets itself up as the dialectical counterpart of masculine reason, as expressed by the Greek philosopher, and has lived, within the bosom of Western culture, in uneasy alliance with the intellect; if complete freedom of will implies ceaselessly repeated acts of creation, rational cognition counters it by setting up scientific laws as specific limitations on the unbounded liberty of willing. The insoluble conflict between freedom and necessity in Western culture is the historical consequence of this uneasy marriage.

Two patriarchal streams converged and joined up when the Persian Emperor Cyrus freed the Jews from their captivity in Babylon and let them go back to Jerusalem to rebuild the Temple in the sixth century B.C. A certain intermingling of creeds inevitably took place, and in the late second century B.C. clear indications of metaphysical dualism appear in Judaism, more especially in the Testament of the Twelve Patriarchs—error against truth, darkness against light—which was sternly rejected by the orthodox rabbis; a great deal of this dualism eventually found its way into Christianity.

It was in post-exilic times that the Torah was established as the law in Israel, with Persia's imperial approval. While many Jews of the Diaspora fell into assimilation with the local populations, a kernel remained in Jerusalem and rekindled the flame of pure monotheism after Alexander the Great swept through the Middle East. This coincided with a revival of Zoroastrianism among the Persians, and this religious parallelism had a great deal to do with their common hostility to Greco-Roman civilization.

3

Greece:
The Intellectual Breakthrough

The Hebrews displayed one essential component of the masculine psyche to the full—dynamic, aggressive willpower. The Greeks emphasized another: emancipation of the discursive intellect, of logic and reason, from the shackles of the dreamlike mythopoeic thought process. The Hebrews were driven to reinterpret and to "patriarchalize" the matriarchal mythologies of former times; the Greeks sought to do away with myth altogether. And unlike the Hebrews, who *believed* in their biblical history with all the strength of willful faith, the Greeks understood their mythologies for what they were—representative symbols and allegories.

But the process of intellectual emancipation itself started well within the confines of mythology, when the new gods of the sunny Olympian pantheon assaulted and defeated the pre-Homeric deities of the land. As Aeschylus's Furies, the defeated goddesses, were to express it in his *Eumenides*,

> The fault's not ours. It lies
> With younger gods who rise
> In place of those that ruled before;
> From stool to crown their throne
> Is stained with gore.
> See, how Earth's central sacred stone
> Has taken for its own
> A grim pollution Justice must abhor.[1]

And they add:

> You mocked primeval goddesses with wine, to break
> The ancient dispensation . . .[2]

Now true and false must change their names
Old law and justice be reversed.[3]

In the legend of the slaying of Medusa by Perseus we have a perfect example of the transposition of actual historical events into instant mythology. Medusa, in her pre-Homeric incarnation, was the enchanting granddaughter of Gaea, Mother Earth; as presented by post-Homeric mythology, she has become the monstrous figure whose hair was made of hissing snakes and whose look turned men to stone. Perseus (king of Mycenae, circa 1290 B.C.) cut off her head—implying presumably that the Hellenic invaders took over the Great Mother's main shrines and " 'stripped her priestesses of their Gorgon masks,' the latter being apotropaic faces worn to frighten away the profane. That is to say, there occurred in the early thirteenth century B.C. an actual historic rupture, a sort of sociological trauma, which has been registered in this myth."[4] The decisive mythological battle was waged when Zeus defeated Typhon, youngest child of Gaea, and put to flight the army of her Titan offspring, hurling them underground into Tartarus, from whence henceforth proceed storms, earthquakes, and volcanic eruptions.

The same archetypes are found all over the lands conquered by the victorious Indo-European warriors—the Vedic pantheon in India is a replica of the Greek Olympus; the victory of the new Aryan god Indra over the cosmic snake Vritra is a duplicate of Zeus's over Typhon. Everywhere, the new demonic antideities are the former cosmic powers of earlier female-oriented mythologies; everywhere, the former cosmic powers of the defeated populations (Pelasgians in Greece, Dravidians in India) have to bow to the new masculine concept of the triumphant warrior-hero. Although in India the victory was not clearcut and, eventually, led to a compromise, in Greece victory was decisive and without appeal—the victory of the principle of free will over earthbound destiny, of individual responsibility and ethical supremacy over the passive worship of the forces of nature and Mother Earth. In this sense, the Homeric Greeks and the biblical Hebrews were moving along parallel lines, setting up masculine stress and tension over the placid and rhythmic feminine cosmic order. As man's attention began to be drawn to an understanding of his own humanity, awe and worship of the life-giving powers of fertility faded into the background.

And yet, even in Greece, the old powers were not utterly destroyed. While the anima sought refuge in the darker recesses of Tartarus and the collective unconscious, the reshaped myths allowed the older, muffled voices of the Bronze Age to be heard. The Great Mother was subdued but not annihilated. The patriarchal deities of Olympus were not as ruthless as the biblical Yahweh; they did not destroy but married many goddesses. There was no struggle of the will in Greece where the goddesses retained, or recovered, the right to be worshiped in many *mysteries,* especially those of Demeter, Persephone of Eleusis, and the Orphics. In Canaan the struggle between the ethical view and the survival of fertility worship was ceaseless until the Hebraic land was laid bare of these cults, but Zeus had no such compunction and zestfully pursued all the nymphs of the Mediterranean—all of which were multiform incarnations of the one and only Great Mother.

Many former matriarchal themes were retained—Demeter; the mournful mother searching for her lost child; the brutal death of Dionysius, followed by his resurrection—but also remolded into a search for a new *individual* salvation. The distance between gods and mortals was reduced sharply, to the point where the initiates of the Orphic mysteries could emerge as gods in their own right after consorting with the Mother Goddess, queen of the dead. In fact, the prestige of all the inhabitants of Olympus, male and female, was far less than their counterparts had been in the Bronze Age—they were not the cosmic creators of the universe, displayed many of the foibles of mere mortals, and had little control over the latter. As Pindar stated it in his Sixth Nemean Ode, "Of one race, one only, are men and gods. Both of one mother's womb we draw our breath; but far asunder is all our power divided, and fences us apart; here there is nothingness, and there, in strength of bronze, a seat unshaken, eternal, abides the heaven."[5] Men were unlucky; that was all the difference.

Female power of inspiration and divination was still respected and feared; sibyls and muses, oracles and pythonesses crowded the Greek landscape, and Greek men rarely overcame their atavistic awe of nature. Probably the mightiest expression of this enduring grasp, the cult of Dionysius, immigrated from wild Thrace, and although its exuberance irritated the devotees of Olympus, its barbaric eruption on the Greek scene could not be stemmed by the sterner patriarchal powers. This savage cult appealed mainly to women and, as Bertrand Russell points out, had in it "a curious element of feminism. Respectable matrons and maids, in large companies, would spend whole nights on the bare hills in dances which stimulated ecstasy, and in an intoxication perhaps alcoholic, but mainly mystical."[6] In spite of their bewilderment and anger, husbands had to put up with it. Never has the cult been depicted with as much power as in Euripides' *Bacchae.*

Against the wild orgiastic Dionysius who knows no limits and for whom excess in itself is the means toward self-enlightenment, the patriarchal Greeks set up the cold and sober Apollo, the deity of self-control and limitation, of *form* in art and *reason* in thought. Apollo is the most masculine deity to appear so far; the masculinity that gives priority to discursive thought and spiritual quest, teaches man to look out at the world and upward at the sun and stars. Essentially he is the god of sublimation who enjoins man to curb his instincts, to store up and save his vital forces for the Promethean conquest of the objectified world.

From now on, as can be seen in the Homeric saga, the male *arete* (pride in excellence) became the leitmotiv of Greek ethics; and woman was reduced to providing men with only limited stimulation—inspiring men to heroic deeds (Athene), marital faithfulness, and plastic beauty of body were to be woman's contributions. Helen, the female "object" over whom the great Trojan War was fought, symbolizes this dramatic devaluation of the feminine element in Greek culture. Only in post-Homeric Greece did man stand alone at the center of the universe—not in the humble position of being cowed under the transcendent divinity of Almighty Yahweh, but self-reliant and confident in his ability to grasp the world through reason and logic. But the price for this was high: the almost total exclusion of woman from the new cultural context.

In the Pandora myth, the great poet Hesiod introduced the new, highly misogynic view of the female sex that was to prevail in classical Greek culture. He developed a theme that was unknown in the days of Homeric chivalry—woman as the root of all evil and source of human misery. According to his version, Zeus, mightily angered by the fact that Prometheus had stolen the sacred fire from heaven, decided to punish mortal man. He ordered Hephaestus to mold a woman out of earth, a woman of such entrancing charm and beauty as would bring misery upon the human race. Thus was Pandora, the "all-gifted" first woman, created: Aphrodite gave her beauty, Hermes speech, boldness, and cunning. Prometheus's brother, Epimetheus, made her his wife, ignoring Prometheus's advice never to accept any gift from the gods. Ignoring also Prometheus's specific instructions not to open a mysterious box which he had left to Epimetheus's safekeeping, Pandora, consumed with curiosity, lifted the lid, releasing all the ten thousand ills that have been plaguing mankind ever since. Only "hope" remained at the bottom of the box. As Hesiod put it in his *Works and Days*,

> For of old the tribes of men lived on the earth apart from evil and grievous toil and sore diseases that bring the fates of death to men. For in the day of evil men speedily wax old. But the woman took off the great lid of the Jar with her hands and made a scattering thereof and devised baleful sorrows for men.[7]

And he adds that "to mortal men, Zeus gave women as an evil," and a punishment for their Promethean spirit. In actual fact, Pandora is but another name for Gaea, formerly Mother Earth, now dethroned and reduced to the status of a plague. She became the Greek counterpart of the biblical Eve, symbol of the widespread belief that the gods were jealous of man's cultural development and revenged themselves by giving him woman as a disturbing companion, responsible for all the evils that befall him and his successors.[8]

Freed from the trammels of a female-oriented outlook, Greek thinkers began their long odyssey leading from mythopoeic understanding to hard-rock philosophy. What led them on was an implicit assumption that the universe was a *cosmos* of course (this had already been established in Mesopotamia when Marduk destroyed Ti'amat), but also *intelligible*. It could be grasped mentally by the intellect and analyzed —not only that a unifying order underlay the chaos of our perceptions, but also that man could understand that order rationally in terms of cause and effect (no longer in terms of symbol and thing symbolized). The speculations of the Ionian thinkers led them gradually into stripping away all the myths, gods, and goddesses in their search for the origin of cosmic creation. Prompted by an unholy curiosity, they removed the problem from the mytho-logical plane and shifted it to the purely logical one. They began seeking for an immanent ground of existence—not a beginning in historical terms but in terms of a "first cause." They had not yet reached the stage of objective, systematic thought process and still couched their intellectual convictions in oracular terms; but they slowly removed the anthropomorphic veil cast over nature by mythological thought. Anaximenes thought that air was the first cause, while Thales stated that it was water and Anaximenes mentioned the "boundless"; Heraclitus boldly suggested fire. The outcome of these cogitations was Democritus's revolutionary theory of atoms.

We must not assume, however, that the Ionian philosophers had completely torn themselves away from mythopoeic thinking. They were intellectual revolutionaries in that, for the first time, they took the major (masculine) *dissociating* step of attempting to divorce the subjective from the objective, but it is doubtful whether they thought entirely in physical or materialistic terms. For many of them, nature still teemed with deities and nymphs; Thales stated so plainly and added that the magnet must be "alive" since it was able to move iron. But they had taken a first and vital step toward objective thought, and if we look at the semantics, we notice that they speak of air, water, and fire in the abstract, not of air gods, water gods, or fire gods. For the first time, regardless of the fact that everything is "full of gods," they saw the external world and its components as detached, autonomous *objects* and began mentally to link these objects with one another, and to bind them into a coherent system of objective relationships. Only boldly self-reliant men would have the courage to do away with religious explanation altogether, move away from Mother Nature, from sentiment and emotion, and, alone in their individual capacity, in an analytical spirit of logical enquiry, attempt to understand nature in a detached, impersonal way.

More remarkable still, when compared with mythopoeic thought processes, is the fanatical logical *consistency* with which they developed their intellectual theories—sometimes in outright conflict with observed facts. What they were really establishing was the *autonomy of thought*, its emancipation from the shackles of the outside world. Attention now focuses not so much on the object of knowledge as on the actual process of knowing it. In the words of Heraclitus of Ephesus, "Wisdom is one thing. It is to know the *thought* by which all things are steered through all things."[9]

It was Heraclitus who called this wisdom Lógos, reason, and it was he who, using the opposites into which Anaximander had sharply divided the components of the phenomenal world—warm and cold, wet and dry, etc.—laid the groundwork for his dynamic philosophy of perpetual motion according to which tension between opposites ultimately made them join together and caused each one of them to change into its opposite. Being was only a Becoming. This is why fire became the Heraclitean symbol for a cosmos in perpetual flux, where nothing ever remained static: a new victory for the masculine ethos.

The Pythagoreans went a step further: the intellect could not remain satisfied with mere qualitative appreciation; they thought with Heraclitus that all things were held together by a concealed measure, what Heraclitus termed "hidden attunement";[10] they wanted to "measure" it, to know it *quantitatively*—hence their emphasis on numbers and proportions, mathematics and geometry. Going to the extreme limit of their doctrine, as is customary with intellectuals, the Pythagoreans held that every phenomenon could be explained by its mathematical proportions—a new victory for the principle of analysis.

With Parmenides, we reach the summit of abstraction. Here pure Being is opposed with absolute conviction to Heraclitus's pure Becoming—denying the fundamental reality of change, movement, and distinctiveness, and thus reaching "the unshaken heart of well-rounded truth"—a philosophical "absolute" that has one thing in common with that of its opponents: it does not take experimental data into account.

Speaking for all Greek speculative thought, Parmenides argued force-fully for the complete autonomy of reason and its primacy over all data conveyed by the senses, "wandering eye or sounding ear or tongue."[11] From now on, Greek logic was on its own, completely detached from gods and goddesses, the world of nature and even of the data of sense perception.

Aristotle devised the logical strait-jacket in which most Western thought was to be imprisoned until the Renaissance. Aristotelian logic rests on two foundation stones: the *principium contradictionis,* according to which contradictions in thought are incompatible; and the basic *principium exclusi tertii,* which states flatly that there is either *A* or non-*A;* any third possibility is excluded. Ironically, contemporary Indian thought had already understood that the pairs of opposites, *dvandva,* were intended to be dialectically overcome by synthesis—but then Indian thought was far more accessible to the female principle of synthesis than the rigidly masculine Greek mind:

> The patriarchal point of view is distinguished from the earlier archaic view by its setting apart of all pairs-of-opposites—male and female, life and death, true and false, good and evil—as though they were absolutes in themselves and not merely aspects of the larger entity of life. This we may liken to a solar, as op-posed to lunar, mythic view, since darkness flees from the sun as its opposite, but in the moon dark and light interact in the one sphere.[12]

The absolute predominance of the *dissociating,* analytical masculine principle in Greek thought is obvious—hence its strength and its weak-ness.

Plato summed up the achievements of Greek thought in the follow-ing way:

> . . . had we never seen the stars, and the sun, and the heavens, none of the words which we have spoken about the universe would ever have been uttered. But now the sight of day and night, and the months and the revolutions of the years, have created number, and have given us a conception of time; and the power of enquiring about the nature of the universe; and from this source we have derived philosophy, that which no greater good ever was or ever will be given by the gods to mortal man.[13]

Whatever the status and position of woman as such in pre-Hellenic times, there was no real sense of opposition between the sexes, since the feminine outlook, unifying and fatalistically passive, dominated. Furthermore, the individual as such was merged in the community and lacked the freedom and autonomy he was to acquire when Greek culture started its development. It was in Greece, first and foremost, that a new conception of the value of the individual emerged—autonomous, free willed, and endowed with reasoning power. For the first time, the respective status, positions, duties, and responsibilities of men and women could become an object of study and controversy. In an unindividualized society, the question does not even arise; both are merged as cooperative entities in a more-or-less harmonious whole, itself imbedded in the world of nature. In Greece, this harmonious outlook on the world and human destiny was shattered by man's freely inquiring mind, and this male-oriented revolution placed woman, as such, in the position of an *object,* of a sexual component of mankind that was being left behind in the clutches of rhythmic nature while man soared mentally into the higher heavens of sheer intellectuality. And, deep down, if there is one thing that revolts the feminine temper, it is objectification, especially when she is the butt of this thought process, that is, when woman is isolated from natural context and viewed as an object, stripped of all her natural connections.

In discovering man the individual, the Greeks did not bother with his subjective self but sought the universal laws of human nature—starting from the "idea" of ideal man, not man as member of a group. We can now proceed from the Homeric ideal of *areté*—excellence in all things—with its connotation of skill in war and athletics and heroic valor, as the true mark of the feudal nobility that began to dominate patriarchal Greece when the Dorian invaders settled down to rule their new domains. As it developed, *areté* came to mean many other things —human effort, love of honor and dignity in the proud man, and more than anything else, love of beauty—to "take possession of the beautiful," implying a capacity for utmost sacrifice of the individual to an ideal, source of the heroism displayed so often in early Greek history.

In this context it became natural for the Greek man to assign a special form of *areté* to woman: physical beauty. The cult of feminine beauty was typical of a chivalrous disposition. It was not only erotic desire but also respect for woman's role as legal mistress of the house —Penelope is the ideal of chastity and wisdom, and also of excellent housekeeping. Still, it is the plastic, erotic beauty of Helen that causes the Trojan War—such a powerful, understandable cause that even the Trojan elders have to blame the gods for the disasters that befall them. All in all,

> Women held a higher social position at the close of the period of Homeric chivalry than at any other time in Greek history.

... The courtesy with which Homeric gentlemen treat all ladies is the product of an old civilization and a highly developed social education. ... The Homeric nobility honors woman as the repository of high morality and old tradition. That is her true spiritual dignity; and it has its effect even on man's erotic behavior.[14]

In an aristocratic age, purity of descent is so prized that women, mothers of the following generation, are entitled to full respect, and all the heroines of the Homeric age bear witness to the high standing enjoyed by women at the time—Penelope, deprived of husband and helpless, is treated by her suitors with considerable respect; Odysseus begs the queen, on Nausicaa's advice, not the king; Arété, wife of a Phaeacian king, is treated like a goddess by her devoted subjects and decisively influences her husband in matters of state. In every respect, Bronze Age ideals still influenced men and women, some of whom were undoubtedly blood descendants of the conquered people. Referring to the refined tenderness with which Odysseus treats young Nausicaa, a scholar can only remark that "the essential good-breeding of the whole scene is produced by the educative influence of woman upon a stern and warlike masculine society ... the intimate relationship of the hero to his divine companion and friend, Pallas Athene, is a most beautiful expression of the feminine power of inspiration and guidance through the trials of the world."[15]

This Achaean society is undoubtedly patriarchal, and yet woman has a power and influence of remarkable scope; her freedom is not yet confined to the gynaeceum nor is she simply a housewife; she moves in society with considerable liberty. All this was to change with the coming of democracy, when Greek culture entered the Periclean age.

With the development of Greek culture came a steady regression of woman's status; from Herodotus to Thucydides, she gradually faded into the home, and Plutarch takes pleasure in quoting Thucydides to the effect that "the name of a decent woman, like her person, should be shut up in the house." Greek literature was suddenly full of disparaging remarks about woman and her innumerable faults—witness the writings of Hesiod, Lucian, Aristophanes, and Semonides of Amorgos.[16] Her legal status deteriorated: inheritance through the mother disappeared; she could not make contracts or incur large debts or bring actions at law. Solon even went so far as to legislate that anything done under the influence of woman could not be legally binding. Furthermore, she did not even inherit her husband's property after his death. She retreated to a virtual purdah, locked in her home and advised not to be seen near a window; she spent most of her life in the women's quarters and never appeared when male friends visited her husband.

Such downgrading at the height of Greek cultural achievements is striking, especially in Periclean Athens. But Pericles himself approved; in his famous Funeral Speech, he summed up his views: "If I must also speak a word to those who are in widowhood on the powers and duties of women, I will cast all my advice in one brief sentence. Great will be your glory if you do not lower the nature which is within you—hers most of all whose praise or blame is least bruited on the lips of men."[17]

The strongly masculine character of Greek culture may in part account for this, but it is also a weird reversal of the basic concepts of sexual creativity. In the old days men were suitably ignorant about their creative role in life. Athenian lore claimed that before Cecrops, the legendary founder of Athens, "children did not know their own fathers."[18] The discovery of their role as sexual inseminators gave them a new pride and stimulated the patriarchal revolution. Now the Greeks went a step further. They fancied that *men alone* were endowed with generative power, women being merely empty vessels or, at best, sort of incubators designed to carry *their* child and nurse it in life's early stages. Like the Persians' divine Ohrmazd, more than one Greek sighed and uttered the famous "If only we could have children without having recourse to women!" This recurring theme of extreme misogynists was echoed again, some two thousand years later, by Thomas Browne: "I could be content that we might procreate like trees, without conjunction, or that there were any way to perpetuate the World without this trivial and vulgar way of union."[19] We shall see what Aeschylus did with this theme in his Oresteian trilogy.

Athenian women were hardly educated, in accord with Euripides' view that women were harmed by an overly developed intellect. In the sixth century B.C., women still contributed somewhat to Greek literature; by the fifth century B.C., they were culturally barren. Having turned their respectable women into bores, men then searched elsewhere for entertainment and inspiration—in the extraordinary development of homosexuality and in the company of the only free women in Athens, the *hetairai*, the "companions," the most accomplished courtesans of the times. Demosthenes summed up the Athenian view of woman's uses in the following statement: "We have courtesans for the sake of pleasure, concubines for the daily health of our bodies, and wives to bear us lawful offspring and be the faithful guardians of our homes."

The only attractive—and therefore influential—women were the *hetairai*, women of some social standing, endowed with a veneer of culture, and capable of witty and learned conversation. They were denied civil rights but were entitled to the protection of their special goddess, Aphrodite Pandemos. Many of them left some mark on Greek history and literature—Aspasia, one of the precursors, who seduced Pericles and opened a school of rhetoric and philosophy; the famous Clepsydra, who timed her lovers' visits with an hourglass; Thargelia, the great spy for the account of the Persians; Danae, who influenced Epicurus in his philosophic views; Archeanassa and Theoris, who amused respectively Plato and Sophocles; and countless others. Some, whose plastic beauty was breathtaking, inspired artists and served as models—Phryne, who appeared stark naked at the Eleusinian festival and posed for Praxiteles' "Aphrodite"; and also Lais of Corinth, one of the great beauties of all time, whose eccentric adventures stunned her contemporaries. In fact, nothing symbolizes more aptly the Greek view of the female sex's social role and value as Praxiteles' two antipodal statues, "The Weeping Wife" and "The Laughing Hetairai."[20]

Greek men held a contemptuous view of the opposite sex; even the best-endowed *hetairai* had a difficult time competing with their clients' male lovers. Even in Sparta, where women enjoyed more prestige and influence than in the rest of Greece, Alcman could pay no greater compliment to his women companions than to call them his "female boy-friends!"[21] The poet-politician Critias stated that girls were charming only to the extent that they were slightly boyish—and vice versa.[22] Homosexuality was both a cause and a consequence of this steady downgrading of the female of the species; and rave against it as they might, the *hetairai* proved unable to curb it. At any rate, the Greek example makes it plain that the prevalence of male homosexuality in any given society is tightly linked with increasing misogyny and the social repression of woman; a kind of *horror feminae* pervades the social atmosphere, springing from the fact that the typical feminine attributes—maternal procreativity and sexual-libidinal endowments—are no longer appreciated. Havelock Ellis quite rightly pointed out the close connection between infanticide (birth control) and homosexuality, a connection that is stamped by an incipient death-wish on the part of any society where they prevail.[23] When the point is reached that woman is rejected, even as a sex object, this society is, psychologically, committing suicide—as the Greek example made plain a few generations after Pericles.

If we dig further, it becomes clear that one main reason for this degradation of the female sex is that, whereas we put the emphasis of love on its object and think of it in terms of the worthiness of the object, the ancient Greeks put it on the urge itself, honoring the feeling even if it happened to focus on an unworthy recipient. This made it easier for the Greeks to restrict their eroticism largely to homosexual relations. Its prevalence was such that it became part of public education in Sparta and Crete; it became the essential element in Greek military formations where pairs of lovers and male beloved ones formed the basic tactical unit, fighting side by side—the Sacred Band at Thebes, presumed to be the finest fighting force in the Hellenic world, was made up entirely of homosexuals.

Most Greeks had only pity for those few men who could fall in love with women with the same passion as with members of their own sex. Even the famous Platonic love is, in fact, sublimated love of an exclusively homosexual nature. In the *Symposium*, Pausanias states:

> There are two goddesses of love, and therefore, also two forms of Eros. The Eros of the earthly Aphrodite is earthly, universal, common and casual. And everything common worships her. Both sexes, man and woman, had part in the creation and birth of the earthly Aphrodite. The higher love comes from the heavenly Aphrodite and she is the creation of man. Therefore all youths and men who are seized with this love strive after their own sex, full of longing for the manly; they love the stronger nature and the higher mind.[24]

Such an outlook was devastating to feminine status, dignity, and influence.

No account of the position of woman in classical Greece would be complete without a more than passing mention of Sparta's extraordinary sociopolitical experiment, perhaps the most far-reaching in recorded history. The astonishing constitution that Lycurgus devised for Sparta endured longer than the others because it synthesized within itself the three classical forms of government—aristocracy, democracy, and monarchy—in a smooth political structure devised to promote the most dedicated and fearful army in Greece. Both males and females were practically slaves of the state; if and when sexual discrimination entered the picture, it was designed not to favor one or the other sex but to serve the state better. Both sexes were trained from birth under the most severe discipline—that is, if they were not thrown off at birth from Mount Taygetus because of a defective physique. Pitiless eugenics were the foundation stone of Spartan physiological excellence. But then, according to Plutarch, Lycurgus stated unambiguously that children did not belong to their fathers but to the all-powerful community.

Both men and women were enjoined to consider carefully the moral and physical health of their future spouse (King Archidamus was fined for marrying too small a wife). There could be no such a thing as adultery or marital jealousy; husbands were sternly warned to let their wives make love to any man of exceptional talent or courage so as to upbreed the race, following Lycurgus' comment that it was absurd to breed selectively dogs and horses without applying the same care to the far more important humans. Spartan girls, always naked in dances and public processions, were advised to become athletic in order to be strong and healthy, making for easy pregnancy and excellent mother-hood; sexual discrimination, however, came in to the extent that Spar-tan girls were spared all forms of mental education. Love, homosexual and heterosexual, was completely free, but kept within the bounds set by the most rigorously disciplined upbringing. At all times, love was subordinated to war, and marriage was considered too important not to be carefully controlled by the state. As for celibacy, it was a crime punishable by withdrawal of civil rights. Once procreation was taken care of, male homosexuality was also held in honor. A Spartan youth usually had a slightly older male lover, his "inspirator" to whom he became a beloved "listener"; in combat they always fought side by side, and this type of homosexual love proved to be perhaps the major ingredient in the military prowess of the Spartans.[25]

Spartan women certainly had a higher status than any other Greek women, which was not difficult. While men fought distant wars or lived frugally at home and ate at their communal dining clubs, women enjoyed relative freedom, could inherit property, and eventually came to own half the wealth of the country. In his chapter on Lycurgus, Plutarch comments that Lacedaemonian women were masculine and strong, often overbearing to their husbands, and he reports that, to a foreigner who accused Spartan women of being the only ones who lorded it over their men, one of the latter replied that, as a result, they were the only ones who gave birth to real men. Even after marriage, the young men lived in their barracks and visited their wives only once in a while, always discreetly at night, as if they were having an illicit affair. This continued for such a long time that their children were often born before they finally set eyes on their wives in daylight for the first time.

Spartan sexual customs were such, claims Plutarch, that they re-mained healthy all their lives, and their marriages were happier and more successful than anywhere else in Greece. But Spartan parents were never allowed to forget that, as emphasized by Lycurgus, children did not belong to their parents but to the state, and that genetically deficient children must be destroyed at birth. All in all, while Spartan life certainly favored women as compared with other parts of the Hellenic world, they paid a high price for the privilege. This totalitarian state did not welcome foreigners and they were usually expelled if they overstayed. Conversely, Spartans were not allowed abroad without permission of the government—precautions which indicate that the slightest whiff of fresh air from other lands of freedom, culture, and prosperity might have been lethal to their discipline.

Lycurgus' revolutionary social structure destroyed all potential for cultural life (after 550 B.C. there were no more poets or sculptors in Sparta) and bred the coldest, most brutal, and inhuman men in antiquity. In this aristocratic socialism, it was specified that Spartan men were debarred by law from trade or manufacture—left to the despised "bourgeois" *perioeci* who had no political rights—and were forbidden to own gold or silver, with the result that the accumulation of movable wealth became impossible. While Spartan women were viewed by the state as procreating creatures, men were trained to be fighting machines. From Sparta's grim reality to Plato's merry utopia was but a step—easily taken, since he never had to live there.

Elsewhere in Greece, freedom was the general rule; even tyrants did not set up totalitarian states. And with freedom came stupendous cultural growth. The emancipation of reason was a steady but gradual process, embedded in the organic development of an entirely new world-outlook. A continuous thread runs straight from the Homeric epics to Ionian natural philosophy; the difference between Homer's concept that the ocean is the original source of cosmic creation and Thales' idea that water is the fundamental principle of the universe is slight—a matter of emphasis, a greater degree of abstraction in Thales. True scientific thought emerges out of its mythological cocoon in a progressive, organic way, and as late as Plato and Aristotle, plenty of mythical thought subsists along with the development of rigorous logic. But this spectacular emancipation of reason from the trammels of mythology represents the Greek miracle, and what is left of myth in Plato or Aristotle is really more poetic license than proper myth.

Every miracle has to be paid for, and pursuing to the limits of its potential the development of logic and rationalism led Greek cultural evolution to a dead end. Mankind simply cannot live without myths, and this applies in our contemporary world as well, no more than he can sleep without dreaming. Myths are an inevitable concession to the anima, repressed as never before in Greece, and now again in our Western civilization. Adapting a statement from Kant, Werner Jaeger claims in his monumental *Paideia* that "mythical thought without the formative logos is blind, and logical theorizing without living mythical thought is empty."[26] This emptiness began to reveal itself in post-Socratic Greece with startling suddenness. Homeric Greeks, that is,

Dorian invaders and Achaean warriors, had set up a male-dominated pantheon of gods; but a successful, lasting mythology (such as that of Hinduism) can rest only on a harmonious combination of rational male and intuitive female elements. The essentially masculine character of Hellenic culture, with its one-sided dedication to abstract logic and reason, precluded the lasting existence of any mythology; masculine skepticism eventually destroyed the Olympian pantheon. When the sun god Helios was understood to be only a ball of fire in the firmament, Olympus collapsed. However, as Carl Jung pointed out,

> It is a futile undertaking to disinfect Olympus with rational enlightenment. The gods are not there; they are ensconced in the shadows of the unconscious, where we cannot uproot them. Whenever a projection of these archetypes is destroyed by rational criticism, the disembodied image returns to its origin, the archetype. There it awaits a new opportunity to project itself.[27]

And in the meantime, it makes its existence felt in a throughly destructive way. Desiccated by an excess of masculine ratiocination, the Greeks lost all faith and began to live for the mere enjoyment of the present.

But, fortunately, a way out of the predicament became available. Greek philosophy had grown out of its initial religious conception of the cosmos by increasingly rationalizing the mythical. Having studied, calculated, and measured the external world, philosophy began to turn around and study the inner nature of man as an *objective* internal cosmos of its own. From the philosophy of an objectified nature to that of an objectified soul was, again, but a step, easily taken. With Socrates and Plato, Greek philosophy at last reached the human soul; from then on, the notion of the soul regained enough vigor to expand outward until ancient classical philosophy exhausted itself in Neoplatonism. The tendency to reduce all being to an exclusively rational system having led to a dead end, the Platonic and Neoplatonic soul was able to reinvade the external world and reconquer a rationalized cosmos. And on that basis new mythologies were built, to culminate in Christianity. The cultural cycle had come full circle.

In order to understand the resurrection of the myth as fulcrum of human consciousness, one must understand the terrible barrenness of sixth-century Greece when its ancestral religious faith evaporated, along with its traditional aristocratic sociopolitical structure, "disturbed by the rise of strange and hitherto unimagined spiritual forces."[28] Pre-Homeric psychological elements, embedded deep in the collective unconscious, were slowly coming to the fore; the anima was attempting to project itself in the outer world again. But unlike India, where the pre-Aryan Dravidian cultural and religious forces were eventually left free to burst out and amalgamate themselves with the Aryan Vedic mythology, the Greek solution was to sublimate them into an original form of collective catharsis—tragedy. So it was that, in an age moving away from myth toward purely discursive thinking, a new form of heroic spirit manifested itself on the stage, giving new life to old, dying mythical tales—but tales fully understood for what they were, legends, symbols of inner human realities.

In Attic tragedy, art, religion, and philosophy were harmoniously amalgamated in symbolic form. Coinciding with the rise and supremacy of Athens and the democratic Athenian empire, tragedy, from Aeschylus through Sophocles to Euripides, unquestionably "furthered the intellectual and moral degeneration which Thucydides correctly asserted to have been the ruin of Athens, just as it had given the state strength and cohesion during its rise and glorified it at the zenith of its power."[29] It must be kept in mind that the ancient Greeks never thought of tragedy in terms of an exclusively aesthetic production but as an integrated, quasi-religious experience of such incisive power that its impact was overwhelming on the cultural, social, and political life of the entire polis—which is the reason for Plato's devastating attack on the freedom of poetry in his *Republic*.

Originating in the state-sponsored dramatic performances at the festival of Dionysius, the tragic play, involving the entire citizenry, appears to have been the yearly climax of the polis's life. The overwhelming strength of the Dionysiac emotion stirred by the somber magnificence of the tragic show revived the old pre-Homeric and Homeric mood, giving original expression to a strange amalgam of Bronze and Iron Age themes.

In this new mode, tragedy answered a question raised by the new predominance of the patriarchal spirit: why does man suffer? The tragic element in tragedy attempted to give an answer to a profoundly metaphysical question. Aeschylus' technique was to use the time-hallowed myths, still fresh in the minds of most Greeks, but to fill them with new content and a structure that gave them universal and timeless meaning—that is, really retrieving the unconscious meaning that had been there all along, but now spelling it out. The one fundamental theme was the implacable inevitability of destiny, with its sudden twists and turns and eventual disaster. In Aeschylus' tragedies, man is not the center of the problem because he is only the bearer of destiny—destiny itself is the fundamental problem, or rather the interplay between destiny and the higher divinity, between dreaded *Até*, the demonic madness of doom, and faith in the everlasting justice of the world's divine rule. The solution to the problem lies in the interplay between the two contrary forces: suffering is pain, but also the one and only road to *knowledge*.

Aeschylus goes all the way back to Homeric mythology and in the *Eumenides* pits the old female-oriented mythical entities against the new patriarchal Olympus. The collision between the two divine realms is shattering. The violent protests of the old feminine powers, the Erinyes, powers of the earth against the gods of the new celestial pantheon, is triggered by an issue of considerable significance: In order to avenge the murder of his father, Agamemnon, by his mother, Clytemnestra, Orestes sheds her blood on orders from the god Apollo. At the trial, presided over by the goddess Athene, Apollo defends the accused against the enraged prosecutors, the Furies (Erinyes)—primal female powers of the earth who guard the cyclical rhythm of nature and prosecute implacably anyone who transgresses them. They clash head-long with Apollo whose shielding of Orestes drives them insane. When Apollo reproaches them for making matricide a far greater offense than patricide and, referring to Clytemnestra's deed, asks, "And when wife kills husband, what of her?" the Furies reply, "They are not kin; therefore such blood is not self-spilt." To which Apollo replies by entering into a significant justification of the new form of marriage introduced by the patriarchal revolution:

> Then you dishonor and annul the marriage-bond
> Of Zeus and Hera, that confirms all marriage-bonds . . .
> Marriage, that joins two persons in Fate's ordinance,
> Guarded by justice, stands more sacred than an oath.[30]

The Furies could hardly care less. They collectively reply:

> You are called great beside the throne of Zeus.
> But I
> Will trace him by his mother's blood, hound him to earth
> And sue for justice on him.[31]

As presented by Aeschylus, the Furies are, of course, bloodthirsty ghouls, elemental powers of nature who show no trace of ethical judgment, blindly chained to the natural cycle of fertility, who, with gory consistency, will suck the last drop of blood from all who flout its laws, regardless of whether their personal intentions were good or bad. In other words, they represent the eternal feminine as seen from the viewpoint of the classical Greeks. Addressing Athene, they describe themselves as "the children of primeval Night, who bear the name of Curses in our home deep under the earth."[32]

Aeschylus depicts with obvious sympathy the sunny spiritual freedom of the new male-oriented Olympus, locked in mortal combat with the dark underground powers of the subdued Earth Mother Gaea. Nature knows only deeds and facts, not human intentions or volitions; it mocks the autonomy of mind and spirit. In the present instance, additional significance lies in the fact that it is his *mother* that Orestes has slain, and all the forces of nature, represented by the Furies, come to bear on him for committing the most unpardonable crime—matricide—just as Olympus is determined to prove the inherent supremacy of fatherhood. Apollo presents its view forcefully and insisting, "mark the truth of what I say," continues:

The mother is not the true parent of the child
Which is called hers. She is a nurse who tends the growth
Of young seed planted by its true parent, the male.
So, if Fate spares the child, she keeps it, as one might
Keep for some friend a growing plant. And of this truth
That father without mother may beget, we have
Present, as proof, the daughter of Olympian Zeus:
One never nursed in the dark cradle of the womb.[33]

This, of course, is a direct reference to Athene who sprang out of Zeus's brow fully clad in armor and never had a mother.

Unappeased and by no means intimidated by this argument, the Furies complain bitterly that Apollo discriminates against the mother in favor of the father, while Apollo attempts to justify the new patriarchal view of moral responsibility: one honorable crime was committed to avenge another foul one; the purpose is what counts, not the factual nature of the deed. The issue is finally settled when the goddess Athene joins the masculine ranks and adopts the male outlook, justifying herself in the following terms:

No mother gave me birth. Therefore the father's claim
And male supremacy in all things . . . wins my whole heart's
loyalty.
Therefore a woman's death, who killed her husband, is,
I judge, outweighed in grievousness by his.[34]

Having spoken, Athene, "who was never nursed in the dark cradle of the womb," breaks the tie vote in favor of Orestes and saves him. Symbolically, this implies that from now on, the law and moral authority of the masculine order replace the implacable retribution of the old matriarchal order, the female earthbound, amoral determination of mere fact that cares nothing for ethical intentions. At the trial's end, Athene herself effects a reconciliation between the old and the new order. Unlike the Hebrews, the Greeks subdued but did not crush the feminine spirit; it remained alive (Demeter of Eleusis was an eloquent witness) and was able, when Greek culture came to a dead end, to reassert itself over and above the dying male gods of Olympus.

While not his greatest tragedy, *Prometheus Bound* is the most significant creation of Aeschylus, essentially the inherent tragedy of creative genius. Here it is not so much blind, destructive, external fate as it is Prometheus's own nature and character that doom him: "By free will, yes, by free will I sinned, I will not deny it: by helping mankind I made my agony," he exclaims, symbolizing the inevitable suffering of all spiritual pioneers.[35] The greatness of Aeschylus stands out strikingly if we compare his interpretation of Prometheus's personality with Hesiod's—essentially an evil one who was justly punished by Zeus for stealing fire from heaven. In Aeschylus' presentation, on the other hand, he becomes the "Bringer of Light" to suffering mankind, and the stolen fire becomes the symbol of civilization. Where Hesiod lamented the five declining ages of a degenerating world and its approaching doom, Aeschylus has faith in "progress"; and Prometheus, inspired by love for mankind, appears as the typical creative male genius without whom progress would be impossible.

While suffering is the main theme of *Prometheus Bound,* the symbolism of the tragedy goes further. Prometheus is a Titan, one of the awful brood of the Earth Mother Gaea who was defeated by Zeus and precipitated into the bottomless pit of Tartarus. But Prometheus had separated from his kin, realizing the futility of their belief in brute force. While the chorus repeats again and again with hypnotic insistence that "the sovereign independence of creative genius knows no bounds,"[36] Prometheus makes his break with the Titans because he has come to understand that creative intellect alone rules the world. But he nevertheless remains a Titan in his excessive love for mankind and in the careless impetuosity with which he flouts the supreme authority of Zeus; his Dionysiac lack of moderation contravenes the harmonious balance required by the Apollonian ideal. When he is finally caught and riveted to his rock by Hermes, messenger of the gods, and mocked as a sophist, a master of discovery, the sight of his ghastly tortures inspires the chorus to chant:

> I shudder to see thee torn by a myriad torments: for without fear of Zeus, in selfwill, thou dost honor mankind overmuch. . . . Hast

thou not seen the feeble dreamlike impotence in which the blind
race of man is fettered? The plans of mortals will never overstep
the accord set up by Zeus.[37]

And in a final acknowledgment of the cathartic effect of the horrendous
sight, the chorus exclaims: "Thus I have learnt from gazing on thy
ruinous fate, Prometheus."

In a very real sense, Aeschylus' tragedy symbolizes the predicament
of the bold masculine spirit of adventure caught in the net of implacable fate. In a strange reversal of mythological roles, it seems almost as
if the Olympian Zeus was attempting to ward off the full consequences
of his patriarchal victory—the unimpeded development of man's intellect and mastery over the forces of nature—from bearing fruit. In the
eternal agony of Prometheus one can detect a partial vindication of the
more gentle and serene feminine mood of the departed Bronze Age.
This is not Aeschylus' intention, however; his tragic message is that the
highest knowledge can be reached only through suffering. But this
message itself is the kernel of masculine thought when spiritualized—
the fruit of conscious *dissociation* and the agonized search for reintegra-
tion, dynamic and excessive force desperately searching for balance
and harmony.

With Sophocles, we turn from grand metaphysical themes to focus
on man himself, and on his soul. Having shaped their bodies, the
Greeks were now concerned with consciously shaping their inner personality. Reaching the concept of soul-structure and the molding of it
by the right kind of poetry, Protagoras claimed that the soul could be
educated into reaching perfect *eurhythmia* and *euharmostia*, rhythm and
concord—concepts borrowed from the plastic arts, especially sculpture. The Greek mind—the Athenian, that is to say—had become
anthropocentric, searching intellectually for the true nature of man.
And now, "for the first time, tragedy shows women as well as men, as
worthy representatives of humanity. . . . Sophocles' power of drawing
strong noble human beings is seen at its highest in many of his tragic
heroines—Antigone, Electra, Dejanira, Tecmessa, Jocasta. After the
great discovery that man was the real object of tragedy, it was inevitable that woman should also be discovered."[38]

This was inevitable. Sophocles had abandoned Aeschylus' concern
with universal themes and focused on individual human problems,
those concerned with the unbroken course of the fate of a family—the
family over several generations being an entity large enough to explain
the workings of fate and divine justice and retribution. And without

taking woman into account, it would have been difficult even to approach this theme since, from time immemorial, the family had been the one domain where woman truly reigned, even as men appropriated for themselves political and social power.

It is in *Antigone*, in fact, that Sophocles pits the two moral orders against one another: the law of the state (masculine) and the rights of the family (feminine), King Creon's dedication to the state against Antigone's desperate defense of family duty. Now women appear as true human beings in Greek tragedy, as concern with humankind prevails over that of religious outlook and cosmic destiny. And all the while, Athenian women remained secluded in their gynaeceum, while men consorted together, forming a unisexed society. Although it was not until Sophocles that women appeared on the stage, it was not until Praxiteles that homage was paid in marble to woman's physical attributes. Greek culture reached a threshold and crossed it in revolutionary fashion; it could not be long before Greek women decided to revolt against the low esteem in which they were held by men.

Toward the end of the Periclean era they did just that, about the time when Greek cultural creativity began to exhaust itself. It became clear in the fifth century B.C. that Greek women, Athenians particularly, were profoundly unhappy in a polis that had become, like most other Greek city-states, an exclusively masculine club. Restless and confused, their unhappiness was sufficiently obvious to puzzle the men:

> . . . they felt, at first vaguely and obscurely and then with gathering clearness, that in their service was not perfect freedom. It did not satisfy all the cravings and instincts of their nature. . . . They were tired of hearing the old traditional story of woman's weakness and subordination. They chafed at being shut out, as inferior beings, from the better part of city life, not only from its active public work, but from its joys and refinements, its music and poetry and discussions. In the last quarter of the fifth century Athens witnessed the rise of a movement for the emancipation of woman.[39]

Euripides, successor of Aeschylus and Sophocles and last of the great tragedians, picked up his cudgels and began speaking up for the weaker sex. This has to be set in its proper cultural context. The new age was seeing the final triumph of the rationalist spirit in a conscious effort, not so much to probe the deepest mysteries of life and destiny, as to portray *reality* as they saw it. With Thucydides, the search for truth was equivalent to demythologization, the dissolution of all myths—just about the most dangerous process in the cultural evolution of any people, but also the process that spurred the tremendous progress made in their rational and mathematical understanding of nature.

Simultaneously, the progress of egalitarian democracy went hand in hand with increasing demoralization and dissatisfaction with social conditions. Citizens wanted to be free from the constraints that their forebears had serenely accepted. They began questioning all their customs and traditions—including marriage, the relations between the sexes, which were now "scrutinized, and found to be a conflict like every other relation in nature."[40] Even in the rise of Greek feminism, the male spirit of *dissociation* triumphs in a sort of negative way.

In *Medea* Euripides showed one of Greece's purest heroes, Jason, as a cowardly opportunist in order to portray the murderess Medea as a tragic heroine. Feeling that woman's fate in general was deplorable, aggravated by traditional mythology's emphasis on masculine prowess, glory, and aggressiveness, Euripides presented an essentially "bourgeois" tragedy based on strictly domestic problems. The unlimited selfishness of the husband pitted against the equally boundless passion of his wife could only fascinate the new audiences that were attuned to the acute problem of marital relations. Medea's complaints about the sad necessity of surrendering oneself in marriage; her equally vehement complaints about the male devaluation of woman's child-bearing obligations and the dangers it entails, which she raises far above those incurred by warriors fighting in battle—everything she said rang true at the time. Jason was presented to the audience as an insufferable prig.

Greek men, in their relentless intellectual quest, had destroyed the patriarchal Olympian pantheon and traditional religion; they were now left to face the feminine consequences. As long as the patriarchal myths had kept a hold on the imagination of Greek women, they had remained suitably humble; but the destructive work of Greek rationalism and skepticism set them free and annihilated the unconscious psychological base on which women's subservience had rested. In Euripides' *Medea* was a striking cry of mythological revolt:

> Back streams the wave on the ever-running river:
> Life, Life is changed and the laws of it o'ertrod,
> Man shall be the slave, the affrighted, the low-liver!
> Man hath forgotten god.
> And woman, yea, woman shall be terrible in story . . .
> The old bards shall cease and their memory that lingers
> Of frail brides and faithless, shall be shrivelled as with fire.
> For they loved us not, nor knew us, and our lips were dumb,
> Our fingers could not wake the secrets of the lyre.

Else, else, O God the singer, I had sung amid the rages
A long tale of man and his deeds for good and ill.[41]

From his *Hippolytus* and *Heracleidae* to the defiant *Bacchae*, Euripides
gives voice to the rising rebellion of Greek women, and this rebellion
came hard on the heels of the collapse of Olympian faith—witness the
great temple of Apollo at Didyma in the Hellenistic period, still unfin-
ished four centuries later, not because of lack of financial means at
Miletus, but for lack of faith and interest.[42]

The feminist rebellion gathered momentum as Greek society started
sliding down the road to decadence. Men did not always appreciate the
new "emancipated" woman, and some reacted with the typical sarcasm
that permeates Aristophanes' *Lysistrata*. But there was no staying a
movement whose roots were sunk deep in the disintegrating religion
of Homeric ancestry. True enough, this had started long ago when
Xenophanes had attacked the Homeric and Hesiodic mythologies; but
now, loss of faith had percolated down to the level of the average
citizen and had become an accepted fact of life. Hecuba, one of Euripides' heroines, no longer knows to whom she should pray—Zeus, the
First Cause of the philosophers, the "mind of man," or nature's laws.

Into this widening void, feminism emerged and set up its own social
goals. Education was spreading, but losing in depth what it was acquir-
ing in extension; in some states (Teos and Chios), coeducational
schools were set up on the model of Sparta. Public games, from being
open to the participation of all citizens, became professional contests;
and from the topmost athletes they had been in their great days of
cultural creativity, Greeks became lazy spectators. Some hidden death-
wish gnawed at the vitals of Greek society. Emphasis was now put on
the seductive attributes of women rather than their worthiness as
mothers; revolt against maternity was the consequence. Abortion and
exposure of infants became highly popular, approved by the philosophers of the day who stated that it reduced the danger of overpopula-
tion—with the result that the deathrate began to overtake the birthrate. Thirst for comfort and pleasure was no longer curbed by religious
fear; Olympus was slowly disappearing behind the philosophers'
clouds of intellectual smoke. All the ingredients of a classical decline
were there; the most striking evidence was the stark shrinking of the
population. Writing about the middle of the second century B.C.,
Polybius claimed:

> . . . the whole of Greece has been subject to a low birthrate and
> a general decrease of the population . . . men had fallen into such
> a state of luxury, avarice and indolence that they did not wish to

marry, or, if they married, to rear the children born to them
... and by small degrees cities became resourceless and feeble.[43]

As Greece was eventually engulfed in a much larger Hellenistic
world in the wake of Alexander's conquests, exotic influences came to
bear on its citizens, many of which filled the void created by a cultural
sterility and lack of faith in traditional symbols. The decline and fall
of the patriarchal pantheon did not drag the surviving Bronze Age
female deities in its wake—quite the contrary. Outside Greece, especially in those areas of the Orient where Hellenistic empires ruled over
vast non-Greek populations, religious faith remained strong and im-
pervious to philosophical criticism; such incarnations of the Great
Goddess as the Ephesian Artemis with her dozen breasts held their
own until Christianity eventually took over.

With the revival or reappearance of the Great Mother's *avatars* came
an increasingly strong influence of the women at the top of the social
ladder. The Macedonian successors of the Diadochi allowed their princesses to wield considerable power; many kings ruled jointly with their
queens, and royal decrees often bore the queen's name as well as the
king's; queen mothers governed as regents. Even in self-ruled cities,
women were sometimes voted into office: in the first century B.C. the
citizens of the large Anatolian town of Priene elected a woman, Phile,
to the highest municipal office; the example of the Hellenistic princesses was contagious.

In Egypt, especially, the Greek Ptolemaic dynasty adopted many
Egyptian customs and, ruling the land as Hellenistic Pharaohs, allowed
their women, from Ptolemy II's Arsinoe to the great Cleopatra, to play
the game of politics alongside the men. Arsinoe II Philadelphus set the
example; her image always appeared on coinage with her royal husband's, and it was not merely for vanity's sake:

> It would seem as if, with a woman like Arsinoe II, ambition left
> no room for anything else; as if she knew her own powers and
> meant somehow to get free scope for them. She got it after her
> marriage with Ptolemy II, when she became co-ruler in name and
> ruler in fact; and the way she pulled round the lost war against
> Antiochus I and turned it into a sweeping Egyptian triumph
> might rank, if we knew the details, as one of the biggest things
> a woman ever did. Even when the dynasties were wearing out the
> women kept their vigour longer than the men; Cleopatra Thea,
> the only Seleucid queen who coined in her own name, almost
> made kings at her pleasure, and the last Cleopatra of Egypt was
> feared by Romans as they had feared no one since Hannibal.[44]

Not surprisingly, Alexandrian social life displayed a strong feminine component that had never existed in Greece proper. Whatever social strata they belonged to, Alexandrian women were not confined to their houses and moved freely in the streets, mingling with the men as Cretan women had, long ago, in the streets of Knossos.

The social and political emancipation of women, triggered culturally in Greece proper by Euripides, was also powerfully influenced by Macedonia's impact on Greece—in stern militaristic states such as Sparta or Macedonia, or in the oligarchic Hellenistic realms that followed, the social status of woman was invariably higher than it was in freedom-loving "democratic" states such as Athens:

> If Macedonia produced perhaps the most competent group of men the world had yet seen, the women were in all respects the men's counterparts; they played a large part in affairs, received envoys and obtained concessions for them from their husbands, built temples, founded cities, engaged mercenaries, commanded armies, held fortresses, and acted on occasion as regents or even co-rulers.[45]

Not only were women of royal birth or high standing influential; middle-class women were affected by a broad change in legislation. Demetrius of Phalerum had caused laws to be passed in Athens in order to keep women "in their place";[46] these laws were repealed when he fell from power, along with most of the antifeminist legislation of the old days. Eventually, all that was left in Greek legislation of former patriarchal times were magistrates known as *gynaeconomi* (supervisors of women) who, in fact, confined their activities to the supervision of girls' schools. Women were now able to get whatever education they desired and could afford, helped to a great extent by the rising influence of Stoicism which was, in all respects, favorable to women's rights. Women began attending philosophers' lectures, such as Epicurus's disciple Leontion; women became poets, such as Aristodama of Smyrna, who lectured and gave recitals throughout Greece, attended by her brother as business manager; some women were noted scholars, such as Hestiaea; some wrote professionally for feminine readership; finally, some even became magistrates, such as Phile, who, having been elected to the highest municipal office in Priene, built aqueducts and reservoirs.

The first historical example of a purely male-oriented culture had come full circle. Exhausted, Greek rationalism gave up the ghost. Everything had been analyzed to death, been proved right and wrong, true and false. Empty ratiocination replaced the great schemes of former times and a feeling of intellectual hopelessness pervaded the Hellenistic world. If anything, the fade-out of Greek cultural creativity demonstrated that a lopsided emphasis on a purely masculine ethos can lead only to cultural sterility. The full acceptance of symbolic thinking alongside abstract discursive thought is vital if a healthy and harmonious balance between conscious and unconscious thought is to be achieved; a satisfactory integration of the personality depends upon it. Indeed, "with the birth of the symbol, the regression of the libido into the unconscious ceases. Regression is converted into progression, damming-up gives way to flowing."[47] Mythology and the symbol are the means whereby the conscious and unconscious are brought into fruitful understanding, avoiding the great danger presented by the accumulation of libido in the unconscious and, eventually, its destructive impact on conscious thought, its flooding and disintegrating influence which exerts itself whenever the symbol has been devalued or destroyed.

Unfortunately for Greek culture, discursive thought did destroy the symbol. Libido accumulated in the collective unconscious during the last centuries B.C.; all the discarded psychological elements started to break through the thin crust of rationalism spread by Greek culture, laying the unconscious groundwork on which new religious creeds and mythologies began to feed. Classical man could no longer "take it" and hitherto repressed feminine emotionalism began to take over. As the center of Hellenistic thought moved from Athens to Alexandria, rational thinking about nature and man faded into the background; philosophers switched to thinking about ethics, theology, and metaphysics.

With Ptolemy the astronomer, we reach the watershed. Scientific thought is put to flight by an overpowering urge to reconcile a resurgent religiousness with the natural laws of the objectified world. With Ptolemy comes the time when rational thought alone no longer suffices, and scientific understanding must lead to some form of mystical understanding of the divine. As Ptolemy put it, "the correspondence we find between the order of divine celestial things and the order of our mathematical propositions encourages students of mathematical astronomy in their love of that divine beauty. . . ."[48] No wonder that he cast aside Aristarchus's uncomfortable discovery of the heliocentric system and put the earth back at the center of the universe, where it remained until Copernicus came along.

Now the leaders of the day were those who concentrated on moral problems, Epicurus and Zeno the Stoic. It was the Stoics who coined the word "logic" and who assigned to the *lógos spermatikós*, "seminal reason," the creative power that makes and rules the universe—with, however, its dialectical counterpart, feminine and emotional, the *eros kosmogonos*, world-creating love. Stoicism represents a return to religious faith, to a form of qualified monotheism that attempts to elevate a moribund Zeus far above the other gods. More important, in its willing surrender to nature and its wisdom, one can detect the awakening of a slight feminine streak in Stoicism; more especially in its pursuit of *apatheia*, an absence of feeling that makes the Stoic invulnerable to the sorrows of life, an apathetic passivity and resignation. The law of the individual's well-being coincides with natural law—we are far from the Promethean spirit and Aeschylus' pursuit of knowledge through conscious suffering.

The creative phase of Greek culture had come to an end. What now passed for Greek thought in Alexandria and elsewhere was, in reality, Oriental elements expressed in Greek. Wars and revolutions had taken their terrible toll, fanned by innumerable intellectual schemes for social betterment that laid the groundwork for revolution. Everywhere, Greeks were urged to live in social concord, *homonoia*, but they rarely took the advice. *Homonoia* was even worshiped as a goddess in such places as Iasos and Priene, but she proved largely ineffective.[49] Utopias were put forth by Zeno, and then Euhumerus and Iambulus who invented a communistic sun-state. The more utopias invented, the fiercer the class wars—the slave rising of Chios in the third century B.C.; the proletarian revolt at Cassandreia under Apollodorus's leadership; the socialistic revolutions in Sparta, Pergamum, Thessaly, and Boeotia—until the Greek revolutionary ferment merged into a nationalistic resistance against the growing might and influence of Rome.[50] But by then it was too late: all Greek intellectual theories and utopias disappeared, crushed under the pragmatic iron heel of the Roman imperium.

CHAPTER

4

Roman Matrons and World Empire

If in Periclean Athens society seemed an exclusively male organization, it was even more so in early Rome. The typical Roman family was patriarchal to the core; the authority of the husband-father was absolute. He alone had legal rights in the early days of the republic, after the overthrow of the monarchy. Only he was entitled to buy or sell property, while a woman could not appear in court in any capacity, including that of witness, and could not claim any dower right to her husband's estate if widowed. The husband had judicial power over his wife if she committed a crime and could sentence her to death for a variety of misdemeanors, including infidelity. The paterfamilias was sovereign in his home; while in virtue of his *patria potestas* he had full power over his children, marriage invested him with the same power, *manus*, in regard to his wife.

In practice, however, his sovereignty was limited by the traditional authority and prestige of the mistress of the household, the *mea domina*, who was not, as was her Greek counterpart, restricted to any gynaeceum. The legal theory was patriarchal but the practice was far more equalitarian. There is every evidence that the early Roman matrons enjoyed the respect and devotion of all the members of their families —honored as they were both as princely wives, *princeps familiae*, and holy mothers, *matronarum sanctitas*. The Roman matron enjoyed far more prestige and influence than her Athenian sister. In the preface to his *Lives*, Cornelius Nepos pointed out that

> many things that among the Greeks are considered improper and unfitting are permitted by our customs. Is there by chance a Roman who is ashamed to take his wife to a dinner away from home? Does it happen that the mistress of the house in any family does not enter the anterooms frequented by strangers and show herself among them? Not so in Greece: there the woman accepts

invitations only among families to which she is related, and she remains withdrawn in the inner part of the house which is called the gynaeceum, where only the nearest relatives are admitted.[1]

Roman women had no legal powers but enjoyed the dignity and influence that goes with respect on the part of fathers, husbands, and sons. Such respect hardly existed in Pericles' Athens.

The legendary glory of Roman matrons was their unsurpassed devotion to their children and the reciprocated dedication of the children to their mothers' welfare. Gaius Gracchus, who initiated the great social revolution in Rome, always surrendered to his mother's judgement in political affairs and withdrew bills that displeased her; in fact, even the Roman state bowed to her and erected at public expense her statue with the inscription *Cornelia, mother of the Gracchi.*[2] Julius Caesar remained under the overpowering influence of his mother, Aurelia, until she died in 52 B.C. Roman character and Rome's historical destiny were definitely molded by the great Roman matrons from whose loins sprang the men who conquered and ruled the civilized world.

It was only natural then that, as time passed and Rome grew and developed, new marital laws were enacted that tempered the ancestral patriarchal severity and better reflected the real situation. A new type of marriage based on coemption set a limit to the legal subjection of the Roman wife and allowed her to use toward her husband the celebrated sentence *Ubi tu Gaius, ego Gaia*—"Where you are master, I am mistress." Common law marriage, *usus*, was also widespread. It is noteworthy that as early as the Twelve Tables, Rome's first legal code, a wife who spent three nights a year outside her husband's home retained the legal position she had had before marrying. In effect, this *usurpatio trinoctii*, whenever kept up year in and year out, guaranteed her legal emancipation and prevented her from falling under the *manus* of the husband.

So long as the old ancestral virtues flourished—that is, as long as Rome refrained from embarking on a career of empire building—evidence shows that marital life was exceptionally happy and successful; evidence of this affectionate companionship appears engraved on many tombstones, where the abbreviation svQ stands for *sine ulla querela.* This happy state of affairs vanished as Rome became an imperial power, discarded its simple, austere way of life, and began to wallow in luxuries resulting from war loot.

In Greece, the emancipation of women came about when Euripides launched his crusade and men became culturally sterile. In Rome, on the other hand, women began their revolt when the Romans embarked on the conquest of the world and became too wealthy for their own good. At first their rebellion was directed at securing all the items of luxury that contact with the Hellenistic Orient made available. Theirs was also an erotic revolt against the stern, puritanical morality of the early republic. As the empire grew, Roman society underwent an extraordinary mutation with uncanny speed, switching from healthy stoicism and simplicity to a life of unrestrained debauchery. In this heady atmosphere it became impossible to maintain the old standards and taboos. All the old values were thrown overboard. As democratic equality progressed after the reforms of the Gracchi, so did the revolt of all the underprivileged. Rome entered an era of simultaneous revolution at home and imperial conquest abroad, culminating in Julius Caesar's one-man rule and ending with Augustus's world imperium.

The rebellion of Roman women has to be seen in its proper context —as part and parcel of a revolutionary process that has many parallels with a similar process going on today. The basis was laid when Rome began interfering in "world" politics and became the prime Mediterranean power after the Punic Wars. "The meek and henpecked Roman husband was already a stock comedy figure in the great days of the Second Punic War,"[3] and became more so as time went on. Within the lifetime of that old curmudgeon Cato the Elder (234–149 B.C.), the metamorphosis of Roman society gathered increasing momentum. Prostitution grew by leaps and bounds; homosexuality was imported from Greece, and women promptly liberated themselves from all constraints. Not content with sweeping away most of the absolute authority of the paterfamilias, Roman women began leaving their homes to play an increasingly important part in the political life of the state, stirring Cato to complain that "all other men rule over women; but we Romans, who rule all men, are ruled by our women."[4]

As in Greece, the evaporation of religious faith stripped marriage of the grand ritual and moving ceremonies that sanctioned it and made it the most memorable event in one's life; increasingly sophisticated and worldly Romans hardly bothered with ceremony, or even marriage. In 195 B.C. Cato made his famous speech in reply to an impassioned plea of the women who demanded the repeal of the Oppian Law (215 B.C.), a prophetic speech in which he virtually predicted the collapse of republican institutions in Rome:

> If we had, each of us, upheld the rights and authority of the husband in our own households, we should not today have this trouble with our women. As things are now, our liberty of action, which has been annulled by female despotism at home, is crushed

and trampled on here in the Forum. . . . Call to mind all the regulations respecting women by which our ancestors curbed their license and made them obedient to their husbands; and yet with all those restrictions you can scarcely hold them in. If now you permit them to remove these restraints . . . and to put themselves on an equality with their husbands, do you imagine that you will be able to bear them? From the moment that they become your equals they will be your masters.[5]

This was a bold speech, but it elicited no echo. Women demanded and obtained the repeal of the Oppian Law; most other laws discriminating against women went down the drain after this initial breach in the patriarchal fortress. From then on, women were free to administer their own dowries, to divorce their husbands at will, and to practice birth control—abortion, infanticide, any form of contraception became morally acceptable, with a resulting decrease in the birthrate, as in the Greece lamented by Polybius. The purpose of sexual congress shifted from procreation to recreation, and the avoidance of what were now viewed as the only three dangers of sexual relations: conception, infection, and detection.

In the last days of the republic, when divorce had become standard procedure among the upper classes and matrimonial alliances were contracted almost exclusively for financial or political reasons, women had achieved practical equality with men. Many engaged in cultural pursuits, learned Greek, studied poetry and philosophy; some practiced law and medicine; others went into business. The leading feminist, the articulate Clodia, wife of Quintus Caecilius Metellus, shocked even the most liberal men of her generation; lampooned by Catullus, she prompted Cicero to attack "her loves, adulteries and lecheries, her songs and symphonies, her suppers and carousing, at Baiae, on land and sea," while protesting all the while that he was "not the enemy of women, still less of one who was the friend of all men."[6]

The fact that the social "liberation" of Roman women took place in an overall atmosphere of moral decadence warped the very nature of their emancipation. Women were emancipated, but for the wrong reasons, amid a widespread breakdown of religious faith, traditions, and respect for authority.

Fruit of the one-sided masculine Greco-Roman culture, this feminist rebellion was marred by a decisive flaw: by revolting against masculine authority and the overstressing of male values on strictly *masculine terms*, Roman women ultimately destroyed the foundations of their own society and civilization. One of the future Fathers of the Church pointed it out clearly when, describing pagan Rome, he exclaimed that some "women put on men's clothing, cut their hair short . . . blush to be women, and prefer to look like eunuchs. . . ."[7] In any given society, women appear to have secured their rightful share of power and influence only through the full acceptance of their inherent femaleness; in a negative way, the Roman example testifies to this.

Roman women unwittingly wrecked with their own hands their feminine strongholds within a patriarchal society; from the proud, dignified and influential mothers they had been in early republican times, they became despisers of their prime biological function in imperial times and began competing with men on men's terms. In this, they were unsuccessful. They made no significant contribution to whatever Roman culture there was; and by failing to reestablish respect for specifically female values, they made their contribution to the corruption of Roman life under the imperial sway of the Caesars—without ever achieving any direct share in political power which fell increasingly under the sway of the legions and the Praetorian guards. In contrast to the Byzantine Empire, they provided not a single ruler; no empress ever ruled in Rome.

Thanks to women's rebellion, a generation gap appeared in the middle of the first century B.C. and, in the words of Guglielmo Ferrero, "the younger generation was . . . wild, scatterbrained and skeptical, emancipated from all family authority, and impatient for the enjoyment of quick and easy profits."[8] The atmosphere was already pregnant with decay in the days of Augustus, prompting Horace to utter his famous ode: "Our fathers, viler than our grandfathers, begot us who are even viler, and we shall bring forth a progeny more degenerate still."[9]

In times of revolution, as we shall see, women determine the pace of change and the eventual stabilization that comes when revolution has run its course. They determine the amplitude of the swings from one extreme to the other; all the more so because, under normal circumstances, they are essentially the *conservative* force that distrusts rapid or violent change.

In Italy, up to that time, it was the women who had preserved the customs and traditions of former generations, who lived in old-fashioned simplicity and preserved the full flavor of the ancient pronunciation of Latin. It was they, in fact, who resisted with all their might the increasingly cosmopolitan, luxurious, and corrupting way of life that wealth and world empire inflicted upon Roman society.[10] But, by the time of Julius Caesar, the dissolution of family life reached its apex, and most of the disciplinary and judicial functions exercised in the old days by the paterfamilias were being transferred to an increasingly bureaucratic state. And the state itself, corroded by revolution and civil war, was in no position to reestablish any respect for authority in the social life of the Romans. The chief sufferers were the virtuous women themselves, often superseded in their husbands' affections by the bolder exotic courtesans of those cosmopolitan times—the famous *ambubaiae* from Syria, for instance.[11] Symbolic of this was the universal pity felt by all Romans for Calpurnia, Caesar's legitimate wife, when he brought Cleopatra to Rome and displayed her with no lack of ostentation. The entire Roman society was in a state of disintegration —the outcome of four centuries of social evolution which had "changed the strength and rigidity of a despotic organization into the freest form of sexual union ever seen in Western civilization. . . ."[12] Now marriage was concluded merely by common consent, without need for ceremony or formalities.[13]

Imperative reasons of state prompted Augustus, now sole master of the "civilized" world, to try to correct these abuses. By promulgating a series of "Julian Laws," he hoped to put a brake on a social dissolution so far advanced that the biological future of the Roman people itself was at stake, threatened by its exceedingly low birthrate. The most important law, the *lex Iulia de pudicitia et de coercendis adulteriis* ("Julian law of chastity and repression of adultery") promulgated in 18 B.C., brought marriage, for the first time, under the supervision of the state. A number of other laws, applicable to certain classes of citizens, attempted to consolidate both marriage and the waning authority of the husband. The two were seen as intimately connected since many "men excused their celibacy by referring to the growing independence of woman, which made her character more imperious, her desires more extravagant and her selfishness more capricious."[14]

When the next piece of legislation, the *lex de maritandis ordinibus* was presented to the Senate, there were violent debates. In order to encourage larger families, Augustus had to gain the women's goodwill; in effect, the mother of three children acquired freedom from the power of the husband, outraging the patriarchally minded puritans, who felt that far too much power had been given away already. Having thus further weakened the power of the husband of a prolific wife, Augustus was asked to add specific riders to the law in order to reinforce the husband's authority at home. He refused and remarked that "it is your business to order and to advise your wives as you please, even as I do mine."[15]

This vast legislative effort was mostly in vain; there were too many legal loopholes, and Augustus came to the conclusion that legislation could not alter disposition and character. He finally attempted to restore religious faith, reviving Rome's traditional creed while trying to restrain the growing invasion of Oriental religions—also in vain.

The old patriarchal order of the republic was never restored in the Roman Empire. Roman women, by and large, retained most of the freedom they had acquired during the revolutionary period. In the prevailing climate of moral anarchy, this became conducive to loose morality, lack of marital affection, instability in the family, adultery, erotic licentiousness, and debauchery Satyricon-style. Writers have left us cynical remarks reflecting the dismal social picture of the times. "Pure women are only those who have not been asked," stated Ovid, and Seneca judged that a married woman who had only two lovers was a remarkably faithful wife. Juvenal, a true misogynist, venomously asserted that there were hardly any women left in Rome who were worth marrying.[16] The Messalinas and Poppaeas of the time certainly justified his sarcasm. And when he condemns the fact that they were allowed to mix freely with men on the benches of the great circuses where the cruelest gladiatorial contests ever devised by man took place, and describes the shattering impact of these spectacles on women's morals, he was probably dead right.[17] Women fully shared in the extraordinary brutalization of life in the Roman world, one which profoundly shocked and repelled the more refined Greek-speaking easterners.

The Antonine emperors legislated away what was left of patriarchal prerogatives concerning wives and children, merely legalizing what custom had made a fact, while still preserving a semblance of patriarchalism. The overall material status of women had improved to such an extent that most of the wealth of Rome had passed into their hands. One striking fact was the growing influence of women in politics, especially at the provincial level. While the authority of the emperors was becoming daily more absolute, and the average citizen's freedom more and more curtailed, women took a hand in local politics—witness the election placards posted by female politicians that were discovered on the walls of Pompeii.[18]

The triumph of the first full-fledged feminist movement known to history had, as ultimate consequence, led to the crippling of Rome's family structure and largely destroyed family loyalty and solidarity. Roman legislation and social evolution steadily eroded what was left of male privileges and responsibilities and, under Domitius Ulpianus's inspiration, proclaimed that women were entitled to the same rights as men—a theory put to practice from Emperor Alexander Severus onward. Meanwhile, corroded by shrinking vitality and depravity, the total population of Italy began to shrink alarmingly. Various emperors (Aurelius, Aurelian, Valentinian, and even Constantine) had to resort to the massive importation of barbarians to compensate for the declining birthrate. Aurelius filled the ranks of the depleted legions with slaves, gladiators, and common criminals. As early as the days of Emperor Septimus Severus, legal documents mention a *penuria hominum,* a catastrophic shortage of manpower.

Unconscious victims of an unwarranted emphasis put by Greco-Roman culture on exclusively male values, "modern" Roman women looked down on childbearing as unworthy of their talents. Unfortunately for them, other women within and without the empire remained immensely fertile. While barbarians and Orientals increased their total numbers at a fast tempo, Italy and Greece saw their populations dwindle. Even Roman Gaul was contaminated by the disease. It had all started with the feminist movement in the upper classes; with the progress of democratic equality under the Caesarian Empire, it had spread downward and outward, to reach the urban proletariat and the rural peasantry. Infanticide was widespread, and sexual lewdness undoubtedly lowered men and women's fertility; marriage was frequently deferred or avoided altogether. At the tail end of this evolution, the western Roman Empire was rapidly becoming, in population terms, an empty shell. The Romans actually committed ethnic suicide.

The collapse of the western Roman Empire was the inevitable consequence. Fast-breeding Teutonic populations eventually overwhelmed it and plunged Europe into the Dark Ages. But before this came about, signs began to appear in the midst of this moral degeneration pointing to a rebirth of ethics and a reconstruction of family life; a revival of religious faith and a renewed search for the meaning of life. The old Roman faith was as dead as the Greek; in both cases their patriarchal pantheons had collapsed. And yet, a religious awakening began sweeping over the entire Roman Empire.

CHAPTER

5

The Religious Awakening

The Great Mother had survived the first onslaught of a patriarchal culture and had outlived, often in subterranean fashion, the dying male gods of Olympus. She had survived mostly in the non-Greek Orient, and when the great Hellenistic empires promoted vast migrations of people around the Mediterranean, her various embodiments made their appearance in the West. About two hundred years before Christ, one of them reached as far west as Rome, where the Great Mother had never had a foothold.

In 204 B.C., as the result of an oracle's prophecy that Hannibal could not be driven out of Italy without her intervention, the Magna Mater was brought to Rome from the Galatian city of Pessinus. In 191 B.C. she was rewarded for her services by being officially enthroned on the Palatine and her cult was adopted by the Roman state.[1] Up till now, the Magna Mater had lived on almost unperturbed by divine male rivals in Asia Minor. Her cult, which went back to the old Neolithic layers, long before the great patriarchal invasions of Dorians and Phrygians, had persisted right through the Greco-Persian Wars into Hellenistic times. Asia Minor and Syria were strewn with multitudes of temple states endowed with great amounts of fertile land, dating back to a pre-Aryan social system based on matrilinear descent, which was utterly foreign to Greek or Persian ideas. Originally they were probably dedicated to the fertility goddesses of Asia and their companion male gods who were simultaneously their sons and consorts.[2] Foreign influence had rarely been able to break down this divine female power and it remained intact, side by side with Greek patriarchalism. It often happens that on Greek inscriptions in Phrygia, the mother alone is named, or precedes that of the husband. Phrygian, Greek, and Persian patriarchal influences had sometimes been able to raise the status of the god-consort; but the Great Mother retained her paramountcy. And from her strongholds she slowly began to spread out until she reached the western Mediterranean.

The Magna Mater of Pessinus and Mount Ida, the first embodiment of the Great Mother to reach Rome, was also the last to survive. Many centuries after her arrival, she became the butt of violent Christian attacks; no pagan cult was so lambasted by Augustine and other Church Fathers as hers. But for a full six centuries, the Magna Mater was worshiped in Rome with a bloody and noisy ritual which cast a spell on the imagination of crowds.[3] This splendidly barbaric cult owed its weirdness to its Phrygian origins and the Dionysiac element of intoxication and rapture that its devotees had injected into it.

As a result of countless fusions and the great syncretism that Hellenistic empires fostered in the Orient, the Magna Mater was also known as Cybele:

> When the tempest was beating the forests of the Berecyntus or Ida, it was Cybele traveling about in her car drawn by roaring lions mourning her lover's death. A crowd of worshipers followed her through woods and thickets, mingling their shouts with the shrill sound of flutes, with the dull beat of tambourines, with the rattling of castanets and the dissonance of brass cymbals.[4]

The climate of Phrygia being one of great extremes, the unhibited wildness of Cybele's cult was remarkable and in a paroxysm of ecstasy, the worshipers wounded themselves. Some even castrated themselves, becoming *galli*, the famous eunuch-priests of the goddess.

Until the fall of the republic, Roman authorities, slightly embarrassed by the vulgar savagery of the cult, severely restricted it. But with the advent of the Caesars, a new embodiment of the Great Mother appeared in Rome, brought back from Asia Minor by Roman soldiers who had fought against the great Mithridates. This was Mâ, the goddess of the two Comanas, whose even wilder worship held Roman crowds spellbound, but also prevented Mâ from becoming anything more than a subordinate deity of the Magna Mater. With the establishment of the empire all the Anatolian goddesses followed in her footsteps and began pouring into the Roman pantheon; and the Magna Mater herself rose in status to be served, now, by castrated *archigalli* who were full Roman citizens. Her male consort, Attis, was also included in the worship—in a distinctly subordinate position at first, then increasingly on a plane of equality, as the monotheistic idea, under Jewish influence, began to remold all the ancient cults. The Seleucides had settled many Jewish colonies in Phrygia and the latter undoubtedly permeated the local creeds with their single-minded monotheism. Under the empire, Cybele and Attis became jointly *om-nipotentes*, "almighty gods."

The steady rise of the monotheistic concept under joint Christian and Jewish influence could only imply the eventual downfall of the Magna Mater and of the concept of the feminine as highest metaphysical entity—and so it turned out. No longer was it the patriarchal Olympus or the rational intellectualism of Greek philosophy that threatened the Great Mother, but the uncompromising patriarchal monotheism of Yahweh. This male-oriented monotheism made headway everywhere, infiltrated every religion—the mysteries of Sabazius, the Phrygian Jupiter, or Dionysius who became identified with "Yahweh Zebaoth," the Lord of Hosts of the Bible, a supreme, almighty male Lord. A further reinforcement came from Persia in the shape of the divine couple, Mithra-Anâhita, the latter fusing in Asia Minor with the Magna Mater.

On the other hand, astrology and the Semitic impulse generated a solar henotheism (one step removed from pure and exclusive monotheism) in Rome. Attis became identified with the sun—"shepherd of the twinkling stars"—and then quite naturally with Bacchus, Pan, Osiris, Adonis, and Mithra. The Magna Mater was slowly becoming a shadow of her former self, gradually emptied of her substance by a rising tide of patriarchal spirit; but it was still her feminine preeminence that was strongly opposed to the Christian concept—the Mother of the Gods stood on a far higher pedestal than would the human mother of Christ, who was not even part of the Trinity.

Before fading away altogether, the Great Mother made her presence felt in many other guises—the great Egyptian goddess Isis, consort of Serapis, identified with Venus because of her tolerance and acceptance of sacred prostitution (Juvenal cursed her as a mere procuress); the Syrian goddess Atargatis who was known as *dea Syria*, the goddess of slaves—the slave revolt that tore Sicily apart in 134 B.C. was led by one of her devotees; the great Baltis, "Our Lady" from Osroene beyond the Euphrates; Astarte, the goddess from Phoenicia, whose reputation for debauchery was even worse than that of Isis. But everywhere, the male impulse challenged them with increasing success. Isis had to contend with Serapis; the more earthly Atargatis began losing out to her consort when Ba'al became an omnipotent *Ba'al šamîn*, "Lord of the Heavens." The Semitic temper, straining toward transcendence, removed divine being above the most distant stars, at the very summit of the vault covering the entire universe, endowed with absolute, infinite, and eternal creative power.

Apuleius had called the Syrian goddess *omnipotens et omniparens*, mistress and mother of all things. But a goddess, because of her femaleness, cannot be truly transcendent; she is by essence immanent, of this earth, Mother Earth, mistress of nature. It was inevitable that the development of transcendental views along with monotheistic concepts would lead to the supremacy of the masculine principle. Ba'al šamîn and not Atargatis could represent full transcendental power. Lord of the Heavens or Master of Eternity—this latter-day monotheistic Ba'al was the result of a coalescence of all the various Ba'als that had come in from Syria. The male consorts of the other goddesses, Osiris and Attis, kept on dying and being resurrected in the cyclical fashion familiar to fertility cults, but the great Ba'al was as eternal as the stars in the constancy of their sidereal revolutions.

But even the fertility gods themselves began to challenge their female consorts' supremacy. Witness the Egyptian Isis, goddess of the heavens and of the dawn, restorer of Osiris (the sun), shifting from her position of complete predominance over him in Pharaonic days, to her far more humble role in Hellenistic and Roman times. In Egypt, her former "importance in the cult far overshadowed that of Osiris; she even had independent shrines, as, for example, the temple of the XXIst Dynasty at Gizeh, called 'the temple of the Mistress of the Pyramids.' "⁵ Centuries later, in the hands of Plutarch, she is mythologically degraded to the status of an inert Mother Earth defined as "that which has an urge to be informed," a mere *receptaculum*, "the negative or female principle which, apart from Osiris, must remain forever barren." Fighting over her are the two dynamic male principles, Serapis (Osiris), principle of orderly growth, and Typho, who is all at once disease, tempest, earthquake, etc. It is the dialectical interplay of these two male principles that fosters the "genesis and composition of the cosmos." Isis herself becomes merely the *object* fought over by two male deities, as well as the mother of the young Horus, "the sensible image of the intelligible world."⁶ As one scholar put it, "Plutarchian transcendentalism begins by widening the gap between God and the universe, the 'intelligible' and the 'sensible' worlds," a definite process of masculinization of the deity.⁷

Preaching along parallel lines, the Syrian priests and the Jews began to introduce the notion of an almighty *deus aeternus*, in full accord with latter-day Greek philosophers. Not only a god without beginning and end in time, but also a *universal* god in space; Ba'al's new title, *mar'olam*, can mean both "Lord of the Universe" and "Lord of Eternity." By looking up at heaven and the stars, the old Chaldean priests made their own patriarchal contribution to the downgrading of Mother Earth; by inventing astrology, an unemotional, mathematical pseudo-science, they dealt a death blow to the old female-oriented fertility cults. All that was left for Christianity to do was to put God Almighty beyond the universe altogether—as the Jews had done with Yahweh—but, with

a subtle twist, to retain some immanent link between the Creator and
His creation by preserving a female component in its theology.

In the first and second centuries of the Roman Empire, the monotheistic idea began to change. It was no longer merely an intellectual
postulate, but became a *moral* imperative; no longer simply the head
of a vast cosmic system, but also an ethical necessity, the supreme God
within the human heart. As subjectivism increased, human beings were
less interested in interpreting the universe than in understanding
themselves and the riddle of life. From Seneca to Marcus Aurelius, this
new conception of monotheism made steady headway; and to this new
vision of things the Magna Mater could contribute nothing. She retained some hold on the inarticulate masses, but none on the male
thinkers. The latter, however, were becoming far more emotional than
their Stoic predecessors. In Seneca, the cold, formal *anima mundi*
becomes a benevolent Creator, Providence, and eventually Father of
man, capable of pity for man's bereavements and repository of absolute goodness. The vast, cold abstractions of the old Stoicism, Law,
Fate, Reason, Necessity, are left behind. In Epictetus and Marcus
Aurelius, the Stoic sage is no longer a proud, solitary being but a
warmer, more humble one depending on an Almighty Being. In other
words, philosophy was slowly turning into religion.

The old Stoic had no object of worship, since pure reason worships
itself and has no religious appeal. But the religious instinct was awakening. Out of the boundless depth of the *Zeitgeist* swelled new tides,
demanding a personal God not only as a voice of conscience but also
as a comforter. More than anything else, it was the new *moral* tone that
strikes the student of history, an ethical purity that was nowhere to be
seen in the wild mystery cults of the times, last refuge of the Great
Mother.

The gory rites of the *taurobolium* with its baptism of blood, the
processions of the effeminate *galli* whose emasculation was a tribute
to Cybele, mother of all the gods, everything that was connected with
these barbaric cults struck the crowds with awe. These Oriental creeds,
focusing on a woman's love and grief, on the punishment and redemption of the male, had brought to Rome a number of elements hitherto
unknown. Filled with terror and hope, they blended asceticism and
gross carnal satisfaction in their temples of prostitution; the exotic
splendor and magnificence of their ceremonies and processions
moved the hearts and overwhelmed the senses; their strange music
hypnotized listeners. Fermented liquor poured down the throat after
a long abstinence gave the illusion of mystic rapture. In a weird blend

of astrology, medicine, mathematics, and magic, they gave the illusion of profound knowledge. Finally, conscience was pacified by mysterious methods of purification unknown in the old national cults; and after the soul had been cleansed of impurities, a promise of blessed immortality was vouchsafed—all through the magic of ritual, bodily purity, and cleanliness acting with sympathetic magic on the soul. Chastity, abstinence, self-denial of all kinds, and physical suffering were the first means, often followed by public confessions; lengthy pilgrimages, macerations, flagellations, and mutilations purged the soul—to be followed by incredible orgies and complete satisfaction of sensual passions of the most depraved kind.

Conscience was satisfied, or at least numbed; but nowhere to be seen was the rigid moral discipline that Judaism or the young Christian Church imparted to its followers. The lewdness and orgiastic nature of these earlier cults, especially those of the Syrian goddess, aroused an extremely dangerous excitability among worshipers, along with displays of unrestrained emotion. In her last attempt to recover her preeminence, the Great Mother fought tooth and nail in an endeavor to emasculate the male spiritually; degraded for centuries, she now attempted to degrade. Her cults were only a caricature of the great symbolism of ancient Bronze Age cults based on the cyclical fertility celebrations.

The cults of Cybele and Isis had always attracted women worshipers; indeed, women were admitted in their clergy. The fast-spreading popularity of the Isaianic cult in Rome had a great deal to do with Cleopatra's extraordinary ascendancy over Julius Caesar and Roman imagination. A temple was consecrated to Isis in Rome in 42 B.C. and her priestesses and worshipers were legion.[8] The extraordinary fascination which the Isis Myrionama, the Isis of "myriad names," exercised in later times almost outstripped that of Cybele.[9]

Desperately fighting for survival in the face of the steady progress of Christianity, the Magna Mater eventually struck an alliance with her complete opposite: the stern, warlike, severely ethical, and exclusively masculine cult of the Persian god Mithra. As a product of Mazdaean mythology, the legends surrounding Mithra could have been created only by a patriarchally oriented pastoral people; this Aryan layer probably antedates the great Aryan invasions of both Persia and India—a Vedic sun god Mitra is to be found as early as the Rg-Veda. On top of this Aryan-Mazdaean layer was a Babylonian-Semitic one, with many increments from Asia Minor; in a sense, it was the warlike Cilician pirates who put Mithra on the Roman map. While his immense success in the western part of the empire was due to his martial qualities and the kind of masculine stiffening needed to save a dying empire, it was also a natural reaction to the debilitating influence of the cults of the goddesses—hence Mithra's enormous popularity in the Roman army. Many of the recruits who flocked to the standards of Roman legions came from Asia Minor, especially from Commagene where Mithraism had sunk its deepest roots, but also from Cappadocia, Pontus, and Cilicia.

That military men required a masculine faith was obvious. The Magna Mater was fine for civilian worshipers, especially women; but men, exposed to the harsh discipline, trials, and dangers of military life, required a male god. The old patriotic cults had died out and the Roman army had become essentially a multinational force protecting the *limes* of the civilized world; a new universal faith was required to supply the need for spiritual maleness as well as for multinationalism. Mithraism fulfilled these requirements. Unlike the devotees of other gods, the worshipers of Mithra did not indulge in contemplative mysticism or sensual debauchery; they were spurred into action under the guidance of a stern code of ethics. Unlike the devotees of Serapis, who believed that the souls of the just dwelt in the depths of the Earth Mother, the Mithraists claimed that those souls lived in the boundless light above the stars. To this day, Mithraic ruins can be found strewn from the Black Sea to Scotland and the Sahara Desert, silent witness to the extraordinary grasp of this faith on Rome's military.

In order to become respectable, in a strictly legal sense, the first Mithraic elements were closely associated with the Magna Mater, an incongruous and yet natural alliance. Mithraists worshiped in sacred crypts built in the shadow of Cybele's vast temples. The fact that only men could worship Mithra hardly bothered the Phrygian priests of Cybele: they enlisted the wives and daughters of the Mithraists as devotees of the Great Mother. Tolerated at first by assimilation with the god Attis, Mithra suddenly emerged as a male deity of the first rank and in his own right under Emperor Commodus (A.D. 180–192), who became a faithful devotee and attended the secret ceremonies of the cult. Thus, the associations of the *Cultores Solis invicti Mithrae* became a major component of the Oriental implantations in Rome.

From then on, worship of the *Sol invictus* was officially encouraged by the emperors; from Severus through Aurelian to Diocletian, Mithra remained the tutelary deity of the empire; even Julian the Apostate, in his efforts to uproot Christianity, turned to the *Sol invictus* for assistance. Under Diocletian, Mithra became officially the *fautor imperii sui*, the patron of his empire; his identification with the sun was coupled with the epithet *invictus* ("invincible") and, like all solar deities of the

Orient, he became "eternal." We are now far from the demythologizing process of the Greek philosophers, who had downgraded the sun god Helios into a mere physical ball of fire. The process of remythologization was in full swing again, strongly encouraged by the autocratic pretensions of the emperors.

Mithraism was a complete religion, with a complex Persian theology attached to it. At the head of the pantheon, and at the origin of everything, was no female principle but Boundless Time, *Kronos*—an inheritance of the Zervanitic Magi, with the addition of some Babylonian astrology. Incorporating on its way a great many fragments of ancient mythologies, the new faith presented itself to the Romans as an exceedingly complex metaphysical system, according to which the generative principle was no longer the female womb; Mithra had no human or even divine mother, but was born from a stone struck by lightning—the "generative rock," *petra genetrix*. The feminine principle was reduced to nought: Mithra's birth was brought about "by the sole heat of the libido"—*solo aestu libidinis*, and in this myth can be found all the basic elements that went into Mother Earth's mythological image—earth, wood (tree) and water—but the actual female component is almost completely abstracted from it.

Not only was the feminine-motherly element absent in this theology, it was also absent from religious worship altogether—a fatal mistake that Mithra's alliance with Cybele could never overcome. The stern militaristic discipline prevented women from being accepted in the sacred cohorts. In the numerous inscriptions that have been uncovered, not a single mention is made of priestesses or women initiates, not even a benefactress.[10]

The wives and daughters of Mithraist devotees had no other choice but to seek refuge with the Great Mother, an easy task considering that Mithra and Cybele often shared adjoining temples: the most ancient *mithraeum* known adjoined Cybele's *metroon* in Ostia. The two worships were obviously conducted in intimate communion with one another, but alliance is a poor substitute for *integration*. Women were offered a sop, not the true spiritual nourishment they craved. Even with all its elaborate mythology cum theology, Mithraism could not offer the Great Mother what women really required—immanentism, the rehabilitation and spiritualization of the flesh, of matter. All it had to offer was a *mythical* redeemer-god, not one of flesh and bones. While men could be content with a mythical god, a mere *idea* or abstract concept, women could not. That early Christianity borrowed many elements from an already mature Mithraism is quite likely; but this takes away nothing from its true originality, the discovery of the mystery of *incarnation*, human flesh sanctified.

Furthermore, Mithraism was theologically tolerant and willing to accept endless accretions, to undergo endless mutations and accept endless compromises. The Mazdaean Mysteries attempted to conciliate paganism, to establish monotheism while accepting a measure of polytheism. The early Christians were sternly opposed to any compromise of a fundamental nature; they decisively enthroned the patriarchal principle as the highest metaphysical entity, while granting women the miracle of an immanentist Incarnation—without mentioning the fact that, far from excluding women from worship, they welcomed them.

So it was that the slow ascent of the male element as the highest mythological, and then metaphysical, principle, worked at with such ardor by the priests and worshipers of Serapis, Ba'al, Attis, and finally Mithra, paved the way for Christianity and its triumph in opposition to them. The day Mithraism lost the protection of the emperors, it was doomed, and it went down the drain of history along with the Roman legions engulfed by the barbarian invasions. As it expired, a last offshoot, Manicheism, had a brief moment of glory. The sect of Mani spread its creed far and wide; it allowed the simultaneous worship of Christ, Buddha, and Zoroaster—a conciliatory syncretism that suffered the historical fate of all such artificial symbiosis. Furthermore, its dualism, unlike the Zoroastrian, which saw good and evil as two antagonistic *spiritual* powers, opposed roughly the intrinsic goodness of all spirit and the evil of all flesh—an ascetic, anti-immanentist viewpoint that could no more satisfy the feminine soul than the unbending masculinity of Mithra. For instance, Mani contended that sexual intercourse was satanic, rejected the claim that Christ was born of a woman (Docetic theory) and denied the fact of Jesus' crucifixion. The Manichean creed, which attracted even the great Augustine for a while, eventually vanished without a trace.

CHAPTER

6

Christianity

The appearance of Christianity did not so much mark the beginning of a new era as the end of an old one. It was the tail end of a long evolution that had more or less prepared its coming, and the success of the creed was the result of its extremely subtle mixture of an uncompromising stand on essentials and remarkable flexibility on minor issues. It is a moot point whether the early stages of its development should be credited to Paul's presiding genius or to more anonymous successors who used Paul as a generic name to lend authority to their concepts. What is of concern is Christianity as a historical phenomenon—as the creative synthesis that took place in the last centuries of classical civilization.

We have already noted the remarkable survival of the feminine principle in religion. The Great Mother had remained active underground, as the persisting deity of the old Neolithic fertility worship under various incarnations, while the old patriarchal religion, in Greece as in Rome, disintegrated—disintegration so patent and obvious that the grave of Zeus was shown to visitors in Crete during the last years B.C., while the body of Dionysius was buried at Delphi next to the golden statue of Apollo—who himself was said to be buried at Delphi.[1] These flourishing mystery cults were linked by a number of common features, most of which eventually became part and parcel of Christianity. These included rites of initiation entailing purification of the soul and rebirth, belief in a redeemer with which symbiosis was effected by the devotee with the help of sacraments, and belief in a new life beyond the grave thanks to this union with the Savior.

The salvation-god mythology sprang from the old fertility cults, the recurring death and rebirth of the seasons—death of the vegetation in winter, its resurrection in the spring—the cyclical, rhythmic lunar-vegetal outlook whose roots were sunk deep in the remote Neolithic past when the Great Mother ruled unchallenged. The mystery cults developed around the theme of the precariousness of the earth's fertility and the vital requirement to renew it regularly. The fields must be seeded and plowed, and their fertility seasonally reinstated by magic ritual—hence the rite of the dying male deity (Attis, Osiris, Adonis, Dionysius, Tammuz) whose spilled blood drenching the ground fertilized the Earth Mother, the universal genetrix, only to be reborn with the next crop. The most explicit mythological account of this ritual depicts the "virgin" Anath, sister of Ba'al, searching for Mot, finding him and, identifying the body of the male god with the grain,

> She seized Mot, son of El,
>> With the sword she cut him up, with the sieve she winnowed him,
>> In the fire she burned him, in the mill she ground him,
>> In the field she sowed him. . . .[2]

Thus, by a form of sympathetic magic, the vernal regeneration of vegetal life was assured. Mother Earth never died; she was eternal, but her son-consorts died and were reborn every year with the seasonal cycle. In the early stages, this was no mere myth but an actual fact in the sense that the slain redeemer was a king or a substitute who was ritually excecuted as a sacrifice. Later, in more civilized times, reproductions were substituted, but the symbolism remained.

However, there occurred a gradual shift from the vegetal cycle of nature to *human* nature: the cosmic power of new life that permeated nature in the spring could also well up in man if he became united with the slain god of fertility; but this same god of fertility now became a *spiritual* redeemer whose work of salvation no longer concerned crops but human souls. The first such redeemer had actually been Zoroaster, who called himself *saoshyant*, the "coming helper." This spiritualization of a hoary sacrificial tradition of the fertility cults was best expressed, much later, by the theology of Athanasius, who described the death of Christ as the "sum of our faith." Redemption implied that Christ delivered mankind from actual physical extinction:

> So the Word by whom man was made came into the world by the Incarnation in order to re-make man, that God's purpose in creation might not be disappointed. . . . Human nature could not finally perish, seeing that the Word united Himself with it.[3]

Furthermore, God had sentenced Adam and his successors to suffer inevitable death; the threat of death, however, was exorcized by Christ's Passion and annulled by the Resurrection of his incorruptible body. Athanasius always refers to the death of Christ as a sacrifice, an offering:

By offering unto death the body He Himself had taken, as an offering and sacrifice free from any stain, straightaway He put away death from all His peers by the offering of an equivalent. . . . Formerly the world as guilty was under Judgement from the Law, but now the Word [Christ] has taken on Himself the condemnation, and having suffered in the body for all, has bestowed salvation upon all.[4]

The magic "spiritualization" of the venerable sacrificial theme of the old fertility cults is evident. In this new scheme of things dominated by the concept of *soteriology* (Greek *soter*, Deliverer), the female principle lost a great deal of its importance. The slain son-consort became the main element. It was *his* sacrifice that redeemed and gave rise to new life—no longer under the overall supremacy of Mother Earth who was merely concerned with vegetal and animal fertility, but entirely on his own, now that what was at stake was the spiritual harvest of human souls. A complex ceremonial marked the rites of initiation, and after temporary burial in the ground or baptism by blood (the *taurobolium*, for instance), the devotee emerged as a *new person* in full communion with the Savior. Some old cults now developed monumental celebrations; one of the more impressive ritual dramas depicted the murder of Attis on the Day of the Blood in March (now the Christian Good Friday), fastened to a tree where he bled to death, was buried in a sepulcher and, after several days of mourning, arose from the dead and was brought out of the sepulcher (Christian Easter). The similarities with the death and resurrection of Christ are obvious.

The general idea of the redeemer was widespread all over the classical world, even in Judea, where the prophet Ezekiel complained that Jewish women wept for the dead savior Tammuz (8:14). That the Jews themselves, in spite of their sharp exclusivism, were not immune to the influence and infiltrations of the mystery cults is certain. All this prepared the ground for the advent of Christianity. Just as certain, in the mystery cults themselves we witness a gradual psychological shift of worship from the female deity to the male redeemer.

It seems probable that it was Paul who attributed the Redeemership to Christ and transferred the symbolism of the Savior-god to Jesus. In all probability, the Apostles saw in Christ merely the Messiah that all Jews were expecting to arise sometime in the future. They did not conceive of the Messiah as a supernatural Son of God but as a mere man of superhuman stature and power. Unlike the devotees of the mystery cults, the Jews did not feel the need for a redeemer. They obeyed the Almighty's command, and whenever they failed to do so, they sinned, but their sin would be forgiven if their repentance was honest and sincere. This was not enough for the weaker-willed mystery cultists, who were more conscious of the *inadequacy* of human nature, of the weakness of the human will: they had to rely on a higher power; they needed a redeemer. It was Paul, drawing on his double background as a Jew who was also a cosmopolitan Greek-speaking Roman citizen, who fused the two concepts—Jewish Messiah and pagan redeemer—into the one person of Christ and gave him universal validity. Paul may have had Jewish precursors among the Essenes who had come to believe that the Messiah would have to suffer and die before his *parousia*, but he seems to be the one who made the actual synthesis of the two concepts.

On the Jewish side, Paul insisted on preserving to the full the severity of the *ethical will.* He was profoundly shocked by converts who brought over from the mystery cults the amoral lasciviousness that so often characterized them, in the mistaken belief that sacramental symbiosis with Christ was sufficient and set them above the Mosaic Law. The fundamental opposition between moral purity and initiatory sacramentalism had always been the root of the mystery cults' great weakness; it did not take a Christian to point it out and, as Diogenes sneeringly remarked, "Pataicion the thief will have a better fate when he comes to die than will Epaminondas, because he has been initiated."[5] The mystery cults did not necessarily foster immorality; they were merely amoral. Christianity, as Paul saw it, was different: here were *both* sacramentalism *and* ethical purity; baptism did not allow the baptized to dispense with morality and steadfastness of character. Jesus the Messiah had superseded the letter of the Law, but not the spirit. Even if theologically permissible, some things remained morally repulsive.

Paul labored hard to merge the two apparently contradictory concepts—the mystery religions' belief that sacramental salvation implied no moral obligation, and the fundamental Jewish belief in the primacy of unadorned ethics. To both, he added a certain dose of asceticism which could not usually be found among the Jews, with the exception of the Essenes—especially in regard to women and sex; the Essenes were all women haters who, according to Josephus, "guard against the lascivious behavior of women, and are persuaded that none of them preserve their fidelity to one man."[6] Very much like them, Paul advised against marriage and against physical contact with women—and yet admitted that it was "better to marry than to burn" in which case both spouses were advised to comply with each other's sexual requirements without discrimination in favor of either sex:[7] "Men ought to love their wives as their own bodies: he that loveth his wife loveth himself."[8]

It was better, however, to have a companion "sister in the Church" and keep her in the position of a "sister-wife" without any sexual relationship. Paul's overall view of women was dim; he saw in them mostly souls to be saved. His emphasis on brotherly love and high ethical standards put a strong masculine imprint on his teaching and on the subsequent development of Christianity.

This masculine imprint was due not merely to its Jewish component; the Greek legacy came in to reinforce it. Thanks to the Diaspora, many more Jews lived outside Palestine than within it. Most of them spoke and thought in Greek, including Paul, so that while the Apostles expressed themselves in Aramaic, and thought in Aramaic, Paul thought out and set down the new law in Greek. Thinking in Greek, the most intellectually advanced language of the time, made it impossible to avoid using Greek concepts. While Hebrew was essentially a language of volition and Aramaic one of emotion, Greek was a highly mental language whose acute precision and power of abstraction made it an ideal vehicle for conveying discursive thought. Although Paul consciously adopted many Hellenic concepts, he absorbed many others unconsciously, by virtue of the fact that he thought in Greek. Had his thinking been done in Hebrew or Aramaic, he could not have elaborated the same doctrine—the Almighty's usual name '*Elohim* translated into Greek *theos* metamorphoses the severe Semitic meaning into a more fluid, Olympian concept. Even after Paul, early Christian theology was thought out in Greek and used a Greek conceptual framework.

All this made it easier to incorporate into the buildup of Christianity various concepts borrowed from Gnosticism, Hermetism, and Stoicism. The contribution of Gnosticism is more theological than ethical, and many basic concepts of early Christianity are directly borrowed from the Gnostics. *Gnosis* is Greek for "knowledge," not scientific knowledge derived from rational thought, but "revealed," and largely esoteric, knowledge. Its complex mytho-theology, set fast generations before Christ appeared, visualized a scheme of salvation that was eventually attributed to Christ—Redeemership of the Son of God. The concepts and terminology of Gnosticism were used to give a coherent explanation of Christ's lifework, message, and suffering. It was largely Paul who adapted Gnostic thought to Jesus' meaning, the central core of which is the idea that evil persists in the world thanks to the fact that evil is returned for evil, according to an implacable *lex talionis*. Christ's martyrdom and crucifixion destroys this vicious circle by returning *good* for evil, putting an end to this otherwise endless chain reaction.

With Christian "love," mercy prevails over strict justice, spiritual grace proves stronger than the mechanical application of strict ethical standards. In turn, this form of *agapē* would have been unthinkable without the sharp distinction drawn by Jewish thought between Creator and His creation; this sharp distinction generates tension between the two, Creator and creature—awe and fear in Old Testament terms, love and aspiration in terms of the New Testament—the same tension-generating distinctions that differentiate the two sexes.[9] In monistic or pantheistic ontology, love would make no sense since there is no basic distinction between Creator and creation: "The essence of the divine is Love," states Unamuno, "Will that personalizes and eternalizes, that feels the hunger for eternity and infinity."[10]

Had the demonic powers of darkness known what they were doing when, through their human agents, they carried out the Crucifixion, they would not have done it—since they were presumably sealing their own doom. Returning good for evil was no Christian invention, but an idea that had been slowly worming its way into consciousness centuries before Christ—in the seventh century B.C. there was an Assyrian saying to the effect that "as for him who doeth evil to thee, requite him with good."[11] Love of God was the equivalent of love of man, of all men, of mankind—a newly discovered concept of broad universality that contrasted sharply with the more narrow, provincial outlook prevailing at a time when, along with widespread slavery on a staggering scale, men of a different nationality were thought of as barely human. These concepts were foreign to strict Jewish thought; only a man thinking in Greek could have formulated this doctrine.[12]

It was mostly in Alexandria that the great synthesis was worked out between the Greek and the Jewish contributions. As early as the first century of our era, the Alexandrian Jews had begun to look upon their Scriptures as symbolism. In order to fit his philosophic doctrine into the procrustean bed of the Bible, Philo had to give up any kind of literal acceptance of the Old Testament and interpret Genesis much as the Greek Stoics explained Homeric legends, that is, as profound allegories in which the historical element is of little consequence. The Fathers of the Christian Church followed in his footsteps. Origen displays a special distrust for literal interpretation because of all the contradictions involved in the biblical account: "Who can be stupid enough to believe that God, like a gardener, tilled the fields of Eden and actually planted a tree named the Tree of Life?"[13] As far as Origen is concerned, Eden is nothing but an allegory of the Church to come; and he claims that, in studying the Scriptures, "We must look for the treasures [of the spirit] hidden behind the letter."[14]

Other Fathers of the Church went along: Hilary, Ambrose, and even Augustine who stated in his Confessions that he heard with great joy Ambrose repeat tirelessly, "the letter destroys and the spirit vivifies and invigorates."[15] But it was Augustine who sternly admonished future generations to retain *also* the literal interpretation and to accept the *historical* validity of the Scriptures: Time and Eternity must be both acknowledged and welded together, failing which the Bible would be understood to be as mythical as the legends of Homer. Valid allegory can only be based on a kernel of historical truth.

Christianity would not have been the successful, creative and all-inclusive synthesis it finally became if it had not found a satisfactory role for the feminine impulse to play. Along with several of the mystery religions, Christianity, first of all, inspired *love*, a new departure in psychological disposition in that this love was ostensibly divorced from sex. This was a reinterpretation of Plato's *eros* or the old Stoic's *eros kosmogonos*, the world-creating love, of which sexual desire is only the lower, earthy aspect that must be sublimated. It is in fact inspiration, the power of poetic and artistic creation through intense emotion rather than mere childbearing, which stands as the counterpart and polar opposite of the *lógos spermatikós*, the fecundating spirit or creative mind. The Savior God loves his worshipers, who in turn are admonished to love one another. This new love was no longer an urbane benevolence such as characterized the best among the Greek philosophies and religions; it was a feeling of overpowering strength, with all the Judaic *will* behind it—but an outgoing, generous will to be concerned with mankind at large. The willful "believer" took precedence over the mere "thinker." In this way, Christianity restored to the feminine element, independent of its treatment of woman as such, a great deal of the emotionalism that had been taken away by classical Greece's masculine culture.

To this new feeling of ardent love was added an original element: unlike Adonis, Attis, Osiris, and countless others, Christ was not a mythical figure, acknowledged as such. He was a real man of flesh and blood; His Crucifixion was not a ritual reenacted year after year, but a "once for all time" historical and unrepeatable event. The grand cyclical theme of the yearly Redeemership was acknowledged, taken over, and incorporated into linear history as a unique event, never to be repeated. In other words, Christianity brought down from the plane of acknowledged mythology the great drama of death and rebirth and introduced it as a *historical event*—Attis was an artificial effigy fastened to a tree; Christ was a real, bleeding human being nailed to an actual wooden cross.

Very much like passing from the dreamlike state to the state of waking being, Christianity set forth a new mystery: the *Incarnation* of the Son of God. There is hardly any doubt that this factor had an immense influence in attracting female devotees. The Gnostics claimed that the actual Incarnation lasted only a few days, and that when Christ was nailed to the cross the divine spirit had already departed from his body—a mere man was therefore crucified, no longer the Son of God, but the overintellectual Gnostics were masculine to the core. A man could worship an abstract Logos; women had to believe that the Word became flesh and manifested itself concretely in this world of sensory perceptions.

Clearly prophesied by the great Judaic prophets, and as clearly imagined mythologically by the mystery cults, the Almighty had finally brought it about in the world of concrete fact, in history. Eternity had been incarnated for a while in the *temporal* world, and Christ was the hinge between the two. Christ was Lord and Savior, both in history and beyond time and space—a temporal event that was ever present in the timeless world beyond. More, He was born of a real woman, also of flesh and blood, and reenacted the endless drama of all the son-consorts of the Magna Mater. Moreover, Mary's virginity and the theme of the virgin birth were restatements of the old theme of the Great Mother Without a Spouse, a symbolic reformulation of the Paleolithic concept of woman being fertilized by a spiritual entity without need of male assistance, *conceptio immaculata.* In Mary, the Mother of God, what was left of the Magna Mater found a lasting reincarnation; in her tragedy the previous mythical *mater dolorosa*, Cybele, Isis, and the others, could witness the reenactment of their own mythical tragedies. But, here again, her tragedy had really taken place in history, in the clear light of day; it was a historical fact, not merely a mythological dreamlike vision.

In the competition that pitted the young Christian Church against rival cults, this element was of cardinal importance. It was not only the higher standard of ethics that allowed Christianity gradually to eliminate them, but a different overall concept of the highest metaphysical principle—a historical event against a self-acknowledged myth, waking-being as against a dreamlike state. This is what made it possible for so many women to transfer their allegiance from the Magna Mater who, as mother of the gods and supreme mythological entity, stood on a far higher pedestal, to Mary, who was merely the Mother of the Son of God—later raised to the higher dignity of Mother of God.[16] As far as women worshipers were concerned, the fact that she was not even a small part of the highest metaphysical entity, the Trinity, was unimportant compared with the fact that she had *existed* as a human being like themselves, and had thus sanctified human motherhood.

Early Christianity refused to make the compromises that all other mystery religions made as a matter of course. Its strongly masculine ethical outlook led to an exclusivism that transcended the nationalistic Judaic one and extended it to the whole human race—but would brook no doctrinal conciliation. The priests of Cybele and Attis would have gladly come to terms with the worshipers of Christ; they had noticed that, with a certain sacred cunning, the Christians had placed their Holy Week at the vernal equinox so as to make it coincide with the *dies sanguinis* during which the *galli* shed their blood and emasculated themselves in honor of Cybele; they claimed that Christian baptism was a watered-down duplicate of their *taurobolium*. They tried in vain to work out some alliance or merger with Christianity, misunderstanding the fact that the Christians were uncompromising and wanted to take *them* over, lock, stock, and barrel—and so they did. At the end of the fourth century, the last *taurobolia* took place in the *Phrygianum* in Rome on the very same spot where the Vatican basilica of Saint Peter stands today.

But while Christianity remained uncompromising in a fundamental sense, it was soon clear that Christ was becoming the psychological heir to all the redeemer-gods of the mystery cults. This inheritance became obvious when the question arose as to his title in the Greek language. "Anointed of the Lord" was unintelligible to the Gentiles; "Son of Man" made sense only to the Jews who were familiar with eschatological literature. He finally became, through the ministrations of Paul, "The Lord" *(Kurios)*, a title that had already been applied to the dying and redeeming Dionysius, although it seems that Christ was already Lord in Aramaic *(Maran)*. Thus he became a Redeemer, not merely a Messiah, who, like all other redeemers, died and was resurrected; the cyclical element of the old fertility cults was preserved and incorporated in the new faith. The Resurrection of Christ caused some subsequent difficulties with skeptics, to whom Clement of Rome retorted that "Day and night are symbols for us of resurrection: the night falls asleep and the day rises; the day passes away and the night succeeds it."[17] This rhythmic conception was typical of the now extinct lunar-vegetal worship of prehistory when the Earth Mother reigned unchallenged by male pretensions.

How little the purely patriarchal creeds understood this new symbolization of the old fertility cults was made plain when the Persian King of Kings, Khusru Parviz, assisted by a body of twenty-six thousand Jews, captured and sacked Jerusalem in A.D. 615. He wrote as follows to the Byzantine Emperor Heraclius:

> Khusru, greatest of gods and master of the whole earth, to Heraclius his vile and insensate slave. You say that you trust in your god. Why, then, has he not delivered Jerusalem out of my hands? . . . Do not deceive yourself with vain hope in that Christ, who

was not even able to save himself from the Jews, who slew him by nailing him to a cross.[18]

Likewise, the forthcoming Muslims, who retained Jesus the Messiah ('Isā'l-Masīḥ) as one of their great prophets preceding Muḥammad, refused to accept the fact that he was crucified and claimed that a substitution was made at the last minute:

> And for their [the Jews'] saying, "We killed the Messiah, Jesus the son of Mary, the messenger of God," though they did not kill him and did not crucify him, but he was counterfeited for them.[19]

These essentially masculine religions saw no symbolic greatness in this reformulation of the antique ritual slaying of the god, indeed found it necessary to deny Christ's crucifixion altogether. This Christian humility, this homage paid to the ghost of the Great Mother and all the cyclical fertility cults of a distant past, repelled rather than attracted the patriarchal Jews, Zoroastrians and Muslims alike.

Christianity retained, with its feminine component, a certain immanentism which the patriarchal religions rejected in favor of uncompromising transcendentalism. In the long run, the Christian God the Father became indeed a Father, much closer to His human flock through Christ's intermediation than the Jewish Almighty who remained at an immeasurable distance. From the fatherly attributes of the Godhead, it was only a step for all Christians to consider themselves brothers and sisters in Christ, who then became metaphorically their "elder brother," whom they wanted to imitate and with whose human nature they attempted to identify. The antisexual character of this terminology, an extension of the incest taboo, is obvious and symbolic of the withdrawal from the world that was characteristic of early Christianity: by making all Christians siblings, true celibacy and sexual continence were raised above all other social ideals.

It now remains to conclude that to say that Christianity was the result of the blending of Greek thought and Jewish messianic faith is an incomplete statement. Christianity went beyond this in that it incorporated all that remained of the female-oriented fertility cults, all the feminine symbolism that had accumulated over the centuries, and still struck a responsive cord in the female soul. It represented a three-way merger, and it is to this successful synthesis that Christianity owed its ultimate triumph.

From the start, Christian teaching made it plain that women should be highly respected as mothers—*mulier tota in utero*—but placed them in a subordinate position.[20] Their dignity was enhanced by the fact that Paul's stern morality condemned the libertinism prevalent in classical society, following Roman women's "liberation." Women were admitted to the congregations and often played important roles; but they were enjoined to lead quiet, submissive lives. They were instructed to avoid all artifices, cosmetics, jewelry, and to come to worship veiled because of the potential seductiveness of their hair. Paul set the new style when he declared:

> Women should keep quiet in church. They must take a subordinate place. If they want to find out anything they should ask their husbands at home, for it is disgraceful for a woman to speak in church. . . . A man ought not to wear anything on his head in church, for he is the image of God and reflects God's glory, while woman is a reflection of man's glory. For man was not made from woman, but woman from man; and man was not created for woman, but woman for man. That is why she ought to wear upon her head something to symbolize her subjection.[21]

Overall, it seems that the strict moral code imposed by Christianity had a definite appeal for women, who are ultimately the main victims of sexual "freedom," and that their "subordination" was quite compatible with an enhanced dignity. Referring to the tight bonds knitting together members of the early Christian communities, Tertullian remarked humorously, as a Christian himself, that "we have all things in common, except our wives; at that point we dissolve our partnership, precisely where the rest of men make it effective."[22] There is little doubt that many women preferred it that way, and that the real burden of sacrifice was on the men, perennially inclined toward promiscuity. Celibacy and virginity were considered the highest ideals. As Freud remarked,

> It is easy to show that the psychic value of the need for love goes down at once, as soon as its satisfaction is made easy. It requires an obstacle to drive the libido up to a high point, and where the natural obstacles to satisfaction are not sufficient, men have at all times interposed conventional ones to be able to enjoy love. . . . In ages in which the satisfaction of sexual desire did not encounter any difficulties, as, for example, during the decline of classical antiquity, sexual love became worthless and life empty, and strong reactive constructions were needed to re-establish the indispensable emotive values. In this context one may claim that the ascetic current in Christianity has created psychic values for sexual love which pagan antiquity had never been able to confer

on it. It attained the highest significance among ascetic monks whose life was almost solely taken up with the struggle against libidinous temptation.[23]

It is the widening gap between desire and fulfillment that is productive, in the sense that it allows for greater sublimation of the libido, for creative tension.

Quite naturally, marriage was allowed by early Christianity mainly as a brake on unlicensed promiscuity, and, waiting vainly for the imminent Parousia, the Second Coming that would put an end to the world, Christians did not lay much stress on family life as a means of perpetuating the human race. Divorce was sternly discouraged, and so was the remarriage of widows or widowers. In a striking departure from the sexual tolerance of the classical world, homosexuality was declared out of bounds: "So far as sex is concerned, the Christian is content with the woman," declared Tertullian.[24]

In actual practice, the early Christians seem to have led the cleanest, happiest lives, based on quiet contentment with their lot, mutual loyalty and marital fidelity, and intense piety in a secure faith—made all the stronger by relentless persecution. The typical Christian conjugal life was as remote from the austere patriarchy of republican Rome as it was from the oversexualized decadence of the empire, based as it was on the sacredness of marital vows and the unimpeachable dignity of the wife and mother. Roman women had finally managed to escape from the stern patriarchalism of early times through sexual emancipation and the virtual destruction of Roman society's ethical framework; Christian women felt no need for this kind of liberation. Shocked by their dignified brand of emancipation and their proud assumption of their conjugal role in life, by the sharing of duties and responsibilities of husband and wife, the male pagans—women despisers, like all sexual libertines—claimed contemptuously that the Christian religion was good only for women.[25] In a sense, they were correct: it was mostly under feminine influence that men converted to Christianity.

High-ranking women and female members of the imperial households were often converts to Christianity who invariably attempted to induce their husbands, fathers, brothers, to join them in the new faith, not always with success. Both Diocletian's wife and daughter were strongly inclined toward the new faith. Diocletian's daughter was married to Galerius, one of the two "Caesars" who assisted him in ruling the empire. And yet Diocletian, probably instigated by Galerius's ardent paganism, launched in the year 303 one of the most violent persecutions that the church had to endure in the early centuries. Emperor Constantine's mother, Flavia Helena, wife of

Constantius Chlorus, had greater powers of persuasion: in 313 he put an end to the persecution and, under her influence, made Christianity the official religion of the empire.

If the mothers, wives, and daughters of the emperors were, as Christians, influential in disposing their male relatives in favor of the church, more than one saint and Father of the Church acknowledged the debt to their mothers and female relatives. Augustine's mother, Monica, was a devout Christian (her husband was converted late in life); without exerting pressure on her son, she let him have his fling at worldly living and then at flirting with Manichaeism before his final and whole-hearted conversion to Christianity. Many others—Ambrose, Jerome, Gregory the Great—testified to the considerable influence exerted by their female relatives and to the fact that they owed a great deal of their Christian vocations to them. Eastern Church Fathers—Athanasius, Basil of Caesarea, Gregory of Nazianzus, John of Damascus, among many others—paid the same homage to their mothers. Women also became actively engaged in charitable works, starting the first hospitals (Fabiola, according to Jerome) and even the first monastic communities; Saint Benedict borrowed many of the institutions of his famous order from the convents previously set up by Saint Marcelle.[26]

It was feminine influence under Christian leadership that changed marital laws, and all the way from Constantine to Emperor Theodosius, these laws which became, in general, more restrictive and binding, gave increasing power and dignity to women as mothers. Constantine put an end to the legal sovereignty of the paterfamilias— already flouted, in practice, for centuries. However severe the new marital laws, they introduced the principle of sexual equality in marriage. What was licit was licit for both sexes; what was forbidden was forbidden to both. Male privileges were discarded.

But when it came to the administrative structure that the church was compelled to set up under the spur of its phenomenal success, authority rested firmly in masculine hands. Priests and bishops were men; only in the eastern part of the empire were there deaconesses in charge of members of their own sex. Christianity, in disciplining men's sexual impulses, gave added protection to women; consolidating the family and imposing strict monogamy gave them additional authority *within* the family and greater influence on their husbands. But women had no direct influence or authority in the social and political life of the church, which remained sternly patriarchal.

By making allies out of women, without giving them any clerical authority, Christianity ensured its temporal triumph. Without including the feminine principle in the Trinity, Christianity gave it its due in \ the world of form and matter. In the long theological controversies that pit orthodox Christians against the two great and durable heresies of the Orient, Monophysitism and Nestorianism, the symbolic bone of contention was always the true nature of Christ and the Virgin. Cyril, bishop of Alexandria, followed in the footsteps of Athanasius and applied to the Virgin Mary the title that had long been in use, *Theotokos*, "God-bearing" or "Mother of God." Nestorius of Antioch, bishop of Constantinople, would have none of this and suggested, instead, the more limited title of *Christotokos*, "Mother of Christ"—restricting her to the role of mother of one member only of the Trinity, that member who had been Incarnated. Her subordination was clearly outlined in the Nestorian Creed. Nestorius's chief disciple, the presbyter Anastasius, warned: "Let no one call Mary the Mother of God (*Theotokos*), for Mary was but a woman, and it is impossible that God should be born of a woman."[27]

In 430 a Roman synod ordered Nestorius to recant or face excommunication; the same year, Cyril convened another synod in Alexandria which concurred with Rome's decision. The Third Ecumenical Council at Chalcedon in 451 ruled for orthodox Christians that the Virgin Mary was indeed *Theotokos*, the acknowledged Mother of God. The importance accorded to the Virgin increased rapidly in the fourth and fifth centuries. Quite clearly, she inherited the remains of the Magna Mater and preserved that type of female-oriented worship within the overall framework of the church.

A far more exclusively masculine trend was now in evidence in the Middle East. The Monophysites, founders of the future Coptic Church, became increasingly important in the Orient, centered around Alexandria: Egypt, Ethiopia, and Syria were rapidly taken over by them —the ancient Orient that was neither Roman nor Greek. They represented a trend of theological thought that was to culminate with Islam: the steady growth of utter *transcendentalism* and the complete extirpation of the feminine principle from religion. Pushing things to an extreme, they determinedly stressed the divine in Christ, at the expense of his humanity. The great asset of Christianity was precisely the idea of *incarnation*, the spirit made flesh, the idea of a Savior who was simultaneously "God, of the substance of the Father," and "Man, of the substance of his Mother," as expressed in the Athanasian Creed.[28] This, however, was disputed all over the East.

The Monophysites threatened the bridge thrown by Christianity over the gap separating the transcending Almighty and His human creation. In their view, Christ, as God, could suffer no pain during the Passion on the Cross; the Crucifixion itself they deemed to be only a *phantasia,* an illusion. By shifting Christ away from His human nature and closer to His transcendent Father, the Monophysites were destroying the profoundly symbolic significance of the Incarnation and removing the godhead halfway to the infinite distance where Muhammad's Allah was to stand: the human nature of Jesus, being eclipsed by the divine, could not be included in it.

For the first time in Western lands, a new creed based on love, charity, humility, and chastity spread like wildfire among the rich and the poor, and especially among women. Revolt against pagan debauchery was in the air; distrust of the essentially masculine ethical severity of Stoicism was widespread. These survivals of a dying Classical Age began to fade away, along with its doomed civilization. Now, women of the empire, fed up with the social and moral disintegration, welcomed with open arms a new, gentle faith based on love and charity for all.

The greatest upheaval brought about by the triumph of Christianity lay in the sexual realm—an end to prostitution that had been condoned by paganism, the same rigid standard of fidelity for both sexes in marriage. Chastity as an ideal, and as a fact in the lives of the leaders of the time, remained the ethical pivot around which Christianity developed. Marriage, however, was fully accepted and raised from a mere social contract to a religious sacrament; with it, matrimony became indissoluble, enhancing the security and dignity of the wife and mother. The famous orator-patriarch John Chysostom ("Golden Mouth") pointed out that an unfaithful husband was just as guilty as an unfaithful wife. The uncompromisingly patriarchal outlook of the Old Testament was amended by the far more gentle and feminine tone of the New Testament; womankind was exhalted in the rapidly growing worship of the Mother of God.

Women being the mainstay of Christianity's growing success, it was inevitable that the church would compromise as far as possible in their favor, even while remaining firmly under masculine authority. The church as a corporate entity even viewed itself as female; as the (probably apocryphal) Pauline *Second Letter to Saint Clement of Rome* states it: "God made male and female; the male is Christ and the female is the Church."[29] And centuries later Augustine added the admonition: "Husbands, love your wives as Christ also loved the Church."[30] In fact, Augustine fought for women tooth and nail, objected to the Voconian Laws because they limited the amount of property women could inherit; he strongly emphasized that "as the honor of the male sex is in the flesh of Christ, the honor of the female sex is in the Mother of

Christ"—possibly remembering his own worthy mother.[31] Devout Christian women—Fabiola, Melania, Paula—repaid the church with monumental charitable work such as was unknown among non-Christians.

Furthermore, by exalting feminine feeling above masculine intellect, the church, in effect, raised feminine qualities over and above masculine ones. Classical culture suffered the consequences; along with the Teutonic invasions and the steady barbarization of the western empire, this exaltation of faith and sentiment at the expense of rational thought was partly responsible for the intellectual regression of the times— some of the great Fathers of the Church notwithstanding.

Before this took place, however, the church had continued its process of growth through synthetic absorption—first of the other religious creeds, then of the administrative apparatus of the western empire itself as it began to crumble under the barbarian onslaughts. In one of the most amazing campaigns ever recorded in the history of religions, pagan deities were transmuted wholesale into saints or angels, introducing a mild form of polytheism through the back door; the most important ones—Horus, Adonis, Attis, Mithra, Ba'al—were absorbed into Jesus, while the Virgin incorporated Demeter, Diana, Isis, Venus, and the Magna Mater. By 431, Cyril, archbishop of Alexandria, had applied to the Virgin Mary, in a celebrated sermon at Ephesus, all the tender epithets hitherto reserved for the goddess Artemis-Diana; in the sixth century the church set up the Feast of the Assumption of the Virgin on August 15, the very same time as the old festival celebrating Artemis and Isis. From then on, Mary became the patron saint and holiest figure of Byzantine Christendom.

And so, Christmas replaced the Saturnalia, Pentecost the Floralia, the Feast of the Nativity the Lupercalia and the celebration of the purification of Isis. The great, ageless theme of the death and rebirth of the male god sacrificed in fertility cults was remade into the Crucifixion, Death, and Resurrection of Christ; even the old festivals of the dead became All Souls' Day. Bit by bit, slowly, octopuslike, the church absorbed into itself and metabolized all the great religious themes of a past that would not be stamped out.[32]

In vain did some Church Fathers protest against the excessively catholic compromises: Augustine warned against treating the saints as gods and dedicating churches and basilicas to them rather than to the one God Almighty; other Fathers warned against the worship of images and relics. But there was no denying the deep-rooted need for emotional outlets for a great variety of religious tempers; and the need met its fulfillment. All in all, early Christianity remained faithful to Vincentius's motto—*Quod semper, quod ubique, quod ab omnibus* ("Believe what has been believed always, everywhere, and by everyone").[33]

At this point, it is essential to recall that Christianity was and remained for a long time an *Eastern* religion with shallow roots in the West, and this up to the collapse of the western empire; that most of its members and clergy were recruited in the Orient, even after the emperors had gone over to the new faith. The first Roman Church was largely a colony of Hellenized Jews and Greek Christians; all the seven great Councils took place in Asia Minor. Even the Fathers of the Western, Latin Church—Irenaeus, Clemens, Hermas, Hippolytus—wrote in Greek; the early popes were Greek, not Italian (the very title "pope" is Greek).

As the western empire began to fall apart, the young Roman Church began to grow fast, out of practical necessity, by attracting the best administrative and political talents that the Western classical world had to offer—in effect substituting for the collapsing authority of the imperial machinery. Something similar happened in the eastern empire when the many priestly families that had ruled the autonomous temple estates (Zela, Cabeira, Comana Pontica) began to provide expert bishops for the new Christian Church[34]—but under far less traumatic conditions. Typical of the Western phenomenon was the career of Ambrose in the fourth century; a man of outstanding ability, he eventually became provincial governor of northern Italy. Called upon to settle a quarrel revolving around the election of the bishop of Milan, he was promptly designated as a compromise candidate. Still unbaptized and protesting, he was, in the short space of a week, christened, ordained to the diaconate, the priesthood, and the episcopacy. He became one of the outstanding Church Fathers; in earlier centuries he would have become an equally outstanding Roman proconsul.

As clerics, these outstanding men had a psychological leverage over the uncultured Teutons which lay officials of the imperial administration lacked; their military power was nil but their magico-spiritual authority, backed by what was left of classical culture, soon overwhelmed the relatively simpleminded barbarians. And, again, they enjoyed plenty of feminine assistance: it was mostly women who worked out the religious conversion of barbarian kings and determined the course of history in Western Europe—as they had, earlier, converted the Roman emperors.

In A.D. 493 Clovis, the victorious king of the Salic Franks in Gaul, married a Christian lady, Clothilde. She soon converted him from his original paganism to Orthodox Christianity. Bishop Remi baptized him in Reims, along with three thousand Frankish warriors; and in alliance with Orthodox Christians throughout Gaul, he eventually defeated his Visigothic and Burgundian enemies. It was largely Queen Clothilde who engineered her husband's triumph and who turned Roman Gaul into the embryo of what was to become France. Upon becoming a widow at the death of Clovis, this high-minded queen retired to Tours, there to serve the rest of her life in the church of Saint Martin. Clothilde was only one of many; one of the last instances was that of Duke Henry of Bavaria's sister, the devout Gisella, who, married to Saint Stephen of Hungary and queen of the realm, can be considered responsible for converting her Hungarian subjects to the Christian faith.

But as wave upon wave of Teutonic invaders poured into what used to be the western empire, the process of barbarization became irreversible and plunged Western Europe into the Dark Ages. A new crop of barbarian women appeared, no longer devout nor retiring, but every bit as savage as their men; women who relished power and domination. The atrocious tales of murders and cruelties that blotted the careers of such eminently ghoulish women as Brunhilda or Fredegunda make chilling reading—the assassination of Sigebert by Fredegunda's agents, of Chilperic by Brunhilda's, the gory tyranny with which the latter ruled Neustria, all testify to the remarkable influence wielded by those ruthless females. Yet the Franks had always enjoyed a strictly patriarchal social organization whose cornerstone was the famous Salic Law that ruled France until the great revolution: "Of Salic land no portion of the inheritance shall go to woman"—an illustration of the gap that sometimes separates theory from practice.

The triumph of Christianity, far more complete at an earlier stage in the East than in the West, was bound to enhance feminine power and influence. For all the emancipation of Roman women, none ever ruled the empire directly, since the state remained largely in the hands of the legions and praetorian guards; things were to prove different in Byzantium. This was so largely because of a basic difference between the Latin Church in the West and the Greek Church in the East. The Latin Church's first objective had been to fight against the moral corruption that had corroded Roman society's fiber; hence, the emphasis on clerical celibacy and the exaggerated praise of virginity and continence. In addition, the Latin Church was soon engulfed by the barbarian invasions and, with little time for pointless theological disputations, had to take over the main burden of preserving what was left of civilization during the Dark Ages.

The Greek Church, ensconced in the far more civilized East, could take a more balanced view of things. Dwelling in richer and more stable lands, its main object was to counteract the violent antisexual attitude of the early Christians. Not surprisingly, the Greek Fathers laid greater stress than their Latin brothers on the basic equality of the sexes, and the fundamental humanity of woman. According to Clement of Alexandria,

> One only is the God of both, one the Instructor and one the Church; theirs is the same temperance and modesty, the same food . . . one and the same is their breathing, their sight, their hearing, their knowledge, their hope, their obedience, everything. . . . Nature is the same in each individual. . . . Woman does not have one human nature and man another. They both possess the same nature. . . .[35]

Clement would not allow any devaluation of the flesh—"that flesh which the Lord himself assumed"—and said of the genitals that "we should not be ashamed to name what God was not ashamed to create."[36]

John Chrysostom asked rhetorically from the pulpit:

> Wouldst thou have thy wife obedient to thee as the Church is to Christ? Take thou thyself the same provident care of her as Christ takes for the Church. Yes, even if it shall be needful for thee to give thy life for her. . . .[37]

And as for man-made legislation that discriminated against woman and allowed man to indulge in his own weaknesses, he added:

> How is it that you demand that which you yourself do not give? How is it that though you are but equally a person, you legislate unequally? If you enquire into the worse—the woman sinned and so did Adam. The serpent deceived them both, and one was not to be found stronger and the other weaker. But do you consider yourself better? Christ saved both in His passion. Was He made flesh for man? So He was also for the woman. Did He die for the man? The woman also is saved by His death.[38]

Not surprisingly, in view of this theological background, Byzantine women behaved with a forceful assurance that their emancipated pagan Latin sisters had never enjoyed. They at all times accepted their actual femaleness, dignified as it was by the Greek Church.

And so, more often than anywhere else, the Greek realm was ruled by women—Pulcheria, sister of Emperor Theodosius, who, at age sixteen, became regent and ruled the empire for thirty-three years, along with her sister-in-law Eudocia, who ruled jointly with her and gave several remarkable decades of peace and prosperity to the realm. Even as early as the fourth century, we find that Dominica, widow of Emperor Valens who had been defeated and killed by the Goths, took it upon herself to organize the successful defense of Constantinople.

A long string of remarkable women punctuated the historical record of Byzantium from then on, but none could ever compare in intelligence and strength of character with the formidable Theodora, wife of Emperor Justinian. Whatever her controversial premarital past may have been, Theodora was one of the great queens of all times. She ruled alongside Justinian and displayed a shrewd understanding of the sinews of political power. She had a decisive influence on the choice of patriarchs and popes, was active in her country's diplomacy, countermanded Justinian's orders at times, and was usually right in doing so. In times of trouble, she proved to be his backbone—during the rebellion of the Greens and the Blues, for instance, when Justinian was preparing to flee, Theodora persuaded him to resist and crush the rebellion. She was perceptive enough to realize the strength of Monophysitism in Egypt and Syria, as well as the fact that on this issue East and West would never meet, and that the future of Byzantium lay in the East. She did much, against Justinian's more orthodox beliefs and against the pope's resistance, to spur the rise of a separate Monophysite Church in Syria and Egypt.

Needless to add, the famous Justinian Code of Laws improved further the legal status of women, largely under church auspices. The old principle that inheritance was transmitted exclusively through males was abolished—a self-serving alteration, since the church received most of its legacies from women. Men were still liable to capital punishment in case of adultery, but for women the penalty was reduced to a life sentence in a convent. The death penalty was also decreed for rape, and the rapist's confiscated property was handed over to the injured woman.

Theodora was the greatest and most notorious, but by no means the last, forceful woman in power in Constantinople. As the orientalist Charles Diehl stated it: "Under few governments have women had a better position, or played a more important part, or had a greater influence upon politics and the government, than under the Byzantine Empire."[39]

Nor was it merely a matter of wielding power *through* men; women often exercised power directly under their own authority as enthroned "Basilissa." In the eighth century, Empress Irene was the prime mover behind the decision to put an end to the Iconoclastic persecution—a masculine, puritan attempt to imitate Islam and banish all images and image worship. Byzantine women would have none of Iconoclasm;

Iconodule to the last, they were fortunate in that Irene became the ruling Basilissa upon the sudden death of her Iconoclastic husband, Emperor Leo IV. From then on, having defeated all the intrigues of her male relatives, she ruled with an iron hand and a ruthlessness to which she sacrificed whatever motherly instincts she may have possessed. A contemporary of Charlemagne in the West, she was his equal in statesmanlike ability, political vision, and willful determination.

In the ninth century the great Basilissa Theodora was canonized by the church for having defeated a new Iconoclastic attempt and restoring orthodoxy. Yet it was quite by chance that she had been picked as wife of a young emperor, Theophilus. Carrying out an old Byzantine tradition, court messengers had scoured all the provinces of the empire in search of the most suitable bride for the ruler. Gathered together in the Pavilion of the Pearl, women were looked over by Theophilus until his eyes came to rest on the prettiest—who, unfortunately for her, was also the cleverest. He began the conversation by remarking that "A woman was the fount and source of all man's tribulations," to which the sharp-tongued Kasia, relying also upon the authority of the Bible, retorted: "And from a woman sprang the course of man's regeneration."[40]

Upon which, frightened by the prompt and witty answer, Theophilus wheeled around and took Theodora for his bride. A few years later, upon his death, she became de facto ruler of the empire.

Far more enigmatic and mysterious, the famous and yet obscure Theophano, loved by three successive emperors, a "young woman of supernatural loveliness, containing in the delicate perfection of her harmony the power that troubles the world," left her own imperishable mark on Byzantium.[41] Having become regent at age twenty-two upon the death of Emperor Romanus II, she used her considerable charms to upset the intrigues of the all-powerful prime minister, the Parakoimomenos Joseph Bringas, even to the point of marrying the unattractive Nicephorus Phocas, the most powerful general of the time, in order to defeat Bringas. Nicephorus became Basileus with the secret connivance of Theophano, who appears to have masterminded the successful revolt against Joseph Bringas. Desperately in love with the beautiful Theophano, Nicephorus Phocas married her in 963; six years later, she had him murdered by his nephew John Tzimisces, whom she hoped to marry but who immediately betrayed her and sent her into exile.

The loves and intrigues of the sensual and passionate Basilissa Zoë the Porphyrogenita make up a tale worthy of the *Arabian Nights*, but at times they shook the Byzantine realm to its foundations. At the age of seventy, her worthy and austere sister Theodora forcibly seized the imperial crown. Warned by Zoë's misfortunes with her husbands, Theodora refused to marry and ruled the realm firmly and well:

> But in the long run, everyone in the capital and the Empire tired of this feminine government that had lasted now for more than twenty-five years. The Patriarch Cerularius, who had become since the schism the Pope, as it were, of the Eastern Church, said openly that it was a shame that a woman should govern the Roman Empire.[42]

They had already been doing so, off and on, for centuries. Fortunately for her, Theodora passed away in 1056 before the antifeminist storm broke out.

But Byzantium was not done with women rulers. The remarkably proud and intelligent Anna Commena hated the brother who threatened to take the throne away from her:

> It was because she believed herself qualified to reign, by right of seniority, that as long as Alexius lived she plotted, agitated, and used all her influence to push forward her husband, Nicephorus, with the aim of recovering the power that she considered herself unjustly deprived of.[43]

Frustrated in her political ambitions, she lived to become perhaps the most cultured woman of her generation. If she finally failed in her grasp for political power, others were more successful. But now, in the last centuries of Byzantine history, the play was taken away from Greek women and delivered to imported princesses from the West, partly as a result of the Crusades. From Bertha of Sulzbach and Agnes of France to Constance of Hohenstaufen and Yolanda of Montferrat, they all found a climate more congenial to feminine power and influence than in their native Western Europe. One of the last Western princesses can even be credited with having dealt a death blow to the empire. In unleashing a bitter and ruthless civil war against John Cantacuzene, the Basilissa Anna of Savoy wrecked what remained of Byzantine power and left the moribund empire an easy prey for the rising power of the Turks; within less than a century, the Ottomans stormed into Constantinople and made it their capital. But, by way of epitaph on the tombstone of a vanishing empire, it still remains that its incredible longevity of about one thousand years must be due in part to the extremely important and "conservative" part played by women in Byzantine public life.

The status of women was higher in Byzantium than in any other civilized society of the time. Both legislation and customs were highly favorable to women, and their influence in politics and affairs of state was at times paramount. Had Saint Paul come back to earth and visited Constantinople, he would have had quite a surprise; yet it was the religion that he helped to found that was responsible for the remarkable feminization of Byzantium. It was Christianity, in its Eastern, Orthodox form, that had evolved such a successful social compromise between male and female attributions; rarely before or since has the female sex enjoyed such power and authority in any civilization.

In some respects, the compromise shifted too far in the feminine direction, and this undue influence of women was partly responsible for some of the least attractive aspects of Byzantine civilization, and for its remarkable cultural sterility after the seventh century—just about when Arab culture began to bloom. Exaggerated feminine influence it was that weakened the moral fiber of these latter-day Greeks and was responsible for the endless hair-splitting that became known as Byzantinism, famously illustrated by its leading theologians going into an endless argument about whether angels could dance on the point of a needle, while Constantinople was besieged and fighting for its existence. In fact, it was probably the most effeminate civilization—almost "Cretan"—ever to appear on earth since the patriarchal revolution, embodied in an imperial state that was raped time and again, by all comers—including the barbaric Crusaders—only to rise from its bed of prostitution and live a while longer, waiting for the next, and fatal, rape by the Osmanli Turks.

If one looks upon the Middle East since the end of classical civilization as one cultural whole, in spite of its obvious diversity, it becomes clear that Byzantium with its Greek Orthodox form of Christianity represents its "Catholic" and Islam the "Protestant" aspect. To put it another way, Greek Orthodox Christianity represents the "feminine" and Islam, the "masculine" pole. The most important feature of this difference is the extreme, almost excessive, ritualism of the Greek Orthodox Church with its impressive pomp and luxurious display of shimmering robes and bejeweled gold ornaments producing an almost magical atmosphere—contrasted with an almost total lack of preaching. Islam emphasizes sermons almost to the exclusion of everything else, very much like the typical denominations of the Western Reformation. Psychologically, this implies that Orthodox Christianity lays very little emphasis on morality and ethics, that most "masculine" element which has little appeal for women who would rather have the magic display and performance of liturgy that strikes the imagination and the emotions.[44] Islam, on the other hand, masculine to the core, stresses utter simplicity in its ceremonial and rigid ethics, at the exclusion of complex ritual, gorgeous paraphernalia, and all the display of emotionalism attached to grandiose ceremonial; it is Eastern Puritanism with its typical emphasis on sermon and ethics. In Byzantium one finds, on the contrary, a compromise between the masculine and feminine principle that shifted slowly, over the centuries, toward the feminine pole to such an extent that it died out as a civilization.

7

India and China

In contrast with the mighty struggle that took place between the male and female elements in the bosom of Greco-Roman culture and finally tore out the guts of the Roman Empire's civilization, Indian and Chinese cultures display a remarkable equilibrium between the two sexual entities. These countries remained patriarchal as far as their socioeconomic structures were concerned, but their cultural values were such that the feminine *principle* received its due recognition in the male-female partnership. Values are what human beings live by, and the value-system of any given culture determines the sense of fulfillment and degree of happiness of its members.

It is therefore not surprising that no record exists of any massive discontent of the female element in either India or China. These cultures never included anything like the Greek overestimation of mental creativity at the expense of the creation of life itself; there never was the devaluation of the female's procreative function which finally induced Roman women, victims of this cultural distortion, to attempt to ape men instead of assuming with pride and dignity their physiological being.

The Eastern civilizations' roots are sunk deep in a profound metaphysical cleavage that began to separate East from West thousands of years before Christ. Creeds and myths antecedent to the Axial period give us the main clue. The first noteworthy but sharp separation appears to have taken place somewhere around 2350 B.C. in Sumer when the respective spheres of man and the higher divinity began to split away from one another; the king is no longer god but the priest of the divinity.[1] He no longer has to *identify* himself with the diety. The religious problem is no longer identification but *relationship*, and the first shadowy contours of the eventual separation between object and subject appear in terms of an I-thou relationship. Already, according to the early Sumerians, man was created for the pleasure of the gods, and in no way does he partake in their essential Being; man does not participate in the divine essence—he is merely human. The Sumerian king is no longer the *incarnation* of the deity but his devoted servant.

This sharp separation triggered a yearning for the reestablishment of the broken connection between the human and divine spheres, by one means or another, a yearning that counteracted and undermined the cyclical lunar-vegetal outlook that had prevailed until then. The end result of this evolution was that, in place of the cyclical view, a new religious outlook focused on historical development in linear fashion, with a temporal direction and without any possibility of recurrence; masculine *tension* replaced feminine *rhythm*. Man began to understand the cosmic process as a progressive and directional development with a once-for-all creation, followed by a Fall and a struggle to overcome the Fall and reach Redemption. The world became the battlefield of a mighty struggle between the powers of good and evil, light and darkness—here again, an essentially masculine and warlike concept of human destiny.

All this was foreign to the concepts of the East, where the cyclical view, either historical (China) or transhistorical (India), prevailed. There is no mighty historical struggle between the spirits of good and evil, light and darkness. In fact, man's problem is not to establish a *relationship* with the divine, but to recognize and realize his true *identity* with the divine, to search for and bring out his inner divinity by peeling off the veils of illusion, *māyā*. Since the separation between man and the divine is only apparent, a result of the interposition of *māyā*, the problem is, by personal striving, to eliminate the mere appearance and rediscover this fundamental identity. In Indian culture, there were no *theological* problems, only *psychological* ones.

In turn, this springs from the fact that the East never separated the objective and subjective spheres as sharply as the West: the umbilical cord joining them was not really severed; the *subject* kept its preeminence and its emotional link and closeness with the nonsubject surrounding it or underlying it—the world of nature, the multifarious gods and goddesses, and life in general in all its manifestations. This closeness and retention of the umbilical cord implied that, in the East, there was no such sharp severance between conscious and unconscious as took place in the West; contents of the unconscious kept on projecting themselves in the outer world and filling it with symbols. As a result, Easterners were less individualized than Westerners, linked as they were, not only by the exchange of rational thoughts and concepts, but also by openly sharing the common symbolism of their collective unconscious, unrepressed and unfrustrated—which, in the West, occurred only within a strictly disciplined religious framework.

This is why Westerners were and are impressed by the unparalleled calm and serenity that pervades so much of traditional Eastern art and religious symbolism—calm and serenity that the Westerner lacks, swinging constantly as he does between his effort to identify and overpower the autonomous *object*, and the correlated need to submit to it. The Easterner neutralizes this anxiety and avoids the struggle by focusing on his subjectiveness and on the denial of the object as ultimately separate; this separation is deemed to be essentially unreal, and the object's only apparent reality resides in its being a mental or emotional projection of the sovereign *subject*.

The unquestionably masculine character of Western religions in contrast to those of the East springs basically from the full acceptance in the West of an objective reality that, in the East, is viewed fundamentally as an illusion: the absolute dissociation of every individual human being from every other, and the equally absolute dissociation of all human beings from the higher divinity. There was in the West (until the advent of psychoanalysis) no conscious problem of identification, of rediscovering one's deeper, divine self; the Western problem was how to *relate* to divine powers *outside* oneself, and how to develop one's ego in the process. In the East the problem was how to extinguish the ego, an essential step on the way to the discovery of one's fundamental identity with the unindividualized divinity within the self. This has striking consequences in terms of the relations between masculine and feminine principles.

According to Indian mythology, the birth of sexual differentiation came about as follows:

> . . . this universe was nothing but the Self in the form of a man
> . . . who still lacked delight . . . and desired a second. He was
> exactly as large as a man and a woman embracing. This Self then
> divided itself in two parts. . . . The male embraced the female, and
> from that the human race arose. . . .[2]

While the predominance of the masculine principle in what is basically an androgynous Self is here affirmed—a psychological consequence of the supremacy of the patriarchal Aryan invader—the metaphysical conclusions reached are quite different from those that obtained in the West where the separation between God and His creation remained sharply in evidence. In Indian lore, after pursuing the female who wondered, "How can he unite with me, who am produced from himself?" and transmuted herself successively into all the female animals of creation, the male exclaimed: "I, actually, am creation; for I have poured forth all this."[3]

Man, therefore, is the sole creator, but since he is also divinity, this creation stands between him and his divine self. Creation itself is a Fall, whereas in the biblical account, the Fall occurs *after* the Creation. The biblical Fall is presumed to be a *historical* event and Redemption is a historical process. The Indian Fall is a metaphysical and transhistorical event, occurring endlessly along with the continuous creation of new life, and redemption is a personal, individual affair completely divorced from history. So, while male predominance is affirmed equally in both myths, the Indian message compromises with the feminine outlook by negating the historical event and placing it on the plane of cyclical timelessness. The biblical one, on the contrary, is uncompromisingly masculine in its affirmation of the irreversible historical process and its ethical tension.

Eastern and Western mythologies diverge in a fundamental sense, the East making far more concessions to the instinctive feminine apprehension of timeless reality, of sheer Being, than the West in its concentration on Doing and Becoming.

The prehistoric roots of Indian culture are barely visible in the archeological remains of the great civilization of Harappā and Mohenjo-daro—"the vastest political experiment before the advent of the Roman Empire," according to Sir Mortimer Wheeler.[4] A noteworthy feature of its religious outlook was the cult of the Great Mother which the patriarchal Aryan invaders scorned and discarded. But this cult never really died out. Even today it survives in the Indian countryside, where the Great Mother, known as *gramadevata,* is worshiped in rustic shrines and temples shaped like female genitalia—and its priests, significantly, are not Brahmins but Untouchables who could probably trace their lineage back to the pre-Aryan Dravidian stock of the Harappā civilization.[5] The little statues portraying the Great Mother are close cousins of the female clay figurines found in' Baluchistan and Mohenjo-daro, or the bas-reliefs of Harappā depicting the Earth Goddess with a plant sprouting from her womb. The worship of the divine *mātṛis* (mothers) is widespread throughout India, each village having its own special guardian mother. The reason for this extraordinary predominance of the female principle and the virtual eclipse of male gods at this elementary level is that

she is held to have a thoroughly feminine nature. She is more easily propitiated by prayer, flattery, and offerings, more ready to defend from evil, more irritable, uncertain, and wayward in her temper and moods, more dangerously spiteful, and prone to inflict diseases, if offended by neglect.[6]

The Great Mother survived all the assaults and invasions of patriarchal warriors; she survived in India despite the Vedic Aryans, and as the multiform, Kālī lived on to be worshiped by the greatest Indian saint of the nineteenth century:

When there was neither the creation, nor the sun, the moon, the planets, and the earth, and when darkness was enveloped in Darkness, then the Mother, the Formless One, Maha-Kālī, the Great Power, was one with Maha-Kāla, the Absolute.[7]

So claimed Ramakrishna.

With the coming of the Indo-Europeans, the Great Mother temporarily faded into the background. Masculine willpower and drive eclipsed the female-oriented outlook based on a cyclical rhythmic order ruling with a nature-imposed determinism against which man's puny will is powerless, an outlook according to which the rhythm of the Great Mother's universal womb regulated inexorably the life-death-rebirth cycle. There is no need to go through the complex, dreamlike metamorphosis of the Vedic pantheon to see the struggle between the invading Aryan male principle and the stubbornly resisting female principle in the process of being overcome; they soon came to terms.

From the start, the Vedic pantheon made room for the two sexual principles—male Heaven (Dyaus) and female Earth (Pṛithivī), from whose union the entire universe, animate and inanimate, proceeds. True enough, the female principle was devalued in this early stage of Aryan settlement in India: the wives of male deities such as Indra and Agni are not associated with their spouses and are not worshiped along with them; the extremely popular Lakṣmī, later on wife of Viṣṇu, is not even mentioned in the Ṛg-veda; Sarasvatī is not yet the consort of Brahmā. It is only much later, when Indian culture went through its "Renaissance" phase—presumably by incorporating submerged elements of the Harappā civilization—that the female principle began its slow ascent toward full recognition. It is in the Brāhmanas and the Upaniṣads that the sexual duality of the Higher Divinity is accepted for the first time.

As Brahmanism turned into Hinduism after undergoing the Buddhist revolution, the metaphysical concept of sexual duality became more sophisticated. According to Vedānta, the separate existence of the eternal masculine Spirit or Self (*ātman*) and of the equally eternal feminine productive force or prolific entity known as illusion (*māyā*) are both recognized as dialectical counterparts. The more abstract-minded Sāṁkhya school of philosophy also recognizes the eternal existence of the two sexual principles—male spirit Puruṣa and female matter Prakṛti—whose union is necessary before any creation can

arise. Later mythology symbolized the perfect union of the two principles in the Ardha-nārī, the androgynous form of the god Śiva, whose
right side is male and left female. But usually the two sexes remained
distinct, symbolized in countless bas-reliefs on Indian temples by the
male and female symbolic trademarks, the *liṇga* and the *yoni*.

It was reserved to the Tantras to give absolute preeminence to the
female principle and teach adoration of the wives of Śiva and Viṣṇu at
the exclusion of their male consorts. The main characteristic of Tantrism was, fittingly enough, a typically female anti-ascetic and antiintellectual attitude, along with contempt for meditation: liberation is
effected, Dionysiac-like, by the full enjoyment of the carnal possibilities of a healthy body.[8] More especially, the followers of what became
known as the "left-hand path" *(Vāma-margīs)* worshiped exclusively the
divine wives, Durgā and Rādhā. It is significant that Tantrism bloomed
essentially in peripheral areas (Bengal, Assam, and southern India)
that had been only slightly Hinduized and where the Dravidian influence of the former Great Mother was still immensely strong.

All the female deities were subsumed under the one great heading
of Ambā or Devī, the great Power (Śakti) of nature, the Great Mother
of the Universe (Jagan-mātā), the mysterious and mighty power that
directs and controls two different operations: "first, the working of the
natural appetites and passions, whether for the support of the body by
eating and drinking, or for the propagation of living organisms
through sexual cohabitation; secondly, the acquisition of supernatural
faculties *(siddhi)*. . . . "[9] Such worship of the female principle could not
remain confined to the realm of religion and metaphysics; inevitably,
it trickled down into the world of social relations. In the Śakta creed,
for instance, every female is conceived of as an actual divinity.[10]

Here we not only have a rebirth of the Great Mother of pre-Aryan
times, along with wonder and awe at the mystery of feminine generative power and its connection with nature's fertility, but we have the
feminine principle as such assimilated into the incomprehensible essence of ultimate spiritual reality, the quintessence of pure Being. The
male deities of the Vedic pantheon are shunted aside and the primordial instincts reassert themselves, blindly unintellectual, in full retreat
from the world-negating mood of the male philosophers of the Vedānta. From the "Apollonian" attitude of Vedānta, the Tantric devotee
travels all the way to the female-oriented "Dionysiac" acceptance of
life with its joys and sorrows, with its refusal to escape from the coils
of a now venerated materialistic Prakṛti.

The result of this unbridled worship of the female principle was also
a remarkable evaporation of all strict moral sense, giving rise to innumerable monstrosities. All the Dionysiac excesses of the Tantric cults

can be traced to it. Among all the goddesses worshiped, the one that stands out is the fearful Durgā who, under her Bengali incarnation as Kālī, venerated by the gentle, saintly Ramakrishna, became also the main inspirer of the greatest criminal conspiracy in history—the Thugs (*thagī*), the robber-stranglers who performed their monstrous deeds without a qualm, feeling that they were proper tributes to Kālī.

It is significant that worship of the female principle in its beneficial aspects was widespread. In the *Tantrasāra*, the following hymn to the Great Goddess in her role as "Ruler of the World," Bhuvaneśvarī, proves conclusively that she survived quite well the early invasions and the Vedic ordeal:

> O Mother! Cause and Mother of the World!
> Thou art the One Primordial Being,
> Mother of innumerable creatures,
> Creatrix of the very gods: even of Brahma the Creator,
> Viṣṇu the Preserver, and Śiva the Destroyer!
> O Mother, in hymning Thy praise I purify my speech.[11]

The masculine imprint, however, remained strong in the early phase of Indian culture's development, right through to Buddha and beyond. The early ascetics distrusted, as they always have throughout the ages and in every land, sex, and hence, woman. The Buddha is reported to have stated that the admission of women to the order would seriously shorten the life span of the Buddhist religion. His overall view of women comes out clearly in the following deathbed conversation with his favorite pupil, Ānanda, who inquired:

> How are we to conduct ourselves, Lord, with regard to women?
> Do not see them, Ānanda!
> But if we should see them, what are we to do?
> Abstain from speech.
> But if they speak to us, Lord, what are we to do?
> Keep wide awake, Ānanda![12]

Ānanda is reported as always speaking up, respectfully, in favor of women. But the Buddha would not be mollified; he once told him:

> Women are soon angered, Ānanda; women are full of passion, Ānanda; women are envious, Ānanda; women are stupid, Ānanda. That is the reason, Ānanda, that the cause, why women have no place in public assemblies, do not carry on business, and do not earn their living by any profession.[13]

With that, one would have thought that women would have shunned such a religious leader. Quite the contrary; they literally flocked to his banner. Reluctantly, he allowed them to become Sisters, establish convents, and join the Order. They remained technically inferior in status to the male brethren, but having escaped from the drudgery of domestic life and "having abandoned a woman's thoughts and cultivated the thoughts of a man,"[14] the Sister obtained from her brethren full recognition as a rational being, a human being rather than a woman. The Psalms make her sing:

Am I a woman in such matters, or
Am I a man? or what am I then?
How should the woman's nature hinder Us?
Speak not to me of delighting in aught of sensuous pleasures!
Verily all such vanities now no more may delight me.[15]

The Jains took an equally poor view of women: "As deceitfulness is natural to women, so are standing, sitting down, roaming about, and teaching the law, natural to sages."[16] The Yoga discipline distrusted the female power with words, since all yogic schools emphasized direct experience and nonverbal realization. A holy text states emphatically:

It is always the mark of a weak, feminine nature to endeavor to establish one's superiority on the issue of a verbal quarrel, whereas it is the sign of a man to desire to conquer the world by the strength of one's own arms.[17]

Since, viewed from the highest metaphysical level, man and woman are not autonomous personalities in the Western sense of the word, endowed with eternally individual souls and free will, the Indian problem was rather to deal with the interplay between the two *sexual principles*, not male and female as such, but maleness and femaleness—both being an outcome of *māyā*, illusory deceit. The individual, male or female, is fundamentally without personality or character in terms of timeless Reality, a misguided, blind slice of timeless Divinity, temporarily trapped in the coils of time and space. Some Indian schools of thought, focusing on asceticism, frowned on the feminine principle as an agent of corruption; others, especially the Tantric, viewed women and sexual congress, as well as intoxicating beverages, as being the "boons that remove all sin."[18] But woman, here, is viewed as an agent of purification rather than an element requiring spiritual realization in her own right. The poet Jayadeva and the Tantric Śakti sects centered their symbolism around the female principle and its feminine human incarnation; others around the male principle.[19] There were cults and worships for all tastes, as befits the most catholic culture in the world.

But Śaktism, in particular, deserves a special mention. It was essentially the worship of power in the shape of a goddess, herself the outcome of the strange nature of the sexless Supreme Being—a self-existent being whose abstract Spirit is Life "without anything to live for, Thought without anything to think about, Joy without anything to be joyful about."[20] As soon as this Supreme Being becomes conscious of *existence,* he becomes a personal God, and, automatically, a bisexual one, partly male, partly female (the left side being the female one). The reason for the preeminence of the female side of the androgyne is due to the fact that

> the male side of the god was believed to relegate all his more onerous and troublesome executive functions to his female counterpart. And hence it has come to pass that the female side of the personal god is often more honored and propitiated than the male.[21]

In absolute terms, however, the virtual equality of the two sexual principles was firmly established, as it never was in the West. This was both the cause and the consequence of the fact that, unlike the Greek philosophers, Indian thinkers never attempted to destroy their traditional mythologies, never cut themselves off from their anima. Distrusting from the start both the limitations of words and linguistic terminology *(nāman)* and the external world of perceived forms *(rūpa),* all Indian schools of thought were unanimous in their conviction that the ultimate goal of thought lies well beyond the world of *nāma-rūpa.* This was in complete contrast with the essentially masculine Greek approach, according to which thought should focus on objective reality, the object of thought being sharply separated from the thinking subject. Pre-Socratic thinkers used the logic of the emerging sciences —astronomy, mathematics, physics—to attempt to depict objective reality, and in the process destroyed their venerable mythology. The Greeks cut off feeling from thinking; the Indians retained the close integration. As a result, Western philosophies progress from thought to thought, from one abstraction to the other, analyzing, deducing, inducing, differentiating, integrating. Indian philosophers progress from one subjective condition to another, from one mode of being to a higher mode of being. Westerners want to *know;* Indians want to *be,* to change the form of their consciousness. In terms of Indian culture, religion implies a personal awareness of Ultimate Reality, not an intellectual theory about it. Under those circumstances, mythological symbolism can be as useful as logical, discursive forms of thought.

This retention of the close working connection between masculine thinking and feminine feeling and intuition reflected the important advice given in the *Bhagavad Gītā:* "Let him not that knoweth much awaken doubt in slower men of lesser wit."[22] Intellectual knowledge should be calibrated to the specific form and degree of intelligence of the individual. The need for this calibration, implying a working connection between anima and animus, feminine mythology and masculine rationalism, must have been in the minds of the Athenian authorities when they banished Anaxagoras in the middle of the fifth century B.C. for teaching that the sun was not the sun god Helios but a physical ball of fire. Socrates had to drink his cup of hemlock because he was accused of lack of faith in the tutelary deities of Athens. And yet, eventually their gods and mythologies collapsed. No such thing ever happened in India: the all-important feminine component of Indian culture would not allow it; the typically analytical, *dissociating*, critical faculty of the masculine mind was kept in check.

Thousands of miles to the north and east of India's Himalayan boundary, another great culture emerged at about the same time in what is now northeast China. The overthrow of the female-oriented Shang realm by the patriarchal Chou accomplished, perhaps less dramatically, a revolution similar to the destruction of the Harappā civilization by the Aryans. Long after this changeover, it was in China as it was, almost simultaneously, in Periclean Athens. According to tradition, Chuang Chou stated that there had been a time when men and women "knew their mothers but not their fathers." The ideogram for a man's family name was and still is formed from the radical for "woman."[23] In fact, the expression for wife means "equal."

As far as one can judge, the patriarchal revolution coincided with the establishment of the Chou feudal system, which began to devalue systematically the social and economic status of women. This degradation proceeded in conjunction with a remarkable cultural development that culminated with Confucius—by which time the power of the father or male head of a clan had become almost absolute. While families and clans owned their land and property in common, the male patriarch had complete authority. In those days, the Chinese paterfamilias could even sell his wife or children into servitude and had power of life and death over them; he ate his meals alone, confined females to separate quarters in his house; the women had only rare social contacts with men other than their relatives. Baby boys and girls were introduced quite differently into the world. According to an old book of legendary songs of the first millennium B.C., the *Shih King*,

> Then a boy is born,
> Put to lie on a bed,
> Robed in a gown

With jade tablets to finger.
And lusty he wails
But one day in red knee-caps shall he walk
Lord or prince, sprung from this house!

Then a girl shall be born,
Put to lie on the floor,
Robed in rags,
With a roof-tile to finger.
No bad thing shall she do,
Nor good thing either.
Enough if she can carry
Wine and plates of food
And give no trouble,
To her father and mother.[24]

No wonder that social and political life was, as in Periclean Athens, almost completely and exclusively male.

Chinese women were honored and respected as mothers and mothers-in-law, rather than as wives. However, the fact is that wherever and whenever family ties are as strong as they were in China, woman's role remains primordial, whatever her apparent subordination. The critical point here is that it was not so much the husband as the *mother-in-law* who had power and authority over the wife. Most of the time, the husband was in no position to protect his wife against his own mother. It was woman against woman rather than a conflict between the sexes, a conflict of generations *within* the same sex—invariably settled in favor of the older one. Behind a patriarchal façade, partly aimed at assuaging male vanity, a real matriarchy was in operation for the benefit of the older generation of women. As in India, and elsewhere in Asia where the concept of "society" in the abstract was extremely vague, as vague in fact as the feeling of "nationalism." Families and clans were entrusted with many tasks and duties that nowadays belong to our modern *social* organization. In China, especially, family discipline and solidarity was all-important; the clan was at one and the same time school, nursery, workshop, government, and police; hence, the vital role played by the relationships within the confines of the clan.

Since there never was any question of competition between male and female—their respective spheres of activity were sharply separated according to tradition—cooperation was the watchword. There was little friction between the sexes, all the friction being reserved for the often abrasive relationship between daughter-in-law and mother-in-law—not unintentionally, the Chinese ideogram for "peace" stands for *one* woman under a roof.[25] Only when women attempted to leave their biologically appointed sphere, only when the "hen crows," as the saying went, did trouble arise between men and women. It was a byword in China that marital happiness, or the lack of it, was largely in woman's hands. The Book of Transformations, the *I Ching*, states categorically that "the happiness of the clan depends on the integrity of woman."[26]

The extraordinary vitality and durability of the Chinese social structure resulted from the immense power of absorption of the Chinese family system which, in due course, swallowed all invaders. While the Chinese patriarch took care of the political and social aspect of government, effective power in this remarkable family structure was mostly in the hands of the older women. In contrast, in the western part of the Roman Empire where the family structure had been shattered, nothing similar could possibly happen; the barbarians were never *biologically* Romanized and were never socially absorbed during the life span of the empire; they remained a separate, alien entity and, eventually, merged with the Latin populations. But only *after* the collapse of the empire, which they helped to bring about.

In the long run, the success of the female principle in China lay in the downgrading of the individual, whether male or female, and the exaltation of the clan and its ancestors. As individuals, he and she were nothing; as members of the clan, they were everything. They were but small units in the flowing stream of Life, looking back and worshiping ancestors, looking forward and generating a posterity that would, in turn, worship them as ancestors. Family solidarity was total: everyone was responsible for everyone else. A collapse of family life such as occurred in Rome never took place in China, and would have been inconceivable. Legislation and the state became all-powerful in the Roman Empire. In China, they remained weak at all times (except during the brief period of the Legalists, and then during the short-lived socialistic experiments); the individual remained completely subordinate to his kinship group, which in turn enjoyed far greater freedom from state-imposed laws in China than in the West.

Woman's social status is invariably enhanced by social and political conservatism. In India as in China, woman's role was debased during the great periods of cultural creativity coinciding with sociopolitical revolutions during the first millennium B.C. Thereafter, more or less petrified in fully crystallized social frameworks (India's rigid caste system, China's clan structure), the feminine ethos began to prevail at the expense of the free, creative, wide-roaming, revolutionary male spirit. Unlike Westerners, the Chinese were not possessed by a Promethean urge to master nature, to conquer and dominate the world. The Chinese were determined to *adapt* to nature, femalelike, not to regulate it. Somehow, Mother Earth retained her hold on the Chinese mind. There were vague masculine attempts during the creative Spring and Autumn era (eighth to fifth centuries B.C.) at overpowering nature, when some Chinese wondered aloud why this Promethean spirit was lacking. The agnostic and rationalist Hsün-tzu asked pointedly:

You glorify nature and meditate on her;
Why not domesticate her and regulate her?
You obey nature and sing her praise,
Why not control her course and use it?[27]

But it was too late. The feminine ethos triumphed in the end, and with it, the Tao. True enough, the official doctrine of the state, the fundamental philosophy of the mandarins, was Confucianism, a stern patriarchal code of ethics; but its very conservatism, its stifling of all individual initiative and free-willing activity, reduced the masculine spirit to complete sterility in the end. Its puritanical outlook, outwardly virile, in fact emasculated the true masculine impulse; whereas its rival philosophy, Taoism, preserved the feminine outlook and inspired most of the cultural output of China, in conjunction, later on, with imported Buddhism. One look at Chinese traditional architecture is enough: while Western architecture is *dynamic* and full of tension, Chinese architecture is essentially *rhythmic*. As Lin Yutang puts it, the spirit of Chinese architecture does not, "like the Gothic spires, aspire to heaven but broods over the earth and is contented with its lot. While Gothic cathedrals suggest the spirit of sublimity, Chinese temples and palaces suggest the spirit of serenity."[28]

At the highest metaphysical level, the Chinese placed a mysterious entity, the Tao—the "Way," etymologically a road, and therefore a process. The basic, elementary entities in the process are emblematic concepts, *yin* and *yang*, and their interplay. In the famous work *Tao Te Ching*—"The Book *(ching)* of the Power *(tê)* of the Way *(tao)*"—the process is defined as follows:

The Tao that can be discussed is not the enduring, eternal Tao;
The name that can be named is not the enduring, eternal name.
From the unnamed sprang heaven and earth;
The named is the Mother of the ten thousand things.[29]

The diagrammatic symbol of the Tao displays geometrically the cooperative interplay between *yin*, the dark, passive, feminine, humid, malignant, and negative; and *yang*, the light, masculine, active, dry, beneficent, warm, and positive. The two principles, *yin* feminine and conceiving, *yang* masculine and creative, represented by a circumference equally divided into two parts by a curved line winding up a diameter, are present in all things and their interplay symbolizes the overall cosmic rhythm. They cannot be judged as morally either good or bad; they simply *are* in all things, in different alternating proportions. In men, the *yang* predominates, and in women, the *yin;* yet they are present in both—an indirect affirmation of the basic androgynous nature of all living beings.

The universe of the ten thousand things is the result of the *cooperative*, not competitive, interplay of the two principles. No real predominance is ascribed to either one; the overall concept is much closer to the Indian, where the original androgynous self splits in two, than to the biblical account: *yin* is created simultaneously with *yang*, unlike Eve who comes *later* than Adam and is merely one of his ribs. Furthermore, and as in India, the Tao is *immanent* as well as transcendant; it permeates all things and all beings.

In the *I Ching*, The Book of Changes, an oracular work made up of trigrams, the masculine *yang* is represented by an unbroken line associated with the heavenly (active, light, dry, and warm), and the feminine *yin* a broken line associated with the earthy (humid, dark, cold and passive), combined in various ways:

 ☰ is Ch'ien, the Creative, strong, implying heaven and
    the father.
 ☷ is K'un, the Receptive, devoted and yielding earth, also
    the mother . . . and so on.[30]

This dialectical interplay also symbolizes the alternating seasons: the *yin* prevails during the wintry cold, the *yang* in the warm summer; both principles meet during the vernal and autumnal equinoxes, when each one takes over the other's former predominance. Both are symbolized by a door—open door for *yang*, symbolizing agricultural production, strength, open-air life, and summer warmth; closed door for *yin*, symbolizing the winter's frost and indoor living when feminine work at home takes precedence. Both sexes were under an antithetical discipline—females indoors *(nei)*, males outdoors *(wai)*, the respective realms of *yin* and *yang*. All the great festivals had a sexual connotation as when, during the equinoxes, all-male and all-female groups met in hollows or valleys, separated from each other by a ritual axis (usually a river or brook), challenging each other in verses, music, and dancing —the males on the sunny side, the females on the dark side: "The *yang* calls, the *yin* answers—the boys call, the girls answer," was the general theme of these hierogrammatic celebrations, expressing the sacred harmony *(ho)* resulting from the interplay *(tiao ho)* of the two sexual principles and the fundamental cosmic unity reached by their union in an ultimate coincidence of opposites—an essentially "organismic" world-outlook.[31] The rhythm of nature and the rhythm of human society were in tune with each other.

As in India, it is the quality of immanence that gives the overall Tao its feminine quality. *Tê* implies "power," more specifically *latent* power, like that of a coiled spring: the power of the Way and order of the universe; and the *Tao Te Ching* now describes the eternal feminine, Chinese style:

> The Valley Spirit never dies.
> It is named the Mysterious Feminine
> And the Doorway of the Myterious Feminine
> Is the root [from which] Heaven and Earth [sprang].[32]

The sexual symbolism of the male convexity and female concavity has endlessly fascinated poets, East and West. In both the *Lao-tzu* book and in *Chuang-tzu*, we find the following verse:

> He who knows the male, yet cleaves to what is female
> Becomes like a ravine, receiving all things under heaven
> [Thence] the eternal virtue never leaks away.
> This is returning to the state of Infancy.[33]

As in India's Tantric cults, and very much unlike the Confucianist tradition to which this was repugnant, Chinese Taoism attributes to the female principle first place in the cosmic hierarchy; Taoist mysticism is rooted in this feminine apprehension of hidden reality. Unlike India, however, where the cultural ethos accepts the laws of nature with quiet resignation and longs to get out of the coils of nature and life altogether, in China there is an optimistic, joyful, and often lyrical acceptance of nature which is delicately expressed in Taoist literature. Nature's right to create and destroy is fully accepted by the Chinese, along with a determination to cooperate with its holy rhythm.

The Indian and Chinese attitudes toward sex—partly a result of their contrasting climates—must be confronted. While *yin* and *yang* appear to be the natural counterparts of the Indian *yoni* and *lingam*, the Chinese symbols are more truly emblematic and ethereal than the grossly suggestive Indian ones. The Chinese make full use of the sexual duality but sublimate it with the help of geometrical patterns. Contrasted one with the other, their respective cultures show the Indians to be always swinging widely between extremes—utter voluptuousness or utter asceticism; the Chinese are masters of a humanistic golden mean, practical, commonsensical, and humorous, but rarely given to exaggeration. What the two have in common, however, as against the West, is full acceptance of both sexual principles as essentially equal although different, and an emphasis on their cooperation in a dialectical interplay in which both principles are equally indispensable.

The Chinese compromise was the result of the Taoist revival of the feminine-oriented ideal, resting on the dim foundation of the pre-Chou matrilineal society when the yin principle had the upper hand[34] —as a counterbalancing force to the strongly masculine Confucian doctrine. As Joseph Needham points out:

> The Confucian and Legalist social-ethical thought-complex was masculine, managing, hard, dominating, aggressive, rational and donative—the Taoists broke with it radically and completely by emphasizing all that was feminine, tolerant, yielding, permissive, withdrawing, mystical and receptive.[35]

In praising the "Valley Spirit," the Taoists ran counter to the masculine Confucian ethos which states in the classic Lun Yü: "The superior man hates to dwell in a low-lying situation, where all the evil of the world will flow down upon him."[36] It was this dialectical interplay between the two philosophies and attitudes to life that created the vital tension in Chinese culture between the masculine and feminine components:

> The recognition of the importance of woman in the scheme of things, the acceptance of equality of women with men, the conviction that the attainment of health and longevity needed the cooperation of the sexes, the considered admiration for certain feminine psychological characteristics, the incorporation of the physical phenomena of sex in numinous group catharsis, free alike from asceticism and class distinctions, reveal to us once more aspects of Taoism which had no counterpart in Confucianism or ordinary Buddhism.[37]

The parallel between female-oriented Taoism in China and Tantrism in India is unmistakable; the link between the two is Buddhist Tantrism which seeped into China in the early centuries A.D. and revivified Taoism, with which it had so much in common—notably a profound interest in the metaphysical significance of sex. Full sexual congress was the quintessence of Tantrism—an orgiastic form of Dionysiac mysticism that is the opposite of the sex-shy traditional mysticism. Tantric metaphysics established that śūnyatā, the freezing emptiness of the void, was a male attribute, whereas karuṇā, "compassion," was female— attributes that had to be brought together through sexual copulation if *advaya,* "unity," was to be achieved.[38] Quite naturally, both Tantrism and Taoism eagerly sought female devotees.

The whole Taoist philosophic outlook is permeated with the fundamental notion that nothing can be achieved without giving woman and the female principle their due. The basic aim (male-oriented, after all) is to use sexual stimulus to accumulate as much life-giving *ching* (sperm) as possible, but without losing it. The *yang* force in man has to be continually strengthened with the adjunction of female *yin;* full control has to be exerted over the emission that results, but Taoism never advocated full continence, which generated neurosis and was absolutely contrary to nature's cosmic rhythm. What was advocated was as great a prolongation of the male act as possible in order to nourish the *yang* with as much *yin* as possible; as for the female orgasm *(khuai),* it was beneficial inasmuch as it strengthened man's vital powers by requiring this prolongation of coitus.[39]

Obviously, while all this was devised by man for man, it also gave the feminine element its due recognition, whose full satisfaction was absolutely indispensable for man's own welfare.

Indian and Chinese cultures, each in its own way, emphasized the basic metaphysical equality between the sexes, but they never granted women the same equality in social and political life; nor is there any evidence that women demanded it. Neither in India nor China is there any trace of a full-fledged revolt of women such as took place in the Greco-Roman as well as the modern Western world. Both Eastern cultures accepted as a fundamental premise that two such different entities could function only through cooperation: in both civilizations, there never was a real striving for *competition* between the sexes. It is within this framework that one must approach the historical changes that took place in the respective status of women in India and China.

As in early Homeric Greece, women in early Vedic India appear to have enjoyed far greater freedom and influence than later on, although even in the early times they were never allowed to attend the tribal councils or state assemblies *(Sabhā).* Women could still choose their mates *(svayamvara),* appeared with men at religious celebrations and festivities, and were allowed to educate themselves. However, while polygyny was tolerated, polyandry was strictly forbidden: according to the *Aitareya Brahmana,* "one man may have more than one wife, but one woman has never more than one husband."[40] Woman's complementary role was constantly emphasized: "As the shadow to the substance, to her lord the faithful wife; and she parts not from her consort till she parts with fleeting life."[41] But in those days there was no purdah, no seclusion; and as a widow, woman was free to remarry. In race-conscious India, the mother was considered far more important for the preservation of caste purity than the father. The *Vashishtha Smriti* put it this way: "The Āchārya is ten times more honorable than an Upādhyāya; the father a hundred times more than the Āchārya, and the mother a thousand times more than the father," recalling the same genealogical-biological premium put on the mother by patriarchal Jews.[42]

As time passed, things changed and woman's status began to shrink. Freedom was increasingly curtailed; woman was enjoined to refrain from education—"For a woman to study the Vedas indicates confusion in the realm," states the *Mahabharata*[43]—and widows were discouraged from remarriage. *Suttee*, the self-immolation of widows on their deceased husbands' funeral pyres, also began in post-Vedic times. These alterations parallel those that took place in Greece between post-Homeric times and Periclean Athens. Under the influence of the austere Jain and early Buddhist movements, an antifeminist trend betrayed itself in India. Manu's great legal code set the tone: "The source of dishonor is woman; the source of strife is woman; the source of earthly existence is woman; therefore avoid woman." The conclusion is metaphysically logical, if the premise is accepted that *all* creation of new life is itself a Fall and that the goal of life is to put an end, once and for all, to the cycle of reincarnations—to life itself, in fact. Furthermore, echoing Cato the Elder in Rome, the Code of Manu displays the perennial fear that man entertains of woman's uncanny wiles: "A female is able to draw from the right path in this life not a fool only but even a sage, and can lead him in subjection to desire or to wrath."[44] But, as happened so often throughout history, there seems to have been a wide gulf between woman's legal subjection according to the formal codes of law and her real position and influence according to contemporary Greek eyewitnesses in Hellenistic days—position and influence of considerable weight in politics and economics, art, and literature.[45]

There was no doubt, however, that the increasingly ascetic, even life-denying, ideal of non-Tantric Hinduism was largely responsible for a certain downgrading of the female principle, and of woman's social status with it, and to the limited extent that the ascetic ideal of the *sannyāsa* kept on prevailing in India, this downgrading remained a permanent feature of Indian civilization. A life-denying outlook will never be kind to the female sex, viewed mostly as the source of all the temptations that keep the soul entrapped in the snares of flesh and matter.

According to Hemacandra, woman was "the torch lighting the way to hell."[46] But those enlightened Indians who reacted against the excesses of the ascetic disposition always made an attempt to rehabilitate the life-creating second sex; in the sixth century A.D. Vārahamihara pointed out that the righteous pursuit of *dharma* depends on woman and that she is essential to human progress. Reacting against Buddhist and Jain-inspired celibacy, Dirghata stated that, in the future, no woman should remain unmarried.[47] But while the idea of womanhood was increasingly respected, and even exalted by poets such as Kālidāsa, Bāṇa, and Bhavabhūti, woman's social freedom was increasingly curtailed—proof, if any is needed, that there may be a complete divorce between social conditions and the overall idealization of womanhood.

In spite of the patriarchal organization of Hindu society (except in some areas of Malabar where matrilinear structures persisted into the twentieth century), women were treated at all times with utmost consideration. Foreign observers, from the Greek Megasthenes several centuries before Christ to the Muslim scholar al-Bīrūnī some fifteen hundred years later, testify to the good treatment wives received at the hands of their husbands, to their often excellent education and their close contact with literature and the arts, especially during the Gupta era.[48] The completely natural attitude of Indians toward sex, and the care with which experts on the subject (for example, Vātsyāyana, presumed author of the *Kāmasūtra*) emphasized the husband's obligations toward his wife, prove conclusively that woman was not treated as a mere object for man's enjoyment but had as much right as he had to share in this enjoyment. She may have been debarred from knowledge of the Vedas, but not from enjoying the pleasures of life. If customs such as the ban on the remarriage of widows became firmly established, it was partly in the name of the ascetic ideal which, deep down, remained the higher aspiration of Hinduism—for men as well as for women. Social pressure compelled women who, through ill luck, found themselves deprived of their helpmate to spend the rest of their lives without replacing him, but woman's position as mother in the joint-family system was secure and honored, and her enforced asceticism was by no means humiliating—she was simply compelled to conform to the highest ideal of the civilization into which she was born.

The result is that sexual morality was higher in Indian civilization than in any other: prostitution, except for a few *devadasis,* was rare; heterosexuality was the rule, and homosexuality as rare as prostitution. By spiritualizing and sacralizing sex, Hinduism removed all traces of that sense of sinfulness that was to plague Western culture. The Hindu woman in public places was never molested or insulted; at the price of severe curtailment of her freedom (not much greater than the curtailment of *his* freedom) she was entitled to a remarkable degree of consideration, and the protection of custom, which was far more effective than that of any legislation. A Western traveler in the late eighteenth century, the Abbé Dubois—who, in other respects, had nothing favorable to report on northern Indian women's treatment after centuries of Islamic rule—stated:

> A Hindu woman can go anywhere alone, even in the most crowded places, and she need never fear the impertinent looks and jokes of idle loungers. This appears to me really remarkable.
> . . . A house inhabited solely by women is a sanctuary which the most shameless libertine would not dream of violating. . . . I have often spent the night in one of the common rest-houses, where the men and women lodging there were lying all huddled together anyhow and almost side by side; but I have never known or heard of any one disturbing the tranquillity of the night by an indecent act or word.[49]

In other respects, the degradation of woman's social position in India was largely the result of the Islamic invasions. For centuries, northern and central India lay under Turco-Afghan and Moghul rule; the severely antifeminist attitude of Muslims could not but influence the social life of the subjugated Hindus. The contrast between the fate of woman in Muslim-dominated northern India and in the south where there was no Muslim occupation was striking. Compared with the Muslim sultanates of the Deccan, the social status and influence of woman in the southern Hindu empire of Vijayanagar was considerable: "Women in general occupied a high position in society, and instances of the active part they took in the political, social and literary life of the country are not rare."[50] Women were often historians, accountants, judges, bailiffs, and even guards in the palace—which would have been unthinkable under Muslim rule. Indeed, with Islam came purdah and many restrictions that had been unknown in pre-Islamic days, and often, for the sake of the protection of the women themselves, Hindu society embraced these restrictions wholeheartedly.

Chinese culture, in full contrast with its Indian counterpart, was essentially life-affirming, humanistic, and areligious. Shunning all extremes, the Chinese sought to live well without bothering overmuch about the hereafter or about spiritual problems in general. Woman was no longer a fellow pilgrim journeying through a vale of tears, as in the humorless Indian cultural framework, but a boon companion in the enjoyment of life—a companion, but a definitely subordinate one. Lin Yutang claims that "the respect for women, a certain tenderness toward the female sex, which was characteristic of the Teutonic races already in their barbaric days, was absent in the early pages of Chinese history."[51] This is a matter of attitude, of psychological disposition which does not necessarily affect the social position of either sex. As a matter of fact, traces of the early matrilinear structure of Shang times survived right through the Chou feudalism, into the Spring and Autumn era; in those days, the family name *(hsing)* was still the woman's name, whereas man had merely a personal name *(shih)* along with his place of birth or official position. As late as the days of Confucius, woman's sexual life appears to have been quite free, including the freedom to choose her mate (as among the southern aborigenes of Kwangsi); divorces were frequent; and widows remarried.

The Confucian *Book of Rights* soon changed all that and led straight to woman's seclusion. A great deal of this doctrine was rooted in the Master's view of women as completely irrational, or rather, unreasonable creatures, largely incomprehensible to men.[52] Confucian philosophy was based on a hierarchical view of society, on the strict observance of authority and obedience within the state as within the family. Strong emphasis on the difference between the sexes was one cornerstone of this hierarchical outlook, and if this emphasis confined woman mostly to home and hearth, it also strongly emphasized, in conformity with the *yin-yang* concept, that this difference was a matter of *complementarity* between two sexual principles rather than fundamental subordination. As in every other field of endeavor, so it was with the relationship between man and woman: the Chinese always put the accent on *cooperation* between polar opposites, not competition between antagonistic elements. Just as they cooperated with nature rather than subduing it in Western fashion, they established cooperation between the sexes, based on a nature-imposed division of labor. If woman wanted power and influence, she had to obtain it *through*, not against, man. That was the *natural* way. As Lin Yutang put it, "women who could rule their husbands knew that dependence on this sexual arrangement was their best and most effective weapon for power, and women who could not were too dull to raise feminist problems."[53]

To state that the clan spirit was strong in China understates the case; in point of fact, the importance of the "sib" can never be overestimated—the sib being, in contrast to the family which is a bilateral group, a *unilateral* one, tracing kinship through either the male or the female parent at the exclusion of the other. Unlike many sibs in different parts of the world, the Chinese one was uncompromisingly patriarchal, made even worse by the fact that while the normal family is a loose organization, the sib is a rigid and permanent structure. As Max Weber pointed out, the sib had completely disappeared in the medieval West, but was completely preserved in China "in the administration of the smallest political units as well as in the operation of economic associations. Moreover, the sib developed to an extent unknown elsewhere—even in India."[54] Village life was entirely ruled by the predominant sib, whose members were bound together by a common ancestor worship. Within the typical sib, all married men were entitled to vote; unmarried ones had no franchise but could be heard in council. As for women, they were excluded altogether, and although they had dowry rights, they were not entitled to inheritance.[55] Male elders collected revenues and distributed both the sib-owned land and the income. At the elementary social level—the self-governing village rather than the walled city in which the imperial mandarin exerted his unlimited authority—women were entirely deprived of authority and power.

The remarkable strength and durability of the clannish sib in China dates from the collapse of feudalism during the Spring and Autumn era and the social reorganization of the newly unified Chinese Empire (third century B.C.) into a bureaucratic state which delegated most of its local authority to patriarchal clans based on bloodlines. The Confucianist view of woman's role came to prevail completely during the Han dynasty (200 B.C.–A.D. 200). Feminine virtues were carefully catalogued by Liu Hsiang, and Pan Ch'ao, a woman writer and author of a *Woman's Guide,* conforming to the numerical mania of the Chinese that still endures in twentieth-century Red China, listed the "three obediences and four virtues" of women, according to the new patriarchal canon.[56] Even at that late stage, widows retained the right to remarry; this was eventually taken away from them and under the Sung dynasty, remarriage became a moral crime.

The steady degradation of her position was obviously not welcome to the Chinese woman who, furthermore, found no emotional appeal in the severely ethical strictures of Master K'ung; they wholeheartedly embraced a new Buddhism imported from India when Chinese society partly broke down with the passing away of the Han dynasty and the subsequent "time of troubles." While Buddhism in India had originally expressed a certain ascetic distaste for the female sex, it appeared in China in its Mahāyāna aspect as a highly emotional creed that merged, more or less, with the remains of Taoism and appealed to women rather than men, who looked upon the imported religion with a jaundiced eye. In spite of male persecutions, Buddhism held its own for centuries. In China as elsewhere, emphasis on ethics always betrays the masculine influence; while masculine Confucianism emphasized ethics, feminine Taoism and Buddhism stressed emotionalism and magic. As Max Weber explained:

> It was almost always through the eunuchs and the harem, the traditional enemies of the literati, that the Taoist sorcerers found their way to the palace. . . . Always the proud, masculine, rational, and sober spirit of Confucianism, similar to the mentality of the Romans, struggled against interference in the guidance of the state when such interference was based upon the hysterical excitation of women given to superstition and miracles.[57]

In conjunction with Taoism, Buddhism began to make the seclusion of women more bearable; they filled the temples of a new and colorful religion in which feminine feeling, repressed under stern Confucianist rule, could express itself. The striking ceremonies with bells and gongs, glitter and pomp, the exciting pilgrimages, the intricate mythology surrounding the Mahāyāna cult, the message of hope and consolation—all these appealed to Chinese women as the new Oriental religions and mystery cults appealed, at the same time, to their sisters in the Roman Empire.

The pendulum swung back again. As time passed, Buddhism lost most of its influence and the Neo-Confucianist restoration set in. The ideal of chaste widowhood became prevalent:

> Worship of chastity . . . became something of an obsession and women were henceforth to be responsible for social morals from which the men were exempted. More than that, women were to be responsible for courage and strength of character also, which curiously the men so admired in the gentle sex, for the emphasis had shifted from women's ordinary routine domestic virtues to female heroism and self-sacrifice. . . . A woman who distinguished herself by committing suicide to guard her chastity had a fair chance of leaving her name in literature in one form or another.[58]

Along with this, however, during the Wei and Ch'in dynasties, both concubinage and the drowning of baby girls increased—one the result of a considerable shift and concentration of wealth in few hands, the other the consequence of the poverty of those who could not afford the extremely expensive wedding ceremonies required to marry off daughters.

These distortions were, by and large, mere pimples on the face of Chinese society; the norm was that Chinese women ruled in the home. And although Chinese social life was almost exclusively masculine—with a generous sprinkling of courtesans—women found ways and means of making their influence felt as mothers, if not as wives: "The more one knows Chinese life, the more one realizes that the so-called suppression of women is an Occidental criticism that somehow is not born out by a closer knowledge of Chinese life."[59] In the famous novel *Red Chamber Dream*, older women are shown to be the real rulers. Marco Polo is an interesting witness to the considerate treatment afforded Chinese women, along with the social framework in which they were ensconced. Referring to the inhabitants of the great city of Kin-sai (modern Hangchow), former capital of the Sung dynasty, he states:

> They are friendly towards each other, and persons who inhabit the same street, both men and women, from the mere circumstance of neighborhood, appear like one family. In their domestic manners they are free from jealousy or suspicion of their wives, to whom great respect is shown, and any man would be accounted infamous who should presume to use indecent expressions to a married woman.[60]

In fact, if Chinese women had any real complaints, it was early in their married life when they were subjected to the whimsical tyranny of their mothers-in-law. Chinese family and social life was geared to absolute reverence for old age, regardless of sex. The real tyranny in China, if such there was, was not that of one sex over another as that exercised by the old against the young—which was closely linked with the tight clannish solidarity, mutual responsibility, and ancestor worship. As the traditional saying went, a man never married a "wife but a daughter-in-law"; when a son was born, the idiomatic expression was "a grandson is born." The daughter-in-law's obligations were toward her in-laws rather than her husband, and if she needed a consoling thought, she had one ready at hand: she, too, would one day become an all-powerful mother-in-law—if she produced sons.

On another level, Chinese art gives us interesting clues to a peculiar appreciation of woman's plastic form; unlike his Western counterpart, the typical Chinese artist depicts the feminine body as he would any other aspect of Mother Nature:

> The whole rhythm of a woman's form is modelled after the graceful rhythm of the weeping willows, which accounts for her intentionally drooping shoulders. . . . For woman's body, as body, the Chinese have no appreciation. . . . Chinese artists fail dismally in the portrayal of the human form, and even an artist like Ch'iu Shihchou [Ming period], famous for his paintings of female life, shows the upper part of the female nude form very much like a potato.[61]

In fact, human forms, male or female, had no appeal for the traditional Chinese artist. In his eyes, the human species did not stand out and apart from nature, as in the West, but was an emanation of it, part and parcel of everything that lived and evolved, was born and died.

What the Chinese admired and revered was a womanly woman, not a girlish, female, or feminine one. Chinese girls' upbringing was far more severe than that of boys; as a result, Chinese women always gave an impression of greater maturity and even strength of character than the weaker-willed men. In spite of all the Confucian customs and taboos, seclusion and feet binding—perhaps, partly because of them —Chinese women often developed steely personalities and ruled de facto with an iron rod. In this connection, the formidable personality of the last Empress Dowager Tzü Hsi, who was still ruling when Mao Tse-tung was born, comes to mind.

More, perhaps, than any other country, China, the longest-lived cultural entity in the world, was kept going and held together by its women rather than its men; and it is largely in their inferior social status and harder upbringing that Chinese women found the well-spring of their extraordinary forbearance. It is also in the peculiar Chinese lack of notion of "society" in the abstract—an essentially masculine creation—that Chinese woman's real power lay: the Chinese mind went straight from the family and clan *(chia)* as the elementary cell to the state *(kuo);* the basic notion was that "when the family is orderly, then the state is peaceful." The concept of society, *kuochia,* was only a derivative. In this atmosphere, where kinship ties were all-important, the Chinese woman, like her Indian counterpart in her caste system, could not fail to make her considerable influence felt; and even though she was excluded from whatever social power and influence there was, she hardly cared. The life of the family was of overwhelming import.

CHAPTER
8

Islam

The cultural trend in the Middle East at the beginning of the Christian era had nothing in common with that which prevailed in India and China. Indeed, it went in the opposite direction, displaying an increasing affirmation of the absolute prevalence of the male principle. And as one of the main components of the great patriarchal revolution that had broken out at the end of the Bronze Age, the Bible's Old Testament had an immense influence, not only on the formation of Judaism, but also on that of Christianity and eventually Islam.

The uncompromising patriarchalism of Judaism began by strengthening the natural patriarchal tendencies of other Semitic populations. The Semitic Middle East was hardly touched by the Greco-Roman feminist movement, nor was it much influenced by the rising status of women in the emerging Byzantine realm. Indeed, the trend was toward eradicating the feminine element from the Divine and exterminating female influence in social life. Within Christianity itself, as pointed out previously, this was unmistakable: the Monophysites emphasized the utter transcendentalism of the Godhead at the expense of the Incarnation.

No wonder that the great Arab conquests were considerably eased by the enthusiastic Monophysitism of most Syrians and Egyptians— Damascus surrendered through treachery, and in many Syrian cities, the enthusiastic populations greeted the Muslim conquerors as saviors with dancing and music, bowing low to the almighty conqueror abu-'Ubaydah.[1] It was Cyrus, bishop of Alexandria, who virtually delivered Egypt to the Arabs and instructed the Monophysites to offer no resistance. The work had already been cut out for Islam before the Prophet was even born.

When Muḥammad, son of 'Abdallah of Mecca, raised his standard in the seventh century, Arabia was in the throes of a profound malaise caused by a momentous shift in the social organization of the Arabs —the shift from a matrilinear to a patrilinear structure. The Arabian peninsula had remained a backwater, remote from the great centers of civilization to the north, east and west, and had retained sturdy matrilinear features that had disappeared in surrounding lands.

But the patriarchal revolution finally caught up with Arabia. The growth of individualism from the middle of the sixth century onward prepared the ground for the advent of Islam by weakening communal ties and promoting trade on a vastly increased scale between cities such as Mecca and the wealthy Syrian north. The Islamic movement was going to be to the Middle East what Calvinism and the Puritan Reformation were later to be to Europe: the antifeudal creed of dynamic merchants and business entrepreneurs, an essentially middle-class bourgeois religion dedicated to the proposition that good business and profits were signs of spiritual worthiness. The Qur'ān is full of praise for the "honest" merchant and his closeness to Allah's throne —and honest mercantilism and banking were precisely the activities of the Prophet's tribe, the Quraysh of Mecca.[2]

Here, therefore, is not only a change in social and economic structures but also a change in the *Zeitgeist*, calling for new spiritual values. Emerging individualism detached men, in a psychological sense, from the collective tribal existence based on female kinship, prompting them to wonder about human destiny, the meaning of life and death. The correlation between the change in the psychological temper and the alteration of the economic and social climate is quite clear.

There is plenty of evidence of the widespread matrilinear features in pre-Islamic Arabia that were beginning to weaken perceptibly in the sixth century. Marriage was usually uxorilocal, and Kitāb al-Aghānī states:

> . . . the women in the Jāhilīyah, or some of them, had the right to dismiss their husbands, and the form of dismissal was this. If they lived in a tent, they turned it round, so that if the door had faced east it now faced west, and when the man saw this he knew that he was dismissed and did not enter.[3]

Obviously, the tent belonged to her family or tribe, and his more-or-less brief sojourn in it depended on her goodwill. It even happened in this matrilocal system that women had several such visiting husbands concurrently.[4]

In the Prophet's days, Medinan society, unlike Meccan, was still largely matrilinear and the pride of its women, summed up in the expression *ghayr,* was legendary and hardly compatible with the new patriarchal *hubris* of the Arab males. Allegedly, Muḥammad would not marry a woman of the Anṣār clan because of that group's haughty *ghayr* and their impatience with polygyny. His successor, Caliph 'Umar, complained:

> . . . we of Quraysh used to dominate [our] women; but when we came among the Anṣār, they proved to be a people whose women dominated them; and our women began to copy the habits of the women of the Anṣār.[5]

And yet, in such matrilinear structures, the women could not own property since it belonged collectively to the tribe and was firmly under the control of uncles and brothers; they had greater prestige and dignity, but no real power. Now, as rising individualism broke up matrilinear tribal collectivism, they emancipated themselves, and the more enterprising among them escaped from the suffocating constraints of tribal collectivism. This new state of affairs produced wealthy women such as Khadījah, Muḥammad's future wife, and Asmā' bint Mukharribah. They enjoyed considerable private wealth and traded in their own name. The importance of this era of transition lies in the fact that it was the crucible in which the Prophet elaborated most of the main themes of Islam.

Although Muḥammad himself was a Meccan and belonged to a patrilinear clan, his example illustrates the fact that his society was still shifting from a matrilinear and matrilocal structure; his mother remained with her family and his father 'Abdallāh had to be content with visiting her from time to time, the typical uxorilocal marriage. Muḥammad himself lived with his mother until she died, and only then did he go to the house of 'Abd al-Muṭṭalib, his paternal grandfather.[6] Whenever his patriarchally minded opponents wanted to insult him— or occasionally when a man from a matrilinear clan addressed him— they called him "Ibn Abī Kabshah" ("Kabshah" being a common feminine name in Medina), reminding him of some presumed matrilinear ascendancy within his family.

Such traces of matrilinear structure disappeared almost completely within a century of the Prophet's death. Men who were known as descendants and sons of females became known as descendants and sons of males. Families soon consisted exclusively of all relatives in the male line; whatever communal property was left shifted to the patri-clan, and individual property was inherited by sons or brothers; females were now restricted to having one husband at a time, whereas males began to enjoy polygyny.

This profound alteration in the social organization of the peninsular Arabs was considerably accelerated by the reforms introduced by Muhammad, as embodied in the Qur'ān. For instance, as long as the matrilinear system endured, children belonged to the woman's family, which implied that paternity in the biological sense was relatively unimportant. As soon, however, as the man became interested in his own children, the physical paternity became all-important and had to be securely established—hence the custom of *'iddah* (or *tarabbus*), that is, the waiting period after a woman has been divorced or widowed before she could remarry in order to ascertain whether she had become pregnant by the previous husband.[7]

In pre-Islamic Arabia, it was highly unusual for a man to have more than one wife in his house; and it is quite certain that polygyny (virilocal) was introduced by Muhammad himself, and that a plurality of wives was actually encouraged by the Prophet within this overall shift toward patriarchalism. What appears to have precipitated this move is that the famous battle of Uhud had left a great many Muslim widows who had to be cared for, along with their children; the link between the proper conduct toward orphans *(yatāmā)* and the encouragement toward polygyny is well established in the Qur'ān. In this fashion the Prophet provided a counterweight to the excesses of selfish individualism and provided honorable marriages for surplus women; in short, polygyny was a rudimentary form of social security for widowed women and orphaned children. It is also evident that Muhammad's plans for Islamic expansion required increased manpower, and that polygyny, in these circumstances, was bound to result in a higher birthrate among his followers. In all likelihood, the Prophet did not foresee that this would ultimately result in the degradation of the status of married women in Islamic society.

Muslim polygyny was firmly established by the following verse of the Qur'ān (4:3):

> If ye fear that ye may not act with equity in regard to the orphans, marry such of the women as seem good to you, two or three or four—but if ye fear that ye may not be fair [to several wives], then one [only]. . . .[8]

The high moral intention is plain and the "social security" aspect unmistakable. In Islamic law the expression *nikah,* usually translated "marriage," implies in fact "a contract for the legalization of intercourse and the procreation of children."[9] This new concept put an end to the looser forms of marriage prevalent in pre-Islamic Arabia, especially in matrilinear and matrilocal societies. Polyandry was now sternly forbidden by Muslim authorities, although some of the more impermanent forms of union had to be tolerated. This was the case for *mut'ah*, known in Islamic legislation as "temporary marriage," although it is actually closer to prostitution than marriage. The relationship is an ephemeral union arranged under contract for a fixed period, a union that comes automatically to an end within a given period without any divorce, but involves payment of a specific "dower" to the woman. Mut'ah was eventually abolished by Caliph 'Umar I, although it persisted among the heretical Shī'ahs.

As a general rule, Qur'ānic legislation tended to abolish all customs and practices according to which the individual was treated as member of a group rather than an independent individual; this to uproot as much as possible tribalism and clannishness as well as matrilinear survivals. Women as well as men benefited from this innovation. In early Islam a woman could not be given away in marriage without her consent and she, personally, rather than her family, received the "dower" paid by the bridegroom.

Muhammad's personal life illustrates strikingly the social position and economic standing of the women of Arabia in the seventh century. Khadījah bint Khuwaylid was a wealthy widow, twice married, who traded on her own account through a network of commercial agents. Muhammad came to her attention because of his praiseworthy moral character and was invited to act as her agent in convoying a caravan to Syria. Highly impressed by his personality, she offered to marry him —she was then forty and he roughly twenty-five. He accepted and found himself in business. There is evidence that she encouraged him unsparingly in his prophetic calling, nursed him tenderly through his epileptic fits, and was sorely missed after her death. The Prophet, however, promptly remarried, and to his next wife, Sawdah, he began adding others, each of whom he set up in a separate apartment within his compound in Medina. It was he who introduced the plural virilocal family system, along with many other new features aimed at protecting his rapidly growing number of wives. Since he was a public personage of considerable importance, his residence was constantly filled with people, and for their own safety, his wives began to wear the "veil" and enjoy a degree of seclusion.

Veiling (Arabic *hijāb*) was actually an exceedingly old custom, widespread throughout the Middle East where it originated in Assyrian times as a status symbol, the privilege of a free woman, wife or daughter of a free man; any servant girl or woman of lowly condition in those remote days could be denounced to the authorities, and punished, for improper use of this mark of social distinction.[10] Through the pre-Islamic ages, the veil continued in usage but was democratically extended to apply to all married women living in cities; this rule never applied to the same extent in the countryside or the desert.

Along with this increased use of the veil in Arabia came other regulations concerning the preservation of "modesty" for Muslim women—casting down their eyes in public, concealing their jewelry, and the like. The general insecurity early in the Islamic era extended these reforms far beyond the Prophet's original intentions as expressed in the Qur'ān and remained a more-or-less permanent fixture of Muslim life thereafter.

The Prophet's growing wealth and the unequal distribution of his favors provoked jealousy among his fast-multiplying wives. Soon enough, they were at each other's throat. At some point, Muhammad left all his wives for a month, threatening to divorce them. This crisis found its reflection in several celebrated verses in the Qur'ān—"O wives of the Prophet, whoever of you commits a manifest indecency, for her the punishment will be doubled twice over. . . ."[11] At any rate, the Messenger of God eventually returned to his harem and divorced a number of its inmates; the rest vowed blind obedience to Allah and His Messenger, and there was no further trouble.

In other respects, the Prophet's marriages followed an ancient Arab custom: they were largely utilitarian and served political ends. He married Sawdah in order to provide for the widow of a loyal follower, but also because he wanted to be on good terms with her former brother-in-law; he took on Zaynab bint Khuzaymah because her deceased husband belonged to the al-Muttalib tribe and she herself served to consolidate his relationship with her own tribe, the 'Āmir b.-Sa'sa'ah—and so on. It is easy to understand why the Prophet had no Medinan wife: their pride, derived from the matrilineal structure of their tribes, would have made life difficult for his other wives, and twice as difficult for him. In general, there was very little intermarriage between Meccans and Medinans.

All told, it is plain that the Messenger of God's major contributions to a social restructuring was squarely to face the fact of the breakdown of the old tribal system adapted to a nomadic way of life but not to the commercial and increasingly urbanized society of the times. In this new "bourgeois" mercantile climate he erected a novel social structure based on the fast-developing individualism of trading and banking communities. It was becoming, also, a strictly masculine society; the social pattern of the future was that of patrilinear Mecca rather than matrilinear Medina. The *umma Muhammadiya*, the great Muslim consensus that was presumed to replace tribal loyalty and solidarity, was uncompromisingly masculine.

The Prophet did not wish to exclude women from worship or social life altogether; after all, he had been put in business by his first wife,

Khadījah, and was not ungrateful. But the increasing patriarchalism of his Meccan followers was becoming too strong to resist. Meccan women had already been wearing the veil and been secluded for some time, and Muhammad's wish to have them share in the spiritual life of the Islamic community met with increasingly fierce resistance, both in Arabia and, later, in the eastern, Persianized part of the expanding realm of dār ul-Islām. Nevertheless, in setting up the new patriarchal structure as embodied in the Qur'ān, he used the individualistic trend of the times to improve women's position regarding inheritance and allowed them free use of their property. But, ultimately, there could be no mistaking the strong patriarchal tone of the new order set up by the Messenger of God and the relegating of women to a secondary position. States the Qur'ān (4:38):

> The men are overseers over the women by reason of what Allāh hath bestowed in bounty upon one more than another, and of the property which they have contributed [i.e., the marriage price]; upright women are therefore submissive, guarding what is hidden in return for Allāh's guarding [them]; those on whose part ye fear refractoriness, admonish, avoid in bed, and beat; if they then obey you, seek no [further] way against them. . . .[12]

Profound social changes such as were taking place in Arabia in the days of the Prophet had their counterpart in a shifting cultural and religious outlook. In spite of its undoubted originality, Islam owed a great deal to Judeo-Christian influence, perhaps more to Jewish than Christian tradition. While apparently no Jews were in Mecca at the time, many lived in Medina side by side with pagan Arabs. Premonitions of monotheism were widespread in Arabia, in spite of strong pagan resistance. Shunning all claims of divine incarnation, Muhammad stated forcefully that he was only a man, although an exceptional one—the Messenger of Allāh, the One, the All-Powerful and All-Merciful. In its uncompromising monotheism, Islam was much closer to Judaism than to the metaphysical complexities of Christianity's trinitarian Godhead; closer, too, in that it was Semites who evolved these two staunchly masculine creeds; it is essentially biblical and haggadic themes that permeate the teachings of the Qur'ān. One need only compare the severity of al-Jāhiz toward the Christians and his leniency toward the Jews at the time when the Caliph Mutawakkil issued in the ninth century his famous edict regulating the status of the "People of the Book" (Christians, Jews, and Zoroastrians) to grasp the much closer connection between the two purely Semitic faiths. As a general rule, Jews have fared far better in Islamic lands than under Christian rule.

It is therefore interesting to note to what a considerable extent the old female-oriented cults had persisted into Muḥammad's time. This is made plain by the curious incident of the so-called satanic verses in the Meccan part of the Qur'ān; idols are mentioned in Sūrat an-Najm, apparently suggested to the Prophet at a time when the Meccans no longer seemed receptive to his teachings.[13] Consciously or unconsciously, he must have believed that some concession to prevailing sentiments was in order; several of the surviving goddesses—al-'Uzzā (who was worshiped by Muḥammad's own tribe, the Quraysh); al-Lāt, the moon-goddess who was worshiped at aṭ-Ṭā'if; and Manāt, who was supreme among the Arab pagans of Medina—were favorably mentioned by him. To the delight of Meccans, Muḥammad stated that "these are the swans exalted, Whose intercession is to be hoped for."[14] And when the Prophet prostrated himself in homage to the goddesses, all Meccans did likewise. With a hint of rude sarcasm, one of them, Abū Uhayhah, added: "At last Ibn Abī Kabshah [Muḥammad's name from his maternal side] has spoken good of our goddesses."[15]

This temporary weakness was eventually corrected and brushed off as being the result of Satan's throwing upon the Prophet's tongue these unsavory verses. Tradition has it that, shortly after, Gabriel came to him and pointed out the grave error he had committed; the satanic verses were promptly abrogated. But they testify to the enduring influence of the female-oriented paganism, and to the Prophet's political acumen in making temporary concessions to gain more adherents among the idolators. Eventually the surviving goddesses were relegated to the role of minor celestial beings, and then to the position of ephemeral *jinns*.

The Prophet's successors steadily widened the male's privileges at the expense of the female's status:

> The elimination of woman from public and social life—a free woman may be seen only by her husband and next of kin within the prohibited degrees—was completed by the time of Hārūn al-Rashīd. While it probably made for easier contact across class lines, it impoverished social life to a remarkable degree.[16]

With the rise of the Abbāsids in Baghdad, the exclusion of women from Muslim social life was achieved. Many women who still played a part in the early days of Islām, before the antifeminist trend had had time to consolidate itself, were not Muslim at all: Maysūn, wife of Caliph Mu'āwiya and mother of the future Caliph Yazīd I, was a Jacobite Christian, for example. And there is hardly any doubt that the success achieved by the Muslims in converting most of the conquered populations to the new faith was due to the appeal that the downgrading of women must have had for many men.

From now on, it was only in court circles that high-ranking women exerted a degree of influence—witness the interference of al-Khayzurān, wife of Caliph al-Mahdī in problems of succession;[17] or Sitt ul-Mulk whose brother was the Egyptian ruler al-Ḥākim—she had him murdered in 1021 and ruled the country with great competence for a number of years thereafter.[18] There is also the curious episode of the Baḥri Mamluks proclaiming a woman, Shajar ad-Durr, as sultan (there is no feminine form, *sultana*, in Arabic), to the great anger of Caliph al-Musta'sim in Baghdad, furious at the idea that a former member of his harem, sent as a gift, should now sit on the Egyptian throne. He ordered the Mamluks to chose a man and added: "If there is not a man left among you whom you can appoint, tell us and we will send you one."[19] She was eventually murdered. There is also evidence that the Georgian and Circassian women taken into the royal harems of the Safavid dynasty in Persia wielded considerable political influence. They were, however, exceptions to the rule. Islamic society, in general, went further than any other in its total exclusion of women from political power and social influence.

This purely masculine Islamic world was multinational and multiracial, and succeeded better than any other civilization in allowing diverse ethnic groups and nationalities to live side by side in relative harmony. But that this masculine exclusiveness was not to everyone's taste was vividly demonstrated when, in outlying districts such as Tabaristan in 783, the conquering Arabs found their native wives joining the ranks of those male natives rebelling against their rule.[20] No other civilization, however, has achieved as remarkable a racial harmony as Islam. Free from sex-related problems, thanks to the complete elimination of women from social and political life, the exclusively male compound of multitudes of disparate societies was able to instill not only a real feeling of democratic equality but also a unique racial tolerance: African Negroes, Aryan and Semitic whites, yellow Chinese and Mongols, Turks, Albanians, Afghans, Pathans and Punjabis, Bengalis, Malayans and Indonesians, all mixed, and still mix, on a plane of perfect equality—which shows up at the mosque where, each Friday, row upon row of believers, kneeling next to one another with hardly any regard for race, social position, or political power, bow in unison to Allāh and knock their foreheads on the ground with military discipline. Nothing like it had been seen since the Mithraic cult. As Richard Burton noted in the nineteenth century, "El Islam seems purposely to have loosened the ties between the sexes in order to strengthen the bonds between man and man."[21] And T. E. Lawrence, in his *Seven Pillars of Wisdom*, added, "woman became a machine for muscular exercise, while man's psychic side could be slaked only among his peers."[22]

We can have no better contemporary witness than the American black leader Malcolm X, a latter-day traveler, who journeyed to Mecca in the early 1960s. His senses sharpened by racial discrimination in the United States, he was able to understand the profound sense of racial tolerance and equality pervading this exclusively masculine complex of multiracial societies known as the Islamic world, whose exclusive maleness he did not notice. Asked what impressed him most, he replied, "The *brotherhood!* The people of all races, colors, from all over the world coming together as *one!*"[23] And he elaborated:

> The *color-blindness* of the Muslim world's religious society and the *color-blindness* of the Muslim world's human society: these two influences had each day been making a greater impact, and an increasing persuasion against my previous way of thinking. . . . Never have I witnessed such sincere hospitality and the over-whelming spirit of true brotherhood as is practiced by people of all colors and races here in this Ancient Holy Land. . . . America needs to understand Islam, because this is the one religion that erases from its society the race problem. . . . I have never before seen *sincere* and *true* brotherhood practiced by all colors together, irrespective of their color.[24]

This explains the remarkable power of expansion of Islam in modern times, in Africa as well as in Asia, which is also invariably accompanied by a stark regression of woman's status. Indeed, part of its power of expansion resides precisely in the fact that under its aegis, woman's status shrinks, just as it did, long ago, with the wildfire success of the Nestorian Church in Asia.

Islamic public law was never really concerned with the state as such but with the *imāma*, the leadership of the community; the concept of the nation-state as a territorial organization within well-defined boundaries and a structure of settled power was alien to the original Muslim world. The whole ethos of the Islamic world remained essentially nomadic—seafaring or desert dwelling—regardless of the permanency of settlement of its faithful; and nothing is more essentially masculine, nothing so unfavorable to the prevalence of feminine values, as nomadism.

New Islamic legislation went far beyond anything the Prophet had dreamed of in cheating women of their rightful portions of inheritance. More especially, the final regulation of the *waqf*, a sort of mortmain or religious foundation, was specifically designed by the rising Muslim middle class to exclude daughters and their descendants from inheritance as specified by Qur'anic legislation, and make them wholly dependent on the founder's patrilinear family.[25] The multiplying number of harems and eunuchs to guard them, finally institutionalized under Caliph al-Walīd II, emphasized the inevitable degradation of womanhood, along with widespread homosexuality; family life lost all affective vitality and cohesion. This in turn had a great deal to do with the cultural decadence and political disintegration that began to afflict the Muslim world.

With the few exceptions mentioned earlier, one searches in vain for outstanding women in thirteen hundred years of Islamic history; the Muslim landscape is bare of any kind of feminine influence. In a sense, Islam's violent antifeminism was as nefarious as the exaggerated effeminacy of Byzantium, and both were jointly responsible for the economic and cultural decay that began to corrode the Middle East within a few centuries of the Prophet's death.

The sternly masculine bias of Islam had a great deal to do with the ethical severity and nomadic character of a peculiar civilization settled astride the great routes of communication between East and West, between Europe, Asia, and Africa. It was a civilization of merchants and traders, constantly plying the deserts and seas with their camels and ships—running muscle was more in demand than sitting fat. Islam's religious structure reflected this masculine yet essentially democratic spirit—no standing clergy but a clerical class of learned doctors, the *Ulamā*, similar to the scribes in Judaism, in charge of interpreting the Law and the Tradition, the Qur'ān and the Hadīth. The Law itself was but the Will of Allāh, revealed through His Prophet, embodied in an informal legal code known as the Sharī'a, the final seal on the complete subjection of the female element.

Faced with an apparently total triumph of the *animus* in the Islamic soul, the frustrated *anima* was bound to reappear under some guise or other. The massive theological superstructure that Muslims elaborated during the first three or four centuries following Muḥammad's death was a replica of the Christian one; but it never satisfied the Muslim soul: "To the great mass of Muslims this dogmatic superstructure was, continued to be . . . a matter of general indifference."[26] Sternly ethical and dryly philosophical, it made no appeal to sentiment, emotion, or intuition. So it was that mysticism soon appeared within the confines of Islam in the guise of Ṣūfism, to enlist the enthusiastic support of the masses. And in Ṣūfism, the frustrated anima of Islam made its reappearance—not expressed directly in the increasingly repressed Muslim women but in the feminine emotionalism of Islamic mysticism.

CHAPTER

9

Prophetism and Mysticism

With the exception of Zoroastrianism, all the great religions of the patriarchal age have generated some form of mysticism—essentially the reappearance of the feminine element in religion, which has been, time and again, overshadowed by the masculine ethical, legalistic, and philosophic or theological aspect. The etymology of the word "mysticism" betrays its feminine affinity, derived as it is from the old Greek mystery cults, themselves manifestations of the repressed, submerged Great Mother Goddess of the Bronze Age.

Prophetism, on the other hand, is a new form of religious expression, corresponding to the new mood generated by the patriarchal revolution. The origin of "prophecy"—to be sharply distinguished from the (feminine) oracular divination—betrays its profoundly masculine character: it springs from the Hebrew *nābī'*, "announcer" of things to come. Hebrew prophetism arose in antagonism to Ba'alism and fertility cults in general, that is, against female-oriented, goddess-worshiping cults, to teach a highly ethical, history-oriented monotheism.[1] Right conduct and moral living, rather than cults and sacrifices, provided the core of prophetic teaching; the emphasis was on morality rather than ritual magic, that same morality that man set up as an artificial substitute for the female emphasis on closeness to nature, indeed *in opposition* to nature.

Prophets also introduced an entirely new concept, an aggressive and militant monotheism that stands in stark contrast to the benevolent tolerance of earlier magic fertility cults, which never rose above the level of henotheism—belief in one supreme god although not at the exclusion of other deities. In this, the prophets went further than Moses or David, who remained mere henotheists. From being "seers" (*rō'eh*) in earlier times, the prophets gradually became listeners and speakers—they were summoned to *call with the throat*.[2] The prophet's organ of perception and communication shifted from the eye to the ear; his world-awareness from space to time, from nature to history. The process of historical development and retribution, centered around the fate of the Hebrew people, became the unfolding of an ethical tale with a moral lesson included in it. Very early, in fact, the prophets shunned and despised the states of mystical ecstasy or rapture connected with the old fertility cults; scorning magic, astrology, and dealing in ghosts and demons, they concentrated on the dynamic issues of historical happenings and their ethical significance. This was the full triumph of the masculine principle over the feminine.

As already noted, in the East, in India and China, the *anima,* far from being repressed, was given its full due; it remained a reality in the consciousness of Easterners, and at times was a reality of far greater magnitude than the *animus.* This explains why prophetism had no place in Indian or Chinese cultures, whereas mysticism had full play in Hinduism, Taoism and Mahāyāna Buddhism; it also explains why, unlike its theology, Islam's Ṣūfism drew its inspiration not from Judaism but from the early Christian mystics—Clement of Alexandria, John Cassian, Ephraim the Syrian, Gregory of Nyssa, Isaac of Niniveh.

As the ultimate expression of the feminine in religion, mysticism represents the full flowering of the *anima* in a religious context that remains, in the West, essentially masculine. But mysticism itself is not one but presents various forms in which the feminine element may be partly subordinated to the masculine. The most completely feminine form is undoubtedly "nature mysticism," a pantheistic interpretation that identifies nature with God, or even eliminates God altogether and seeks merely the "oneness of Being"—a form of mysticism that William James has profusely described in *The Varieties of Religious Experience.* In this form of "downward transcendence" the mystic does not seek to *advance* toward knowledge of, and union with, God but rather regresses toward the "security of the infantile state and the pre-natal condition in which there is real identity of subject and object in the shape of the embryo enclosed in the mother's womb," a regression to the dim state of consciousness of the child who cannot distinguish itself from the mother who gave it birth.[3] All the typical symbols used by nature mystics—ocean, sea, air, trees, water—are feminine, both mythologically and psychologically. For example, the mystical experience of identification with the drop of water dissolving in the ocean symbolizes this regression toward the unconscious state in the security of the womb—Mother Earth reclaiming her child and attempting to cancel the upthrusting male spirit. The fact that similar mystical experiences represent, on the contrary, such an outward expansion of the personality that it seems about to absorb into itself the whole world, does not invalidate the first type of experience. Fundamentally, it amounts to the same thing—whether the mystic reenters Mother Nature or whether Mother Nature enters the mystic, the end result is a merging of the two; without and within are one, death loses all meaning. As the Chinese Taoists put it: "The Valley Spirit never dies, it is named the Mysterious Feminine."

Summing up his survey of the mythologies of the world in his *Psychology of the Unconscious*, Carl Jung claimed that mysticism represents "in unmistakable symbolism, the confluence of object and subject as the reunion of mother and child"; in other words, a return to the undifferentiated state of the collective unconscious.[4] Jung was still under the influence of Freud when he wrote this in the light of Freudian "mother fixation." Later, however, he stumbled on a higher form of mystical experience which, far from regressing from the ego-dominated consciousness as nature mystics do (along with all consumers of hallucinogenic drugs), progresses *beyond* that stage toward *individuation* or "integration of the personality"—that is, the fruitful integration of the conscious and unconscious. This represents an acceptance of the fact that all human beings are psychologically androgynous. This is probably what the French poet Rimbaud implied when he exclaimed,

> Elle est retrouvée!
> Quoi? L'éternité.
> C'est la mer mêlée
> au soleil.[5]

Sun and sea mingle, symbolizing the integration and fusion of the male and female principles. The integrated personality is both active and passive, lets things happen to itself without rejecting anything, accepts to the full the workings of the feminine anima without letting it extinguish the male principle, rational and individuating. This process of integration has been well depicted in the Chinese classic *Secret of the Golden Flower*. Following a summary of the branching out of the Tao, the common stem, into *yin* and *yang*, and then into feminine *K'un* and masculine *Ch'ien* principles, it proceeds to outline a process of integration that takes place entirely through the *yang* or male principle. As summed up in annotated translation,

> In the personal bodily existence of the individual they (*yin* and *yang*) are represented by two other polarities, a *p'o* soul (or *anima*) and a *hun* soul (or *animus*). All during the life of the individual these two are in conflict, each striving for mastery. At death they separate and go different ways. The *anima* sinks to earth as *kuei*,

a ghost-being. The *animus* rises and becomes *shên*, a revealing spirit or god. *Shên* may in time return to *Tao*.

If the life-forces flow downward, that is, without let or hindrance into the outer world, the *anima* is victorious over the *animus;* no "spirit-body" or "Golden Flower" is developed and, at death, the ego is lost. If the life-forces are led through the "backward-flowing" process, that is, conserved, and made to "rise" instead of allowed to dissipate, the *animus* has been victorious, and the ego persists after death. It is then possessed of *shên*, the revealing spirit. A man who holds to the way of conservation all through his life may reach the stage of the "Golden Flower," which then frees the ego from the conflict of the opposites, and it again becomes part of *Tao*, the undivided Great One.[6]

In short, integration of the personality implies that the mystical experience should be under the control of the masculine intellect, following which the male, rational and conscious, and the female, instinctive and unconscious, are truly and harmoniously integrated. This being the case, the highest level of mysticism also implies the overcoming of the mere "nature" mysticism with its exclusive emphasis on the feminine, its ecstatic manifestations and ultimate evaporation of the self, and bringing it under the control of the rational, masculine element—the transition leading in Ṣūfism from the wild ecstasies of Abū Yazīd of Biṣṭām who thought he had achieved complete identity with the Godhead ("I am He, Glory be to me"), to the far more sober and controlled mysticism of his leading critic, Junayd.[7] Even Ghazālī, greatest of Islam's mystical philosophers, had to dismiss Abū Yazīd's monistic ecstasies as mystical "drunkenness." So that if, at the start, the mystical experience represents in truth the manifestation of the female principle, it can achieve its supreme goal only in harmonious conjunction with the rational male principle.

However, the feminine element appears to triumph in one important respect—the claim of all mystical experiences to transcend morality and ethics, to lead to "a strange and lovely land beyond individuality, and incidentally beyond good and evil, since the opposites are reconciled, and the peace that passes all understanding rules supreme."[8] This is clearly implied in the land where mysticism ruled supreme without interference from prophetism, India, where some of the greatest holy books, such as the *Upaniṣads*, describe at length this passage beyond good and evil as a result of mystical rapture. There, the triumph of the female principle is absolute; it can lead with equal ease to the monstrous cult of the goddess Kālī's thugs as to the gentle exaltation of Ramakrishna's "Mother" as supreme spiritual entity.

Once integration of the personality is achieved, the theistic mystic, unlike the nature mystic or pantheist, must play the part of the bride in his relationship with God. He must be mostly passive and receptive, and fully accept his inherent femininity. According to Meister Eckhart, "If man remained always a virgin, no fruit would proceed from him. If he is to become fruitful, he must necessarily be a woman. 'Woman' is the most noble word one can apply to the soul, more noble than 'virgin.' " Likewise, Suso always refers to himself, in his autobiography, in the feminine gender. Even Ghazālī claims that sexual congress is a foretaste of heaven.[9]

It was the fate of Ṣūfism to give up early its efforts at personality integration and yield uncompromisingly to the feminine element in mysticism by assuming that all ecstasy is divine; this was almost inevitable inasmuch as Islam's official creed remained implacably prophetic and masculine. Almost for the last time, Qushayrī pointed out the vital distinction to be made between *basṭ* (feeling of endless expansion of the self) and actual communion with God, which supposes prior integration of the personality.[10] As Ṣūfism triumphed decisively in Islam after the eleventh century, it came to rely more and more on the ecstatic possibilities induced, as among dervishes, by music, dance, and drugs, and causing a "downward transcendence" rather than an upward one. In the centuries-long conflict that pitted the orthodox *ulamās*, doctors of the law and theologians, against the Ṣūfis, one can detect the opposition between the masculine rational and conscious intellect with its secondhand knowledge (*'ilm*) of the theologians, and the feminine, emotional, and intuitive direct "experience" (*ma'rifa*) of the mystics. As a further but natural compensation, the Ṣūfis became increasingly hostile to women and sex; in the first centuries of Islam, most were married—by the twelfth century, few were.[11]

The struggle between Ulamās and Ṣūfis became fierce in the second and third centuries of the Hijrah; at the beginning of the fourth, the famously cruel execution of Mansūr al-Hallāj, accused of heresy for having identified himself with Allāh, set an example. He upheld the concept of *hulūl*, "incarnation," which Islam had violently rejected, and claimed:

> I am He whom I love, and He whom I love is I.
> We are two spirits dwelling in one body.
> If thou seest me, thou seest Him,
> And if thou seest Him, thou seest both.[12]

By way of consequence, he also popularized the widespread notion of *fana'*, extinction of personal consciousness. After his execution, Mulism mystics were careful to explain that *fana'* did not imply complete destruction of the personality, but only loss of human attributes, not of human essence.

Persecution, however, was in vain. In the end, Ṣūfism defeated and routed the *Ulamās*. Later Muslim mysticism adopted the language of earthly love to express mystical ecstasy, to the point where Muslim scholars themselves began to wonder whether the mystical poets were describing human or divine love—especially the pantheistic Ṣūfism of such Persians as Jalāl ad-Dīn ar-Rūmi and Jāmi. As Islam expanded and began to include converted populations who came into the fold with their own customs, Ṣūfism occasionally included women in the ranks of its devotees—the oldest Turkish mystical order, the Yesavīya, allowed women to take part in the *dhikr* (liturgical recitation) unveiled —which was unheard of among Arabs or Persians.

To sum up. The feminine nature of mysticism is obvious—the surrender to nature or to God, the passive attitude waiting for the spiritual blessing and uplift up to ecstasy, essentially quietist, contemplative, and resigned—an expression of femininity as experienced through the feminine side of all human beings. As the *Theologia Germanica* puts it: "Behold, in such a man must all thought of Self, all self-seeking, self-will and what cometh thereof, be utterly lost and surrendered and given over to God."[13] The human soul must always be passive and receptive in relation to the Almighty; as Abū Yazīd of Bisṭām described his own personal experience, "For thirty years I looked for God, but when I paused to think, He was the seeker and I the sought."[14] It should be stressed, however, that mysticism is also endowed with a certain noetic quality, that it is not only a state of feeling but one of knowledge—of a knowledge immediately apprehended but unavailable to the discursive intellect.

The "prophetic" aspect of religion, on the other hand, is uncompromisingly masculine: demonstrating a self-assertive will to live, active, aggressive, and ethical. Here is no passiveness, no surrender, no delicate feeling. Prophetism is essentially militant and intolerant, essentially "personality affirming," believing in God-given revelation rather than individual ecstasy, and seeing the handiwork of the Almighty as revealed through the historical process rather than the more poetic spatial display of nature, through time rather than space. As Meister Eckhart, one of the great mystics of all times, stated it, in justification of mysticism: "The Soul is created in a place between Time and Eternity: with its highest powers it touches Eternity, with its lower Time."[15]

The prophetic outlook could not be more diametrically opposed: mysticism gives priority to timeless Being, prophetism to active

Becoming—which brings us back to the age-old dichotomy between the female, who identifies herself easily with the mother who gave her birth and, therefore, places the emphasis on Being; and the male, who places emphasis on Doing, on actively differentiating himself from the female sex that generated him. Two completely opposed life-attitudes that condition, each in its own way, all religious dispositions and outlooks.

Part III

THE RISE OF THE WEST:
WOMAN AND CULTURE

❁

CHAPTER

I

The Barbarian Woman

The collapse of the Roman Empire raises an interesting question: why did Rome crumble under the assaults of the Teutonic hordes when another contemporary empire, the Chinese, withstood all barbarian invasions and several dismemberments of its "universal" state without any loss of cultural continuity? Indeed, it is not so much the political breakup of the western empire that ushered in the Dark Ages as the almost complete *disintegration of its civilization* and loss of cultural continuity. One explanation is certainly biological and statistical: since before the reign of Augustus, the birthrate had fallen catastrophically in Italy. The lack of manpower was unconsciously symbolized when the famous Roman legions, the XVIIth, XVIIIth, and XIXth, slaughtered in the Teutoburger Wald disaster, were never replaced. There remained a permanent gap in the army list—until the Roman army itself ceased to exist.

The erosion of family spirit, the widespread use of all available contraceptives as well as infanticide, and the desire for social emancipation on the part of Roman women dealt a death blow to Roman biological fertility. Arguments familiar to us today were already used to justify this Malthusian attitude—the unwisdom of bearing children in times of political troubles, imperialistic wars, urban congestion, and widespread immorality. As early as the second century B.C., both Cato and Polybius remarked on the declining birthrate and on the inability of the authorities to raise such armies as had defeated Hannibal only a few generations ago. In the third century A.D., after the Marcomannic War, the situation took a turn for the worse; the depletion of Roman manpower was fast turning into a major disaster: "By the age of Marcus Aurelius there was little left of the virile population of ancient Greece or of the best breeding stocks of Rome and Italy."[1] Ethnic suicide appears to have been one of the long-term results of Rome's

207

feminist movement. While the Roman Empire was rapidly becoming an empty shell, at the far end of the world Chinese society did not seem to suffer from any such internal ailment. The family system was preserved throughout Chinese history and was able to absorb biologically most barbarian invaders by "Sinifying" them and thus preserving Chinese civilization intact into the twentieth century.

The historical fact is that the first barbarians who sought refuge behind the Roman *limes* (Rome's rudimentary "Great Wall") and entered Rome's military service wanted nothing as much as to *preserve* the Roman Empire and its civilization; they were out not for destruction but for conservation. For a long time, the barbarian infiltrations, officially encouraged by the Roman authorities from Marcus Aurelius on, continued at a steady pace. To an increasing degree, the actual defense of the empire was entrusted to half-civilized Teutonic warriors. But at no time were they ever absorbed by the increasingly sterile Italian or Gallo-Roman populations. Intermarriage between civilized Roman citizens and Teutonic barbarians was forbidden by law, as it was between free men and slaves, until the empire itself collapsed. Had they been in China, the barbarians would soon have been civilized and absorbed into the immensely strong clan structure, to disappear eventually as droplets in the swelling Chinese ocean.

A loss of moral dignity and civic pride and courage corroded the inner fiber of the civilized people of the western empire. The more authoritarian the imperial government of Diocletian, the more reluctant were the citizens to abide by their civic duties. Reluctance to bring children into a darkening world increased steadily. In earlier days the Romans had been able to vanquish, civilize, and absorb the Celts of Cisalpine Gaul as successfully as the Chinese "Sinified" their barbarians. Several centuries later, worn out and without biological vitality, the Romans were in turn overwhelmed by Germanic barbarians who, far from being civilized by Romans, barbarized Rome completely. Healthy and simple-minded, the prolific Goths, Saxons, and Franks delighted in rearing large families and respected the tribal sanctity of marriage; so did the Vandals, Ostrogoths, Visigoths, Lombards, and Alemanni. Settled in the midst of the civilized populations as "hosts" or "federated" (*foederati*) allies, they were at first awed by Rome's legendary power, by a civilization they did not begin to understand, yet attempted to grasp. The Visigoths and Burgundians of the fifth century even applied themselves to imitate the outward style of life of the effeminate populations in whose midst they dwelt. The more savage Franks made no such effort and, under their rule, the barbarization of Gallo-Romans proceeded swiftly. The Dark Ages settled on Europe.

There is every evidence that the Teutonic tribes were organized in a highly patriarchal society—all social power and authority to the men but with a fearful male respect for woman. Tacitus has left us a highly colored description of the first Germans encountered by the Romans: lazy when it came to agricultural work, but exceedingly warlike, especially when encouraged by their womenfolk, who often joined them in battle. Roman historians, alarmed and prophetic, compared the simple and vigorous nature of the barbarians with the slothfulness of the decadent Romans, corroded by too many years of peace and luxury.[2] In his *Germania* (A.D. 193), Tacitus told his Roman contemporaries that "the German women live in inviolable chastity, with no lascivious shows or provocative banquets to lure them to vice; secret love-letters are unknown to either sex. . . . That is a land where no one has an indulgent smile for immorality or calls seducing or being seduced 'the spirit of modern times.' "[3]

As soon as the soil was exhausted by extensive farming, the Germans moved on to other lands, which they conquered with the sword. Women were bought from their parents to serve as wives, and husbands had power of life and death over them—but only with the approval of the tribal assemblies. Nevertheless, women were highly regarded and even feared for their alleged magic powers. Adultery was extremely rare, as is the case in most tribal societies; and although they were apparently free to practice abortion, they rarely did so and usually bore many children.

In *The Golden Bough* James Frazer notes that "the ancient Germans believed that there was something holy in women, and accordingly consulted them as oracles. . . . But often the veneration of the men went further, and they worshipped women as true and living goddesses. For example, in the reign of Vespasian a certain Veleda, of the tribe of the Bructeri, was commonly held to be a deity, and in that character reigned over her people, her sway being acknowledged far and wide."[4]

Goddesses, in the flesh or otherwise, were prominent, usually associated with soil and planting and harvesting. Whether they worshiped Mother Earth, Nerthus, or Hertha, like the Angles, or the Mother of the Gods, like the Aestii, they all stood in awe of womanhood—an attitude that largely disappeared upon their becoming Christians. The Celtic druids held the same view and saw in woman something mysterious and unfathomable, partaking of divinity; Celts and Teutons were both close to their Bronze Age Neolithic roots. As for the male gods mentioned at the time, Thor, Wodan, or Tyr, they all sprang from the Earth Mother, children of the predominating female principle.

When the western empire finally collapsed under the barbarian flood, all legal and biological barriers between invaders and invaded broke down. In Gaul, the most prosperous and populated part of the former empire, Frankish chieftains began to intermarry with daughters of the old Gallo-Roman senatorial and landowning classes; from these faraway seeds sprang the feudal nobility that was to rule France. Elsewhere, in Spain and Italy, the same process was repeated. While the Angles and the Saxons invaded Britain where the Roman veneer was much thinner than in Gaul, they in turn were eventually doomed to become the serfs of the Danes, and then of the Normans. In Gaul the Franks laid down, once and for all in the sixth century, the famous Salic Law, excluding women from the inheritance of any portion of Salic (i.e., Frankish) land—which may explain why, pseudo-paradoxically, women have been more influential in France than in any other European country. Frankish women in early Merovingian days were certainly not cowed by the Salic Law. As in previous Dark Ages, after the collapse of former civilizations and the consequent barbarization leading to virtual anarchy, women play a conspicuous role in an extremely virile setting, which they eventually forfeit when culture and civilization rise again—witness Greek women in Homeric times and their steady decline in status thereafter, down to the days of Pericles.

As regent, and then as queen of Mercia, King Alfred's daughter Ethelfled ruled with greater wisdom and strength of purpose than any ruler of her generation—granted that hers was a relatively small realm. War between the Angli and the Warni broke out because of Radiger's repudiation of his marriage contract with the English king's sister. If we are to believe Gregory of Tours, the Burgundian kingdom's destruction was the result of Hlothhild's urging her sons to revenge the murder of her parents; and because she claimed to be ill treated by her husband, the Visigothic king Amalaric, Hlothhild's brother Hildeberth invaded Spain. The jealous pride of Amalaberga, wife of Irminfrith, was instrumental in bringing about the collapse of the Thuringian kingdom. In short, we have to accept the fact that

> unless we are prepared to shut our eyes to the plain evidence of history we are bound to recognise that the personal feelings of queens and princesses were among the very strongest of the factors by which the politics of the Heroic Age were governed.[5]

Other women played an important part in Italy. Theodora, wife of Theophylact, a prominent official at the papal court in Rome, arranged for the election of Pope John X early in the tenth century. Her daughter Marozia had shown her the way when she procured the election of her lover as Pope Sergius III; then, married to the Duke of Tuscany, she had Pope John X (her mother's choice) thrown in prison and secured the election of her bastard son by Sergius III as Pope John XI.

Dark as those ages were, and obscure as the records may be, there is enough evidence to show that, regardless of their legal status, women could exert enormous influence on the course of affairs, both lay and ecclesiastical, both for good and ill. The great German nun Hroswitha made her mark in literature during the tenth century with her poetic lives of saints, and her prose comedies. In other lands, women continued the religious work that so many of their predecessors had started in the last phase of the Roman Empire: as mothers or wives, to convert their pagan relatives to Christianity. King Ethelbert of Kent's wife, who was a Frankish Christian, had no trouble proving to her husband that conversion to the most sophisticated creed of the time was the easiest means to achieve a higher degree of civilization. At a time when the Roman and Celtic churches were struggling for supremacy in Britain, Oswy, king of Northumbria, was persuaded by his wife to abandon the Church of Iona and join Rome, a decisive event which broke the back of the Celtic Church and brought, not only the English, but eventually the Scottish, Irish and Welsh churches to join the Roman fold.[6]

On the whole, most women worked hard to promote the cause of Christianity. As elsewhere on the Continent, manners and morals were coarse in Anglo-Saxon England; lechery and adultery were widespread, and women lived in constant insecurity—an inevitable consequence of the breakdown of stern tribal traditions and taboos. Along with their children, women could be sold into slavery by their husbands and fathers; husbands could divorce their wives at will and remarry whenever they pleased. It was only after the strong admonition of the Synod of Hertford (673) that the church was gradually able to enforce a certain stability in marital relations—which is, basically, what most women were striving for.

Of great importance to the social position of women was the hectic transition from tribal to feudal society. This transition did not occur all over Europe simultaneously but depended to a large extent on the temper of the tribesmen themselves, and on the degree of civilization that had survived among the native populations. The breakup of the Frankish tribes, permeated soon enough by the surviving Roman municipal tradition, was far swifter than that of the Anglo-Saxons in England—who, themselves, were moving away from tribalism far more rapidly than the Celts. In fact, one reason why Northumbria's King Oswy joined the Church of Rome was his desire to expel tribalism from his realm and introduce a Roman-type ecclesiastical hierarchy as a substitute for the old, deceased imperial bureaucracy.[7]

Usually, not always, feudalism arises out of the contact between invading barbarians and conquered but civilized populations—as in Homeric Greece, Vedic India, or Chou China. Following the invasions, government and administration collapse; what is left of the civilized apparatus is no longer able to protect its subjects against unlawful aggression and military power is monopolized by small tribal war bands and powerful landowners. As a consequence, trade comes almost to a standstill and large economic integration breaks down— conversely, highly organized trade usually inhibits the rise of feudalism. The devolution of political and military power from decaying central government to increasingly powerful local magnates and tribal chieftains becomes unavoidable; and the feudal structure arises from contact and alliance between invading tribal chiefs and native local magnates.

What happens then is easy to grasp: the kernel of tribal political organization lies in the overall and ultimate authority of tribal councils, over and above that of the chiefs. This democratic supervision, bolstered by venerable traditions, curtails to a great extent the power and authority of the elected chieftains, who can be deposed by the tribal councils whenever they see fit. When the entire tribe moves into a new area of higher civilization, however, it begins to lose, sooner or later, its internal cohesion through contact with alien populations and higher cultures. The tribal chiefs, anxious to emancipate themselves from the tribal council's control, strike up *personal* alliances with the local magnates, often marry their daughters, while the bulk of the tribesmen do likewise with the smaller gentry and landholders. The tribe begins to disintegrate and detribalization is on its way when tribal chieftains, allied with the local magnates, surround themselves with nontribal followers recruited from outside the tribe, and pledged to *personal* allegiance to them. This new personal support enables them to free themselves from the public control of the councils; and the first ghostly contours of the complex feudal system become visible, erected on the ruins of tribal law and tradition. Its essence now resides in the vassal-lord relationship based on a personal oath of fealty.[8]

In other words, the binding force that now holds society together is not kinship but pledged loyalty between vassal and suzerain. This amounts to a substitution of one set of relationships for another, the substitution of blood relationship as a binding force for personal pledges based on an entirely new sense of individual honor, loyalty, and personal commitment. Both landed magnate and emancipated tribal chief become leaders of war bands; their interests become merged through intermarriage, by an exchange of women similar to that originally devised by the incest taboo; the long-range consequence is the biological emergence of a new generation of leaders. As time goes on and the small "fief" appears as the basic autonomous administrative cell, an in-group faces all other out-groups; relationships between fiefs are conducted, on a long-term basis, by intermarriage, and the exchange of women acquires its political significance. In contrast with the barbarian woman, the feudal woman's status is much lower.

This social metamorphosis is fatal to woman's influence in all post-Heroic Age epochs. Regardless of the type of tribal organization that is superseded, whether cognatic or agnatic, woman's power and influence are always greater where blood relationship rules, and so is her feeling of being protected by tribal tradition. A striking symbol of this social metamorphosis is the far greater prevalence of strife between relatives, which is rare in a tight tribal structure. Women become prizes to be wrested (the abduction of Helen of Troy, Haethcyn's kidnaping of the Swedish queen), at the risk of generalized warfare: woman becomes an object.

With the rise of feudalism, a new hierarchy took over. The transition from primitive or tribal to feudal implied an increasingly sharp division of labor, unknown in tribal times, between fighting man and farming man, or between political man and economic man. Social specialization permeated the complex structure based on the feudal system of contracts and entailed that women, too, had their specific functions to perform. They could no longer substitute for men as they did, occasionally, in the Dark Heroic Ages; they became mostly a medium of exchange between in-groups that were, hitherto, indifferent or hostile to one another.[9]

More than that, they became, in a sense, what they had been at the dawn of prehistory: in a barbarized land where, by and large, communications and trade had broken down, women became again *signs* or symbols whose purpose in life was to be *communicated.* The exchange of women was used to *bind* men together.[10] Earlier, this social function was the outcome of the rules of exogamy and the prohibition of incest. In medieval times women were less rooted in the soil than men were; few were expected to marry within the limited confines of the little group in which they had been raised. They were usually destined to travel far and wide and cement new relationships and alliances between relatively distant lands.

If we start at the top of the feudal ladder, that is, with the ruling princes, we must keep in mind the fact that a princess sent to a distant land for marital purposes became the head of a vast expedition with its own clerks and household staff, along with a great deal of authority over the expenditure of her often considerable financial resources. She could be expected to bring an alien influence with her which was often upsetting to local customs and traditions but was also a powerful agent of cross-cultural fertilization. The marriage of King (and future Emperor) Henry III of Germany with Agnes de Poitou in 1043 is a case in point. While local German churchmen complained that "now we see the shameful habits of French folly introduced into our kingdom," it was the start of a remarkable career for her. As one historian points out:

> The career of Agnes illustrates the way in which a woman in a great secular position could overcome the local limitations, which pressed more hardly on a man, and could absorb more easily than a man, with his more exacting political responsibilities, the disturbing ideas of the time.[11]

After thirteen years of marriage, at age thirty Agnes became a widow and regent of the Holy Roman Empire for her son's benefit. Six years later she was ousted and retired to Rome, where she became the major intermediary between the two greatest powers of the time—the pope and Emperor Henry IV, her son. She was at the heart of the historical struggle between empire and papacy and had to witness the emperor's humiliation at Canossa.

As they traveled to and fro, moving from father or brother to husband and son, women became the main agents of cultural diffusion and dissemination—witness Judith, sister of the Count of Flanders, married to Tostig, Earl of Northumbria, who soon left her a widow; then remarried to Duke Welf of Bavaria, to whom she brought an extraordinary collection of English relics and manuscripts gathered during her first marriage. This collection, eventually willed to the monastery of Weingarten, became a prime source of information and inspiration to artists and scholars during the Middle Ages.

What gave further importance to women as means of communications was an extraordinary tightening of the rules governing incest. This stiffening of the regulations resulted from the fact that, after the collapse of the empire, the church's Canon Law became the main legal influence in shaping the new family structure, often owing as much to barbarian feeling as to Roman legislation.[12] In the ninth century, what became known as the Isidore-Mercatus *False Decretals* (a largely spurious code of Western Canon Law) imposed the Teutonic method of counting degrees of kinship from a common ancestor instead of the Roman method which traced them to a common ancestor and back again.[13] As a result, the prohibited degrees of marriage were so considerable that, the greater the status of the future husband, the farther afield he had to look for a wife—thus spreading an immense net over the European continent that went as far as Russia and Constantinople.

Until well into the middle period of the medieval era, the prohibited degrees were seven in number; in other words, from the ninth to the twelfth century, at the peak of extreme difficulties in travel and communications, men and women were within the prohibited degrees if they had had a common ancestor during the previous seven generations—when, most of the time, their ancestral knowledge and records hardly reached the fourth or the fifth. For instance, Henry I of England wanted to give one of his daughters in marriage to William of Warenne, Earl of Surrey. Compelled to submit a genealogical tree to Archbishop Anselm, it was discovered that they had a common ancestor some two hundred years before, and the marriage was forbidden.[14] It was not until the Fourth Lateran Council in 1215 that the doctrine of the False Decretals was rejected and the prohibited degrees limited to the first four generations springing from a common ancestor; the Roman accounting of relationship degrees was reinstated—but not before the cross-cultural consequences of this far-flung exchange of women had come to fruition.

The fact that women occasionally found themselves in a position of influence and even political power was not gracefully accepted by all men. In a sense, women's position was further weakened when the medieval world began its slow retreat from the essentially concrete outlook on political power of the Dark Ages and early Middle Ages. In the thirteenth century, the twin ideas of political freedom and the rule of law cropped up in the thinking of philosophers and theologians. It all started with the English barons who initiated the Magna Carta: freedom was the outcome of the rule of law; and what is law but applied reason? Tyranny is merely the absence of the rule of law; any man who lives outside the realm of law is fettered by the shackles of servitude. Quite naturally, thirteenth-century Franciscan chronicler Fra Salimbene lists the five kinds of rule which disgrace men: the rule of women, serfs, fools, boys, and enemies, all of which destroy rational order. As a historian points out pertinently:

> The inclusion of women in this list deserves notice, because it emphasizes the point that rule over free men should be rational. . . . But equally in the theological and chivalric conceptions of the time, women stood for that which was either below or above reason: woman, in the person of Eve, was the agent by which sin came into the world, and, in the person of the Virgin, the agent by which Salvation came; in courtly literature, women stood at

once for that which was below reason—caprice—and for a higher principle than reason—love. But liberty, at least in this world's affairs, was a product of the masculine quality of reason, as expressed in law.[15]

Nothing illustrates better the changing outlook of early medievalism than the metamorphosis of the conception of the Virgin Mary from the ninth to the twelfth century, for instance, the transformation of the theme of the Virgin and Child and its gradual *humanization*. Western Christendom was already familiar in the eleventh century with the dignified and slightly hieratic Child, seated on his Mother's knee as if on a throne, holding up his right hand as a sign of benediction, and with his left holding either a book (symbol of wisdom) or an orb (symbol of dominion). Then, gradually, the Child's expression becomes more mobile: He laughs, plays with a ball or apple, caresses His Mother, or is even being fed from his Mother's breast. Such humanization had long been known in the more civilized East; in the barbarized West, it was quite unfamiliar. It reached the West from Byzantium, along with Greek inscriptions acknowledging the Virgin as *Theotokos*, "Mother of God." Humanization proceeded slowly—the Mother began to lose her remoteness, the Child began to give up his symbols of wisdom and authority. A sign of this altered status of Mary is her progressive emergence as a miracle maker. Until the twelfth century, she had hardly ever been portrayed in that role; from then onward, miracle stories of the Virgin begin to appear, again largely inspired by imports from Byzantium. The collection of Mary stories grew by leaps and bounds in a medieval society that had been addicted, until then, to masculine legends.

Along with this, a new type of religiosity typified by Saint Anselm and Saint Bernard introduced an emotionalism that was absent in the rough barbaric hearts of the Dark Ages. More than anyone, Saint Francis gave added meaning to the subjective psychological quest of Anselm and Bernard—the reconciliation of faith with reason, the sublimation of carnal desire, the spiritualization of earthly longing for the other sex. The increasing discipline of monastic life that started with the foundation of Cluny triggered, in counterpart, a remarkable humanization of the great symbolic themes of Christianity. One need only go back to the famous Song of Roland, swan song of the Dark Ages, to see how things had changed between the sexes—the Song of Roland portraying a one-sided masculine society whose members are exclusively dedicated to the male group to which they belong rather than to a subjective quest of their own hearts. In this atmosphere—which pervaded Western Europe in the heroic days of the great dukes of Normandy such as William the Conqueror and counts of Anjou such as Geoffrey Greymantle—when priests, monks, and bishops battled, axe in hand, alongside warriors and knights, and the feudal system was being built up on the basis of pledges, oaths, and loyalties tying men to one another, women were referred to "only in the crude way of the camp." Men thought of their earthly possessions and power far more than their loves; in fact, their simple and primitive souls knew far more about lust than love:

> The dying Roland had no thought to spare for his betrothed [Aude], though she straightaway died on hearing of his death. And when the heroes think of their lands, they think also of the ancient holy places of France, and call upon St. Michael or St. Denis—never on the Virgin.[16]

But now, a new age was dawning.

The Medieval Lady

Everything changed in the twelfth century. The works of Chrétien de Troyes no longer focus on the exaltation of the ties of lordship and vassalage, the sacred bond of comradeship and the foulness of treason and betrayal; Chrétien focuses on love. His is the secular counterpart of the emotional piety of the new monkish order of Citeaux; both his romances and the new orientation of the Cistercian monks are on love —profane and sacred, earthly and divine. The introduction of love as the main object of interest in worldly affairs as well as in religion entails an entirely novel concentration on subjective states of mind and feeling. Love is a lonely, personal emotion; Chrétien's knight no longer seeks the companionship of his peers but the solitude required by his often desperate quest. Regardless of the community to which he is compelled to belong, he can find his true self only by occasional flights into some wilderness. The extraordinary solidarity of the knights of Charlemagne and his successors contrasts, in the remarkable simplicity and complete lack of introspection of the Carolingian barons, with the far more delicate and refined subjectivity of the twelfth-century knight seeking his love and just as likely to find the enemy in one of his fellow knights—unthinkable in the days of the *Chanson de Roland*—as in a Saracen.

In Chrétien's new world, the soul sets out on a pilgrimage of love, the longing of the heart set on some member of the opposite sex. There is a close connection between the rebirth of a new cult of the Virgin, a new emotionalism in the religious feeling of the times, the purely secular longing for love à la Chrétien de Troyes and the new ideal of knighthood that it entailed; all men worth their salt were thenceforth offered one or another form of love as the ultimate worthy pursuit: secular or religious, love of woman or love of God. Chrétien de Troyes wrote in the second half of the twelfth century. Only fifty years before, the collection of stories known as the *Miracles of the Virgin* began to appear. Until then, practically all miracle stories were connected with the concrete, physical remains of a saint in a specific geographical location and a specific historical context. Relics were the most prized possessions of churches and monasteries. With the startling appearance of the Virgin, this changes completely; instead of being merely the spiritual assistant of a local saint, she becomes what she already was in the Eastern church—the greatest healer and dispenser of miracles, the feminine principle in its boundless love and charity.

With this, in a widening world in which travel and communications were becoming easier and safer, both time and place lost their importance. The Virgin's power is unlimited, universal and eternal. Somehow, "like the rain, this protective power of the Virgin falls on the just and the unjust alike—provided only that they have entered the circle of her allegiance."[1] Unlike the saint who specializes in protecting a specific place, church, or convent, or in being the greatest expert at curing some particular ailment or safeguarding some given trade or profession, Mary's power has universal applications; she saves souls, individual souls longing, in fact, to reenter the womb of the long-ago Great Mother of Neolithic times.

Already in the eleventh and twelfth centuries, the Almighty was frequently addressed as "God, son of Holy Mary." This was the religious counterpart of the new exaltation of love with which the church itself had no choice but to cooperate, and attempt to coopt by encouraging a new form of Mary worship in order to channel and control this novel devotion to the feminine ideal. Even in its most patriarchal guise, the church simply could not stop this popular groundswell of "Mariolatry" which placed the Virgin on a higher emotional plane than the purely masculine Trinity. There was considerable ecclesiastical reluctance stemming from an inveterate distrust of woman and feminine influence. Bernard of Clairvaux, for instance, was dead set against Mariolatry. Thomas Aquinas stated firmly:

> The woman is subject to the man on account of the weakness of her nature, both of mind and of body. . . . Man is the beginning of woman and her end, just as God is the beginning and end of every creature. . . . Woman is in subjection according to the law of nature, but a slave is not.[2]

And he did not spare the Virgin, conceived, in his view, in sin, but actually *redeemed* by her Son. But even he could not put a brake on the new trend. Mariolatry dispelled the traditional image of Eve, the symbolic temptress, and substituted the image of Mary as the spiritual counterpart of the medieval lady for whose heart the courtly knight pined away.

The Virgin was often thought of as the highest and most merciful judge, and more than one must have echoed the prayer of a Cistercian lay brother threatening Christ in the following terms: "Lord, if Thou free me not from this temptation, I will complain of Thee to Thy mother."[3] Mary soon became *Regina Coeli*, Queen of Heaven, and popular imagination often pictured Jesus as being jealous of His mother on account of her worship. This new Gospel of Mary, carved in stone in every Gothic cathedral consecrated to "Our Lady," swept Western Christendom, compelling the church to yield and sanctify it. Great festivals came into being celebrating the main events of the Virgin's life—the Annunciation, the Visitation, Candlemas, the Assumption and, eventually, the Immaculate Conception, which freed Mary of the taint of original sin, deemed to be the inescapable lot of all human beings since Adam and Eve. In fact, in the thirteenth century, one author bluntly declared that "God changed sex."[4]

Nothing did more to civilize the coarse and brutal world of early feudalism than the institution known as chivalry, defined as "a body of sentiment and practice, of law and custom, which prevailed among the dominant classes in a great part of Europe between the eleventh and sixteenth centuries."[5] Chivalry was all at once a new spirit and a code of etiquette grafted onto feudalism by the church—unable to do away with feudalism altogether, the church found it easier to attempt to curb it by spiritual means. In order to understand the metamorphosis brought about by the appearance of chivalry, it is essential to keep in mind the sharp outlines of early feudalism as it emerged slowly out of the barbarian Dark Ages—the knight in early Norman times who held a plot of land in exchange for military service under his lord suzerain, a fearless warrior but treacherous and undisciplined, faithless in religious outlook, brutal and cruel, and utterly lacking in respect for women and the weak and defenseless. Nothing could curb the senseless violence of the contemporaries of the idealized knights of the "Chansons de Gestes," Ogier the Dane or Raoul de Cambrai, or the atrocious Geoffrey de Mandeville—men who mercilessly murdered unarmed men, raped and burned nuns in their convents, Nietzschean beasts of prey who cared nought for anything save their appetites of the moment. The great goddess of their tribal ancestors was no more; the medieval lady-goddess was not yet. All documents of the time testify to their contempt for women, their utter distrust for their advice and lack of interest in the fair sex, as well as their exclusive passion for handsome horses and good swords. Wives were often brutally beaten by their impetuous and short-tempered lords and masters, and were usually expected to thank them for it.[6]

By the eleventh century, feudalism had actually achieved its prime historical mission—the defense of Europe and Western Christendom against Saracens, Magyars, and Norsemen after the collapse of Charlemagne's ephemeral empire. But the feudal lords were still there in their impregnable castles, guarded by their invincible metal-sheathed horsemen, looting, burning, and raping to their heart's content, untamable by priest, monarch, bourgeois, or peasant. However, the Western church, at first pacifist, had become far more militant when Islam appeared on its doorstep, and even more so when the Turks wrested Muslim leadership from the Middle Eastern Arabs in the tenth and eleventh centuries. To an extent, the church had become militarized, and this militarization had enabled it to attempt to join with a reformed feudalism in a common cause—the war of the Cross against the Crescent. This historic fusion had come to a head at the Council of Clermont in 1095 when the First Crusade was proclaimed. Simultaneous with this proclamation, a general injunction was issued, commanding that every male person of knightly birth and training should, at the age of twelve, take a solemn oath before a bishop that "he would defend to the uttermost the oppressed, the widow and the orphan; and that women of noble birth should enjoy his special care."[7] On this foundation stone arose Christian chivalry to tame the barbaric feudal knighthood and transform knightly brigands into idealistic Crusaders and gentlemanly protectors of the weak.

The ideal was set but rarely reached in practice. Most Crusaders retained the savagery of their ancestors—witness the great cargo of sliced-off noses and thumbs sent by Bohemund of Antioch to the Byzantine emperor. Nevertheless, the church set about its new task with true religious zeal and, over the centuries, was successful in converting unmitigated savages into rudimentary gentlemen. It was even able to merge completely the dedication to religious pursuit and the warlike fanaticism of the times by establishing the great Crusading Orders—the Templars, Hospitallers, and Teutonic Knights. The apparently incongruous association of war and religion in a homogeneous whole rested on a remarkable exercise in self-discipline; the Templar, for instance, was a warrior-monk of the most austere type, disciplined by Cistercian asceticism, pledged to blind obedience, chastity, and absolute poverty.

Their lay compeers, meanwhile, were not restrained by such ascetic vows and plunged into the erotic atmosphere generated by a newly discovered art of gallantry. This was made possible by a considerable change in life in Western Europe after the taming and conversion of Normans and Danes—and the dwindling importance of the Crusades after the first flush of universal enthusiasm had evaporated. In a new atmosphere of relative peace and increasing prosperity and refinement, southern influences from the warm Mediterranean wafted toward the north with the marriage of Louis VII and Eleanor of Aquitaine. The baronial castle became a center of social intercourse, not merely a military fortress; and, with a modicum of peace such as had been unknown for centuries, music, poetry, painting, and countless minor arts began to flourish again. Feminine influence gained immensely.

While the priests tamed the knights, the troubadours "captured womanhood for romance."[8] Again it must be emphasized that the growth of religious feeling and of mundane love were closely interrelated and developed along parallel lines. Before chivalry, early feudalism was as implacably an enemy of romance as it was of true religion; love and marriage were as completely divorced as was religious faith from ecclesiastical office. A man "married a fief" by way of a bride who was the inevitable burden that went with the prize:

> The wife of the knight or baron of the dark post-Carolingian age was a serf and a chattel. But, like her husband, she was also a ferocious savage, capable of murderous cruelty, satanic blasphemy, and bestial lust.[9]

The names of some of these high-powered women have come down to us—Adelaide de Soisson, Blanche de Navarre, the Chatelaine de Cahusac, Mable de Montgomery—all of whom displayed true masculine vices and virtues as befitted such an age. But with the dawn of chivalry, new conditions appeared that once again brought forth true femininity. Hordes of trouvères, troubadours, minstrels, and minnesingers descended upon lonely dames and damsels to praise the ecstatic joys of love—not love of husbands, since marriage remained under chivalry what it had been before, mostly a business transaction, but of lovers and paramours, of the dangers and excitement of illicit affairs, of intrigues and devices whereby jealous husbands could be outwitted. In this atmosphere of established bigamy, a new relationship began to prevail in the erotic world. While legitimate marriage remained what it had been before, every husband and wife was expected to have mistress and lover, and between mistress and lover, the sexual roles were reversed; she almost always took the initiative. She was the goddess and he the humble wooer.[10]

In Germany, the ancient poet known as the Kürenberger had celebrated the man as lord and master, the fierce falcon for whom woman sighs; now the relationship was turned upside down and shifted the man to the position of a lowly vassal and the *vrouwe* (lady) to that of a lordly suzerain. Now *he* sighs for her and serves her humbly to win her favor. Although inspired by the troubadours of Provence, the Teutonic minnesingers expressed this love-service in a purely Germanic tone of lament and melancholy. All over Europe, minstrels sang the praise of their ladies' perfection and craved their approval. Knights no longer fought for the sake of fighting but to win their ladies' hearts; in fact, the idea gained ground that there could be no perfect knight who was not a perfect lover, that is to say, a perfectly *courteous* lover such as depicted in the subtle poem, "Lay of the Shadow."[11]

The zenith of this form of chivalric courtesy was reached during the Hundred Years' War when the knight's only acknowledged spur to action was his lady's love; most challenges to combat were flung in her name. The great chronicler Froissart claims that King Edward, victor at the battle of Cressy, was moved exclusively by his passionate love for the Countess of Salisbury. As Geoffrey of Monmouth, describing England in those days, put it:

> The Knights in it that were famous for feats of chivalry, wore their clothes and arms all of the same colour and fashion; and the women also, no less celebrated for their wit, wore all the same kind of apparel; and esteemed none worthy of their love, but such as had given a proof of their valour in three several battles. Thus was the valour of the men an encouragement for the women's chastity, and the love of the women a spur to the soldier's bravery.[12]

This was "gallantry," which set the rules for the art of love, as chivalry set those for the art of war; and although frowned upon by the church, it persisted until medievalism itself came to an end.

The church fought hard and long, and on the whole successfully, to compel men to consider their wives as equal "in everything, except in hierarchical rank."[13] Woman now began to be considered man's peer. A few monkish chroniclers still suspected woman of being endowed with diabolic influence, but, by and large, she was highly regarded. This was even more true in northern climes where home and hearth meant more during the interminably long, windy, and frosty winters than in the sunnier and warmer south. In the north, huddled together near the fire, men and women developed an intimacy unknown in Mediterranean lands; women acquired more influence over their men through long and close contact than was possible in the south where the gynaeceum and sexual segregation still prevailed, however unofficially. But regardless of clime and latitude, the church had good reason to fight for woman's dignity, since she was extremely instrumental in taming and civilizing medieval man. The church reached him more easily through her than directly, and more than one man replied to his wife's entreaty as Girard de Fraite did to Ameline when she converted him to the faith: "Wife, I want to become connected with God," with the implication that he could best do so with her as connecting link.[14]

Once again, woman became a means of communication, a transmission belt, but with the spiritual world this time. Love, purified of its lustful element, was now the main agent of man's spiritual salvation and this love could be secured only through the agency of woman as a supreme object of desire whose carnal seduction had to be overcome and sublimated—Tannhäuser dying with the certainty that a short but intense emotion felt with Saint Elizabeth was worth infinitely more than many hours of sexual passion in the Venusberg cave. But love first came to him with Venus—and the hard climb from Venus to Saint Elizabeth, from plain lust to spiritualized love, was interrupted by many relapses. In short, medieval woman was expected to be to medieval man what the stained-glass window was to the Gothic church—a wonderfully multicolored, translucent prism through which light filters in from the boundless space of the spirit, letting into his heart the spiritual light generated by sublimated love.

With woman once more raised up on a pedestal—not only as mother as in other civilizations but as prime object of love—the amatory arts developed speedily. True, gallantry did not usually flourish at home between husband and wife, yet men's illicit but gallant relationships were with women of the same social strata, not professional *hetairae*, and if the woman felt unfulfilled or sacrificed as wife, she was usually *also* the mistress, in reality or imagination, of a gallant lover who worshiped her. But European medievalism introduced something new in the concept of love: *l'amour courtois* was far more than a physical relationship with all the polite trimmings invented by an increasingly sophisticated age. For the first time in history, there developed a passionate interest in *unfulfilled desire*, a total sublimation of love, a thirst for a fusion with the principle of beauty itself, an absorbing fascination for the idea of love as almost a religion in itself and for which actual physical attraction between the sexes was nothing more than a convenient trigger. To be worthwhile, the object of love had to be immensely distant—the Provençal *amor lonthana*, faraway love—and preferably unattainable.

In formalizing the amatory art and framing it within a complex system of rules and aesthetic considerations, the medieval romantic movement went a long way toward its spiritualization; man loved woman, but also loved *through* woman a higher spiritual entity. Love was thus formalized according to a largely artificial code. Andrew the Chaplain, the celebrated author of the *Treatise on Love and Its Cure*, put forth thirty-one propositions or "Laws of Love," the first of which states emphatically that marriage, with all its trials and tribulations, is no excuse for rejecting love. This was based on the decision made by one of the most famous women of the time, Marie de Champagne, who, when asked whether real love was possible between husband and wife, replied negatively, claiming that true lovers give freely without being compelled by external circumstances such as prevail in the married estate. One is reminded of Ambrose Bierce's cynical definition of "love" in *The Devil's Dictionary:* "A temporary insanity curable by marriage"—precisely the point made by the courts of love when they severed one from the other. Medieval lovers simply did not want to be cured.

Many highly placed dames maintained celebrated courts of love—the Viscountess of Narbonne, the Countess of Flanders—where they sat in judgment and saw to it that the code of love was respected by both sexes. Among some of the Laws of Love, the most noteworthy were the following: "Love never stands still: it either increases or dwindles." "It is impossible to love two people simultaneously." "Possession should be difficult, not easy; difficulty stimulates love."[15]

In February 1401 the Duke of Burgundy founded the most famous of all courts of love at the Hotel d'Artois; both Philippe le Hardi and Louis de Bourbon asked the king to institute a royal court of love during a plague in order "to spend part of the time more graciously, and in order to find awakening of new joy." Ancestor of the future literary salons, the court was established to uphold humility and fidelity in "service of all noble ladies"; headed by the "Grands Conservateurs" and a Prince of Love (Pierre d'Hauteville), it sponsored debates "in the form of amorous lawsuits," following which the ladies distributed prizes to the winners.[16]

All in all, the medieval ideal of womanhood was highly complex, made up of apparently incompatible parts. On the one extreme was the more sensual view of Jean de Meun's continuation of the *Roman de la Rose;* at the other end of the spectrum a certain asceticism that sublimated mundane love and often led to a mild contempt for marriage; and in the middle, an attempt to raise above all else the true sort of love worthy of a God-fearing knight who would, nevertheless, not be deprived of his sexual enjoyment. Nowhere, it seems, can we find a trace of a love and respect for motherhood for its own sake, divorced from romantic love—except perhaps in Germany where, closer to old

tribal roots, the greatest of the minnesingers, Walther von der Vogel-
weide, moved away from the artificial standards set by the French
trouvères and troubadours, and sang the praise of the womanly
woman; contrasting favorably the *wîp* (woman) with the *vrouwe* (lady),
he reacted against the conventional praise of dames and, claiming that
German women are the best, praised them as human beings rather
than mere objects of love.[17]

There is ample proof that women all over Western Christendom
were not waiting for some gallant knight to worship and protect them
but were often quite prepared to defend themselves when peculiar
conditions compelled them to do so. While her husband was away on
duty or war, the wife became suzerain in the eyes of the vassals. She
often undertook the defense of her husband's castle, supervised the
administration of his affairs, and held court. Heiresses were in constant
danger if widowed, and often fought back with all the available weapons, legal or otherwise:

> Women in the thirteenth century were great litigants. No one can
> read English Plea Rolls of the second half of that period without
> being struck by their legal acumen and independence, qualities
> evidently necessary if dower rights were to be preserved.[18]

Other women made a living with their writing—witness the remarkable Christine de Pisan, born in Italy in 1364 but a lifelong resident
of France, who became a widow early in life, worked hard to support
her family, and produced probably the best treatise on the art of war
in her time. Celebrated and extremely influential, she lived long
enough to praise Joan of Arc as the liberator of France. That chivalry
still remained an important moral force in the latter part of the Middle
Ages is proved by her *Epistle to Othea* in which she gave many precepts
of knightly conduct approved by a woman. It was in those days (1398)
that Marshall Boucicault, an authentic champion of true courtesy,
founded the Order of the White Lady, dedicated to the defense of
oppressed women and more particularly of maidens in distress; he had
probably been encouraged to do so by Christine de Pisan's praise of
his ardent defense of ideal courtesy.

It was also Christine who assumed the defense of women against the
gallant male admirers of the *Roman de la Rose* and its salacious atmosphere; assisted by the great theologian Jean Gerson who hated the
"vicious *romaunt of the rose*"[19] and, along with the entire church, poured
maledictions on all forms of erotic love, she fought her opponents
tooth and nail in defense of female honor and put forth a moral version
of true chivalry that was far removed from its corrupted form in the
late Middle Ages:

Whence, exclaims Gerson, come the bastards, the infanticides, the abortions, whence hátred, whence poisonings? Woman joins her voice to that from the pulpit: all the conventions of love are the work of men: even when it dons an idealistic guise, erotic culture is altogether saturated by male egotism: and what else is the cause of the endlessly repeated insults to matrimony, to woman and her feebleness, but the need of masking this egotism? One word suffices, says Christine de Pisan, to answer all these infamies: it is not the women who have written the books. . . . Indeed, medieval literature shows little true pity for women, little compassion for her weakness and the dangers and pains which love has in store for her.[20]

In spite of chivalry and the increasingly popular cult of the Virgin, theology, relying mostly on Aristotle, took a dim view of the female sex. Johannes Scotus Erigena, that ninth-century Irish beacon shining in the Dark Ages, had already propounded the thesis that originally mankind was sinless and therefore without distinction of sex; it was as a result of sin that human beings were divided into males and females, the female embodying mankind's sensual and sinful nature. For Thomas Aquinas woman was an inferior human being, defective and accidental (deficiens et occasionatum), a male that was askew, the result of a weakness in the procreative powers of the father. Aquinas remained faithful to the old concept of classical Greece (as interpreted by Aristotle) that woman provides only inert matter to her offspring while man provides the spiritual entity, the active form. Woman is mainly a sexual appetite, while man is better balanced; weaker in every respect—in will, mind, and body—she is to man what the physical senses are to reason. Her sole purpose is procreation, since man can do everything better than she does—even her domestic chores. Unable to occupy any important position in either church or state, she is meant to look up to man as her natural lord and accept his authority without question.

With all this, the most surprising thing is that Canon Law was actually more generous to woman than civil law. True, the wife was instructed to obey her husband, in exchange for his protection, since man rather than woman was made in God's image; but the church insisted on monogamy, imposed equal moral standards on both sexes, and granted woman the right to inherit property. Civil law, on the other hand, stated that the word of woman was not to be admitted in court because of her unreliability, and, while depriving her of political rights, ruled that marriage gave the husband full use of property his wife owned at the time of marriage. As for wife beating, both codes of law permitted it; only in the thirteenth century did the "Laws and Customs of Beauvais" instruct husbands to beat their wives "only within reason" and with moderation.

Regardless of laws and legal inferiority, medieval women held their own against men, and the literature of the times testifies to the numerous instances of matriarchal families. With relative peace and increasing prosperity, family life became more stable—at all times an element favoring greater feminine influence. Men began to lose their warlike virility and became softer. Furthermore, hereditary transmission of noble rank started around the fourteenth century, giving women, as vessels of biological transmission, that much more importance.[21] From the eleventh to the thirteenth centuries there was no nobility of blood; social fluidity, in these unstable days, was considerable. In the fourteenth century, however, a new nobility based on secure bloodlines began to assert itself, demanding social privileges by virtue of its real or presumed ancestry. Bloodlines became all important; the aristocratic class began to close up; and, thereafter, only royal decrees could make a man noble, not alone his deeds and personal ability, as in former times. This new rigidity in social stratification gave some privileged women far more power and importance than they had enjoyed in the former chaotic, brutal and warlike era.

With the close of the Middle Ages, it is time to examine the peculiar nature of its *Weltanschauung*—the world-outlook, not merely of a new society, but of a new breed of human beings resulting from the biological intermingling of invaders and invaded, civilized and barbarian. The result of this cross-fertilization was raw, youthful humanity on a much lower cultural level than its Muslim antagonists or its Byzantine cousins and fellow Christians. To medieval man, the outlines of all things were far more clearly marked than they were to be to his more cultured descendants; the contrast between opposites—pain and joy, tenderness and cruelty, health and illness, wealth and misery, and more than anything else, male and female—was violent, and so were their convictions, qualities, and faults, their laughter and their tears. This was not a jaded, satiated society of cynics and skeptics but a violently alive and passionate one. Medieval men and women were organically and exuberantly young in a world full of ever-present danger which made the slightest bounty appear truly miraculous. Each event was important and was surrounded with solemn, expressive celebrations and ritual in an atmosphere of passionate excitement. Everything and everyone was different from anything and anyone else, and had unique value; from lepers and beggars to bourgeois and lords, every order and estate and profession was clad in its own colorful garment. Processions were frequent, and so were the innumerable pilgrimages; bells pealed from one end of Europe to the other and their sound faded away only on the periphery of Christendom, the borderlands with Islam, where they were replaced by the proud and plaintive chant of the *muezzins* calling their own faithful to prayers from atop their minarets.

The Middle Ages, like every other healthy society, had a passion for order and organization, pushed at times to a ludicrous degree: dogma, human knowledge, society, and art were all organized in complex organic wholes whose parts were interdependent. Nothing reveals the essence of the medieval soul as clearly as Gothic art in its hieratic greatness. Art was not so much a means of aesthetic enjoyment as a teaching and education in holy lore; the cathedral was the "Bible of the poor" in which Old and New Testaments were depicted symbolically and allegorically; even the slightest detail had symbolic significance. Gothic architecture was just as much "frozen music" as the literature of the times, and Dante's heaven was just as much a symphony as the frontage of the cathedral at Chartres—music in which every note had allegorical meaning.

The Middle Ages revered "numbers" and the plainest arithmetic had symbolic value, whether it be Dante's *Divina Commedia* which is entirely constructed around numbers or the seven tones of Gregorian music, or the twelve columns in the nave of a church corresponding to the twelve apostles and the twelve months of the year. Gothic art was all at once a holy script, an arithmetic, and a symbolism of profound harmony, reflecting the medieval concept that the universe was a *thought* of God the Father, actualized by the Word, that is, His Son. It was Christ who carried out the transformation of potential into actual, and He it was, according to Gothic art, who actually both created, and then redeemed, the world.

If, in truth, the universe was no more than an *idea* in God's mind, actualized by the Logos, there was not much room for the feminine principle, but this was promptly remedied by the depiction of the Twelve Virtues in the shape of lovely chaste women, often armed and in combat with the equally female vices. The famous mystical ladder stretching from earth to heaven displays, close to the top, a woman about to reach Paradise while all the men have fallen off. It was quite clear that in the organismic world-picture of the Middle Ages, the sexes were viewed as organically interrelated in a way that implied no fundamental superiority or inferiority of either sex in religious terms —regardless of the views of Aquinas. Since the Bible, for instance, could be understood on four different and distinct levels—historically, as describing real happenings; allegorically, as portraying the New

Testament as a mirror image or replica of the Old Testament; tropo-logically, as displaying the moral truth hidden behind the Holy Scrip-ture; and anagogically, as depicting the eternal blessings of life beyond death (the four meanings of the word Jerusalem, for instance)—so could the medieval conception of the respective roles of the sexes, inferior or superior, depending on the level of understanding.[22]

The medieval spirit was essentially naïve, and in its youthfulness always sought to give concrete expression to every sentiment and every idea. As time went by, and the Middle Ages grew older, the fantastic proliferation of images, observances, celebrations, religious interpretations of all and sundry began to crush medieval society un-der its increasing weight. Religion was at the center of everything, true, but everything—good, bad, or indifferent—was also connected with religion. The mutual interpenetration of the sacred and the profane had its dangers to the extent that the holiest of holies lost some of its remoteness and mysterious magic; religious feeling became that much more shallow, sinking to the level of the commonplace. The endless multiplication of relics and amulets, images and reproductions, sacra-ments and special indulgences began to crowd out true spiritual sig-nificance. Religious orders, especially mendicants, swarmed over the land; superstition intruded in religious thought and feeling, warping everyday life—coronations, battles, and inaugurations had to be put off because of inauspicious signs, prompting Jean Gerson to claim that it proceeded *èx sola hominum phantasiatione et melancholica imaginatione*—disorder of the imagination due to lesions of the brain, in turn pro-duced by diabolically inspired illusions.[23] Reformation was inevitable, and sooner than later.

The medieval outlook rested on one broad principle: only the "uni-versals" are real; individual man is not as real as the estate to which he belongs—the individual priest or monk is nothing, the church is everything; the knight is nought as compared with the principle of knighthood. This was why the great cathedral builders and Gothic artists were usually anonymous. In such an organic conception of things in which the individual paled into insignificance, there was and could be no room for any concept of man as a separate, autonomous entity—and therefore of woman as a separate entity either, let alone in opposition to man. Both were different types of organic cells, merged in a much vaster spiritual superorganism.

The Middle Ages came to an end when this world-picture disinte-grated under the impact of a new philosophic outlook, generated by scholastic cogitations: Nominalism, first introduced by Duns Scotus but developed to its full potential by his most famous disciple, William of Occam. From the Nominalist viewpoint, the universal could not exist in things but only in the ratiocinating mind. Duns Scotus still claimed that concepts were copies of things, but Occam stated firmly that they were only *signs* that we use in our relations with things. Five centuries of Scholastic development ended in destroying scholasticism itself. With this development, the entire medieval world-picture collapsed into its opposite: from now on, only singular, discrete concepts and ideas, and discrete sensual moments, are real; all collective concepts and universals become merely convenient fabrications of the mind.

This "nuclear" destruction of the medieval organic outlook in turn generated a complete disorientation and a profound pessimism, along with a loss of religious faith that spilled over well into the Renaissance. Every traditional institution disintegrated—the empire and the church found their authority eroded when several emperors and popes appeared on the scene simultaneously. In 1409, for instance, there were no less than three popes. All the social and political bonds loosened drastically; the time-hallowed traditions faded away, along with the medieval values. Love and sex, and the relationship between men and women, changed accordingly. Medieval, chivalric love had so completely hypostatized its object that it had become unattainable—erotic yearning was so insatiable that love became as much an expression of infinite longing as the Gothic cathedral with its flying buttresses, stained-glass windows, and elongated spires became an expression of infinite space. Sublimated erotism, deprived of its spiritual goal by loss of faith, slowly turned into raw sexuality. Woman was no longer an idealized means to spiritual fulfilment but a means of sexual enjoyment: she became a sex object—but also, rid of her apotheosized figure, a true human being seeking, as man was also seeking, to become an emancipated individual:

> She was infected by the general urge towards emancipation, her attitude was bolder, her rightful position in the family and in public was acknowledged: indeed, she may be said in the period to have held the spiritual and moral primacy.[24]

In this picture, the virago of the Renaissance is clearly foreshadowed.

CHAPTER

3

The Virago

The Renaissance implied an apparent rebirth of the classical Greco-Roman spirit, a return of the European center of gravity from the cold Gothic north to the Mediterranean. Gothic art began to be looked upon as barbaric, weird, and unintelligible. Medieval symbolism faded away like northern mist warmed by the Mediterranean sun; and with Petrarch and Dante, the Middle Ages drew to a close.

With *La Rinascita*, the European *locus in quo* shifts to Italy. The material basis was a remarkable increase in wealth, the result of trade with the Orient; merchants and bankers were in a position to buy the old manuscripts, the study of which gradually dispelled the medieval haze and revived pride in the Italian roots of classical Rome. The fall of Constantinople in 1453 and the final collapse of the Byzantine Empire prompted numerous Greek scholars to flee to Italy and revive classical Greek literature. In fact, some years before, in 1439, Greek scholars had attended the Council of Florence to debate the great ecumenical issue—the reunion of the Eastern Greek and Western Latin churches; Florentine literati flocked to the scholarly lectures of Greek delegates to the conference, many of whom settled down in Florence after the fall of Constantinople.

The growth of universities, the rise of a new middle class, and remarkable business acumen set the stage for one of the greatest outpourings of artistic creativity ever seen. And with it all, a new skepticism in matters religious, an erosion of faith in Christian dogmas which infected even popes and clergy, dispelled the cosmic fear and hope that had all at once haunted and warmed medieval men and women. Renaissance man began to focus without restraint on the plastic beauty of the human body, searching now for the *superhuman* rather than the supernatural; sexual life began to pattern itself on a revived paganism without much restraint from religion. In the process,

232

the church became more catholic but far less Christian: the classical Greco-Roman component almost eliminated the Jewish biblical one, in spite of the violent reactions of the likes of Savonarola.

All in all, the Renaissance was lopsidedly creative in the artistic sphere and delighted in shaping forms and mixing colors; very little of that creative genius was left over for philosophy or science, except for Leonardo da Vinci whose genius was protean. Actually, the Italian Renaissance was not comparable to Periclean Athens in overall scope; but from the renewed study of classical culture came the expression *umanisti*, a label that humanists bore proudly, implying a revived interest in humanity. Man, rather than God, became the prime object of study—man in all aspects, his physical strength and beauty, his intellect and cultural creativity. Focusing on man rather than the Almighty, the Renaissance was bound to bring to the fore, once again, the problem of the relationship between the sexes. Focusing on man implied, inevitably, focusing also on woman. Thus was born the *virago*.

In spite of occasional antifeminist satires in the manner of Ariosto, Jacob Burckhardt, the great historian of *The Civilization of the Renaissance in Italy*, is quite firm in his opinion that

> we must keep before our minds the fact that women stood on a footing of perfect equality with men. . . . The education given to women in the upper classes was essentially the same as that given to men . . . with education, the individuality of women in the upper classes was developed in the same way as that of men. . . . In Italy, throughout the whole of the fifteenth century, the wives of the rulers, and still more those of the Condottieri, have nearly all a distinct, recognizable personality, and take their share of notoriety and glory. . . . There was no question of "woman's rights" or female emancipation, simply because the thing itself was a matter of course. The educated woman, no less than the man, strove naturally after a characteristic and complete individuality.[1]

Under the warm sun of the Renaissance, Italian women began to retrieve some of the emancipation that their Roman ancestors had acquired in the last stages of the Roman Republic. The career of the first woman to whom the term *virago*, then a praiseworthy epithet, was applied, the famous Caterina Sforza, wife of Girolamo Riario, exemplifies the forcefulness and boldness of these women who would dare wage battle against a Cesare Borgia. Whether they were celebrated patronesses of the arts like Isabella Gonzaga, or writers such as Cassandra Fedele and Vittoria Colonna, viragos made their personality felt directly as autonomous individuals rather than through the intermediary of powerful men.

The courtesan, la grande putana, played a vital part in the social life of the times. Courtesans seem to have had an impact on the cultural life of the Renaissance comparable to that of the ancient Greek hetairae —Rome's famous Imperia de Cugnatis was fluent in Latin and Greek and was painted by Raphael as Sappho; the beautiful Isabella de Luna, the celebrated Milanese Caterina di San Celso, golden-haired Tullia d'Aragona—women known as cortigiane oneste were treated with great respect and consideration, displaying as they did great intelligence and vast culture along with undoubted femininity.[2] As Burckhardt points out, the contrast is stark between women of that type in the fifteenth century—who displayed no such talent and left no trace—and those glittering female personalities of the early part of the sixteenth century who left an indelible mark on their times, implying a sharp rise in feminine power and influence within a single generation.

In spite of the loose morals triggered by the Renaissance, family life was happier and more rationally organized than during the Middle Ages. At the height of chivalry, the wandering knight was away from home most of the time, his love and homage always given to women other than his wife, leaving her to her own devices in the castle:

> The spirit of the Renaissance first brought order into domestic life, treating it as a work of deliberate contrivance . . . the chief cause of the change was the thoughtful study of all questions relating to social intercourse, to education, to domestic service and organization.[3]

Social life began to move out of the walled cities and fortified castles where medieval insecurity had confined it, and in the new Italian country houses (villas), an entirely novel style of carefree life developed. In spite of numerous wars, the relative peace and security of the Italian countryside, along with a vast increase in wealth, enabled the Italian woman to achieve a degree of independence and influence unknown in the rest of Europe at that time.

Symbolic of this higher status was the religious recrudescence of Mariolatry, an enormous extension of its popularity in the late Middle Ages. Nowhere in the north was the worship of the Virgin as widespread as in Renaissance Italy where "the number of miraculous pictures of the Virgin was far greater, and the part played in the daily life of the people much more important. . . . The popular craving for the miraculous, especially strong in women, may have been fully satisfied by these pictures, and for this reason the relics been less regarded."[4]

True, the educated classes did not share in Mariolatry, which was essentially a popular worship; but it remained the great inspirer of art and literature in the early part of the Renaissance. Never had sculptors and painters glorified the Madonna as they did at the time, in works of plastic beauty that even the uneducated could appreciate. But in literature, Dante's great work is the last tribute paid to the Virgin Mary; in the religious poems and hymns written at the end of the fifteenth and beginning of the sixteenth centuries, such as those of Lorenzo the Magnificent and Vittoria Colonna, the atmosphere is almost Protestant —predominance of the Almighty, deliverance wrought by Christ's sufferings, and strong sense of sin. The Mother of God appears rarely.

Side by side, Renaissance Italy displays two contradictory strains in sexual relations as in religion: on the one hand, the renaissance of feminine power and prestige, along with a new pagan outlook on sexual matters; and in religion, a considerable development of Mariolatry that went counter to a pre-Reformation spirit that inspired the almost Puritan revolt of Savonarola against the corruption and loose morals of the times. The pagan outlook on sex, fruit of the rediscovery of ancient Greece and Rome, could not help but foster the rise of homosexuality among men. Leonardo's dislike for women is only one of the more notorious instances; and the prevalence of homosexuality was such that Leonardo never forgave Florence for singling him out and arresting him on charges of sexual depravity when so many others went scot-free. While he portrayed men far more often than women, he knew and understood the latter well, and it would be impossible to accuse the creator of the *Mona Lisa* and the *Virgin, Child and St. Anne* of being insensitive to feminine beauty and personality.

Humanists commented favorably on homosexuality and, according to Ariosto, most if not all of them were homosexuals. Aretino stated that homosexuality was widespread in Rome, and San Bernardino was shocked by its prevalence in Naples. In the middle of the fifteenth century the Venetian authorities raved against "the abominable vice of sodomy" and took steps to curb it. Only with the Counter-Reformation did homosexuality began to fade away—about the time when Spanish influence seeping in from the south began to undermine feminine emancipation and put an end to Italian viragoism altogether.

The virago brought forth by the Renaissance in Italy was not unique: viragos have cropped up at different times and in different places, whenever conditions were favorable. Etymologically the epithet implies a strong masculine component in the makeup of such women, and an autonomous strength of character not usually associated with what is presumed to be the weaker sex. At its best, it implies highly mature women who find themselves in unusual positions of power and authority in an essentially aristocratic society; this was frequently the case during the Italian Renaissance where equality of education for both sexes was instrumental in developing women's natural potential.

The career of Lucrezia Borgia is an outstanding instance. After Rodrigo Borgia had been elected pope under the name of Alexander VI, he often made use of his talented daughter Lucrezia in papal affairs, occasionally promoted her to the governorship of a city or induced her to make love to some ruling prince or other to further the interests of the Vatican. Twice, when compelled to leave Rome on affairs of state, he left her in complete charge of the Vatican, with full authority to open his mail as well as transact routine business. This delegation of power to a woman was unusual in ecclesiastical Rome, although frequent in other parts of Italy—Urbino, Mantua, Ferrara, for instance. Despite this, such gifted women did not object to having their fathers choose their husbands for them in traditional fashion, as when Pope Alexander picked Giovanni Sforza as husband for Lucrezia because of his family ties to the Duchy of Milan, only to have the marriage annulled and a new one set with Don Alfonso, duke of Bisceglie, with whom she fell in love. Nor did she object openly, in spite of her tender feelings, when her brother Cesare Borgia had Alfonso murdered and her father arranged a new match with Duke Ercole of Ferrara—an important state in Alexander's political strategy. She accepted her role as political pawn with good grace, and while her astute father and diabolically clever brother wrecked the power of the Borgias, she escaped from the crumbling edifice and was enthusiastically accepted by her adopted countrymen in Ferrara, acclaimed by all as an exemplar of true feminine excellence. She bore her husband five children and developed Ferrara into a cultural center by attracting leading artists and poets, which did not prevent her from acting temporarily as regent, to everyone's satisfaction—including that of her dour husband. Lucrezia was only thirty-nine when she died after a very full life—the paragon of viragos.

However, viragoism also developed some harmful side effects that historically seem to occur when the female of the species begins to negate her sexual personality and metamorphoses herself into its opposite: the beast of prey. Consider the case of the women of the ruling House of Anjou in Naples whose first notorious female, Queen Joanna I, had to be strangled with a silken cord by Charles of Durazzo because of her dangerous eccentricities. Better still, consider ruthless Joanna II who was already forty when she reached the throne in 1414. Married three times, she banished her second husband and murdered her third.

Faced by an uprising against her outrageous rule, she called upon the assistance of King Alfonso of Aragon, adopted him as son and heir in 1420, then disowned him three years later and finally picked upon René of Anjou as her rightful heir—with the immediate result that the two rulers fought over the Kingdom of Naples, and the more remote consequence that the French eventually invaded and devastated part of Italy.

The virago gone wrong is a special type of inverted female—perfectly normal physiologically but psychologically warped by special social circumstances and upbringing. Borderline types, they have that settled ambiguity characteristic of all that is wildly extreme—in this case, the preying instinct normally associated with the male. Only at the top of the social strata are such women to be found—women whose exalted social position compensates, largely, for the usual inferior status of their sex in a patriarchal structure. In this environment, granted a modicum of inherited or delegated power, they seem to ape men at their preying worst. So we have the Salomes and the Cleopatras and Eleanors of Aquitaine who prove to be more ruthless and deadly than the male at their own game of power politics.

Usually brought up and educated in an atmosphere of great or even absolute power, pampered beyond reason, all distinction between desire and fulfillment is erased in their minds; by any means, fair or foul, they usually get what they want. To the extent that their talent and energy remain unused for useful purposes, they become generators of dangerous frustrations. Being, as a rule, far more practical and flexible than the men in their adaptation to the reality of any given situation, women take charge, most of the time, of that share of married life that calls for those qualities. But at the summit of the social pyramid where women are often both pampered and idle, a curious psychological inversion takes place in the virago: since paucity of creative imagination appears to characterize feminine psychology, she begins to seek or provoke odd situations in concrete reality, rather than imagining them in her brain and making mental constructions. She works on the flesh rather than the spirit—distortions must become incarnate. Suffering the frustrations of unused, bottled-up talent and energy, her daydreaming becomes the most important part of her being—which is not the case with most active women—and the virago's personality undergoes a dangerous masculinization.

Sexually normal, with no trace of lesbianism, the virago is quite prepared to surrender herself—but only fully to creations of her extravagant delusions, usually a flesh-and-blood man whom she misunderstands completely and phantasmagorically bloats to suit her own psychological purposes; and woe be it to the passing male who attracts her fantasy and is then fitted into the procrustean bed of her fancied desire. No real man can ever suit her dream; he merely gives a concrete embodiment to the dreamlike male to whom she wishes to surrender —her femininity longs to surrender to the vision conjured by her inherent masculinity, her *animus.*

The virago type, brought to full bloom in Italy during the Renaissance, is as eternal as the species, and European history, not to mention other civilizations, is full of viragoes—Queen Elizabeth I of England who deliberately set her face against marriage for the sake of safeguarding her political power; Queen Christina of Sweden who mercilessly dragooned her chancellor and mentor, Axel Oxenstjerna, and compared herself with the queen of Sheba. Her vigorous masculinity—short hair, love of fencing and hunting—was so apparent that she was rumored to be a hermaphrodite—a reputation she once attempted to destroy by deliberately overturning her carriage, lying on the ground with her skirts pulled up, crying out to those who were rushing to her rescue: "Don't be shy! Come closer and convince yourself that I am no hermaphrodite."[5] Upon her abdication, she left Sweden dressed in masculine attire under the name of Count Dohna.

But what of Peter the Great's female brood! Compare the male weaklings—Tzars Peter II and III—to the formidable women who, in effect, ruled Russia throughout most of the eighteenth century. When Catherine I, daughter of a plain Lithuanian mujik and second wife of Peter the Great, was illegally raised to the throne on her husband's death in 1725, she became the first woman ruler Russia ever had—to the considerable irritation of many Russian males, who claimed that it should be their wives, and not they, who should swear allegiance to the empress. As Peter's second wife, Catherine had proved to be a very strong personality in her own right and Peter always credited her courage and steadfastness with saving the situation during the disastrous campaign of the Pruth. As empress, her wildly extravagant but unusually shrewd personality was on full display during her two-year reign—far too short to accomplish anything noteworthy.

Empress Elizabeth Petrovna, youngest of Peter's daughters, who seized the throne in 1741 after driving to the barracks and commandeering the Preobrazhenski Guards, proved an exceedingly capable ruler with some of the remarkable talents of her pharaonic father. Her rule came as a ray of light after the disastrous ten-year reign of Empress Ann, former Duchess of Kurland. Elizabeth's twenty-year rule was noteworthy for the remarkable extension of the Russian Empire. Abolishing the cabinet council system in favor of the senate as it had been under her father, she launched into the fateful Seven Years' War; from 1759 to 1761, it was Elizabeth's iron will that prevented the heterogeneous anti-Prussian coalition from disintegrating and drove Frederick the Great to the edge of irremediable disaster. He should have known better: Elizabeth came into the war not so much for reasons of state and grand geopolitical designs, as because of the disparaging remarks made incautiously by Frederick about her private life.[6] Nevertheless, her foreign policy was both clever and audacious, and it was only her death in 1762 that saved the exhausted Prussian monarch from utter ruin—in 1760, a Russian force of Cossacks and Kalmuks had actually reached the outskirts of Berlin.

Catherine the Great is, like Cleopatra and Theodora, a household word, the epitome of female rulership at its greatest. German-born, she arrived in Russia at the age of fourteen, already mature and boundlessly ambitious; much later, she stated that she knew from the very beginning that she would, one day, become the "autocratic Empress of Russia." She had been married to the foolish and incapable Peter III, who became tzar upon the death of Elizabeth in 1762. The same year, enlisting the assistance of the Ismailovsky and Semenovsky regiments, Catherine dethroned her husband (and possibly had him murdered by Alexis Orlov) and became empress in her own right. As a ruler, she proved to be the equal of Peter the Great, with the slight but typical feminine difference that she was far more flexible and realistic in the sense of adapting to concrete situations as they happened to present themselves. Not only did she have countless lovers but she used most of them as her ministers and advisers in affairs of state; however, true virago that she was, she never let herself be dominated by any of them. She enjoyed lovemaking, but politics and intellectual pursuits were her main passion. Her love letters "might almost be those of man to man, with the difference by which Catherine herself characteristically explained her amours, that 'one of the two friends was a very attractive woman.' "[7]

But Catherine was no bloodthirsty Salome. She was profoundly humane, and during the disastrous Pugachev rebellion she urged her subordinates who were crushing the revolt to avoid any unnecessary bloodshed; she herself insisted that Pugachev not be tortured during his trial. She was also farsighted; and this rebellion had shown her, and she never tired of repeating it, that the social conditions of the time would lead Russia to some revolutionary catastrophe if reforms were not undertaken in time. She was also shrewd enough to exploit all the prerogatives due to her sex in her diplomatic dealings with male monarchs.

Her female contemporary and royal colleague, Maria Theresa, queen of Hungary and Bohemia, archduchess of Austria, was a different type. More than Catherine, she made full use of her sex and beauty when she seduced, for instance, the Hungarian Magnates at the Diet of Pressburg in 1741. Legend has it that they were so moved when she appeared with her infant son in her arms that they rose in unison, shouting *Moriamur pro rege nostro Maria*—the Magnates were all men; women Magnates might have seen through her wiles and been less impressed. She was a cautious but able ruler, whose true femininity showed during the ruthless, shameful partition of Poland, against which she protested in vain although offered a large slice of Galicia. As Frederick the Great stated it sneeringly, "the more she wept for Poland, the more she took of it."[8]

If the Renaissance brought out the type in bold relief and coined the name, the virago is, in fact, of all times and all places. She has been and always will be that exceptional woman who is more than a match for her male rivals, especially when she preserves to the full all the assets of her femininity in her struggles against them—which presupposes, of course, that she operates in a completely male environment in which she can bring to bear the advantages of her double personality: femininity along with masculine power. Against other women, she might become powerless, and usually shuns them like the plague. The virago is an autonomous female, clever at manipulating men; but she can and does succeed in her own right, and does not, unlike other women, always have to operate *through* a man in order to assert herself. To a degree, she is also the result of historical developments. By breaking up the medieval concept of organic social harmony and cooperation which makes all the individual members of society focus on their social rather than individual role, on the different but specific parts they play in the whole social organism, the Renaissance let loose vast forces of social metamorphosis that were to lead to a complete reorganization along national lines. But it is the Renaissance's emphasis on the liberation of the individual per se that, to an extent, freed woman from her preordained gender role as set in the organic concept of the social body.

Inevitably, men's attitude toward women also began to change. Gone were the medieval concepts of chivalry and courtesy, of moral obligation on the part of the strong sex toward the weak. The attitude of the Humanists, the intellectual aspect of the Renaissance, is quite revealing in this respect. Just as they prefaced, to an extent, the religious upheaval that was going to take place with the Reformation, they revealed in advance the change in the male attitude toward the female in post-medieval times. The breakdown of traditional Christian morality and ethics that the Renaissance triggered with its revival of classical

Greco-Roman culture was, in the long run, unfavorable to women; a great deal of what the church had done for them came apart. But that was not all. The Humanist movement of the Renaissance was essentially male-oriented and socially elitist; medieval culture aimed at universalism, attempted to educate *all* people into an allegoric consensus —the humblest serfs and peasants, women and children, all were trained to understand the Gothic symbols. The Humanists despised crowds as well as women, looked down upon the vulgar plebs that medievalism had incorporated in its organic conception of the integrated social body. Humanistic literature was aristocratic, reserved for a refined elite.

Only those rare Humanists whose admiration for classical antiquity had not extinguished their Christian feelings bothered with female education. Juan Luis Vivès is a perfect example. This pioneer in the realm of psychology, who became famous for reintroducing induction as a method of philosophical disputation and psychological discovery, educated the four daughters of Isabella la Catolica, the remarkably forceful and virtuous queen of Castille who was farsighted enough to bankroll Christopher Columbus. Vivès then followed Catherine of Aragon to England and was appointed preceptor to Mary, princess of Wales—and fell out of favor when he opposed Henry VIII's divorce from Catherine. His entire life was devoted to the education of women and he dedicated his celebrated *The Instruction of a Christian Woman* to Henry's estranged wife. Vivès was not alone; Erasmus wanted women to be educated on a par with men and asserted that feminine intelligence was fully the equal of man's.

But all those Humanists who rebelled against the church and advocated a return to the epicurean ideals of classical culture looked upon women and female bodies as the highest instruments of man's pleasure rather than as equal human beings: for instance, Lorenzo Valla, for whom Luther had a high regard (Cardinal Bellarmine even went so far as to label him *praecursor Lutheri*), and whose famous *De Voluptate* became the bible of the new epicureans. Valla asserted that prostitutes were far more useful than nuns and that the highest social ideals enjoined female promiscuity. In his *Hermaphrodite*, Antonio Beccadelli praises woman's intelligence only to the extent that it becomes an adjunct of her sensual awareness. Giovanni Pontano's erotic writings synthesized better than any other the sheer paganism of the Renaissance's outlook: woman's intelligence must and can only be that of Sappho of Lesbos and Aspasia, a mental extension of their flesh designed specifically for man's erotic pleasure. Woman's soul is now sacrificed to her body, whose sole object and purpose is to satisfy man's craving. So, at least, claims Leonardo Bruni.[9]

The new post-medieval literature testifies to this changed outlook on the roles of the sexes in social and cultural life. In the days of the virago, Rabelais discourses at great length on education—but only for men. As far as intelligence is concerned, woman is never mentioned. Even Petrarch, the founder of Humanism, with his roots deep in medieval Christianity, and still quite unwilling to substitute a pagan for the Christian ideal, viewed woman with distrust, not as an object for the sensual pleasure of man (his pathetic and platonic love for Laura appears to be a masterpiece of sublimation) but as a reincarnation of the eternal Eve. In his *Epistle to Posterity* he states that "enemy of peace, source of impatience, cause of quarrels which destroy tranquillity, woman is a real devil."[10]

It was left to his Humanist followers to set up an epicurean, pagan ideal in place of the Christian one; and where medieval Christianity had allowed plenty of room for an important feminine role in public life, the Renaissance was essentially man-made, for males only; woman, unless she was a virago, once again became an object rather than a subject in her own right. Famous medieval women were usually highly moral, virtuous females such as Blanche de Castille who was all at once a masterfully energetic wife and regent, a saint, and the mother of a saint. With the Renaissance, we enter an era of famous courtesans and mistresses. Freed from moral duty by the Renaissance and its looser ethics, woman's spiritual symbol shifted back from the Virgin to Eve.

In Italy, birthplace of the modern "emancipated" woman, the virago eventually passed away, largely because of the Spanish conquests and the spread of Moorish-Hispanic influence; Italian women were resubjugated and lost most of their public influence in the land.

CHAPTER

4

The Witch

The fade-out of the Middle Ages and the disintegration of its symbolic world-outlook triggered large-scale outbreaks of collective insanity—typical of any society, whether primitive or civilized, whenever its traditional mythology loses its credibility. If one should attempt to pinpoint a date for the beginning of this strange phenomenon, 1349, that of the outbreak of the plague which, under the name of Black Death, devastated Europe from one end to the other, would undoubtedly fit the bill. This catastrophe generated several waves of mass hysteria, the most remarkable being the exalted flagellant monks who toured the Continent, singing, praying, and beating themselves into bloody pulps, preaching in a heretical vein against the sins of clergy and laity alike. Like so many magnets, they promptly attracted assorted crowds of lunatics, criminals, and fanatics who joined their dreadful processions. But certain forms of collective madness had made their presence felt even before the Black Death; what became known to us as Saint Vitus's dance had already become widespread—men and women dancing around the clock like Muslim dervishes, foaming at the mouth and falling to the ground in a state of cataleptic exhaustion. Another phenomenon was the extraordinary Crusade of the Children of Schwäbisch-Hall who were prompted under hypnosis to go and pay their respects to Archangel Michael in faraway Normandy. Even anti-Semitism became virulent, and countless Jews were slaughtered as a result of the collective madness generated by the flagellants.

What was happening, largely as a result of the general breakdown of medieval ideals and values and the waning of faith in God, was an exuberant revival of faith in evil, in the Devil. This outbreak of Satanism was a profound mental trauma, a collective neurosis impressively depicted in Hieronymus Bosch's tortured, almost surrealistic *diableries.* Somehow, many people came to believe that the days of Antichrist were at hand and that they were living in a nightmare from which escape was impossible. Gripped by this collective terror, European crowds became far more gullible than they had ever been during the Middle Ages when even belief in the most extraordinary legends was largely a matter of understanding the symbolic meaning concealed behind the myths. Now that the old myths were evaporating before the increasing clarity of thought of the Humanists, man was delivered psychologically naked to all the atavistic fears and cosmic terrors springing from the unconscious.

The frenzy with which men and women threw themselves into sexual enjoyment betrayed a form of moral ataraxia, an ethical blindness or indifference produced by the chaotic state of the world during this age of transition when all the traditional moorings were set loose. Down to the humblest village, special establishments dedicated to debauchery suddenly appeared in which married and unmarried men and women bathed naked in large groups, operating as places of rendezvous for those who did not want to go to the equally innumerable brothels strewn all over Europe. In fact, the chief complaints of brothel keepers and whores was that their business was being ruined by the keen competition of the convents; those were the days when nun and whore were almost synonymous expressions. The general belief was that the Devil ruled the world: the stage was psychologically set for the forthcoming hysteria against witches.

It was not by pure coincidence that witch-hunting on a large scale began with the Renaissance. Sorcery had always been recognized as an evil delusion during the Dark and Middle Ages, but witch-hunting had never become a major issue and the object of collective insanity as it became during the Renaissance and the Reformation. What distinguished sorcery from previous magic practices was that, first of all, it testified to a rebirth of pagan, pre-Christian cults going all the way back to the Bronze Age. Essentially it was a popular movement spreading among the lower social strata of society, away from cities and often in those remote corners of Europe where Christianity had not penetrated in depth. Furthermore, most witches were not men but women, and the viciousness of the witch-hunts indicated a rebirth of male fright at the closeness of females with the still uncontrollable forces of nature. This fear had never really died but had remained latent, visible in such things as the horror of menstrual blood whose presumed dangerous properties included destroying grass, tarnishing mirrors, dissolving asphalt, blasting the buds of the vine, and so on, all of which was asserted by such noteworthy scholars as Rodericus a Castro and Lemnius.

The rise of heresies eventually compelled the church to label all attempts to deal with the unknown as diabolic, implying a compact between the would-be sorcerers and the Devil. Fascination with the occult had long and far more alarmed the church than plain unbelief and practical agnosticism; the Humanists themselves made an important contribution with their literary revival of Greco-Roman superstitions.

The fatally dangerous transition was that from the witch who merely divines and prophesies in oracular fashion, to the witch who becomes an active magician, proficient in the malignant arts—exciting love or hatred between the sexes, destroying cattle, causing the sickness of small children, casting fateful spells on adults.[1] In happier medieval times, as Giovanni Ponto illustrates in connection with the famous sorceress of Gaeta, witches could settle the matter by paying a fine; they could afford this because their profession was often lucrative. But belief in, and fascination for, the deeper occult began to grow like an epidemic; spells were cast, incantations came into increasing use, every object, number, and letter was believed to be endowed with magic power. Satan began to appear to humans' feverish imagination with increasing frequency, and not always as an object of terror.

In the fifteenth century Carmelite monks in Bologna began to teach that there was no harm in learning from devils; Pope Sixtus IV promptly put an end to that line of thought in 1474. But as witchery appeared to grow like a poisonous weed, Pope Innocent VIII decided to put out a papal bull that forbade any resort to witches and put the Inquisition in charge of official witch-hunting. For three hundred years, this incredible obsession accounted for thousands upon thousands of helpless women being tortured and executed throughout Europe and the Americas. Those who had been skeptical as to the reality of witchcraft before began now to believe in it since the pope himself had taken official notice of the diabolic ploy.

This was quite a new departure. The church had always taken the attitude that most aspects of sorcery and magic were mere conjurers' tricks with no basis in objective reality. Yet, such superstitions were widespread and had always been, from India to Israel to Europe. The female witch flying nightly on a broomstick to attend the Sabbath, hair floating in the air (hair carefully combed and knotted deprived her of her magic power), was familiar to the Hebrews.[2] In the ninth century in Europe, at the close of the Dark Ages, a diabolic illusion is mentioned for the first time—that certain perverse women, enticed by demons, truly believe and claim that they fly in the dead of night with an innumerable host of similar females led by Diana, their leader, or

Herodias, the witch-queen:[3] the shadow of the Bronze Age Great Goddess of long ago extending into the European Middle Ages!

Ecclesiastical authorities adamantly refused to accept the objective reality of such things and treated this belief as the result of subjective nightmares provoked by diabolic influence: true faith implied knowledge of God, not Satan. All medieval theologians (Regino, Ivon, Burchard, Gratien) upheld this doctrine. Diana's name linked the belief in witchcraft with Greco-Roman antiquity; Diana, goddess of women in ancient Roman times, identified with the moon and presiding genius of the darkness of night, was a pagan survival known in the northern parts of Europe as the southern *daemonium meridianum*. Pope John XXII identified her as *succubus*.[4] All other pagan strains came in to join this one: Bishop Burchard identified her with Diana Holda, the Teutonic goddess who is an occasional follower of Wotan. But try as it may, the church could not stifle this growing and spreading belief in the power of witches; indeed, it developed steadily through the late Middle Ages along with the Dianic cult and the revival of what was known in Italy as *la vecchia religione;* but the church remained firm in its attitude of complete skepticism as to the objective reality of witchcraft.

Other developments, however, were to compel even the church to change its attitude. Rumors of secret societies and mysterious nocturnal gatherings had begun to spread early in the Middle Ages, along with the far more startling news that heretics were taking part in them —the Cathars in the eleventh century, later on the Templars. Here sorcery became linked with heresy, no longer a laughing matter from the ecclesiastical standpoint. By the middle of the fifteenth century, the church began to treat such beliefs in the occult as heresy, without however giving up its contention that it had no objective reality. Saint Antonio, archbishop of Florence, asked all confessors to inquire from their faithful whether they truly believed that women could be changed into cats, fly throughout the night, and suck the blood of small children —all tales in which, he claimed, only insane persons could believe. Thirty years later, Angelo de Chivasso and Bartolommeo de Chaimis followed in his footsteps and gave out the same instructions. But the belief was too firmly implanted to be destroyed by ecclesiastical efforts and pronouncements; even these were often half-hearted, and a number of orthodox theologians began to entertain beliefs in Satanic powers—the Dominican Thomas de Cantimpré as early as the thirteenth century, for example.

Actually, witch-hunting had humble beginnings. The first detailed description of sorcery appears in 1337 in Nider's *Formicarius*, just about the time when ordinary conjurers' tricks began to metamorphose themselves into diabolical witchcraft. At about that same time,

Judge Bartolo, a great legal authority, sentenced a woman in Novara who had confessed to worshiping the Devil and killing children merely by looking at them. There was no mention of any Sabbath. But this new, quite uncommon type of sorcery so puzzled the learned judge that he was compelled to seek the assistance of expert theologians. In 1353, witches' mad dancing at night was mentioned at a trial.[5] Bit by bit, the popular lore of a new form of vicious witchcraft began to build up and take shape.

Heated controversies between theologians in the fifteenth century brought the church around to a new interpretation: these things were indeed objectively real. Witchcraft had to be accepted as an objective reality and its link with the Devil made theologically secure. Satan suddenly found himself credited with new and unsuspected magical powers, in addition to that of creating psychological illusions; his powers were further increased when it was asserted that he could act physically on human beings. In 1458 the Inquisitor Nicolas Jaquerius promoted the thesis that contemporary witches had nothing in common with the old-fashioned ones; they were an entirely new breed, belonging to a recently created secret society. Witches were now presumed to attend physically, and not merely in dreams or imagination, the diabolic Sabbaths and to consort personally with Satan. In such circumstances, Satan took on the appearance of a billy goat who impressed with his hoof the famous and indelible *stigma diabolicum* on the skin of the neophytes.

New evidence emanating from the overheated imagination of the times was coming in as to the deadly reality of witchcraft; Pico della Mirandola, the Inquisitor Bernard of Como, and the famous Sprenger added lurid details concerning the behavior of witches with assorted devils. In vain did the learned jurist Gianfrancesco Ponzinibio prove in his treatise on sorcery that it was all fiction; his opponents had an irrefutable argument—it was true enough that the church, in former days, had stated officially that it was all an illusion, but the fact remained, according to them, that an entirely new type of witch had recently appeared, in the year 1404 as a matter of fact, to which ancient theological statements did not apply—a new type that was physically present at those mysterious Sabbaths. Soon enough, the debate came to an end and witchcraft was officially acknowledged as a powerful reality and an evil to be extirpated with Pope Innocent VIII's bull *Summis desirantes affectibus*, promulgated on December 9, 1484.

What is of utmost interest in this matter is the sexual aspect of this modern belief in a new type of witchcraft. The new witch had nothing in common with run-of-the-mill sorcerers and magicians; the latter merely made a living performing more or less valuable services, good or bad. The witch was essentially evil because she was always in league with, and enslaved to, the Devil. This compact with Satan is fundamentally sexual; whatever his officially sexless status, the Devil is always presumed to be male, and the witch, being female, fell far more easily than a male under his sexual spell. At the Sabbath, after rendering homage to Satan in his incarnation as a billy goat (occasionally as a dog or a monkey) and kissing him under his tail while holding a lighted candle, the witch offered herself physically to him. The Sabbath then proceeded with wild dancing and sexual orgies until dawn.

In point of fact, this secret Dianic cult, celebrated four times a year (Candlemas Day, Rood Mass Day, Lammas Day, and the eve of All Hallows), and often on nights of the full moon in isolated meadows, involved some man who became, for the occasion, the incarnation of the horned god of the Dianic cult (now labeled Satan), who was equipped with a mask worn beneath an animal's tail on his backside and a metallic phallus for ritual copulation with the female devotee (now labeled a witch). The reality of some such Sabbaths was attested by well-known personalities who witnessed them, though few lived long enough to tell the tale. Around 1450 the Inquisitor of Como, Bartolomeo de Homate, the Podesta (city manager) Lorenzo da Concorezzo, and the notary Giovanni da Fossato attended such a Sabbath near Mendrisio; their presence was discovered and they were so badly beaten up that they all died within a fortnight.[6]

As time passed, further lurid details were added to the already horrifying statements about witchcraft. One can read all about them in what became the gospel of witch-hunting, Protestant as well as Catholic, for several centuries: the *Witches' Hammer* or *Malleus Maleficarum*, which tells us that in the first year after the promulgation of Pope Innocent VIII's bull, forty-one witches were burned at the stake in Como alone. Published in 1487 by the papal inquisitor Jacob Sprenger, the *Malleus Maleficarum* looked upon its topic with the cool detachment of a new technical spirit and proceeded to display its pseudo-scientific approach by adopting a question-and-answer format: Is it possible that men be procreated by *incubi* (devils who lie upon women shaped as men) and *succubi* (the reverse)? Is it possible that witches can deal magically with the *membrum virile* in such a way as to detach it from the body? The authors then proceed to give a detailed account of the way in which witches raise hail and thunderstorms, destroy cattle, produce abortions, and so on.

But what is of exceptional interest is that the *Malleus Maleficarum* asserts flatly, in full agreement with all the other demonologists, that

Satan attracts far more women than men, giving the work an anti-female bias that has rarely been matched in literature. Jacob Sprenger's rationale for this state of affairs is interesting and ingenious. After stating the exceptional vulnerability of the "fragile sex," and the eagerness of women for explanations on this topic, he elaborates:

> Now the wickedness of women is spoken of in *Ecclesiasticus XXV:* All wickedness is but little to the wickedness of a woman. . . . What else is a woman but a foe to friendship, an unescapable punishment, a necessary evil, a natural temptation, a desirable calamity, a domestic danger, a delectable detriment, an evil of nature, painted with fair colors! Therefore if it be a sin to divorce her when she ought to be kept, it is indeed a necessary torture . . . since they are feebler both in mind and body, it is not surprising that they should come more under the spell of witchcraft . . . they have slippery tongues, and are unable to conceal from their fellow-women those things which by evil arts they know; and since they are weak, they find an easy and secret manner of vindicating themselves by witchcraft. . . . Terence says: Women are intellectually like children . . . the natural reason is that she is more carnal than a man, as is clear from her many carnal abominations. And it should be noted that there was a defect in the formation of the first woman, since she was formed from a bent rib, that is, rib of the breast, which is bent as it were in a contrary direction to a man. And since through this defect she is an imperfect animal, she always deceives. . . . Women also have weak memories; and it is a natural vice in them not to be disciplined, but to follow their own impulses without any sense of what is due. . . . Justly we may say with Cato of Utica: If the world could be rid of women, we should not be without God in our intercourse. For truly, without the wickedness of women, to say nothing of witchcraft, the world would still remain proof against innumerable dangers . . . a woman is beautiful to look upon, contaminating to the touch and deadly to keep.[7]

This is Pandora all over again. We can spare ourselves the trouble to read the few encomiums Sprenger is compelled to pay out to the Virgin and assorted women saints; in the view of the authors of the *Malleus Maleficarum,* the female of the species is the natural agent through which Satan is enabled to contaminate the world. Once again, man's ancestral, atavistic fear of woman sprang up—a pathological fear of the corruption and sinfulness underlying sexual intercourse; but also the old cosmic terror of the self-contained, convex, and cerebral male in front of the wide-open concave female who is linked with mysterious nature, who is a chameleonlike being, opened to all possibilities, capable of all metamorphoses, attuned to all natural phenomena which baffle men. These two intermingled themes underlay the extraordinary explosion of sexual hatred resulting from the loosened morals of the Renaissance and the "liberation" of the individual of both Renaissance and Reformation.

The *Witches' Hammer* finally comes to its concluding point:

> To conclude: All witchcraft comes from carnal lust, which is in women insatiable. . . . Wherefore for the sake of fulfilling their lusts they consort even with devils. . . . And in consequence of this, it is better called the heresy of witches than of wizards, since the name is taken from the more powerful party. And blessed be the Highest Who has so far preserved the male sex from so great a crime: for since He was willing to be born and to suffer for us, therefore he has granted to men this privilege.[8]

This is the famous, most authoritative work that for roughly three hundred years "lay on the bench of every judge, on the desk of every magistrate. It was the ultimate, irrefutable, unarguable authority. It was implicitly accepted not only by Catholic but by Protestant legislatures."[9]

The question now arises, Why did witch-hunting crop up with such viciousness at that particular time when Western Europe was slowly emerging from the Middle Ages? The reason is to be sought in the remarkable development of Mariolatry at the end of the medieval era, an extraordinary enhancement of the cult of the Virgin which almost eclipsed the worship of saints and holy relics. The excesses of this cult, as any excess will, signified that its symbolic meaning was slowly passing into reverse: far from symbolizing an increase in male respect for woman, it began to imply an increase in fearful contempt. In order to understand this phenomenon, we must go back to the medieval, chivalric conception of the *service of woman* which, as Carl Jung points out, symbolizes the *service of the soul*—Dante who acts as the spiritual knight of Beatrice who, in the process, is exalted to the rank of mystical Mother of God in Canto xxxiii of the *Paradiso:* "Of Virgin Mother, daughter of Thy Son, More lovely, more sublime than any creature!" helping Dante, disguised as Saint Bernard, in his discovery of his own being. And Goethe's Faust ascending from Margaret to Helen and then to the Mother of God, metamorphosing his soul as he goes along until he utters his prayer to the Virgin Mother, introducing it with the exclamation, "Supreme and sovereign Mistress of the world! . . . Oh

Virgin, in the highest sense most pure, oh Mother, worthy of all worship, our chosen Queen, equal with the gods."[10]

The pioneer who first explored the psychological path leading from the service of woman to the service of the soul was an early Christian, Hermas, whose famous work, *The Shepherd* (circa 140), described this spiritual road in a dreamlike succession of visions and revelations. Welling up from the depths of the collective unconscious at the dawn of Christianity, the Great Mother sought to reestablish herself within the context of the new faith. How this was done psychologically is explained by Jung; referring to Hermas's vision, he states:

> His mistress appears before him, not in an erotic phantasy, but in "divine" form, seeming to him like a goddess in the heavens. This fact indicates that the repressed erotic impression in the unconscious has activated the latent primordial image of the goddess, which is in fact that archetypal soul-image . . . if, against the wholly overwhelming power of passion . . . the psyche succeeds in erecting a counterposition, whereby at the summit of passion it severs the idol from the utterly desired object and forces the man to his knees before the divine image, it has thereby delivered him from the curse of the object's spell . . . preserves him in a practical way against that most dreaded possibility, the loss of the soul, with its inevitable sequel of diseases or death.[11]

The practical effect of the loss of one's soul can be seen in the case of many primitive men, throwing them off balance into self-destructiveness—running amok or berserk. The purpose of exorcising ritual is to bring back the lost soul and drive the libido back into the unconscious by destroying the erotic bondage to the object—the real flesh-and-blood woman. This erotic impulse in turn is tranferred to the "sovereign lady," that is, the soul-image upon which all his passion is lavished, now that the primitive sensual bondage has been destroyed: the soul acquires a far greater degree of reality than any concrete object.

As we pass from Hermas and the first centuries of the Christian era to the European Middle Ages, we find the same theme metamorphosed into the famous legend of the Holy Grail whose main symbolism is connected with the "holy vessel," a leftover from pagan times which "indicates a strengthening of the feminine principle in the masculine psychology of that time" by bringing into play the primitive notion of the uterus.[12] The erotic impulse is spiritualized by this symbolization, holding back some of the libido that would otherwise be expended in sexual activity; part of it finds its way into the spiritualized expression, the rest sinks into the unconscious where it activates "corresponding images of which this vessel symbolism is the expression. The symbol lives through the holding back of certain libido forms, and then, in turn, becomes an effective control of these libido tendencies."[13]

The power of adequate symbolism to constrain and discipline the erotic impulse is not only obvious but of vital importance. In this case, the Holy Grail is a perfect example, with its age-old vessel symbolism (the magic caldron of the Celts as well as the *vas virtuum* qualification attributed by the Gnostics to the Virgin—in short, the hoary theme of female concavity) sublimating the erotic impulses of medieval man. What is important, as a general theme of which the present instance is merely an example, is the psychological power of symbolism in general, at all times and in all places:

> The dissolution of the symbol is synonymous with a dispersal of libido along the immediate path, or at least with an almost irresistible urge towards direct application. A symbol loses its magical, or if one prefers it, its redeeming power, as soon as its dissolubility is recognized.[14]

To be effective, a symbol must therefore be proof against dissolution by the critical mind, and embody the best possible expression of a given world-outlook: it must be unanalyzable, superior in its power of suggestion to the critical mind that seeks to destroy it and, far from least, of such superior aesthetic value that it moves feelings as compellingly as it convinces the intellect.

This brings us back to witch-hunting. The actual depreciation of the service of woman, that is, of real flesh-and-blood woman, in favor of the service of the soul, was the first result of the intensification of Mariolatry. Translation into the general symbol entailed the loss of the individual soul since it also implied the disappearance of the individual mistress through whom the soul could be reached and identified. Individual differentiation went by the board, to be replaced by a collective symbolical expression. Largely in order to free himself from his early dependence on the mother, medieval man had begun to idealize the untouched woman, the Virgin, the sublimated object of the *amour courtois*. Concrete woman as such was secretely despised and feared. As long as medieval symbolism prevailed, these Satanic tendencies were kept in check; but with the gradual dissolution of this symbolism at the dawn of the Renaissance, the psychological dam collapsed and they were let loose in the real world.[15]

Within the time-span of a few generations, a tidal wave of hysterical witch-hunting began to sweep over Europe. The night skies suddenly filled with broomstick-riding, long-haired witches sliding down shafts of moonlight who, like Shakespeare's apparitions, were forever doubling and troublemaking, with fires constantly burning and caldrons bubbling. These "secret, black and midnight hags," as Macbeth calls them, became the object of dreaded but fanatical belief. Ever ready to connive in weak mortals' criminal intensions and deeds, quick to pounce on their broomsticks to "hover through the fog and filthy air," after uttering the magic formula "fair is foul and foul is fair" (reminiscent of the *Eumenides* of Aeschylus), these ghostly witches poisoned the imaginations of otherwise sensible human beings. Women were often suspected of belonging to some secret "weird sister" group, and those women that did not were often presumed to call, like the murderous Lady Macbeth, on unknown diabolic powers to give them the evil strength they lacked: "Come you spirits/ That tend on mortal thought, unsex me here,/ And fill me, from the crown to the toe, top-full of direst cruelty!"

Many women began to entertain an unshakable belief in the reality of witchcraft, along with an almost masochistic faith in their own talents for sorcery. Torture helped mightily in the process. The confessions extracted from one and all suspects, shaped and streamlined by theological lore, eventually amounted to a highly colorful, consistent, and comprehensive account. It is significant that in England, where judicial torture was not allowed, witch-hunting started much later. Each new confession extracted under horrible duress strengthened the previous ones until it became almost impossible to doubt the objective reality of sorcery. In fact, it became extremely dangerous to do so, whatever one's intimate belief, but few, even the mightiest minds, had any doubts on the score—even a scientific genius such as Kepler claimed that it was impossible to deny the reality of witchcraft. In 1487 the University of Cologne gave its official seal of approval to the *Malleus Maleficarum* and stated that whosoever denied the reality of witches and witchcraft should be prosecuted for raising obstacles to the Inquisition's labors.

The Holy Office set to work with diabolic energy. According to Paramo, a century and a half after the presumed appearance of the new Satanic type of witch, over thirty thousand wretched women had been burned at the stake. Nor were witches all old and decrepit like Macbeth's "midnight hags"; according to the expert Sprenger, many were young and attractive women whose love had been spurned and who sought revenge on society by making the famous compact with Satan.[16] Nor was witch-hunting a monopoly of ecclesiastical authorities and inquisitors; it had the full support of public opinion, and on numerous occasions, the crowds, frightened by natural catastrophes, took matters in their own hands without waiting for official sanction and killed scores of unfortunate women. More than once, public authorities had to step in and protect the helpless victims. In the summer of 1644, the Parlement of Dijon had to send two special commissioners and a force of police to put an end to the massacre of "witches" by inhabitants of several villages near Beaune.[17]

But if this psychological epidemic ravaged all Europe, its main seat and source of malevolent power was in the Holy Roman Empire and areas under its influence or authority. Innocent VIII's notorious bull *Summis desiderantes* specifically designates Teutonic lands as the main countries infected with the disease; quite likely, the local inquisitor Jacob Sprenger was his main source of information. While the disease spilled over the borders of German-speaking lands into northern and eastern France and northern Italy, it was in the Holy Roman Empire that witch-hunting had a field day and a seemingly endless supply of victims; German Dominicans became the leaders of this type of persecution. In Italy, it affected only the north (the Dominican province of Lombardy, Cremona, Brescia, Bergamo and the Alpine valleys, all under strong Teutonic influence); in the rest of the country the relatively harmless *stregheria* remained the traditional psycho-magical craft it had always been. The Italian witch practiced a trade and, as Jacob Burckhardt put it: "We find nothing about her of the hysterical dreams of the Northern witch, of marvellous journeys through the air, of Incubus and Succubus; the business of the *strega* was to provide for other people's pleasure."[18]

Was there a connection between the great hysterical witch-hunting in German lands and the coming Reformation? Certainly, as the center of gravity of European history-in-the-making moved from the Italy of the Renaissance to the Germany of the Reformation, the historical conception of feminine role and status underwent a considerable change for the worse. Perhaps the prevalence of witches in Teutonic lands had something to do with preparing the grounds, psychologically, for Luther and his struggles with Satan.

At any rate, the Reformers themselves, Luther and Calvin at their head, entertained exactly the same beliefs regarding witchcraft as Roman Catholics, and persecuted witches with as much fanaticism as their Catholic antagonists. Witch-hunting started later in England, but eventually became as fierce as it was on the Continent. The Statute of 1541 mentions witchcraft as a crime for the first time; others followed in due course, up to the Statute of Elizabeth in 1562 which described it as a heinous crime but punishable by death only when it could be proved that the witch had made an attempt on someone's life. Persecution started in earnest, however, to reach its climax, not under the relatively lenient Church of England, but under the fanatical Puritans; the number of Englishwomen who were burned without ever having been brought to trial will never be known but must have been considerable. King James VI was not far behind Pope Innocent VIII and Sprenger in his persecuting zeal, a zeal that no land in Europe was spared, regardless of the religious denomination of its inhabitants.

CHAPTER

5

The Reformed Woman

From the start, the autonomy and authority of the church vis-à-vis raw political power had found ardent supporters among women, who always tended to side with the pope whenever he entered into conflict with secular princes, rulers, kings, and emperors. When Pope Gregory VII had his famous headlong clash with Henry IV, ruler of the Holy Roman Empire, it was his friend and ally Matilda, countess of Tuscany, who assisted him, offered him refuge in her fortified castle at Canossa when the pope feared armed aggression from Henry, and finally witnessed the humiliating backdown of the emperor. To make sure that the papacy would have greater means with which to defend its political autonomy and moral authority, she even bequeathed it her dominions. At a later date when, in order to free itself from the German emperor, the papacy sought refuge in Avignon and gave itself up to the no-tenderer mercies of the King of France, another remarkable woman assisted in freeing itself after sixty-eight years of "Babylonian Captivity" under French protectorate. Catherine of Siena prevailed upon Pope Gregory XI, not only to return to Rome where the papacy would be truly independent, but also to give up warfare in favor of peaceful diplomacy. In moving terms she implored Gregory to renounce war and its barbarity, even in defense of a just cause. Gregory heeded her plea and gave up fighting after returning the Holy See to Rome.

In counterpart, the church had fought for women's rights, defended the sanctity of marriage, women's rights to equal education and to work as members of guilds—as a result of which there were many professional females including doctors and university professors. The Crusades and the consequent depletion of manpower had also allowed women to substitute for men in many trades. When the French provinces sent representatives to the "états," local legislative assemblies, women were granted the right to vote: in 1576, for instance, as many

256

as thirty-two widows were elected to the États of Franche-Comté, then under Spanish domination.

With the Reformation in sixteenth-century Germany, a new trend started. Under Luther's auspices, Protestantism proceeded to destroy that division of power between spiritual and political authority, between church and state, for which so many women had toiled. Luther unhesitatingly accepted the subordination of spiritual to political authority and made the first outstanding contribution to the divinization of the state that culminated with Hegelian philosophy and the Prussianization of Germany. The old medieval division of power had, at least, curbed the usual male appetite for tyranny and untrammeled autocracy. It was feminine influence that had raised the prestige of the papacy against the many princes and kings, imposed a modicum of charity in a barbaric age, protected the weak against the strong. Who was it but his wife, the queen, who, kneeling before England's King Edward III in 1347, begged him to spare the lives of the six "bourgeois de Calais" after the fall of the city, and saved them.

All this came to an end when Luther raised the standard of rebellion against a Roman papacy that had become decadent and half pagan during the Renaissance. Not surprisingly, like the Renaissance, the Reformation implied a rebirth of strong individualism—another masculine phenomenon. Man now took a personal view of things, against tradition and the socialized view of the community. When Luther stated "Here I stand, I cannot do otherwise," he triggered the rise of individual conscience and the predominance of the ethical outlook; masculine morality put to flight the feminine integrating emotionalism of the Middle Ages.

In another sense, the Reformation was also a companion piece of the Renaissance. While the latter implied a revival of the classical pagan and Mediterranean element in European culture, the Reformation implied a rebirth of its strictly Hebraic, anticlassical component. With Luther, it was an odd marriage between the revival of Teutonic nationalism against the Roman civilization that the church had imposed on its barbarian ancestors, and of Old Testament themes from the Middle East—the main link between them being the antifeminist attitude of both the Hebraic and Teutonic traditions. Like the Arabs when triumphant Islam began sweeping through Christian lands in the Middle East, the Lutherans began closing down all monasteries and convents, echoing Muḥammad's often quoted command that there was to be "no monkery in Islam."[1] Lutheranism thus put an end to the widespread charitable work that had been the lot of women's convents. By abolishing celibacy for the clergy, the members of the Reformed Church were bound to take their own, male, side, however unconsciously, whenever there was any issue dividing the sexes.

Protestant women went back to the home and kitchen from which the Roman Church had offered them an escape, whenever they wanted it badly enough. Luther blasted as a dangerous thinker the celebrated Humanist and educator Juan Luis Vivès, who advocated equal education for both sexes and never tired of repeating that woman should be restricted to reading and writing, while the rest of her labors should be devoted to hearth and home. In his eyes, the Lord intended woman to confine her activities to childbearing, cooking, and sewing. Some samples of his thoughts on the subject: "Take women from their housewifery, and they are good for nothing."[2] "If women get tired and die of bearing, there is no harm in that; let them die as long as they bear; they are made for that."[3] "I wish that women would repeat the Lord's Prayer before opening their mouths."[4] Nuns were chased out of their convents and released from their vows, but each Protestant home became a private convent in its own way and a woman was not encouraged to step out of it into the wider world. She was born to be and to remain throughout her life man's subordinate; a strict limitation of her education, by making her inescapably dependent, ensured that she did not forget this subordination.

One point deserves specific mention: the Reformation was, to an extent, a logical derivative of the Satanism that pervaded the witch-hunting era. Evil and fear dominated Protestant themes with their hellfire and brimstone atmosphere; rather than the love of God, it is the fear of the Devil and of sin that culminated in the Puritans. In Luther's view, the Devil actually rules the world as *Princeps Mundi*—this god of evil which was always associated with a sulphurous stench—the Devil, who as father-surrogate actually symbolizes the masculine in its worst female-hating aspect. In this age of prevalent diabolism, fear had replaced medieval love as the dominant sentiment, and the Reformation was, along with witch-hunting, its most representative feature. When Melanchton accused Luther of Manichaeism, he quite correctly linked the two woman-hating creeds that diabolized the world of creation and against which the Greek Orthodox and Roman Catholic traditions consistently fought, with women as their most fervent supporters.

Luther's sermons are full of references to the Old Testament, to Eve's Fall and the divine curse. Gone is the redeeming feature of Roman Catholicism, the consoling cult of the Virgin as a counterpoise to the terrors of hell and damnation. The old Hebraic conception of the respective roles of the sexes here joins with the Teutonic atavistic conception of woman's subordination to man. The legal concessions that had gradually been granted to German women could be traced only to the influence of Roman law; according to the oldest Teutonic legislation, the right of inheritance was either severely restricted or denied to woman altogether. Right through the Middle Ages the legal inequality between the sexes in Germany remained striking; only in the thirteenth century did German women receive a limited right of inheritance. In Scandinavia and Frisia, in fact, women inherited nothing, neither movable nor immovable property—as the saying went, "the man enters into inheritance, the woman leaves it." The Reformation was going to do little to improve this condition. Luther tirelessly repeated that the wife was God-given to man, that she should fear him, listen and obey, and refrain from arguing. More than ever, the Teutonic *hausfrau* became chained to the three traditional Ks—*kinder, küche, und kirche*—with a great deal of the churchly service being performed now at home under the supervision of the husband lord and master without clerical intermediation.

Even marriage lost its status as a sacrament and the door was opened slightly to some form of sophisticated polygyny. When the powerful Landgrave Philip of Hesse, a supporter of Luther, expressed the desire in 1539 to take Margaret of Saale for second wife, he suggested to the Protestant leader that his new religion, heavily indebted as it was to the Old Testament, should, like it, condone some form of polygamy, or at least bigamy. Luther, who had already suggested bigamy to England's Henry VIII as a way out of his marital difficulties, was hard put to refuse such an important patron as Philip of Hesse—who had also hinted that, if he did refuse, he might defect to the imperial or even papal camp. Luther agreed and the Landgrave was married secretly in 1540 in the presence of two eminent Protestant theologians, Melanchton and Bucer. The news leaked out and the scandal was such that Luther, on the defensive, had to argue that, while he did not usually advocate this solution for other men, he had to state that he could not condemn men who wanted several wives simultaneously and that Holy Scriptures had nothing to say against it. Bucer added that it was obvious that polygamy was necessary for some men.[5]

The communist-leaning Anabaptists began to carry out in practice what Luther preached. In Münster, on the basis of biblical precedent, it was decided that unattached women could become "companions of wives"—a convenient euphemism for second wives. But this was going too far: the Anabaptist rebellion was a rare issue on which Luther had to agree with the Roman Catholics.

This new biblical-Teutonic attitude toward the female sex implied a decisive regression from medieval standards, already low in German-speaking countries. It can therefore come as no surprise to hear that in one year, 1595, fifty doctoral theses were presented at Wittenberg in which women were denied the dignity of being a human person.[6] Islam had never gone quite that far!

The church of the Middle Ages had viewed Holy Scripture mostly as a vast *symbolism* rather than literal truth. Not only was the Bible divided chronologically into Old and New Testaments, but the Old was viewed as an exact prefiguration of the New. Gothic art plainly demonstrates this extraordinary concordance between the two sections, and many a cathedral fresco makes a pointed parallel between scenes of the Old Testament and scenes of the Gospels. There was a profound, preestablished harmony and parallelism between the two, as if, in the Old testament, Truth was seen under a veil which Christ's martyrdom and death tore apart to let Truth shine in all its splendor —symbolized by the curtain of the Temple being torn at the precise moment when Jesus gave up the ghost. What the Gospels reveal under the clear light of the sun is seen in the Old Testament under the uncertain light of the moon and stars; in other words, the Old makes sense only when connected with the New.

The Gothic Age, so often depicted in the forthcoming Age of Enlightenment as naive, saw that nature as well as history should be understood fundamentally as a symbolism—and implicitly stated that man is, first and last, a symbol-making animal. This viewpoint has become understandable again in our century thanks to the development of analytic psychology. The rediscovery of the unconscious, of its importance in the makeup of the human personality; the discovery that all dream images have to be understood and interpreted symbolically rather than literally—these are the fundamental discoveries that have changed our understanding of the human personality.

Many past cultures, however, were quite familiar with this dream symbolism; not only in China and India, in Egypt and Chaldea, but the Bible itself is full of such insights—Joseph interpreting Pharaoh's dreams, for instance. What psychology rediscovered is that there is a vast difference between *literal* truth and *psychological* truth and that the latter is no less important than the former: the dream that arises from a part of the mind that is inaccessible to our waking-being consciousness, and is made up of a series of apparently contradictory or meaningless images, is, in fact, a reality per se.

All this is fully in keeping with the insights of the Fathers of the Church whose exegesis was entirely based on symbolism. But the time was coming when the conflict between symbolism and allegory, on the one hand, and rational logical thought, on the other, had to end in the victory of one or the other—as it had in Greece when the gods on Olympus were shattered by discursive thought. There was no possibility, at the time, of seeing those two modes of understanding coexist on two different mental planes, as in Hindu culture—and which was eventually made possible in the West by the discovery of the psychology of the unconscious. Thus Luther, although no champion of rational thought, blasts symbolism away in a virulent attack against the greatest theologians of the Middle Ages—Bonaventura, Denis the Carthusian and Gerson:

> These allegorical studies are the work of people who have too much leisure. Do you think I should find it difficult to play at allegory-making about any created thing whatsoever? Who is so feeble-witted that he could not try his hand at it?[7]

In fact, the Reformation's exclusive reliance on a *literal* interpretation of Scriptures implied a massive step backward. Gone was the remarkable insight of fifteen hundred years of symbolic understanding. What proved, in other respects, an extremely rewarding psychological change—the development of a new critical attitude and the beginning of scientific thinking—proved disastrous from the standpoint of religious faith. Even the Roman Catholic Church finally joined the Protestants; from the Counter-Reformation and the Council of Trent onward, the Church shunted aside symbolic interpretation—indeed, hardly understood it anymore.[8] Medieval art and literature became an enigma for Catholics and Protestants alike and no longer awakened any echo in the *Zeitgeist* of the new era—hence the barbarous and contemptuous epithet "Gothic" applied to an archaic art and an incomprehensible symbolism. In the eighteenth-century Enlightenment, Gothic cathedrals had become as mysterious and unfathomable as the temples of India; some scholars believed that the signs of the zodiac at Notre Dame of Paris proved the solar origin of all religions; others thought that the bas-reliefs devoted to Saint Denis represented the legend of Bacchus![9]

While Luther cleared the path for subsequent reformers, his was not the most historically significant movement. John Calvin's influence was ultimately greater and more extensive. By stripping the Reformation of its exclusively Germanic flavor, Calvin gave it an international appeal that spread his brand of Protestantism far and wide under different guises to France, England, Scotland, America, Switzerland, Holland, Hungary, and even Germany. Both modern democracy and capitalism sprang from this new faith which, unlike Lutheranism, favored universal education for all. The creed was essentially masculine, hard and stoical, one that inspired the English and Dutch Puritans, the Scottish Covenanters, and the Pilgrims of New England.

It was one of Calvin's disciples, Scotland's John Knox, who defined the new creed's attitude toward women with the most drastic eloquence. His *First Blast of the Trumpet against the Monstrous Regiment of Women* (1558) indeed blasted the extraordinary number of more-or-less remarkable and colorful women rulers who were then enthroned or in power in many countries—Mary Tudor, Mary Stuart, Elizabeth, Mary of Lorraine, Catherine de Médicis. It was not only on religious grounds that he objected to them, as he made plain in the following excerpt:

> To promote a woman to bear rule, superiority, dominion, or empire above any realm, nation or city is repugnant to Nature, contumely to God, a thing most contrarious to His revealed will and approved ordinance; and finally it is the subversion of good order, of all equity and justice. . . . For who can deny but it is repugnant to Nature that the blind shall be appointed to lead and conduct such as do see? That the weak, sick and impotent persons shall nourish and keep the whole strong? And finally that the foolish, mad and phrenetic shall govern the discreet and give counsel to such as be of sober mind? And such be all women, compared unto men in bearing of authority. . . . Woman in her greatest perfection was made to serve and obey man, not to rule and command him: As Saint Paul doth reason in these words: Man is not of the woman but the woman of the man.[10]

Knox went on to curse Mary Tudor as a monstrous and cruel "Jezebel," and in a work printed in Geneva and distributed throughout England, he urged rebellion against "the monstrous empire of a cruel woman." In a following tract, he urged the Scots to rise in revolt against Mary of Lorraine. Like Luther, Knox despised and feared both nature and reason: "Nature and reason," he stated, "do lead men from the true God. For what impudence is it to prefer corrupt nature and blind reason to God's Scriptures?"[11]

Turning its back on the medieval exaltation of virginity for women and monkish chastity for men as the true religious ideal, the Calvinistic attitude favored the married estate, as well as dedication to business. The Protestant ideal was a thoroughly religious home and private Bible reading; and the endless pounding of biblical themes, with their raw Hebraic patriarchalism, was well calculated to instill in women a subtle but effective inferiority complex vis-à-vis the male. The stronger the Puritan streak, the greater the subordination of woman to man, and wife to husband. Even in early colonial America,

. . . American women were almost treated like Negro slaves, inside and outside the home. Both were expected to behave with deference and obedience towards owner or husband; both did not exist officially under the law; both had few rights and little education; both found it difficult to run away; both worked for their masters without pay; both had to breed on command, and to nurse the results.[12]

In a sense, the Reformation represented a return to the pure sources of the past; but just as the Renaissance did not represent an actual rebirth of classical Greco-Roman culture—it used it simply as a prop for the expression of its own specific spirit—the Reformation was essentially a movement sui generis. Lutheranism revived a form of Mosaic ethics and triggered the rise of the modern autocratic state, and Calvinism, especially in its Puritan garb, became a latter-day Islam, expansionist, imperialistic, and the ultimate source of both capitalism and Marxism. Cromwell, as Lord Protector, was a latter-day Caliph, an antimonarchist Commander of the Faithful—neither king nor emperor but leader of the Puritan devotees.

The masculine ethos came to prevail completely in northern Europe and the American colonies—the male divisive "ego" principle, wilful in Luther, rational in Calvin. While Calvin's successful blend of Bourse and Bible was going to generate modern capitalism with its extraordinary force of economic expansion and technological inventiveness, Luther's destruction of the Roman Catholic clergy's countervailing force in Prussia led straight to the modern Bismarckian state. All the colorful, legendary, mythical side of life that had prevailed for centuries gradually disappeared from adult life, to give way to an essentially masculine mode increasingly founded on logic and systematic efficiency—dry, cool, and slightly inhuman.

In Protestant lands, all the archetypes of the unconscious which found expression in Catholic symbolism were left without any outlet or form of expression; the *anima* was thrown back into the unconscious and remained, until our day, as a festering sore—a psychological penalty for the Promethean success of the modern Protestant West.

CHAPTER

6

The Cultured Woman

The fifteenth century was the century of the Renaissance in Italy; the sixteenth, of the Reformation in Germany. During the two centuries that followed, the European center of gravity shifted to France where the Classical Age of European culture bloomed and spread outward to encompass most of the Continent. And it was in France that woman's involvement with culture flourished as it never had before; for this remarkable fulfillment of her destiny, woman could thank the Frenchman's peculiar psychology.

The French are rightly credited, even today, with being Cartesian— which does not mean that they follow Descartes' philosophy to the letter. Descartes' main contribution to Western philosophy was his epistemological emphasis on the primacy of consciousness—his famous *Cogito, ergo sum* ("I think, therefore I am"). The mind apprehends and knows itself better and more directly than it can know anything else; its understanding of the "external" world is indirect and relies on sensations and perceptions impressed on the mind. This was the cornerstone of Descartes' doctrine and his elaborate logical structure was built around it; he conceived the world of reality as divided into two ultimate and irreducible elements, two homogeneous substances underlying, one all forms of mind, and the other all forms of matter. He proceeded to explain everything except God and the soul by exclusively rational and logical means—mechanical and mathematical laws. Having given the initial cosmic impulse in creating the universe, God had then allowed every nonmental process to take place according to strictly mechanical principles, including all bodily functions and movements: everything in the universe is a machine except God without and the human soul within. Founder of analytical geometry, Descartes captured and froze into permanency the flux of reality, using a fixed network of lines of reference—his famous Cartesian coordinates which

threw a steely mathematical network on nature's fundamentally irrational and incalculable reality: first analysis and dissection, then
method and construction.

This mechanistic approach and interpretation of reality was a landmark in the history of philosophy and mathematics and exerted a
profound influence in the seventeenth century. Henceforth, reality is
what can be grasped logically by human reason; only rationality as
conceived by the conscious mind actually exists. Since everything is
now considered a machine except the Almighty and the indwelling
soul, it follows naturally that all of Creation, nature, and even animals
are mechanical and soulless. That this concept was prevalent in
France, and not merely Descartes' idea, is seen in seventeenth-century
French literature which largely ignores nonhuman nature, except occasionally as background for human nature. Witness the great classi-
cists, Molière, Corneille, and Racine, whose plays are restricted to the
narrow spatial dimensions of a hierarchical society in a largely urban
environment; compared with them, Shakespeare's plays seem penetrated by the cosmic thundering power of raw nature with all its profound and impenetrable mysteries. Indeed, one look at the geometric
patterns imposed upon the natural growth of vegetation in the *jardin
à la française* is enough to convince anyone that the French imposed
Cartesianism upon wild nature itself; they see nature through the eyes
of an architect with compass and ruler, not those of a gardener.

French thinking, unlike English, German, Italian, or Spanish, sets
man apart from nature as an autonomous mental entity in its own
right; whether believer in God or not, the man who thinks in this
manner is divorced from his natural environment as drastically as the
Hebraic God was divorced from man. Hegel's complaint that Descartes cut the world in two with a hatchet is quite valid; by sundering
the sphere of thought from the sphere of extension, Descartes left the
mind operating, as it were, in a vacuum.

French thought is essentially analytical; it enjoys tinkering intellectually with the machine, taking it apart in abstraction, understanding the
logical connections between each element, and putting it all back
together as a harmonious whole. Analysis is essentially precise vision
—*faisons la lumière* is one of the most characteristic French expressions.
English thought, practical and empirical, focusing on the concrete,
enumerates and inventories, and takes from the concrete object what
it requires; German thought is essentially synthetic and takes from the
concrete object what it yields. But French thought is not interested in
taking, only in seeing and analyzing. Hence, the French emphasis on
definition—rigorously separating the concrete object under analysis
from its environment (English thinking, respecting life in its impreci-

sion, leaves it partly submerged in its surroundings). Also, an equal emphasis on *clarity*, on the preservation of clear intellectual vision, regardless of the distortion inflicted on its representation of concrete reality: what is important is not that the mental picture should be a true reflection of some external reality but that it should be a clear, harmonious, symmetrical, and well-proportioned mental construction. French cogitation appears to be utterly cold and scientific, as detached from the object as it can possibly be. French thought is essentially visual and geometric, abstract and precise; there is very little of what Pascal called *l'esprit de finesse*, the intuitive element that underlies so much of English and German thought. The French seek knowledge in an entirely conscious way, analyzing, classifying, applying as much discriminating power as it possibly can with microscopic precision: it is basically methodical, which justifies the title of Descartes's main opus, his *Discours de la Méthode*.

But such thinking entails as many drawbacks as assets. It can be and often is a superb piece of mental machinery, but it is totally unequipped to cope with the irrational. Cold detachment from the object may clarify the mental vision, yet it inevitably distorts its picture of reality. Purged of all the vital, imprecise elements with blurred contours that cannot be projected into its intellectual framework, French thought is often disconnected from external reality, and begins to think for the sheer pleasure of thinking; hence the fact that France is the home of the *faux esprit*—great discursive and analytical power, almost invariably starting from false premises. In other words, French thought processes are rarely *geared* to reality . . . unless feminine flair and intuition reestablish the connection.

The peculiarity of the Frenchman's psychology and mental processes thus presented the Frenchwoman with an opening wedge with which to exert a cultural influence almost unmatched in history. French history, in spite of the Salic Law, is more bisexual than that of any other land, and this for the simple reason that Frenchmen are among the few men who need women, not only emotionally and sexually but also *mentally*. They need them in an intellectual sense as a blind man needs his dog. And throughout history, their women have met them more than halfway, providing them with all they lack—warmth, feeling, intuition, affinity for life and everything that germinates and lives, the flexibility and adaptability of a sex that is essentially protean and can metamorphose itself in any number of ways. French thought processes would always remain on the level of useless abstractions were it not for that indispensable feminine touch that gears them to reality. The development and achievements of French culture are the only ones that cannot be explained without taking into account the vital impact of female contribution.

In turn, few women in history have reached a feeling of fulfillment comparable to that of Frenchwomen, and from the start of France's Classical Age, they have taken by the hand and guided, sometimes misguided, their male consorts, lovers, and admirers through the jungles of nature in the raw, the labyrinth of the irrational, the twists and turns of the unconscious; they polished them, disciplined them, and controlled them, gave them a sense of measure and balance lacking in more gifted men of other nations. They also curbed them and cut them down to a more neutral size where talent may bloom to the full but where genius is rare; there is no French equivalent of creative giants such as Dante, Shakespeare, Cervantes, or Goethe. The general cultural level was much higher in France than anywhere else; genuine talent was more widespread than in any other nation. But the outstanding, wholly original genius was seldom seen.

It all started in the seventeenth century at the Hotel de Rambouillet. Until then, feminine influence in French literature was slight, almost unknown in the male-oriented worlds imagined and described by Montaigne and Rabelais. In the salon presided over with remarkable skill and taste by Catherine de Vivonne, Marquise de Rambouillet, most of the literary giants of the day gathered and willingly put themselves under the discipline established by their hostess. It was there that the last traces of Humanism and its pedantic reliance on Greco-Roman models were disposed of; there, where a certain type of feminine polish was coated onto a previously coarse literature and supplied a "preciosity" that remained throughout the centuries; and there also where the French language was "purified" of most of its medieval wealth of rich, concrete words and expressions and made into a language of admirable clarity and precision, almost geometric in its grammatical structure, but with a limited vocabulary, impoverished by the loss of its Rabelaisian power. While the anonymous landscapers of the English language operated as careful gardeners—off with a twig here, chop away a branch there—preserving as much flowering richness as they could, the French linguistic architects *simplified*, shortening and flattening Latin words (*anima* into *âme, cathedra* into *chaise, Augustus* into *août*, and so on), schematizing, cutting down to essentials—*abstracting* to the utmost, almost diagrammatizing according to the simple and frugal dictates of *ordre, économie, et choix.* The French language became a perfect Cartesian mode of expression, admirably suited to express what was clearly conceived by the conscious mind but totally inadequate when it came to deal with the unconscious or the irrational. Locked in his linguistic Cartesianism, man in France found himself, and remained, at the mercy of woman's feeling and intuition.

Feminine influence in French literature was not always good. Linguistic expurgation had an ennobling effect, but separated popular and educated use of the French tongue far too sharply. This purification did preserve a real wealth of expression in all that concerned social life, but it crippled that part of the vocabulary that had to do with imagination and philosophic thought—as Germaine de Staël noted long ago, comparing the French and German tongues.[1] The bisexual setup was instrumental in the establishment of the famous *République des Lettres* as an almost autonomous and official state within the state, with its academies, uniforms, literary prizes and unparalleled prestige. But a new feminine preciosity gave an artificial and often superficial flavor to French cultural output, and launched a type of drawing-room literature that had its own characteristics. In her *ruelle* at the Hotel de Rambouillet, Catherine de Vivonne mixed harmoniously, on a plane of perfect, if temporary, equality, people from all walks of life—ambassadors, generals, aristocrats, literary figures, and attractive women—and shaped the new style that has remained typical of a large part of France's literary output: a certain superficiality, a mania for treating serious topics lightheartedly and vice versa, shifting the focus of attention away from profound themes onto trivial matters, emphasizing stylistic elegance and witticisms at the expense of depth of meaning, snuffing out individual originality in favor of a more "social" average mean, destroying true lyricism and personal expression. Catherine de Vivonne sternly forbade the use of vulgar terms, ruled out archaic expressions, erudite references to antiquity, provincial terminology, obscure technical words. Prodding here, enticing there, she finally had her way, and over the decades had a great deal to do with reshaping the French tongue. It did wonders for the art of conversation, developed a brilliant epistolary style (the *Maximes* de la Rochefoucauld, the *Lettres* of Madame de Sévigné, the *Caractères* of La Bruyère), and gave great impetus to the psychological novel; indeed, Madame de La Fayette became the first true novelist in France when she wrote *La Princess de Clèves*.

Catherine's daughter, the immensely spoiled Julie d'Angennes, did a great deal to heap ridicule on the Hotel de Rambouillet and became the prototype of Molière's *Précieuses Ridicules*, but it was too late to roll back the feminine tide. As Rambouillet passed away, many more salons took its place, with an equivalent impact on French culture. The *précieuses* had set an indestructible style and had compelled men to treat them with the respect to which women were entitled in civilized society. There was some male resistance, as usual in the coarse and ironic vein, on the part of such as Guez de Balzac and Voiture, but on the whole the feminine style set by the *précieuses* was respected by the men, and female influence became ineradicable. Politeness, courtesy, and ready wit became the main standards for acceptance in any salon, and built bridges over which men of vastly differing talents and social condition could meet and communicate. Excessive literary individualism inspired caricatural styles known as *gongorism* in Spain, *euphuism* in England, and *marinism* in Italy, all of them symbols of purely masculine expressions in lands where women had little cultural influence; but French literature fell completely under the spell of social standards and requirements set by Frenchwomen, and few such excesses marred its expression. French literature became the expression of general and common views to which individual talent had to adapt and conform. This is probably the reason for the universality of its appeal—focusing on the general common mean rather than the individual output of a particular genius; in other words, on the transferable rather than the untransferable.

Even France's relatively fluid social structure made its contribution. Germaine de Staël, comparing it with Germany's, where a rigid caste system was firmly entrenched, where everyone knew his permanent rank from birth and no one had to or could struggle up the social ladder regardless of talent, pointed out that this French socialization of culture, this deliberate shunning of depth of meaning and true originality, often favored the mediocre at the expense of the truly talented, intellectual conformity at the expense of creativity. Added to this, the typically French terror of appearing ridiculous; as Germaine de Staël put it, "A Frenchman would no more want to be alone in his opinion than he would want to be alone in his room!"[2]

The typical French salon had no equivalent in any other European society. Who but Madame de la Sablière could have devoted such literary friendship to Madame de Sévigné and Madame de La Fayette, and encouraged countless others of lesser talent with no trace of jealousy or resentment toward those more talented than herself? Madame de Tencin, another great hostess, was unsuccessful in her efforts to seduce the regent of France, Philippe d'Orléans, that incestuous roué who was one of the few misogynists of the time; but, undaunted, she struck up a fruitful friendship with the depraved prime minister, Cardinal Dubois, and became mixed up in the scandalous financial schemes and eventual collapse of her lover John Law. But she was astute enough to sell her Mississippi stock before the crash. In fact, she meddled in everything with tireless energy—politics, diplomacy, finances, the Court—arranged countless marriages, decided upon the elections at the Academy, in other words ruled French society as a queen, and a sometimes contemptuous one at that. "The greatest error is to underestimate the stupidity of men," she often claimed.[3]

Her successor and friend was Madame Geoffrin, who inherited most of the personalities who had fallen under Madame de Tencin's spell. This extremely clever but uneducated daughter of a former valet became a focal point not merely of French but of European society. She was in regular correspondence with the Russian empress; King Stanislaw-Augustus of Poland called her Mother; she could not spell and was profoundly ignorant but knew how to listen to chatterboxes as well as inspire genuine literary talent. She was also an extremely competent businesswoman whose wealth was largely invested in the failing Companie de Saint-Gobain at its low ebb; her feminine instinct picked the talented employees who restored the firm to sound financial health. Her salon attracted as many painters, engravers, and sculptors as literary figures. Having chosen an archaeologist, M. de Caylus, to replace her deceased husband as host, she could also be credited with having had a decisive influence on the course of French painting and sculpture at the end of the century, especially in encouraging its proclivity toward themes drawn from classical antiquity. Between 1750 and 1770, she personally ordered and bought over sixty major paintings, although she occasionally had some trouble imposing her determined tastes on artists such as Boucher and Greuze.[4]

Madame Geoffrin also picked her young friend and part-time collaborator, the sensitive Julie de Lespinasse, as her successor, and it was she who patronized the most ambitious intellectual undertaking of the times, the famous *Encyclopédie*. Alongside such other luminaries as Marie du Deffand, the Maréchale de Luxembourg, Madame Lambert, Madame d'Epinay, Madame Necker, and Voltaire's great good friend, the Marquise du Chatelet, she continued a tradition that was now a century and a half old. One and all, these women regulated the cultural life of the country, gave talent its due, disciplined the often tempestuous behavior of their male guests, curbed their unjustified pride, and occasionally encouraged those rare birds who were unduly humble and shy. At all times they made sure that their guests, whatever their social standing and their profession, could *communicate* fruitfully with one another on a plane of complete equality and perfect courtesy. They also knew how to stimulate creativity by the use of appropriate encouragement and praise: the *abbé* de Saint-Pierre, astounded at his unexpected success and popularity in Madame Geoffrin's salon, admitted that he was merely an instrument in her skillful hands.[5] Far better psychologists than the cocksure males, and also basically more realistic and modest, hostesses spoke little and listened a great deal, knowing with their usual flair how to bring dull conversation delicately to an end. But talented men were always encouraged and came away quite surprised to discover that they were far more witty in this kind of environment than elsewhere.

The unfortunate counterpart of an excess of feminine influence, however, was an overwhelming premium given to superficial brilliance. Tension, passion, and true emotions were ruled out of order; everyone had to be gay and witty, and lightheartedness (and often lightheadedness) held undisputed sway. Women eventually became tired of such emotional sterility, felt decadence in the air, and, shortly before the Revolution, went over to Rousseau's sentimentalizing with enthusiasm—they "returned to nature," their more normal habitat, however ersatz. Having made a major contribution to the destruction of the ancien régime by inducing its male leadership to adopt a frivolous attitude toward the profound social problems of the times, they switched from culture to nature—Queen Marie-Antoinette's farm at the Petit Trianon, the *jardins à l'anglaise* at Ermenonville and Bagatelle—making France safe for the greatest social upheaval in man's memory.

The great Revolution came and went. In the quarter of a century when wars and upheavals destroyed the social basis of the salon, feminine influence in France's cultural life was slight. There was not much room for it during the Terror of Robespierre, nor under the imperial despotism of Napoleon Bonaparte. Storm and stress over, however, Madame Récamier picked up the scepter and reigned over French culture for thirty years. Poor and of modest social extraction but intelligent and beautiful, Juliette Récamier drew to her salon practically all the celebrities of Europe and enchanted them with the delicate refinement and subtlety of her conversation.

But the great days were over. France's cultural preeminence passed away, and with it, the remarkable bisexual collaboration that had made it possible.

The eighteenth century was the French century; French cultural supremacy was acknowledged all over Europe and French court life was imitated, down to the minutest details, from Berlin to Dresden, Vienna and Saint Petersburg. Everywhere, small Versailles were erected, complete with all the luxury, etiquette, and paraphernalia required by French-style ceremonial. But Versailles and Court life

were a bore; Paris was the stimulating place. Where could one duplicate these extraordinary Parisian salons where sparkling conversation
and stimulating refinement presupposed generations of bisexual cultural collaboration? Nowhere else, in fact, because in no other country
were women equipped to handle the role that talented Frenchwomen
played with such consummate skill in their heyday; foreign imitations
were always artificial and stilted because only in France were creative
men in real *need* of women's cultural collaboration.

A pilgrimage to Paris was a sine qua non for all cultured Europeans
and admission to the "kingdom of the rue Saint-Honoré" (Madame de
Tencin's) was more prized than being presented to Court at Versailles:
nowhere else in the world could one find this clever swordplay of
words, this mental fencing with witticisms, and this quick brushing
over all topics of interest, flitting rapidly from one to the next.

No wonder foreigners streamed into Paris from all quarters; the
prevailing disease in the France of the ancien régime was indeed
xenophily, the love of foreigners who flocked to pay homage to the
cultural stimulus of French womanhood—kings, crown-princes, ministers, ambassadors, writers, artists. "I spent one half of my life longing
to see Paris," said Prince Henry of Prussia. "I will spend the second
half missing it," he added.[6]

What could even remotely compare with it? Englishwomen in the
seventeenth and eighteenth centuries could barely spell and were totally unlike their predecessors in Elizabethan times who were often
well versed in poetry, music, mathematics, and classical literature. In
the days of Dr. Johnson, women hardly existed in England's cultural
life. Only with Fanny Burney did Englishwomen make their timid
entrance into literature; and while, later, Macaulay saluted her respectfully as the first English novelist of her sex, Samuel Johnson called her
with affectionate condescension his "little character-monger." It is
symptomatic that she spent most of her time in France after having
married French General d'Arblay, regardless of the fact that Napoleonic France was at war with England. As for literary salons in England, those that began to appear in the second half of the eighteenth
century were pale replicas of the French ones—the "blue stocking"
gatherings of Elizabeth Vesey, or Elizabeth Montagu's "Queen of the
Blues," and the philanthropic Hannah More's. Along with those of
Mrs. Chapone, they were usually dull and spiritless, and attracted
noted writers only with the greatest of difficulty. Sarcasms poured on
the hapless blue stockings whose pseudo-literary meetings simply
could not compete with the all-male club founded in 1764 by Samuel
Johnson, where one was likely to meet all the famous names of the day
—Goldsmith, Reynolds, Burke, Gibbon and Garrick.

German women, so brilliantly analyzed by Germaine de Staël in her work on Germany, were less shy and retiring than Englishwomen because, she claimed, they rarely met men who were superior to them. Happier than Frenchwomen in that complete loyalty was a dominating trait of the German male and true love was therefore less dangerous for women,[7] they were, however, slower-witted, unable to stimulate cultural creation, and their contribution to German cultural output was negligible. Sexual polarity in German social and cultural life was total; women worked harder than men—as they had already done in old Teutonic tribal days—leaving the men free to pursue cultural creation unhindered and unassisted by feminine influence. Goethe, who drew such remarkable portraits of women in his masterworks, and who loved women, had only this to say in his celebrated conversations with Eckermann:

Women are silver dishes into which we put golden apples. My idea of women is not abstracted from the phenomena of actual life, but has been born with me, or arisen in me, God knows how. The female characters which I have drawn have therefore all turned out well; they are all better than could be found in reality.[8]

As Germaine de Staël points out, Frenchwomen paid a price for their considerable influence. She traces the downfall of true feeling of love in France to the decline of the spirit of chivalry; in its stead came what she calls *l'esprit de fatuité,* the typical masculine self-conceit of the Gallic rooster which, "far from protecting women, seeks only their destruction; and far from despising trickery, takes pride in using guile against these weak creatures."[9] And she adds: "I would even venture to say that, of all countries in the world, France is perhaps the one where women's heart was least happy. France was called a paradise for women because they enjoyed great freedom, but this very freedom sprang from the ease with which men abandoned them."[10] French-style love became a witty but cruel game at which men were more adept than women—hence Frenchwomen's eventual rejection of an artificial and decadent culture in favor of a "return to nature" where one need not be ashamed of displaying true feelings.

Any trend that comes to the end of its course reverses itself—as the exaggerated worship of the Virgin Mary finally triggered witch-hunting. Eighteenth-century Frenchmen, unlike their forebears in the seventeenth, were less favorably disposed toward women—as if resentful of all they owed to them. Even Rousseau, forerunner of the Revolution, stated flatly that "woman is intended to please man: and if man must, in turn, be pleasing to her, it remains true that it is less directly necessary; his worth lies in his power, and he pleases merely by being strong."[11] The female is implicitly subordinate to the male and should merely be taught what a mother and housewife should know to please and serve her consort and offspring. Rousseau thought little of woman's cultural ability and in his *Lettre à d'Alembert*, favorably quoted by Schopenhauer, he declared that "women have, in general, no love of any art; they have no proper knowledge of any; and they have no genius."[12]

Voltaire was the darling of women throughout his life—from Ninon de Lenclos, through Russia's Catherine the Great, to Madame du Châtelet, his lifelong mistress and possibly the most intellectually gifted woman of the age. Yet he rarely displayed any real gratitude. Even his tearfully ironic epitaph for the Marquise du Châtelet betrays a secret contempt:

> She was a great man whose only fault was in being a woman. A woman who translated and explained Newton, and who made a free translation of Virgil, without letting it appear in conversation that she had done these wonders; a woman who never spoke evil of anyone, and who never told a lie; a friend attentive and courageous in friendship—in one word a very great man whom ordinary women knew only by her diamonds—that is the one whom you cannot hinder me from mourning all my life.[13]

In fact, esteem for, and gratitude to, woman was never a Frenchman's characteristic. There was, at all times, an undertone of resentment at their dependence upon them.

The nineteenth century was no longer France's in a political, economic, and social sense, but French literature retained its productivity and prestige, and contributed more female writers of the first order— Germaine de Staël and George Sand, for example—than the eighteenth century. The bisexual character of French cultural life remained throughout with the assistance of numerous salons patterned after the prestigious one of Madame Récamier.

But this bisexuality was not restricted to literature and culture in general. What made Frenchmen dependent to such an extent on feminine influence and guidance applied just as much to political life; this explains how the long line of royal mistresses, the "left-hand queens" of France inaugurated by Charles VII's delightful Agnès Sorel, played a role in politics and influenced statesmanship to a degree unknown in other lands. Russia's Catherine the Great had many male lovers, yet her statesmanship was never profoundly influenced by any of them, not even by Lanskoy, Orlov or Potemkin. In contrast, no French king's policy remained uninfluenced by his favorite of the time—and, more often than not, the left-hand queen was the real ruler of the land. The subtle struggle between Diane de Poitiers (who often attended meetings of King Henry II's cabinet) and her rival, Catherine de Médicis, the lawful queen, also proves that a royal woman can play, as a mother, an even greater part than a mere mistress—if it so happens that she is the mother of a minor when she becomes a widow and, perforce, a regent of the realm. When this happened to Catherine de Médicis, this throwback to the viragos of the Renaissance promptly eliminated her rival and seized the reins of power. She ruled a country torn apart by the Wars of Religion; presided over meetings of the Council of Ministers and rarely bothered to consult her sons; and was largely responsible for the gory massacre of the Saint-Barthelemy in which eight thousand Protestants were butchered. This mother of nine had more energy than most men but her statesmanship achieved nothing constructive. The assassination of her last son, Henry III, opened the way for the accession to the throne of the remarkable Henry IV, one of France's greatest rulers. A man of unbounded vitality who enjoyed during his lifespan no less than fifty-six recorded mistresses, he fell eventually under the spell of the extraordinary Gabrielle d'Estrées. Of all the historical deeds for which she was responsible, the Edict de Nantes, which guaranteed freedom of worship to the Huguenots and put a temporary end to religious strife in France, was the greatest, the crowning achievement of her long struggle in favor of religious tolerance. Her children by the king were legitimized and a decree proclaimed her to be the King's Titulary Mistress; she reconciled her lover with Pope Clement VIII and achieved a position of such power and authority that her brother wrote in his memoirs: "My sister was more powerful than the king at this time, His Majesty's faith in her being so great that he left in her hands many matters that otherwise would have required his personal attention."[14]

Subsequent events were to demonstrate eloquently that, in the absence of strong men, women could rule almost directly, in spite of the Salic Law, and then that they could rule indirectly as well under strong rulers by using their feminine wiles. When Henry IV died, his widow, Marie de Médicis, became regent with full power and authority; her son, the future Louis XIII, was only nine. Untalented, Marie misruled the country with the assistance of her Italian adventurer friends and was eventually eliminated by her grown-up son. To the latter, however, she bequeathed the great Cardinal de Richelieu, France's outstanding statesman, whose skill remained unmatched until the Revolution, and one of the few who remained immune to feminine influence. Then, again, a new regency befell France at the death of Louis XIII and his widow, Anne d'Autriche, took over. More fortunate than her female predecessor in her choice of premier, she appointed her lover, the subtle and devious Cardinal Mazarin, who ran France tolerably well for two decades and enjoyed Anne's full support during her lifetime, thanks to which he became as "powerful as God the Father on the eve of Creation." This, however, was the end of female regencies in France. A new age of royal mistresses—*maitresses en titre*—dawned.

With Louis XIV's exceedingly long reign, royal mistresses reappeared. It would be no exaggeration to say that the different phases of this absolute monarch's rule were powerfully influenced by whatever mistress prevailed at the time. In particular, when this otherwise imperious ruler fell under the influence of Madame de Maintenon's rigid and bigoted Catholicism, he did something he would have been unlikely to do under another's influence: the revocation of the Edict de Nantes which was followed by savage persecution. What one woman (Gabrielle d'Estrées) had done, another (Madame de Maintenon) proceeded to undo, both using their royal lovers as de facto puppets. Hundreds of thousands of extremely talented Huguenots emigrated and this hemorrhage dealt a shattering blow to the nation, from which it never really recovered. In many ways, Madame de Maintenon's influence was more profound that that of her predecessors— Louise de la Vallière and Madame de Montespan. She bears a large share of responsibility for the catastrophes that befell France in the last years of the Sun King's reign; cabinet ministers were accustomed to discuss all political affairs with her before they saw the king, and whatever her remarkable moral dignity and elevated character, her influence was often disastrous.

With Louis XIV's great-grandson and successor, the role of *maîtresse en titre* acquired its full dimensions, as distinct from mere *dames du lit royal.* Louis XV was no fool, but he was sensual, selfish, and weak-willed—predestined to fall under the sway of women, even temporarily under that of his worthy wife, Maria Leszczynska, in the early days of his marriage. Soon enough, she was replaced by a mistress, the Duchesse de Châteauroux, who was not able to exert her influence for long and was eventually dismissed. The fate of France was determined when Louis met the ravishing Jeanne Antoinette Poisson at a ball given by the city of Paris in 1744. She was promptly transmogrified into the Marquise de Pompadour—a name that was destined to become a household word, the epitome of the professional *favorite.* It was she, in fact, who ruled France during the two decades that followed, and the most amazing aspect of it is that she was only forty when she died in 1764. In effect, the most populated and powerful nation in Europe was ruled by a young, inexperienced woman. She dealt with everything

—in literature she played the part of a Maecenas, befriending Voltaire and the chief Physiocrats; in foreign policy, which fell completely into her hands, she picked the cabinet ministers, brought Belle-Isle and the Abbé de Bernis into office, and corresponded directly with the generals in command of armies in the field. Maria Theresa of Austria corresponded directly with her, bypassing the king's cabinet—and swung her to her side; and it was Pompadour who initiated the complete reversal of France's traditional opposition to the Habsburgs of Austria and triggered the disastrous Seven Years' War. Her power in internal politics was even greater, close to being absolute: she was the effective ruler of the country, her control over the mind and will of Louis being total. All she had to do to remain in power was to introduce young, beautiful ladies to the king in the famous Parc aux Cerfs, and while he took his erotic pleasures with others, she was left free to enjoy unchallenged power in France.

The vacuum created by her death was promptly filled when Lebel, Louis XV's valet, introduced Jeanne Du Barry. The political leadership soon changed; the Duc de Choiseul refused to acknowledge her and was disgraced in 1771, to be replaced by her lover, the Duc d'Aiguillon, with dire consequences for the country. Just as alarming, Comptroller-General Terray actually put the Treasury at her private disposal in order to secure her political backing, with the result that she promptly emptied it and drove the country to the edge of bankruptcy. But the far-reaching consequences of Louis XVI's marriage with Marie-Antoinette, Princess of Austria, were even direr. A great deal of the king's inept behavior at the beginning of the Revolution can be credited to her. For a change, this Louis had no mistress and fell completely under the spell of his foolish wife, and she, in turn, can be considered to have a large share of responsibility in the dramatic development of a revolution that might have taken place far more peacefully if it had not been for her catastrophic *politique du pire*—playing both ends against the middle.

The tale in the nineteenth century is not so compelling and there are no more Pompadours; but the susceptibility of Frenchmen to feminine lures and influence remained unimpaired. Consider the influence exerted by a semisecret agent of the skillful Italian statesman Cavour, the beautiful Virginia de Castiglione, on Louis Bonaparte who, as Emperor Napoleon III, swung the policy of France in favor of Italy's *Risorgimento*. But it was his legitimate and strong-willed consort, Eugenie de Montijo (who became his wife by refusing to become his mistress), who was primarily responsible for the two disastrous wars of France's Second Empire: the Mexican expedition and the fatal Franco-Prussian War of 1870 which cost them the imperial throne. It would be difficult to guess who wanted the war most, Bismarck or Eugenie; at any rate, contemporaries quoted her as having stated at the time, "This is *my* war."[15]

One may wonder with Schopenhauer, "May it not be the case in France that the influence of women, which went on increasing steadily from the time of Louis XIII, was to blame for the gradual corruption of the Court and Government, which brought about the Revolution of 1789, of which all subsequent disturbances have been the fruit?"[16] Quite possibly, but then, it was the peculiar temper of the French that dictated this type of bisexual cooperation.

Skipping over Madame de Bonnemain, whose company the would-be dictator General Boulanger chose in preference to absolute political power in 1889 (and saved France from a coup d'état), one comes straightaway to ambitious Hélène de Portes, mistress of French Premier Paul Reynaud during the dark days of 1940 and the German invasion. Madame de Portes' ascendancy over Reynaud was almost as great as that of Pompadour over Louis XV, and is all the stranger because their political views frequently diverged. But she invariably managed to make hers prevail in the end, and the fact that she became increasingly anti-British during the war had incalculable consequences as far as France's policy during the military collapse is concerned:

> Perhaps the most baneful feature of her relationship with Paul Reynaud was that she held him totally her prisoner, and chivvied him relentlessly until he was simply worn out. Together they lived in Reynaud's bachelor flat near the Assembly, where much business of state was transacted. She was constantly intervening and interfering, and even in his office Reynaud was never immune from her endless telephone calls. On at least one occasion, Madame de Portes was found actually seated at his desk, presiding over a gathering of generals, deputies and government officials. Once when André Maurois criticised a political appointment made by his friend, Reynaud admitted, "It was not my choice, it was hers."[17]

Hélène de Portes never left Reynaud during the crisis of France's collapse and the last negotiations with the British; with relentless energy, she interfered and, more often than not, imposed her views, not only on her lover but on other members of the cabinet as well:

> Paul Baudouin, who was completely her man and came to represent her will within the Cabinet, wrote with the utmost restrained chivalry: "If she acted as the controller of the Cabinet her one desire was to save the country by defending and fortifying the

man she admired." Certainly the impression one gets from those others who were present is that Reynaud was never for a moment left alone, never allowed to make a decision or an appointment without Hélène de Portes being party to it. In the middle of deliberations of the War Cabinet she would ring him on his private telephone; if in despair he should disconnect it, she would summon ushers to take in written messages to him; and finally she would often burst into the council chamber herself.[18]

On at least one occasion, a vital secret telegram that was missing was eventually retrieved from under her bedsheets. To hear Britain's General Spears tell it, he wrested Paul Reynaud's signature on a highly important document (for the creation of an indissoluble union between France and Britain) and went over to the adjoining secretary's room to have it typed; there he found Hélène de Portes:

> As I handed a secretary the paper, she stepped behind him and read over his shoulder, holding his arm to prevent his turning the pages too fast for her to read them. It was difficult to tell from her expression whether rage or amazement prevailed. But both feelings were apparent. As she went on delaying the secretary to read herself, I told him curtly the message must be typed without a moment's delay.[19]

The astonished indignation of a Britisher, unaccustomed to women without official position meddling in such matters, is understandable. At any rate, she won the game. Worn out, Paul Reynaud gave in; Britain's "Declaration of Union" was not put to a vote and he resigned, leaving the field open to those who were going to seek an armistice with Germany. A few weeks later, Hélène de Portes was killed in an automobile accident. Apprised of her demise, Paul Reynaud, now ex-premier of France during the country's greatest national catastrophe, said sadly: *"Elle était la France."*[20] Indeed, she was the eternal Mariane.

The main gauge of feminine influence in a body politic is its society's attitude toward ethics—that essentially man-made code of morality superimposed on human nature's atavistic reflexes. The strict ethical standards imposed by Protestantism in general, and more especially Puritanism, were unknown in France, except to the Huguenots. France's social life was essentially characterized by considerable moral tolerance—with its inevitable counterpart, political intolerance; the great Revolution with its orgy of blood and terror made this plain. The feminization of France's social life was such that there never was any need to interfere with the private individual's morals so long as they conformed to the well-established patterns of traditional *amorality* and in no way threatened the social organism. Such moral tolerance was socially sound and fitted the intellectual pattern of French thinking— the open admission that it is an individual's right to interpret the moral code as he pleases, thus avoiding the hypocrisy that plagued Protestant societies. Because of this refined hedonism, the French saw in sexual activity a tool of the intellect that it was imperative to keep at all times under rational control; hence, it was more a matter of self-regulation than of repression. Sexual passion, regulated by the intellect, could always be proclaimed openly because it was always *sous contrôle* of the rational faculty.

This in turn explains why the French, with a certain cold detachment, displayed such talent in explaining lucidly states of mind and emotion, ideas and sensations, as a surgeon explains to his students the physiological complexity of the human body. No other nation could have produced a Stendhal, with his subtle analysis of the *grandes passions*, his cool and detached delineation of characters, his extraordinary psychological insights and depictions of the innermost recesses of the soul. Who but Stendhal would define his *De l'Amour* as "simply an accurate and scientific treatise on a type of madness which is very rare in France"? Precisely because of the scarcity of true love in Gallic land, French writers could take the irrational life force and break it up intellectually into its component parts in a completely objective way— feminine influence completing the job by taking care of the nonrational components. Love, French-style, is essentially dispassionate and usually devoid of the sentimental attitude that so often cloys sexual relationships in other, more northerly climes. Nor is it the mixture of lustful passion and jealousy that characterizes southern love, Mediterranean-style. It focuses essentially on the relationship between the physical and the mental, with the mental in full control. Nowhere else in Europe did culture master nature to such a degree—and nowhere else could woman achieve, for both good and ill, this unparalleled emancipation from her mental bondage to nature.

Part IV

THE MODERN AGE:
WOMAN AND CIVILIZATION

CHAPTER

I

Woman in Search of an Identity

Late in the eighteenth century, when the gate of history swung on the hinges of the industrial and French revolutions and opened wide to usher in the modern age, Western man's understanding of mankind's destiny changed completely under the spur of a profound alteration in the nature of knowledge. This epistemological mutation brought forth a new *Weltanschauung* that is still with us today.

All through the post-medieval era, a coherent world-picture had linked the theory of representation with that of language, natural order, wealth, and value. From the early nineteenth century onward, the theory of representation (discourse that unrolls representation into a static picture) disappears as foundation of all conceivable mental organizations. Language, as a spontaneous and nature-given picture of a cross-ruling pattern of things and an essential liaison between being and representation, disappears along with it: the spiritual supremacy of the Logos comes to an end. When Sprenger in his *Malleus Maleficarum* based his verdict on woman by appealing to the God-given structure of language, for example, he was doing only what every other theologian and philosopher did at the time: "all this is indicated by the etymology of the word; for *Femina* comes from *Fe* and *Minus*, since she is ever weaker to hold and preserve the faith.[1]

It never occurred to Sprenger, or to anyone else, that language is man-made and evolves ceaselessly in response to alterations in the *Zeitgeist*. Instead, along with his contemporaries, Sprenger viewed the world as teeming with signs and symbols, given once and for all at the time of Creation, to be unraveled, interpreted, and classified according to affinities and similitudes. Nature itself was a continuous canvas of interrelated things, words and signs, forms and symbols, pointing to permanent identities and distinctions.

Now, suddenly, historicism begins to pervade everything, disconnects what used to be connected, and places all the newly isolated elements of knowledge in the stream and perspective of time, along with a new form of mental organization based on historical background rather than pseudo-affinities. Temporal continuity gives a coherence to this new order of knowledge that makes previous mental organizations appear incongruous. Everything is now in motion: the study of static wealth is replaced by that of dynamic production, that of taxonomy by the study of living organisms, and language itself loses its privileged position as a gift from heaven or nature, becoming merely one more historical feature with its own past evolution and future becoming.

Thanks to the new science of philology and comparative grammar, the Word is suddenly shifted out of its purely representative function and is integrated in an evolving grammatical structure that becomes the predominant element; it alone allows the Word to mean what it intends to mean in that particular context. As Friedrich von Schlegel, the great Sanskritologist, was to put it in his memorable *Uber die Sprache und Weisheit der Indier* (1808):

> . . . the decisive element that will shed light on everything is the inner structure of languages or comparative grammar, which will give us brand new solutions to the genealogy of languages, just as comparative anatomy has thrown a great deal of light on natural history.[2]

In fact, his pioneering work on philology destroyed the static view of language and introduced the philological concept of linguistic historicity. It was the same in the field of legislation, where the founder of the "historical" school of jurisprudence, Friedrich Karl von Savigny, stated that all laws arise "in the way that the prevailing linguistic usage, as a customary law, indicates for it . . . by inner, stilly working forces and not by the arbitrary will of the legislator."[3] In other words, legislation is only the crystallization and codification of customs and mores that spring up spontaneously. The key word now is "comparison," an extension to the history of every field of Cuvier's epoch-making *Anatomie Comparée*, a revolutionary method which, analyzing the connection between character, structure, and function, inspired all the seminal philological works of Jacob Grimm, Friedrich Diez, and Wilhelm von Humboldt, as well as the comparative geology of Karl Ritter.

As a consequence, *Man* for the first time enters the world-picture of Western knowledge as a separate, autonomous entity. Post-medieval understanding did not conceive of the study of man in terms of a specific, separate area of knowledge, nor did it conceive of life as opposed to nonlife; it was aware of living things, classified hierarchically along with all the other things, inanimate as well as animate, of the universe. Only when "Life" appeared as a specific entity was natural history able to metamorphose itself into biology. There could be no science of man because post-medieval thought linked in an unconscious dialectical opposition nature and human nature—nature, the difference in the continuum of being; human nature, the continuity in the disorderly chain of representations. Human nature and nature were so completely intermingled through the dialectical mechanics of the understanding that man alone, as first and foremost reality, found no place in this scheme of things. Man as a separate entity and topic of epistemological study existed no more before that time than the productivity of work, the dynamics of living organisms, or the historicity of language.

Just as natural history became biology, the study of wealth was replaced by that of economics, thought about language became philology, and the *discourse* where being and representation had found a common ground faded away. Man began to appear in his modern, ambiguous position: as the *object* of knowledge, but also as knowing *subject*—man's position shifted to that of a separate object of scientific investigation. And the day man became a specific, isolated object of knowledge, the tail end of a long process of individuation and intellectual emancipation that had started with the Renaissance, so did *woman* —no longer in conjunction with man and as his nature-appointed partner, but as his human equal. This, we recall, is what happened in Greece, in a more rudimentary way, when classical tragedy turned anthropocentric with Sophocles and Euripides: the search for the identity of man triggered a similar search for that of woman.

Most expressive of this new mode of thought was the Romantic movement. The eighteenth-century Enlightenment had been rooted in an optimistic view of the present, the past being a mere preparation leading up to it, and the future an idealized version of it. Romanticism, however, looked upon historical eras and people—viewed as a joint production of nature and history—as slowly evolving organisms to be understood in their own specificity; the present qua present suddenly narrowed down to a razor-thin edge separating a meaningful past from an unforeseeable future pregnant with possibilities.

Industrialization, increasing urbanization, the population explosion, and the rise of democracy all combined to shape the rise and nature of modern feminism. Man's new, tentative image of himself was bound to trigger a search for its counterpart in woman. As a contemporary feminist states it: "It was the need for a new identity that started women, a century ago, on that passionate journey, that vilified, misinterpreted journey away from home."[4] What had, until then, been accepted as a matter of course by both men and women—that mankind as a whole was not an end in itself but merely the materialization of a higher cosmic purpose—was now rejected. The erosion of religious faith and the raising of Man onto a historical pedestal from which spiritual significance was banished, destroyed the *organic* link between the sexes as members of a higher spiritual *whole*. Just as feminism would have been inconceivable a century before, it would now have been inconceivable for such a movement not to have arisen.

Germaine de Staël is eminently representative of this new trend in an age of transition—not that she was ever an ardent feminist, but she stood on the threshold between the old and the new worlds, part prerevolutionary, part modern. She felt welling up in her a new consciousness of women's potential which she only dimly understood, a feeling of the latent power of womanhood in the now dawning world, which she could only partly actualize.

Favored by birth and circumstances, this extraordinary young woman began her career by taking over her mother's Paris salon a few years before the Revolution. Madame Necker's establishment was changing with bewildering speed under the darkening clouds of a prerevolutionary atmosphere. The great literary lions (Voltaire, Rousseau, D'Alembert, Diderot) were dead; the *philosophes* who had laid the intellectual groundwork for the Revolution were gone. In their stead came men primarily concerned with the deteriorating political climate of their day—budget, deficit, and taxation. Although her husband had at one time been Louis XVI's finance minister, Madame Necker had lost her bearings in this new field of interest; her daughter, on the contrary, felt quite at home. Germaine was probably the greatest conversationalist of her day, and could live happily only in Paris; to be exiled was a fate worse than death—and yet, what with the Terror of Robespierre and Napoleon's hostility, she spent a great deal of her life roaming over Europe.

Her remarkable energy and lack of tact aroused most women's hostility, and that of not a few men, but she was never too shy to fight back, and plunged recklessly into the stormy politics of her time—as an energetic man would, but with all the combined advantages and disadvantages due to her sex. As Byron was to state it: "She thinks like a man, but alas! she feels like a woman"[5]—a masculine viewpoint widely shared at the time. Germaine, much like another volcanic woman of great talent, George Sand, had a great heart and did far more good than harm; to an extent, in spite of the numerous flaws in her character, it was her truly feminine passion and exalted idealism that gave practical weight to her rational mind and swayed powerful men who could not have been influenced by members of their own sex. She it was who acted as liaison between Bernadotte, by then de facto ruler of Sweden, and Tzar Alexander of Russia; during her stay in Stockholm, the anxious French chargé d'affaires sent news that "she calls on the Prince Royal [Bernadotte] at all hours; he tells her everything and she sometimes advises him."[6] Although she alone was not responsible for the formation of the Fourth Coalition against Napoleon, she alone was responsible for the timing of Sweden's accession to it—timing fatal for Napoleon, insofar as the Swedish army in northern Germany robbed Napoleon of the fruit of his victories and gave his opponents time to bring Austria into their coalition. "A Frenchman held the destiny of the world in his hands; he was one of the principal direct causes of our misfortunes,"[7] Napoleon stated at Saint Helena, referring to Bernadotte—and behind Bernadotte stood Germaine de Staël. Looking back wistfully from Saint Helena's tropical heat, Napoleon thought of Madame de Staël enthroned in Coppet's plush exile from 1804 to 1810 during the heyday of his imperial rule and of the part she played in his eventual downfall: "Her house at Coppet became a veritable arsenal against me. One went there to win one's spurs."[8] In a sense, no man, however brilliant or powerful, could have so relentlessly harmed Napoleon in the way that this superior woman did.

She did not come by her political influence easily. More than once, insults were heaped on her simply because she was a woman. She had played an important part in Bonaparte's coup d'état on September 4, 1797, and was rewarded in the press by articles such as this:

> But who intrusted you with the mission you are carrying out among us? Who has asked you to meddle in matters of no concern to you? . . . Miserable hermaphrodite that you are, your sole ambition in uniting the two sexes in your person is to dishonor them both at once![9]

She was soon to regret whatever assistance she had given to Bonaparte's cause. On December 6, 1797, she met him for the first time and began her grotesque attempts to seduce him—Bonaparte, the Corsican misogynist who, in reply to her blunt question, "Who is the greatest woman, alive or dead?" shot back, "The one that has made the most children."[10] At one point she asked to see Napoleon at his home, rue Chantereine; upon being told that the citizen general was naked in his tub, she cried, "No matter. Genius has no sex."[11] However hard she tried, there was no seducing Bonaparte, who could not abide viragos, much as she praised his genius. The growing rift between them did not endear her, however, to the royalists. One royalist newspaper, published abroad, ruthlessly pinned her down: "She writes on metaphysics, which she does not understand; on morality which she does not practice; on the virtues of her sex, which she lacks."[12] She got it from all sides; the Jacobin *Journal des Hommes Libres* threw at her: "It is not your fault that you are ugly, but it is your fault that you are an intriguer. . . . You know the road to Switzerland."[13]

Germaine, thick-skinned as she was, began to feel strongly about the consistently antifeminist persecution she provoked from right, left, and center. Her literary output testifies to her growing resentment at a society that was not only unjust and cynical but deliberately stifled all attempts on the part of its female half to develop its full potential. She already felt this on the eve of the Revolution; to her great disappointment, she felt it even more strongly during and after that cataclysmic upheaval. In her *De La Litérature,* she stated indignantly that "the entire social order . . . is arrayed against a woman who wants to rise to a man's reputation."[14] Berated by her critics, she cried out, "Oh, if I could make myself into a man! How I would settle accounts with those *antiphilosophes* once and for all!"[15] She left us, however, no clue as to what difference it would have made—and she would have lost the undoubted advantages that her femaleness brought in its train. But other women, only slightly less talented, could not abide her either. Madame de Genlis, former mistress of the duke of Orléans and governess of his children, knew Germaine well, thought her a "most embarrassing person," conceited and rude, and wrote a vicious satire about her, *Mélanie, or the Female Philosopher* (1803).[16]

One should not be left with the impression that Germaine was a crusading feminist; she was nothing of the kind. She did sense a certain injustice in her treatment at the hands of a male-controlled society, but she never hesitated to use to full advantage the rather mediocre endowments of her female figure—a usually uncovered but voluptuous bosom, fat arms always bare, and shapely but massive legs. Her real means of seduction, however, were conversation and wit, and she used them to the full in France and wherever anyone was willing to listen to her and fall under her spell. She had less success in Germany; her French form of intelligence ran headlong into the awakening German intellect. Schiller did claim that she represented "French intellectual culture in its purity," but Goethe blamed her for her rather light treatment of profound topics.[17]

The German mind had never been exposed to the experience of the French salon under feminine chairmanship, and even though she thought as a man, as Byron stated, Germaine retained enough femaleness to "provoke the evil genius" in Goethe, who then proceeded to deal with the topics raised by her "dialectically and problematically," which infuriated her.[18] On her part, she perceived with acuteness what was wrong, and even dangerous, in the German cultural and social setting:

> The two classes of society—the scholars and the courtiers—are completely divorced from each other. As a result, the scholars do not cultivate conversation, and mundane society is absolutely incapable of thought. . . . The thinkers are soaring in the empyrean, and on earth you only find grenadiers.[19]

German philosophic thought had just embarked on its trail-blazing career that was going to revolutionize political and social thinking all over the world, and in Germaine de Staël we have a remarkable witness to its launching, one endowed with a sharp understanding of its nature. In her brilliant *De l'Allemagne* she states that the Germans, searching for truth for its own sake regardless of its practical applications, talking to the clouds and enjoying contemplation, were "the scouts of the human spirit's host; they try for new roads, they attempt to use means hitherto unknown; how could one be indifferent to what they have to say when they return from the infinite?"[20] She lays part of the responsibility for their character, their independence of spirit and individual originality, on the political balkanization of German lands and, as a consequence, the futility of political ambition in small principalities. But she becomes almost prophetic when, comparing their original individuality with the prevailing conformity of the French "who are all-powerful only when in a large body," she warns: "How much harm this spirit of conformity would do to the Germans"—something of which the following century became painfully aware.[21]

She was also quite capable of debunking some excesses of German philosophers. On one of her most hilarious encounters with Teutonic profundity, she was introduced to the abstruse Fichte:

> He had scarcely been introduced when she invited him to explain his Absolute Ego [*Ich-Ich*] "as briefly as possible, in a quarter of an hour for instance." Fichte swallowed, spoke for a few minutes, then was interrupted by Germaine: "Oh, that will do, Monsieur Fisht," she remarked with a charming smile, "I understand you completely. Your system may be illustrated admirably by one of the tales of Baron Munchausen." While Fichte looked thunderstruck and the guests studied their shoes, she explained how Baron Munchausen, having come upon a large river, had managed to cross it by firmly taking hold with his right hand of his left sleeve and swinging himself to the other shore. "This, if

I understand you correctly, Monsieur Fisht, is exactly what you have done with your I."[22]

A perfect illustration of the old saying that while the great merit of German philosophic thought is to go to the bottom of things, its great drawback is that it usually stays right there.

One can wonder what would have happened to German philosophic thought if feminine influence had made itself felt in German culture; there is little trace of it, however, and in the most profound philosophic thought of the nineteenth century, there was hardly any sympathy for femaleness or womanhood. Goethe was an exception. For the creator of the incomparable Faust who, through sheer masculine strength of will, is spared the necessity of repentance because he can rise from a lower to a higher plane of being, woman is what she is to the medieval soul—a mediator, a convenient object on which to focus temporarily while man's spirit aims beyond at eternal salvation. Faust rises from flesh-and-blood Margaret to ghostly Helen to the Virgin Mother, undergoing several figurative deaths, and finally escapes from the clutches of the Devil, in great part thanks to their spiritual mediation. As Faust's soul rises up to the ethereal regions beyond death, it first traverses the intermediate masculine spheres where rule the holy anchorites (*Pater Extaticus, Pater Profundus, Pater Seraphicus*), where the blessed souls of the dead shed their last remaining impurities. But on reaching the highest sphere, Faust's soul enters the sublime realm of the *Mater Gloriosa*, the realm of the eternal feminine where the three great penitents—*Magna Peccatrix, Mulier Samaritana* and *Maria Aegyptiaca*—plead with the Holy Virgin in his favor, followed closely by the soul of Margaret longing for her earthly lover. Faust is forgiven because of this intercession and, forever blessed, dwells henceforth in eternity.

The poetic mind has always been more sensitive to the feminine than the philosophic or scientific one. Faust was saved because he refused to turn his back on nature and reject life; his inquiring mind lived on in spite of his broken heart—and for the first time Mephistopheles becomes worried and wonders whether, after all, his prey is not going to escape him—worry that increases when Faust, transmogrified as a Gothic knight, finds himself in command of a fortress of another medieval age, that of pre-Homeric Greece. There he defeats Menelaus and accepts Helen as his lady and queen, treating her with a chivalrous courtesy unknown to the ancient Greek world, but very similar to that of Dante's spiritual knightly service to Beatrice, for whose sake he undertakes his journey in the lower and upper invisible realms. Helen is not slow in responding to this new treatment; honored and respected as she never was in antiquity, she helps Faust through his ghostly metamorphosis.

Goethe's view of femininity, however, was far different from that of other German thinkers. Where the poetic insight disappears along with its mystical undertone, male philosophic criticism takes over. In *The Phenomenology of Mind*, Hegel views womanhood through a thoroughly masculine prism; contrasting the conflicting claims of the social community and the narrower interests of the family—"the community gets itself subsistence only by breaking in upon family happiness"—he claims that this very same community

> creates its enemy for itself within its own gates, creates it in what it supresses, and what is at the same time essential to it—womankind in general. Womankind—the everlasting irony in the life of the community—changes by intrigue the universal purpose of government into a private end, transforms its universal activity into a work of this or that specific individual, and perverts the universal property of the state into a possession and ornament for the family. Woman in this way turns to ridicule the grave wisdom of maturity, which, being dead to all particular aims, to private pleasure, personal satisfaction, and actual activity as well, thinks of, and is concerned for, merely what is universal; she makes this wisdom the laughing-stock of raw and wanton youth, an object of derision and scorn, unworthy of their enthusiasm. She asserts that it is everywhere the force of youth that really counts; she upholds this as of primary significance; extols a son as one who is the lord and master of the mother who has borned him. . . . The community, however, can preserve itself only by suppressing this spirit of individualism.[23]

This thoroughly Germanic outlook of the spiritual father of totalitarianism is rooted in the Germanic conviction that women belong by natural destiny to home and hearth, whose family instinct is permanently and irretrievably in conflict with the male-ruled social community. As for the connection between women and the generation gap, we shall refer to it again.

With Schopenhauer, whose doctrine of the primacy of the will was in direct conflict with Hegel's idealism, we reach a stage of antifeminist bitterness that goes well beyond the usual Teutonic diatribes against the second sex—a bitterness that heralds the dawn of a new age in terms of a direct conflict between the sexes that would have been meaningless in preceding centuries. In his *Studies in Pessimism,* he berates "our old French notions of gallantry, and our preposterous system of reverence—that highest product of Teutonico-Christian stupidity. These notions serve only to make women more arrogant and overbearing; so that one is occasionally reminded of the holy apes in Benares, who in the consciousness of their sanctity and inviolable position think they can do exactly as they please."[24]

In order to understand the violent misogyny of most German males, it must be kept in mind that the German inner spirit is essentially one of *pathos,* a basically feminine characteristic which is so easily betrayed by the very structure of their language—indefinite and imprecise, emotional, unrestrained and anarchical, romantic and sentimental, still close to its Gothic roots. It is essentially the language of brooding and introspective people, which has been shaped by, and then shaped in its turn by a feedback process, German psychology. As Hermann Keyserling explains it:

> In every feminine person the masculine element which is always present supplies the inferior function. It is typical that precisely this function should be overemphasized through the urge toward psychological compensation. Thus the German emphasis on the masculine is just what betrays the feminine character. And the fact that the prime masculine model is presented in the character of the drill-sergeant again demonstrates the inferiority of the masculine function.[25]

From this springs the German male's overemphasis on the will to power and contempt for woman which implies an unconscious contempt for the exceptionally important feminine component in his own makeup. The German is rarely his own master and requires the dictate of externalized and objectified ideas as a compulsive framework. The German stress is always on yielding oneself up to externally imposed organization and discipline, and his feminine component will stress nature, primitivism, and romanticism against what is artificial, the fundamental instinctive against form, shape, clarity, and style, the gigantic and colossal as against the harmonious balance dictated by good taste. To an extent, all this reflects the Germanic stress on inner experience as against outgoing living.

This peculiar character of the German also explains how as an introverted individualist, he can become, if at all gifted, an exceptionally creative man. German abstract thought has dominated the nineteenth and twentieth centuries, German philosophy that ranges from Kant and Hegel to Schopenhauer and Nietzsche has no equivalent in other Western lands. Distinctly German also are the thought processes of Marx, Engels, Freud, Jung, and Einstein who, in their respective fields, revolutionized the world. And German pathos has given the world its greatest music from Bach to Wagner and beyond. All the great intellectual and artistic productions of the Germans, as well as their pharaonic distortions in the political world, are the result of this uneasy marriage within the bisexual German male's soul between the masculine and feminine principles. To take only the latest instance of this Germanic mode of thought, listen to Adolf Hitler's *Mein Kampf:*

> Like a woman . . . who will submit to the strong man rather than dominate the weakling, thus the masses love the ruler rather than the suppliant, and inwardly they are far more satisfied by a doctrine which tolerates no rival than by the grant of liberal freedom; they feel at a loss what to do with it, and even easily feel themselves deserted.[26]

A rather shrewd analysis of Teutonic mass feeling.

At any rate, German women certainly did not prove Hitler wrong. It is well known that "at the beginning of his political career he owed much to the encouragement of women. . . . Many women were fascinated by his hypnotic powers; there are well-attested accounts of the hysteria which affected women at his big meetings, and Hitler himself attached much importance to the women's vote."[27] And they did not disappoint him.

Schopenhauer's typical misogyny becomes more understandable against this background. His violent attack against the female sex came a few decades after the first feminist blast sounded in England. Coinciding with the beginning of the French Revolution and in the midst of England's own industrial revolution, Mary Wollstonecraft's pioneering work, *Vindication of the Rights of Women* (1792), was the first clarion call for the forthcoming battle of the sexes, the first appearance and explicit statement of a problem that had not existed previously in Western consciousness—since the distant days of Greco-Roman antiquity. "Let us consider women," she pleaded, "in the grand light of human creatures, who in common with men, are placed on this earth to unfold their faculties."[28] It was her opinion, forcefully stated, that biological facts were unimportant and that education made all the difference. She raved against Rousseau's statement according to which woman was *by nature* subordinate to man: "Rousseau exerts himself to prove that all *was* right originally . . . and I, that all will *be* right."[29] In her previous *Thoughts on the Education of Daughters* (1787), she stoutly maintained that nature had made the sexes equal and that education should strive to develop that equality. A pupil of the eighteenth-century *philosophes*, she also entertained a passionate belief in the power of human reason and spurned religious feeling. The main butt of her argument was that marriage was servitude, and she proceeded to justify her thesis by entering into "no-marriage" arrangements with several men—only to capitulate and eventually marry William Godwin in 1797 in order to safeguard the interests of their children. Quite apart from her personal eccentricities, Mary Wollstonecraft's thoughts and activity implied a sense of profound change; they betrayed the fact that a revolutionary undercurrent was about to break into the open and violently upset the traditional relationship between the sexes in Western civilization.

Of this, men became conscious too, and some were not slow in responding in kind, sometimes with the violence of those who feel that some monstrous danger lurks underfoot. Goethe and Hegel, in this respect, remained faithful to the old concepts, basically unaware of any impending change. Not so Schopenhauer who went into battle fully clad in armor, displaying with great talent and some insight the very pettiness in his own personality which he held against the female sex:

> . . . it will be found that the fundamental fault of the female character is that it has *no sense of justice*. This is mainly due to the fact, already mentioned, that women are defective in the powers of reasoning and deliberation; but it is also traceable to the position which Nature has assigned to them as the weaker sex. They are dependent, not upon strength, but upon craft; and hence their instinctive capacity for cunning, and their ineradicable tendency to say what is not true. . . . And since women exist in the main solely for the propagation of the species, and are not destined for anything else, they live, as a rule, more for the species than for the individual, and in their hearts take the affairs of the species more seriously than those of the individual.[30]

Therefore, the proper place for women in any social structure is on the lower rung of the ladder:

> They form the *sexus sequior*—the second sex, inferior in every respect to the first; their infirmities should be treated with consideration; but to show them great reverence is extremely ridiculous, and lowers us in their eyes. . . .[31]

Finally, with Nietzsche we reach a nadir in the German male's estimation of the human female. It is a shame that he could never have met Germaine de Staël, who represented everything he detested in woman. Her *De l'Allemagne* offended him deeply, and in his *Beyond Good and Evil,* he says: "let us call to mind . . . that it is not so very long ago that a masculinized woman could dare, with unbridled presumption, to recommend the Germans to the interest of Europe as gentle, good-hearted, weak-willed and poetical fools."[32] Nietzsche's low opinion of women was based on no greater personal acquaintance with them than that of his devoted sister. Unlike Schopenhauer, he does not rationalize his contempt, merely states it flatly, Zarathustra-like:

> Man shall be trained for war and woman for the recreation of the warrior. All else is folly. . . . Thou goest to woman? Do not forget thy whip. . . . Woman has so much cause for shame; in woman there is so much pedantry, superficiality, schoolmasterliness, petty presumption, unbridledness and indiscretion concealed . . . which has really been best restrained and dominated hitherto by the *fear* of man.[33]

But, unlike Schopenhauer the pessimist, Nietzsche's more optimistic life-affirming views make him see the good points of woman as object: "We take pleasure in woman as a perhaps daintier, more delicate, and more ethereal kind of creature. What a treat it is to meet creatures who have only dancing and nonsense and finery in their minds! They have always been the delight of every tense and profound male soul."[34]

He blames Rousseau for having made women interesting—the same Rousseau who had such a low opinion of them. But he is right in the sense that Rousseau's "return to nature" philosophy was bound to revive an interest in that half of the human race that is closest to Nature. However, it was in philosophy that the reappearance of the feminine principle was most noteworthy—in the triumph of Hegelian dialectics over the Cartesian mechanistic outlook. Nietzsche's analysis of the German character gives us a clue to the psychological roots of this momentous philosophic innovation when, speaking of his compatriots, he says that "they belong to the day before yesterday and the day after tomorrow—*they have as yet no today.*"[35] In his *Beyond Good and Evil,* he explains:

> The German himself does not *exist:* he is *becoming,* he is "developing himself." "Development" is therefore the essentially German discovery and hit in the great domain of philosophical formulas.[36]

Hegelian dialectics is, as it were, formal logic in motion; it adds a new, temporal dimension to classical logic as it was understood from Aristotle to Descartes. In no way does it contradict or cancel formal logic, any more than Einstein's revolution in physics and cosmology contradicted or canceled the Newtonian universe: Newton's astronomical concept was absorbed and incorporated in a vaster and more comprehensive system, becoming merely a *particular case* within the much broader concept formulated in the general theory of relativity. In a similar vein, dialectic logic is related to formal logic as higher mathematics to elementary arithmetic; it is all a matter of scale. Inasmuch as it conforms to natural processes, it is closer to nature. As the great Indianist Heinrich Zimmer put it in his *Philosophies of India,*

. . . 1 plus 1 logically is 2, never 3 or 5, and can never shrink to 1. Yet things are not that way in the field of the vital processes of nature, where the most alogical developments take place every day, on every side, as a matter of course. The rules of life are not those of logic but of dialectics; the reasonings of nature not like those of the mind, but rather like those of our illogical belly, our procreative faculty, the vegetable-animal aspect of our microcosm. In this sphere, the sphere of biological dialectics, the illogical sphere of nature and life forces, 1 plus 1 is usually far from remaining 2 for very long.[37]

The tremendous impact of dialectics on modern philosophy is precisely due to its synthetic approach and its far greater connection with the biological and reproductive processes of nature than formal logic. Being is no longer a static state but a dynamic process of Becoming. In this sense, the birth of Hegelian dialectics is at one with the profound mutation in the nature of knowledge early in the nineteenth century when historicism came to pervade every intellectual discipline. This "historicization" of all fields of knowledge added a new dimension to human understanding and depth to its new four-dimensional world-picture.

By overcoming the more limited and essentially masculine Aristotelian-Cartesian formal logic, it reestablished a "feminine" element at the very core of discursive thinking with the *synthesis* that gathers together, and overcomes eventually, the merely logical opposition between thesis and antithesis in a *coincidentia oppositorum.* Starting from his psychological investigations in *The Varieties of Religious Experience,* William James arrives at an examination of mysticism (the feminine component of the religious temper) and cannot avoid pointing out the mystical sentiment which, deep down, supports and feeds dialectic thought. In his own words, he came to the definite conclusion, after personal experience, that

. . . our normal waking consciousness, rational consciousness as we call it, is but one special type of consciousness, whilst all about it, parted from it by the filmiest of screens, there lie potential forms of consciousness entirely different. We may go through life without suspecting their existence; but apply the requisite stimulus, and at a touch they are there. . . . Looking back on my own experiences, they all converge towards a kind of insight to which I cannot help ascribing some metaphysical significance. The keynote of it is invariably a *reconciliation.*[38]

Here we have, clearly, the intrusion of the reconciling feminine element in human consciousness, keynote of all mysticisms.
   He then proceeds to dialectics:

It is as if the opposites of the world, whose contradictoriness and conflict make all our difficulties and troubles, were melted into unity. Not only do they, as contrasted species, belong to one and the same genus, but *one of the species,* the nobler and better one, *is itself the genus, and so soaks up and absorbs* its opposite into itself. . . . I feel as if it must mean something, something like what the hegelian philosophy means. . . .[39]

And, in a footnote, he adds:

What reader of Hegel can doubt that that sense of a perfected Being with all its otherness soaked up into itself, which dominates his whole philosophy, must have come from the prominence in his consciousness of mystical moods like this, in most persons kept subliminal? The notion is thoroughly characteristic of the mystical level, and the *Aufgabe* of making it articulate was surely set to Hegel's intellect by mystical feeling.[40]

   The unmistakably "sexual" imagery of James' "otherness soaked up into itself" unconsciously suggests the female cell soaking up into itself, as it were, the male sperm in order to start a new life in the womb of time.
   The last step in the reintroduction of the feminine principle at the heart of philosophic thinking was the reemergence of cyclical interpretations of history, contrasted with the traditional, strictly linear, eschatological, and masculine interpretation—to which Marxism's apocalyptic vision remains faithful in spite of its dialectical interpretation. One of the first portents of this new trend was Nietzsche's theory of "eternal recurrence," the metaphysical theory that humankind has been, is, and will forever be undergoing the same life course from beginning to end, thus rejecting simultaneously the Christian doctrine of an afterlife and the fashionable belief in endless progress that was inaugurated by the Enlightenment. For all his ranting against woman,

Nietzsche was by far the most "feminine" of the nineteenth-century philosophers—including his preaching the advent of the iron-hard superman upon whose forthcoming appearance he looked with all the longing of a palpitating female heart.

The cyclical concept had, actually, never quite died out. In the twelfth century, the monk Joachim de Floris had applied the theological concept of the Trinity to the historical process, which he divided into three parts or stages (that of the Father, the Son, and the Holy Ghost or future time); he demonstrated that, allegorically, the New Testament reenacted the Old, and that the same thing would apply to the third and last stage of historical development under the aegis of the Holy Ghost. Next came Giambattista Vico in the eighteenth century with his theory of *ricorsi*, historical returns, which introduced the notion of parallel life courses in the history of all nations. At the end of the nineteenth century, the American Brooks Adams tried his hand at it in *The Law of Civilization and Decay*, patterned after a strictly mechanical model; previously, the Russian Nikolai Danilevsky had propounded the biological model of historical cycles encased in quasi-zoological laws. Finally, we reach Oswald Spengler and his massive opus *The Decline of the West*, the most uncompromising cyclical statement of them all.

In this counter-traditional trend, one cannot fail to see the survival, however muted, of a stubborn feminine streak which, in its resistance to the traditional patriarchal *linear* vision, displays the unconscious expression of the old cyclical, rhythmic lunar-vegetal outlook. But to this day it has remained a minority report and the masculine linear viewpoint remains firmly in the saddle: the unalloyed triumph of scientific thinking in the nineteenth and twentieth centuries with its materialization of seemingly endless technological progress could only bolster this viewpoint.

2

Industrial Revolution: The Birth of Feminism

New historical developments are, by definition, initiated by those societies that are the most progressive in their time. Quite logically, it was mostly in English-speaking countries (and to an extent in Scandinavia) that feminine self-consciousness first manifested itself. To assist matters further, the very fact that English nouns have no gender implies that the "sexualization" of the objectified world that comes naturally in other Western languages has no place in English-thinking consciousness.

England was the first to engineer and experience the industrial revolution whose consequences impacted the world at least as much as France's Revolution. Starting in 1760, an avalanche of technological inventions came tumbling out—the flying shuttle in 1760, closely followed by Hargreaves' spinning jenny in 1764, Watt's steam engine in 1768, Compton's mule in 1779, and Cartwright's power loom in 1785. As a result, England's standard of living early in the nineteenth century was far higher than that of any country on the Continent in terms of hygiene, cleanliness, clothing, and leisure. The English upper-class style of life was possibly less refined than elsewhere, but the rich were far more vigorous and forward-looking; their houses were less elegantly furnished than French houses, but their plumbing was better. At the fall of Napoleon, London was lighted entirely by gas. Nowhere on the Continent was the postal service as prompt and reliable; not since Roman times had roads been kept in such good repair. Iron was already in much greater use in Britain than abroad and in the century's first decade, five thousand steam engines were working in England as against a mere two hundred in France at the height of its Napoleonic glory. And when Waterloo struck down the would-be unifier of

Europe, steamships were already in use in Great Britain's coastal waters and Stephenson had built his first locomotive. In short, in "civilized" terms, England stood head and shoulders above the rest of the world. And so, inevitably, it was in England that woman's search for a new identity began.

It would have been almost impossible to conceive Frenchwomen as taking the lead in this matter (although a few revolutionary firebrands attempted it), since they had always assumed, as a matter of course, that they could exert an almost unlimited influence on their men. If they felt inclined to do so, they could even challenge them successfully on their own masculine grounds—witness Germaine de Staël and cigar-smoking George Sand who were very different from the demure Jane Austen—"one of the happy authors who have no history"—or colorless George Eliot, the advance guard of what Hawthorne chose to call the "damned mob of scribbling women."[1] Frenchwomen were "personalities" in their own right who could not possibly comprehend the necessity for a feminist movement. George Sand, who had long pondered on the relations between the sexes, never even came close to advocating political equality for her sex, convinced as she was that public life was simply not compatible with motherhood.[2] She lived as a man yet remained quite conscious of the ineradicable difference, merely complaining about the rather contemptuous attitude of the men of her time toward the fair sex in general.

In the twilight of her life, she commented: "That women differ from men, that heart and intellect are subject to the laws of sex, I do not doubt. . . . But ought this difference, so essential to the general harmony of things, constitute a moral inferiority?"[3] She was undoubtedly troubled by a certain awareness of her sex's social inferiority—something that would not have occurred to her had she lived two or three generations earlier, but she refused to advocate feminism as it was beginning to develop in her own time, in other lands. She did not want political equality but legal and sexual equality—in her view, sex was inseparable from love, the physical from the emotional.[4]

She became furious when Flaubert, in defense of the old lecherous critic Sainte-Beuve, wrote to her that "woman, for all members of my sex, is a groined archway opening on the infinite. That may not be a very elevated attitude, but it is fundamental to the male."[5] She rebuked him firmly:

> I am *not* a Catholic, but I do draw the line at monstrosities! I maintain that the old and ugly who buy young bodies for cash are not indulging in "love," and that what they do has nothing in common with the Cyprian Venus, with groined arches or infini-

ties or male or female! It is something wholly against nature, since it is not desire that pushes the young girl into the arms of the ugly dotard, and an act in which there is neither liberty nor reciprocity is an offense against the sanctity of nature. . . .[6]

But she persistently refused to be drawn into a feminist position and claimed that "for a woman to cease being a woman is productive only of inferiority." In fact, she was quite conscious of the fact that true femininity has in itself elements of superiority over the male that should not be sacrificed by an exaggerated desire for equality:

Education will in time be the same for men and women, but it will be in the female heart par excellence, as it always has been, that love and devotion, patience and pity, will find their true home. On woman falls the duty, in a world of brute passions, of preserving the virtues of charity and the Christian spirit. . . . When women cease to play that role, life will be the loser.[7]

George Sand's viewpoint is quite clear: having refused all her life to knuckle under to masculine authority, she yet refused to minimize the distinction between the sexes. She wanted the freedom for women to dispose of their bodies and souls as they saw fit without masculine compulsion, yet never advocated political equality for them. A forceful woman, a throwback to remote antiquity, a reincarnation of the Great Goddess, she viewed her male lovers as a mother views her children —love for her was essentially matriarchal, and her long-lasting lovers were all weak men. She did not want to turn women into men but demanded more dignity and influence for the female half of the human race. Men should not be allowed to smother women's intelligence in order to rule them, and women should emancipate themselves not as pseudo-males but as females. George Sand had behind her centuries of French tradition of collaboration between the sexes, of mutual interdependence; her revolt could take place only within the traditional framework of her country and culture. This traditional context, however, did not exist in more northerly climes, in other lands where the Protestant ethos had clung for a long time to a stern biblical patriarchalism—hence, a far more pronounced rebellion on the part of their repressed females.

The Protestant Reformation, considerably intensified by Calvin and brought to its dynamic apex by the Puritans, was definitely antifeminist in its essence. It was not only the sexual asceticism of the Puritans which, after all, deprived men as well as women, but also the Calvinistic concept of predestination—which, inevitably, included a rigorous view of sexual predestination. Along with continence went a veneration for hard and continuous work—*laborare est orare*—a natural counterpart. As Max Weber put it:

> The sexual asceticism of Puritanism differs only in degree, not in fundamental principle, from that of monasticism; and on account of the Puritan conception of marriage, its practical influence is more far-reaching than that of the latter. For sexual intercourse is permitted, even within marriage, only as the means willed by God for the increase of His glory according to the commandment "be fruitful and multiply." Along with a moderate vegetable diet and cold baths, the same prescription is given for all sexual temptations as is used against religious doubts and a sense of moral unworthiness: "Work hard in your calling."[8]

Whenever sexual asceticism prevails in a given society, woman gains in dignity but loses in power—inevitably since, to a great extent, her power has been derivative and dependent upon her influence over men through her sexual leverage. She is no longer a sex object, but soon enough she becomes an economic tool. This was even more true in the Calvinistic Puritan context since this new creed provided the spiritual foundation for the birth of the industrial revolution and capitalism. Puritanism elevated work into a sacrament—unwillingness to work was a consequence of a lack of spiritual grace. Unlike the Lutheran who bows to fate and submits in an almost passive way to external authority (the German streak), the Calvinistic Puritan is dynamic and works at first for the greater glory of God, then increasingly for the sake of his own economic welfare. Individualistic and impatient of all forms of authority, the Puritan is a natural republican who sees in the free play of private economic interests a Providential character. The combination of thrift and hard work is explosive: the sharpening of the acquisitive activity along with stringent limitation of consumption can lead only to an extremely high rate of saving and accumulation of capital, that is, to *stored power*—to the extent that it is reinvested in business instead of being wasted away in superfluous consumption. When Calvin legitimized banking and interest rates, he merely accepted an inevitable financial development, acceptable if the fruit of hard toil was dedicated to the Lord. The Puritans went one step further and looked upon work and profitable business as a spiritual calling, and economic prosperity as proof of the Lord's blessings. Success in this world was to be as much the reward as the symbol of moral superiority. As a Puritan advocate stated: "No question but it [riches] should be the portion rather of the godly than of the wicked, were it good for them; for godliness hath the promises of this life as well as of the life to come."[9] No time was to be expended on leisure or enjoyment; only ceaseless toil served to increase the glory of the Lord —waste of time was the greatest of all sins. Idle talk, sociability, sex and idolatry of the flesh, luxury, even too much sleep entailing loss of time were to be shunned. It was a way of life as hard as it was productive, and pregnant with the accumulation of economic power.

That the most determined of the Puritans had to sail away to the American colonies does not mean that Puritanism as a way of life died out in England and Scotland; to a greater or lesser extent it pervaded British, Dutch, and French Huguenot social customs and way of life, both in respect to sex and to business. John Wesley was not blind to the inescapable drift of such a worship of worldly economic success toward the evil of crass ethical materialism; yet the founder of Methodism, spiritual precursor of the industrial revolution, stated emphatically that "we must exhort all Christians to gain all they can, and to save all they can; that is, in effect, to grow rich."[10] The moral conclusion is plain: the rich are the righteous people, the poor are the damned; economic prosperity gradually replaces the Christian quest for salvation of the soul. As the French historian Taine put it, referring to England in the birth pangs of the industrial revolution: "A preacher here is nothing but an economist in priest's clothing who treats conscience like flour, and fights vices as if they were prohibitions on imports."[11]

All that was now needed to activate and enormously multiply the stored savings and accumulated capital was the industrial revolution, and the concomitant birth of modern capitalism. The intensely dynamic and competitive system that was beginning to unfold, fruit of the Calvinistic Puritan ethic, was profoundly masculine; no room was left in it for the display of feminine qualities. Puritan women themselves had long ago acquired unfeminine traits that distinguished them sharply from their Roman Catholic sisters. On the one hand, this new ethos, like that of Islam a thousand years before, led directly to a far more democratic concept of fundamental social equality—stopping short, however, of sexual equality. Society was no longer viewed as a hierarchic organism on the model of the human body, that is, made up of different and interdependent organs and members with their own specific and different functions. Instead, it became a machine made up of similar, interchangeable and equal pieces of machinery, the only major, fundamental, and unbridgeable difference being that of sex— a difference all the greater in that it replaced the others.

At the same time, this intensely dynamic creed was responsible for the terrible social consequences of the birth pangs of capitalism during which most of the lofty spiritual goals of Calvinism evaporated, leaving only an ethical materialism in their wake—for, as Goethe observed, "the man of action is always ruthless; no one has a conscience but an observer."[12] This exacerbated masculine spirit of unrestricted competitivity, along with the mobilization of savings and new sources of fresh capital, led straight to the industrial revolution and the collapse of the old order of things. The Puritan spirit had long ago frozen out the remnants of old "Merry England" and now its harvest, the "dark satanic mills," began to spread over the British landscape.

Arthur Young, the celebrated agronomist, neatly encapsulated the social ethics of budding capitalism when he stated that "everyone but an idiot knows that the lower classes must be kept poor or they will never be industrious."[13] It became accepted as self-evident that wages had to be kept to a strict minimum; for whatever distress and abject poverty existed, society was not held responsible. This general attitude, along with the extraordinary social dislocation triggered by the industrial revolution, set the framework within which the forthcoming feminist movement was to grow.

This dislocation entailed the breakup of the family as an integrated economic unit, and the daily exile of the husband—and often of wife and children too—to hard work in distant factories. The home became divorced from the work place; the formerly integrated functions of producing, selling, and consuming were sundered, and relocated in different areas. Until that time, both sexes usually worked at home; women always had plenty to do—household care, embroidery, spinning wool and flax, needlework, cooking, preserving and curing, preparing medicines from herbs, in addition to helping out their husbands in whatever branch of cottage manufacturing they were engaged. In Stuart and early Hanoverian England, cottage manufacturing had undergone a remarkable development which kept the family unit intact as a cooperative undertaking. The revolutionary introduction of increasingly sophisticated machinery resulted in an almost sudden and startling collapse of cottage industries. The small rural household, whose precarious budget had always been balanced by the leisurely work of women and children during the winter when agriculture was slack, began to disintegrate. Agricultural concentration ruined many small farmers, and big farmers began to employ gangs of women, especially during the Napoleonic War, in hosing and weeding. Employing women had the great advantage that it kept the wages of men lower, and during the first half of the nineteenth century the vicious circle remained unbroken: men could not support their families on their meager wages, compelling their wives to work outside all the year round—and the fact that women worked competitively with men prevented the latter from increasing their earning power. Furthermore, they were together far less often, working separately, and often drifted apart.

The net result of this evolution can be summed up as follows: The wife as husband's productive partner and fellow worker disappeared forever; the family as the cooperative unit of production faded away, never to return. The one exception was agriculture which retained the family as a unit of production, but the gradual shrinking in the number of farms and increasing urbanization so reduced the farming population in the industrialized countries that, in terms of numbers, it became a marginal element. Housewives were gradually deprived of most of the work that had been traditionally done in the home; most of that work was now moved to industrial plants. The increase in the speed of communications and the new mobility of labor, the growth of great urban centers and the increasing complexification of industrial production stripped the traditional home of its productive usefulness. Part of woman's traditional housekeeping, nurturing, and child-raising activities were shifted out of the home to socialized centers. Working women had less time for domestic chores, although they were still expected to keep house for the family. Needless to add, it is not these working women who had time to engage in feminist activities; they were far too busy to even think of such matters.

The economic dislocation of the family as a productive unit and the fact that women, working separately in field or factory, gained financial independence, set husband and wife apart, sometimes in competitive positions. Wage-earning women, long before legal changes permitted them the full property of their money, began to give food for thought to middle-class "ladies of leisure" who no longer had anything to do and became bored to distraction. In the past *all* women, as well as all men, had worked; now, some worked independently of their husbands, and some, the privileged women of bourgeois background who could afford it, worked not at all. It is from this disparity that the first elements of the feminist movement arose:

> By the middle of the nineteenth century, members of the leisured classes like the Brontë sisters and Florence Nightingale were beginning to feel that the independent factory hand, earning her own bread, was setting an example that might be of value to the "lady."[14]

Regency and early Victorian "ladies" had often strictly nothing to do except seek, as china dolls and household pets, the approval of their lordly husbands; it was the male breadwinner or property holder who decided everything and enjoyed almost absolute power. The vast increase in wealth in Victorian times and great upward social mobility rapidly increased the numbers of the middle and upper classes, along with the growing idleness of their womenfolk. Both physically and mentally, bourgeois women were totally wasted and suffered intensely from it. With the birth of the so-called nuclear family, the middle class nonworking woman's role became restricted to "wife and mother"; in turn this sharpened considerably the contrast between the feminine and masculine roles in social life, by narrowing the existence of the bourgeois woman to the point where "the 'Victorian' version of the 'good woman' pattern may be considered a parallel of monasticism for men."[15] She was not only confined or restricted to the family but also was expected to be uninterested in the erotic aspect of marriage—which turned, often enough, into outright frigidity. Life held for them no greater purpose than the mimicking of Walter Scott's and Byron's heroines:

> The upper-class woman was being devitalized and cut off from life and its interests, as a result of the increasing wealth of her men folk and the more artificial conditions of modern life. In the old self-supplying manor-house, with its innumerable jobs to be done within and without doors, the ladies of good family, like the Pastons and Verneys, had had their allotted tasks. But now it became the hall-mark of a "lady" to be idle.[16]

This was an entirely new departure in historical terms—the idea of one sex being entirely supported by the other, this strange masculine aberration that required that women be useless, mere consumers of the goods men produced. Even rich farmers' wives began to consider that it was unladylike to work. The new bourgeois mentality of the rising middle classes began to look upon the idle wife as a badge of social success, the new status symbol—very much as purdah, the seclusion of Oriental women, had become a status symbol of social superiority, regardless of the harm it inflicted on Muslim society. In other words, the new bourgeois woman produced by the industrial revolution was induced or compelled to sacrifice her natural *femaleness*, which has proverbially included hard work in any society, for an artificial *femininity* defined by the new canons of industrial society. The Victorian concept was that man's work alone should support the family and that there could not be two breadwinners—this was good only for the lower classes. The middle-class wife's pride and self-respect depended upon the status *he* achieved or inherited, not upon her own autonomous one—since her autonomous usefulness had been taken away from her.

Since, from time immemorial, idleness is the mother of all evils, a sense of profound dissatisfaction began to creep into the minds of these women who had plenty of time to think about their condition and the purposelessness of their lives. To compound the social malaise, the industrial revolution worked against the status of women in another respect—they lost out on property rights. In the past some women had enjoyed considerable power in the aristocracy, and among the landed gentry and independent craftsmen; in the new types of investments in industry, commerce, and business generally, they found themselves squeezed out in an exclusively masculine world which they barely understood and into which they were no longer invited as legitimate partners.[17] Their dissatisfaction grew in an unsettled political environment which fostered the claims of the "rights of man," the exaltation of the common *man* and the steady drive toward increasing social equality. Budding feminism became a camp follower of all these movements and adapted its methods and tactics to theirs, often finding justification in male social protests for their own protestations.

In the eighteenth century, Sir William Blackstone, greatest of all English jurists and fellow of Oxford's All Souls, stated unambiguously that "the husband and wife are one and that one is the husband."[18] Biblical tradition and common law had relegated woman to a state of wardship that left her little or no power—no control at all over her property, liability to husbandly beatings sanctioned by custom, inability to sue alone in the courts, and the impossibility of leaving the home without facing the risk of being treated almost like a runaway slave. In the rare instances when divorce was permissible, she jeopardized everything—home, children, and property. Both in England and in the colonies, where Blackstone's prestige was even higher than in his own country, wives were deprived of almost all rights. In the United States it was easy to get rid of a troublesome wife by having her committed to an insane asylum—witness the case of a Massachusetts state senator's wife.[19]

Education, an essential lever of power, was almost completely denied to English and American women of this period. In England, girls' secondary education was largely nonexistent, while all the resources of the parents were devoted to paying for the boys' expensive boarding schools. "Ladies" were far more ignorant than they had been in Elizabethan times; most of them were taught to read, write, and sew by their mothers. Jonathan Swift commented that "not one gentleman's daughter in a thousand should be brought to read her own natural tongue, or be judge of the easiest books that are written in it."[20] Men were conscious of this educational disparity between the sexes, but often defended it as essential to the maintenance of wives in proper subjection. In the United States it was only when Emma H. Willard, an ardent feminist and self-educated schoolteacher, opened the Troy Female Seminary in 1821 that proper high school education for American women began. An audacious move, indeed, it sought to initiate girls in "men's subjects" such as science, mathematics, and philosophy which, until then, were thought to be too severe for women's "delicate" brains and would deprive them of their charm and refinement.

In short, in English-speaking countries, where women's power and influence had always been greatly inferior to those of their sisters in prerevolutionary France, and where the social dislocation of the industrial revolution started earlier—much earlier in England than in America—conditions were ripe for a feminist revolt.

Mary Wollstonecraft pioneered when she brought out her works late in the eighteenth century, but decades went by before they began to have an impact—and that impact was swifter and greater in the United States than in England. There was good reason for this. A certain amount of feminine emancipation had become a tradition on America's mobile and constantly shifting frontier, largely because of the scarcity of females and their all-important economic role in these exceptionally rough surroundings. As a result, frontier women's social status was always higher than that allowed by common law in more settled areas; married women often enjoyed the right to make contracts and sue in the courts, or receive land grants as heads of families, and were always favored by judges, who defended them against personal abuse, enforced conjugal rights, and recalled runaway husbands —rights and privileges unheard of in the American East or in England. Yet frontier spirit and customs sometimes found their way east and gave to men-women relations in America a distinctive imprint that began to differentiate them from the British.

Early in the nineteenth century, Alexis de Tocqueville shrewdly observed the vast difference in status between unmarried girls and married women which put a peculiar stamp on American feminism and its connection with a weaker family structure. He stated that "nowhere are young women surrendered so early or so completely to their own guidance" and continued:

> Long before an American girl arrives at the marriageable age, her emancipation from maternal control begins: she has scarcely ceased to be a child when she already thinks for herself, and acts on her own impulses. . . . An American girl scarcely ever displays that virginal softness in the midst of young desires or that innocent and ingenuous grace which usually attends the European

woman in the transition from girlhood to youth. It is rare that an American woman, at any age, displays childish timidity or ignorance. Like the young women of Europe she seeks to please, but she knows precisely the cost of pleasing. If she does not abandon herself to evil, at least she knows that it exists; and she is remarkable rather for purity of manners than for chastity of mind.[21]

To an extent, the American girl's early emancipation merely paralleled that of her brothers and, rather than being a specific training for girls, it reflected the early emancipation of American children of both sexes. De Tocqueville added:

In America the independence of woman is irrecoverably lost in the bonds of matrimony. If an unmarried woman is less constrained there than elsewhere, a wife is subjected to stricter obligations. The former makes her father's house an abode of freedom and of pleasure; the latter lives in the home of her husband as if it were a cloister. Yet these two different conditions of life are perhaps not so contrary as may be supposed, and it is natural that the American woman should pass through the one to arrive at the other.

Religious communities and trading nations entertain peculiarly serious notions of marriage: the former consider the regularity of woman's life as the best pledge and most certain sign of the purity of her morals; the latter regard it as the highest security for the order and prosperity of the household. The Americans are at the same time a puritanical people and a commercial nation; their religious opinions as well as their trading habits consequently lead them to require much abnegation on the part of woman and a constant sacrifice of her pleasures to her duties, which is seldom demanded of her in Europe. Thus in the United States the inexorable opinion of the public carefully circumscribes woman within the narrow circle of domestic interests and duties and forbids her to step beyond it.[22]

Nevertheless, while the Englishman as father and husband remained in firm control when the feminist movement got underway, his American counterpart soon saw his power begin to slip out of his hands. Early in the century, it had become common practice in the United States (outside the South) to settle seduction and breach-of-promise suits in the woman's favor. Mixed audiences were already addressed as "Ladies and Gentlemen" rather than the traditional "Gentlemen and Ladies" that prevailed elsewhere. Here was the beginning, not of equality, but of a favored status for American woman—however much deprived she still was in other matters. In America, as elsewhere, women were still kept socially within the tight confines of Puritan proprieties, just as they were physically in their cagelike steel ribs and whalebone corsets, but their menfolk were so busy building a new country that they left their women to tend to cultural tasks and pleasures that remained largely male concerns in Europe. Contemptuous of art, culture, and the refinements of life, American men concerned themselves largely with finance, trade, and industry. Complaining as early as 1855 about the collective power of wealthy American women, the New York poet-editor N. P. Willis wrote:

> It is the women who regulate the style of living, dispense hospitalities, exclusively manage society, control clergymen and churches, regulate the schemes of benevolence, patronize and influence the Arts, and pronounce upon Operas and foreign novelties, and it is the women . . . who exercize the ultimate control over the Press.[23]

This was a far cry from conditions obtaining in England and on the Continent. Furthermore, one could see that the Puritan society was steadily transforming itself, in one respect at least; the old, frugal, ascetic Puritanism was undergoing a metamorphosis. For men, work, competition, and success were still uppermost, but women were beginning to revolt against the traditional asceticism and frugality. The United States was fast becoming a country dominated by eager consumers—that is, largely by women. One of the great badges of worldly success for men became their ability to provide their wives with spending money; in Europe, money was preferably spent on mistresses. Protestant doctrine had always exalted the married estate—"a prescribed satisfaction for irrational heat," as Milton put it—along with business life, and did not tolerate adultery (except in the slave-owning South); this premium put on marriage implied that male bachelors were almost as despised as female spinsters, entailing a considerable social pressure on all men to marry early and provide for a family. Inevitably, American wives began to benefit from the vast increase in wealth provided by America's rapid economic expansion; men worked hard and women began to consume equally hard.

CHAPTER

3

The Victorian Age

The feminist movement was essentially a middle-class one, a reflection of the swiftly rising standard of living of a substantial part of Western society and of the new, unnatural idleness of middle-class women. It developed in England and America along somewhat parallel lines, with many personal contacts established between feminists on both sides of the Atlantic.

Things were different elsewhere. After the French Revolution, France fell under the sway of the Code Napoléon—the most advanced and comprehensive legal monument of the times, but regressive as far as women's rights were concerned. Frenchwomen were legally better off in the eighteenth century than in the nineteenth. Along with the metric system, the Code Napoléon swept most of the civilized world and firmly implanted the idea of the wife's subordination to her husband and total obedience to his wishes (article 213). She was compelled to live in the domicile of his choice and follow him wherever he chose to reside (article 214); she could not dispose of her personal estate without his permission (article 217). In case of divorce, the husband kept the children (article 267). In case of adultery, the husband's only punishment was to be forbidden to marry his mistress—which came as a great relief to many guilty husbands; but if the wife was the guilty party, she could be jailed for a period lasting from three months to two years (article 298). This code was so conveniently precise that it lacked all flexibility and could be altered only with the greatest difficulty. It was only after the Second World War, for instance, that the French began to alter the articles concerning women in order to establish equality before the law for both sexes.

English-speaking nations, on the other hand, reshaped their common law gradually throughout the Victorian era; and it was through this remodeling that the feminist movement began to acquire its momentum—witness New York State's Married Women's Property Act of 1848 that led straight to the first women's rights convention and the official birth of a feminist movement in America.

Differences between the two major Anglo-Saxon movements reflected the disparity in their social structures—the more sharply defined social hierarchy in England in contrast with the greater drive toward democratic equality in the United States. In Victorian England, at the peak of its imperial splendor and power, both the male and the aristocrat were far more powerful than their American counterparts, and, as an English feminist put it at the time, "American women do not dislike men as much as English women do."[1] Women already had far more power in America where the democratic dogma was firmly rooted in the prevailing ideology, the only major distortion being, for a while, the problem of slavery in the South. In England, however, monarchy and aristocracy introduced considerable social distinctions between men which blunted the sharp edges of the feminist movement. Englishwomen were entitled to inherit titles and wealth in the absence of sons or brothers; on the other hand, an Englishman's right to vote was curtailed by property qualifications until the end of the Victorian era. Moreover, many English liberals failed to lend their full support to the feminist movement out of fear of women's traditional conservatism in social and political matters—"Girls and widows are Tories, and channels of clerical influence," stated Lord Acton[2]—and social considerations often overruled male prejudices, inducing conservatives to favor giving the vote to women of means. English ladies endowed with large estates could enjoy considerable local power, nominate Members of Parliament in rotten boroughs, vote in church and municipal matters. This was not the case in the United States; in a democratic society, the feminist issue was far more clear-cut.

As elsewhere, until the nineteenth century, women in England had never been politically discriminated against in a conscious way. It never occurred to anyone that there could be such a thing as a feminist problem. The law had never expressly forbidden women to sit in Parliament, for instance; it remained true that none had ever done so. Symbolic of the change in consciousness, the word "male" appeared for the first time in English legislation in the First Reform Bill of 1832, extending franchise to large sections of the new industrial middle class; this was in answer to the claim put forth by a wealthy spinster from northern England that women of substance should be entitled to vote.[3] Voting was thus specifically and officially restricted to qualified "male persons"; the political battle of the sexes was joined.

Both in America and in England, the feminist movement was an outcrop of the antislavery struggle. Outrage at the slave trade had pricked the conscience of both sexes in the rising middle classes; for the first time, Englishwomen began to organize themselves in groups in view of political action. The antislavery movement became powerful enough to enlist the active support of such conservative women as Hannah More, who wanted nothing to do with feminism per se. The antislavery contagion swiftly spread to the United States where abolitionism became the cradle of feminist activities. As one of the early feminists and abolitionists put it: "We have good cause to be grateful to the slave for the benefit we have received to *ourselves,* in working for *him.* In striving to strike his irons off, we found most surely, that *we* were manacled *ourselves.*"[4] But it was not so much with *him* that the female abolitionists identified as with *her*—the female slave who was used and abused by most plantation owners in a perversion of the medieval *droit de cuissage.* Feminine feelings about rape could easily cause hatred for the patriarchal planter and transfer that hatred to all men who had imposed the "slavery of sex"; the harm done to black women was figuratively extended to all women, regardless of race and social status.

Antislavery action on both sides of the Atlantic gave the initial impulse to the forthcoming feminist struggle, but always with England leading the way. The successful abolition of the slave trade, thirty-two years before slavery itself was wiped out in America, left Englishwomen free to devote their organizational talent to their own cause; in the United States, the two movements remained intertwined until the end of the Civil War, when the feminist issue appeared in all its nakedness and fury: the final outrage was committed when the Negro *male* received, however nominally, the suffrage while *all* women were still disbarred. One black feminist declared in 1867 that "if coloured men get their rights, and not coloured women theirs, you see the coloured men will be masters over the women, and it will be just as bad as it was before."[5] For the first time in the United States, in the Fourteenth Amendment to the Constitution, the word male appeared in an official document, sealing the legal "humiliation" of the feminists whose dedication had been instrumental in putting an end to slavery.

It was at the world antislavery convention of 1840 that Englishwomen abolitionists had imparted the feminist ideology to their American cousins. Aristocratic Englishwomen had real social power and therefore considerable leverage in the struggle for women's rights. Along with the rising and prosperous but dissenting middle class in the industrial cities of northern England who resented their political impotence, they were able to enlist the support of an increasing number of individuals of both sexes, leading to the inclusion of female franchise in the electoral platform of the Chartists—the first such demand ever made by a political party. This was contagious, and in 1848, prompted by the fact that American wives could not legally keep their wages from their husbands, the first women's rights convention gathered in Seneca Falls to list their grievances in the fighting style of a "Declaration of Sentiments and Resolutions." Denial of suffrage was among these grievances, of course, but also the status of civil death and wardship for wives, the limited economic and educational opportunities for their sex, the unfair divorce laws, the exclusion of their sex from church business, and the double moral standard. The opening sentence of the Declaration was symptomatic of the new mythology that was springing up: "The history of mankind is the history of repeated injuries and usurpations on the part of man toward woman having in direct object the establishment of an absolute tyranny over her."[6]

The struggle was on in America under the leadership of Susan Brownell Anthony and Elizabeth Stanton, to win, bit by bit from grudging legislators, all the legal and political rights that had been denied them, to culminate temporarily in 1920 with the passage of the Nineteenth Amendment and the grant of female suffrage.

Both in America and in England, local geographical and social considerations determined and shaped the feminist style of combat. In the United States, these considerations were the frontier and the equalitarianism of the western states where distrust of the East was widespread. In England, the determining feature was the rapidly industrializing north, centered around London-hating Manchester— now the second city in the land, industrial, wealthy, Puritan, and proud. And it was in Manchester that the first female suffrage organizations saw the light of day, shortly before the first women's rights convention in America. From Manchester, these organizations spread to Bristol, London, and Edinburgh and fused into a national movement before any suffrage organization was founded in the United States. It should, of course, be kept in mind that England was already largely industrialized and urbanized, while the United States was still mostly made up of small towns and rural communities. England was geographically compact, America extremely decentralized with its populated centers widely scattered over an enormous continental spread.

In one area of the United States, the South, women received special treatment; here the planters still worshiped the "sheltered female" in Victorian bourgeois fashion rather than the ancient aristocratic one. Southern women, although they had wills of their own, were also household pets, high-ranking members of an oriental harem, rather than companions for their profligate husbands. Plantation patriarchalism set up the cult of pure southern womanhood and in later, post-Civil War times, used it as an excuse for the countless lynchings of Negro males. Shifting from the plantation to the all-white mountains, the cult became the "code of the hills" in whose name blood feuds between clans perpetuated a style of life that made woman a prize to be protected and fought over by males.

As already noted, the changing impact of mere words is an important clue to changing psychology. The Second Reform Bill that granted the franchise to lower segments of the English middle class dropped the expression "male person" and substituted "man," while the American legislators adopted "male" in their turn. With prescience, John Stuart Mill suggested substituting "person" for both these expressions, thus including both females and males in the reform bills, but he soon lost his seat in Parliament and his advice was discarded. At any rate, the debate over the Second Reform Bill fired the imagination of Lydia Becker, destined to become England's leading feminist. "There are three sexes, Male, Female and Lydia Becker," as the saying went. She founded the Manchester Women's Suffrage Committee and struggled twenty years through her mouthpiece, the *Woman Suffrage Journal.* Thanks largely to her, year after year the House of Commons debated woman suffrage and three times granted a majority of its votes to a bill enfranchising propertied women—to no avail because of the indifference of the British government.

The irony of the situation was that England was ruled by a woman and that the feminist cause had no greater opponent than Queen Victoria. When the influential Lady Amberley demanded the vote for women, Her Majesty was so outraged that she made her feelings known in the following terms:

> The Queen is most anxious to enlist everyone who can speak or write or join in checking that mad, wicked folly of "Woman's Rights" with all its attendant horrors, on which her poor feeble sex is bent, forgetting every sense of womanly feeling and propriety. Lady Amberley ought to get a *good whipping.*[7]

Feminine jealousy and rivalry have always been, and are likely to remain, the bane of every feminist movement. Again, the problem has never been whether "sisterhood" is powerful but whether it exists at all. As Schopenhauer pointedly if unkindly expressed it:

> The natural feeling between men is mere indifference, but between women it is actual enmity. The reason of this is that trade-jealousy—*odium figulinum*—which, in the case of man, does not go beyond the confines of their particular pursuit but with women

embraces the whole sex; since they have only one kind of business. Even when they meet in the street women look at one another like Guelphs and Ghibellines.[8]

While Queen Victoria was expressing the undoubted sentiment of a majority of the English population of both sexes, she also, along with all other female rulers in history, much preferred ruling an exclusively male society to having to contend with the dangerous wiles of her own "poor feeble sex." She undoubtedly had some influence on both Disraeli and Gladstone, and spurred the latter in his implacable hostility to all the suffragist bills introduced in Parliament.

But the progress of the movement could not be stopped. Englishwomen could already vote in local elections and were becoming increasingly politically minded, far more so than American women. In spite of differences in timing on both sides of the ocean, the feminist movement at the end of the nineteenth century had remained what it was at its inception: a middle-class phenomenon whose exponents were anything but revolutionary. The leading feminists in both countries wanted merely limited suffrage for middle-class women of means. With the assistance of dedicated religious associations, they wanted to improve social conditions. They had begun their training in the anti-slavery struggle; they went on to fight for temperance. What they profoundly believed was that women's suffrage would "increase the decent vote in society" and wrest political power from the hands of immoral, power-hungry male politicians.[9] They definitely believed that they could better uphold the values of civilization than their male counterparts—although they rarely stated this in so many words. In the meantime, their increasingly spectacular methods amazed, and often shocked, Victorian society—hunger strikes, stone throwing and window breaking, picture slashing and physical assaults on the police force. Militant suffragists were actually few, but they made up for their lack of numbers by their extreme aggressiveness, prompting an English Member of Parliament to state: "It is no longer a joke. It is a sex war. . . . The whole movement is but part of the effeminate superficiality of this generation. This superficiality finds its consummation in the present masculine abasement now witnessed in America."[10]

The sentiments of this latter-day Cato the Elder found their reflection in the fact that repression was far more brutal in England than in America where, as Lord Bryce noted, "the American man is exceptionally deferential to women."[11] England was then, and has largely remained, a man's country, and whenever militant suffragists behaved violently, they got every bit of it back upon themselves, with plenty to spare. Well-bred English ladies were treated with condescending chivalry, but women in general were treated with far less courtesy than in France or the United States. Most female suffragists, however, would rather have the brutal treatment of the English male than the semisarcastic tolerance of his American counterpart. As one American feminist put it, "We are up against a hard proposition in the American man. Now, in England, its different. There, they take us seriously. They deny us our rights, but they don't put us away as if we were spoiled children ... the police put us off the streets; they send us to jail!"[12] And Emeline Pankhurst echoed: "All the American men I met seemed to regard the movement as something of a joke.... We have had definite opposition to encounter on the part of the English male, and I don't know but what it is preferable to this half-amused indifference which I see in the men of America."[13] Then as today, and probably tomorrow, the great fear of dedicated feminists was to be taken too lightly by men and treated with ridicule.

In fact, as Bryce testified at the turn of the century, the proportion of women who wanted the suffrage was far smaller in the United States than in England, and in many American states where the suffrage issue was coming to a head, powerful Women's Anti-Suffrage Associations sprang up spontaneously.[14] One reason for the lesser feminist pressure in the United States was that American women were beginning to enjoy far greater civil rights than Englishwomen, even though the latter sometimes had a municipal franchise of which their American counterparts were deprived. English feminists reacted violently against the obsessively masculine atmosphere of Victorian England with its exclusive male clubs, its educational system tailored almost exclusively to fit masculine upbringing and the half-Oriental exclusion of women from a meaningful social life dedicated to the rule of a global empire.

Looking back at the whole span of feminist activity on both sides of the ocean during the Victorian era, it is clear that women militants were fighting not only to redress their sociopolitical inferiority, but they also hoped, with increased political leverage, to improve general conditions in a world slowly drifting toward world war—a world irresistibly led by male leaders imbued with an excess of aggressive virility toward some global catastrophe already looming in the distance. Some subterranean undercurrent was obviously powering the movement and inflecting the feminist cause toward pacifism. In fact, the proportion of pacifists among feminists was remarkably high, and Julia Ward Howe spoke for all of them when she stated that "peace and woman suffrage go together, masculine government being founded on the predominance of physical force."[15] That woman's suffrage was not the sole answer is clear after two world wars and countless minor ones.

Yet, they hoped in those days to bring about universal peace through female suffrage and many ardent suffragists were enraged at the militants who used violent means to convey their demands, feeling instinctively that they were, thereby, playing man's game on his own, and not their, terms. As one of them pointed out, "Women never show up their real weakness so much as when they attempt force."[16]

The feminist movement in the United States aimed at far more than equal rights with men. First and foremost, it wanted to change male attitudes toward the weaker sex and polish the rough edges of their male pioneers who, in a new country, had often sloughed off centuries of European tradition. Until the Civil War, few American feminists wanted to be elected to political office alongside the uncouth wild men who dominated the political scene. In 1852, Elizabeth Stanton wanted women to vote but not hold office. As she explained it:

> I disclaim all desire or intention to meddle with *vulgar* politics . . . to sit in council with vulgar, rum drinking, wine bibbing, tobacco chewing men, with thick lipped voluptuaries, gourmands and licentiates, who disgrace our national councils with their grossness and profanity, their savage rudeness, and uncurbed ferocity. . . . No, until a new type of man be placed at the helm of the ship of state, rest assured we women shall decline all nominations for office.[17]

Many feminists believed that reform should start at the beginning, at the root of contemporary evil, that is, with the institution of marriage. The same Elizabeth Stanton, less cautious than her colleagues Susan B. Anthony and Lucy Stone, stated emphatically:

> The right idea of marriage is at the foundation of all reforms. . . . A child conceived in the midst of hate, sin, and discord, nurtured on abuse and injustice, cannot do much to bless the world or himself. . . . Man in his lust has regulated this whole question of sexual intercourse. Long enough! Let the Mother of Mankind, whose prerogative it is to set bounds to his indulgence, rouse up and give this whole matter a thorough fearless examination.[18]

Unlike her colleagues, she was imbued with the idea of a latent war between the sexes. Far more important than the denial of political rights was the fact that the man-made law gave rights to the husband over his wife's body, children, and estate. It was largely through her ceaseless campaigning that marriage and divorce laws were progressively liberalized.

Almost as important, and far more difficult to achieve, was the physical emancipation of women from the constrictions of the whalebone corsets in which they had been imprisoned for almost a century. Women had become status symbols whose mere appearance had to indicate that they were women of leisure, and "the dress of women," as Thorstein Veblen pointed out, went "even farther than that of men in the way of demonstrating the wearer's abstinence from productive employment."[19] Nowadays, there are more practical ways of displaying affluence that do not endanger women's health. In those days the corset, as Veblen stated it, was "in economic theory, substantially a mutilation, undergone for the purpose of lowering the subject's vitality and rendering her permanently and obviously unfit for work."[20] In the state of near idleness to which middle-class women were confined, a new emphasis was put on their delicate and fragile nature; they hardly exercised and the muscular atrophy which resulted from an artificial and unhealthy style of life deprived them of freedom of movement and squeezed out their breath, taught many of them "the *poetry* of dependence."[21] Addressing the National Council of Women of the United States in 1891, Frances Willard said:

> . . . be it remembered that until woman comes into her kingdom physically she will never really come at all. Created to be well and strong and beautiful, she long ago "sacrificed her constitution, and has ever since lived on her by-laws." She has made of herself an hour-glass, whose sands of life pass quickly by. She has walked when she should have run, sat when she should have walked, reclined when she should have sat. . . . She is a creature born to the beauty and freedom of Diana, but she is swathed by her skirts, splintered by her stays, bandaged by her tight waist, and pinioned by her sleeves until . . . a trussed turkey or a spitted goose are her most appropriate emblems.[22]

So, while fashion and custom imprisoned her physically as she had never been before and reduced her to the dependent status of a Chinese woman with bound feet, the suffragists were forcefully propelling all women toward legal and political emancipation. If she kept the tight corset, it was not so much because it produced "delicious sensations, half pleasure, half pain";[23] it was the inveterate snobbishness of the times that made these female sufferers feel more ladylike than those healthy female bodies that had to work all day long, unfettered by cage ribs, squeezed feet, and cramped livers. It was a badge of higher social status, the badge of the fast-rising bourgeois class. For generations, feminist leaders attempted to reform women's clothes, with hardly any success during Victoria's lifetime. As a reformer sighed in the 1870s, "The second nature of conventionality has always appeared stronger to women's mind than nature at first hand."[24] It took the First World War to accomplish this physical liberation, along with the discarding of all the moral taboos of the Victorian-Edwardian era.

Another problem plagued the movement—the fact that it had arisen in Protestant lands where religious faith was still vigorous and based exclusively on Holy Writ. At the women's rights convention in Syracuse (1852), suffragist Antoinette Brown suggested basing women's rights on the authority of the Bible—to the horror of freethinking rationalists who had no trouble pointing out the antifemale bias of the Scriptures—"Thy desire shall be to thy husband and he shall rule over thee . . . the head of every woman is man." Others suggested rewriting the Bible itself, a task eventually undertaken boldly by Elizabeth Stanton. Although an agnostic personally, she was haunted by the idea of a female deity and, anticipating Freud, wrote that "the love of Jesus, among women in general, all grows out of sexual attraction. The Virgin Mary appeals in the same way to her male worshippers."[25] She attacked the Old Testament for being the "mere history of an ignorant, underdeveloped people"[26] which should be expurgated before being put in the hands of women and children—something the Roman Catholic Church had done many centuries before by putting it under the Index. She further began to fasten onto the new discovery of ancient "matriarchy," quoting from the now outdated theories of Bachofen and Morgan, pointing out that "all along from the beginning until the sixteenth century, when Luther eliminated the feminine element wholly from the Protestant religion and brought the full power of the Church to enforce woman's complete subjection, we find traces of the matriarchate."[27] But all this did not touch the core of the fundamental problem of feminism which was, as one of them stated it, "ethical and religious. Freedom, true freedom, must come from within."[28]

The fact that women suffragist leaders were overwhelmingly Protestant meant that the movement was affected by the controversy introduced by Darwin and his adherents. Feminists quoted him gingerly, since they realized that Darwinism and natural selection did not appear to operate in their favor. While it destroyed the moral authority of biblical patriarchalism, it replaced it with another male-oriented credo that made "woman simply a lesser man, weaker in body and mind—an affectionate and docile animal, of inferior grade. That there is any aim in the distinction between the sexes, beyond the perpetuation of the race, is nowhere recognized by them."[29] In fact, Darwinism merely dressed up the dethroned biblical patriarchalism in a new, scientific, and therefore that much more dangerous, affirmation of nature-imposed male supremacy.

Caught in the welter of intellectual contradictions generated by fast-multiplying scientific discoveries, feminism found it impossible to elaborate a consistent doctrine; but it did spark some interesting off-shoots. For instance, the problem of woman's place in religion was solved at one stroke for her followers by Mary Baker Eddy when she founded her church. Christian Science, which is hardly Christian and completely nonscientific, aims at achieving moral excellence by simply ignoring inconvenient facts, however scientifically established, that do not fit into its theological framework. Founded by an outstanding woman, this was of course an ideal religion for women, freeing them from fear of illness through blind faith and providing an outlet for religious requirements not available in other, male-dominated, and sterner churches. Mary Baker Eddy had little doubt as to her role and importance: she was a "God-like woman, God-anointed." Jesus Christ, she conceded, was a "God-like man" but hardly superior to herself; and often enough, "Mother Mary" claimed for herself part of the worship granted by Roman Catholics to the Virgin; this was undoing Luther and Calvin with a vengeance.[30]

Other problems impinged on American feminism. Biological progress appeared to have disclosed that "the first manifestation of life is feminine,"[31] but new biological discoveries strengthened the fears of the leading suffragists (most of whom were WASPs) that the new flood of immigrants would degrade the old American stock. Vote or no vote, motherhood was again restored to first place, for eugenic and patriotic reasons. In 1912 *Woman and Social Progress* trumpeted that "woman is the race . . . is at the top of the human curve from which the higher superman of the future is to evolve. . . . Her whole soul, conscious and unconscious, is best conceived as a magnificent organ of heredity."[32] Except for advocating fewer children and smaller families, most leading feminists agreed.

A century of feminist activity in England and America eventually led, in both countries, to a rough equality of the sexes in education, legal status, and political rights. Progress in both countries usually started on the geographical peripheries—the American West and the British dominions beyond the seas—where young struggling societies looked upon women, often scarce, as indispensable helpmates in a hard life rather than the social ornaments they had largely become in the more settled and bourgeois societies at the centers. Women in New Zealand were granted suffrage as early as 1893 and in Australia in 1902; Canadian women first received the vote in the western provinces whereas Quebec had to wait until the Second World War to be on a par with the rest of the country. The same development took place in the United States: by the end of the nineteenth century, Wyoming, Colorado, Utah, and Idaho had granted the vote to women. More states might already have adopted woman suffrage by then if it had not been for the fear that women were all more inclined toward temperance and would vote dry. Rather than antifeminism, it was the male fear of not being able to hit the bottle that retarded the process; California turned down female suffrage in 1896 for precisely this reason.

Political equality would have been meaningless if woman's legal status had not improved and kept pace with political progress. American women reached legal equality sooner than British women, who had to wait until the Married Woman's Property Act of 1870 to be released from financial bondage to their husband, if they had any property of their own. A second act in 1882 completed the first one and emancipated them completely—remarkable progress considering that common law had completely disallowed property rights to wives, except upper-class women who had been protected since the time of Henry VIII by the Chancery Courts. Most of the rights granted by these British acts had already been secured by American women as early as 1848.

Progress in American women's education kept abreast of these developments, from the day in 1821 when the Troy Female Seminary was founded by Emma Willard. Here again, the West pioneered: before the Civil War Iowa State and Wisconsin universities had already been opened to women, to be followed by many others in California, Michigan, and Illinois after the war, on a coeducational basis. In the East, however, colleges were founded for women alone, on a segregated basis, and as for the South, higher education was almost completely unavailable there to females. Progress was slower in England than in America, but both societies were moving in the same direction. Real progress in the education of Englishwomen was made only in the last thirty years of the Victorian era when women's colleges were founded at Oxford and Cambridge. Liberal sentiment, if not yet ready for female suffrage, was strongly in favor of greater educational opportunities for women. Thomas Huxley, for instance, was in no uncertain mood; in a letter to Sir Charles Lyell he wrote:

> I am far from wishing to place any obstacles in the way of the intellectual advancement and development of women. On the contrary, I don't see how we are to make any permanent advancement while one-half of the race is sunk, as nine-tenths of women are, in mere ignorant parsonese superstitions; and to show you that my ideas are practical I have fully made up my mind, if I can

carry out my own plans, to give my daughters the same training in physical science as their brother will get. . . . They, at any rate, shall not be got up as man-traps for the matrimonial market. If other people would do the like the next generation would see women fit to be the companions of men in all their pursuits—though I don't think that men have anything to fear from their competition.[33]

Even in a man as liberal as Thomas Huxley, there was still a touch of Victorian condescension, reemphasized when he added at another time that "nature's old salique law will never be repealed, and no change of dynasty will be effected."[34] A firm believer in man's natural mental superiority, he nevertheless insisted that this superiority was no reason to deprive women of the benefit of equal education and that "whatever argument justifies a given situation for all boys justifies its application to girls as well."[35] And he added:

> Without seeing any reason to believe that women are, on the average, so strong physically, intellectually, or morally as men, I cannot shut my eyes to the fact that many women are much better endowed in all these respects than many men, and I am at a loss to understand on what grounds of justice or public policy a career which is opened to the weakest and most foolish of the male sex should be forcibly closed to women of vigor and capacity.[36]

No one went further than John Stuart Mill in giving the feminist movement its bible, when his work *On the Subjection of Women* was published in 1869. The fact that he acknowledged the strong influence of his wife, Harriet Taylor, the first political feminist and Mary Wollstonecraft's intellectual heiress, is of course of some importance. The main point, however, is that Mill was a trained philosopher and logician and a lucid thinker who expressed the feminist viewpoint with far greater persuasiveness than any woman militant—even when he was wholly unconvincing.

Far more interesting than his feminist avocation, although by no means unconnected with it, was his original interest in the distinction between culture and civilization. In his *Logic*, Mill stated that "a volume devoted to explaining what civilization is and is not, does not raise so vivid a conception of it as the single expression that Civilization is a different thing from Cultivation."[37] Civilization was a new word, barely a century old and ill defined—used in 1812 for the assimilation of common law to civil law. That granting women full equality with men would improve the tone of morality and civilization was undoubtedly in Mill's mind; referring to the prevalent Victorian idea that women were mostly valued for their reproductive function, Mill stated that "little advance can be expected in *morality* until the producing of large families is regarded in the same way as drunkenness or any other physical excess."[38] Those were the days when Lord Birkenhead viewed mothers as mere "conduit pipes" whose physiological happenings were of importance only insofar as the welfare of the newly born was concerned—a truly Athenian viewpoint of the times of Pericles, against which Mill was determined to set his face.

John Stuart Mill's viewpoint was the one that was going to prevail, as we know from hindsight. And if one had to pick the decisive moment in English literature when feminine emancipation became a literary fact of primary importance—in terms of the search for woman's new identity—we would have to settle on that product of the remote Haworth parsonage, Charlotte Brontë's *Jane Eyre*, a landmark in Victorian literature inasmuch as, for the first time, here was a fictional woman confronting fictional man on equal terms. The "man's woman," the masculine viewpoint which had been the only one expressed hitherto, now had to contend with the "woman's woman." *Jane Eyre* was the first truly modern English novel in which woman feels free to rebel and to express her true feelings without reservations; for the first time, the feminine *ethos* came out in the open in this fictional counterpart of John Stuart Mill's treatise. In a sense, both of them announce the beginning of the end of Victorian patriarchalism.

It would be inexcusable to omit, by way of intermission, a reference to one of the most unusual social experiments made in the Western world: the polygamy of the Mormons. The leaders of the Church of Jesus Christ of Latter-Day Saints trekked west across the Great Plains in order to be free to enjoy polygamy away from the more conventional societies of the East and Middle West. The remarkable fact is that their austere but flourishing settlements around the Great Salt Lake attracted single women immigrants from the East Coast and even Europe, and that few of them were disappointed by living conditions among the Latter-Day Saints. Women were not allowed to remain single in Mormon land and virgins were presumed to be barred from heaven—therefore, no prostitutes and no spinsters. Every plural wife had or was supposed to have a house of her own and became a sister to the other wives of their single husband; they all felt much freer than single wives in that they were liberated from excessive male lust and free to raise smaller families. One woman state senator in Utah put it this way: "A plural wife isn't half as much of a slave as a single wife. If her husband has four wives, she has three weeks of freedom every single month."[39] To the famous explorer and translater of the *Arabian Nights*, Sir Richard Burton, we owe a fair description of the polygamy he saw at work in *The City of the Saints:*

> The Mormon household has been described by its enemies as a hell of envy, hatred, and malice—a den of murder and suicide. The same has been said of the Moslem harem. Both, I believe, suffer from the assertions of prejudice or ignorance. The temper of the new is so far superior to that of the old country, that, incredible as the statement may appear, rival wives do dwell together in amity. . . . They know that nine-tenths of the miseries of the poor in large cities arise from early and imprudent marriages, and they would rather be the fiftieth "sealing" of Dives than the toilsome single wife of Lazarus.[40]

Another impartial observer, the French botanist Jules Remy, had no trouble interviewing many local wives and was quite "amazed when he found that the greatest approval for plural marriage came from the Mormon women."[41] The plain fact is that, although some women left the Salt Lake area in disappointment, most defended their system and institution against the American government and stood their ground on biblical authority. The men felt so certain that they had the allegiance of their wives that, although they were outnumbered by them three to two, they unhesitatingly gave them the vote in 1870, a year after the Cullom Bill was introduced in Congress, making polygamy illegal in the United States. They were not disappointed. Mormon women upheld their institutions; and Congress, refusing to sanction plural marriages, temporarily stripped them of the suffrage for "failure to emancipate themselves!"[42]

By the middle of the nineteenth century, something quite significant was happening in the United States that was going to widen the gap between the respective positions of American and European women. Hitherto, clergymen and legislators following in their train usually emphasized the inherent sinfulness of woman as justification for her lowly sociopolitical status. Then, sometime before the Civil War broke out, a subtle change came over the psychological landscape and men began to stress women's spiritual, rather than animal, nature. To achieve the same practical result, that is, to eliminate women from meaningful social and political activity that might corrupt or harm them, emphasis was now put on their natural goodness, sensitivity and delicacy. What had previously been advocated because of her presumed natural inferiority was now advocated because of her equally presumed superiority. Now it was woman's God-given moral supremacy that had to be shielded from the temptations and dangers of public life, from the rough-and-tumble of politics and the crass business of building a continent. The myth of the Goddess of Liberty was born and her concrete likeness was soon erected in 1876 on Bedloe's Island, brimming with maternal kindness and solicitude. At last, the mythological Uncle Sam (the negative embodiment of stern government, police, and taxation) had his positive female counterpart, as loving and generous as his aggressive maleness was mean and demanding.

The idea of woman's moral superiority implanted itself deep in American consciousness, justifying the males' feeble attempts to keep them in their place for the sake of "protecting" them, but also justifying, more than ever, the women feminists' revolt and struggle for sociopolitical equality. As Elizabeth Stanton hyperbolically put it, man was "infinitely woman's inferior in every moral virtue, not by nature, but made so by a false education. In carrying out his own selfishness, man has greatly improved woman's moral nature, but by an almost total shipwreck of his own. Woman has now the noble virtues of the martyr."[43]

American man's obsession with business and politics had left the American woman free to devote herself to teaching, cultural activities, and child rearing for which man had a barely disguised contempt. In this new dispensation, men were meant to deal with *things*, and women with *people;* to this day, the American male strongly resents feminine intrusion in the world of things he considers his exclusive domain, quite removed from the influence of feminine morality. Thus, while in most of Europe both sexes blended their activities in some form or other of joint cooperation, they found themselves sharply separated in America in a functional sense—and therefore in a moral sense. The separate spheres of activity for the sexes became as drastically separated as they were racially between black and white. The American male made the American woman conscious of the specificity of her sex and praised her for it; in turn she began to consider herself ethically superior to the naturally immoral male. Even antifeminist ideology in America stressed the "high and holy sphere for which both nature and the God of nature intended woman," thus supplying grist to the feminist mill in that it riveted the notion of female superiority, however unconscious it may have been.

Swift progress in terms of legal and political equality between the sexes proceeded along with the enthronement of the new Goddess of Liberty. This equality became a free gift in the sense that American women did not give up the idea of their superiority nor the practical perquisites that went with it.[44] British women progressed toward equal status more or less at the same pace but were never enthroned. The men of Wyoming were only fooling themselves when, on the day their women were granted suffrage, they drank a toast to the "lovely ladies, once our superiors, now our equals"; the ladies *remained*, in many respects, their social superiors because of the vital part women had come to play in education, in the upbringing of both sexes and in the fact that they had gradually come to substitute for an increasingly vestigial father.

At a time when a great deal more was going on in the world, Henry James set about to write *The Bostonians* on the premise that "the most salient and peculiar point" in American social life at the end of the century was "the situation of women, the decline of the sentiment of sex, the agitation on their behalf."[45] His work depicted the profound change that was coming over the social landscape in the last years of the Victorian era—the beginning of the emancipation of youth "in the age of obedient parents"[46] and, with the increasing absence of strong paternal influence, the inability or unwillingness of American parents to control their children. The gap between the stern and still-patriarchal English upbringing and the increasingly permissive atmosphere in the United States was widening considerably. American women were changing, both in real life and in fiction; the young girl was on the way to becoming the post-World War I flapper and the older woman the typical American mother of the twentieth century. Rebellious girlhood and feminism were now approved by the late Victorians. For the first time in the land, women novelists of substantial talent appeared and began to exert a great deal of influence on behalf of their sex's emancipation.

In the relatively short span of a century, American society was transformed from an unadulterated patriarchy into an incipient matriarchy —a metamorphosis that did not take place in other new countries such as Australia into which poured European immigrants of the same ethnic background. While the perennial shortage of women in the West suggests one reason for this state of affairs, it would seem that this social transformation was also due to some obscure telluric impact of the American land itself—which must have had some influence, originally, on the American Indians' setting up the closest thing to real matriarchates that have ever been recorded in history.

CHAPTER

4

Culture and Civilization

If we look at Western culture from the early Gothic to the present century, there seems to be no question that women have remained, at all times, on the periphery of cultural *creation*—just as they have in every other society. With the exception of their contribution to literature, mostly confined to novels and poetry, their *original* output has been slight because they lack creative imagination. In days when they provided great rulers such as Elizabeth I of England, Christina of Sweden, Maria Theresa of Austria, and Catherine the Great of Russia, they produced not a single noteworthy philosopher, painter, sculptor, mathematician, architect, scientist, or composer. Nor was social pressure, lack of education, custom, or tradition responsible for this— social pressure never prevented them from becoming such successful writers as Jane Austen, George Eliot, and the Brontë sisters, no more than it prevented women from enjoying enormous political power and authority.

The explanation lies, rather, in their own physiological being; it is as if nature had purposefully equilibrated the sexes by giving the male the power of mental creativity, reserving physiological creation for the female. There is growing evidence that mental functions are influenced by sex and that female brains do not operate as male brains do. That creative genius often lies close to insanity has been a theme of traditional wisdom for centuries; but only recently has this fact been established on scientific grounds. Statistical evidence, based on objective tests, reveals that while *average* intelligence scores for males and females are roughly equivalent, the *variations* in scores are far greater for males, who are more prone to be either mentally retarded or unbalanced, or worthy of classification in the genius category. There are more men in both the lowest and highest brackets.[1]

At any rate, the historical fact is that paint and canvas were always as much at the disposal of women as needle and thread; but there were no female Rembrandts nor Leonardos. Clay and marble were as available to them—but no female Michael Angelo or Rodin ever appeared. Musical instruments were plentiful, and women often used them—but invariably to play male composers' works; they almost never enjoyed the gift of musical or any other major artistic creativity. They needed only pen and paper to become philosophers or mathematicians, but they were rarely interested in abstract creation. They seldom enjoyed the gift of *mental* creativity. This has been true to this day, throughout history.

Even in the field of scientific discovery and progress, with its tremendous acceleration in the nineteenth and twentieth centuries, woman is largely absent; in mathematics and physics and chemistry, in astronomy and biology, few feminine names of any consequence are to be found. One exception always springs to one's lips whenever this topic is mentioned: Marie Curie, the co-discoverer of radium. But even here, it is not so much that this exception proves the rule; it is not even an exception in the sense that she was not alone but worked in close collaboration with a husband of great talent who was already widely recognized before they had ever met. Furthermore, he was that rare type of man who can work with a woman in a spirit of teamwork and whose knowledge of womanhood was acute. Long before he married Marie, Pierre Curie wrote:

> Woman loves life for the living of it far more than we do: women of genius are rare. Thus, when we, driven by some mystic love, wish to enter upon some anti-natural path, when we give all our thoughts to some work which estranges us from the humanity nearest us, we have to struggle against women. . . . The struggle almost always is unequal, for women have the good side of it: it is in the name of life and nature that they try to bring us back. . . .[2]

He could have added that it is only in our Western culture, with its distant roots in Greek culture, where abstract *Thought* is valued higher than *Life* itself, where the part that emanates from the whole is considered greater than the whole that gave birth to it—in other words, where masculine power of mental creation is more highly valued than the female physiological gestation from which it proceeds. Hence Western woman's painful feeling that her prime function in life—motherhood—is crassly undervalued by a Western man who has fallen in love with his own cerebration.

To come back to the Curies. After he had picked her doctoral thesis for her, they began to work together—again, in that French atmo- ·

sphere where cultural bisexual cooperation is far more the norm than it is in any other country. As their daughter, Eve, points out in her mother's biography:

> We cannot and must not attempt to find out what should be credited to Marie and Pierre during these eight years. It would be exactly what the husband and wife did not want. . . . From this moment onward it is impossible to distinguish each other's part in the work of the Curies. . . . We therefore have formal proof that in the fusion of their two efforts, in this superior alliance of man and woman, the exchange was equal.[3]

This, of course, is hardly proof that Marie could have made it on her own; Pierre was a scientist of near genius in his own right, long before he married, and all her creative work took place in collaboration with him. After his death, "Marie Curie the widow unflinchingly carried the weight of a new science and conducted it, through research, step by step, to its harmonious expansion."[4] But it was largely elaboration of the fundamental discovery made in *his* lifetime.

The standard explanation that "woman never had a chance" simply does not stand up. This would be forgetting under what sometimes fantastic handicaps creative men have worked and generated master-pieces—deafness, blindness, lack of formal education, poverty, political persecution, ridicule—and kept going at it with invincible will-power, prompted by an inner Promethean fire that few women have ever possessed. In many instances, women have been provided with greater educational opportunities than men in specific areas—musical training, for instance, which was part of every young girl's education and for which most boys simply did not have the time or the opportunity. Yet all the music composers were men. Or even cooking, which generations of young girls have been taught, while all the great cooks have been men. A noteworthy feminist, Havelock Ellis is reluctantly compelled to point out:

> It is forgotten that for more than a thousand years, all over Europe the cloister delivered women from the fetters of the hearth and the family, and it was certainly the most gifted and developed women who sought the cloister. No prejudice hindered them from devoting themselves to science, art, and literature; in fact, they so devoted themselves. Yet all the famous names in the annals of the cloister are men's names.[5]

Even in their typical fields, which hardly require any genius—domestic architecture, interior decorating, furniture styling, women's fashion

—all the major inventions and discoveries are the work of males. If social "oppression" alone is responsible for depriving women of their rightful share of public power and authority, it certainly cannot account for the fact that 98 percent of all patents for new inventions are delivered to men and only 2 percent to women.[6] It is almost invariably men who invent the "new mousetraps" and all the domestic items that women have traditionally used daily; housewives almost never come up with new inventions in what is their primary field of occupation, and no patent office can seriously be accused of practicing sexual discrimination.

In many societies, women have been more appreciative of art and literature, because they have been more perceptive and receptive than men; they can *preserve* culture, not create it. When it comes to actual creation *ex nihilo*, to the invention of new forms abstracted from the brain, involving the analytical assimilation of the old as well as the bringing to mental birth of the new, they are nowhere to be seen. Women are geared to the subjective, personal and concrete, and they lack the biological aggressiveness, the totally uninhibited drive and ambition, as well as the power to objectify that ambition, which is typical of the creative male.

This is not to suggest that women are totally uncreative, but that they cannot create without man, or rather that they can create only *through* man—through their power of inspiration or motherhood. Man's power of inspiration springs from his mind, from his imagination, and woman's from her emotional being. It is not a matter of intelligence, that is, of intellectual *understanding;* women are as intelligent as men, but that is not their prime function. It is not their physiologically ordained way of understanding—which is why the typical woman's intellect appears so often disconnected from the vital depths of her personality. Even such an ardent feminist as Bernard Shaw had to point out the basic differences between the mental functions of the sexes:

> In actual experience, the first shock to rationalism comes from the observation that though nothing can persuade women to adopt it, their impatience of reasoning no more prevents them from arriving at right conclusions than the masculine belief in it ... saves men from arriving at the wrong ones. When this generalization has to be modified in view of the fact that some women are beginning to try their skill at ratiocination, reason is not re-established on the throne; because the result of Woman's reasoning is that she begins to fall into all the errors which men are just learning to mistrust. The moment she sets about doing

things for reasons instead of merely finding reasons for what she wants to do, there is no saying what mischief she will be at next.[7]

Intellect, in any case, is only a piece of machinery, utterly dependent on what stands behind it and puts it to work. If man's intellect so often seems to be much more closely connected with his fundamental creative function than is the case with woman, if he has so often displayed mental inspiration amounting to the utmost creativity of a genius, it is essentially because woman's creativity is of an entirely different order and lies on a different plane which is not accessible to the masculine rational faculty. Woman's creativity is fundamentally mysterious, a creative power admirably depicted by the Hindu symbol of Śakti, a magic, spell-casting charm which Rabindranath Tagore defines as the power of woman over man, an intangible and undefinable element springing from the source of life itself: "Deprived of Śakti the creative process in society languishes, and man, losing his vitality, becomes mechanical," comments Tagore.[8] Indeed, if man is not somehow fertilized by this awesome irrigating power, this yin to his yang, he stands to lose whatever potential creativity he may have. Man is the fecundator on the mental as well as the physical plane, but at a deeper level, that of the intangible spirit or soul which stands back of the unconscious, it is the woman who is the fecundator; it is she who provides the vital feelings and emotions that underlie every one of man's cultural achievements. She inspires, and he, pregnant with the idea, gives birth to the masterpiece.

It now becomes easier to see that, even if woman alone rarely proves to be intellectually or artistically creative, man cannot create without her; hence, her part in the cultural process, however indirect, is vital. The most appropriate symbol of the mutual interdependence that binds the two sexes together is to compare male and female to the two poles of an elliptic field of magnetic forces. The *correlation* between the two poles provides the creative power; no one pole, male or female, can achieve anything without the contribution of the other.

This being so, what happens when man's talent for original creation evaporates—when a historical phase, such as the prodigious Periclean age in Greece, comes to a close and gives way to the utilitarian and culturally uncreative "Roman" era, an era of road builders and aqueduct engineers? Clearly, a profound alteration in the relationship between the sexes. We have seen it in the Greco-Roman world; we are now seeing it in ours, two thousand years later. We live in an era of transition, and it is often felt as such by some of the most creative men of the past hundred years. As Nietzsche pointed out, decadence is in the air. After centuries of relatively continuous and fruitful cultural evolution without any major break, centuries of accumulation of masterpieces, the sheer weight of this cultural inheritance threatens to overwhelm and choke contemporary cultural creativity—hence the desperate search for new forms and new styles. This cultural inheritance stands between the artist and the new world that the industrial revolution's technological offshoots are endlessly creating and destroying; the past has to go, with all its traditions, concepts, and styles. As Pablo Picasso pointed out:

> Today we are in the unfortunate position of having no order or canon whereby all artistic production is submitted to rules . . . as soon as art had lost all link with tradition, and the kind of liberation that came in with Impressionism permitted every painter to do what he wanted to do, painting was finished . . . there was no more painting; there were only individuals. Sculpture died the same death.[9]

The greatest sculptor of the century confirmed Picasso's statement. In reply to Anatole France's remark upon the low estate of decorative arts, Auguste Rodin exploded:

> If it were only our decorative arts! But it is art, art pure and simple, which has dwindled to nothing. No distinction can be made between decorative art and art. To make a very beautiful table or model the torso of a woman, is all one. Art always consists in translating dreams into forms. We no longer dream! . . . machinery has put dream to flight.[10]

The fact is that art, which stood for centuries at the very center of Western man's activity, is slowly moving toward the periphery of his concerns. Art has renounced its importance, abandoned its former role as kingpin of culture, and is gradually yielding to technology, politics, and economics its former preeminence.

Pure science is another great culture form of the West; here, too, signs of exhaustion are cropping up. Science no longer appears to be an endless frontier. As a former president of the American Association for the Advancement of Science stated in 1970:

> More and more scientists, publishing more and more papers, fill in missing details and extrapolate in quite predictable directions. The great conceptions, the fundamental mechanisms, and the basic laws are now known. For all time to come, these have been discovered, here and now, in our own lifetime. . . . There are still

innumerable details to fill in, but the endless horizons no longer exist.[11]

The observable universe is finite and radiotelescopes are reaching its limits; the universality of the genetic code, the distinctive features of proteins, are now known. And Dr. Bentley Glass adds: "It is in fact becoming more and more difficult, as scientific knowledge grows, to make a totally new and unexpected discovery or to break through the dogmas of established scientific views." This gradual leveling off will, he states, result in the reaching of a plateau of knowledge and a state of affairs in which human beings will begin to live like ants, bees and termites, locked in the same endless routine, with atrophied emotions and a withering away of consciousness itself.

This is the usual dream-nightmare that has haunted Western thinkers ever since science fiction began its attempt to peer into the misty future. They have tried to imagine the structure that Western culture's Promethean drive would eventually raise and see in it, with horror, total dehumanization—which, Dr. Glass suggests, could perhaps be overcome by using genetic tools to produce a new man, capable of transcending his present nature. Meantime, a great deal of tinkering and technological improvement remains to be done—but this will be merely engineering, designed to raise the overall level of civilization. The age of great scientific discoveries, requiring creative imagination on a gigantic scale, appears to be over.

The decline of contemporary cultural creativity is of a piece with the trend that stripped away Victorianism, gradually abolished all sexual restraints, developed the cult of the human animal's body and, inevitably, promoted the new cult of youth—since only the young body is as truly beautiful as the mature mind. In Victorian days, as in traditional China, youngsters could hardly wait to become old and respectable; in post-Victorian days, supposedly mature adults cannot try enough to imitate the manners of a long-departed youthfulness—overlooking the fact that youth is only the physiological stuff out of which mental maturity is eventually made. The increasing glorification of man's bestial origins and nature leads to the increasing infantilism of Western society, and admiration for man's sheer animality is bound to lead to a cultural dead end and to barbarization.

In turn, the cult of youthfulness implies a great increase in feminine influence. Recall Hegel's verdict in *The Phenomenology of Mind*, in which he states that woman "asserts that it is everywhere the force of youth that really counts; she upholds this as of primary significance; extols a son as one who is the lord and master of the mother who has born him."[12] In short, *her* creation. The connection between the cult of youthfulness and rising feminine influence is extremely close, so that this trend and the granting of female suffrage after World War I are closely interrelated and connected with the belief that mankind was about to make a new departure toward a better world, toward "making the world safe for democracy."

The decline of cultural creativity has profound implications as far as the relationship between the sexes is concerned. It is the creative man, chief exemplar of psychological virility, who harmonizes best with woman because they complement each other; and it is the uncreative one who most resents woman's intrusion into what he considers to be man's privileged domains, because she can then compete with him on equal terms—he becomes to woman what the southern "poor white trash" was to the black. As in the Greco-Roman world in decline, Western cultural creativity is slowly evaporating, its cathartic impact spent, to give way to the rising preeminence of "civilization" on a global scale.

The fact that the greatest advance made in woman's progress toward political equality came hard on the heels of a devastating World War was not accidental. It was as if the male-directed world, having seemingly fallen apart, longing for greater political stability, had induced man to give woman her fair share of political power. Western women, in that sense, were the real winners of the century's great world wars.

In 1918, under Prime Minister David Lloyd George's leadership, the Representation of the People Act granted married women, women householders, and female university graduates over thirty years of age the franchise in Great Britain. This reform was completed in 1928 when the age of women electors was lowered to twenty-one so as to put women on a plane of complete equality with men. American women had to wait for the final ratification of the Nineteenth Amendment in 1920 to receive their full political rights. The Weimar Republic extended universal suffrage to German women in 1919, and article 109 of its constitution asserted the equality of "all Germans, male and female," before the law.[13] With relatively few exceptions (Frenchwomen and Canadian women in the Province of Quebec had to wait until the end of World War II), suffrage was granted to women in Western democratic states, in the partly unconscious hope that feminine influence would prove to be politically beneficial and conducive to peace. Women were presumed to be on the side of clean government and morality, law and order; their motherly influence was required to exert a civilizing influence. Jack London epitomized this viewpoint:

> I voted that women might vote, because I knew that they, the wives and mothers of the race, would vote John Barleycorn out of existence and back into the historical limbo of our vanished customs of savagery. . . . The women are the true conservators of the race. The men are the wastrels, the adventure-lovers and gamblers, and in the end it is by their women that they are saved. . . . The women know.[14]

What they did not know but discovered after half a century of experience with female suffrage is that it made not one whit of difference. By and large, women voted like their men; few women ran for political office in any country, and fewer still were elected; the political world remained firmly under masculine control, and although in most countries registered women voters outnumbered the men, they never voted along gender lines. It could be surmised that in some marginal situations greater feminine preference made some difference as to the outcome, but on the whole, it would be difficult to prove that the difference was ever significant. Indeed, many great political machine bosses in the United States longed for female suffrage on the assumption that women's vote could be more easily manipulated than men's. In other lands, all strong male political leaders with greater or lesser dictatorial tendencies found it easier to appeal to female emotionalism than to overcome male skepticism.

Urbanization, an inevitable consequence of the industrial revolution, was growing fast, along with an increasing division and specialization of labor, the invention of the typewriter, the rapid development of department stores, the endless multiplication of business offices, and the shift toward "service" economies—all of which fostered in the early 1920s the "emancipated woman." The old patriarchal family disintegrated; "extended" family ties loosened up with the increasing mobility of the population and the steady emigration out of rural areas, and all that was left was the nuclear family with its built-in instability and rising divorce rate. Birth control became popular, releasing women's energies for other, still undefined, purposes.

In this general atmosphere, women's civilizing influence made itself felt in social activities to a far greater extent than at the ballot box. Women's clubs and organizations fought against bars and saloons, as the main causes of immorality, poverty, and broken homes; they fought for decent housing, improvement in public health standards, the introduction of new legislation protecting women and children workers. But for all that, women's direct political influence reached its peak with the suffrage issue; never again were they able to enlist the massive support of their sex in such dramatic form. The old politicians' fear that they would have to deal with female bloc-voting disappeared almost overnight; female political leverage evaporated and, by and large, female voting was seen as a mere extension of the male vote. According to reliable American polls taken after World War II, less than 5 percent of the wives polled stated that they voted independently of their husbands and most specified that they followed their husbands' choice: female suffrage was merely a "multiplication table."[15] More fundamental still, women voters proved Schopenhauer right in their ingrained reluctance to vote other women into office and in often preferring anti- to pro-feminist politicians. Women remained influential at the local level, but rarely at the national level in any country— unless they inherited, as widows or daughters, the political position and influence of their former husbands or fathers.

When John Stuart Mill introduced his seminal distinction between culture and civilization, he was probably imbued with the idea that the raising of woman's social and political status would improve the quality of contemporary *civilization*. Both terms came into increasing use in history, anthropology, and sociology in the nineteenth and twentieth centuries, each of them rather arbitrarily endowed with multiple meanings, depending on the authors' tastes and viewpoints.[16] In the present context, we will simply assume that culture and civilization represent distinctive phases in the historical life course of a given society. Although there is always a certain amount of overlapping, these terms should be understood as being linked by organic succession, of youth (culture) followed by maturity (civilization).

Culture predominates in new societies awakening to life under specific conditions (post-Homeric Greece, Vedic India, China during the Spring and Autumn era, Europe's Middle Ages), growing like vigorous organisms and developing entirely new *Weltanschauungs*. Cultural growth implies essentially the creation of *new* religious symbolism and artistic styles and values, *new* ethical codes, *new* intellectual and spiritual structures. Essentially culture, as a historical phase, emphasizes *original* creation rather than preservation and duplication, favors prototypes rather than mass production; culture is essentially trailblazing.

Civilization represents exactly the reverse trend, that is, nothing less than the crystallization, on a much larger scale, of the preceding culture's deepest and greatest thoughts. It lives out of the multiplication of petrified stock forms, is basically uncreative and culturally sterile, dedicated to some form or other of social democratization, mass production, and technological proficiency. Culture represents *organic growth;* civilization embodies *mechanical extension.*

A given society transiting from culture to civilization undergoes a revolutionary crisis that can last generations or even centuries—an era of political and social convulsions, world wars, and fundamental revolutions, before settling down to some form of civilized stability. In our Western society, it can be assumed that this phase of transition started with the French and industrial revolutions—the conjunction of political, social, economic, technological, and intellectual upheavals that are still with us today, almost two hundred years later.

The fact that the problem of feminism arose at the beginning of this phase of transition is no mere coincidence. The problem of the emancipation of woman is part and parcel of this reorientation of modern society, and perhaps its most important aspect, because it raises the problem of woman's relationship, no longer with culture, but with civilization. In any society where the emphasis is put increasingly on materialistic extension and multiplication rather than on original creation, on social organization and structure rather than the full flowering of the creative individual, woman's natural endowments in those domains will begin to assert themselves.

Time and again, throughout history and in all societies, woman proved herself to be a born ruler and competent administrator and organizer; what she performs naturally in her own household is what the ruler is supposed to perform for the benefit of the state as a whole. Few women have been granted the opportunity to rule large states or empires, but most of those who did outperformed most male rulers, save for a few exceptional, and not always beneficent, geniuses. From Cleopatra to Russia's Catherine the Great and India's Indira Gandhi, they have proved that they were matches for their male rivals; and this for an obvious reason: an effective ruler governs by suggestion rather than coercion, and that rule by suggestion presupposes a social sensitivity and a consideration for others which men often lack. The fact is that woman, basically, is the working, rather than playing, part of mankind; she is the serious, responsible, altruistic element, while man remains the selfish gambler, player, and adventurer—the eternal child, often irresponsible and frequently dangerous element. The idea that woman should be a stay-at-home toy, a doll-like creature destined to amuse the male, is one of the great fallacies of the new bourgeois ethics generated by the industrial revolution. That woman, who is the more *civilized* portion of the species, should eventually revolt against this stigmata was a foregone conclusion.

Whenever civilization tends to prevail over culture, woman tends to assert her autonomy and, in some areas, her predominance—predominance that becomes a plain fact to the extent that the malelike original, inspired, mentally and artistically creative, gives way before the femalelike capacity for routine labor, precise organization, emphasis on economics, security (social and otherwise), and conservatism. Thanks to two world wars, woman has quite naturally expressed a new mode of being and a new attitude in the relationship between the sexes. But the change is more fundamental: it is largely the masculine tendency toward waywardness and instability, that is, toward variation, that has upset the world, so it is woman who now asserts her right to work for stability and security. Although outwardly more independent, man is in fact less well equipped to resist the influence of woman if she decides, however emotionally or obscurely, to exert it in earnest.

The granting of suffrage to woman, the steady alteration of legislation in her favor, all the social and political rights extended to her, have not only practical significance but also symbolic value: they imply nothing less than the male-acknowledged bankruptcy of a world out of control. Even if rigid patriarchalism had been preserved, the inevitable drift toward welfare statism, rising antimilitarism in Western nations, the increasing preoccupation with ecological and pollution problems, imply the irresistible ascendancy of the female principle of conservation. Having fouled his planetary nest, Western man now has to contend with the aroused spirit of Mother Earth—generator, like the multifaceted goddess Kālī, not only of civilized stability but, occasionally, of revolutionary anger.

Part V

BEYOND HISTORY:
WOMAN AND REVOLUTION

CHAPTER

I

The Dream of Anarchy

With the twined French and industrial revolutions, Western society embarked on a series of social upheavals and armed conflicts that have engulfed the entire planet.

The inception of this revolutionary epoch took place when the Renaissance and the Reformation swept most of Europe—the first signs of masculine rebellion against medieval concessions to the feminine ideal. The Reformation broke the medieval mold and, laying the major stress on man as individual rather than as member of a social organism, also laid upon him a heavy burden of personal responsibility, stripped of all the consoling symbolism of Mariolatry. In its reckless demythologizing, the Reformation—with its spiritual offspring, the eighteenth-century Enlightenment—proved to be a fundamentally virile manifestation. From the early conquistadors and scientific discoverers of the secrets of nature to the latter-day explorers and great business entrepreneurs, it stamped the imprint of Western civilization on the whole world. Western man had listened to the rhythm of nature and applied his logic to the elaboration of a steely web of mathematical laws, prodded on toward the discovery of mastery of the physical world by his inborn Promethean urge. From the simple use of nature's available forces he shifted to the creation of the machine, an independent cosmos that became the materialization of his mathematical dream, an animated universe in miniature made, by man's creative genius, out of inorganic matter—the concrete manifestation of the *lógos spermatikos*. With this new world at his command and his power increased tremendously, Western man hurled the machine at the rest of the world, smashing and destroying other civilizations. Domination over the forces of nature went hand in hand with political domination. With unlimited vigor, Western man threw immense networks of railroads and steamship lines over the world, and with levers and screws fastened his grip on every corner of the globe, holding Mother Earth in tight bondage. Never had the masculine Logos seemed so potent, and never had the devaluation of the specifically female function been so total.

But times change and potentials exhaust themselves when they become actual. Protestantism, especially its Puritan offshoot, generated capitalism, industrialism, and mechanism; it spent its initial religious impulse in concrete accomplishments and began to shift toward an ethical materialism concealed behind the outworn religious forms of Victorianism. Finally, it generated its antithesis—world revolution, a violent upsurge that has spread from its small geographical nucleus in Western Europe to the whole world—revolution in a spirit that is as masculine as the Western capitalist society it is attempting to overthrow. And in the process, woman, whose increasing dissatisfaction and social rebellion becomes one of the major dissolvents of contemporary Western society, becomes deeply involved. Today we are reenacting, on a much larger scale, the social drama that, from Euripides on, shook the Greco-Roman world to its foundations, and eventually destroyed its civilization from within before the barbarians invaded the empire from without.

The Euripides of the West was undoubtedly Henrik Ibsen who, of all modern playrights, comes closest to the pattern of classical Greek playwriting, especially in pure tragedy, where the sense of implacable destiny predominates. Suzannah Thoresen, Ibsen's forceful wife, stiffened his weak backbone and gave him the strength of character he lacked; she probably enhanced his profeminist views. Like his Greek predecessor, Ibsen set out to shatter, no longer myths and mythology —Western Society had by then largely metamorphosed them into ideals and ideologies—but all the traditional preconceived ideals set up by bourgeois society. To achieve this, Ibsenism used the emancipation of woman as a battering ram with which to knock down the Victorian fortress of respectability; the liberation of woman from the concept of duty to an ideal would also liberate the man. Any typical Ibsen play transmogrifies the impeccably conventional idealist—good, pure, strong, and brave—into a subtle villain, while his female heroines are, from a Victorian standpoint, typically unfeminine.

In one of his early dramatic poems, "Brand," he shows us an idealistic priest whose very saintliness, admired and worshiped by the crowd, destroys his wife and child and causes more intense suffering to others than a half-dozen devils. In A Doll's House he really comes to grips with the problem of woman, although he did not intend to depict Nora as a feminist. From the viewpoint of bourgeois morality, his idealistic Torvald is beyond reproach; in point of fact, from a purely human viewpoint, he is a coarse, selfish, and cowardly husband. Ibsen's main theme here is the struggle between society and the individual's private right to live and love, and in describing a woman's tragic destiny, Ibsen relied on the idea that woman takes a more *personal* view of life than man who is forever abstracting and generalizing. His main target is Torvald's view that a sin against society is more serious than the destruction of love—a view Ibsen abhorred. Ibsen's was the individualistic anarchistic outlook, which is the other side of the same coin—the feminine-personal-antiethical outlook.

For Ibsen admirers who thought Nora should have become reconciled to duty instead of abandoning home and hearth, he next produced *Ghosts*, a ferocious attack on marriage as a totally useless sacrifice for all concerned. Alving, the idealistic nonhero, is a sensuous man whose dutiful wife drives him to spend most of his time in the arms of a housemaid. No Nora, Mrs. Alving decides to remain with husband and child, although this implies soul-destroying concealment. She sends her son abroad, fearing that his ideals might collapse as he grows older and finds out the truth. Finally, after years of sorrow, she is freed by the death of her husband. His reputation, thanks to her deceit, is that of a thoroughly honorable gentleman. Now comes the bitter reward for years of martyrdom: the son comes home, and being his father's son, starts to behave like the deceased. The tragedy is that, while she never loved her husband (they had made a marriage *de convenance*, very much like Ibsen's own matrimonial arrangement), she adores her son. She realizes she has no right to sacrifice him to the ideals that ruined her own life. But these ideals take their dramatic toll: having indirectly compelled the father to lead a sordidly secretive love life, she learns that the son has inherited the disease that such a way of life often breeds and that, forewarned, he carries poison with which to destroy himself when he becomes insane. The play ends in an intensely tragic scene wherein the mother dispatches her mad son to the netherworld with her own hands.

Victorian audiences were stunned and outraged by this powerful onslaught on all standard ideals, and a great deal of the message was lost in the sheer amount of vituperation thrown at it. A publication called *Truth* flung the following epithets at Ibsen's masterpiece: "The sexless. . . . The unwomanly woman, the unsexed females, the whole army of unprepossessing cranks in petticoats. . . . Effeminate men and male women. . . . A wave of human folly."[1] Obviously Ibsen had pricked a raw social nerve not only in English-speaking nations but in his native Norway. But he went even further.

In *Hedda Gabler*, he depicts a frigid woman incapable of love and, therefore, a castrating type who transcends the mere war of the sexes and who, bored to death, deprived of idealism, and unencumbered with the concept of duty to God or others, is left only with that of duty to herself. Unable to discover what this consists of, she makes an ideal of vice. She ends by destroying herself; Hedda is a true reincarnation of Euripides' Medea.

Undismayed by the mounting criticism, Ibsen went on doggedly. In *When the Dead Awaken*, his last play, he left a literary legacy to feminism that no other writer has provided before or since—one with such insight and power that it raises the problem of the meaning of civilization itself in the form of a devastating indictment. Basically, the play contrasts two couples, one made up of a cultured and refined pair of human beings, at the height of Western culture; the other, basically primitive, from the exclusively sports-minded, hunting crowd. The question asked, and to which the play replies in the affirmative, is whether primitive men and women enjoy a more fruitful and humane relationship in which she fully shares the joys and passions than a highly cultured modern couple in which the woman's soul is degraded, sucked dry to stimulate man's creative genius, and then wasted and thrown away.

In the play, the sculptor Rubeck finds the beautiful model he was always looking for, enthralls her by telling her about his vision of the perfect statue. Grasping his inspiration, she poses for him and helps him in every way with utter devotion. The statue at last achieved, he callously indicates that he has no more use for her—she has been only a means to an end. She leaves him and becomes insane. Soon enough, Rubeck marries a totally unsuitable primitive woman, who nevertheless influences him sufficiently so that he no longer sees the perfection of his statue—which he now proceeds to alter and, gradually, destroy as a work of art, reshaping it into a monstrosity that satisfies the public's taste and makes him famous. Rubeck eventually loses his wife to a more suitable primitive man who makes her happy; his former model, cured of her insanity, comes back into his life. Seeing that for all the harm he had done her, he had actually crippled himself, she comes to believe that a miracle can undo the damage, that indeed the dead can awaken if and when the two sexes can work out a relationship in which they do not sacrifice and destroy each other. But, ascending an allegorical mountain where they meet the primitive couple, they climb up to their figurative death while the caveman saves his primitive woman. This work, which Ibsen viewed as an epilogue, appeared symbolically in the last days of December 1899, at the close of the century which it could aptly terminate—in the words of its antihero, "When we dead awaken, we shall see that we have not lived."

The incisive power of Ibsen's work springs from the fact that his human creations are more real than real people, as if his surgical eye could see right through the innermost recesses of their souls and the structures of the personalities. His profundity shows in his portrayal of the ambiguities and impenetrabilities of life. Out of the mists of the far north came the most penetrating dramatist since Shakespeare, a Scandinavian poet who stated through his mouthpiece, the skald Jatgejr in *The Pretenders*, "No song is born in full daylight." This massive interpenetration of symbolism and realism was more believable and far more striking than any concrete reality, a miraculous display of logical irrationality that could delineate the spiritual and psychological complexities of both sexes as no other writer ever could. True to life, Ibsen bulldozed all the artificial Victorian ideals and conventions out of his way, and was labeled immoral for so doing.

No one in the English-speaking world was so consistently a feminist as Bernard Shaw, and he, too, used the theme of the emancipation of woman with which to attack the Victorian edifice he abhorred. Even more than Ibsen's, Shaw's plays resemble Euripides' in their dissolution of the stern dramatic form into psychology and philosophy, accompanied by essays or prefaces on any number of topics, especially feminism. Just as Ibsen, Shaw is, in his own words, "on the side of the prophets in having devoted himself to showing that the spirit or will of Man is constantly outgrowing the ideals, and that therefore thoughtless conformity to them is constantly producing results no less tragic than those which follow thoughtless violation of them."[2] But, in fact, Shaw's wit proved more immediately effective than Ibsen's somber and tragic genius; society will always laugh itself to destruction if its demise is presented to it with adequate humor.

It would seem that once again, as in the Middle Ages when man used woman as a means to his own spiritual salvation, modern man was using woman as a convenient revolutionary tool with which to smash a social structure whose ideological underpinnings were becoming intolerable. Victorian conventionality was smothering the "need for freedom of evolution," which justifies the need for toleration. Along with Schopenhauer, Nietzsche, Ibsen, and Strindberg, Shaw wanted to strip away the artificial strait-jacket of Victorian moralistic conformity; but with Ibsen, and unlike Schopenhauer, Nietzsche, and Strindberg, Shaw believed that the easiest, most convenient way to do so was to produce a social "nuclear" explosion by liberating the imprisoned female energy, instead of isolating it as Strindberg would have it:

The sum of the matter is that unless Woman repudiates her womanliness, her duty to her husband, to her children, to society, to the law, and to everyone but herself, she cannot emancipate herself. But her duty to herself is no duty at all, since a debt is cancelled when the debtor and creditor are the same person. Its payment is simply a fulfilment of the individual will, upon which all duty is a restriction, founded on the conception of the will as naturally malign and devilish. Therefore Woman has to repudiate duty altogether. In that repudiation lies her freedom; for it is false to say that Woman is now directly the slave of Man: she is the immediate slave of duty; and as man's path to freedom is strewn with the wreckage of the duties and ideals he has trampled on so is hers. . . . A whole basketful of ideals of the most sacred quality will be smashed by the achievement of equality for women and men . . . the destroyer of ideals, though denounced as an enemy of society, is in fact sweeping the world clear of lies.[3]

In Strindberg's plays, man is displayed as the victim of married life and the woman as the tyrannical soul-destroyer; Shaw will see in the emasculating woman only the twisted result of man's own behavior. Strindberg was a woman hater of the first order who attempted to arouse men out of their slothful idealization of the female sex—which, to him, was but the hypocritical rationalization of their sensual impulses. His tragic inability to establish a meaningful relationship with his wives darkened his outlook on woman and gave his work the quality of a mirror image of Ibsen's, for whom the absolute and final tragedy was the denial or destruction of love, usually sacrificed on the altar of "social necessity." Both Ibsen and Strindberg were the spokesmen of *individualism*, and it is in its name that they inveighed against the increasingly oppressive weight of a complex social structure.

Long before Bernard Shaw decided to encapsulate Ibsen's message in comic form, George Meredith had used his comic talent to describe the double war between the generations and the sexes—two conflicts that are, in reality, one, inasmuch as woman, the true procreator of the species, always upholds the young against the old if free to do so. Meredith was one of the first modern male writers who depicted women of intelligence and character *(The Egoist)* who were the equals in most respects of men. But Shaw conveyed the message most convincingly, although not without an ulterior purpose in mind—to expound, after Schopenhauer, the primacy of will over reason. Here again, woman is used to condemn the tyranny of utter rationalism; woman *because she herself* uses feeling and intuition rather than discursive logic. As far as Shaw is concerned, woman, when willing to follow her impulse and instincts rather than ratiocinate, demonstrates conclusively the limitations of mere logic and the primacy of the will.

Shaw stood in no need of Ibsen to formulate his views on womanhood, and his influence in the English-speaking world made itself felt more quickly, directly, and forcefully. Shaw's outlook can be summed up succinctly: the root of the war between the sexes is the masculine idealization of woman's self-surrender in love; he points out that the "infatuation of passionate sexual desire" repels even the object of that infatuation and that love loses its charm when it is compelled—either by custom, law or mere sensuality. "The desire to give inspires no affection unless there is also the power to withhold."[4] Thus, contemporary marriage, with all its legal compulsions, is wrong, and is doomed to disappear as "the responsibility for the maintenance and education of the rising generation is shifted from the parent to the community."[5] Fortunately Shaw, unlike Jean-Jacques Rousseau, never had any children of his own with which to experiment.

Nevertheless, marriage, in all its degrading aspects, remained the pillar of the social structure in which woman was imprisoned. "This being so, it is not surprising that our society, being directly dominated by men, comes to regard Woman, not as an end in herself like Man, but solely as a means of ministering to his appetite"[6]—a sex object. This, of course, was untrue in former centuries when the religious outlook did not allow man to look upon himself as an end but rather as a means with which to glorify God and the universe He created. In that case, *both* men and women found themselves to be respective means in the higher metaphysical sense, establishing a cooperative equality and a spiritual integration of sorts between the sexes. The collapse of the all-pervading religious outlook made man an end in himself, but having substituted for the Almighty, he now looked upon woman as a means to his own enjoyment rather than a fellow human being engaged in the same earthly pilgrimage toward mutual spiritual salvation. The metaphysical equality and partnership of former times was destroyed. The rebellion of woman became an inevitable consequence of this new state of mind. As Shaw put it, "to treat a person as a means instead of an end is to deny that person's right to live. And to be treated as a means to such an end as sexual intercourse with those who deny one's right to live is insufferable to any human being"[7]— this, of course, presupposing that most women, in those late Victorian days, found no erotic enjoyment of their own in sexual intercourse. "Woman, if she dares face the fact that she is being so treated, must either loathe herself or else rebel. . . . Does she then loathe herself? By no means: she deceives herself in the idealist fashion by denying that the love which her suitor offers her is tainted with sexual appetite at all."[8]

When disillusionment sets in, "the self-respect she has lost as a wife she regains as a mother, in which capacity her use and importance to the community compare favorably with those of most men of business."[9] But this redeeming role depends entirely on the greater or lesser natural vocation she may have for a purely domestic life: "The domestic career is no more natural to all women than the military career is natural to all men. . . . If we have come to think that the nursery and the kitchen are the natural sphere of a woman, we have done so exactly as English children come to think of a cage as the natural sphere of a parrot: because they have never seen one anywhere else."[10]

These were almost revolutionary views when Shaw propounded them, although many have become commonplace. But revolutionary social change was precisely what Shaw was aiming at, and the emancipation of woman was largely a means to an end, pointing toward "Man's repudiation of duty by way of Woman's." Shaw's revolution, however, was not so much socialistic as a purely individualistic rebellion in a Nietzschean or Schopenhauerian sense. The ultimate good was not the perfect society but that particular social organization that allowed maximum freedom of expression and individual development to all human beings.

This is essentially libertarian thinking, the intellectual foundation of anarchism. In turn, libertarian thinking has an old ancestry and is always connected with an instinctive feminine revolt against an outdated authority—and therefore against all authority and artificial moral constraints; usually unfettered by intellectual dogmatism, woman goes to extremes once her traditional moorings have broken loose. Sensing intuitively that she will never really be able to wrest public power from the hands of man, woman's thinking along revolutionary lines always ends in some form of utopian anarchism, aiming at the total destruction of power, pure and simple.

As early as the late Middle Ages, for example, with the church's traditional authority greatly eroded, religious sects like the Anabaptists expounded similar libertarian views. In the thirteenth century, groups of mystical women inspired by ecstatic visions gathered together spontaneously and formed convents; they soon became known as Béguines, the famous Sisters of the Free Spirit. Before long, they were joined by male Beghards and celebrated orgies of pantheistic mysticism followed. They were all thoroughgoing anarchists, claiming total freedom for all individuals, inasmuch as God dwells in each individual soul and therefore the individual will of each was the Will of the Almighty. In their preaching the Brethren and Sisters of the Free Spirit advocated outright collectivism, community of goods, personal equality, and the destruction of any kind of authority—the modern libertarian program of Bakunine and Kropotkin in toto, except for the acknowledgement of the Almighty.[11]

What is remarkable here is that this movement was started spontaneously by women—which is actually not so remarkable insofar as females usually start great historical trends, even when they are formulated and led by males. Man, in his one-sided intellectualism, is far more a self-contained, autonomous and well-defined entity, often the prisoner of his intellectual framework. Women usually appear to have an intuitive flair for the secret germination of new trends that are going to shape the future, an uncanny telepathic sense for the forthcoming that is the natural counterpart of their basic conservatism. They are far more plastic and adaptable and flexible than men, closer to ever-changing nature. So it was with the medieval libertarian Sisters of the Free Spirit; and so it was on the threshold of the Age of Revolution with their lay descendants.

Not by chance, Bernard Shaw was in a direct line of intellectual descent from William Godwin, first articulate exponent of the anarchist credo, and often better remembered as the husband of Mary Wollstonecraft, the first outspoken feminist. This odd couple jointly ministered to the birth of both libertarian and feminist thinking, symbolizing in the flesh, as it were, the obscure but close relationship between the two trends. Only a year after Mary Wollstonecraft published her *Vindication of the Rights of Woman* (1792), her future husband's startling work, *Enquiry Concerning Political Justice,* appeared. A striking philosophico-political study, it set forth all the arguments in favor of anarchism—rejection of any kind of social organization dependent upon government and of all authority, in favor of an utterly decentralized social organism founded upon a voluntary sharing of material goods on a plane of complete equality:

> Anarchy awakens mind, diffuses energy and enterprise through the community, though it does not effect this in the best manner. ... But in despotism mind is trampled into an equality of the most odious sort. Everything that promises greatness is destined to fall under the exterminating hand of suspicion and envy.[12]

Actually Godwin refused to call himself an anarchist in order to divorce himself from the negative anarchists of the contemporary French Revolution. But in essence he was an anarchist of the Bakunin type, prefiguring the libertarian trend of the following centuries, and while he refused to go as far as to trust the presumed innate goodness of the uneducated people's spontaneous instincts (he believed that only education could truly free the individual), he anticipated anarchism's rejection of government and its vision of society as a naturally developing organism in need of neither authority nor coercion. This seminal ancestor was no believer in force or violence and stated emphatically that "revolutions, instead of being truly beneficial to mankind, answer no other purpose than that of marring the salutary and uninterrupted progress which might be expected to attend upon political truth and social improvement."[13] Unlike some believers in violence (the radical Chartists, Auguste Blanqui), most of the leading theoreticians of libertarian revolution (Owen, Saint-Simon, Proudhon) shared Godwin's peaceful views and followed in his intellectual footsteps.

In his day, Godwin's popularity and influence were enormous; in Hazlitt's words, William Godwin "blazed in the firmament of reputation."[14] His doctrine later filled with enthusiasm generations of Romantic poets from Coleridge to Shelley. The idea that both society and government exist solely for the convenience of the individual, without any valid claims or rights of their own, was novel in those days, but Godwin's originality was to break away from Locke's and Rousseau's concept of a basic social contract as a foundation of political justice because of its binding, legalistic nature which prevents the full flowering of the individual's exercise of private judgment and instinctive commitment to truth and justice.

The fact that the founders of anarchism and feminism became husband and wife is, again, highly symbolic. In an intellectual sense, Godwin's message inspired many latter-day male thinkers who were wholeheartedly in favor of feminism, and its influence can be traced easily in Oscar Wilde's *The Soul of Man under Socialism* and H. G. Wells' *Men Like Gods*.[15] In *Back to Methuselah*, Bernard Shaw treated a Godwinian theme, and in his study on Ibsen, Shaw pointed out with greater acuteness than anyone else the revolutionary impact of the anarchistic-individualistic trend as compared with socialism of the Marxist type. In a noteworthy paragraph, Shaw explains the paradoxical irony of the Victorian outlook on socialism:

> The credit of our domestic ideals having been shaken to their foundations, as through a couple of earthquake shocks, by Ibsen and Strindberg (the Arch Individualists of the nineteenth century) whilst the Socialists have been idealizing, sentimentalizing, denouncing Capitalism for sacrificing Love and Home and Domestic Happiness and Children and Duty to money, greed and ambition, yet it remains a commonplace of political journalism to assume that Socialism is the deadliest enemy of the domestic ideals and Unsocialism their only hope and refuge. In the same

breath the world-grasping commercial synthesis we call Capitalism, built up by generations of Scotch Rationalists and English Utilitarians, Atheists, Agnostics and Natural-Selectionists, with Malthus as the one churchman among all its prophets, is proclaimed the bulwark of the Christian Churches.[16]

Time has proved Shaw correct, and proved socialism, Marxist or otherwise, essentially conservative in its attitude toward social duty, morality, marriage, domestic life, and the traditional relationship between the sexes.

With Pierre-Joseph Proudhon, Godwin's intellectual successor, the anarchistic strain becomes evident. Proudhon was a strong super-individualist who stood in lonely pride, spurned parties and political sects, and set such store by individual freedom that even a mild expression such as "association" was suspect in his eyes. He viewed the individual as the ultimate concern, but conceded that the individual's personality had to be shaped by, and find fulfilment in, society. In other words, society was not the individual's enemy but the inevitable matrix within which the individual's personality could temper itself and find its true function. Proudhon's impact on nineteenth-century thought was enormous—in fact, second only to Marx's. From Baudelaire and Flaubert to Sainte-Beuve and Victor Hugo, most writers of the century who were interested in social matters fell under his spell. Even Tolstoy borrowed not only his greatest novel's title from Proudhon's *La Guerre et la Paix*, but also many of his views. Famous for having coined the greatest slogan of the century when, in answer to the question title of his first work, *What Is Property?* he concluded, "Property Is Theft," this dynamic revolutionary was also one of the leading anti-feminists of the century.

Proudhon's attitude toward woman illustrates one of the paradoxes of the individualistic-anarchistic trend: inasmuch as man is already by nature more individualized (even embryologically) than woman, any added emphasis put on individualism will strengthen his masculine character, and that of any society which emphasizes and encourages individualism. Like many arch-individualists and anarchists after him, Proudhon appeared to set more store by the actual struggle than by the ultimate victory, by the means than by the end, as if it was in the crucible of conflict that the individual forged his personality and achieved true personal freedom. In this almost joyful acceptance of tension and stress as inevitable, the virile side of anarchism stands out in bold relief. And yet, in its antisystematic and antiintellectual approach, and in its refusal to set up a consistent doctrine, in its shunning of an intellectual paraphernalia and its reliance on instinctive behavior, its feminine side betrays itself. In his last letter to Karl Marx, which was to break up their relationship, Proudhon stated defiantly:

> . . . I make profession in public of an almost absolute economic anti-dogmatism. . . . Let us give the world the example of a learned and farsighted tolerance, but let us not, because we are at the head of a movement, make ourselves the leaders of a new intolerance, let us not pose as the apostles of a new religion, even if it be the religion of logic, the religion of reason. Let us gather together and encourage all protests, let us brand all exclusiveness, all mysticism. . . .[17]

There could be no meeting of the minds between them.

This strong, solitary revolutionary, however, did not look upon woman as a companion and fellow worker in the cause, but as an inferior being, physiologically condemned to home and kitchen, and to ultimate dependence on the strong male, for whom the "true woman" was the devoted housewife and mother, and the rest harlots and prostitutes. There was in him an ascetic strain similar to that of the early Buddhist or Christian saints—in particular in his elimination of love from marriage because it destroys the love of work, cripples domestic respect, and harms the performance of social duty. The historian Michelet, who was at all times under the spell of women, attacked Proudhon on this point and stated that he disagreed with his view that woman was only receptive; she was also productive "through her influence on man"—although he admits that, by herself, she is largely uncreative.[18]

Proudhon appears to have been an exception in his attitude toward woman. As far as his anarchist successors were concerned, equality of the sexes was taken for granted, but their libertarian views were also slightly different. For the greatest anarchist, Michael Bakunin, the absolute individualism of Proudhon had to give way to free associations. What for Proudhon had been a reluctant concession to necessity, a mere *means* of coping with fast-increasing industrialization, became for Bakunin the pivot of all socioeconomic organization: it is the productive collectivity, the group of workers rather than the isolated individual, that becomes the cornerstone of a suitable economic structure. From here on, anarchism sloughs off the rigid individualism of its forebears to become a libertarian, antiauthoritarian *collectivism*. Bakunin lays stress on individual freedom but not that kind of bourgeois freedom that springs from Rousseau's theory in *Du Contrat Social*—that "vile book" as he termed it.[19] There never were entirely free individual men who joined together in order to create society; in fact, the community existed before the individual and the concept of freedom is unthinkable outside the community. Primacy belongs to the group; as he stated it:

> I am only free when all human beings around me, men and women, are equally free. Other people's freedom, far from putting limits on, or being the negation of, my freedom, is, on the contrary, both necessary and the confirmation of it.[20]

Like all anarchists, Bakunin wanted to destroy the state; but he put far greater emphasis on *society,* the indispensable medium for the full flowering of the individual personality. And again, like most of his successors, Bakunin saw clearly the growing artificiality of life springing from the industrial revolution and the bourgeois society issued from it: everything good—customs, public opinion—is *natural,* perhaps the key word of the whole anarchist movement. The libertarian emphasis on destruction springs from this inner conviction that once the artificial barriers that separate men from one another are swept away, nothing will prevent wholesome social organisms from cropping up. Just as his Spanish successors were to hark back, unconsciously, to the free, quasi-independent communities that prevailed in medieval Spain, Bakunin undoubtedly had in mind the small peasant communities of Russia and the natural collectivism of the *mir;* similarly, his worthy successor Peter Kropotkin was to look back wistfully upon the medieval manor and guild, the *obshchina* and *artel'.*

Basically, anarchism, then and today, was a reaction against the brutal excesses of industrialism, a longing for a simpler if more austere way of life that prevailed in the nonindustrial past. Anarchism did not want to deal with "the masses" as Marxists did, but with small groups and communities in which human rights—and, even more important, human *dignity*—could really be protected. In anarchism one could find a true reincarnation of one aspect of medieval Christianity, its respect for the fundamental equality of all human souls in the eyes of the Lord —and now that the Lord was denied, of all human beings. And the bitter violence with which anarchism turned anticlerical at times demonstrated its profound, quasi-religious conviction that the Christian churches had betrayed a sacred ideal.

In the same vein is Bakunin's emphasis on the rejection of a priori ideas or preordained, preconceived laws in favor of his own emphasis on "purely instinctive" doctrines—here again, a feminine attitude.[21] His distrust of abstractions extended even to science and he proclaimed a "revolt of life against science, or rather, against the rule of science," against Auguste Comte's Positivism as well as against Marxists, the "priests of science."[22] Some of his successors, the Russian brothers Gordin, for instance, rejected both religion and science outright: "The rule of heaven and the rule of nature—angels, spirits, devils, molecules, atoms, ether, the laws of God-Heaven and the laws of Nature, forces, the influence of one body on another—all this is invented, formed, created by society."[23] One important aspect of anarchism is its revolt, not only against scientific determinism and its implied threat to human freedom and autonomy, but also against the tremendous power that the technology derived from it can accumulate in a very few hands; and one reason for the persistence of anarchist tendencies today (masquerading under some of the New Left labels) is that technological concentration has made some traditional forms of political and economic power almost unbearable.

For the same reason, Bakunin profoundly distrusted the Marxist dictatorship of the proletariat and affirmed that it would inevitably end in "the rule of scientific intellect, the most autocratic, the most despotic, the most arrogant, and the most contemptuous of all regimes." He understood Marxism quite accurately and was prophetic when he wrote:

> According to the theory of Mr. Marx, the people not only must not destroy [the State] but must strengthen it and place it at the complete disposal of their benefactors, guardians, and teachers —the leaders of the Communist party, namely Mr. Marx and his friends, who will proceed to liberate [mankind] in their own way.[24]

On the contrary, power, all forms of power of man over man, must be destroyed.

The general attitude of anarchism toward woman was a logical corollary of this outlook; in Spain, for instance, the first general gathering of the anarchistic *Alianza de la Democracia Social* in 1872 put at the head of its program:

> 1. The Alliance desires first of all the definite and complete abolition of classes, and economic and social equality of individuals of both sexes. . . .
> 2. It desires for the children of both sexes equality of education, of food and social position. . . .[25]

In other words, all anarchists echoed the brothers Gordin in advocating "gynantropism"—the emancipation and humanization of woman.

Unlike the Marxists, who emphasized doctrinal orthodoxy and dialectics, strict discipline, and the Jesuitical approach of sacrificing moral principles to expediency, the anarchists relied entirely on their spontaneous instincts. Like the Marxists, they hated the greed of the capital-ists; but they hated even more the love of power displayed by most Marxists, especially the Soviet dictatorship in Russia. When the test came for anarchism, the Spanish Civil War, it was able to show its true mettle.

Shocked by the hypocritical morals of Spain's bourgeoisie, the anarchists proceeded to apply their ideals to the concrete situation as it was evolving: anarchism was not merely something to believe in but something that had to be *lived*. Far from wishing to abolish the family, they wanted it "to be based on love and on feelings of honorable reciprocity."[26] The collectivist village communes that were set up in July 1936 in anarchist districts were administered by assemblies consisting of every able-bodied man and woman belonging to the working class: except for the inclusion of women, these were much like the medieval *concejo abierto* and *cabildo* of the communes of medieval Spain. And as far as morals were concerned, already in 1918 the anarchists of Andalusia neither smoked nor drank, opposed cock and bull fights, often favored naturism and vegetarianism, and stood for the protection of a slightly incongruous medley of "women, children, old men, trees and animals."[27]

Yet atavism remained strong, especially in a country such as Spain. The Latins in general and Spaniards in particular have never had much use for the concept of sexual equality; when the revolutionary pinch came, they reverted to type. George Orwell, describing Barcelona under anarchist rule in the early days of the Spanish Civil War, tells us:

> There were still women serving in the militias, though not very many. In the early battles they had fought side by side with the men as a matter of course. It is a thing that seems natural in times of revolution. Ideas were changing already, however. The militiamen had to be kept out of the riding-school while the women were drilling there because they laughed at the women and put them off. A few months earlier no one would have seen anything comic in a woman handling a gun.[28]

Even though Pablo Picasso joined the French Communist party after the Second World War and had always displayed his left-wing views in political matters, he made no secret of the fact that, as far as he was concerned, "there are only two kinds of women—goddesses and doormats." And one of his faithful female companions adds that "whenever he thought I might feel too much like a goddess, he did his best to turn me into a doormat." Only a Spaniard such as Picasso, whatever his political persuasion, could claim that "there's nothing so similar to one poodle dog as another poodle dog and that goes for women, too."[29]

In the last resort, anarchism displays its innermost femininity in its overall approach to life and behavior: the anarchist wants to *be*, whereas the communist wants to *do*, and from all times woman has placed greater emphasis on *being* and man on *doing*, on proving that he *differs* from the females that nursed him into life. At heart, and except for the anarcho-syndicalists, anarchism was essentially a retrograde movement, a more-or-less unconscious desire to return to a simpler, purer and more natural past—which explains the far greater destructive element in its makeup than can be found in Marxism. In its nostalgia for the past, it sees destruction as inherently constructive: paradoxically, violence will lead to the extinction of compulsion and to the rule of freedom. With the idea of the *Siglo de Oro*, the Golden Age of the past, in his mind, an anarchist commented on the burning of Málaga during the Spanish Civil War in the following terms:

> Yes, they are burning it down. And I tell you—not one stone will be left on another stone—no, not a plant nor even a cabbage will grow there, so that there may be no more wickedness in the world.[30]

Nestor Makhno, the formidable Ukrainian anarchist guerrilla leader, organized his rural communes in 1919 on the pattern of the Andalusian agricultural communes and handicraft cooperatives, but with the age-old examples of the Russian *obshchina* and *artel'* in mind. He was essentially a town hater, an implacable enemy of urban civilization longing for natural simplicity.[31] This "return to nature" theme, whether played by Queen Marie Antoinette at the Petit Trianon or by twentieth-century anarchists in their communes, is basically feminine, an atavistic unwillingness to cope with the challenge presented by the Promethean development of contemporary civilization. And yet, from William Godwin to Peter Kropotkin, anarchist leaders always preached the virtues of scientific and technological progress in the belief that the machine would free the worker from drudgery and soul-destroying exhaustion. But, in the long run, no anarchist movement was ever able to reconcile two diametrically opposed views of life. In the end, the anarchist does not want to conquer power but to destroy it; basically, woman in revolt adopts the same position, not so much out of innermost conviction as because she feels that she can never exert direct power for long before man wrests it away from her—except in the rare instances when an individual woman is born to it or inherits it from a close male relative.

To sum up: The contemporary technological revolution has made the problem of raw power more acute than ever—and therefore will keep the issue of anarchism as a philosophy alive for the foreseeable future—in that it has immensely accentuated the accumulation of power in the hands of the contemporary bureaucratic structures that rule the world. Such ubiquitous power of investigation, control, manipulation, and destruction of other human beings is vested today in the hands of the most democratic government that it would dazzle Genghis Khan at the height of his power. This technologically induced concentration of power has made many aspects of its exercise almost intolerable in our contemporary world and increased not only women's but many men's distrust of it.

CHAPTER

2

Revolution in Action

The French Revolution, the first great social conflagration in the history of Western civilization and the prototype of many others, did nothing to improve the condition of woman. The early revolutionary legislators were caught in a dilemma: having abolished the limited female suffrage in the prerevolutionary *États Provinciaux* and *États Généraux*, along with all other social privileges, they failed to follow through logically by setting up a universal suffrage because they were fundamentally afraid of woman. Two females, in particular, scared them: the hated Austrian Queen Marie Antoinette, and the fanatical Charlotte Corday who assassinated revolutionary leader Marat. The great men of the Revolution, Mirabeau, Danton, and Robespierre, were antifeminist to a man. Robespierre, in particular, the cold-blooded, tyrannical puritan dictator, disliked women in general and detested women of "loose morals." Of course, the great intellectual precursor of the Revolution and political mentor of Robespierre was Jean-Jacques Rousseau, whose revolutionary egalitarianism was reserved for men and did not extend to women. All of them labored for the emancipation of man, not woman whose "delicate constitution," in the words of the lecherous Mirabeau, "while perfectly suitable for the perpetuation of the species . . . restricts them to modest household chores and the sedentary inclination that this type of work requires."[1]

Yet, women did acquire equal rights in one respect—the right to have their heads chopped off, like those of their male counterparts. From Queen Marie Antoinette and Madame du Barry to high-minded revolutionaries like Madame Roland and Lucile Desmoulins, they were one and all carted off in the dreaded tumbrils to have their delicate necks severed with a total lack of elementary courtesy. One can understand why the widow of the philosopher Condorcet, in reply to Bonaparte's stinging remark that he did not like "women who meddled in

360

politics," should complain that "in a country where their heads are cut off, it was natural that they should want to know why."[2]

The irony was that many women had welcomed the Revolution. On August 7, 1789, Parisian women generously poured all their jewelry into the "Patriotic Gifts" coffers; as Carlyle put it, "unfortunate females give what they 'have amassed in loving.' "[3] But the more they gave to the budding Revolution, the less they received. Yet, without their active participation, there would have been no Revolution at all. Spontaneous revolutions cannot take place without a deep-seated discontent among the rank and file of women—which usually manifests itself in the shape of female mobs taking matters into their own hands and, with elemental power and determination, carving out a revolutionary path along which emboldened men eventually follow. In the first great riots in Paris, the bolder men joined the females, but cautiously disguised as women.[4] Woman, Mother Earth, is the ground man walks on, and when this naturally cautious, prudent, conservative element is shaken by uncontrollable anger, the effect on man is almost telluric, akin to a psychic earthquake. Female mobs can be terrifying, as they were in the French Revolution; as Carlyle painted it: "Your mob is a genuine outburst of Nature; issuing from, or communicating with, the deepest deep of Nature."[5]

Carlyle drew a remarkable picture of these enraged crowds that swept into the Hôtel de Ville of Paris before surging on as a tidal wave toward Versailles:

> A thought, or dim raw-material of a thought, was fermenting all night, universally in the female head, and might explode. In squalid garret, on Monday morning, Maternity awakes, to hear children weeping for bread. Maternity must forth to the streets. . . . In one of the Guardhouses of the Quartier Saint-Eustache, a "young woman" seizes a drum—for how shall National Guards give fire on women, on a young woman?· The young woman seizes the drum; sets forth beating it, "uttering cries relative to the dearth of grains." . . . All women gather and go; crowds storm all stairs, force out all women. . . .[6]

No one has described with greater eloquence the irresistible power of women's revolt, born of hunger and outrage at social injustice, propelling the more timid and oratorical men into concrete revolutionary action:

> And so, like snowbreak from the mountains, for every staircase is a melted brook, it storms; tumultuous, wild-shrilling, towards the Hôtel de Ville. . . . Grand it was, says Camille, to see so many

judiths, from eight to ten thousand of them in all, rushing out to search into the root of the matter! Not unfrightful it must have been; ludicro-terrific and most unmanageable. . . . The National Guards form on the outer stairs, with levelled bayonets; the ten thousand judiths press up, resistless. . . . The National Guard must do one of two things; sweep the Place de Grève with cannon, or else open to right and left. They open; the living deluge rushes in. . . .[7]

Led by the famous red-clad amazonian Théroigne de Mericourt, and knowing full well that the soldiers would hesitate to strike them, they sweep through the Hôtel de Ville, followed by the more timorous male rioters. Then on to Versailles, possessed by a particular hatred for a rival female, the Austrian queen, swearing that they will behead her, stick her head on a spear, and make cockades out of her guts; but when Lafayette appears on the balcony in order to save Marie Antoinette from the wild mob and bravely kisses her hand, a lightning change of mood takes place: the bold gesture is greeted with thunderous and tearful applause.[8]

Once the Revolution was on, however, there was no stopping it until it had come full circle. Now fully controlled by the males, once the female mobs had physically overthrown the remains of the ancien régime, the Revolution showed its true colors in reply to Théroigne's efforts to raise female battalions. In a striking article, the influential publication entitled *Révolutions de Paris* stated in February 1791:

Political freedom and civil rights are, so to speak, useless for women and therefore must not be granted to them. Destined to spend their entire lives in their father's house or that of their husband's, born in a condition of absolute dependence from birth to death, they have been endowed with only private virtues. . . . A woman belongs only to her home and family. Of all that takes place outside, she is entitled to know only what her parents or her husband choose to tell her.[9]

To a more forceful demand on the part of feminists for equal rights, the revolutionary leaders replied by an increasingly vocal expression of their own antifeminism. For Olympe de Gouges, the most representative feminist of the times who wrote a "Declaration of the Rights of Women," male revolutionaries had nothing but scorn when she moaned, "O my poor sex, O women who have in no way benefited from this revolution."[10] But when Charlotte Corday assassinated the dreaded Marat, the left-wing revolutionaries—"Montagnards"—reacted with an antifeminist violence born of atavistic fear; Olympe de

Gouges tried in vain to explain that by slamming the door to power and prestige in women's face, male revolutionaries condemned them to open "the door to crime." It was too late. On October 30, 1793, the all-powerful Convention, the revolutionary legislative assembly, closed all women's clubs and organizations, putting an end to any kind of organized feminist movement, just as it was getting into the full swing of the "Grande Terreur."[11]

A striking feature of the political slant of active feminism up to that time was its formal alliance with those left-wing revolutionaries who advocated a thoroughgoing social, as well as political, revolution. The *Républicaines révolutionnaires* struck up, against Danton and Robespierre, an alliance with the extremist "Club des Cordeliers," prompting their Girondin opponents to accuse them of being anarchists.[12] On October 29, eve of the suppression of all women's political organizations, Fabre d'Eglantine pointed out that these organizations were not made up of "mothers, daughters or sisters, but of adventuresses, emancipated girls, harlots and female grenadiers."[13] To which the Convention replied with thunderous applause. The remarkable ugliness of the *Républicaines révolutionnaires* horrified many of these worthies, and a police commissioner pointed out that "the Jacobins were fools to have enlisted the support of such strikingly repulsive women in defense of the revolution."[14]

Napoleon nailed woman's inferior social status in his enduring legal code, even though, at one point, he had to appeal to Frenchwomen's assistance to get one of his most unpopular measures through: the signing of a concordat with the pope, a step that even some of his most trusted and loyal military companions criticized violently.

Napoleon's genius had promptly understood what generations of forthcoming socialists would, in their turn, meditate upon: in the end, the French Revolution was defeated by the women's obstinate resistance, because it had neglected to take them into account. The basically religious and conservative outlook of the bulk of France's female population could not be overcome, and on that stubborn obstacle the French Revolution eventually foundered. In his work *La Femme*, the historian Michelet relates the revealing outburst of a young Frenchman:

> Frenchwomen are brought up to hate and despise what all Frenchmen love and believe in. Twice, Frenchwomen embraced, then abandoned and killed Revolution: once, in the sixteenth century [the Reformation], when it was a matter of freedom of

conscience; then again, at the end of the eighteenth century, when political freedom was concerned. They are chained to the past, without knowing too much about it.[15]

In order to be successful, forthcoming revolutions would have to enlist women's support or be doomed to failure. Even on tactical grounds, the presence of numerous women was advisable, inasmuch as it prevented police or armed forces from handling crowds too brutally—as was made symbolically evident when they stormed the Hôtel de Ville in Paris; this point was not lost on socialist leaders in many countries. The man who best understood this truth was the German socialist August Bebel, who shook a whole generation of patriarchally minded German workers by insisting that feminism was not a mere whim of spoiled bourgeois women but a profound historical necessity if social democracy was ever to succeed. Most of his fellow socialists derided his profeminist views, some with outright anger. But with the publication of his *Die Frau und der Sozialismus* (whose opening sentence reads, "From the beginning of time oppression has been the common lot of woman and the laboring man"),[16] he eventually won over to his side most of his colleagues, many of them undoubtedly moved by the pragmatic view that Bebel summarized by stating, in a speech to the Reichstag, that "victory will lie wherever woman takes a stand in the great social movement."[17]

This idea does not seem to have struck Karl Marx very forcibly. One searches in vain in his monumental *Das Kapital* for references to a specifically feminist problem; once in a while he will mention women along with child labor in order to make a point and will comment upon the fact that "woman's true qualities are warped to her disadvantage, and all the moral and delicate elements in her nature become the means for enslaving her and making her suffer."[18] But the true Marxist villain is capitalism, not patriarchalism or masculine privileges. God knows that Marx owed everything, except his talent, to his brave and self-sacrificing wife, Jenny von Westphalen, an aristocratic heiress who gave up wealth and social position out of love for "the Moor," as he was known to his intimates. He himself acknowledged that it was her determination that clinched their marriage: "My fiancée has fought for me the most bitter fights—fights which have almost undermined her health—against her pietistic, aristocratic relatives, to whom the Lord in Heaven and the Lord in Berlin are alike objects of worship."[19] Her reward was a life of misery and suffering, which she endured because of her love for him. Yet, when he began to expound his materialistic theories to her, she expressed typically feminine doubts as to the real value of philosophic systems in general and his in particular, as well as apprehension of his inclination toward extremism. To his claim that economics was the exclusive cause of everything, she could only wonder: "For what economic reasons had she married him? Obviously one must be motivated not by economic reasons alone."[20] She had long believed that revolutionary philosophers truly wanted to enthrone reason and science in place of myths and superstition; now she slowly discovered that, in typical masculine self-deception, they were in the process of creating a new form of mythology, a metaphysical ideology masquerading in the guise of a materialistic "scientific socialism." Her feminine realism saw through the sham performance and its probable consequences but "she smiled at the prospect with a tender, good-humored irony . . . that was his affair. She had married him, not his philosophy."[21]

Friedrich Engels, rather than Marx, is the one who looked deeper into the problem of woman and developed a comprehensive theory of *The Origin of the Family* based, unfortunately for his theory, on the now outdated speculations of the anthropologist Lewis H. Morgan, who claimed that the monogamic family was a late development, preceded by the sib.[22] From these false premises, Engels' imagination took its flight and wove a theory centered around the idea that masculine and feminine characteristics were merely the result of capitalistic society. The savage capitalistic male had, at some point in the transition from matrilinear to patrilinear society, brought about the overthrow of mother-right which "was the world-historical defeat of the female sex."[23] From this, Marx was led to conclude that "the modern family contains in germ not only slavery but . . . it contains in miniature all the contradictions which later extend throughout society and its state."[24] And he added: "Social progress can be measured with precision by the social position of the female sex"[25]—which is why it is usually higher in the most primitive societies!

As a result, they all chorused the same litanies. "Marriage is sexual slavery" (Bebel); "Marriage differs from prostitution in that one is purchase and the other hire" (Engels).[26] In the *Communist Manifesto*, Marx and Engels took the bull by the horns:

> Abolition of the family! Even the most Radical grow hot over this shameful intention of the Communists. On what does the present bourgeois family rest? On capital, on private gain. It exists in its complete development only for the bourgeoisie; but it finds its complement in the proletariats' forced want of family life, and in public prostitution. . . . The bourgeois ways of speaking about the family and education, about the sacred relation of parents and children, grow the more sickening, the more, in consequence of

the progress of industry, all family bonds are torn asunder for the proletariat. . . . The bourgeois sees in his wife a mere instrument of production. He hears that instruments of production are to be exploited in common, and naturally cannot imagine but that women will share the same fate. He does not guess that this is the very problem, to abolish the position of women as mere instruments of production.[27]

And, ironically, the bourgeois was doing just that—abolishing the position of women as mere instruments of production and, on the contrary, idling them and raising them up to be passive, nonworking status symbols. But then, neither Marx nor Engels ever let facts stand in their way when they wanted to prove a doctrinal point. In fact, one should not take too seriously the sincerity of these apostles of revolution; the *tactical* advantage of marrying feminism and the cause of socialism was not lost on them. As one of them expressed it, "Let Socialists espouse the emancipation of women and women will be the foes of capitalism and devotees of socialism."[28]

This tactical policy paid off handsomely. If Jenny von Westphalen had married Karl Marx the man and not his philosophy, other women married Marxism without reservation. It was in the very Russia that Marx feared and despised that a woman, Vera Zasulich, founded the first Russian Marxist organization with Plekhanov and Axelrod; and it was in Russia, in 1917 Petrograd, that his brainchild came to violent birth as a concrete historical phenomenon when women workers organized an all-female meeting at the Lesnoy textile plant to plan the inevitable insurrection.

It sounds like a replay of the early stages of the French Revolution when female mobs routed the National Guard. The Bolsheviks and other left-wing parties had condemned the forthcoming revolution in advance, as doomed to inevitable failure. But, never mind, the female workers took matters into their own hands. On March 8, 1917, women workers poured out of the textile factories of Petrograd and enlisted the assistance of male workers who had just been locked out of the Putilov plant. A few hours later, a powerful mob made up almost exclusively of women managed to break through police barriers and pour into the Nevsky Prospekt, looting the bakeries. All the male left-wing political leaders were caught by surprise and most of them rushed in to join the revolting crowds. On March 9, the Mezhrayonka —a Social Democratic organization dedicated to bringing together the feuding Mensheviks and Bolsheviks, and also the most influential with female workers—issued a call for a general strike, but it was the infuriated women who had started it all and had given the men courage enough to defy the police and the Cossacks.

Even then, however, the men who joined the crowds lacked leadership since the revolutionary leaders themselves had not foreseen the power of the spontaneous female rising. In his exile in Zurich, Lenin remained skeptical for a long time; and even after the tzar's formal abdication, he wrote to one of his women followers, Alexandra Kollontai, that no change of any great importance had taken place in Russia. It took the men a while to join the female-initiated movement. Having triggered the insurrection, Russian women workers then let the men take over the more brutal aspects of the unfolding revolution. But they remained active, on both sides of the civil war. Female battalions defended the Winter Palace against the Bolsheviks, and women political leaders emerged, such as Maria Spiridonova, who led the Left Social Revolutionaries in their attempt to block the dictatorial takeover of the Bolsheviks.

But if the Bolshevik takeover was finally successful, it was largely the result of the mass action of other revolutionary women, shaped and organized by the first conference of working and peasant women held in Moscow in November 1918. Women were enlisted for military service and actually took part in combat on numerous occasions; the repeal of the attacking White Guards at Lugansk was mostly women's work. The women of Petrograd played an important part in the repeal of General Iudenich's White Army; organized in regular battalions, women dug trenches, organized nursing corps, strung barbed wire on barricades, provided the famous "stopping detachments" which turned deserters around and sent them back to the front. On this Petrograd front alone, over fifteen hundred women were killed, wounded, or captured.[29]

Women revolutionaries who stood apart from the crowd and became political leaders in their own right usually displayed typical feminine traits—a certain abhorrence for useless violence, unless fired by some hysterical passion (Maria Spiridonova killing General Luzhensky and masterminding the assassination of the German ambassador, Count Mirbach, for instance). They displayed a taste for changes along evolutionary rather than brutally revolutionary lines, impatience with dogmatic hair-splitting and empty intellectualism, a lesser emphasis than men on political differentiation and a greater one on the unifying basics of the revolutionary movement. They also focused their feminine intuition on personalities and on concrete issues—bread, shelter, fuel, peace—rather than abstract ones. At the 1907 International Congress in Stuttgart, the great Rosa Luxemburg pointed out Lenin to

Clara Zetkin, a fellow German Communist leader: "Have a good look at that man. That's Lenin. Observe his obstinate, self-willed skull." As Clara Zetkin stated later, "Rosa was distinguished by her accurate artist's eye."[30] When a nebulous peace conference was suggested at the 1907 Russian party congress in London, Rosa Luxemburg poured scorn on this suggestion of a platform for endless debates:

> At this conference, naturally, only a handful of fighting cocks living abroad would rival in clamoring for the ear and soul of the German trustees, and to expect anything of these cocks is pure delusion. They are already so involved in quarrels and so embittered, that a general confab will merely give them an opportunity to unburden themselves of their old, oldest and freshest insults.[31]

But when Soviet terror became an established and permanent feature of the new communist regime in Russia under the leadership of the dreaded and dreadful Djerzhinsky, she was profoundly indignant and protested: "Terror has not crushed us. How can you put your trust in terror?" And she exclaimed with anguish, "But how can Joseph—Djerzhinsky—be so cruel?"[32]

Rosa Luxemburg was of Polish Jewish extraction, a naturalized German. Impatient with the bourgeois moderation of Germany's prewar Social Democrats, she gathered around her the nucleus of the future Spartakusbund in which Clara Zetkin was entrusted with the organization of women followers. Rosa fought against the First World War tooth and nail, believing it to be fatal to the welfare of the European labor movement; in which she proved to be far less perceptive than Lenin who correctly foresaw the unique opportunity afforded by this collapse of the old social order for decisive revolutionary change. Regardless of the shortcomings of her forecasts, Rosa remained both a true revolutionary and a humane one, who was soon horrified by the dictatorial grip of Soviet terror in Russia; perhaps earlier than anyone, she saw what was coming and delineated the inevitable process:

> In place of the representative bodies created by general, popular elections, Lenin and Trotsky have laid down the Soviets as the only true representation of the laboring masses. But with the repression of political life in the land as a whole, life in the soviets must also become more and more crippled. Without general elections, without unrestricted freedom of press and assembly, without a free struggle of opinion, life dies out in every public institution, becomes a mere semblance of life, in which only the bureaucracy remains as the active element . . . such conditions must inevitably cause a brutalization of public life.[33]

This from the leading German Communist, but a feminine one; at heart, she was an anarchist who was too intelligent to believe that anarchism could work.

Disregarding her merciless criticism, Lenin could not help remarking that "in spite of her mistakes she was—and remains for us—an eagle."[34] Lenin and Rosa Luxemburg—male and female revolutionaries, the contentious, differentiating, masculine *doer;* and the profoundly humane, instinctive, feminine *being.* Rosa, had she ever reached power, would have trusted the people; Lenin could not. Even Karl Kautsky, Rosa's German Communist partner, could not, and he agreed with Lenin that "Socialist consciousness is an element imported into the proletarian class struggle from outside," that is, from the (usually male) intellectuals who are the true "revolutionary bacillus."[35] In short, the proletariat is not so much a mass of impoverished and suffering humanity in need of uplift as the inert raw material to be shaped and used unsparingly in the concrete realization of the intellectuals' wildest dreams; no true woman could take that view. The typical self-alienation of modern man that Marxist thinkers blame on the capitalist mode of production is, in fact, a typically masculine phenomenon—the alienation man already feels as a child when he begins to realize that he must differentiate himself from the person closest to him, that is, in the nature of things, a woman. Where the little girl feels with utter certainty "I am" and identifies with the mother, the boy comes to understand that he is *not* a female and that he must struggle, with greater or lesser success, toward self-identification: he must *become.* In that sense, ideological revolution comes easily to the masculine mind but not to the feminine mentality which can only be moved by specific, concrete grievances—but once moved, will not stop until the old order is destroyed. In another part of the world, in India for example, it was largely the women who arose against the British Raj and signified, in the early 1930s, that its rule was eventually doomed. Jawaharlal Nehru was a witness to this:

> Our women came to the front and took charge of the struggle. Women had always been there, of course, but now there was an avalanche of them, which took not only the British government but their own menfolk by surprise. Here were these women, women of the upper or middle class, leading sheltered lives in their homes, peasant women, working class women, rich women, poor women, pouring out in their tens of thousands in defiance of government order and police lathi. It was not only that display of courage and daring, but what was even more surprising was the organizational power they showed.[36]

As this instance exemplifies, along with the French, Russian, and other revolutions, all great revolutionary movements are triggered by earthquaking shifts in women's feelings—when their natural conservatism shifts to indignation and desire for fundamental change—only to be promptly and invariably usurped by male leadership which directs them into the procrustean beds constructed beforehand by their intellectual doctrines.

CHAPTER

3

The Communist Reality

Contemporary political ideologies are the psychological equivalents of the departed mythologies of former times. A myth can be defined by its connection with a temporal system: a myth always deals with past events, but events of such great symbolic importance that they have permanent validity and combine in one timeless whole past, present and future. A political or socioeconomic ideology can be seen under the same light: while historians deal with the dead, irreversible past, political ideologies see this past as having present and even future value, permanently efficient to the extent that it conditions and throws new light—however distorting—on present and future events.

But the *revolutionary* nature of contemporary ideologies introduced some fundamental differences. The concept of revolution, in the modern sense of the word, is deeply rooted in the Zoroastrian-biblical-Christian tradition. Revolutionary ideologies actually spring from the most uncompromisingly masculine trend of thought which was launched by the Persians and the Hebrew prophets at the beginning of the Iron Age, and which put to flight the cyclical myths of the female-oriented Bronze Age—the *linear* aspect of historical development, the eschatological view that there is a beginning and an end of the world, that the world will undergo a complete upheaval of revolutionary proportion, and that what matters is the final outcome of the process at the end of time, rather than the painful stages leading up to it—hence the revolutionary propensity to sacrifice the means to the end. In short, historical evolution moves from initial evil to final good, thanks to a long struggle between the powers of light and those of darkness, implying violence, and a long, patient, chiliastic waiting for the ultimate millennium. Even stripped of former religious transcendentalism, the ideological belief of Marxism betrays its uncompromisingly prophetic origins, betrays also its apocalyptic vision—an imminent catastrophe ending, thanks to devastating ordeals, in ultimate redemption—now viewed as the classless society and the mythical withering away of the state.

Thus in Marxism we have in concentrated and pseudo-scientific form the masculine ideology that has been able to capitalize on the revolutionary discontent of modern womenfolk, provoked by the dislocation of traditional social structures and modes of living, and able to siphon its energy into the concrete actualization of its ideology. In reward, modern communism has granted women a new status, different from the "bourgeois" status inherited from the early days of the industrial revolution, a status modeled on that of the most successful and durable totalitarian state of antiquity, Sparta.

In the Spartan model, man the citizen becomes a slave of the state, and so do woman and child. A rough equality of sorts is established between them, not because her status rises up to his, but because his sinks down to hers; they are both equal in their total subordination to the state. This is amply illustrated by the fate of woman in the Spartan regimes established by the twentieth century's great revolutions.

The clearest indication of what the Spartan model implies, outside a Marxist context, is furnished by the brief experiment made in Germany under National Socialism. Contrary to widespread belief, Hitler had no intention of reestablishing the strong patriarchalism that would have stood as a protecting barrier between the individual and an all-powerful state. He did encourage women to turn themselves into pro-creating cows, in the racial interest of the German nation—how could he get a sufficient number of soldiers if the women did not produce? But he also attempted to destroy the autonomous family as effectively as Sparta did, enslaving both males and females as individuals in the overriding interest of the Third Reich. German women were no more repressed than the men and, on the whole, were the most ardent admirers and supporters of National Socialism, irrational and hysterical pseudo-romanticism. A wartime economy had to make full use of every ounce of energy that members of both sexes possessed and no family considerations stood in the way. *Mutatis mutandi,* the same principle applies in every totalitarian state, whether reactionary or revolutionary, fascist or Marxist.

Russia, on the other hand, was the first country to go through the Marxist-Leninist mill and the specifically Russian relationship of the sexes, as historical tradition had shaped it, had some bearing on the course of the revolution itself. Until Peter the Great, Russian women were treated, by and large, very much as Muslim women; locked up in their haremlike *terems*, they had seen their social status and influence decline sharply since the old days preceding the Mongol invasions and their orientalization under the dominion of the Golden Horde. It was Peter the Great, the first Russian revolutionary, who abolished their seclusion, forced them to mingle with men in public and take part openly in social life—this as a means to Westernize his barbaric realm. The fact that Russia was spared the historical phases through which Western Europe had to proceed—Middle Ages, Renaissance, Reformation—made this improvement easier to achieve in spite of the fierce resistance of the boyars.

The long succession of empresses who followed in Peter's footsteps promoted education for women and in all respects attempted to train Russia's upper class to imitate the French pattern in its social relations between the sexes. However artificial this may have been, this steady upgrading of the Russian woman in the eighteenth century paved the way for the appearance of a new type of self-reliant female in the following century, a woman endowed with a strong personality and a spirit of initiative rarely displayed in history.[1] With the coming of the Decembrists and such dedicated women as Maria Volkonskaya, the movement for the emancipation of Russian females became part and parcel of the general revolutionary movement. There never was a specifically feminist movement in opposition to, and against the will of, menfolk as in the West; Russian women were far more energetic and dedicated to overall causes and ideologies than their Western sisters, quite prepared to fight for whatever they believed in—and not only with pen and ink, but also with fire and blood in an atmosphere of autocratic oppression. Maurice Hindus put it this way:

> I can think of no other movement in history where men and women lived on such terms of intimacy and camaraderie, of mutual respect and trust, and worked with such sublime selflessness for a common purpose. There were no discriminations or rivalries between the sexes. . . . Under such circumstances feminism in Russia never could assume the narrow form that it did in other lands—that is a battle against the domination of men.[2]

Russia's Byzantine inheritance had something to do with this better understanding between the sexes, if only because of the extensive feminine component of Byzantine culture and the respect of Greek men for their women in Constantinople. Unfortunately, the feminine nature of Orthodox Christianity, its one-sided emphasis on gorgeous paraphernalia, on glittering robes, ikons, and jewelry, on all the ecclesiastical magic and mystery of Babylonian splendor at the expense of moral sermonizing and inner spirituality, also doomed it as a bulwark and support for the Russian soul in times of great stress. The mere fact that Russian Orthodoxy dispensed with sermons and moral preaching symbolizes the fact that it had no ethical content. It had definite emotional appeal for women, but none for men. They were longing for a new ideological code of ethics, a new morality that would give meaning to their lives in place of the debased magico-mystical atmosphere of an ultraconservative and petrified church that had no message whatsoever to impart—in fact, that never even sent missionaries to evangelize other people.

In short, the Byzantine legacy that had done so much to elevate the Russian woman as an individual was also responsible for the lack of ethical framework that men absolutely require. A masculine reaction, a new Islam, was in order and it came with the 1917 October Revolution, along with a new Marxist-Leninist code of Spartan ethics in which the masculine element predominated absolutely.

Although a puritan in sexual matters, one who was actually shocked by the outspoken views of some of his female allies in politics on the matter of free love—more especially those of Inessa Armand and the beautiful Alexandra Kollontai—Lenin at first lost no time in launching the legal emancipation of Russian women by striking down the major bulwark of civilized "bourgeois" life: the family, the one sociobiological entity that could stand as a protective shield between the individual and the all-destroying revolutionary state. He issued two decrees, in December 1917 and October 1918, establishing civil marriage as the only legally recognized form—an entry in the public marriage register was all that was needed—and making divorce a mere formality, obtainable immediately at the request of one of the partners—the famous "postcard" divorce. Children, however, were taken under the paternalistic wing of the state with no distinction made between legitimate and illegitimate; the law was no longer concerned with adultery. Starting in 1920, abortions were allowed without any restrictions whatsoever. Needless to say, males lost all their former prerogatives and the legal emancipation of women was bolstered by their economic liberation when they were put to work outside the home; a few nurseries and day-care centers were established to assist them, along with extensive maternity leaves with full salary. The long-range goal was to emancipate the younger generation from parental influence and make it amenable to systematic Marxist-Leninist indoctrination. The Communist party became the surrogate father of all children, and to the party were transferred all the patriarchal privileges hitherto belonging to the males. Parents of both sexes were stripped of all legal authority over their children, who were induced to show no respect for them. A young woman who went to school in Moscow testified:

> In Moscow in 1921 there was a positive Soviet approach. . . . I was nine and we were left alone. We worked on the Dalton plan. The teacher had no authority whatsoever. We were broken into units of four or five of our own choosing. . . . The children in school had the feeling that they couldn't rely on their families. There was no such thing. The government encouraged it and said that it was the government who was supposed to take care of the children. We were completely liberated from our parents. We felt no responsibility to them.[3]

And as early as 1919, Soviet authorities decreed that "the family has ceased to be a necessity both to its members and for the state."[4]

In those days, the sexual-ethical radicalism of Alexandra Kollontai held full sway; women had been "nationalized" along with all the other means of production. Although her numerous written works on the topic of free love repelled Lenin personally, his political designs compelled him to go along with the movement, insofar as it was the quickest and easiest way to destroy in depth the old society which he abhorred.[5] It is worth recalling, incidentally, that Alexandra Kollontai was no proletarian but the daughter of a tzarist general and came from a genuine "bourgeois" strata; no real proletarian woman could have thought in terms of "sexual" liberation along those lines.

In a few short years the great experiment began to fall apart. Men, stripped of their former paternal power and responsibilities, became neglectful toward their families and left the burden of the upbringing of the younger generation to the women—wives and mothers, usually assisted by the irreplaceable *babushkas*, older female relatives, who substituted for the planned but usually nonexistent collective day-care centers. The collapse of family solidarity resulted in the mushrooming of juvenile delinquency on a staggering scale, and far from raising the status of woman, the revolution proved to be utterly demoralizing. Rather than freeing woman, it had freed *man* from sexual restraints and domestic responsibility, the two great gifts of stable marriage to woman. The male revolutionary leaders had their pat justification: "Lust is the collaborator of atheism; it will destroy social and bourgeois prejudices and regenerate feminine psychology."[6] In fact, the new Soviet female was sexually oppressed as she had never been before. A perfect illustration of the revolutionary male attitude toward woman is the official decree of the Soviet of Saralof which stated, in February 1919:

Beginning with March 1, 1919, the right to possess women between the ages of 17 and 32 is abolished. . . . The former owners of women retain the right to use them without awaiting their turn. . . . By virtue of the present decree no woman can any longer be considered as private property and all women become the property of the nation. . . . All women thus put at the disposition of the nation must, within three days after publication of the present decree, present themselves in person at the address indicated. . . . Male citizens do not have the right to use women more often then prescribed, that is, three times a week and for three hours each time. . . . Any man who wishes to make use of a nationalized woman must hold a certificate issued by the administrative Council. . . . [7]

If ever woman has become a purely sexual object for the male, it is in such revolutionary circumstances. In 1918, for example, the Soviet of Vladimir decreed that males could choose their conjugal partners "regardless of the latter's consent."[8]

Woman became not only a sexual object but an economic tool as well. The new Soviet woman was compelled to work eight hours a day outside the home—in addition to bearing and raising children, cleaning house, cooking, washing, and searching for largely nonexistent food and clothing. As recently as a half century after the October Revolution, it is estimated that women in Moscow still spend 50 percent of their off-work time shopping, cooking, and washing laundry. Since party membership was overwhelmingly male, there was little or no sympathy wasted on the overburdened females, and male political careers in the Communist party usually progressed on the wreckage of discarded wives and mistresses. In exchange for a few formal rights, Soviet women have been among the most exploited human groups in our century. A startling statistic given out in the Moscow Kommunist of November 1963 reveals that at the turn of the century, the average lifespan of a Russian woman was two years less than that of the average man, and that in the early 1960s, it was eight years less. The author of the article places the responsibility for this relative reduction of Soviet woman's life expectancy squarely on multiple abortions and "the traumas of living conditions and working conditions."[9]

Meanwhile, with the consolidation of the revolution under Stalin, the collapse of the sexual revolution became institutionalized into a formal counterrevolution. The bezprizorny, juvenile delinquents, the tragic result of the breakdown of family life, who roamed large areas of Russia in wolflike packs and terrorized their elders, were hunted down and massacred without pity; the death sentence was applied to all delinquent children above the age of twelve. Many voices were now fearlessly raised in favor of a reestablishment of strict laws to protect the family system; it became clear that the social chaos resulting from this catastrophic license would doom the Five-Year Plan on which Soviet Russia's hopes were based. Discipline was restored in the schools. The same witness quoted previously tells us that, around 1928,

> the teacher's authority became greater and greater. . . . As time went on—my later experiences in school—the political situation changed and it became something that was imposed on you. The democratic method [of choosing student representatives] was abolished. The representatives of the Party were assigned to the school.[10]

Even the Soviet writers began a long campaign against free love "which can never be really free and always ends in disappointment and harmful situations."[11] The brutal contempt of Soviet men for their victimized female consorts was vividly portrayed in the novels of Nikitin, Gladkov, and Pilnyak—along with the hoary theme of the female seductress whose sexual wiles emasculate men and divert them from their productive tasks and ideals. The stage was set for a full-fledged restoration of the old family virtues and even Lenin's well-known dislike for sexual promiscuity was invoked. Premarital chastity and conjugal fidelity were openly praised; marriage-breakers and promiscuous men were likely to be expelled from the party and find their careers ruined. Soviet writers began to shun descriptions of passionate love; even the chastest kiss was hardly mentioned and all new editions of the novels of the early phase of the revolution were carefully expurgated. The new puritanism actually did as much to restore dignity to the Soviet woman as the total lack of sexual restraint in the early 1920s had done to degrade her. Formerly known as a "bourgeois capitalistic slave invention," marriage was now officially extolled:

> The State cannot exist without the family. Marriage is a positive value for the Socialist Soviet State only if the partners see in it a lifelong union. So-called free-love is a bourgeois invention. . . . Moreover, marriage receives its full value for the state only if there is progeny, and the consorts experience the highest happiness of parenthood.[12]

Reverence for the elders was similarly enjoined:

Young people should respect their elders, especially their parents. . . . The respect and care of parents is an essential part of the Comsomol morale.[13]

All experiments with the raising of children in state institutions were declared failures, justifying the revival of the old-fashioned monogamic family:

Under our present conditions there is no doubt that the home offers a more stimulating environment for the development of the infant than the asylum. Not only have we decreased the death rate in this way [by placing the institutional children in private homes] but we have insured normal development to a much larger proportion of babies, since in almost every case our asylum-trained babies were both mentally and physically backward.[14]

On June 27, 1936, new legislation was promulgated reestablishing the family officially as the nuclear basis of the state. Divorce became more difficult to obtain; tax exemptions and various subsidies helped families with many children—the declining birthrate, in Great Russia especially, alarmed Soviet leaders, as it still does today. Abortion became again a criminal offense, except for strictly medical purposes; oddly enough, this decision was put up for free discussion in plants, offices, and kolkhozes, and was vigorously criticized by the women; the law was promulgated nevertheless. Obviously, Stalin wished to strengthen the Soviet state, increasingly threatened by Germany's armed might. By encouraging women to breed more frequently, the terrible gap made in the population by the revolution, the civil war, and the political purges could be partly filled. In addition, the strengthening of marital and family ties made it possible to apply the principle of collective responsibility for the behavior of one of its members to the entire family, which became a virtual hostage of the state.

On August 4, 1943, the Soviet authorities declared that coeducation on the elementary and secondary levels would be abolished, justifying this decision by the following comment:

A boy must be prepared for service in the Red Army while he is still at school. He receives special physical and purely military training for a stern soldier's life. . . . What of the girl? She is essentially a mother. School must give the girl special knowledge of human anatomy, physiology, psychology, pedagogy and hygiene.[15]

The realities of wartime circumstances made such a startling change in outlook inevitable; with it went an intensification of the affective bonds within the family, as enjoined in a textbook issued to teachers in the 1940s:

> The feeling of love for father and mother is the first noble feeling which arises naturally in a child and which plays a central role in the life of every individual . . . our children must appreciate how honorable is the title of mother in our land. Only in the Soviet Union has the state established the title of "mother-heroine" [to those who have ten children or more] and the bestowal of orders and medals on mothers of many children.[16]

In other words, Soviet woman had reverted to the role of prize cow and no professional achievement could bring her the honors that biological fertility brought in its train.

From then on, laws were passed, altered, or repealed without taking too much into account the specific welfare of women; only the welfare of the Soviet Union came into consideration. If the rulers in Moscow feel that the birthrate is too low, women are invited to breed more and induced to do so by new financial advantages. After World War II, the authorities adopted, for a while, a more indifferent attitude in population matters. Abortion was allowed again in 1956, although not encouraged—its legalization was designed to put an end to far more dangerous black market operations. In the early 1970s, however, there are signs that Soviet leaders are becoming alarmed at the rapidly declining birthrate of the ethnic Russians and other Slavs. Early in 1971, demographer Viktor Perevedentsev quoted the following statistics in *Literaturnaya Gazeta:* in the decade of the 1960s, the Russian population had increased by 13 percent while the Central Asian Muslims increased by 52 percent; he added that while only 8 percent of Byelorussian women married as early as eighteen, 54 percent did so in Turkmenia.[17] Conclusion: Russian women were invited to get to work producing more children by marrying earlier, strongly encouraged to do so by the institution of the order of "Motherhood Glory" and the granting of the "Motherhood Medal."[18]

As in Sparta twenty-five hundred years ago, bachelorhood is almost a crime in the contemporary Soviet. In Sparta bachelors were excluded from the rolls of voting citizens and were compelled to remain nude in public, even in midwinter; *Literaturnaya Gazeta* virtually accused them of being traitors to Soviet society, selfish men who rob those who are married and support children,[19] and, for a clincher, stated that they suffer from special neurosis and a shorter lifespan—a medical fact confirmed in Western societies.

Thus, in the Spartan model, women are made full use of to the point of being downright exploited. This, in spite of the fact that Marx had accused the bourgeois of looking upon his wife as "nothing but an instrument of production," and had added: "He never dreams for a moment that our main purpose is to ensure that women shall no longer occupy the position of mere instruments of production."[20] He should visit Soviet Russia today. Ironically, Soviet women almost appear to enjoy it; busy night and day, dog tired after a hard day's work, they are too exhausted even to think about their plight. Nor is it different in other Marxist lands; in Red Albania's textile factories, 90 percent of the labor force is female; most of the field hands are also females. Meanwhile, according to a foreign observer, Tirana's "cafés are crammed with men who can stretch a doll's cup of Turkish coffee throughout a whole steaming morning. They stand on their hundreds of street corners idly gossiping for hours on end, presumably waiting until their women get through doing the work."[21]

Whatever equality between the sexes is achieved in Marxist lands is due merely to the fact that their relatively inefficient regimes cannot afford the supreme capitalist luxury: a large idle female population, a wasteful policy made possible by far greater overall productivity in Western societies. The result is that womanpower in Soviet Russia is a far more essential component of the national economy than it is in "bourgeois" countries. In fact, almost half the jobs are held by women —but what jobs! While it is true that some are engineers and technicians, the fact remains that women are mostly confined to low-paying manual work: street sweeping, bricklaying, garbage collecting, coal mining, ship loading; they are steamfitters, riveters, welders. In fact, the truth seems to be that labor is divided, by and large, along sexual lines; in many instances, women do the work and men oversee it. Labor laws discriminate in women's favor to the extent that they get day-care centers for their children and paid leave of absence for pregnancy, but they usually do the heavy work while male workers operate the machinery—fork lifts, cranes, bulldozers, trucks, mechanical diggers. Eighty percent of Soviet women are engaged in sheer physical labor—justified in the immediate postwar period when manpower was scarce but still true in the 1970s when the same need no longer exists.

Soviet women rarely reach positions of power and authority in their chosen field; in such positions as foreman or shop steward, men outnumber women seven to one. As one Western journalist put it, "In practice the Soviet woman is a drudge whose work has given her face the complexion and texture of tanned cowhide and her fingers the look of raw carrots just pulled from the ground."[22] As for political power, women can vote for the single-candidate slates like the men—but of real power at the top, women's share of the Communist party's Central

Committee in the 1960s was merely 3 percent!

One fact, evident in our Western societies as it has been in all societies throughout history, seems just as true in Soviet Russia and other communist states; a sort of Gresham's Law applies to the job market as it does to finances where "bad money drives out good." Any profession in which women are numerous or in a majority is socially devalued and brings in lesser financial rewards. The Soviet statistics are eloquent: out of approximately 600,000 medical practitioners, 75 percent are women; whereas in the United States, only 7 percent of the medical doctors are female. While the medical profession commands prestige and high remuneration in Western countries, it enjoys low status in the Soviet Union where the starting salary of the average physician barely amounts to more than half that of a skilled worker. Male physicians are far from being considered the cream of Soviet manpower: "This was why . . . a man with a suspicious social background could get into medical school although he couldn't get into an engineering school or scientific institute."[23]

The same applies, of course, to schoolteaching, in which women also outnumber men. A study of the situation reveals the following:

> The doctor is next to lowest paid of professionals; only school teachers are lower. The cream of Soviet manpower is encouraged to go into other work, and in recent years it has become something of a matter of apology for a male student to enter medical school, such an action being interpreted as an indication either that he had not the ability to become an engineer, or that he is politically unreliable. This is largely the explanation of the fact that since the Revolution the proportion of women doctors has risen from ten per cent to over seventy-five percent.[24]

This is not all; even *within* the medical corps, sexual discrimination is blatant:

> Perhaps fewer than twenty percent of doctors are members of the Party. These Party members are almost exclusively medical administrators. The administrators, in turn, are also predominantly male. The pattern which is evolving is that of a medical profession which is composed of non-Party, female, practicing physicians, and Party, male, medical administrators.[25]

Still, medicine is about the highest the average woman can reach; the majority are field hands on the collective farms, "the most poorly rewarded and most exploited of any except the residents of forced labor camps. The woman collective farmer has the least attractive life of any of the rank-and-file Soviet citizens."[26]

The Soviet Russian male is firmly in the saddle, in full control of the party apparatus and of the Soviet social structure. Soviet women have become again, willy-nilly, what they have always been: beasts of burden. But we must introduce an important caveat; it would be a mistake to overlook what some shrewd foreign observers of Soviet Russia have pointed out: the remarkable resemblance between modern Soviet women and the picture drawn by Tolstoy in *The Cossacks:*

> The Cossack looks on woman as an instrument of his well-being: he permits young girls to gad about, but he compels his peasant woman to work for him from youth even to advanced old age, and he regards a woman with an Eastern demand to submission and labor. As the result of such a view, the woman who develops intensively both physically and morally even though she is externally submissive, obtains, as generally in the East, an influence and weight in domestic life that is beyond comparison greater than in the West. . . .
>
> [The man] feels confusedly that everything he uses and calls his own is the product of this [woman's] work, and that it is in the power of the woman, mother or wife, whom he counts his serf, to deprive him of everything that is of any use to him. Moreover, the continual masculine, heavy work and the worries that are entrusted to her hands have given a particularly independent, masculine character to the . . . woman and to a surprising degree have developed in her physical strength, decisiveness and firmness of character.[27]

This appears to be the case with most Soviet women today.

Revolution struck China in a different context. Unlike half-Westernized and Christian Russia, China had an immensely old civilization whose disintegration early in the century was a far more traumatic event than even Russia's social revolution: it was the collapse of a completely autonomous, self-contained civilization stretching all the way back to the dawn of the Iron Age. It was a long drawn-out process which started with the overthrow of the Manchu dynasty in 1911 and is still going on in the 1970s, more than two decades after the communists seized power. Chinese civilization and its essentially Confucian core began to fall apart early in the century under the impact of Western civilization, long before Marxism made its influence felt. This disintegration struck the cities rather than the immense countryside where the rural populations went on living as before, faithful to the old traditions, to the extent permitted by the appalling anarchy and warlordism that had settled on the land. The basic innovation of Mao

Tse-tung's Red regime was to provoke in the countryside the same sociopolitical upheaval that the impact of the West had spontaneously provoked in the urban centers, an immense tidal wave that engulfed the hundreds of millions of Chinese peasants for whom the disappearance of the Son of Heaven from Peking's Forbidden City had been, until then, a remote and nebulous event.

The fundamental self-appointed task confronting the new rulers in the early 1950s was the metamorphosis of a thoroughly decentralized people, enjoying self-rule to the utmost thanks to the autonomy of its clans, into a unified nation, forcibly propelled into a new form of civilization by an all-powerful centralized state. This task could only be fulfilled by the complete destruction of the traditional kinship system and the ideology that upheld it. In short, the Chinese Reds were faced with the same problem that confronted the Russian Bolsheviks when they came to power: in order to sweep away the old order, they had to pulverize the traditional family structure by freeing women from their traditional obligations as wives (and privileges as mothers and mothers-in-law) and by setting the younger generations against the old in the great Cultural Revolution of the late 1960s. Here again, the "liberation" of woman was designed to destroy the old fabric and emancipate youth from its traditional reverence for oldsters, without really giving woman greater scope for her talents in the new structure to come.

Traditional Chinese society had been completely centered around its kinship system of clannish relations, and therefore divided into innumerable autonomous and mutually exclusive kinship cells—the opposite of the mass society that prevails increasingly in the West and that Marxism attempts to bring about forcibly whenever it comes to power. The Chinese kinship system was based on its peculiar matrimonial concepts; marriage implied basically that the husband's family acquired a daughter-in-law *(ch'u hsi fu)* against payment to her family of a "body price," whose control over her, and therefore protection, then lapsed forever.[28] In Hopei Province, a common saying had it that "in a betrothal, when a daughter goes out, an ox comes in."[29] There could be no divorce, and all the bride could look forward to was motherhood, as many sons as possible, and, eventually, the satisfaction of becoming a mother-in-law in her turn. In this "patriarchal" context, tension was, in fact, rather between mother and daughter-in-law than between husband and wife. The gradual introduction of divorce in the cities after the overthrow of the Manchus, and its swift implementation throughout the countryside after the Reds took over in 1949, implied the potential liberation of woman—not so much from the male tyranny of her husband, as liberation from the future half of her own self as potential mother-in-law. But this was consonant with the complete destruction of the traditional kinship system with its clan and extended family.

The process of erosion of the traditional structure was already under way in the 1920s when Mao Tse-tung started his political career in the Chinese countryside. Considerably shaken by the anti-Confucian revolution triggered by the noncommunist intellectuals in Peking and the hysterical destruction of the old culture's values and landmarks, women began to feel uncertain. The great impoverishment of millions of rural homes caused by the swiftly spreading anarchy and endless civil wars further undermined the venerable traditions. In March 1927, Mao was moved to comment:

> As to the authority of the husband, it has always been comparatively weak among the poor peasants, because the poor peasant women, compelled for financial reasons to take more part in manual work than women of the wealthier classes, have obtained more right to speak and more power to make decisions in family affairs. In recent years rural economy has become even more bankrupt and the basic condition for men's domination over women has already been undermined. And now, with the rise of the peasant movement, women in many places have set out immediately to organise the rural women's association; the opportunity has come for them to lift up their heads, and the authority of the husband is tottering more and more every day. In a word, all the feudal and patriarchal ideologies and institutions are tottering. . . . The abolition of the clan system, of superstitions and of inequality between men and women will follow as a natural consequence of victory in political and economic struggles.[30]

The innate conservatism of women, however, had to be overcome and their traditional beliefs and loyalties destroyed; more than once, Mao remarked that "in places where the power of the peasants is predominant, only the older peasants and the women still believe in gods," but wherever the action of his rural soviets was successful, women rebelled against time-hallowed traditions:

> The old rule that forbids women and poor people to attend banquets in the ancestral temple has also been broken. On one occasion the women of Paikwo, Hengshan, marched into their ancestral temple, sat down on the seats and ate and drank, while the grand patriarchs could only look on.[31]

Wherever they were, the communists worked hard at undermining the traditional kinship system. But, again, a great deal of destruction had already been accomplished by their rivals before they came to power. The first and second drafts of the new marriage laws, in 1911 and 1915, provided that only the consent of the parents was required; in 1916, the consent of the marital partners was tacked on; and finally in 1931, the Kuomintang decided to do away with parental consent altogether, leaving only the consent of the partners—and legalizing divorce. In effect, the urbanized and partly Westernized Chinese had already begun the work of destruction of the patriarchal clan. The communists had their work started for them; all they had to do was extend it throughout the countryside. But it was only when they actually came to power all over China in 1949 that they struck hard and immediately at what was left of the old social structure.

On May 1, 1950, the Chinese Communists promulgated the new Marriage Law; while it provided for greater equality between husband and wife, it also contained a retroactive clause: the Government Administrative Council issued a directive which specified that "large-scale complaint meetings must be held to expose those marriages which do not comply with the provisions of this new Marriage Law."[32] As Professor Chow Ching-wei, a former high-ranking member of the Chinese Communist party who took part in the drafting of the law, says, "I found out too late that the motives of the CC for doing anything are seldom what they seem, and the passing of the Marriage Law was no exception."[33] Soon enough, communist cadres persuaded millions of naive housewives to complain against husbands and in-laws at widely publicized public meetings; Professor Chow states:

> The result was that marriages which had been arranged by heads of families or in which cash payments were involved were annulled and millions of families were broken up. In doing this the CC also incidentally gathered detailed information about every household, which they used to . . . carry through the Land Reform Movement.[34]

This is what they were really aiming at: with the destruction of the traditional family system, nothing more stood between the isolated individual, male or female, and the all-powerful, monolithic state and party. Chow Ching-wei, a participant and eyewitness, adds:

> During this period, in almost every village in the country, there was tumult in every household. The trials and tribulations of the struggle meetings were responsible for many a suicide and even murder. Wives who were forced to complain against their husbands came back from struggle meetings and hanged themselves. Others, who went to cadres to seek help for divorce, came back

and were killed by their husbands. . . . I remember from the reports received at the Committee on Political and Legal Affairs in Kiangsu province alone, fifteen thousand people died because of the Marriage Reform in the month of August in 1952. The total number of deaths all over the country for which the Marriage Reform was responsible must have amounted to hundreds of thousands.[35]

This "nuclear" social explosion was by no means designed to "free" the Chinese woman but to enslave her to the state, and individually, often enough, to the more important male party members: "During this time, cadres took advantage of the new provisions which allowed a person to 'love' anyone of his choice, to chase girls, especially those from landlords' families and make these victims sleep with them."[36] Another analyst reported:

> What these little despots in the villages did with the women was so low and contemptible that it shocked the not-oversensitive leaders in Peking. Party members ordered husbands and wives to separate, and if any resisted, they were sent to jail as counterrevolutionists, or were handed over to the village militia, which soon became notorious for its licentious behavior. . . . Those not themselves philanderers indulged in the nation-wide sport of "fornicator-catching," confessions being extracted from women by physical torture. No wonder suicides and violent deaths amongst women showed a rapid increase.[37]

Meanwhile, in 1952, the Three-Anti and Five-Anti movements began to sweep the urban areas; wives were mobilized to persuade their husbands to confess to various assorted crimes. Too talkative for their own good, wives often unwittingly betrayed their family secrets to the authorities. Former kinship loyalties were forcibly shifted to the Red state; now it was wife against husband, sister against brother, son against mother, and all the while a long drawn-out explosion was tearing apart the kinship fabric of Chinese society.[38]

This could not go on forever, and eventually Peng Chen informed the Committee on Political and Legal Affairs that "the situation in rural areas has become chaotic. Too many people have died because of the Marriage Reform. We must try to stop it." Chow Ching-wei adds: "But by that time, the CC had achieved their purpose, which was to break up millions of homes and isolate individuals to make them turn to the CC for help. This helped them to push through the Land Reform and other movements."[39]

Nothing could stop the party juggernaut; the authorities organized the All China Democratic Women's Federation and in April 1953 its Second National Congress convened, not so much in order to air Chinese women's long-standing grievances as to convince them (consciousness-raising) that these grievances were real and should be put at the service of the party—yet, the *People's Daily* had to admit in 1954 that "the women in the countryside have been in the forefront in resisting socialization."[40]

Conditions had finally become so dismal that the Department of Justice of the Northeast Regional Government had to point out that "the People's Government is not promoting divorce, and the Marriage Law is not a divorce law. Those who take 'freedom of divorce' for 'divorce at will' are committing a grave error."[41] Worse still, this chaos gravely affected production and even party discipline, to the point where divorce became almost unobtainable whenever it threatened economic productivity or the morale of the members of the armed forces.[42] After 1953, there was a partial return to the old values, even on the part of party members, and more than once the situation was such that, rather than the husband's or the mother-in-law's opposition, it was the "obstacle of the cadres" that was the hardest to overcome. They had come back full circle to the view that "good women hang themselves [as a result of family discord], only bad women seek divorce."[43] In 1955, they were advised to recognize the social value of being a "family woman":

> If women who stay at home can encourage their husbands and children to take part in socialist reconstruction, and educate their children to become members of the next shift in the work of socialist reconstruction, then their domestic service already contains revolutionary and social value, and the salaries and income of their husbands and other family members already contain their own labor.[44]

It would have been too much to expect that men, whether revolutionary or reactionary, would agree to grant full equality to women; further, by raising women's expectations beyond any possibility of fulfillment, the new laws had greatly increased the social chaos generated by the breakdown of the traditional clans. This was grave since the main purpose of the "liberation" of Chinese women was to put them to much harder work than they had been accustomed to in the bad old days. Womanpower was put to full use in the wheat, rice, and cotton fields, as well as in the small commune industries. Most of the time, farm hands were paid with "work points," a system which invariably favors men who, being physically stronger, accumulate more points. Chinese women apparently were not as strong as Russian women and their health began to deteriorate sufficiently to alarm the authorities. Early in 1971, an article in the *People's Daily* quoted a survey taken in a random county in Kiangsu Province, to the effect that 20 percent of the women could not assume a normal share of the collective work, and that half of all women had some kind of ailment.[45] Such loss of labor power could not be tolerated and medical treatment was started on a massive scale. Working women are precious chattel in Red China.

Inevitably, there was a steady retreat from the earlier revolutionary profeminist stance; the rebellion of women, such as it was, had fulfilled its main task: to destroy the traditional clan system and family solidarity which stood as the main obstacle on the road to socialization and the supremacy of the state. Now the time had come for the reconstruction of the new society. In the last part of 1955, a communist directive began to stress that the "building of a democratic and harmonious new family, united for production and devoted to the cause of socialist reconstruction," was woman's main responsibility.[46] Household work was increasingly "socialized" with the creation of millions of nurseries and kindergartens, public mess halls and dormitories, presumably freeing women from child care, cooking, and other household chores so as to enable them to contribute to the collective work.

Although the Marriage Law did not stipulate it, young Chinese were discouraged from marrying early because of its disturbing effect on study, work, and even health—the puritanical authorities frowning on "excessive sexual activity."[47] Having fulfilled their purpose as male-directed revolutionary instruments, Chinese women were firmly enjoined to give up any kind of "militant struggle" for the exclusive betterment of their sex's social position.[48] But at no time have the communist authorities indicated that they wanted to do away with the family altogether. Far from it. Even if they had wanted this, the staggering cost, in terms of economic disruption, and the unending conflicts this would entail, would have prevented them from attempting it. The main objective, all along, was the destruction of the socioeconomic power of the clan and the kinship loyalty which stood as a powerful screen between the state and the individual; having reached this goal with remarkable dispatch, the two- or even three-generation family could be left in peace. But even where the extended family structure remained intact, and where the conjugal couple remained with parents or in-laws, the latter had lost all power of coercion; the constant exaltation of youth and ruthless contempt for impotent old age had done away with the old gerontocratic supremacy. Now that economic self-interest in the clan cooperative community had disappeared, only ties based on mutual affection could keep a Chinese extended family together. In terms of social, economic, and political power, the old kinship system and structure based on a hierarchy of generational levels has ceased to exist in Red China.

As in Russia, sexual segregation at work is striking. The raising of children in nurseries and kindergarten is exclusively done by women; jobs that have not been mechanized are allotted to women. But most of the highest-paid jobs or those that are the most prized in the educational system are given to men. In the summer of 1971, a group of American scholars, fresh out of the Western atmosphere pervaded by women's liberation arguments, were quite surprised that

> When we asked why these differences between male and female employment continue, we were usually told that women are by nature better suited to some tasks, such as gentle care of the sick, patient rearing of children, and meticulous sewing or inspection tasks where perfection is required. Neither the men nor the women seemed to question the assumption that there are these sorts of inherent differences between men and women.[49]

What struck them most is not only the fact that higher education is largely a male prerogative but that all leadership jobs are "disproportionately" male:

> With one or two exceptions, this means that every commune, every school, every factory, every hospital, every local government branch which we visited had many more men than women in its revolutionary committee. . . . We found that even in factories where the workers are mostly female, the leadership is heavily male.[50]

At the top, the Central Committee of the Chinese Communist party has only 15 women out of 170 members—just about the same ratio as in most other Communist parties, in or out of power. A significant incident illustrates the fact that, deep down, the Red Chinese find this overwhelmingly male leadership normal. Having put the question "How many men are on your revolutionary committee and party committee, and how many women?" at Peking University,

> The people speaking to us, many of them members of these leadership committees, looked at us blankly and said that they had never noticed. Since women and men are completely equal in China now, who would think to ask that question, they said. We persisted . . . so somebody went off to look it up, and came back a little sheepishly with the information that the revolutionary committee has five women and thirty four men and the party

committee has five women and forty two men. Three of the five
women on each committee are the same, so really only seven
women in all get to participate in top leadership at Peking University.[51]

When it came to investigating the problem of household chores, it
was more of the same: "The old patriarchal division of labor which
relegated all the household tasks to women has not been very much
modified in the People's Republic of China . . . almost everywhere
when we asked who washes the clothes by hand, who takes care of the
children after they come home from school, who buys the food, who
cooks the meals, who cleans the house, who does the sewing, the
answer was, 'The wife, of course.' "[52] But the visiting scholars were
also witness to the strong family feelings that still persist, regardless
of the disintegration of the traditional clans. Three and sometimes
four generations live together or as close together as they can. And
they were struck by another fact:

> . . . it was obvious wherever we went in China that parents,
> grandparents and children have close relationships and enjoy
> doing things and going places together. Far from weakening the
> family, the employment of women and the child-care facilities
> that permit this have really strengthened it.[53]

Put in succinct terms, the Red Chinese woman has been emancipated from the tutelage of the traditional clan only to fall under that
of the party and state, both of which are almost entirely male-controlled. As in Russia, some women hold minor positions of leadership
in the apparatus, partly as window-dressing; but the higher echelons
are invariably in men's hands. Those few women who do play a role
are usually related to high officeholding males who enjoy direct power,
and their influence is merely derivative. For instance, Tsai Chang, who
was for years the highest-ranking woman as member of the Central
Committee and chairman of the Woman's Federation, also happened
to be the wife of Deputy Premier Li Fu-chun. Mao Tse-tung's fourth
wife, the notorious Chiang Ching, cannot be omitted, if only because
of the part she played in the Cultural Revolution; but another aspect
of her influence must be noted—her rivalry with, and hatred for, China's former Chief of State Liu Shao-chi's wife, which became legendary. Beautiful and brilliant Wang Kuang-mei, for long Red China's
"first lady," waged a relentless war against Chiang Ching, and a great
deal of the turmoil of the Cultural Revolution can be laid at the door-
steps of these two ruthless ladies, both worthy successors of that paragon of female ruthlessness, the Dowager Empress Tzü Hsi.

All in all, except for some wives of powerful men, few women play any important part in Red China. Only a small fraction of the leadership, at any level, is female, and the closer one gets to the hard core of power, the less direct influence women possess; females occupy the lower rungs of the revolutionary ladder. What is traditionally known as "big mannism" prevails in Red China as it does in Soviet Russia, and there are no real signs that it is waning. Womanpower was successfully used as a battering ram against the old Confucian fortress; now that the fortress has collapsed, it is used as productive economic power. As for the rest of it, regardless of pious wishes and forecasts, the "socialist liberation" of Red Chinese womanhood, one can only quote a familiar Chinese expression: "a light breeze that leaves no traces at all."

In an article published in the early 1970s, Simone de Beauvoir, no mean feminist of extreme-left political persuasion, wrote that "socialism has brought no benefits, or practically none, to women."[54] She is quite correct. The Marxist revolutions of the twentieth century, in adopting the Spartan model, have cunningly made full use of womanpower, in both a destructive and then constructive sense, but without giving woman per se any greater share of ultimate power or responsibility. Freed from subservience to patriarchal families, they have collectively fallen under the domination of their successors: male-ruled totalitarian societies organized on a pharaonic scale. Usually puritanical in sexual matters once their power is secure, Marxist regimes have, to a marked degree, enhanced the dignity of womanhood, as had the early Christians in the dissolving Roman Empire. But dignity can be granted at the expense of power or influence; by its very nature, revolution is masculine in spirit, in a direct line of descent from all the monotheistic creeds in which historical development progresses, not smoothly along evolutionary lines, but in spasmodic fashion by way of sudden restructuring of the entire social and political order. The Marxist creed, in particular, endowed, as Bertrand Russell expressed it, with "a cosmic optimism which only theism could justify,"[55] is essentially a prophetic faith which subordinates the means to a more-or-less mythical end, allowing the simultaneous coexistence of a good conscience and evil instincts. Chief among those means is the full use of womanpower in a subordinate way, in marked contrast with Western societies in which so much of the enormous middle-class component is wasted away, without even the consoling illusion of working toward that elusive millennium.

In between the West and the Marxist worlds lies the rest—the far-flung Third World strung around the globe's tropical and equatorial belts, made up of widely disparate elements. We can start with the Arab countries, where left-wing socialist revolution often, if not usually, signifies a return to pure, puritanical, and antifeminist traditions. Modern Islam has had, to a modest extent, its feminists and advocates of woman's emancipation—the Egyptian Qāsim Amīn whose *Emancipation of Woman* stirred middle-class Arab women, and another popular Egyptian Muslim who advocated liberating and putting to social and economic use what he chose to call the Arab world's "unused lung."[56] But, by and large, Muslim women remain more or less where they have always been: in the virtual seclusion of the kitchen and the nursery. They are likely to remain there for the foreseeable future, especially in the more revolutionary Arab states such as Algeria and Libya where a return to a puritanical but traditional Islamic past works to women's ultimate disadvantage.

In contrast, India, still faithful to its traditional civilization, socially conservative to a large extent, grants far more prestige and influence to its women than Red China, for instance. It is in its inherent social conservatism and its persisting endogamic caste system that Indian womanhood finds the true source of its enduring influence.

In all other lands, Asian, African, or Latin American, where military dictatorship has become the almost normal form of government, except in Argentina, the all-male military establishments effectively block any access women might have to positions of power and influence.

Out of the socialist trend that became immensely strong at the turn of the century in Eastern Europe's Jewish communities emerged what is perhaps the most creative social experiment of the century: the Israeli *kibbutz* ("group" in Hebrew), a utopia come true—in Martin Buber's words, "the only experiment which did not fail."[57] To go from the gigantic pharaonic empires such as Soviet Russia and Red China to minute social organisms consisting of a few hundred people is like going from macrocosm to microcosm. Basically, however, the difference is that the macrocosm is based on enormous concentrations of power in few hands, and therefore on coercion for the rest, whereas the microcosm has done away with all forms of concentration of power and domination of one human being over another. It is unique in its amalgam of collectivism and complete freedom, and this without in any way falling into anarchism—quite the contrary.

Over sixty years have now gone by since the first collective settlement was established in Degania (then part of the Ottoman Empire) by East European settlers escaping from the *shtetl* ("ghetto") way of life and its typical Jewish patriarchalism. An outcrop of the socialist ideology that swept through Europe in the nineteenth and twentieth centuries, and of the opening of Yiddish culture to Western influence, this peculiar brand of Zionism embodied to the full the age-old characteristic of the Hebrew-Jewish spirit—that of the irresistible *will* produced by the messianic drive. It is largely the predominance of this will that explains why the kibbutz way of life is "the only experiment that did not fail," unlike all the other communal utopias tried and given up by weaker-willed Europeans and Americans.

From the start, the feminist component loomed large in the formulation of the kibbutz ideology—the revolt against the tight-knit, money-conscious patriarchal family of the ghetto. According to this ideology, there was to be no real family in the kibbutz, and the sexes were to be completely equal in every respect.[58] One should emphasize again that feminism as such can arise only in societies that are aggressively masculine, such as the Jewish one. The early ideology of the movement laid great stress, however, on "the biological tragedy"[59] of woman and, in one pamphlet, mention was made of the fact that "the only obstacle in the way of achieving true equality of the sexes was the unfortunate physical differences between men and women."[60]

In any patriarchal society, the feminist rebellion takes place wholly unconsciously within a masculine framework—since it understands no other—and always lays stress on the "greater value" of man's work: hence, in the early kibbutzim, women were to work alongside the men and share equally in their labors; pursuits considered typically feminine, such as household work, services, and rearing children, were immediately socialized; all kibbutzniks eat together in a communal dining hall, and children are entrusted to professional guardians, the *metapelets*, who raise them in separate children's houses. Thus, according to the theory, female kibbutzniks would be free to devote themselves to "productive" (i.e., masculine) work on a par with the men.

Some six decades have gone by since this ideology was first materialized in concrete collectives. Second and third generations have appeared, and that the movement is still very much alive is proved by new collective settlements springing up all over Israel, many of them started by recruits from the youth movement. But the movement is alive only because it faced realities—foremost among them, the enduring "difference" between the sexes. Pragmatic, ever adapting to new circumstances without being fettered by dogmatism, the kibbutz movement is about the only organic social entity that actually lives its dream freely and from which valuable lessons and conclusions can unquestionably be drawn. The first noteworthy conclusion that can be made is that the present-day kibbutz reality is very far from the vision beheld, in terms of sexual equality, by the early Zionists in Eastern Europe.

After a short period of hesitation and free love in the early settlements, the family structure was promptly reestablished and the marital bonds strengthened. Today, sixty years later, both are stronger than ever. Their own "Center for Social Research on the Kibbutz" in Givat Haviva states it this way:

> Today the family fulfills an important role in the social structure of the kibbutz. The family has no economic role, and no role in consumption. It has only a partial role in the process of socialization and education but it fulfills important functions in the social and emotional integration of the kibbutz and especially is a link between generations. . . . Our contention is that the kibbutz is changing from a society in which the family did not receive full legitimation as the basic social unit to a society placing more and more stress on the family group.[61]

Even in the left-wing, Marxist-oriented group of the Kibbutz Artzi, it is claimed that

> experience has strengthened the conviction that the parents are the most important factor in the education and healthy development of their children. Collective education does not question the unique emotional tie between parent and child, so that the problem has not been how to weaken them, but on the contrary —how to make them into a more stable and permanent source of security, and how to integrate them into education for communal life.[62]

The rate of divorce is very low in the collectives, far lower than in society at large. It should also be emphasized that in sexual matters, kibbutzniks display a very strong puritanical streak.

In fact, there is absolutely no contradiction between the strengthening of the family bond and the other two great loyalties that stamp the kibbutz way of life: the strong emotional attachment of the individual members to the peer group with which they were brought up, and the equally strong sentimental link with the entire kibbutz which represents "home" to most of the younger members of the second and third generations. What the kibbutz really represents in historical terms is a way of overcoming the deficiencies of the modern nuclear family's selfish isolation, loneliness, and brittleness, and of reintegrating it in a much larger, if artificial, extended family. That a healthy collective is indeed a vast family is quite obvious to any outsider who spends any length of time in one of them. All the adults behave toward all the children of the kibbutz like so many affectionate uncles and aunts, grandfathers and grandmothers, with the typical warmth of members of a tribal group—similar in some ways to the Andaman Islanders whose married couples often exchange their children. In effect, the Andaman child acquires several sets of parents who all share the responsibility, love, and affection that the natural parents are expected to devote to them.[63] In fact, there is some evidence that the entire kibbutz movement may represent a retribalization, with a new set of unformulated rules of endogamy (kibbutz youngsters often prefer to marry other kibbutzniks) and endogamy (they rarely marry *within* their own kibbutz). This also explains in part why there are almost no Oriental Jews in the kibbutzim— they still live in their own extended families.

Meantime, what has happened to the woman's role in kibbutz life? The first striking thing about it is that the daughters of the pioneering first generation of feminists are no longer feminists per se; they show no particular preference for typically masculine work. Quite the contrary. What was bound to happen, happened: sex-typed roles, in terms of work and social activity, slowly reestablished themselves. As one authority pointed out:

> Kibbutzim are finding that the goal of freeing women from household tasks is becoming increasingly unworkable. . . . As the community grows older, a tremendous pressure develops to put more people to work in child care, to improve the dining-room service, to provide more clothing. . . . The women, therefore, are pulled out one by one, often against their will, from whatever else they are doing and placed in the services.[64]

The fiction of equality is still maintained, to an extent; such subtle euphemisms as the distinction between "mechanical equality" and "qualitative equality" are often used when work is distributed along gender lines. But,

> . . . it may well be that the accepted orientation today is that there are basic differences between the sexes in abilities, characteristics, aspirations and social roles so that each should have its own particular and separate sphere of activity . . . in practice it is usually found that inequality does in fact arise as a result of this differentiation.[65]

There was, at the start, an implicit contradiction between the movement's overall aspirations and the harsh reality of an ascetic way of life; in the early stages, preference was inevitably given to productivity at the expense of the services in which women were, later, asked to serve —thereby increasing sexual differentiation and some feeling of deprivation among the women. Yet, as recent investigations have shown, this particular character of the feeling of deprivation in the spheres of work and social activity also explains the fact that we found only very few expressions of competition and rivalry between the sexes. . . . To the extent that complaints against men or against the institutions exist, these do not usually refer to deprivation but rather to the lack of sufficient encouragement.[66]

In sum, the old dream of the pioneering feminists has vanished, in spite of all the masculine goodwill that it incorporated, and sexual work roles have been reestablished de facto. It is striking that the older the kibbutz, the less egalitarian the sociosexual structure; the younger ones still attempt to keep the egalitarian dream alive:

The egalitarian attitude will be most strongly entrenched in the younger kibbutzim, least in the veteran settlements and the mid-position will be held in the intermediate type of kibbutz. Since the processes of differentiation in the older kibbutzim will be accepted as natural by the second generation, women of this generation will be the least egalitarian.[67]

The trend toward strengthening family bonds (at the insistence of the women themselves) is so strong that some of the younger kibbutzim are now allowing mothers to raise their children at home, and no longer in special children's houses under the guardianship of the metapelets. It seems that the experience has come full circle and returned to its point of departure by reestablishing the strong family structure of the typical Jewish family, but without sacrificing the great advantage of integrating it in the artificial, nonbiological extended family which the kibbutz life style offers. All the statistical evidence garnered by sociological students of the movement indicates that "the interest and aspirations of the women, according to the respondents, concentrate on the family in the wider sense of the word; this sphere is not mentioned at all for men, whose alleged spheres of interest are wider and more variegated."[68] By and large, male kibbutzniks are more satisfied with their work than the women for whose sake the services have considerably improved and many unprofitable or non-profit-making types of work (poultry farms, orchards, etc.) have been maintained, in the hope that these undertakings will keep them happy within the kibbutzim.[69]

Thus it is that the boldest and most creative social experiment of the century teaches us that there is no social organization that can guarantee more than a "qualitative equality" between the sexes; and that pair-bonding, marriage, and the family are, in the long run, indestructible in a *healthy* society.

CHAPTER

4

Cultural Revolution in the West

Shifting from the "communist reality" to the West is like moving from the consequence to the cause, from the twisted duplicate to the original. Marxism, as a *historical phenomenon,* is a militant doctrine based on rigid organization, blind discipline, hierarchy, and efficiency applied to the tactical conquest of power and the strategic use of that power. Its revolutionary aspect is a means to an end—the elimination of Western power and influence throughout the non-Western world, a counter-imperialism to answer Western imperialism. In fact, the West is where the *true revolution* is taking place because it is there that the trouble started in the first place—in the only cultural organism that was, and still is, evolving freely rather than compulsively. The rest of the world has been essentially *reacting to the Western impact* in one guise or another and has originated nothing really new in the process. For example, feminist problems in the non-Western world—to the extent that there are any problems, aside from the utilization of womanhood as a revolutionary tool—are merely projections of Western influence, not sui generis problems—the Israeli kibbutzim are essentially a Western experiment carried out in the Middle East. Only in the West is there constant innovation and, therefore, constant revolution. In depth, what is the nature of this cultural revolution?

When Nietzsche, with prophetic prescience, proclaimed the death of God, he was really proclaiming the death of man. Man was the mere raw material out which superman can eventually make himself. If, as acknowledged by contemporary radical theologians, man killed God, the Nietzschean vision is correct: man killed God by an act of man's free will and man must now assume personal responsibility for his own finiteness. Nietzsche's implication is that the death of God implies the death of the murdered, and of the murderer himself—the end of man and the beginning of a new cycle of Eternal Recurrence.

When contemporary radical theologians assert that the death of God is a historical event that has happened in our lifetime, that we should not shrink from facing the fact, what they are really saying is that the traditional Western relationship between man and God has broken down—the religiously oriented man no longer "feels" the Almighty's presence and can no longer communicate with Him. The Almighty no longer exists for *us*—but this is merely another way of saying that man no longer exists. Basically, these theologians take their cue from Nietzsche who, two thousand years after the ancient Greeks had located and identified the tomb of the dead Zeus, exclaimed: "What are these churches now, if they are not the tombs and monuments of God?"[1]

The process of theological disintegration is easy to follow. Starting from Karl Barth's absolute separation between the divine and the secular, the Death of God school dismissed the former, separating Christianity from religion and focusing exclusively on Jesus Christ the man. Paul Tillich contributed the rejection of theism and Bultmann the rejection of mythology. Theology was thus reduced to Christ, the historical figure, and to man's self-understanding—a topic that might as well have been left to professional psychologists. In other words, with the death of God, true *theo*-logy simply evaporated.

Advanced Muslim thinking does the same thing—dismisses Allah and focuses on the historical reality of Muḥammad and the moral teaching of the Qur'ān; even Israeli Marxists, atheists to the core, enjoin their youngsters to study the Old Testament thoroughly as a prime *historical* document propounding basic ethical values.[2] In other words, far from focusing on what unites all religions and all human beings, that is, on the fundamental identity of God, Allah, Yahweh, contemporary theologians and religious leaders focus on the specific and *divisive* historical roots of their respective creeds.

This is the tail end of an evolution that began with the collapse of the medieval outlook. By stripping the Godhead of feminine attributes, the Christian Reformation unwittingly altered completely the meaning of Creation, which could no longer be conceived ex nihilo. If the Godhead is not bisexual, that is, *beyond* sexual opposition, *matter* has to be credited with some kind of preexistence and endowed with the powers of maternity—hence, the natural and easy transition from Judaic-Protestant theism to Marxist materialism.

We are today in the throes of a fundamental negation, and because of this we have lost all creative contact with the holy and sacred—the "Dark Night" of the Western soul. Some seek refuge in Gnosticism with its rejection of the world and the profane. Others embrace the contemporary profanity in the dialectical hope that, by doing so, they will ultimately retrieve its *very* opposite—the holy and sacred. Their general attitude can be summed up this way:

Our waiting for God, our godlessness, is partly a search for a language and a style by which we might be enabled to stand before him once again, delighting in his presence. In the time of waiting we have a place to be. It is not before an altar, it is in the world, in the city, with both the needy neighbor and the enemy.[3]

The destruction of the mythological outlook prompts many to seek a nonreligious theology, if there can be such a thing, and a nonreligious interpretation of the Gospels. But the destruction of the mythological outlook really implies the cutting off of all deliberate contact between man's conscious thinking and his symbol-making unconscious. This is what Bultmann does when he claims that only two types of thinking are permissible—scientific and existentialist—because they operate on two different and unconnected planes, along with the reinterpretation of mythical thinking in existential terms—again, an exacerbation of the masculine divisive principle.

But the human mind is as steeped in unconscious symbolism and mythology as an iceberg is nine-tenths submerged in water; from deep in the unconscious it draws its imaginative nourishment, without which it is mentally sick. Symbol making is man's most profound and necessary mental activity; an exaggerated striving after objectification must destroy symbolism because symbols are subjective. But, as a product of the collective unconscious, they are also intersubjective and just as psychologically *real* as any object found in nature outside human consciousness. To demythologize—as the Greeks eventually did—is to deny this intersubjective reality and suffer the psychological consequences: the death of artistic and cultural creativity, the disruption of the connection between conscious and unconscious, and disharmony in the relations between the sexes. Unless this link is reestablished, contemporary man's, and woman's, self-identification will disintegrate. Some indications that this is happening are already at hand.

In *Beyond Freedom and Dignity,* B. F. Skinner makes it quite plain that in the world-outlook of the behaviorist school, man no longer exists as an autonomous, free-willing entity—if he thinks he does, this is only an illusion. Nothing specifically human remains in the Skinnerian world but bundles of environmental influences with no man to control or experience them: "To man *qua* man we readily say good riddance."[4] In an earlier work, *Science and Human Behavior,* Skinner firmly rejected the existence of such things as mind and ideas, and added that they had been "invented for the sole purpose of providing spurious explanations." And he added: "Since mental or psychic events are asserted to lack the dimensions of physical science, we have an additional reason for rejecting them."[5] This is the logical outcome of the process of objectification that started with the classical Greeks and ends in the utter destruction of the knowing and feeling subject. This nightmarish "behavioral utopia" is based on the arbitrary assumption that man is merely the focus of environmental forces, nothing more; there is no mental being, no autonomous personality, no free will, ego, character, mind, or soul. Behavioral technology, based on the notion that behavior is determined from without and not from within, will alter the environment rather than the human being, who will change as his environment changes.

Pushing scientific materialism to its absurd, yet logical, consequences, Skinner faithfully represents one important intellectual trend of our times and gives striking expression to the fundamental psychological trend of the contemporary West: the gradual disappearance of man qua man as he had been thought of for some two centuries, through the dislocation of his twin-being as knowing subject (now eliminated) and object of knowledge. This disappearance of man would, eventually, entail the simultaneous disappearance of woman and of the present tension between the sexes. This in no way implies that Skinner's ratlike perspective of human destiny will survive; far from it. It is only one episode in a process of intellectual breakdown. But Skinner's destructive vision corresponds to the increasing profanity of the age—a succinct and forceful expression of the ever-increasing technological nightmare that threatens to de-soul Western man to the point where he is ready for the Skinnerian vision of hell on earth.

What is luminously clear, right now, is the progressive disintegration of Western civilization's values through the general collapse of its traditional mythology, and consequently the breakdown of Western man's means of communication with his own unconscious—which he tries desperately to recapture with drug-induced trances and ecstasies. Contemporary man appears to have forgotten what Goethe stated toward the end of *Faust*—reality depends entirely on symbolic significance, the true symbol being, as Goethe had described it earlier, "the representation of the general through the particular, not, however, as a . . . shadow, but as the revelation of the unfathomable in a moment filled with life."[6]

What is now happening to Western civilization, its true cultural revolution, is what has happened, time and again, to self-enclosed communities suddenly exposed to the chilly influence of an overpowering alien culture: they fall apart when their traditional *Weltanschauung* is destroyed, when their myths are overthrown, their symbols exploded, their cosmologies blown to bits. In other words, when man's most precious possession, *mental coherence,* is shattered. This shattering of his world-picture drives man to some form or other of insanity, and in the long run, having lost all will to lead a meaningless life, to suicide. Westerners have seen it happen to exotic civilizations as well as primitive communities for centuries; now it is happening to their own civilization, not through the brutal intrusion of an alien culture, but through the working out to its utmost logical conclusions the inner drive of their own culture.

This drive is Promethean, the essentially one-sided masculine force of aggression striving for endless expansion and conquest which started, in Western Europe, when the Gothic spires shot up toward the sky, the flying buttresses challenging the laws of gravity and the stained-glass windows incorporating outer space in the Gothic structure; when the conquistadors circled the globe, destroying "heathen" empires and grabbing whole continents; when scientific inquiry began to discover the inner mathematical structure of Nature and technology began to overpower her, given the means to do so by the industrial revolution. Now, like a steamroller out of control, the masculine principle in Western civilization is in that state of exacerbation characteristic of all that is about to die. All the components of a virility pushed to caricature are present in our societies: collapse of the traditional mythologies and rejection of the *anima;* exasperation of the desiccating cerebral in art and literature at the expense of the emotional; triumph of loveless and depersonalized sex in the traditionally masculine rather than feminine mode; contentious emphasis on exaggeration, on pushing theories, artistic and literary techniques, ideologies, and every other category to the limits of the absurd.

Chasing away the sacred and the holy and stripping love from sex, all point the same way—the way symbolized by the apostles of the death of God when they substitute what they call an Oresteian for the former Oedipal theology and claim that

> the mother must be destroyed, the mother who represents security, warmth, religion, authority, but who has become corrupt and an evil bearer of all that she is supposed to represent.[7]

It is fitting that, in its last gasp, the patriarchally oriented death-of-God Protestant ethic should all at once reject the Oedipal outlook with its tension between father and son—and the gap between them in which woman finds her place—and move to an Oresteian one where, in matricidal fashion, all that remains of the warm, unifying, and soothing feminine element that still lingers in what is left of Christianity is rejected[8]—an exacerbation of the masculine pushed to the limits of self-destruction.

This is an aging, almost decrepit Prometheus in his late Protestant-Puritan garb, unsteady and faltering. He is attempting to accelerate the destructive flight forward, toward ever more pointless activity, aggressiveness, and competition, trying in a last gasp to sweep the world bare of what is left of love, warmth, beauty, and security. It is Eros put to flight by Thanatos, the spirit of death. Against this, Miguel de Unamuno upheld what is left of the more feminine form of faith in the *Tragic Sense of Life:*

> It is not . . . rational necessity, but vital anguish that impels us to believe in God. . . . To believe in God is to long for His existence and, further, it is to act as if He existed; it is to live by this longing and to make it the inner spring of our action. This longing or hunger for divinity begets hope, hope begets faith, and faith and hope beget charity. Of this divine longing is born our sense of beauty, of finality, of goodness.[9]

This is true faith, as opposed to the contemporary mania for the believing-to-be-true; but few hear this contemporary voice from an immensely remote and almost enigmatic past.

Nietzsche prophesied the inevitable doom of European culture, the collapse of all traditional values, and the triumph of nihilism, along with the triumph of the Dionysian spirit—the full acceptance and, eventually perhaps, the transcending of decadence. Today, we can see and feel the decadence, but certainly not the overcoming of it. The Western Promethean drive is coming to an end, and all its components are beginning to fall apart. Quite naturally, one of its most important components, the relatively harmonious relations between the sexes, is also falling apart: now that Prometheus's sons are faltering, Pandora's daughters revolt—not gently, in womanly fashion as they did some generations ago, but with cold, revolutionary fury, in the *masculine* mode.

CHAPTER

5

Pandora's Daughters

Nineteenth-century feminism died in the early 1920s; with the granting of suffrage to women in most countries in Europe and America, it
died the natural death that comes with fulfillment. From today's revolutionary standpoint, however, it appears that it was not a natural
death but the result of a "wave of reaction" that swept through the
social landscape:

> We got sidetracked and discovered to our astonishment that
> when you got the vote you were not thereby made a full-fledged
> citizen. It was a horrible discovery.[1]

The "horrible discovery" was that granting suffrage to women made
no overall difference. Few women were elected in the legislatures;
fewer still acceded to top political office; women's share in the liberal
professions tended to shrink; they remained virtually absent from the
higher echelons of business and totally absent from the higher ranks
of the increasingly influential armed forces. Even in those labor unions
where women outnumber men—by three to one, for instance, in the
American unions (The International Ladies Garment Workers Union
and the Amalgamated Clothing Workers)—nine out of ten members
of the boards are men. In fact, women rarely favor the election of
members of their own sex.

At times, and in marginal situations, woman's suffrage makes some
difference in the selection of successful male politicians. Women seem
to pay more attention to the candidate's personality and background
than the more abstract-minded male voters who concentrate on ideas
and party labels. The female vote is largely responsible for the rise of
"independents" outside the regular party framework, favoring often
the "strong man" in times of crisis. In the French presidential election
of 1965, for instance, Charles de Gaulle was reelected by the women

while a majority of the men voted against him. Female votes are usually more conservative, against foreign commitments everywhere, more focused on practical issues and local affairs. Often the more conservative, right-wing men favored female suffrage, for this very reason. When Pope Benedict XV stated in 1919 that he favored the vote for women, he symbolized this conservative viewpoint—female suffrage as a stabilizing, conservative force—which prompted the left-wing French radical-socialists to stand against it.

In English-speaking nations, after the first flush of feminist victory in the early 1920s the Great Depression struck, relegating feminist claims to the background; too much time and effort were spent merely surviving to bother about a redistribution of gender roles. The trauma of World War II reinforced this trend by giving new life—as armed conflicts always do—to the old traditional sexual stereotypes of Anglo-Saxons: the search for happiness, so arduous in the difficult decades of the 1930s and '40s, was narrowed down to the search for sexual companionship within the framework of the typical bourgeois nuclear family. Writing in the early 1950s, Margaret Mead noted with astonishment:

> . . . a half-century ago the eyes of the specially able girl who went to college faced ahead towards a profession, towards a career. The idea of marriage was often pushed aside as a handicap. Today, the girl of the same ability is usually willing to admit that she wants to marry, and seems more willing to sacrifice her career to marriage than to sacrifice a chance for marriage to her career. . . . Success for a woman means success in finding and keeping a husband. This is much more true than it was a generation ago.[2]

In a sense, and for a while, happiness of a dull sort was achieved by many.

But something had been happening below the surface, a hidden traumatic development that had begun at the turn of the century and now lay concealed under the superficial jollity of the early postwar era; the full psychological consequences of the industrial revolution, and its technological sequels, began to make themselves felt in the realm of intersex relations. The industrial revolution had, of course, already destroyed the hoary concept of the family as a productive economic unit, but it had left it free to enjoy itself as a consuming unit. But something far more dangerous was taking place stealthily: the sexes were moving at full speed away from one another in all realms, except that of physical relations, because the ever-expanding *machine* had interposed itself between them. As the machine developed, expanded, and began to devour the earth, it entrapped man, its creator, into devoting increasing time and care to its sustenance.

First of all, the machine had to be thought out in man's brain; as a technician, scientist, or engineer, the husband began to find it difficult to communicate with his wife about his work. Not only was it a matter of lack of scientific and mathematical education for women; it was the well-attested fact that, by and large, women are less interested in abstractions than in concrete issues, less concerned with general problems than with people. Man, however, fell in love with his abstractions. Even as a young boy, he fell in love with mechanical gadgets and would trade girls any day for his mechanical toys; later, as a technological husband, he would find that he had little to say to his nontechnological wife. The full-scale flight into ever-increasing specialization and the increasingly abstruse nature of these special fields of interest have raised the interconjugal barriers higher still: in an age of growing specialization, increasing gender specialization became inevitable.

In some ways, just as at the beginning of the prehistoric hunting way of life, a psychological and social dimorphism between the sexes appeared and began to increase at full speed. A highly specialized man's world, unknown in former, nonmechanical centuries, has grown within contemporary life styles, made up of all the multifarious activities to which men give themselves with passion, and from which most women are rigidly excluded. A feeling of intense solitude and increasing, hopeless alienation has gripped many women since this trend started —as if males and females were living on different planets moving away from one another. Man, given to the passion of his professional endeavors, does not feel this alienation, although he should to some extent—this new way of life is shattering whatever harmonious relations there ever were between the sexes. An increasingly technological environment is slowly destroying the former pride that both males and females found in the specific tasks of their respective sexes; it destroys the romanticism that used to pervade their relationship, the magic attached to mystery, the stimulating tension due to restraint, the dignity of both, disrupting the human sexual ecology and compelling women to attempt to metamorphose themselves into pseudo-men. Indeed, whatever B. F. Skinner may think, many Western men and women are already beyond freedom and dignity. What kind of a society advises young, ambitious business executives that "the man who goes to the top has got to be slightly dissatisfied with his marriage" and "should be able to put his marriage 'in neutral' when his job becomes unusually demanding"? Or that "the really successful executive has distressingly little time for his family" and that "if you want a full home life, you'd better be content with a lesser job"?[3]

When Western man fell in love with the machine, he indeed began to alienate his soul, to dehumanize himself. As his subjective self, his inner life, began to shrivel, he increasingly sought refuge in the external object—the social consequence being the rise of the consumer society. This love of the object, of the machine, became a substitute for the love and affection that should be directed at other human beings. For Western man, increasingly trapped in the steady routine of jobs, compelled to lead a sedentary life in which social ritual has programmed in advance all the synthetic values, duties, and pleasures that are his lot, the machine becomes a substitute, giving him the illusion of control and power, and, worst of all, the illusion of masculinity—a masculinity he no longer displays for the benefit of the opposite sex. Just as little boys are surrounded with mechanical toys, the male adult, remaining in a state of perpetual adolescence, now surrounds himself with power tools and gadgets, identifies with them, and ends by destroying his relationship with the female sex.

Karl Menninger encapsulated the problem as follows:

> If I were to try to express in a single word the accusation brought by wives against husbands and by children against fathers, as I have learned in my clinical experience, I should say the chief sin of men with reference to their wives and children is not harshness, not parsimony, not tyranny or injustice or eccentricity but PASSIVITY: and under this I should include overdependence, inattentiveness, helplessness, overmeekness, indifference, neglect. . . . Many a wife tells a story something like this: "My husband is good, kind, loyal, but he just takes me for granted. He is really not interested in me except as part of his surroundings. It seems to me I compete unsuccessfully with his business interests, his hobbies, and even with the children, although he takes little enough interest in them. . . ."[4]

Medieval man reached out for God through love for woman; now, godlike, man has created the machine, as God created the universe *ex nihilo*—hence the theology of the death of God. The Almighty is no more needed now than the eternal feminine. Woman has no part in this creation; all she is supposed to be left with is her biological function. In narcissistic fashion, man's love and emotions are wrapped up in the machine. This unconscious reification includes human beings as well and invests woman with all the attributes of a strictly material object.

One must also keep in mind that by the middle of this century, the spread of social equalitarianism and the leveling of educational opportunities, the vastly increased number of college graduates and the increasingly keen competition that comes with improving social equality of opportunities—putting all the onus for success or failure on the individual himself, and depriving him of the convenient alibi provided by a fatalistic acceptance of traditional social inequality—added greatly to the nervous strain of middle-class men. Inevitably, this strain was reflected back at home upon the hapless wives.

Finally, in an age of increasing, insectlike professional specialization, it was a foregone conclusion that sexual differentiation would be included in an increasingly complex distribution of roles: specialization splits up knowledge in an ever-greater number of watertight compartments, age groups in the professional activities, and the sexes in their allotted social tasks.

To make matters worse, but part and parcel of the same trend, the postwar era saw a considerable acceleration of middle-class emigration to suburbia's psychological wastelands. In the United States, especially, ever since the WASP social elite began looking down on the common immigrating herd, a proto-caste system, flexible and yet rigorous, was set up, and segregation became the general pattern. The races were segregated and the ethnic groups and minorities isolated, despite the traditional American melting-pot policy. In the land of perpetual adulation of youth and all things youthful, the age groups were segregated, since the suburban nuclear family could not encompass a three-generation tier, and justified its rigid isolation by a flight from presumably obnoxious in-laws; this, in turn, implied isolating older people in senior-citizen centers, areas and cities of their own, sunny subtropical ghettos from where they could no longer disturb the younger generation, regardless of the dramatic loneliness inflicted on millions of oldsters. Ironically, having virtually atomized the social structure and the traditional extended kinship system, within which all age groups with their ramifications learned to live together, help, love, or hate each other, proposals are now made to undo this age segregation which is just as harmful for the young as for the old:

> At the very least, we should interrelate senior-citizen centers with day-care centers. An obligation of healthy senior citizens should be, without pay, to care for the next generation.[5]

How? By having them commute between Florida and Ohio, for example? It might have been simpler to retain the old kinship system and tailor business life and industry to fit the purpose.

Finally, in the glorious land of suburbia, the income groups were also socially and geographically segregated from one another, thanks to zoning laws and club-membership requirements. Segregation not only had to be rigid, it also had to shift its caste membership along with the evolution of the husband's business and social status, regardless of the emotional harm inflicted upon his family: "The wife has no choice. She can be downright dangerous if she insists on keeping close friendships with the wives of her husband's subordinates."[6] And, "when the husband of a friendly couple receives a promotion, then we can no longer socialize." Even the children "are affected by an unstated need to avoid children of people their father has surpassed."[7]

Yet, in the midst of this ritualized segregation caused by a typological mania—society should be as neatly structured as machinery in a plant or personnel in an office where everyone becomes a potential spare part—the worst of all was overlooked for a long time: the virtual segregation of the sexes. Not only were men keeping themselves busy in their professions and the new technological world they had carved up for themselves at the exclusion of women, but they also retained unconsciously, from the early days of the industrial revolution, the idea of the idle housewife as status symbol. And this, more than half a century after Thorstein Veblen had pertinently remarked that "woman is endowed with her share—which there is reason to believe is more than an even share—of the instinct of workmanship, to which futility of life or of expenditure is obnoxious."[8] The evident futility of the middle-class suburban woman's parasitic life began to weigh intolerably.

The less there was to do in the home, thanks to the absence of cumbersome relatives, the presence of new technological gadgetry, and the fact that most of what used to be performed at home was now done outside, the more they were expected to stay home, improve their housekeeping standards in terms of child raising, cleanliness, cooking, and to confine their external activities to socializing with other status-symbolizing wives. And, if the husband happened to be a business executive, to be the proper corporate wife from the right social, religious, and ethnic background, respectful of the right pecking order prevailing among the wives of the other executives, capable of displaying the right social skills, ready to accept the husband's long absences for "business" purposes without displaying resentment. They also had to be ready to move their home, in an age of increasing business and labor mobility, to wherever he happened to be transferred; if possible, to be without a private income (earned or unearned) of their own (which increases ambition, dependence upon, and loyalty for, the firm); keep an idyllic home free from pressures where the husband-warrior could relax and recuperate under their tender care; and be ready to take a back seat, along with the children, whenever business considerations became imperative.

Living, unlike most Europeans, in glass houses with extremely limited privacy—a way of life with deep historical roots—it was almost inevitable that American wives should become a prime concern of their husbands' business partners and be compelled, for the good of their husbands' careers, to kowtow to business requirements. Meanwhile, their husbands have precious little time or energy to spare to fulfill both their conjugal and parental roles. Paradoxically, more women than ever went to college in the 1950s, and less went on to a career or profession than before—campuses and their surroundings became for them matrimonial meeting grounds, from whence they could take off in their "flight into femininity," which often enough turned out to be a flight into limbo.

Soon, the greatest disease that can afflict the human being began to spread like an epidemic among housewives, taking a terrible toll and spiritually destroying those who were not quite dull enough to enjoy this "objectified" parasitic and meaningless existence: shattering boredom. From boredom to revolt is but a step, and in the 1960s, the step was taken.

What in most other lands, with stronger family feelings and ties, comes as a matter of course in a wholly natural way—full acceptance of the existence of a biological difference along with all its social consequences—has now been put up for public discussion, especially in the United States, where tension between the sexes is greatest. In the rest of the Western world, where new middle classes tend to adopt the American way of life, there are also shifts from the traditional kinship groups and extended families to the narrow, unstable nuclear family living in growing urban and suburban areas.

Once again, the traditional psychological relationship between black people and women reasserted itself in America. As long as the black male had the vote (however theoretically in the South) while women, black and white, were deprived of it, his masculine pride and sense of dignity were preserved. The adoption of female suffrage made it increasingly clear to him that his race was still the least-favored group and compounded the virtual matriarchy in which he lived (since black women were more easily employed than he was). As one historian points out:

> The surprising thing is that the Negro revolt has been so long in coming—fully four decades after the emancipation of women. Part of the reason has been the principle of matriarchy in Negro society. Negro women, like all women, tend to conservatism and opposition to violence.[9]

In the early 1960s, however, American blacks became restless and the civil rights movement swung into high gear; a resurgence of feminist agitation could not be far behind. The first sign of it was the rather sudden appearance of the "generation gap" and the revolutionary mood on college campuses. The generalized mood of women as mothers at any given time finds its echo in their children's generation; to quote again Hegel's *Phenomenology of Mind*, the frustrated wife will invariably attempt to rouse her children against their father. In the 1950s, how many American mothers felt and behaved like those "many wives who feel that they are losing their husbands to the company [and] try to turn their sons against their fathers with admonitions not to 'be like him' "?[10]

This is the ground-root of true revolution: when woman, who is basically conservative, becomes so frustrated by her unsatisfactory relationship with the other sex that, through the powerful influence of motherhood, she abandons her usual resignation and rouses one generation against another. In turn, this is easy to accomplish because what the industrial revolution has done in terms of separating the sexes, it has also done in separating the generations. If one looks at children in sixteenth- or seventeenth-century paintings, the most striking item is the fact that they dress like small adults and that even their faces are portrayed with adult expressions—symbolic of the fact that as soon as they abandoned their swaddling clothes, they lived as grown-ups, partaking in the same chores as their parents, eating the same food, playing the same games, living in the same rooms. There was no generation gap in those days because there was no concept of a prolonged childhood and extended adolescence. Everyone lived in a narrow geographical space, and life was a continuous stream of births and deaths in which the individual, infant or adult, was but a droplet. Work was not specialized by age groups. The family was, among many other things, a cooperative economic unit in which all ages and sexes shared to the best of their ability; even labor and amusement were not as sharply separated as they are today. All this changed with the industrial revolution.

The life and work of adults has become increasingly complex, difficult to understand for children. What the machine did to separate the sexes, it did even more to separate the generations, so that there is an intimate correlation between the revolt of women and the generation gap, the second one feeding on the first. Only one type of society has been spared this dramatic dilemma: the Israeli kibbutz which duplicates, in a rural setting but at a much higher technological level, the traditional life style of the preindustrial age. There, children engage, as soon as possible, in productive work without in any way neglecting their academic studies; they are made to feel *useful* from the beginning of their lives. In Western societies, studies are prolonged beyond all reasonable standards, forcing masses of young people to lead, and to know that they lead, a useless, parasitic, irrelevant existence in colleges and universities. Here again is a point of contact with the feeling of emptiness and uselessness of their largely idle, status-symbolizing mothers. Thanks to rising affluence in Western societies, it became possible to extend public school and college life, in terms of both time and numbers of students, through the whole of adolescence, postponing for years the start of productive work and the need to earn a living. This is poison in the body social.

The male adolescents of the 1960s began to suffer from, and display violently all the signs of, an intense crisis of self-identity, largely the result of the unwillingness or impossibility of identifying with their fathers. The young females, on their side, became terrified at the prospect of having to duplicate their frustrated mothers' lives. The generation gap opened wide, and with it, the first stirrings of the woman's liberation movement.

One of Pandora's most distinguished daughters, Simone de Beauvoir, created quite a stir in the early 1950s when she brought out *The Second Sex* and reopened the proverbial box. A true bluestocking, she produced a work far more notable for its commendable literary style than for the accuracy of her data or the soundness of her judgment. As far as she is concerned, there is no eternal feminine, only a historical one imposed by male-induced social conditioning; this thesis was neatly wrapped up in the existentialist jargon borrowed from her mentor, Jean-Paul Sartre. Implicitly and explicitly, she claims that both sexes are historically guilty, man for having made an object of woman, and woman for having accepted this objectification. From the start, then, relations between the sexes have been characterized by hostility and conflict, never by communion or even cooperation—a tragic, and historically unfounded, view of human destiny which agrees well with the morbid existentialism of the nature-hating author of *La Nausée*.

Sartre's hatred for nature springs from a concept of existentialism that commands man to build himself up and acquire his autonomy by conquest over his human nature; nature hating automatically implies female hating, a repulsion for the very nature of femaleness. Sartre's female disciple has made hers his feelings toward nature and femaleness, and her descriptions of her sex's physiological processes reek with disgust because they are *natural*. Inasmuch as nature is related to life as expression is to meaning, he who hates nature hates life and embodies implicitly a longing for death. Denying the reality of human nature implies automatically the denial of any kind of feminine nature, which accords well and fully with Sartre's dictum that Existence precedes Essence: a human being is not born female or anything else but *becomes* one under social pressure: "It is by denying Woman that we can help women to assume the status of human beings."[11] Beauvoir has nothing but contempt for maternity contrasted with man's external creative activities, as if giving birth to new human life was not the essence of creation in the full sense of the word.

This prevalent devaluation of motherhood entails, implicitly, a devaluation of life itself—a logical outcome of the masculine overemphasis on the mind and on abstract thought. Beauvoir's concept of femalehood is inseparable from Sartre's brand of existentialism, as made plain in her *Ethics of Ambiguity*—an existentialism derived from all the great ambiguities of life: man's desire to live but his certainty of the inevitability of death, his discovery of nonbeing while searching for being, his assertion of the preeminence of the subject while making the others his objects and becoming himself an object for them. Even the freedom man prizes and glorifies turns out to be absurd because it involves freedom from everything, including the acceptance of an objective set of values which he has not elaborated himself.[12] With Sartre, French philosophic thought reaches its nadir. Absurdity, culled from the undigested Germanisms of Marx, Heidegger, and Nietzsche, takes over; Beauvoir's view of the female of the species fits perfectly in his overall scheme of absurdity.

In *The Second Sex,* one can find encapsulated all the contradictions that are going to plague the new women's liberation doctrine: affirm that nothing is natural but only social, yet be compelled to accept the overpowering impact of the reality of physiology; assert yet deny some kind of anatomic destiny; accept that the given situation depends on physiology and yet claim simultaneously that physiology depends on the situation; deny the female's inherent passivity but accept it in all sexual matters; refuse to accept that woman's personality is affected by endocrine secretions yet accept their interrelatedness; demand that the sexes be neutralized, and in the same breath, assert that this is impossible.[13] Never mind; *souvent femme varie.* She steamrolls on, undeterred by contradictions and inconsistencies, toward her main goal: the famous *difference* does not exist generically; woman and femininity must be denied. By and large, within the general context of a cultural exacerbation of the one-sided masculine, this is the position on which the forthcoming extremists of the "liberation" movement are going to take their stand. In a world in the throes of a multiplicity of simultaneous revolutions on different levels, the "difference" is to be repudiated, since it is a *social* monstrosity perpetrated by the males; the complementarity of the sexes is hogwash, and so is the cooperation based on it; childbearing is almost demeaning. All that derives from the "difference," social institutions, the state, marriage, family, sexual restraints, traditions, must go by the board. And with the world stripped bare of all its former structures, the happy dream of anarchy can at last come true: power and hierarchy will be destroyed.

The similarities between the atmosphere of the contemporary Western world and that of the Roman Empire in the throes of decadence are startling—the same loss of true religious faith and ethical purpose, the same cultural degeneracy and lack of creativity, the same brutalization and cult of purposeless violence. The Roman circus in which gladiators shed their blood for the sadistic satisfaction of the crowds is now replaced by the ubiquitous cinema and television screens; and the blood formerly shed on the sand of the circus has become the ketchup splashed on our screens for a contemporary, sophisticated type of psychopathic crowd. But the psychological significance is identical in both instances. Even the rebellion of women in both civilizations has identical connotations and portends the same ultimate destruction for both societies, because in both instances woman revolts *within the masculine framework* instead of displaying a creatively feminine approach to the fundamental problem of how to restore woman's power and influence without destroying society, how to give the feminine component of our collective being its due place. Instead, the woman's liberation movement looks forward to achieving complete equality with man in the political, social, and economic fields without regard to retrieving, not only women's fast-fading femininity, but *womanly values*, which have almost completely disappeared from our exclusively male-oriented Western society. Their "liberation" resembles the attempt of artists engaged in interior decorating while the building's foundations are crumbling. What did it avail the "liberated" women of Rome when Alaric's Visigothic hordes swept through the city, sacking it and raping them? Instead of countering the male tendency to aggress and dislocate, the liberation movement makes it their own and aims at the destruction of all the cultural values and social institutions that have traditionally protected women. As Margaret Mead states in reference to a primitive community:

> This Manus example is very instructive because it represents a case where women do not enjoy being women, not because public rewards given males are denied to them . . . but because the sensuous creative significance of the female role of wife and mother is so undervalued. . . . When all achievement is outside the home, women of enterprise and initiative hate to be told that

they must confine themselves there, but when the home itself is undervalued, then also women will cease to enjoy being women, and men will neither envy nor value the female role.[14]

As with the Manus, so with the Westerners.

It is true that the Western social structure has been grievously defective in idling a large portion of its middle-class womanpower as an industrialist deactivates his obsolete machinery—women should be, as they always were in the past, the flywheels of economic production. What Western women have been longing for quite naturally is not an innovation but

> to regain the position of economic productivity and the sense of social usefulness they had lost when the center of production moved from the home to the factory . . . in fact they were not striving for a new thing but for the restitution of their lost share in the scheme of economic affairs.[15]

To complicate matters further, female life expectancy is so much greater today than it was a few generations ago that "the women of today have not only one but two adult lives to dispose of."[16] The Western woman could hardly make full use of one life; what is she to do with two? In his utter concentration on his Faustian destiny, Western man has forgotten that woman is not only a status symbol and a convenience (or inconvenience) but also a specific human value; it is entirely his own fault if this specificity has become lost and if woman finds herself unable or unwilling to retrieve it. Yet, if she does not, there is no future for Western society as we know it.

Nothing illustrates more poignantly the implicit contempt for and anger at femalehood in America than the celebrated attack on "momism" by Philip Wylie some decades ago in his *Generation of Vipers:* "Mom is the end product of She," he proclaimed. "Mom is an American creation. Her elaboration was necessary because she was launched as Cinderella."[17] True enough, in compensation for her deactivation as a piece of obsolete social machinery in the economically productive sector of American life, she was granted several privileges: she became the all-consumer and set the pace and tastes of consumption; being longer-lived than the male, she came to own well over half of the nation's wealth; and as a salve for her wounded dignity as economically unproductive, her motherhood was exalted whereas elsewhere motherhood comes as much as a matter of course as crops and the weather, good or bad. At times, this condition of privilege, granted to compensate for having become a status symbol, maintained a precarious social equilibrium between the sexes. But it was all make-believe on the part of the men, still resentful of being tied to Mom's apron strings as youngsters, and later contemptuous, in their heart of hearts, of femaleness. Philip Wylie articulated this mixture of contempt and resentment with drastic eloquence:

> I give you mom. I give you the destroying mother. I give you her justice—from which we have never removed the eye-bandage. I give you the angel—and point to the sword in her hand. . . . We must face the dynasty of the dames at once, deprive them of our pocket-books when they waste the substance in them, and take back our dreams which, without the perfidious materialism of mom, were shaping up a new and braver world. . . . Our society is too much an institution built to appease the rapacity of loving mothers . . . never before has a great nation of brave and dreaming men absent-mindedly created a huge class of idle, middle-aged women.[18]

Obviously, but having created this huge class of idle women, Wylie then sought to strip away the one consolation that soothed their offended dignity without offering them anything in return. This is precisely the condition against which the next generation of women—the present one—decided to rebel. However, the road back from socio-economic obsolescence is not an easy one, as the feminine reaction *against* the Amendment on Equal Rights suggests. One of the most articulate female opponents of this legal abolition of all forms of sex discrimination has pointed out that "equal rights" would be a "step down for women, who 'already have the status of special privilege.' " Such privileges many women want to keep and preserve: "the right not to take a job and the tradition that awards children to the mother in divorce cases," along with extremely substantial alimonies from the male partner.[19]

In a nutshell, many contemporary women would like to have their cake and eat it too—share with the men the status, power, and privileges that they apparently enjoy in social and professional life, while keeping all the special privileges that were allotted to women as compensation for having been virtually idled by the machine. This, of course, will never come to pass.

Beyond the technical problem, involving some socioeconomic restructuring, of allowing women full scope for the use of their natural talents (including, if need be, a compulsive *numerus clausus* in political institutions) without harming their offspring or antagonizing their male partners, at a much deeper level, the basic problem lies in changing Western man's one-sided virile outlook and discarding those patriarchal values that now, pushed to an extreme, undermine his society's foundations. This would require an entirely new breed of women who could see beyond the mere, and largely futile, struggle for equality—which, in reality, is a struggle for *sameness*. They would have to discard the artificial femininity foisted upon their sex after the industrial revolution and retrieve the deeper values of womanliness; they would also have to put a brake on the cult of an artificial masculinity and enhance the more stabilizing characteristics of femaleness. In other words, let the frustrated *anima* of our society enjoy free scope to project itself, even if it implies a profound reorientation of our social goals.

The basically androgynous nature of all human beings implies that, whether male or female, they must periodically alternate their modes of being, shifting from the masculine to the feminine style, and back again. Any effort to suppress one of the elements of bisexuality can only cause psychic trauma. If this is true within the individual, it is even more true within the social organism. The contemporary revolutionary mood is rooted in the present psychic distortion of the Western soul: it is the revenge of the frustrated *anima*, a spontaneous, unplanned, uncoordinated revolt which does not understand itself and persists in remaining *within* the confines of male-oriented values instead of breaking out of them. In essence, it is a rebellion against the superficial effects rather than the root cause—hence, doomed to failure.

Contemporary eroticism attempts to free woman sexually but according to a *masculine* conception of sexuality. Shifting the purpose of sexual activity from procreation to recreation symbolizes this decadent emphasis on an exclusively masculine mode of being. The present rehabilitation of the erotic in its purely sexual, loveless aspect is completely at variance with the truly feminine conception. Even the prophets of the New Left fall into this error, followed by hordes of deluded females, unable to free themselves from the shackles of the ancestral patriarchal outlook. Freud correctly assimilated the purely sexual, loveless erotic with the desire for release and, consequently, with an ultimate striving toward dislocation, destruction, and death—Thanatos—as against Eros, the love-filled erotic, unifying and conservationist. Libidinous energy can overcome its built-in self-destructiveness only by focusing on an external being, on the *other*, by overcoming its tendency toward deadly narcissism.

Ultimately, this overemphasis of the masculine component in Western society threatens to destroy its foundations. As one psychologist states it, contemporary women are often afraid to be considered mere women, while men are often terrified that their maleness will be judged insufficient—a vicious circle of pseudo-virilism out of which it is difficult, but essential, to emerge.[20] There can be no salvation in the new revolutionary movements, all of which represent, almost by revolutionary definition, the exacerbation to the point of caricature of the masculine outlook at its most destructive. The humorless women's liberation movement leads nowhere either because it does not even attempt to break the fetters of the all-powerful male outlook; rather, it wraps them more tightly around itself and compounds its social destructiveness. All it really does is contribute further to the self-dislocating Promethean drive by the blind fanaticism of many of its members and their uncompromising determination to become their own lunatic fringe.

Western women's only real hope, as it has been throughout history, is to change the male-manufactured "feminine identity" to which they seem to object, by using their motherhood effectively and influencing their offspring, developing in their children what they consider to be the desirable attitude in the matter. This should be all the easier since mothers face little masculine competition in the child-raising business, the father having become almost vestigial in middle-class society. The actual overprotecting, oppressive mother, doubling up as surrogate father, producing infantile sons because she has nothing better to do, and becoming a tyrant in the home, must disappear. In a sense, the strange paradox is that while the power structure of Western society remains entirely in the hands of men, the latter have lost all power in the home, and therefore all influence over the next generation—a fundamental imbalance that must be redressed.

All this presupposes, of course, that the family is not to be destroyed —that, as the experience of the Israeli kibbutzim has demonstrated, the family simply *cannot* be destroyed without wrecking society altogether. The liberation's lunatic fringe, starting with Beauvoir, wants to do away with it altogether; but the solution of the problem raised by the nuclear family's deficiencies does not lie in its dissolution, but in *overcoming* its narrowness and its selfish shrinking of affective life by reintegrating it in a larger organic whole—some form of extended family that can generate far greater human warmth than is possible within the restricted confines of the nuclear group.

As usual, the greatest victims are the children, next to be "liberated" from any kind of compulsion, discipline, hierarchy, tradition, parental authority, sexual restraint, learning, and education. What, unfortunately, they have been liberated from is parental concern and affection —just as their fathers and mothers are actually liberating themselves from deep concern for each other. Western middle-class life, with its work patterns, social obligations, and housing facilities, allows little adult time to be devoted to children; in turn, the latter are condemned to live largely with their peer groups, suffering in fact from age segregation as much as the oldsters. It is striking to see how much more time and concern are devoted to children by parents in Israeli kibbutzim, or even in Soviet Russia or Red China where lack of housing space throws everyone together and social activities integrate, rather than segregate, sexes and age groups. The whole style of Western living, made possible by affluence, town-planning, architecture, commuting, seems to be designed for the express purpose of isolating children's activities from those of their parents. A certain selfishness and dryness of heart is now afflicting a large part of Western society, which is well reflected in the contemporary cultural output. This affliction is at the root of the so-called permissiveness which is nothing but the inevitable consequence of indifference, lack of concern, and a low level of affectivity. Children are to be let loose in an exclusively materialistic universe devoid of cosmic meaning, a vacuous nirvana in which they will truly become "liberated" through spiritual evaporation.

CHAPTER

6

The End of the Iron Age

The disintegration of Western culture, by itself, does not entail the end of the world; the human race can still live on and prosper under the aegis of other ideals and values. But what is coming to an end with it is a five-thousand-year historical cycle that started at the end of the Bronze Age with the patriarchal revolution. The reason for this is obvious—the far-reaching consequences of the technological revolution. Like wheels within wheels, the end of Western culture's life course is also coinciding with the end of all other separate cultures, with the end of the Iron Age and, hopefully, with the establishment of a global, humankind-wide civilization.

An essential component of this profoundly traumatic change in human conditions, the biological revolution is an earthquaking event no matter how one looks at it. As scientific investigation comes ever closer to the biological roots of life itself, the possibilities of an entirely new biological technology loom on the horizon of knowledge—the potential for integrating living tissue with machinery, injecting biological life into the lifeless machine, merging parts of human beings with artificial mechanisms, altering their genetic inheritance and changing the human body entirely. In fact, there seems to be no limit, save ethical, to the potential for physiological and embryological engineering. Already, researchers at Cambridge University have been able to fertilize human eggs outside the body, growing the resulting embryo up to the blastocyst stage when it normally attaches itself to the uterine wall.[1] The potential for purely genetic engineering is startling: deletion or insertion of genes through microsurgery, using lasers or X rays beamed through DNA molecules and slicing them as required, or introducing specific molecules into the DNA chain's protuberances. This potential for modifying the complex store of information contained in the genes with the possible help of specific viruses to carry the desired information, enzymes that copy genetic material, nuclear graft, or simply taking a DNA chain from one egg and injecting it into another egg to fertilize it, is already at hand. In the latter instance, it would enable woman to fertilize herself without any male assistance. At any rate, it seems clear that, within a generation or two, it will be possible to program cells with synthesized information.

Perhaps the most terrifying prospect lies in *cloning*, a form of reproduction by division of a body cell rather than fusion or conjugation of two sex cells, which results in the production of genetically identical "carbon copies" of the single parent who donates the body cell. Even if a woman were still required to provide the uterine environment and the egg-cell cytoplasm for the development of the fetus, she would not be the biological mother of the child but merely the empty vessel that the Greeks of Periclean times had hopefully imagined.

Of course, cloning can just as well use a female body cell as a male one, producing a child without a biological father. From there to doing away with the need for a female womb altogether is but a step; babies could be conceived and nurtured entirely outside any woman's uterus. The political, social, and ethical implications—not to mention the psychological and emotional ones—of the biological revolution are staggering.

Thus, what the political, economic, social, and cultural revolutions cannot achieve—changing in depth and scope the present relations between the sexes—may perhaps be achieved by the biological revolution, which is in the process of freeing woman from her natural impedimenta. By exorcizing the threat of unwanted pregnancies, regulating or eliminating the menstrual cycle, radically separating the sexual act from procreation, it could ultimately destroy all the shackles that bound woman to nature and the lunar cycle. Hormonal injections and genetic engineering could further alter her strictly female characteristics and bring her closer to the masculine type. The trend toward homogenized androgyny in contemporary Western societies is clearly in evidence, and could undoubtedly lead to the creation of an insect-like third sex through hormone implantations in the early stages of pregnancy, just about the time when the male or female neural circuits are in the process of being activated, masculinizing a female fetus or vice versa.

With this, the Iron Age will truly come to a close. There is already plenty of evidence that, quite apart from short- and long-term physiological considerations, the biological revolution is already having a profound *psychological* impact on younger women and, *mutatis mutandi*, could well be the contemporary equivalent of man's discovery of his biological paternity eons ago. Some ardent liberationists claim that "as soon as woman has mastered her procreative functions, the future of the world is hers."[2] Is it? Aside from the still largely unknown long-term physiological consequences of such a state of affairs, it is obvious that such innovations as the biological revolution can cut both ways. All these developments, fruits of man's mental cogitations, are in the hands of males, not females. Nevertheless, psychologically exhilarated by this new physiological freedom and closer to the masculine model, the woman of the future may well decide to challenge man on what he considers his own grounds, forgetting that all the elements of power —except that of motherhood—are in his, and not her, hands. Her masculinization would undoubtedly aggravate him far more than her present challenge. Any large-scale threat to man's self-imposed concept of his masculinity could trigger a counter-move, a violent reaction that would aim at relocating the female of the species where the male thinks she belongs. The recent rise of sexual impotence among young American males, for instance, could do it if it threatened to become a permanent feature. A report published early in 1972 in the *Archives of General Psychiatry* blames this alarming rise on the fact that "newly freed women demand sexual performance," in a "reversal of former roles."[3]

What is important in this respect is the possible collision between new sociosexual mores and the, so far, inescapable biological and psychological realities of the present. Patterns of sex recognition and attraction simply cannot be overthrown or discarded overnight, and always vary from one sex to the other. Every species has a pattern of sex recognition that is phylogenetically rooted, and the usual pattern combines sex drive and aggressiveness in the male, sex receptivity and submission in the female.[4] Any sociocultural tampering with these patterns can mean disaster for the survival of the social group concerned. It could well happen that an angry male backlash would use genetic engineering and hormonal treatment for the opposite purpose, that is, to *refeminize*, rather than masculinize, human females. It can work both ways. The idea that men would willingly let women challenge them on their own reserved grounds can only germinate in a totally unwarranted optimistic view of human nature as it really is.

Beyond the male-female relationship, all this raises an even graver issue—the problem of the freedom of biological research in the future, which may well be curtailed by international agreement as being more dangerous than the entire nuclear arsenal on this earth. For instance, referring to the problem of test-tube babies and the artificial growth of human embryos outside a maternal womb, molecular biologist James Watson of *Double Helix* fame, testifying before the House Subcommittee on Science in Washington, advocated the prohibition of any kind of research on human embryos and cell fusion.[5] In 1972, the American Medical Association called for a moratorium on experiments on cloning and the implantation of embryos in women's wombs, stating that "representatives of various disciplines should be assembled to discuss once again the thorny issues raised by the genetic engineers."[6]

At some point in the future, the profound conservatism of the human race—embodied in the great majority of its females—is likely to reassert itself under the science-born threat of total dehumanization. Genetic engineering, like nuclear experiments for military purposes, may come to a dead stop by universal agreement. Recoiling in horror before the prospects, man will call a halt to the accumulation of fatally dangerous knowledge, heeding Nietzsche's advice: "Man ought not to know more of a thing than he can creatively live up to."[7] Or, as Konrad Lorenz put it: "It is the unripe fruit of the tree of knowledge that proves to be dangerous."[8]

What is evident is that the trend toward a drastic reduction in the sexual difference and the purposeful drive toward the unisexual, far from being progressive, is essentially *regressive;* this has proved to be true in evolution since sexual differentiation started at the unicellular level. Margaret Mead states it succinctly:

> Every adjustment that minimizes a difference, a vulnerability, in one sex, a differential strength in the other, diminishes their possibility of complementing each other, and corresponds—symbolically—to sealing off the constructive receptivity of the female and the vigorous outgoing constructive activity of the male, muting them both in the end to a duller version of human life, in which each is denied the fullness of humanity that each might have had.[9]

It is the sublimation of the sexual urge that has brought mankind to its present level of knowledge and self-consciousness, created the cultures we enjoy, and brought us closer to an understanding of the mysteries of cosmic creation. To cut off at the root this urge and this sublimation is suicidal. While the new freedom conferred on woman is all to the good, since it enhances true femininity by making it a free choice rather than an imposed obligation, the present drive toward a neutralization of the sexes by shrinking the difference and the creative tension between them denotes a social death wish—implicit in the depreciation of motherhood that is becoming so prevalent and is, again, too easily justified by the threat of a global population explosion.

The greatest error made by Western man since the days of Aristotle, repeated and emphasized by Thomas Aquinas and many others, is precisely to slur over the "difference" and mistakenly see woman as a defective, incomplete, lower-grade male who *lacks* something—*un homme manqué;* to see what is essentially the other as basically the same, but misbegotten and of lesser quality. As Thomas Browne expressed this traditional view: "Man is the whole World, and the breath of God; Woman the Rib and crooked piece of man."[10] This mistake was never made in civilizations such as the Indian and the Chinese where the difference never implied ultimate superiority or inferiority. If Western woman now attempts to become a pseudo-male, it is largely because Western man invented this concept long ago, instead of granting female specificity the full recognition and respect it deserves—result of an overvaluation of cerebral creation at the expense of the physiological maternal creativity that gave birth to it.

As a result, female "liberationists" are only too prone to assert that "after a long period of celebrating the differences between men and women, we are heading into an androgynous world."[11] But, if this is the case, it is only Western civilization that is heading in that deadly direction. Decrease in differentiation is devitalizing and would threaten Western society with biological extinction. The burden of the Promethean drive will have spiritually exhausted its civilization by depriving it of any further reason to live. The sons of Prometheus will simply have forgotten that just as man lives and woman *is* lived, just as man attempts to control destiny and the future, woman *is* destiny and the future. Men make history; Pandora's daughters *are* history.

Notes and References

PART I BEFORE HISTORY: THE ETERNAL FEMININE

Chapter 1 Anthropoids and Humans

1. Montagu, *The Human Revolution*, p. 85.
2. Ibid., p. 102.
3. L. Tiger, in *Impact, Science and Society* (Unesco) 20, no. 1 (1970): 38–40.
4. R. Fox, in *Encounter*, July 1970, p. 38.
5. Morris, *The Naked Ape*, p. 32.

Chapter 2 Incest and Communication

1. Malinowski, *Sex, Culture and Myth*, p. 33.
2. Hagen, *Realm of the Incas*, p. 125.
3. Mead, *Sex and Temperament in Three Primitive Societies*, p. 84. Also, *Male and Female*, p. 200: " 'If you married your sister,' say the Arapesh, 'you would have no brother-in-law. With whom would you work? With whom would you hunt? Who would help you?' And anger is focused on the antisocial man who will not marry off his sister or his daughter, for it is a man's duty to create ties through the young females of his household."
4. Lévi-Strauss, *Les Structures Elémentaires de la Parenté*, p. 43.
5. Ibid., p. 45.
6. Ibid., p. 47.
7. Ibid., p. 61.
8. Ibid., p. 135.
9. The position of the maternal uncle, in particular, is remarkably strong. For instance, in the mid-twentieth-century Nzakara kingdom where filiation is actually patrilinear, the term *kǫlǐ* designates the object (bride) or "reason of exchange," and *kǫlǐ-ma*, the maternal uncle, is the one who has given his sister to "my" father, "who thereby made it possible for me to be born." The maternal

uncle is such a complex personality that he enjoys several kinship titles, whereas the noncomplex paternal aunt enjoys only one. On the other hand, the brother-in-law, "he who has given me his sister, is the one I fear since he can refuse the exchange and wreck my marriage." (E. de Dampierre, in *Kinship and Culture*, ed. F. L. K. Hsu, pp. 252–53).

10. *Encyclopedia of Religion and Ethics*, 9:256.
11. Lévi-Strauss, pp. 352–53.
12. Ibid., p. 354.
13. Ibid., p. 561.
14. Ibid., pp. 567–68.

Chapter 3 The Rise and Fall of the Great Mother

1. Breuil and Lantier, *The Men of the Old Stone Age*, p. 260.
2. Campbell, *Primitive Mythology*, pp. 314–15.
3. Eliade, *Myths, Dreams and Mysteries*, pp. 156–67.
4. *Encyclopedia of Religion and Ethics*, 5:130.
5. Campbell, pp. 315–18.
6. Lissner, *Man, God and Magic*, p. 209.
7. Campbell, p. 325.
8. Ibid., p. 324.
9. Lévi-Strauss, *Anthropologie Structurale*, pp. 218–19.
10. Campbell, p. 321.
11. Eliade, p. 155.
12. Campbell, *Occidental Mythology*, p. 7.
13. Childe, *What Happened in History*, p. 64.
14. Mellaart, *Çatal Hüyük*, pp. 67–68.
15. Ibid., p. 72.
16. Ibid., p. 176.
17. Eliade, *Patterns in Comparative Religion*, p. 258.
18. Campbell, p. 46.
19. Kramer, *Sumerian Mythology*, p. 74.
20. Campbell, *Oriental Mythology*, p. 37.
21. Eliade, *Myths, Dreams and Mysteries*, pp. 169–70.
22. Ibid., p. 184.
23. Hall, *The Ancient History of the Near East*, pp. 47–48.
24. Campbell, *Primitive Mythology*, p. 69.
25. Childe, *The Dawn of European Civilization*, p. 78.
26. Mead, *Male and Female*, pp. 143–44.
27. Ibid., p. 86.
28. Ibid., pp. 174–75.
29. Vaughan, *The House of the Double Axe*, p. 198.

30. Eliade, *Patterns in Comparative Religion*, p. 244.
31. Ibid., p. 207.
32. Zimmerman and Cervantes, *Marriage and the Family*, p. 517. See also Montagu, *Sex, Man and Society*, pp. 203–15.
33. Montagu, p. 209.
34. Ibid., pp. 217–18.
35. Zimmerman and Cervantes, p. 400.
36. Karen Horney, quoted in Zimmerman and Cervantes, p. 400.
37. Vaughan, p. 198.
38. Kramer, *History Begins at Sumer*, p. 147.
39. Lévi-Strauss, *La Pensée Sauvage*, p. 24.
40. Ibid., pp. 16–17.
41. Lévi-Strauss, *Anthropologie Structurale*, p. 218. This also explains that a certain congruence between sex and procreation appears to have been established relatively early in the Neolithic era (see Mellaart, *Çatal Hüyük*, illustration 83, facing p. 149), although it did not imply an actual understanding *causal* of the relationship.
42. Lévi-Strauss, *La Pensée Sauvage*, pp. 122–23.
43. Ibid., p. 139.
44. Ibid., p. 141.
45. Lévi-Strauss, *Les Structures Elémentaires de la Parenté*, p. 430.
46. *Encyclopedia of Religion and Ethics*, 2:18.
47. Eliade, p. 259.
48. Ibid., p. 259.
49. Jung, *Psychology of the Unconscious*, p. 130.
50. Campbell, *Oriental Mythology*, pp. 93–94.
51. Ibid., p. 53.
52. Kramer, *History Begins at Sumer*, p. 194.
53. Ibid., p. 196.
54. Kramer, *Sumerian Mythology*, p. 74.
55. Albright, *From the Stone Age to Christianity*, p. 195.
56. Breasted, *The Dawn of Conscience*, pp. 34–35.
57. Campbell, *Occidental Mythology*, pp. 23–24.
58. Ibid., p. 158.

Chapter 4 The Past That Survives

1. Lowie, *Primitive Society*, p. 191.
2. *Encyclopedia of Religion and Ethics*, 8:851.
3. The *Encyclopedia of Sexual Behavior*, p. 669.
4. Wallace, in *Kinship and Culture*, ed. F. L. K. Hsu, pp. 368–72.
5. Lowie, pp. 187–88.

6. Ibid., p. 194.
7. Ibid., p. 201.

Chapter 5 The Biological Roots

1. Auerbach, *The Science of Genetics*, pp. 217–22.
2. Beck, *Modern Science and the Nature of Life*, p. 259.
3. Auerbach, p. 108.
4. The *Encyclopedia of Sexual Behavior*, p. 132.
5. Montagu, *Sex, Man and Society*, p. 82.
6. *Encyclopedia of Sex*, p. 133.
7. Ibid., p. 766.
8. *Gray's Anatomy*, p. 1015.
9. Lilar, *Le Malentendu du Deuxième Sexe*, p. 281.
10. S. Levine, "Sex Differences in the Brain," *Scientific American*, April 1966, pp. 2–7
11. *Encyclopedia of Sex*, p. 110.
12. U. Mittwoch, "Sex Differences in Cells," *Scientific American*, July 1963, pp. 2–8.
13. P. Bakan, in *Psychology Today*, April 1971, p. 96.
14. The *Encyclopedia of Sexual Behavior*, p. 116.
15. Lilar, p. 285.
16. Jung, *The Integration of the Personality*, p. 18.
17. T. Alexander, "There are Sex Differences in the Mind, Too", in *Fortune*, February 1971, p. 134.
18. E. Maccoby, in *Impact: Science and Society* (Unesco) 20, no. 1 (January-March 1970): 19–20, quoting H. A. Witkin, et. al., *Personality Through Perception* (New York: Harper & Row, 1954).
19. Maccoby, p. 21.
20. Ibid., p. 28.
21. L. Tiger and R. Fox in *Psychology Today*, February 1972, pp. 23–32.
22. Ibid., p. 28.
23. L. Tiger, "Possible Biological Origins of Sexual Discrimination," in *Impact: Science and Society* (Unesco) 20, no. 1 (January–March 1970): 49.
24. Mead, *Male and Female*, p. 8.
25. Beauvoir, *The Second Sex*, pp. 28–30.

Chapter 6 Sex and Psyche

1. Jones, *The Life and Work of Sigmund Freud*, 1:315.
2. Lilar, *Le Malentendu du Deuxième Sexe*, p. 236.
3. Ferenczi, *Problems and Methods of Psycho-Analysis*, 3:84.
4. Jastrow, *Freud : His Dream and Sex Theories*, pp. 201–2.

5. Jones, 2:300–301.
6. Ibid., p. 291.
7. Jung, *The Integration of the Personality*, p. 12.
8. Ibid., p. 13.
9. Ibid., pp. 13–14.
10. Ibid., p. 23.
11. Ibid., p. 3.
12. Fordham, *An Introduction to Jung's Psychology*, p. 18.
13. Jung, p. 24.
14. White, *God and the Unconscious*, p. 45.
15. Jung, p. 25.
16. Reich, *Character Analysis*, p. 189.
17. Jung, p. 52.
18. Quoted in Brown, *Life Against Death*, p. 13.
19. Jung, p. 54.
20. Ibid., p. 73.
21. Fordham, p. 57.
22. Jung, p. 95.
23. Ibid., pp. 76–77.
24. Ibid., pp. 78–79.
25. Ibid., p. 81.
26. Ibid., pp. 87–88.

PART II   THE AXIAL PERIOD: WOMAN AND RELIGION

Chapter 1 The Patriarchal Revolution

1. Frankfort, *Before Philosophy*, p. 16.
2. Ibid., p. 187.
3. Ibid., p. 188.
4. Ibid., p. 194.
5. Kramer, *Sumerian Mythology*, p. 39.
6. Dewar, *The Holy Spirit and Modern Thought*, p. 3.
7. Ibid., p. 12.
8. Frankfort, p. 237.
9. Hall, *The Ancient History of the Near East*, p. 205.
10. Moscati, *The Face of the Ancient Orient*, pp. 168–69.
11. Gurney, *The Hittites*, p. 139.
12. Breasted, *A History of Egypt*, p. 269.
13. Ibid., p. 273.
14. Ibid., p. 320.
15. Bell, *Egypt*, p. 139.
16. Albright, *From the Stone Age to Christianity*, pp. 201–7.
17. Eberhard, *A History of China*, p. 25.

Chapter 2 Iran and Israel: The Spiritual Breakthrough

1. Jaspers, *The Origin and Goal of History*, p. 3.
2. Aurobindo, *The Ideal of Human Unity*, p. 309.
3. Jaspers, p. 3.
4. Ibid.
5. G. Van Der Leeuw, in *Man and Time*, p. 347.
6. Nietzsche, *Thus Spake Zarathustra*, p. ix.
7. *Encyclopedia of Religion and Ethics*, 12:864.
8. Zaehner, *The Teaching of the Magi*, p. 19.
9. Ibid., p. 31.
10. Ibid., p. 43.
11. Ibid., p. 44.
12. Ibid., p. 100.
13. Ghirshman, *Iran*, p. 44.
14. Frye, *The Heritage of Persia*, p. 93.
15. Campbell, *Occidental Mythology*, p. 106.
16. Smith, *The Religion of the Semites*, pp. 156–58.
17. Vaux, *Ancient Israel*, p. 39.
18. Ibid., p. 40.
19. The *Encyclopedia of Sexual Behavior*, pp. 577–78.
20. Montagu, *The Human Revolution*, p. 133.
21. Unamuno, *The Tragic Sense of Life*, p. 113.
22. Agus, *L'Evolution de la Pensée Juive*, p. 31.
23. Kohn, *The Idea of Nationalism*, p. 34.

Chapter 3 Greece: The Intellectual Breakthrough

1. Aeschylus, *The Oresteian Trilogy*, p. 152.
2. Ibid., p. 172.
3. Ibid., p. 164.
4. Campbell, *Occidental Mythology*, p. 152.
5. Frankfort, *Before History*, p. 249.
6. Russell, *A History of Western Philosophy*, p. 33.
7. *Encyclopedia of Religion and Ethics*, 6:670.
8. *Ibid.*, 5:709.
9. Frankfort, p. 255.
10. Ibid., p. 258.
11. Ibid., p. 261.
12. Campbell, pp. 26–27.
13. Frankfort, p. 262.
14. Jaeger, *Paideia*, 1:23.
15. Ibid., p. 24.
16. Ibid., p. 122.

17. Zimmern, *The Greek Commonwealth*, p. 338.
18. Harrison, *Prolegomena to the Study of Greek Religion*, pp. 260–62.
19. Browne, in *Harvard Classics* 3:323.
20. Zimmerman and Cervantes, *Marriage and the Family*, p. 450.
21. Ellis, *Studies in the Psychology of Sex*, 6:134.
22. Jaeger, 1:346.
23. Zimmerman and Cervantes, p. 451.
24. Friedell, *A Cultural History of the Modern Age*, 2:348–49.
25. Zimmerman and Cervantes, p. 453.
26. Jaeger, 1:152.
27. Jung, *The Integration of the Personality*, p. 23.
28. Jaeger, 1:244
29. Ibid., p. 246.
30. Aeschylus, p. 154.
31. Ibid., p. 155.
32. Ibid., p. 162.
33. Ibid., pp. 169–70.
34. Ibid., p. 172.
35. Jaeger, 1:262.
36. Ibid., p. 264.
37. Ibid., p. 265.
38. Ibid., p. 280.
39. Zimmern, p. 336.
40. Jaeger, 1:344–45.
41. Zimmern, p. 337.
42. Tarn, *Hellenistic Civilization*, p. 337.
43. Polybius, *Histories* 2. 17.
44. Tarn, p. 56.
45. Ibid., p. 98.
46. Ibid., p. 99.
47. Jung, *Psychological Types*, p. 325.
48. Toulmin and Goodfield, *The Fabric of the Heavens*, p. 144.
49. Tarn, p. 91.
50. Ibid., pp. 124–25.

Chapter 4 Roman Matrons and World Empire

1. Ferrero, *The Women of the Caesars*, p. 3.
2. *The Legacy of Rome*, ed. Bailey, p. 219.
3. Cowell, *Cicero and the Roman Republic*, p. 219.
4. Ibid., p. 219.
5. Livy, *History of Rome* 1. 34. See also Plutarch, *Lives*, chapter on Cato the Elder.

6. Plutarch, *Lives*, loc. cit.
7. Jerome, *Selected Letters* 22. 13, 27.
8. Ferrero, *Greatness and Decline of Rome* 1. 152.
9. Horace, *Odes* 3. 6: Aetas parentum pejor avis tulit nos nequiores, mox daturos progeniem vitiosiorem.
10. Ferrero, *The Women of the Caesars*, p. 34: ". . . woman, in periods commanded by strong social discipline, is the most beneficient and tenacious among the cohesive forces of a nation; and . . . in times when social discipline is relaxed, she is, instead, through ruinous luxury, dissipation, and voluntary sterility, the most terrible force for dissolution."
11. Hitti, *History of Syria*, p. 302.
12. Ferrero, *Greatness and Decline of Rome*, 4:194.
13. Ferrero, 4:195: "Henceforth in the family the woman was almost entirely free and equal to the man . . . the unfortunate husband in the days of Augustus was but a shadow of caricature of the old Roman *paterfamilias* with his terrible austerity. Power he had none, except that of squandering part of the dowry. . . ."
14. Ibid.
15. Ferrero, 5:65.
16. Ferrero, 5:67.
17. Dill, *Roman Society from Nero to Marcus Aurelius*, p. 86.
18. Ibid., 211. Also p. 81: "In the reign of Tiberius, Caecina Severus, with the weight of forty years' experience of camps, in a speech before the Senate, denounced the new-fangled custom of the wives of the generals and governors accompanying them abroad, attending reviews of troops, mingling freely with the soldiers, and taking an active part in business, which was not always favorable to pure administration."

Chapter 5 The Religious Awakening

1. *Encyclopedia of Religion and Ethics*, 4:377.
2. Tarn, *Hellenistic Civilization*, p. 138.
3. Dill, *Roman Society from Nero to Marcus Aurelius*, p. 547.
4. Cumont, *Oriental Religions in Roman Paganism*, p. 49.
5. *Encyclopedia of Religion and Ethics*, 7:435.
6. Cochrane, *Christianity and Classical Culture*, p. 170.
7. Ibid., p. 171.
8. Dill, p. 565.
9. Ibid., pp. 569–70.
10. Cumont, *The Mysteries of Mithra*, p. 173.

Chapter 6 Christianity

1. Frazer, *The Golden Bough*, p. 265.
2. Albright, *From the Stone Age to Christianity*, p. 232.
3. *Encyclopedia of Religion and Ethics*, 2:170.
4. Ibid.
5. Enslin, *Christian Beginnings*, p. 188.
6. Ibid., p. 122.
7. Davies, *The First Christian*, p. 146.
8. Zimmerman and Cervantes, p. 474.
9. Tresmontant, *La Métaphysique du Christianisme*, p. 113.
10. Unamuno, p. 181.
11. Hitti, p. 329.
12. Other concepts began filtering into the Christianity that was preached by Paul and his successors. For one, some influence must be ascribed to Hermetic teaching, here again an essentially mental, unemotional, and nonsacramental creed. In its most important work, the *Poimandres*, the devotees of Hermes Trismegistus were taught that God is Mind *(noûs)* and the Son of God the Word, *lógos;* the beginning of John's gospel is essentially Hermetic. Follows a description of the Fall of the archetypal man which is closely similar to Paul's own description of the "first Adam"; and it continues with an account of man's ascent toward God. In Hermetism, there is no concession to feeling and emotionalism; it is purely abstract thought. Nor is there any greater feminine accent in Stoicism, either in its ethical severity or in its high-minded philosophy. Stoicism viewed the Almighty as both the Soul and Mind of the universe, and visualized, in truly masculine fashion, the cosmos as replete with *logoi spermatikoi,* "seed-concepts." Other ascetics such as the Essenes and the Therapeutae of Alexandria contributed other essentially masculine elements to Christianity.
13. Mâle, *L'Art Religieux du Treizième Siècle en France*, p. 136.
14. Ibid.
15. Ibid., p. 137.
16. Cumont, *Oriental Religions in Roman Paganism*, p. 70.
17. Guignebert, *Jesus*, p. 531.
18. Sykes, *A History of Persia*, 1:482.
19. Watt, *Muhammad in Medina*, p. 317.
20. Zimmerman and Cervantes, p. 232.
21. Paul, I Cor., 11:3.
22. Tertullian, *Apologeticus* 39. 11–12.
23. Kaufmann, *Critique of Religion and Philosophy*, pp. 420–21.
24. Tertullian 46. 10.

25. Broglie, *L'Eglise et l'Empire Romain au Quatrième Siècle*, 1:160.
26. Lamy, *La Femme de Demain*, p. 58.
27. O'Leary, *How Greek Science Passed to the Arabs*, p. 183.
28. Bell, *Egypt*, p. 107.
29. Zimmerman and Cervantes, p. 486.
30. Ibid., p. 493.
31. Ibid., p. 494.
32. From the standpoint of this remarkable continuity, the history of Ephesus is particularly symbolic: the Ionians, who conquered it eight centuries before Christ, found a shrine dedicated to the Neolithic Mother Goddess, who was promptly renamed Diana (Artemis); John the Evangelist succeeded in transmuting Diana into the Virgin Mary and eventually the first basilica to Mary was built in place of the former Neolithic shrine and the sanctuary of Diana: through all these metamorphoses, the Great Mother's presence remained unimpaired—a fact that fascinated Freud, who even wrote a paper about it (Jones, 2:349).
33. Stanley, *Lectures on the History of the Eastern Church*, p. 41.
34. Tarn, p. 141.
35. Zimmerman and Cervantes, pp. 497–98.
36. Ibid., p. 498.
37. Ibid., p. 500.
38. Ibid., p. 501.
39. Diehl, *Byzantine Empresses*, p. 6.
40. Ibid., p. 95.
41. Ibid., p. 114.
42. Ibid., p. 173.
43. Ibid., p. 185.
44. Stanley, p. 268.

Chapter 7 India and China

1. Campbell, *Oriental Mythology*, p. 6.
2. Ibid., pp. 9–10.
3. Ibid., p. 10.
4. Wheeler, *Early India and Pakistan*, p. 98.
5. Piggott, *Prehistoric India*, p. 202.
6. Monier-Williams, *Brahmanism and Hinduism*, pp. 222–23.
7. Campbell, p. 165.
8. Eliade, *Yoga, Immortality and Freedom*, pp. 202–5.
9. Monier-Williams, pp. 185–86.
10. Ibid., p. 187.
11. Campbell, p. 39.

12. Humphreys, *Buddhism,* pp. 38–39.
13. Coomaraswamy, *Buddha and the Gospel of Buddhism,* p. 162.
14. Ibid., p. 164.
15. Ibid., p. 165.
16. Campbell, p. 237.
17. Eliade, pp. 39–40.
18. Campbell, p. 359.
19. Ibid., p. 361.
20. Monier-Williams, p. 180.
21. Ibid., p. 181.
22. Coomaraswamy, p. 105.
23. Needham, *Science and Civilization in China,* 2:108.
24. *Shih King* 2. 4, 5, in Wilhelm, *The Soul of China,* p. 324.
25. Wilhelm, in *The Book of Marriage,* ed. Keyserling, p. 132.
26. Ibid., p. 131.
27. Hu Shih, *Development of the Logical Method in Ancient China,* p. 152.
28. Lin Yutang, *My Country and My People,* p. 296.
29. Needham, 2:37.
30. *I Ching, or Book of Changes,* trans. Wilhelm, 1:1–9.
31. Granet, *La Civilization Chinoise,* pp. 140–142.
32. Needham, 2:58.
33. Ibid.
34. Granet, p. 142.
35. Needham, 2:59.
36. Ibid.
37. Ibid., 2:151.
38. Ibid., 2:427.
39. Ibid., 2:149.
40. *The Legacy of India,* ed. Garratt, p. 145.
41. Rawlinson, *India,* p. 37.
42. *The Legacy of India,* p. 147.
43. Sidhanta, *The Heroic Age of India,* p. 160.
44. Tod, *Annals and Antiquities from Rajasthan,* 1:604.
45. Majumdar, *An Advanced History of India,* p. 76.
46. Radhakrishnan, *Religion and Society,* p. 143.
47. Ibid., p. 145.
48. Rawlinson, p. 214.
49. Dubois, *Hindu Manners, Customs and Ceremonies,* p. 340.
50. Majumdar, p. 376.
51. Lin Yutang, p. 131.
52. Weber, *The Religion of China,* p. 161.
53. Lin Yutang, p. 133.
54. Weber, p. 86.

55. Ibid., p. 89.
56. Lin Yutang, p. 134.
57. Weber, p. 203.
58. Lin Yutang, pp. 134–35.
59. Ibid., p. 139.
60. Polo, *Travels*, p. 299.
61. Lin Yutang, pp. 143–44.

Chapter 8 Islam

1. Hitti, *A History of Syria*, p. 415.
2. Rodinson, *Islam and Capitalism*, p. 33.
3. Watt, *Muhammad at Medina*, p. 381.
4. Ibid., p. 272.
5. Ibid., pp. 381–82.
6. Ibid., p. 375.
7. Ibid., p. 274.
8. Ibid.
9. Ibid., p. 277.
10. Contenau, *La Vie Quotidienne à Babylone et en Assyrie*, p. 22.
11. Watt, p. 286.
12. Grunebaum, *Medieval Islam*, p. 175.
13. Watt, *Muhammad in Mecca*, p. 101.
14. Ibid., p. 102.
15. Ibid., p. 103.
16. Grunebaum, p. 175.
17. *The Cambridge History of Islam*, 1:114.
18. Ibid., 1:187–88.
19. Ibid., 1:210. See also Dunlop, *Arab Civilization to* A.D. *1500*, p. 264.
20. Grunebaum, p. 35.
21. Brodie, *The Devil Drives*, p. 105.
22. Ibid.
23. Malcolm X, *Autobiography*, p. 334.
24. Ibid., pp. 338–40.
25. *The Cambridge History of Islam*, 2:561.
26. Gibb, *Mohammedanism*, p. 127.

Chapter 9 Prophetism and Mysticism

1. *Encyclopedia of Religion and Ethics*, 10:384.
2. *The Legacy of Israel*, p. 11.
3. Zaehner, *Mysticism, Sacred and Profane*, p. 39.
4. Ibid.
5. Ibid., p. 79.

6. Ibid., p. 113.
7. Ibid., p. 114.
8. Ibid., p. 116.
9. Ibid., p. 151.
10. Ibid., p. 200.
11. Gibb, *Mohammedanism*, p. 138.
12. Grunebaum, *Medieval Islam*, p. 136.
13. Smith, *Early Mysticism in the Near and Middle East*, p. 5.
14. Zaehner, p. 147.
15. Underhill, *Mysticism*, p. 65.

PART III THE RISE OF THE WEST: WOMAN AND CULTURE

Chapter 1 The Barbarian Woman

1. Fisher, *A History of Europe*, 1:87.
2. Seneca, *De Ira* 5. 10: "To those vigorous bodies, to those souls unwitting of pleasures, luxury, and wealth, add but a little more tactical skill and discipline—I say no more; you [Romans] will only be able to hold your own against them by returning to the virtues of your sires."
3. Dudley, *The World of Tacitus*, pp. 221–22.
4. Frazer, *The Golden Bough*, p. 97.
5. Chadwick, *The Heroic Age*, p. 338.
6. Trevelyan, *History of England*, p. 61.
7. Ibid., p. 62.
8. Coulborn, *Feudalism in History*, pp. 196–97; and Chadwick, p. 443.
9. Chadwick, pp. 337–38.
10. Lévi-Strauss, *Les Structures élémentaires de la Parenté*, p. 565.
11. Southern, *The Making of the Middle Ages*, p. 80.
12. Zimmerman and Cervantes, *Marriage and the Family*, p. 16.
13. Ibid., p. 27.
14. Southern, p. 83.
15. Ibid., p. 115.
16. Ibid., p. 252.

Chapter 2 The Medieval Lady

1. Southern, *The Making of the Middle Ages*, pp. 257–58.
2. Aquinas, *Summa Theologica*, Supplement 39. 3.
3. Coulton, *From St. Francis to Dante*, p. 119.
4. Gautier, *La Chevalerie*, p. 360.
5. *Chivalry*, ed. E. Prestage, p. 2.

6. Gautier, pp. 349–50.
7. *Chivalry*, p. 9.
8. Ibid., p. 16.
9. Ibid., p. 13.
10. Ibid., p. 18.
11. Ibid., p. 97.
12. Ibid., p. 170.
13. Gautier, p. 359.
14. Ibid., p. 360.
15. Huizinga, *The Waning of the Middle Ages*, p. 116.
16. Ibid., p. 117.
17. *Chivalry*, p. 100.
18. Ibid., p. 52.
19. Huizinga, p. 118.
20. Ibid., p. 128.
21. Southern, p. 116.
22. Mâle, *L'Art Religieux du Treizième Siècle en France*, p. 107.
23. Huizinga, p. 156.
24. Friedell, *A Cultural History of the Modern Age*, 1:109.

Chapter 3 The Virago

1. Burckhardt, *The Civilization of the Renaissance in Italy*, pp. 240–41.
2. Ibid., p. 242.
3. Ibid., p. 243.
4. Ibid., p. 299.
5. Friedell, *A Cultural History of the Modern Age*, 2:120.
6. Pares, *A History of Russia*, p. 238.
7. Ibid., p. 247.
8. Ibid., p. 275.
9. Lamy, *La Femme de Demain*, p. 89.
10. Ibid., p. 90.

Chapter 4 The Witch

1. Burckhardt, *The Civilization of the Renaissance in Italy*, pp. 324–25.
2. Lea, *A History of the Inquisition in the Middle Ages*, 3:493.
3. *Malleus Maleficarum*, tr. Summers, p. 36.
4. Lea, 3:494.
5. Ibid., 3:534.
6. Ibid., 3:501.
7. *Malleus Maleficarum*, pp. 112–21.
8. Ibid., pp. 122–23.
9. Ibid., p. 21.

10. Jung, *Psychological Types*, pp. 273–74.
11. Ibid., pp. 277–78.
12. Ibid., p. 291.
13. Ibid.
14. Ibid.
15. Ibid., pp. 292–93.
16. Lea, 3:539
17. Huxley, *The Devils of Loudun*, p. 149.
18. Burckhardt, p. 327.

Chapter 5 The Reformed Woman

1. Gibb, *Mohammedanism*, p. 48.
2. Maulde La Clavière, *The Women of the Renaissance*, p. 467.
3. Maritain, *Three Reformers: Luther, Descartes, Rousseau*, p. 184.
4. Bainton, *Here I Stand: A Life of Martin Luther*, p. 301.
5. Lamy, *La Femme de Demain*, p. 100.
6. Ibid., p. 101.
7. Huizinga, *The Waning of the Middle Ages*, p. 215.
8. Mâle, *L'Art Religieux du Treizième Siècle en France*, pp. 134–35.
9. Ibid., p. 2.
10. Knox, *Works*, ed. Laing, 4:373–74.
11. Muir, *John Knox*, pp. 148–49.
12. Sinclair, *The Emancipation of the American Woman*, p. 4.

Chapter 6 The Cultured Woman

1. Staël, *De L'Allemagne*, p. 67.
2. Ibid., p. 62.
3. P. Reboux, in *Les Grands Salons Littéraires*, p. 103.
4. Ibid., p. 129.
5. Ibid., p. 143.
6. Réau, *L'Europe Française au Siècle des Lumières*, p. 307.
7. Staël, p. 28.
8. Eckermann, *Words of Goethe*, pp. 278–79.
9. Staël, p. 31.
10. Ibid., p. 33.
11. Lamy, p. 116.
12. Schopenhauer, *Essays: Studies in Pessimism*, p. 68.
13. Edwards, *The Divine Mistress*, p. 268.
14. Lewis, *Lady of France*, p. 251.
15. Germain, *Les Grandes Favorites*, p. 77.
16. Schopenhauer, p. 74.
17. Horne, *To Lose a Battle*, pp. 178–79.

18. Ibid., p. 570.
19. Benoist-Méchin, *Sixty Days That Shook the World*, p. 367.
20. Horne, p. 596.

PART IV THE MODERN AGE: WOMAN AND CIVILIZATION

Chapter 1 Woman in Search of an Identity

1. *Malleus Maleficarum*, p. 117.
2. Foucault, *Les Mots et les Choses,* p. 292.
3. Friedell, *A Cultural History of the Modern Age*, 3:34.
4. Friedan, *The Feminine Mystique*, p. 73.
5. Herold, *Mistress to an Age*, p. 475.
6. Ibid., p. 431.
7. Ibid., p. 432.
8. Ibid.
9. Ibid., p. 179.
10. Ibid., p. 181.
11. Ibid.
12. Ibid., p. 221.
13. Ibid.
14. Ibid., p. 233.
15. Ibid.
16. Ibid., p. 229.
17. Ibid., p. 263.
18. Ibid.
19. Ibid.
20. Staël, *De L'Allemagne*, pp. 111–12.
21. Ibid., p. 63.
22. Herold, pp. 269–70.
23. Hegel, *The Phenomenology of Mind*, pp. 496–97.
24. Schopenhauer, *Studies in Pessimism*, p. 70.
25. Keyserling, *Europe*, p. 120.
26. Fromm, *The Fear of Freedom*, p. 192.
27. Bullock, *Hitler, A Study in Tyranny*, pp. 391–92.
28. *British Encyclopedia*, 1960, 23:705.
29. Sinclair, *The Emancipation of the American Woman*, p. 49.
30. Schopenhauer, pp. 65–67.
31. Ibid., p. 69.
32. Nietzsche, *The Philosophy of Nietzsche*, pp. 511–12.
33. Ibid., p. 512.
34. Russell, *A History of Western Philosophy*, p. 792.
35. Nietzsche, p. 549.

36. Ibid., p. 555.
37. Zimmer, *Philosophies of India*, p. 352.
38. James, *The Varieties of Religious Experience*, p. 298.
39. Ibid.
40. Ibid., pp. 298–99.

Chapter 2 Industrial Revolution: The Birth of Feminism

1. Sampson, *The Concise Cambridge History of English Literature*, p. 668.
2. Maurois, Lélia, *The Life of George Sand*, p. 324.
3. Ibid., p. 321.
4. Ibid., p. 200.
5. Ibid., p. 429.
6. Ibid.
7. Ibid., p. 324.
8. Weber, *The Protestant Ethic and the Spirit of Capitalism*, p. 158.
9. Tawney, *Religion and the Rise of Capitalism*, p. 267.
10. Weber, p. 175.
11. Friedell, *A Cultural History of the Modern Age*, 2:188.
12. Weber, p. 151.
13. Tawney, p. 270.
14. Trevelyan, *English Social History*, p. 487.
15. T. Parsons, in *Kinship and Culture*, p. 424.
16. Trevelyan, p. 489.
17. Myrdal and Klein, *Women's Two Roles*, p. 7.
18. Wish, *Society in Early America*, p. 416.
19. Ibid., p. 417.
20. Trevelyan, p. 312.
21. De Tocqueville, *Democracy in America*, 2:198 – 99.
22. Ibid., 2:201.
23. Wish, p. 418.

Chapter 3 The Victorian Age

1. Sinclair, *The Emancipation of the American Woman*, p. 277.
2. Ibid.
3. Ibid., p. 279.
4. Ibid., p. 37.
5. Ibid., p. 184.
6. Zimmerman and Cervantes, *Marriage and the Family*, p. 161.
7. Sinclair, p. 283.
8. Schopenhauer, *Essays*, p. 67.
9. Sinclair, p. 283.
10. Ibid., p. 285.

11. Bryce, *The American Commonwealth*, 2:610.
12. Sinclair, pp. 285–86.
13. Ibid., p. 286.
14. Bryce, 2:610.
15. Sinclair, p. 288.
16. Ibid.
17. Ibid., p. 66.
18. Ibid., p. 72.
19. Veblen, *The Theory of the Leisure Class*, p. 121.
20. Ibid.
21. Sinclair, p. 105.
22. *National Council of Women, 1891*, ed. Avery, p. 45.
23. Sinclair, p. 104.
24. Ibid., p. 106.
25. Ibid., p. 199.
26. Ibid., p. 200.
27. *National Council of Women, 1891*, p. 218.
28. Sinclair, p. 203.
29. Ibid., p. 235.
30. Ibid., p. 270.
31. Ibid., p. 236.
32. Ibid., p. 237.
33. Huxley, *Life and Letters of Thomas H. Huxley*, 1:228.
34. Ibid., 1:283.
35. Ibid.
36. Ibid., 1:449.
37. Mill, *Logic* 4, chap. 4, quoted in Meadows, *The Chinese and Their Rebellions*, p. 500. See also Mahdi, *Ibn Khaldun's Philosophy of History*, p. 184.
38. Sinclair, pp. 131–32.
39. Ibid., p. 213.
40. Burton, *The City of the Saints*, pp. 482–83.
41. Muller, *The Mormons*, p. 171.
42. Sinclair, p. 215.
43. Ibid., p. 255.
44. Ibid., p. 356. See also Keyserling, *America Set Free*, p. 309.
45. Ibid., p. 263.
46. Ibid., p. 265.

Chapter 4 Culture and Civilization

1. *Psychology Today*, July 1973, p. 16. See also Robert Lehrke's theory on the possible genetic origin of mental retardation and learning

disorders (*American Journal of Mental Deficiency* 76, no. 6).

2. Curie, *Madame Curie*, p. 120.
3. Ibid., pp. 159–60.
4. Ibid., p. 159.
5. Zimmerman and Cervantes, *Marriage and the Family*, p. 263.
6. U.S. Department of Commerce, Patent Office: personal communication to the author, June 25, 1973.
7. Shaw, *Selected Prose*, ed. Russell, pp. 551–52.
8. *The Book of Marriage*, ed. Keyserling, p. 116.
9. Gilot and Lake, *Life with Picasso*, p. 74.
10. Gsell, *The Opinions of Anatole France*, p. 186.
11. *New York Times*, 29 December 1970.
12. Hegel, *The Phenomenology of Mind*, pp. 496–97.
13. Scheele, *The Weimar Republic*, p. 53.
14. Sinclair, *The Emancipation of the American Woman*, p. 323.
15. Ibid., p. 344.
16. Kroeber and Kluckhohn, *Culture, a Critical Review of Concepts and Definitions*, p. 15. Originally, "civilization" came from the Latin *civis*, "citizen," from whence *civitas*, "city" and *civiltas*, "citizenship." In the Middle Ages, we have *civitabilis*, i.e., entitled to citizenship, urbanizable. On the other hand, anthropology has largely used "culture" for more primitive societies, close to nature and the earth, whereas "civilization" applies to far greater aggregates of human beings, and especially to their more *urban* character—for example, Chinese civilization and Yakut culture. Among the various ways of contrasting these two terms, here are a few definitions that come fairly close to our interpretation of these terms: "Civilization is 'impersonal and objective' . . . Culture, on the other hand, is thoroughly personal and subjective. . . . It is this basic difference between the two fields which accounts for the cumulative nature of civilization and the unique (noncumulative) character of culture" (p. 23). Alfred Weber contrasts them this way: "Civilization is simply a body of practical and intellectual knowledge and a collection of technical means for controlling nature. Culture comprises configurations of values, of normative principles and ideals, which are historically unique" (p. 22). Adopting a time-sequential approach, Sumner and Keller state that "the adjustments of society which we call civilization form a much more complex aggregation than does the culture that went before" (p. 19). John Cowper Powys emphasizes that culture implies spontaneity rather than formal education, the expression of individual personality rather than the shackles of custom and tradition (p. 55).

PART V BEYOND HISTORY: WOMAN AND REVOLUTION

Chapter 1 The Dream of Anarchy

1. Shaw, *Selected Prose*, p. 607.
2. Ibid., p. 660.
3. Ibid., pp. 574–75.
4. Ibid., p. 568.
5. Ibid., p. 569.
6. Ibid., p. 571.
7. Ibid.
8. Ibid.
9. Ibid., p. 572.
10. Ibid., p. 573.
11. *Encyclopedia of Religion and Ethics*, 1:420.
12. Woodcock, *Anarchism*, p. 57.
13. Schwartzschild, *Karl Marx, The Red Prussian*, pp. 80–81.
14. Woodcock, p. 58.
15. Ibid., p. 86.
16. Shaw, p. 541.
17. Woodcock, p. 111.
18. Michelet, *La Femme*, p. 257.
19. Brenan, *The Spanish Labyrinth*, p. 133.
20. Ibid., p. 134.
21. Avrich, *The Russian Anarchists*, p. 92.
22. Ibid., p. 93.
23. Ibid., pp. 177–78.
24. Ibid., p. 93.
25. Brenan, p. 167.
26. Ibid., p. 200.
27. Ibid., p. 201.
28. Orwell, *Homage to Catalonia*, p. 11.
29. Gilot and Lake, p. 84.
30. Brenan, p. 189.
31. Woodcock, p. 396.

Chapter 2 Revolution in Action

1. Lamy, *La Femme de Demain*, p. 119.
2. Lacour, *Trois Femmes de la Révolution*, p. 91.
3. Carlyle, *The French Revolution*, 1:237.
4. Taine, *Les Origines de la France Contemporaine*, 2:128.
5. Carlyle, 1:248.
6. Ibid., p. 249.

7. Ibid., p. 250.
8. Taine, 2:137.
9. Lacour, p. 261.
10. Ibid., p. 76.
11. Ibid., p. 62.
12. Ibid., p. 353.
13. Ibid., p. 355.
14. Ibid., p. 356.
15. Michelet, pp. xxii, xxiii.
16. Zimmerman and Cervantes, *Marriage and the Family*, p. 170.
17. Lamy, p. 189.
18. Beauvoir, *The Second Sex*, p. 114.
19. Schwartzschild, *Karl Marx*, p. 75.
20. Ibid., p. 113.
21. Ibid., p. 115.
22. Lowie, *Primitive Society*, pp. 147–51.
23. Zimmerman and Cervantes, p. 171.
24. Ibid., p. 139.
25. Ibid.
26. Ibid., p. 172.
27. Russell, *German Social Democracy*, p. 95.
28. Zimmerman and Cervantes, p. 170.
29. Füelöp-Miller, *The Mind and Face of Bolshevism*, pp. 202–3.
30. Fischer, *The Life of Lenin*, pp. 58–59.
31. Ibid., p. 71.
32. Ibid., p. 318.
33. Fischer, *Stalin and German Communism*, p. 50.
34. Ibid., p. 27.
35. Monnerot, *Sociology of Communism*, p. 35.
36. Nehru, *The Discovery of India*, p. 29.

Chapter 3 The Communist Reality

1. Hindus, *Humanity Uprooted*, pp. 284–85.
2. Ibid., pp. 286–87.
3. Gorer and Rickman, *The People of Great Russia*, p. 109.
4. Zimmerman and Cervantes, *Marriage and the Family*, p. 173.
5. Rauch, *A History of Soviet Russia*, p. 140.
6. Zimmerman and Cervantes, p. 526.
7. Ibid., pp. 526–27.
8. E. Pawel, "Sex under Socialism," in *Commentary*, September 1965.
9. Fischer, *The Life of Lenin*, p. 555.
10. Gorer and Rickman, p. 110.

11. Füelöp-Miller, *The Mind and Face of Bolshevism*, p. 292.
12. Zimmerman and Cervantes, p. 529.
13. Ibid.
14. Ibid., p. 530.
15. Ibid., p. 173.
16. Gorer and Rickman, pp. 110–11.
17. *New York Times*, 24 April 1971.
18. *The Encyclopedia of Sexual Behavior*, p. 992.
19. *New York Times*, 24 April 1971.
20. Mills, *The Marxists*, p. 63.
21. *International Herald Tribune*, 9 August 1971.
22. Ibid., 9 January 1971.
23. Bauer, *Nine Soviet Portraits*, p. 50.
24. Ibid., p. 177.
25. Ibid.
26. Ibid., p. 175.
27. *The Encyclopedia of Sexual Behavior*, p. 989.
28. Yang, *Chinese Communist Society: The Family and the Village*, p. 64.
29. Ibid., p. 110.
30. Mao, *Selected Works*, 1:46 – 47.
31. Ibid.
32. Chow, *Ten Years of Storm*, p. 145.
33. Ibid.
34. Ibid.
35. Ibid., pp. 145–46.
36. Ibid., p. 146.
37. Walker, *China Under Communism*, p. 90.
38. Yang, p. 180.
39. Chow, p. 146.
40. Walker, p. 40.
41. Yang, p. 78.
42. Ibid.
43. Ibid., p. 81.
44. Ibid., p. 210.
45. *International Herald Tribune*, 13 March 1971.
46. Yang, p. 136.
47. Clubb, *Twentieth Century China*, p. 404.
48. Yang, p. 136.
49. *China: Inside the People's Republic*, Committee of Concerned Asian Scholars, p. 271.
50. Ibid., pp. 273–74.
51. Ibid., p. 276.
52. Ibid., p. 282.

53. Ibid., p. 291.
54. *Le Nouvel Observateur* (Paris), 6 March 1972.
55. Russell, *History of Western Philosophy*, p. 816.
56. Cragg, *The Call of the Minaret*, p. 14.
57. Rosner, *The Kibbutz as a Way of Life*, p. 8.
58. Bettelheim, *The Children of the Dream*, p. 33.
59. Ibid.
60. Ibid., p. 34.
61. Rosner, pp. 17, 65.
62. Leon, *The Kibbutz, A New Way of Life*, p. 98.
63. *The Encyclopedia of Sexual Behavior*, p. 398.
64. Bettelheim, p. 206.
65. Ibid., p. 58.
66. Rosner, p. 87.
67. Ibid., p. 71.
68. Ibid., p. 85.
69. Leon, p. 41.

Chapter 4 Cultural Revolution in the West

1. Altizer and Hamilton, *Radical Theology and the Death of God*, p. 39.
2. Leon, *The Kibbutz*, p. 108.
3. Altizer and Hamilton, p. 53.
4. Skinner, *Beyond Freedom and Dignity*, p. 191.
5. Koestler, *The Ghost in the Machine*, p. 7.
6. Heller, *The Disinherited Mind*, p. 165.
7. Altizer and Hamilton, p. 55.
8. Ibid., p. 54.
9. Unamuno, *Tragic Sense of Life*, pp. 84–85.

Chapter 5 Pandora's Daughters

1. *International Herald Tribune*, 24 August 1970.
2. Mead, *Male and Female*, p. 323.
3. Packard, *The Sexual Wilderness*, pp. 64–65.
4. Zimmerman and Cervantes, *Marriage and the Family*, p. 303.
5. *Psychology Today*, January 1972, p. 62.
6. Packard, p. 252.
7. Ibid., p. 170.
8. Veblen, *The Theory of the Leisure Class*, p. 232.
9. Sinclair, *The Emancipation of the American Woman*, pp. 351–52.
10. Packard, p. 253.
11. Beauvoir, *The Second Sex*, p. 202.
12. Heinemann, *Existentialism and the Modern Predicament*, p. 211.

13. Lilar, *Le Malentendu du Deuxième Sexe*, pp. 127–28.
14. Mead, p. 92.
15. Myrdal, *Women's Two Roles*, p. 7.
16. Ibid., p. 13.
17. Wylie, *Generation of Vipers*, pp. 194–97.
18. Ibid., pp. 199, 215.
19. *New York Times*, 15 January 1973.
20. Packard, p. 118.

Chapter 6 The End of the Iron Age

1. *New York Times*, 1 May 1972.
2. Sullerot, *Demain les Femmes*, p. 50.
3. *New York Times*, 15 March 1972.
4. Lorenz, *On Aggression*, p. 99.
5. *Washington Post*, 29 January 1971.
6. *New York Times*, 1 May 1972.
7. Heller, *The Disinherited Mind*, p. 84.
8. Lorenz, *On Aggression*, p. 255.
9. Mead, *Male and Female*, pp. 371–72.
10. *Harvard Classics*, 3:323.
11. Bird, *Born Female*, p. ix.

Bibliography

AESCHYLUS. *The Oresteian Trilogy.* Translated by P. Vellacott. Penguin ed. Baltimore, 1969.

AGUS, J. B. *L'Evolution de la Pensée Juive.* Paris, 1961.

ALBRIGHT, W. F. *From the Stone Age to Christianity.* New York, 1957.

ALTIZER, T., and HAMILTON, W. *Radical Theology and the Death of God.* Penguin ed., Baltimore, 1968.

A New Way of Life. Edited by N. Bentwich. London, 1949.

AQUINAS, T. *Summa Theologica.* 22 vols. London, 1920.

AUERBACH, C. *The Science of Genetics.* New York, 1961.

AUROBINDO. *The Ideal of Human Unity.* New York, 1953.

AVRICH, P. *The Russian Anarchists.* Princeton, 1967.

BAINTON, R., *Here I Stand: A Life of Martin Luther.* New York, 1950.

BEAUVOIR, S. de. *The Second Sex.* Translated by H. M. Parshley. New York, 1953.

BEBEL, A. *Woman Under Socialism.* New York, 1923.

BECK, W. S. *Modern Science and the Nature of Life.* Penguin ed. Baltimore, 1961.

BELL, H. I. *Egypt, From Alexander the Great to the Arab Conquest.* Oxford, 1948.

BENOIST-MECHIN, J. *Sixty Days That Shook the West.* New York, 1963.

BERENSON, B. *The Italian Painters of the Renaissance.* London, 1959.

BETTELHEIM, B. *The Children of the Dream.* London, 1971.

BIRD, C. *Born Female.* New York, 1969.

BLAKE, W. *Prophetic Writings.* 2 vols. Oxford, 1926.

BREASTED, J. H. *A History of Egypt.* New York, 1954.

————. *The Dawn of Conscience.* New York, 1933.

BRENAN, G. *The Spanish Labyrinth.* Cambridge, England, 1943.

BREUIL, H. and LANTIER, R. *The Men of the Old Stone Age.* London, 1965.

BRODIE, F. M. *The Devil Drives: A Life of Sir Richard Burton.* New York, 1967.

BROGLIE, A. de. *L'Eglise et L'Empire Romain au IVie Siècle.* 6 vols. Paris, 1867.

449

BROWN, N. O. *Life Against Death.* New York, 1959.

BRYCE, J. *The American Commonwealth.* 2 vols. New York, 1912.

BULLOCK, A. *Hitler, A Study in Tyranny.* New York, 1964.

BURCKHARDT, J. *The Civilization of the Renaissance in Italy.* London, 1951.

BURTON, R. F. *The City of the Saints.* London, 1963.

CAMPBELL, J. *Primitive Mythology.* New York, 1959.

————. *Oriental Mythology.* New York, 1962.

————. *Occidental Mythology.* New York, 1964.

CARLYLE, T. *The French Revolution.* London, 1900.

CARR, E. H. *The October Revolution.* New York, 1969.

CHADWICK, H. M. *The Heroic Age.* Cambridge, England, 1967.

CHILDE, G. *What Happened in History.* Penguin ed. Baltimore, 1950.

————. *New Light on the Most Ancient East.* London, 1954.

CHOW CHING-WEN. *Ten Years of Storm.* New York, 1960.

COCHRANE, C. N. *Christianity and Classical Culture.* New York, 1957.

COMMITTEE OF CONCERNED ASIAN SCHOLARS. *China: Inside the People's Republic.* New York, 1972.

CONTENAU, G. *La Vie Quotidienne à Babylone et en Assyrie.* Paris, 1950.

COOMARASWAMY, A. *Buddha and the Gospel of Buddhism.* London, 1928.

COULTON, G. G. *From St. Francis to Dante.* London, 1908.

COWELL, F. R. *Cicero and the Roman Republic.* London, 1948.

CRAGG, K. *The Call of the Minaret.* New York, 1956.

Culture: Man's Adaptive Dimension. Edited by M. F. A. Montagu. New York, 1968.

CUMONT, F. *The Mysteries of Mithra.* Translated by T. J. McCormack. New York, 1956.

————. *Oriental Religions in Roman Paganism.* New York, 1956.

CURIE, E. *Madame Curie.* Translated by V. Sheean. New York, 1937.

DAVIES, A. P. *The First Christian.* New York, 1957.

DE TOCQUEVILLE, A. *Democracy in America.* 2 vols. New York, 1953.

DIEHL, C. *Byzantine Empresses.* New York, 1963.

DILL, S. *Roman Society From Nero to Marcus Aurelius.* London, 1925.

DUBOIS, J. A. *Hindu Manners, Customs and Ceremonies.* Translated by H. K. Beauchamp. Oxford, 1928.

DUDLEY, D. *The World of Tacitus.* Boston, 1968.

DUNLOP, D. M. *Arab Civilization to A.D. 1500.* London, 1971.

EBERHARD, W. *A History of China.* London, 1948.

ECKERMANN, J. P. *Words of Goethe.* New York, 1949.

EDWARDS, S. *The Divine Mistress.* New York, 1970.

ELIADE, M. *Myths, Dreams and Mysteries.* Translated by P. Mairet. New York, 1967.

————. *Yoga, Immortality and Freedom.* Translated by W. R. Trask. London, 1958.

————. *The Myth of the Eternal Return.* Translated by W.R. Trask. London, 1954.

————. *Patterns in Comparative Religion.* Translated by R. Sheed. New York, 1958.

ELLIS, H. *Studies in the Psychology of Sex.* 6 vols. Philadelphia, 1911.

EMERY, W. B. *Archaic Egypt.* Penguin ed. Baltimore, 1961.

Encyclopedia of Religion and Ethics, ed. J. Hastings. 13 vols. Edinburgh, 1908–21.

ENSLIN, M. S. *Christian Beginnings.* New York, 1956.

FERENCZI, S. *Sex in Psychoanalysis.* Translated by E. Jones. 3 vols. New York, 1950.

FERRERO, G. *The Greatness and Decline of Rome.* Translated by A. Zimmern. 5 vols. New York, 1910.

————. *The Women of the Caesars.* New York, 1911.

FISCHER, L. *The Life of Lenin.* New York, 1964.

FISCHER, R. *Stalin and German Communism.* Cambridge, Mass., 1948.

FISCHER, H. A. L. *A History of Europe.* London, 1949.

FLEISCHMANN, H. *Robespierre et les Femmes.* Paris, 1909.

FORDHAM, F. *An Introduction to Jung's Psychology.* Penguin ed. Baltimore, 1953.

FOUCAULT, M. *Les Mots et les Choses.* Paris, 1966.

FRANKFORT, H. *Before Philosophy.* Penguin ed. Baltimore, 1954.

FRAZER, J. *The Golden Bough.* London, 1950.

FRIEDAN, B. *The Feminine Mystique.* New York, 1963.

FRIEDELL, E. *A Cultural History of the Modern Age.* 3 vols. New York, 1953.

FROMM, E. *The Fear of Freedom.* London, 1955.

FRYE, R. N. *The Heritage of Persia.* New York, 1963.

FÜELÖP-MILLER, R. *The Mind and Face of Bolshevism.* New York, 1965.

GAUTIER, L. *La Chevalerie.* Paris, 1884.

GERMAIN, A. *Les Grandes Favorites.* Paris, 1950.

GHIRSHMAN, R. *Iran.* Penguin ed. Baltimore, 1954.

GIBB, H. A. R. *Mohammedanism.* Oxford, 1950.

GIBBON, E. *The Decline and Fall of the Roman Empire.* 3 vols. New York, n.d.

GILLOT, F., and LAKE, C. *Life with Picasso.* New York, 1964.

GORER, G., and RICKMAN, J. *The People of Great Russia.* London, 1949.

GRANET, M. *La Civilization Chinoise.* Paris, 1929.

Gray's Anatomy, ed. T. B. Johnston. London, 1958.

GRUNEBAUM, G. E. von. *Medieval Islam.* Chicago, 1956.

GSELL, P. *The Opinions of Anatole France.* New York, 1922.

GUIGNEBERT, C. *Jesus.* Translated by S.H.Hooke. New York, 1956.

GURNEY, O.R. *The Hittites.* Penguin ed. Baltimore, 1954.

HAGEN, V. W. von. *Realm of the Incas.* New York, 1957.

HALL, H. R. *The Ancient History of the Near East.* London, 1957.

HARRISON, J. E. *Prolegomena to the Study of Greek Religion.* Cambridge, 1922.

Harvard Classics, ed. C.W.Eliot. 50 vols. New York, 1937.

HEINEMANN, F. H. *Existentialism and the Modern Predicament,* New York, 1958.

HEGEL, G. W. F. *The Phenomenology of Mind.* London, 1949.

HELLER, E. *The Disinherited Mind.* Cambridge, England, 1952.

HEROLD, J. C. *Mistress to an Age.* New York, 1958.

HINDUS, M. *Humanity Uprooted.* New York, 1930.

HITTI, P. K. *History of Syria.* London, 1957.

HORNE, A. *To Lose a Battle.* Boston, 1969.

HUIZINGA, J. *The Waning of the Middle Ages.* Penguin ed. Baltimore, 1955.

HU SHIH. *Development of the Logical Method in Ancient China.* Shanghai, 1922.

HUXLEY, L. *Life and Letters of Thomas Huxley.* 2 vols. New York, 1901.

HUYGHE, R. *Dialogues avec le Visible.* Paris, 1955.

I CHING. Translated by R. Wilhelm. 2 vols. London, 1951.

JAEGER, W. *Paideia, The Ideals of Greek Culture.* Translated by G. Highet. 3 vols. Oxford, 1954.

JAMES, W. *The Varieties of Religious Experience.* New York, 1958.

JANEWAY, E. *Man's World, Woman's Place.* London, 1972.

JASPERS, K. *The Origin and Goal of History.* London, 1958.

JASTROW, J. *Freud, His Dream and Sex theories.* New York, 1948.

JEROME. *Selected Letters.* Loeb Library ed. Cambridge, Mass., n.d.

JONES, E. *The Life and Work of Sigmund Freud.* 3 vols. New York, 1955.

JUNG, C. G. *Psychological Types.* Translated by H.G. Baynes. London, 1953.

——. *The Integration of the Personality.* Translated by S. Dell. London, 1963.

——. *Psychology of the Unconscious.* Translated by B. M. Hinkle. London, 1951.

KAUFMANN, W. *Critique of Religion and Philosophy.* New York, 1961.

——. *Nietzsche.* New York, 1968.

KEYSERLING, H. *Europe.* New York, 1928.

——. *America Set Free.* London, 1930.

Kinship and Culture, ed. F. L. K. Hsu. Chicago, 1971.

KNOX, J. *Works.* Edited by D. Laing. 6 vols. Edinburgh, 1854.

KOESTLER, A. *The Ghost in the Machine.* London, 1967.

KOHN, H. *The Idea of Nationalism.* New York, 1944.

KRAMER, S. N. *Sumerian Mythology.* New York, 1961.

——. *History Begins at Sumer.* London, 1958.

KROEBER, A. L., and KLUCKHOHN, C. *Culture, A Critical Review of Concepts and Definitions.* New York, 1952.

LACOUR, L. *Trois Femmes de la Révolution*. Paris, 1900.

LAMY, E. *La Femme de Demain*. Paris, n.d.

LATOURETTE, K. S. *A History of Christianity*. New York, 1953.

LEA, H. C. *A History of the Inquisition in the Middle Ages*. 3 vols. New York, 1888.

LEON, D. *The Kibbutz, A New Way of Life*. London, 1969.

Les Grands Salons Littéraires. Paris, 1928.

LÉVI-STRAUSS, C. *La Pensée Sauvage*. Paris, 1962.

———. *Anthropologie Structurale*. Paris, 1958.

———. *Les Structures Elémentaires de la Parenté*. Paris, 1958.

LEWIS, P. *Lady of France*. New York, 1963.

LILAR, S. *Le Malentendu du Deuxième Sexe*. Paris, 1969.

LIN YUTANG. *My Country and My People*. London, 1956.

LISSNER, I. *Man, God and Magic*. New York, 1961.

LIVY, T. *History of Rome*. 6 vols. Everyman's Library. New York, n.d.

LORENZ, K. *On Aggression*. New York, 1970.

LOWIE, R. H. *Primitive Society*. New York, 1961.

MAJUMDAR, R. C. *An Advanced History of India*. London, 1953.

MALE, E. *L'Art Religieux du XIIIie Siècle en France*. Paris, 1923.

MALINOWSKI, B. *Sex, Culture and Myth*. London, 1963.

Man and Time, ed. J. Campbell. 3 vols. London, 1958.

MAHDI, M. *Ibn Khaldun's Philosophy of History*. London, 1957.

MAO TSE-TUNG. *Selected Works*. 5 vols. London, 1954.

MARITAIN, J. *Three Reformers: Luther, Descartes, Rousseau*. London, 1950.

MAULDE LA CLAVIERE, R. de. *The Women of the Renaissance*. New York, 1905.

MAUROIS, A. *Lelia: The Life of George Sand*. New York, 1953.

MEAD, M. *Male and Female*. London, 1950.

———. *Sex and Temperament in Three Primitive Societies*. New York, 1935.

MEADOWS, T. T. *The Chinese and their Rebellions*. Stanford, n.d.

MELLAART, J. *Çatal Hüyük*. New York, 1967.

MICHELET, J. *La Femme*. Paris, 1960.

MILLS, C. W. *The Marxists*. Penguin ed. Baltimore, 1963.

MONIER-WILLIAMS, M. *Brahmanism and Hinduism*. London, 1887.

MONNEROT, J. *Sociology of Communism*. Translated by J. Degras and R. Rees. London, 1953.

MONTAGU, A. *The Human Revolution*. New York, 1965.

———. *Sex, Man and Society*. New York, 1969.

MORRIS, D. *The Naked Ape*. London, 1968.

MOSCATI, S. *The Face of the Ancient Orient*. London, 1960.

MUIR, E. *John Knox*. London, 1920.

MULLEN, R. *The Mormons*. London, 1967.

MYRDAL, A. and KLEIN, V. *Women's Two Roles*. London, 1962.

NATIONAL COUNCIL OF WOMEN OF THE UNITED STATES. *Transactions.* Edited by R.F. Avery. Philadelphia, 1891.

NEEDHAM, J. *Science and Civilization in China,* vols. 1 and 2. Cambridge, Mass., 1954–56.

NEHRU, J. *The Discovery of India.* New York, 1946.

NIETZSCHE, F. *Thus Spake Zarathustra.* Modern Library ed. New York, n.d.

O'LEARY, D. L. *How Greek Science Passed to the Arabs.* London, 1951.

ORTEGA Y GASSET, J. *The Dehumanization of Art.* New York, n.d.

ORWELL, G. *Homage to Catalonia.* Penguin ed. Baltimore, 1966.

PACKARD, V. *The Sexual Wilderness.* New York, 1968.

PARES, B. *A History of Russia.* New York, 1953.

PIAGET, J. *Le Structuralisme.* Paris, 1968.

PIGGOTT, S. *Prehistoric India.* Penguin ed. Baltimore, 1952.

PLUTARCH. *Lives.* 3 vols. Everyman's Library ed. New York, n.d.

POLO, M. *Travels.* London, 1930.

POLYBIUS. *Histories.* 6 vols. Loeb Library ed. Cambridge, Mass., n.d.

POWELL, L. P. *Mary Baker Eddy.* New York, 1930.

RADHAKRISHNAN, S. *Religion and Society.* London, 1956.

———. *Eastern Religions and Western Thought.* Oxford, 1940.

———. *Indian Philosophy.* 2 vols. New York, 1956.

RAUCH, G. von. *A History of Soviet Russia.* Translated by P. Jacobsohn. London, 1957.

RAWLINSON, H. G. *India.* London, 1954.

REAU, L. *L'Europe Française au Siècle des Lumières.* Paris, 1938.

REICH, W. *Character Analysis.* Translated by T.P. Wolfe. London, 1958.

RODINSON, M. *Islam et Capitalisme.* Paris, 1966.

ROSNER, M. *The Kibbutz as a Way of Life in Modern Society.* Givat Haviva (Israel), n.d.

RUSSELL, B. *A History of Western Philosophy.* London, 1948.

———. *German Social Democracy.* New York, 1965.

SAMPSON, *The Concise Cambridge History of English Literature.* Cambridge, 1959.

SCHEELE, G. *The Weimar Republic.* London, 1946.

SCHOPENHAUER, A. *Essays.* Translated by T.B. Saunders. London, 1951.

SHAW, B. *Selected Prose.* Edited by D. Russell. New York, 1952.

SCHWARTZSCHILD, L. *Karl Marx, The Red Prussian.* New York, 1947.

SINCLAIR, A. *The Emancipation of the American Woman.* New York, 1966.

SKINNER, B. F. *Beyond Freedom and Dignity.* New York, 1972.

SMITH, M. *Studies in Early Mysticism in the Near and Middle East.* London, 1931.

SMITH, W. R. *The Religion of the Semites.* New York, 1959.

SOUTHERN, R. W. *The Making of the Middle Ages.* London, 1959.

SPEARS, E. L. *Assignment to Catastrophe.* 2 vols. London, 1954.

SPRENGER, J. *Malleus Maleficarum.* Translated by M. Summers. London, 1971.

STAEL, G. de. *De L'Allemagne.* Paris, 1839.

STANLEY, A. P. *Lectures on the History of the Eastern Church.* Everyman's Library ed. New York, 1924.

SULLEROT, E. *Demain les Femmes.* Paris, 1965.

SYKES, P. *A History of Persia.* 2 vols. London, 1951.

TAINE, H. *Les Origines de la France Contemporaine.* 6 vols. Paris, 1876–94.

TARN, W. W. *Hellenistic Civilization.* London, 1953.

TAWNEY, R. H. *Religion and the Rise of Capitalism.* London, 1948.

TERTULLIAN. *Apologeticus.* Loeb Library ed. Cambridge, Mass., n.d.

The Book of Marriage, ed. H. Keyserling. New York, 1926.

The Cambridge History of Islam, ed. P.M. Holt. Cambridge, Mass., 1970.

The Encyclopedia of Sexual Behavior, ed. A. Ellis and A. Abarbanel. New York, 1961.

The Essential Works of Anarchism, ed. M.S. Shatz. New York, 1971.

The Legacy of India, ed. G.T. Garratt. Oxford, 1951.

The Legacy of Israel, ed. E.R. Bevan and C. Singer. Oxford, 1953.

The Legacy of Rome, ed. C. Bailey. Oxford, 1951.

The Meaning of the Death of God, ed. B. Murchland. New York, 1967.

THOMAS, E. *The Women Incendiaries.* New York, 1966.

TOULMIN, S. and GOODFIELD, J. *The Fabric of the Heavens.* New York, 1961.

TRESMONTANT, C. *La Métaphysique du Christianisme.* Paris, 1961.

TREVELYAN, G. M. *English Social History.* London, 1946.

UNAMUNO, M. de. *Tragic Sense of Life.* Translated by J.E.C. Flitch. New York, 1954.

UNDERHILL, E. *Mysticism.* New York, 1956.

VAUGHAN, A. C. *The House of the Double Axe.* New York, 1959.

VAUX, R. de. *Ancient Israel.* New York, 1961.

VEBLEN, T. *The Theory of the Leisure Class.* New York, 1953.

WALKER, R. L. *China Under Communism.* New Haven, 1955.

WATT, W. M. *Muhammad at Mecca.* Oxford, 1953.

———. *Muhammad at Medina.* Oxford, 1956.

WEBER, M. *The Religion of China.* Glencoe, Ill., 1951.

——— *The Protestant Ethic and the Spirit of Capitalism.* New York, 1956.

WHEELER, M. *Early India and Pakistan.* New York, 1959.

WHITE, V. *God and the Unconscious.* New York, 1961.

WHISH, H. *Society and Thought in Early America.* London, 1953.

WYLIE, P. *Generation of Vipers.* London, 1955.

WOODCOCK, G. *Anarchism.* London, 1963.

X, MALCOM. *Autobiography.* New York, 1966.

YANG, C. K. *Chinese Communist Society.* Cambridge, Mass., 1965.

ZAEHNER, R. C. *The Teaching of the Magi.* New York, 1956.

_____. *Mysticism, Sacred and Profane.* Oxford, 1957.

ZIMMER, H. *Philosophies of India.* Edited by J. Campbell. London, 1951.

ZIMMERMAN, C. C., and CERVANTES, S. J. *Marriage and the Family.* Chicago, 1956.

ZIMMERN, A. *The Greek Commonwealth.* Oxford, 1924.

Index

Index